The Sporting News

The Author

Joe Gergen, a native of Brooklyn, has worked for Long Island-based Newsday for the last 19 years, covering a variety of sports and writing a general column.

Gergen was raised in Queens and attended Boston College, graduating in 1963 with a bachelor's degree in English. After college, he began working for United Press International in New York, remaining there for five years before joining the Newsday staff.

Gergen, who has covered every Final Four Tournament since 1975, has written three other books: "Kiner's Korner," "Roger Staubach of the Dallas Cowboys" and "Dr. J: The Story of Julius Erving."

The Photographs

A majority of the photographs appearing in this publication came from the extensive basketball files of Malcolm Emmons, who has been covering the NCAA Tournament since 1961. Other contributors: Bill Smith, the University of Oregon, Indiana University, the University of Wisconsin, Stanford University, the University of Wyoming, the University of Utah, Oklahoma State University, Holy Cross College, the University of Kentucky, City College of New York, the University of Kansas, La Salle University, the University of San Francisco, the University of California and UCLA.

Jacket design by Mike Bruner
Of The Sporting News

Inside design by Bill Perry
Of The Sporting News

The Sporting News

THE FINAL FOUR

By JOE GERGEN

ACKNOWLEDGMENTS

As with any subject relating to the past, this book is dependent on the memories of the men who lived it. The scores and statistics are a matter of record. The flavor of the times is a matter of personal observation and recall by the men whose heroics helped to make the Final Four what it is today.

Therefore, this book is their book. My thanks to the participants who shared their experiences with me, often at great length: John Dick, Bob Dro, John Kotz, Gene Englund, Howie Dallmar, Ken Sailors, Arnie Ferrin, Wat Misaka, Henry Iba, Bob Kurland, George Kaftan, Wallace (Wah Wah) Jones, Ralph Beard, Floyd Layne, Frank Ramsey, Cliff Hagan, Clyde Lovellette, Bob Leonard, Tom Gola, Hal Perry, Bob Dalton, Tony Yates, Ed Jucker and Jerry Harkness.

The author acknowledges a debt to Newsday and Sports Illustrated and the assistance provided by the following books: "Second Wind," by Bill Russell and Taylor Branch; "Goliath: The Wilt Chamberlain Story," by Bill Libby; "Mr. Clutch," by Jerry West with Bill Libby; "Hondo," by John Havlicek and Bob Ryan; "Giant Steps," by Kareem Abdul-Jabbar and Peter Knobler; and "The Walton Gang," by Bill Libby. Special thanks is due Prof. Barbara Dunlap, the archivist at the City College of New York.

Also, the accuracy of the material is the result of painstaking research by Mike Nahrstedt and Joe Hoppel of The Sporting News, who challenged each fact and kept the author in line.

—Joe Gergen

Published in the United States by THE SPORTING NEWS Publishing Co., 1212 North Lindbergh Boulevard, St. Louis, Missouri 63132.

Library of Congress Catalog Card Number: 87-61216

ISBN: 0-89204-276-1
10 9 8 7 6 5 4 3 2 1

First Edition

FOREWORD

By
Al McGuire

It all started in 1939 when the Oregon basketball team won the first NCAA Tournament by beating Ohio State. A message had gone out the year before, after the first National Invitation Tournament was held in Madison Square Garden.

Every hoop junkie knew that the NCAA's postseason tournament was a potential grand slammer. The championship game of that first tourney was played in a rather small arena at Northwestern University in Evanston, Ill., only eight schools competed in the initial tournament and teams reached their destinations most often by train. We've come a long way—to huge playing facilities, air travel and 64 teams. That's 64 and, possibly, counting.

No doubt about it, the NCAA Tournament is the greatest annual amateur sports event in the world. The ides of March automatically means the NCAA extravaganza. The tourney captures the sporting world for almost a month, and the Final Four ranks with the World Series and Super Bowl as an event expressed in two words that fit headline space.

The media blitz has become greater than that accompanying a summit conference, and television networks dig deeper into their treasure chests for the opportunity to get even a piece of the action. For the next three years, CBS has paid an unbelievable $166 million for the rights to televise. Ticket prices have reached Broadway-show levels (even for Bob Uecker seats), and the NCAA Tournament's sponsors have ranged from bus lines to car-rental agencies to soft-drink companies.

About the only thing the tournament doesn't have is John Madden. The excitement is contagious, with the level of performance matching the combined efforts of Bruce Springsteen, Michael Jackson and Barbra Streisand in concert.

As I look back over the last decade or so of tournaments, my memories flash to the coaches—especially to their reactions at that final buzzer. Immediately coming to mind are Rollie Massimino, Jim Valvano, Dean Smith, Bob (as he prefers to be called) Knight, John Thompson, John Wooden and Denny Crum. Even yours truly.

Rollie made it a family, Jimmy V looked to hug somebody, Dean sighed, Bobby smiled, John hugged and I cried. Wooden made it monotonous, and Crum made it tingle.

Each year has brought innovations in the game itself. In 1978; Kentucky won when Joe B. went to space-eaters. Coach Hall's use of grunt players started a trend in physical power play. The game that really moved the NCAA Tournament to another level of awareness, though, featured Magic and Special K (Greg Kelser) clipping the Bird's wings in 1979. In that game, Magic Johnson and the Michigan State Spartans reintroduced the matching zone against Larry Bird and Indiana State. And in 1987, Knight proved that coaches can adjust to the times by picking up his third NCAA title with a mixture of junior-college players, zone defenses and an Adidas sweater.

You've got to remember that a coach's whole season and the team's dedication are based on playing in the tournament. The season is like the shrimp cocktail and the tourney is a steak or lobster. Reputations are made by winning just one game. Take 1987, when Austin Peay beat Illinois; or the year before, when Arkansas-Little Rock defeated Notre Dame and Cleveland State eliminated Indiana. If a coach makes it to the Yellow Brick Road—the Final Four—he gets speaking engagements, clinic invitations, a 100 percent increase in his basketball-camp enrollment and endorsement offers for everything from cookbooks to sneakers to hair spray.

On the other side of the coin, players with a hot hand in March have been picked in the first round of the NBA draft in June and then received guaranteed, megabuck contracts for three to five years. Even the zebras who work the finals can count on instant recognition in their private careers and increased dates on the whistle circuit.

The tourney also creates new philosophies and styles of play that immediately plug into the country's high schools, as well as the junior colleges, the NAIA, NCAA Division II and III schools, YMCA ball, church ball and industrial teams.

What is the future for this blockbuster? First of all, I see it coming to permanent sites for regional games based on the size and location of the city, its hotel facilities and whether its chamber of commerce is willing to work on the event for a full year. Obviously, all sites will have to be close to a modern hub airport. Perhaps the ticket crunch means that only domed arenas are suitable prospects for future Final Four sites, with a minimum seating of 30,000, but for me that destroys the amateur nature of the sport. There's nothing as charming as the Lexingtons of the world—college towns with frat rows and laundromats, where you couldn't get a cab if your life depended on it.

As for the game itself, I expect the three-second lane to be widened a la international rules and the three-point distance to be moved nearer the NBA mark. Superstars in the 1990s will not foul out of a game; after their fifth foul, the opponent will go to the free-throw line and also get the ball at half-court. An athlete will not be locked into wearing the basketball shoe from a company that has a personal contract with his coach.

You'll see the NCAA grow stronger in its discipline of coaches for on-bench misconduct because of the psychological edge that prominent coaches have over the less-visible coaches. And in the future there will be more prime-time coverage on TV, but you will not see beer sponsorship in the tournament. For the past few years I've been expecting a rule for drug-testing of players, and that time is now upon us.

You'll see the NCAA Tournament selection process taken out of the smoke-filled rooms of the power-brokering commissioners in the top six conferences. (At the present time, the six power conferences are Big East, Atlantic Coast, Big Ten, Southeastern, Big Eight and Pacific-10, and almost half of the 64 competing teams come out of those leagues each year.) In the future, a set criteria will determine the participating teams. The final list probably will come from a computer that has been fed the won-lost record, difficulty of schedule, prominent injuries, eligibility record and probation status of each school.

Eventually, the revenue generated from the tournament will be split equally among all Division I schools. The teams winning the Final Four get so much exposure through the tube and other media, that giving them more than $1 million along with all the publicity is creating super-rats, and their recruiting edge prolongs dynasties. What happened to football is now happening to basketball. Each year you have the same teams in the Top 20, only their positions change. We have created haves and have-nots, and we are going to have to assist the "Third World" teams with an equal distribution of monies.

In addition, adequate TV exposure will have to be ensured during the regular season for the struggling schools, to allow them to compete in the recruiting battles for the blue-chip high school athlete.

My three wishes for the NCAA Tournament of the '90s are: First, that all teams would qualify and that the postseason conference tournaments would be eliminated. (There is no purpose for the league tourneys and they make the regular season look like a warmup.) Second, that half of the ticket allotment to schools in the Final Four would go to the student body. And third, that some of the hundreds of millions of dollars down the road be returned to all the student-athletes in the form of monthly allotment checks. This could amount to $100-$200 a month for nine months of school and should be administered through the NCAA rather than the colleges. Let's be realistic. Many of these players don't have any pocket money and are extremely vulnerable to street games and the breaking of NCAA rules.

The NCAA Tournament has improved my station in life, given me opportunities to walk on the moon and has put a calliope in my ear. I share the dream the Greek runners and Roman gladiators had and the dream that the shoeshine boy still has today—that of being called "Champ."

Contents

INTRODUCTION

Try these numbers on for size. The total attendance for all sessions of the first two NCAA Tournaments was 51,905. That figure was exceeded by 13,054 at a single game in 1987, the championship contest between the Indiana and Syracuse basketball teams.

Here's another indication of the tournament's growth. Indiana won the second event staged in 1940 and received $750, plus expenses. Forty-seven years later, the champion Hoosiers earned $1,056,027, minus a fine because of Coach Bob Knight's tantrum at the Midwest Regional final.

Eight teams competed for the top prize in 1939, which was awarded in a modest gymnasium on a college campus before 5,500 witnesses. Now the field numbers 64 and the championship game is routinely staged in domed stadiums and televised throughout the nation. The crowd total of 64,959 for each of the two sessions of the 1987 Final Four in the Louisiana Superdome established a record, but by no means does it represent the outer limit. Three of the five Final Fours from 1988 through 1992 have been awarded to domes in Seattle, Indianapolis and Minneapolis. And you can bet that New Orleans hasn't seen the last of college basketball's showcase event.

It wasn't until 1951 that the NCAA Tournament was expanded to 16 teams. The first Final Four as we know it, with representatives from four playoff sites gathering at one arena, occurred the following year in Seattle. From 1953 through 1974, the field varied from 22 to 25 teams. The figure grew to 32 in 1975 when, for the first time, more than one representative from a conference was invited to participate.

Additional conference teams were dispatched to distant sites, so as not to overload a regional. The format had the effect of balancing the tournament, a goal that officials later endorsed through a national seeding process (with the result that many high-ranking teams receive assignment to regionals out of their geographic area). The number of teams admitted was increased to 40 in 1979, 48 in 1980, 52 in 1983, 53 in 1984 and finally set at 64 in 1985.

At the outset, the NCAA Tournament wasn't even the nation's foremost postseason tourney. The National Invitation Tournament was the more prestigious of college basketball's postseason competitions for many years, due largely to the heavy media attention it received as a New York-based event. Of course, an automatic trip to the Big Apple was, in itself, a lure to the nation's top teams and players (many of whom opted for a taste of the big city and its basketball tradition over participation in the NCAA Tournament).

It was the success of the first NIT at Madison Square Garden in 1938 that led Harold Olsen, the coach at Ohio State, to propose a national event sponsored by the colleges in a letter to George Edwards, the president of the National Association of Basketball Coaches.

Edwards placed the matter before the coaches' annual convention in April 1938 at Chicago and, encountering no major objections, assigned a committee to investigate the feasibility of such a tournament promoted and managed by the coaches under the NCAA banner. The committee, which included Olsen, returned with a positive verdict and the proposal was submitted to the NCAA. That group, which already conducted national championship events in track, swimming, boxing, wrestling, tennis and golf, voted in October 1938 to authorize a championship basketball tournament commencing the following spring.

"It is entirely fitting that the 'prestige' of college basketball should be supported, and demonstrated to the nation, by the colleges themselves, rather than that this be left to private promotion and enterprise," stated William B. Owens of Stanford, the president of the NCAA. "It is also fitting that the suggestion for such a tournament, under college auspices, should come from the National Association of Basketball Coaches, an organization of college basketball coaches which cooperates with the National Collegiate Athletic Association in seeking to improve and develop the game in the colleges. Their suggestion was timely and was promptly accepted."

And so began the battle for attention and public recognition. As late as 1950, the NIT boasted a larger field (12 teams to eight) and uniformly larger crowds. It wasn't until the 1951 point-shaving scandal, which was particularly damaging to New York basketball, and the enlargement of the NCAA Tournament field that the NCAA's postseason meet began to emerge as a major event on the sports calendar. Now it stands with the World Series, the Super Bowl, the Kentucky Derby and the Indianapolis 500 as a national attraction.

Of course, the game has changed appreciably along the way. In 1939, most players were anchored to the floor when they attempted field goals and anything over .300 was an outstanding shooting percentage. Now basketball is played above the rim and no team expects to win unless it makes 50 percent of its shots. The first tournament entrants traveled by train; now they crisscross the country in jet planes.

What remains from the earliest days, however, is

This was the scene at the railroad station in 1939 when the victorious Oregon team returned to Eugene with college basketball's first national championship.

an intense spirit of competition and a pride in accomplishment.

"We didn't have television and we didn't have the press coverage they do now," said Gene Englund of Wisconsin's 1941 championship team, "but it was a big thing to us. It was a big thing in our lives."

It has been so for thousands of athletes, from a Kansas reserve named Dean Smith (one point in two championship appearances) who would someday coach an NCAA titlist to a Princeton star named Bill Bradley (58 points in a consolation game) who was destined to become a U.S. senator. No school has enjoyed the opportunity more than UCLA, whose 10 championships in 12 years under John Wooden stand as a monument in American sports.

My first Final Four coincided with Wooden's last (1975). He was saying goodbye while I was saying hello. In Wooden's absence, the tournament has become a democratic institution. Although I have seen Knight win three titles and Louisville's Denny Crum two in that time, no champion other than Georgetown has returned to the final game the following year. And Georgetown lost on that occasion.

The decade of the 1980s has been particularly fertile for the improbable outcomes that stamp events so indelibly in our minds. No one who was there will ever forget the shocking comeback and last-second victory by North Carolina State over a physically awesome Houston team in 1983 or the near-perfect performance by upstart Villanova against Georgetown two years later. Michael Jordan's title-winning shot for North Carolina in 1982 was one for the memory banks, as was Keith Smart's for Indiana in 1987. There has never been a shortage of heroics in college basketball, and now they can be shared by more people than ever before.

"The National Collegiate Athletic Association basketball tournament," Owens wrote in 1939, "should become a classic, a fitting annual climax in the program of this great American sport." His prediction was right on target, a two-hand set shot that drew nothing but net.

Even to someone who believes that the best basketball arena in America is the Palestra and who remains unconvinced of the wisdom of the three-point field goal, the Final Four is better now than it has ever been. As the NCAA prepares for its 50th tournament in 1988, one can only wish the event a happy anniversary and many more years.

Joe Gergen
New York
June 1987

To Lynne, Bryan and Baby G.,
a fortunate man's Final Three.

1939 The Beginning: Oregon Is King

College basketball's first NCAA Tournament champions hailed from the University of Oregon. Seated (left to right) are Wally Johansen, Slim Wintermute, Bobby Anet, Coach Howard Hobson, Laddie Gale and John Dick. Standing (left to right) are Bob Hardy, Red McNeeley, student manager Jay Langston, Ford Mullen, Matt Pavalunas, trainer Bob Officer, Ted Sarpola and Earl Sandness.

Few college basketball teams have traveled longer or farther in pursuit of a championship than the Oregon Ducks of 1939.

The train ride from San Francisco, home of the Western playoffs, to Evanston, Ill., site of the first NCAA title game, wasn't the half of it. The Ducks had spiced the early part of their schedule with the equivalent of a national tour.

The previous year, Oregon had lost to Stanford in the North-South playoff that determined the Pacific Coast Conference championship. Without the mechanism of a national tournament, Stanford was acclaimed in some quarters as the best team in the nation. While the graduation of the fabled Hank Luisetti seriously weakened the Indians for the 1939 season, the Ducks returned all five starters.

Assessing the strength of teams throughout the nation, Madison Square Garden basketball promoter Ned Irish offered Oregon a place in one of his intersectional doubleheaders in December 1938.

Howard Hobson, the Ducks' cerebral coach who left nothing to chance, saw the trip as an opportunity to toughen his team for the season ahead and expose it to different styles of play and officiating. It seemed like the ideal preparation for possible participation in the new NCAA Tournament, which had been approved by NCAA officials in October on the condition that management of the event be handled by the National Association of Basketball Coaches.

So Hobson booked games for Oregon not only in New York, but also in Philadelphia, Buffalo, Cleveland, Detroit, Chicago, Peoria, Ill., and Des Moines before winding up with a New Year's Eve engagement against Stanford in San Francisco.

It was no small achievement for the Ducks to fold themselves into sleeping berths night after night as they lurched from city to city. With a 6-foot-8 center in Urgel (Slim) Wintermute and a pair of 6-4½ forwards in Laddie Gale and John Dick, Oregon was among the taller teams in the country. L.H. Gregory, sports editor of the Oregonian in Portland, referred to the Ducks as the "Tall Firs," and the New York newspapers attempted to outdo each other in lining up the players for photographs accentuating their height.

Oregon's performance at the Garden was less than a smashing success. The Ducks, confused by the officials' interpretation of legal and illegal screens to the moving picks set by City College of New York, fell far behind and rallied too late, losing 38-36. They lost twice more on the trip, to Bradley when Wintermute was troubled by a sprained ankle and to Stanford on the last night of the nearly three-week journey.

The Ducks returned to Eugene exhausted but confident in their ability to play against any team anywhere. They were enormously successful in conference competition, winning 14 of 16 games and defeating a strong Washington team four times (the Huskies lost only one other game all season). As the first-place finisher in the league's North Division, Oregon qualified to meet South representative California in Eugene in a best-of-three playoff to decide the Pacific Coast championship and the conference's first entrant in the national tournament.

It would be a tight schedule if the teams required a third game in Eugene on Saturday night. The Western competition was set for the pavilion at Treasure Island on San Francisco Bay, site of a world exposition, starting on Monday night and the trip by train required 24 hours. But Oregon solved that problem by beating the Bears, a team its own size, in the first two games, 54-49 and 53-47. The Western playoffs weren't nearly as tough.

As it developed, the Ducks had more difficulty with the portable floor installed in the pavilion, site of livestock shows, rodeos and various pageants, than they did with either Texas or Oklahoma. Oregon dismissed Texas, 56-41, and then routed Oklahoma, a victor over Utah State in the other first-round game, 55-37. The Ducks' fast break, directed by 5-8 Bobby Anet and 5-11 Wally Johansen, was at its best in the Western final.

Meanwhile, a continent away in Philadelphia, Ohio State had triumphed in the Eastern playoffs by overpowering Wake Forest, 64-52, and Villanova, 53-36, at the Palestra. That the Buckeyes qualified for the NCAA title game was poetic justice. It was Harold Olsen, the Ohio State coach, who had pushed for a national tournament to be run by the colleges.

Irish had used the foundation of his popular intersectional doubleheaders to convince Madison Square Garden management to underwrite the first National Invitation Tournament in 1938. While Olsen thought a postseason tournament was overdue and applauded the exposure it gave college basketball, he was not pleased to see an outside organization profit from the college sport. Olsen proposed his idea to the coaches' association, which submitted the plan to the NCAA. Once the concept was approved by that body, Olsen was appointed chairman of the first tournament committee.

Among matters requiring attention was the selection of facilities for the games. It wasn't until three weeks before the final that Olsen sought and received permission to stage the championship game at Patten Gymnasium on the campus of Northwestern University. It was a small field house by the standards of the Big Ten and the Pacific Coast conferences, but Olsen was operating on a tight budget and Evanston, just north of Chicago, was centrally located no matter what the identity of the opponents.

Two more nights on a train weren't about to bother the Oregon players, whose trips were so meticulously planned by Hobson that the Ducks ordered from their own limited menu at off-hours in the dining car. Hobson, an Oregonian who held a master's degree from Columbia, addressed the same attention for detail to his coaching. He charted shots not only in games, but also in practices and adjusted his offense to take maximum advantage of his players' abilities.

Offensively, the Ducks liked to run whenever possible. Smaller opponents invariably attempted to slow the game, which led Hobson to lobby for a shot clock. A guard in his playing days at Oregon, he also advocated a three-point field goal, placing Hobson decades ahead of his time.

Unlike most teams in 1939, Oregon did not rely solely upon a man-to-man defense or a zone. It played a combination defense, adjusting to the offense it faced. That defense baffled an Ohio State team that had displayed its offensive firepower in the Eastern playoffs.

Following an exhibition of basketball depicting the development of the game from the days of the peach basket, presented by a group of Northwestern athletes, the Ducks brought a crowd of 5,500 up to date as they bolted to a 6-0 lead. A free throw and a basket by Jimmy Hull, the Ohio State captain and Big Ten scoring champion, keyed a five-point run by the Buckeyes before Oregon stepped up the pace. With Anet and Johansen triggering the fast break, the Ducks opened an 18-11 lead. The margin at halftime was 21-16.

"We felt then we had the game well in hand," Dick said, "even though that was one of our poorest shooting nights."

One reason for the Ducks' confidence was their balance. Ohio State focused its defense on Gale and Wintermute, opening the floor for the other Oregon starters.

"I was a decoy," said Gale, the leading scorer in the Pacific Coast Conference. "Wherever I went, Ohio State sent two men."

Dick seized advantage of the overplay and scored a game-high 15 points, and the swift Anet, usually content to feed his taller teammates, added 10 points. The Buckeyes closed the deficit to a single point at the outset of the second half on two baskets by Hull, but four quick field goals by Oregon, including two by Dick, ended the suspense. The Ducks won as they pleased, 46-33.

Proponents pronounced the tournament a success, at least aesthetically. But a turnout of 6,000 for the two nights of the Western playoffs and a combined attendance of only 3,500 at the Palestra resulted in a net loss of $2,531. Since the coaches did not have that much money in the treasury, they requested that the NCAA underwrite the deficit and assume fiscal and organizational responsibility for future tournaments. The NCAA agreed.

As a pioneer in a brave, new world, the championship team was not overburdened with mementos. There was no outstanding-player award, nor were watches presented to the participants as they would be at future championships. Back in Dick's hometown of The Dalles, a community on the Columbia River east of Portland, the citizens proposed to do something about it.

On the day following the championship, a collection was taken and a gold watch was purchased and suitably engraved. Civic leaders then proposed to a railroad official that the train from Chicago make an unscheduled stop so they might present Dick with a token of their esteem. The official rejected the proposal.

But the residents were not easily discouraged. The fans contacted his superior and then another until they finally were granted an audience with the president of the line. They told him if he did not agree to stop the train, they would barricade the track. Reluctantly, he agreed. He gave them 10 minutes.

And so at 5 o'clock on a morning in early spring, 1939, between 2,000 and 3,000 people assembled at the train station in The Dalles. Dick stepped off the train in the company of Hobson and Anet and received the first championship watch in NCAA Tournament history. Clearly, the event was an idea whose time had come.

1939 Tournament Results

First Round	Semifinals
Villanova 42, Brown 30	Ohio State 53, Villanova 36
Ohio State 64, Wake Forest 52	Oregon 55, Oklahoma 37
Oklahoma 50, Utah State 39	**Championship**
Oregon 56, Texas 41	Oregon 46, Ohio State 33
Regional Third Place	
Utah State 51, Texas 49	

Howard Hobson was the cerebral coach of the NCAA's first championship team.

STATISTICS

1939 OREGON

Head Coach—Howard Hobson   **Final Record—29-5**

Player	Pos.	Hgt.	Wgt.	Cl.	G	FG	FGA	Pct.	FT	FTA	Pct.	Reb.	Pts.	Avg.
Laddie Gale	F	6-4	195	Sr.	34	145	...	....	117	...	....	...	407	12.0
Slim Wintermute	C	6-8	195	Sr.	31	124	...	....	61	...	....	...	309	10.0
John Dick	F	6-4	200	Jr.	34	90	...	....	49	...	....	...	229	6.7
Wally Johansen	G	5-11	155	Sr.	34	74	...	....	45	...	....	...	193	5.7
Bobby Anet	G	5-8	175	Sr.	33	56	...	....	67	...	....	...	179	5.4
Wimpy Quinn	F	6-2	180	Jr.	1	2	...	....	0	...	....	...	4	4.0
Bob Hardy	F	6-3	180	Jr.	30	46	...	....	22	...	....	...	114	3.8
Ted Sarpola	F	6-2	160	Jr.	27	37	...	....	17	...	....	...	91	3.4
Matt Pavalunas	G	6-0	170	Jr.	33	38	...	....	12	...	....	...	88	2.7
Red McNeeley	G	6-2	180	So.	18	9	...	....	5	...	....	...	23	1.3
Ford Mullen	G	5-8	165	Jr.	29	13	...	....	9	...	....	...	35	1.2
Earl Sandness	C	6-4	190	So.	12	4	...	....	0	...	....	...	8	0.7
Don Mabee	G	...	...	...	5	0	...	....	2	...	.500	...	2	0.4
Oregon					34	638			406				1682	49.5
Opponents					34	...			...				1304	38.4

1939 OHIO STATE

Head Coach—Harold Olsen   **Final Record—16-7**

(Full-season statistics unavailable; individual statistics are for NCAA tourney.)

Player	Pos.	Hgt.	Wgt.	Cl.	G	FG	FGA	Pct.	FT	FTA	Pct.	Reb.	Pts.	Avg.
Jimmy Hull	F	5-11	178	Sr.	3	22	...	....	14	15	.933	...	58	19.3
Richard Baker	F	5-11	168	Sr.	3	12	...	....	5	8	.625	...	29	9.7
William Sattler	C	6-6	188	Jr.	3	8	...	....	3	9	.333	...	19	6.3
Robert Lynch	G	6-0	176	Jr.	3	6	...	....	4	7	.571	...	16	5.3
John Schick	C	6-3	185	Jr.	3	5	...	....	1	2	.500	...	11	3.7
Gilbert Mickelson	F	6-1	165	So.	3	2	...	....	2	2	1.000	...	6	2.0
Jack Dawson	G	5-10	160	So.	3	3	...	....	0	3	.000	...	6	2.0
Robert Stafford	F	6-2	185	Jr.	2	1	...	....	0	0	.000	...	2	1.0
Richard Boughner	G	6-0	180	Sr.	3	1	...	....	0	0	.000	...	2	0.7
Don Scott	G	6-2	215	So.	2	0	...	....	1	1	1.000	...	1	0.5
Charles Maag	C	6-4	210	So.	2	0	...	....	0	0	.000	...	0	0.0
Jed Mees	G	6-0	175	So.	1	0	...	....	0	0	.000	...	0	0.0
*Ohio State					23	...			..		....		999	43.4
*Opponents					23	...			..		....		908	39.5

*Full season.

1939 OKLAHOMA

Head Coach—Bruce Drake   **Final Record—12-9**

(Full-season statistics unavailable; individual statistics are for NCAA tourney.)

Player	Pos.	Hgt.	Wgt.	Cl.	G	FG	FGA	Pct.	FT	FTA	Pct.	Reb.	Pts.	Avg.
Jimmy McNatt	F	...	...	..	2	10	...	....	4	6	.667	...	24	12.0
Garnett Corbin	F	...	...	..	2	6	...	....	2	2	1.000	...	14	7.0
Herbert Scheffler	C	...	...	..	2	3	...	....	5	6	.833	...	11	5.5
Ben Kerr	C-F	...	...	..	2	3	...	....	4	4	1.000	...	10	5.0
Marvin Mesch	G	...	...	..	2	4	...	....	1	2	.500	...	9	4.5
Gene Roop	F-G	...	...	..	2	2	...	....	4	6	.667	...	8	4.0
Marvin Snodgrass	G	...	...	..	2	3	...	....	1	1	1.000	...	7	3.5
Matthew Zollner	G	...	...	..	2	1	...	....	0	1	.000	...	2	1.0
Roscoe Walker	G-F	...	...	..	2	1	...	....	0	1	.000	...	2	1.0
Bill Richards	G	...	...	..	1	0	...	....	0	0	.000	...	0	0.0
Vernon Mullen	C	...	...	..	2	0	...	....	0	0	.000	...	0	0.0
Ralph Bollinger	G	...	...	..	..	..	...	....	..	..	....	...	...	...
Hugh Ford	C	...	...	..	..	..	...	....	..	..	....	...	...	...
*Oklahoma					21	..			..		....		862	41.0
*Opponents					21	..			..		....		829	39.5

*Full season.

1939 VILLANOVA

Head Coach—Alex Severance   **Final Record—20-5**

(Full-season statistics unavailable; individual statistics are for NCAA tourney.)

Player	Pos.	Hgt.	Wgt.	Cl.	G	FG	FGA	Pct.	FT	FTA	Pct.	Reb.	Pts.	Avg.
John Krutulis	G	...	...	...	2	8	...	....	3	4	.750	...	19	9.5
Paul Nugent	G	...	...	...	2	8	...	....	2	3	.667	...	18	9.0
James Montgomery	F	...	...	...	2	6	...	....	3	6	.500	...	15	7.5
George Duzminski	F	...	...	...	1	2	...	....	2	3	.667	...	6	6.0
Michael Lazorchak	F	...	...	...	2	5	...	....	0	1	.000	...	10	5.0
Louis Dubino	C	...	...	...	2	3	...	....	0	3	.000	...	6	2.0
Arthur Vigilante	G	...	...	...	1	1	...	....	0	0	.000	...	2	2.0
William Sinnott	F	...	...	...	2	1	...	....	0	0	.000	...	2	1.0
Lloyd Rice	C	...	...	...	2	0	...	....	0	0	.000	...	0	0.0
Charles Yung	G	...	...	...	2	0	...	....	0	0	.000	...	0	0.0
Ernest Robinson	F-C	...	...	...	2	0	...	....	0	1	.000	...	0	0.0
Walter Burlington	.	...	...	...	.	.	...	....	..	..	....	...	...	...
Bernard McAloon	.	...	...	...	.	.	...	....	..	..	....	...	...	...
John Murphy	.	...	...	...	.	.	...	....	..	..	....	...	...	...
Anthony Vinci	.	...	...	...	.	.	...	....	..	..	....	...	...	...
*Villanova					25	..			..		....		1013	40.5
*Opponents					25	..			..		....		755	30.2

*Full season.

1939 FINAL FOUR

Semifinals
At Philadelphia

Ohio State	fg	ft	fta	pf	tp
Hull	10	8	8	1	28
Baker	2	0	0	2	4
Schick	3	1	1	3	7
Dawson	1	0	2	1	2
Lynch	0	0	1	3	0
Mickelson	1	0	0	0	2
Stafford	1	0	0	0	2
Sattler	3	2	3	1	8
Maag	0	0	0	0	0
Boughner	0	0	0	0	0
Mees	0	0	0	0	0
Scott	0	0	0	0	0
Totals	21	11	15	11	53

Villanova	fg	ft	fta	pf	tp
Lazorchak	2	0	1	4	4
Montgomery	1	1	3	4	3
Dubino	1	0	3	3	2
Krutulis	2	1	1	2	5
Nugent	7	2	3	2	16
Duzminski	2	2	3	3	6
Sinnott	0	0	0	0	0
Rice	0	0	0	0	0
Robinson	0	0	0	0	0
Yung	0	0	0	0	0
Totals	15	6	13	15	36

Halftime: Ohio State 25-10. Officials: Kennedy and Walsh.

At San Francisco

Oregon	fg	ft	fta	pf	tp
Gale	3	5	7	4	11
Hardy	0	3	3	1	3
Sarpola	0	0	0	0	0
F. Mullen	0	1	2	0	1
Dick	6	2	2	1	14
Wintermute	4	2	2	1	10
Johansen	4	0	1	3	8
Pavalunas	1	0	0	1	2
Anet	1	4	5	2	6
Totals	19	17	22	13	55

Oklahoma	fg	ft	fta	pf	tp
McNatt	5	2	3	1	12
Roop	1	1	2	2	3
Walker	1	0	1	0	2
Corbin	1	0	0	0	2
Scheffler	2	2	2	4	6
V. Mullen	0	0	0	1	0
Kerr	3	3	3	0	9
Mesch	1	0	1	4	2
Zollner	0	0	0	2	0
Snodgrass	0	1	1	1	1
Totals	14	9	13	15	37

Halftime: Oregon 21-14. Officials: Leith and Bailey.

Championship
March 27
At Evanston, Ill.

Oregon	fg	ft	fta	pf	tp
Gale	2	4	5	1	8
Dick	5	5	5	3	15
Wintermute	2	0	1	1	4
Anet	4	2	3	3	10
Johansen	4	1	2	1	9
F. Mullen	0	0	0	0	0
Pavalunas	0	0	0	0	0
Totals	17	12	16	9	46

Ohio State	fg	ft	fta	pf	tp
Hull	5	2	2	2	12
Baker	0	0	1	0	0
Schick	1	0	0	1	2
Dawson	1	0	0	4	2
Lynch	3	1	3	3	7
Maag	0	0	0	0	0
Scott	0	1	1	1	1
Boughner	1	0	0	0	2
Sattler	3	1	2	0	7
Mickelson	0	0	0	2	0
Stafford	0	0	0	0	0
Totals	14	5	9	13	33

Halftime: Oregon 21-16. Officials: Getchell and Clarno.

1940 Hoosiers Win, In a Hurry

The Hurryin' Hoosiers of 1940 literally ran away with the second NCAA basketball championship. Seated (left to right) are Jim Gridley, Herm Schaefer, Bob Dro, Marv Huffman, Jay McCreary, Curly Armstrong and Ralph Dorsey. Standing (left to right) are Coach Branch McCracken, Chet Francis, Bill Menke, Andy Zimmer, Bob Menke and assistant coach Ralph Graham.

They were always in a hurry. At the insistence of Branch McCracken, their vigorous young coach, the Indiana Hoosiers played basketball at a pace that, in the days before World War II, was breathtaking to behold. They ran and they ran and then they ran some more.

If they didn't beat opponents with their speed and quick ball movement, then the Hoosiers beat them with their conditioning.

"You're going to beat them in the last 10 minutes," McCracken told his players. And a great many teams wilted under the pressure of Indiana's tempo.

"We always had a fast break," said Marv Huffman, Indiana's standout guard. "His (McCracken's) contention was that you get down before them and you get back on defense before them, so we were fast-breaking both ways. We just ran like mad."

It didn't take long for McCracken's teams to be dubbed the "Hurryin' Hoosiers." Nor did it take them long to impose their will on the Big Ten Conference.

McCracken, a former All-America player at Indiana who possessed a courtside manner as intemperate as that displayed by Bob Knight about three decades later, was an immediate coaching success.

His first team, the 1939 Hoosiers, won 17 of 20 games overall and finished second in the conference behind NCAA Tournament finalist Ohio State. In McCracken's second season, the Hoosiers again were 17-3 in regular-season play. And again they finished second in the Big Ten, with Purdue taking the league title.

The difference in 1940 was that Indiana defeated Purdue in both games between the intrastate rivals. Additionally, Purdue's esteemed coach, Ward (Piggy) Lambert, was no fan of postseason competition. As a result, the selection committee for District 4 in the Upper Midwest tapped the Hoosiers to represent the area in the second national tournament.

"Look," McCracken told his team, "there's no point in going if we're not going to win it."

It was a supremely confident group that made the short trip to the Butler University field house in Indianapolis for the NCAA Eastern playoffs, whose opening games would match Indiana against Springfield and Duquesne against Western Kentucky.

The Hoosiers weren't particularly tall, but they didn't stand in one place long enough to be mea-sured. Even Bill Menke, Indiana's 6-foot-5 center, "could run forever," according to forward Bob Dro. The other forward was Paul (Curly) Armstrong, with Huffman and Herman Schaefer at the guards.

McCracken wanted his players to handle the ball like a hot potato, keep it moving at all times. He abhorred dribbling when it wasn't necessary.

"I remember at one of our first practices," Huffman said, "I got a rebound and dribbled it a couple of times. Well, Branch blew his whistle and threw two balls up on the boards. I got one and dribbled it before I passed and he took the other one and just threw it downcourt. Then he looked at me and said, 'OK, now which one got there faster?' I said, 'You made your point,' and that was the last time I ever dribbled the ball."

The Hoosiers weren't reluctant to fling a court-length pass if a teammate was open.

"If you took the chance and threw wildly," Dro said, "so be it. But we got pretty good at those passes."

Branch McCracken was the fiery architect of Indiana's run-and-gun basketball.

Springfield didn't stand a chance. The Massachusetts school, where the sport had been born, was no match for the Hoosiers in its only NCAA Division I tourney appearance. Indiana led, 30-11, at halftime and McCracken cleared the bench in the second half en route to a 48-24 victory.

Duquesne edged Western Kentucky for the other berth in the Eastern final, setting up a rematch of a taut contest during the regular season in which the Hoosiers edged the Iron Dukes, 51-49, in Pittsburgh. What the Hoosiers feared most about Duquesne was its zone. The key was to beat the Dukes downcourt before they could align themselves in the defense. This Indiana did often enough to open a 25-13 lead at halftime as Menke scored 10 points.

Rattled by the pace, Duquesne made only four of 26 shots from the field. Although the Dukes cut into the deficit in the second half, they never threatened to take control and Indiana won, 39-30.

The next stop was Kansas City, where the Kansas Jayhawks had emerged from the more competitive Western playoffs. The Jayhawks had defeated Rice, 50-44, and then rallied to upset Southern California, 43-42, on Howard Engleman's corner set shot in the waning seconds. The Trojans had beaten Colorado in the opening round for their 20th victory in 22 games and were favored to represent the West in the national title game.

This second national tournament, the first under the direct supervision of the NCAA, would be very much a Kansas production. Dr. Forrest (Phog) Allen, the venerable Kansas coach, had promoted the idea of holding both the Western playoffs and the championship contest in Kansas City's modern Municipal Auditorium. In fact, he was serving as the manager of both events. Of course, the proximity of Kansas City to the Kansas campus in Lawrence ensured a partisan crowd.

In addition, a pregame ceremony honored the late Dr. James Naismith, who had invented basketball at Springfield in 1891. Naismith had died at his home in Lawrence on November 28, 1939. He had been affiliated with the University of Kansas for the last 40 years of his life and had been Allen's mentor.

Against this tide of sentiment, the Hoosiers had their fast break and a belief in themselves. That belief was tested at the outset of the game when Kansas jumped to a 10-4 lead. Indiana called a timeout, but the rules prevented the team from huddling with its coach.

Instructions were not necessary. The Hoosiers had been schooled well enough to recognize their deficiencies.

"We knew what we had to do," Huffman said. "We tightened up our defense and got our fast break going."

The reversal was dramatic. Indiana rallied to force ties at 11-11, 12-12 and 14-14 and then overran the cautious, probing Jayhawks.

"If you get that shot," McCracken had told his team, "put it up and everybody go to the board except one. Let it go, don't hesitate."

And that's exactly what the Hoosiers did. They shot 39 times in the first half and made 13 field goals, and they left Kansas dazed and trailing, 32-19. Nevertheless, the Jayhawks stayed with their ball-control offense in the second half, continuing to play what Dro called a game of "cat and mouse." Even when the lead rose to 20 points, Kansas took its time looking for the perfect shot.

Indiana won easily, 60-42. It would be 10 years before another team scored as many points in an NCAA championship game. And basketball observers marveled at the fact the Hoosiers made 34.7 percent of their field-goal attempts.

So sure was Allen of his system—a style, after all, handed down from on high—that, in a perverse sense, he believed he had won the game. His players had done what he had asked them. They had controlled the ball. McCracken, remember, believed in putting the ball in the basket and not in an Indiana player's hands.

"They had the ball twice as long as we did," Dro contended. But the championship was decided on points, not on time of possession.

Ironically, the game's leading scorer was Bobby Allen of Kansas, the coach's son. He had 13 points, one more than teammate Engleman. Huffman (12), Jay McCreary (12) and Armstrong (10) paced Indiana. The outstanding-player award—the first such honor bestowed in the NCAA finals—went to Huffman, the captain, although a number of Hoosiers were equally deserving.

As much as Indiana's success was a victory for the players, so it was a triumph of strategy. The 10,000 fans in attendance were buffeted by a fresh, new breeze in college basketball—although a Kansas City newspaper, in a burst of hyperbole, described it as a tornado.

"That tornado was us," Huffman said. "We just blew them out of the stadium."

The second-place team from the Big Ten was going back to Bloomington with the big prize. But the major winner may have been the tournament itself. With a total attendance of 36,880 at the five sessions, the NCAA was pleased to announce a small profit after expenses. No longer was the future of the event in doubt.

1940 Tournament Results

First Round	Semifinals
Duquesne 30, W. Kentucky 29	Indiana 39, Duquesne 30
Indiana 48, Springfield 24	Kansas 43, Southern Cal 42
Kansas 50, Rice 44	**Championship**
Southern Cal 38, Colorado 22	Indiana 60, Kansas 42
Regional Third Place	
Rice 60, Colorado 56 (ot)	

STATISTICS

1940 INDIANA

Head Coach—Branch McCracken   **Final Record—20-3**

Player	Pos.	Hgt.	Wgt.	Cl.	G	FG	FGA	Pct.	FT.	FTA	Pct.	Reb.	Pts.	Avg.
Paul (Curly) Armstrong	F	5-11	170	Jr.	23	78	...	...	48	...	...	...	204	8.9
Herman Schaefer	G-F	6-0	175	Jr.	23	77	...	...	30	...	...	...	184	8.0
Bill Menke	C	6-5	175	Jr.	23	71	...	...	35	...	...	...	177	7.7
Bob Dro	F-G	5-11	190	Jr.	23	66	...	...	14	...	...	...	146	6.3
Jay McCreary	F	5-10	145	Jr.	21	40	...	...	15	...	...	...	95	4.5
Marv Huffman	G	6-2	185	Sr.	23	41	...	...	16	...	...	...	98	4.3
Andy Zimmer	C	6-4	175	So.	18	13	...	...	6	...	...	...	32	1.8
Chet Francis	F	6-1	170	Jr.	14	9	...	...	2	...	...	...	20	1.4
Bob Menke	C-F	6-3	165	Jr.	18	10	...	...	5	...	...	...	25	1.4
Ralph Dorsey	F	5-10	175	Sr.	20	8	...	...	7	...	...	...	23	1.2
James Gridley	G	6-0	170	Jr.	18	7	...	...	5	...	...	...	19	1.1
Bill Torphy	G	6-0	175	So.	12	5	...	...	2	...	...	...	12	1.0
Bill Frey	F	6-1	175	So.	4	1	...	...	1	...	...	...	3	0.8
Jack Stevenson	F	6-1	175	Sr.	7	1	...	...	3	...	...	...	5	0.7
Clarence Ooley	G	6-2	190	Sr.	3	1	...	...	0	...	...	...	2	0.7
Tom Motter	F	6-1	175	Jr.	8	1	...	...	1	...	...	...	3	0.4
Norman Hasler	G	5-11	165	So.	3	0	...	...	0	...	...	...	0	0.0
Harold Zimmer	F	5-8	145	Jr.	1	0	...	...	0	...	...	...	0	0.0
Everett Hoffman	C	6-3	190	So.	1	0	...	...	0	...	...	...	0	0.0
Russell Clifton	G-F	6-1	165	Jr.	1	0	...	...	0	...	...	...	0	0.0
Cliff Wiethoff	F	6-0	165	So.	1	0	...	...	0	...	...	...	0	0.0
Indiana					23	429	...		190				1048	45.6
Opponents					23	288	...		238				814	35.4

1940 KANSAS

Head Coach—Forrest (Phog) Allen   **Final Record—19-6**

Player	Pos.	Hgt.	Wgt.	Cl.	G	FG	FGA	Pct.	FT.	FTA	Pct.	Reb.	Pts.	Avg.
Ralph Miller	F	...	...	So.	25	85	...	...	58	...	...	...	228	9.1
Bob Allen	C	...	...	Jr.	25	66	...	...	46	...	...	...	178	7.1
Don Ebling	F	...	...	Sr.	25	63	...	...	48	...	...	...	174	7.0
Howard Engleman	F	...	...	Jr.	21	53	...	...	20	...	...	...	126	6.0
Dick Harp	G	...	...	Sr.	25	48	...	...	27	...	...	...	123	4.9
Bruce Reid	F	...	...	Sr.	11	17	...	...	7	...	...	...	41	3.7
Bruce Voran	G	...	...	Sr.	24	27	...	...	21	...	...	...	75	3.1
John Kline	G	...	...	Sr.	24	13	...	...	1	...	...	...	27	1.1
Bob Johnson	F	...	...	So.	17	8	...	...	2	...	...	...	18	1.1
T.P. Hunter	G	...	...	Jr.	14	2	...	...	7	...	...	...	11	0.8
William Hogben	G	...	...	Sr.	12	4	...	...	0	...	...	...	8	0.7
Jack Sands	C	...	...	Sr.	10	2	...	...	0	...	...	...	4	0.4
Kansas					25	388	...		237				1013	40.5
Opponents					25	...	...		...				868	34.7

Other members of squad who did not score: James Arnold (Jr.), Miller Cameron (So.), Jack Engel (So.), Jack Floyd (So.), John Krum (So.), Dunn Musser (So.), Ted Moser (So.) Bob O'Neil (So.), DeWitt Potter (So.), Bob Woodward (So.), Charles Walker (So.).

1940 DUQUESNE

Head Coach—Charles (Chick) Davies   **Final Record—20-3**

(Full-season statistics unavailable; individual statistics are for National Invitation Tournament and NCAA Tournament.)

Player	Pos.	Hgt.	Wgt.	Cl.	G	FG	FGA	Pct.	FT.	FTA	Pct.	Reb.	Pts.	Avg.
Paul Widowitz	G	...	...	...	5	21	...	...	5	...	...	...	47	9.4
Morris Becker	F	...	...	...	5	12	...	...	8	...	...	...	32	6.4
Ed Milkovich	F	...	...	...	5	12	...	...	8	...	...	...	32	6.4
Bill Lacey	C	...	...	...	5	12	...	...	6	...	...	...	30	6.0
Rudy Debnar	G	...	...	...	5	4	...	...	9	...	...	...	17	3.4
Lou Kasperik	F-C	...	...	...	4	5	...	...	2	...	...	...	12	3.0
Lester Reiber	G	...	...	...	2	1	...	...	0	...	...	...	2	1.0
Sparky Adams	G	...	...	...	..	..	...	...	..	...	...	...	..	...
Huck Hartman	C	...	...	...	..	..	...	...	..	...	...	...	..	...
Charles Kristofak	G	...	...	...	..	..	...	...	..	...	...	...	..	...
John Scarry	F	...	...	...	..	..	...	...	..	...	...	...	..	...
Joe Yankitis	F	...	...	...	..	..	...	...	..	...	...	...	..	...
*Duquesne					23	...			...				935	40.7
*Opponents					23	...			...				772	33.6

*Full season.

1940 SOUTHERN CALIFORNIA

Head Coach—Sam Barry   **Final Record—20-3**

(Full-season statistics unavailable; statistics shown are for Pacific Coast Conference Southern Division games.)

Player	Pos.	Hgt.	Wgt.	Cl.	G	FG	FGA	Pct.	FT.	FTA	Pct.	Reb.	Pts.	Avg.
Ralph Vaughn	F	6-0	174	Sr.	12	53	...	...	32	...	...	...	138	11.5
Dale Sears	C	6-2	190	Sr.	12	39	...	...	27	...	...	...	105	8.8
Jack Lippert	G	5-11	170	Jr.	12	37	...	...	9	...	...	...	83	6.9
Tom McGarvin	G	6-0	190	Sr.	12	29	...	...	21	...	...	...	79	6.6
Jack Morrison	F	6-0	180	Sr.	12	24	...	...	11	...	...	...	59	4.9
Joseph Reising	G	...	...	...	..	..	...	...	..	...	...	...	..	...
Keith Lambert	F	6-1	195	...	..	..	...	...	..	...	...	...	..	...
John Luber	G	...	...	So.	..	..	...	...	..	...	...	...	..	...
Guelff	...	...	...	...	..	..	...	...	..	...	...	...	..	...
Bob Matthews	...	...	...	...	..	..	...	...	..	...	...	...	..	...
Steve Miletich	...	...	...	...	..	..	...	...	..	...	...	...	..	...
Carl Patton	...	...	...	...	..	..	...	...	..	...	...	...	..	...
Jack Barton	..	6-3	190	Jr.	..	..	...	...	..	...	...	...	..	...
Leonard Berg	..	...	...	So.	..	..	...	...	..	...	...	...	..	...
Robert Ormsby	..	...	...	Jr.	..	..	...	...	..	...	...	...	..	...
*Southern California					23	...	...		...				1099	47.8
*Opponents					23	...	...		...				821	35.7

*Full season.

(Vaughn led full-season scoring with 265 points in 23 games for 11.5 average.)

1940 FINAL FOUR

Semifinals
At Indianapolis

Indiana

	fg	ft	pf	tp
McCreary	0	0	3	0
Schaefer	2	4	3	8
W. Menke	4	2	4	10
Dro	2	1	2	5
Huffman	2	2	3	6
Zimmer	1	1	0	3
Dorsey	0	0	0	0
Armstrong	2	3	0	7
Totals	13	13	15	39

Duquesne

	fg	ft	pf	tp
Becker	2	2	4	6
Milkovich	4	2	4	10
Lacey	1	0	3	2
Debnar	0	2	2	2
Widowitz	3	1	3	7
Reiber	0	0	0	0
Kasperik	1	1	1	3
Totals	11	8	17	30

Halftime: Indiana 25-13. Officials: Kennedy and Adams.

At Kansas City

Kansas

	fg	ft	fta	pf	tp
Ebling	2	4	8	1	8
Engleman	3	0	1	1	6
Allen	3	2	2	2	8
Miller	2	2	4	2	6
Harp	6	3	4	3	15
Voran	0	0	1	0	0
Kline	0	0	0	0	0
Totals	16	11	19	9	43

Southern California

	fg	ft	fta	pf	tp
Vaughn	2	2	5	2	6
Morrison	0	0	0	3	0
Sears	8	3	4	2	19
McGarvin	3	0	0	4	6
Lippert	4	0	1	3	8
Lambert	0	1	2	2	1
Luber	1	0	1	0	2
Totals	18	6	13	16	42

Halftime: Southern California 21-20. Officials: Curtis and Vidal.

Championship
March 30
At Kansas City

Indiana

	fg	ft	fta	pf	tp
Schaefer	4	1	1	1	9
McCreary	6	0	0	2	12
W. Menke	2	1	2	3	5
Huffman	5	2	3	4	12
Dro	3	1	1	4	7
Armstrong	4	2	3	3	10
Gridley	0	0	0	0	0
R. Menke	0	0	0	0	0
Zimmer	2	1	1	1	5
Dorsey	0	0	0	0	0
Francis	0	0	0	1	0
Totals	26	8	11	19	60

Kansas

	fg	ft	fta	pf	tp
Ebling	1	2	5	0	4
Engleman	5	2	3	3	12
Allen	5	3	4	3	13
Miller	0	2	2	4	2
Harp	2	1	3	1	5
Hunter	0	1	1	0	1
Hogben	2	0	0	0	4
Kline	0	0	0	0	0
Voran	0	1	2	0	1
Sands	0	0	0	0	0
Johnson	0	0	0	0	0
Totals	15	12	20	11	42

Halftime: Indiana 32-19. Officials: O'Sullivan and McDonald.

1941 Badgers Deliver Crowning Blow

The Wisconsin Badgers reached national prominence by winning the 1941 championship. Seated (left to right) are Bob Alwin, Bob Sullivan, Fred Rehm, John Kotz, Gene Englund, Charles Epperson, Ted Strain, Harlo Scott and Ed Scheiwe. Standing (left to right) are team manager Morris Bradley, Walter Bakke, Ed Downs, Bob Roth, George Affeldt, Warren Schrage, Don Timmerman, Ted Deppe, John Lynch, Edward Jones, Coach Bud Foster and assistant Fritz Wegner.

Once upon a time, the Wisconsin Badgers were the scourge of the Big Ten Conference. To the members of the 1941 Wisconsin team, however, that was ancient history.

Under Doc Meanwell, an English-born and American-educated physician who never played basketball on a competitive basis, Wisconsin had dominated its conference in the second decade of the 20th Century. Meanwell's offense, which stressed short passes, the crisscrossing of players and the use of screens, revolutionized the sport. The so-called "Wisconsin system" helped to transform a roughhouse game into one of precision and finesse.

Meanwell won his last league title in 1929 with a team featuring Bud Foster. After several years of playing professional basketball, Foster returned to Madison to coach his alma mater. His team finished in a first-place tie in the Big Ten in 1935, but a drought ensued.

The Badgers placed a woeful ninth in the conference in 1940 and their overall record of 5-15 repre-

sented a low point in the school's proud basketball history. The addition of sophomores Johnny Kotz and Fred Rehm to the varsity offered hope, though, as Foster assembled his team for the 1941 season. But it wasn't long before Wisconsin followers were led to expect the worst.

In their first conference game, at Minnesota, the Badgers failed to make a single field goal in the second half and suffered a dismal defeat.

"We were just awful," said Gene Englund, the senior center. Foster did not dispute the claim.

But Foster continued to preach his system, the one handed down by Meanwell. The coach was convinced he had the personnel to be successful once the players were able to work in unison. Although prominent programs at Purdue and Indiana were championing the radical new fast break, Wisconsin traditionally employed a set offense.

"We have stuck to our guns and we still feel that we are stressing the short-pass game and using a defense similar to the one Wisconsin teams have

Badgers (left to right) Ted Strain, Gene Englund, Charles Epperson, John Kotz and Fred Rehm wear championship smiles after defeating Washington State.

used for several years," Foster explained. "In lean years our critics point out that the set-play days are over and that we must change our offense to the racehorse game. But these fans are all for this type of play when a winning team uses it. In the same vein, when we lose, the defense is no good, but is a dandy when we win. We know that this is just human nature, but it is a very interesting fact nevertheless."

What the fans found more interesting was the team's reaction to the Minnesota game. Instead of collapsing, the Badgers revived.

"It woke us up," Englund said.

In short order, Wisconsin began to gain attention throughout the Big Ten, sometimes through its play, sometimes through its antics. At Purdue, forward Charlie Epperson decided he had taken just about enough abuse. So, during a stoppage in play late in the game, he stood in the middle of the court and thumbed his nose at the crowd. He drew a technical foul, but apparently it was worth it. In addition to the satisfaction he derived from the gesture, the Badgers won the game.

The opponent the Badgers pointed for was Indiana. The Hoosiers had won the national championship the previous year and still were regarded as the class of the conference. Indiana's only two defeats of the '41 season had been to Southern California on a West Coast swing and at Purdue. And the Hoosiers hadn't lost a game in Bloomington in three years.

Wisconsin won handily, 38-30, on Indiana's home court, holding the Hoosiers to their lowest point total of the season and justifying Foster's faith in Meanwell's tactics. The Badgers did not hold the ball, but instead repeatedly ran a series of set plays until a man popped open.

"We'd make 10-12 passes before we'd shoot," Kotz said. Yet, Wisconsin led the Big Ten in total points that season.

Remarkably, after losing their first game in such desultory fashion, the Badgers swept undefeated through the rest of the conference schedule. Their first Big Ten title in six years qualified them for a berth in the third NCAA Tournament, one that would establish a precedent of sorts.

Hoping to increase profits, the NCAA considered several sites for the Eastern playoffs and settled upon Madison. It so happened that the Badgers had one of the largest on-campus arenas in the nation and often filled it to its capacity of 13,000.

It was difficult to say what the home-court advantage was worth because Wisconsin had such a difficult time against Dartmouth and Pittsburgh. The Badgers trailed both teams at halftime and had to rally in the final minute to subdue Dartmouth, 51-50. The Badgers earned the right to participate in the NCAA championship game by overcoming Pittsburgh, 36-30.

To find itself in such a position was a most pleasant surprise for Wisconsin. At the start of the year, the Badgers hadn't looked beyond the Big Ten season. But now they were only one victory from a national championship. Since Ohio State had been a finalist in the first tournament and Indiana had won the NCAA title the previous year, there was no shortage of confidence in Madison.

"We thought the Big Ten had the best basketball," Kotz said.

Washington State, featuring massive 6-foot-8 center Paul Lindeman, had won the Western playoffs in convincing fashion by defeating Creighton, 48-39, and Arkansas, 64-53, in Kansas City. Since the championship game also would be played in the Missouri city, the Cougars waited around for the better part of a week.

"I think it hurt them," Kotz said.

The Badgers arrived by train on the day before the final. They came with a plan for bottling up the 230-pound Lindeman and slowing Washington State's fast-paced attack. Although scouting was not widely practiced in 1941, Wisconsin assistant coach Fritz Wegner had attended the Western playoffs and mapped out a strategy.

The standard defense practiced at Wisconsin was the shifting man-for-man passed down from Doc Meanwell. It called for extensive communication among players on the court.

"We feel that using the voice on defense is all-important and, aside from calling shifts, we yell at shooters," Foster said. "We have earned the name of having the loudest defense in the country."

In addition to taunting the opposition, the Badgers planned to position the 6-4 Englund behind Lindeman and drop back a guard to help out at all times.

One order of business for the Wisconsin team after checking into the President Hotel was a tour of a sporting goods factory. Among the items on display was the outstanding-player award for the championship game.

"The year before," Kotz said, "they had given out a trophy about four feet high. This time they offered a medal about as big as a silver dollar. I

Wisconsin's Charles Epperson (38) goes high for a shot despite the defensive effort of Washington State's Kirk Gebert (8) in the 1941 final.

thought, 'If I play well tomorrow night, I might win that.'"

Many of the 7,219 fans in attendance at Municipal Auditorium had taken the train down from Madison. Although that figure was little more than half of what the Badgers had drawn for the Eastern final, the sense of a hometown celebration was perpetuated by a reunion in Kansas City of the 1916 Wisconsin team, the finest in Doc Meanwell's tenure.

For the first time in the tournament, Wisconsin started fast. Two baskets by Rehm and another by Englund provided the Badgers with a 6-0 lead. Washington State came back to tie at 6-6 and 8-8, then forged ahead, 12-9. A nine-minute scoreless streak by the Cougars enabled Wisconsin to regain the lead at 17-12. Washington State's Kirk Gebert scored the next five points, but Wisconsin accounted for the last four points of the half and seized a 21-17 lead.

The Badgers' defense had completely shut off the West Coast team's inside game. Lindeman, in Englund's words, "didn't get to see the ball much." That left the Washington State offense in Gebert's hands.

The guard shot the Cougars into a tie at 24-24 after four minutes of the second half. But Wisconsin scored the next six points and was never headed.

Washington State drew within two points at 34-32 late in the game, but Kotz's basket sealed the 39-34 victory. Kotz finished with 12 points, one fewer than Englund, who limited Lindeman to three free throws for the entire game. Although Gebert led all scorers with 21 points, the "most valuable" medal was awarded to the 6-3 Kotz for his overall play.

A huge crowd was at the station in Madison to meet the returning heroes. Unaware of plans for a parade, Englund had gotten off in his hometown of Kenosha to report to his draft board. Kotz was amazed—and fearful—at the greeting.

"They put us on a fire wagon," he said. "There were thousands of people. I jumped off because I thought we were going to be mobbed to death."

It's a problem other Wisconsin teams have not encountered. The Badgers have won just one Big Ten crown, in 1947, since their national championship season. And, in '47, Wisconsin lost in the first round of the NCAA Tournament.

The triumphant Badgers take Coach Bud Foster on a joy ride after their victory over Washington State.

1941 Tournament Results	
First Round	**Semifinals**
Wisconsin 51, Dartmouth 50	Wisconsin 36, Pittsburgh 30
Pittsburgh 26, North Carolina 20	Washington State 64, Arkansas 53
Washington St. 48, Creighton 39	**Championship**
Arkansas 52, Wyoming 40	Wisconsin 39, Washington State 34
Regional Third Place	
Dartmouth 60, North Carolina 59	
Creighton 45, Wyoming 44	

STATISTICS

1941 WISCONSIN

Head Coach—Harold (Bud) Foster   Final Record—20-3

Player	Pos.	Hgt.	Wgt.	Cl.	G	FG	FGA	Pct.	FT.	FTA	Pct.	Reb.	Pts.	Avg.
Gene Englund	C	6-4	193	Sr.	23	103	...	.....	98	...	.....	...	304	13.2
John Kotz	F	6-3	200	So.	23	80	...	.....	47	...	.....	...	207	9.0
Theodore Strain	G	5-11	158	Sr.	23	38	...	.....	35	...	.....	...	111	4.8
Charlie Epperson	F	6-1	192	Jr.	22	37	...	.....	25	...	.....	...	99	4.5
Frederick Rehm	G	6-2	175	So.	21	22	...	.....	33	...	.....	...	77	3.7
Robert Alwin	G	5-10	155	Jr.	21	19	...	.....	19	...	.....	...	57	2.7
Harlo Scott	C-F	6-3	185	Jr.	13	10	...	.....	9	...	.....	...	29	2.2
Donald Timmerman	C	6-10	209	Sr.	22	14	...	.....	13	...	.....	...	41	1.9
Raymond Lenheiser	F	6-1	165	So.	13	9	...	.....	6	...	.....	...	24	1.8
Warren Schrage	F	6-4	180	Jr.	12	8	...	.....	2	...	.....	...	18	1.5
Edward Scheiwe	G	5-11	168	Jr.	17	10	...	.....	4	...	.....	...	24	1.4
Theodore Deppe	F	6-1	193	So.	3	2	...	.....	0	...	.....	...	4	1.3
Frank Siewert	G	5-11	170	So.	1	0	...	.....	1	...	.....	...	1	1.0
Robert Roth	G	5-10	175	So.	7	2	...	.....	2	...	.....	...	6	0.9
Robert Sullivan	F	6-1	176	So.	5	1	...	.....	0	...	.....	...	2	0.4
John Lynch	G	6-1	165	Jr.	5	0	...	.....	0	...	.....	...	0	0.0
George Affeldt	F	5-11	165	So.	1	0	...	.....	0	...	.....	...	0	0.0
Edward Downs	F	5-9	153	So.	1	0	...	.....	0	...	.....	...	0	0.0
Bill Mayer	...	...	...	...	1	0	...	.....	0	...	.....	...	0	0.0
Harry Stoll	...	...	...	...	1	0	...	.....	0	...	.....	...	0	0.0
Art Wellman	...	...	...	...	1	0	...	.....	0	...	.....	...	0	0.0
Wisconsin					23	355	...	.....	294	...	.....	...	1004	43.7
Opponents					23	310	...	.....	215	...	.....	...	835	36.3

1941 WASHINGTON STATE

Head Coach—Jack Friel   Final Record—26-6

Player	Pos.	Hgt.	Wgt.	Cl.	G	FG	FGA	Pct.	FT.	FTA	Pct.	Reb.	Pts.	Avg.
Paul Lindeman	C	6-8	230	Sr.	32	132	...	.....	62	111	.559	...	326	10.2
Ray Sundquist	G	6-1	...	Sr.	32	85	...	.....	48	85	.565	...	218	6.8
Kirk Gebert	G	5-9	165	Jr.	27	83	...	.....	12	24	.500	...	178	6.6
Vern Butts	F	6-2	...	Sr.	29	70	...	.....	25	44	.568	...	165	5.7
Dale Gentry	F-C	6-3	...	Sr.	28	60	...	.....	28	49	.571	...	148	5.3
Marv Gilberg	F	6-2	185	So.	31	63	...	.....	22	35	.629	...	148	4.8
Jim Zimmerman	F-C	6-2	185	Sr.	32	38	...	.....	13	27	.481	...	89	2.8
John Hooper	F	6-2	190	Jr.	28	26	...	.....	8	15	.533	...	60	2.1
Owen Hunt	G	6-1	165	So.	32	26	...	.....	5	20	.250	...	57	1.8
Frank Adkkins	G	5-10	...	Jr.	25	18	...	.....	7	19	.368	...	43	1.7
Elvin Bergquist	G	6-2	...	Jr.	4	1	...	.....	3	3	1.000	...	5	1.3
John Harrington	.	...	...	.	3	2	...	.....	0	3	.000	...	4	1.3
Chuck Dosskey	G	6-0	...	Jr.	11	5	...	.....	2	4	.500	...	12	1.1
Don Mason	...	...	...	...	2	1	...	.....	0	1	.000	...	2	1.0
Phil Mahan	G	5-11	150	So.	29	9	...	.....	6	9	.667	...	24	0.8
Jack Kelleher	G	6-0	...	So.	4	0	...	.....	0	0	.000	...	0	0.0
Washington State					32	619	...	.....	241	449	.537	...	1479	46.2
Opponents					32	...	...	.....	...	...	.....	...	1235	38.6

1941 PITTSBURGH

Head Coach—H.C. (Doc) Carlson   Final Record—13-6

(Full-season statistics unavailable; individual statistics are for NCAA tourney.)

Player	Pos.	Hgt.	Wgt.	Cl.	G	FG	FGA	Pct.	FT.	FTA	Pct.	Reb.	Pts.	Avg.
Eddie Straloski	F	...	...	Sr.	2	9	...	.....	0	3	.000	...	18	9.0
George Kocheran	F	...	...	Sr.	2	3	...	.....	4	4	1.000	...	10	5.0
Tay Malarkey	G	...	...	So.	2	4	...	.....	2	2	1.000	...	10	5.0
Mel Port	C	...	...	Sr.	2	1	...	.....	6	10	.600	...	8	4.0
Sam Milanovich	G	...	...	Sr.	2	3	...	.....	1	1	1.000	...	7	3.5
Larry Paffrath	G-C	...	...	Jr.	2	1	...	.....	1	1	1.000	...	3	1.5
Jimmy Klein	G	...	...	Sr.	1	0	...	.....	0	0	.000	...	0	0.0
John Swacus	F	...	...	So.	1	0	...	.....	0	0	.000	...	0	0.0
James Egan	F	...	...	Jr.	1	0	...	.....	0	0	.000	...	0	0.0
Lefty Ziolkowski	G	...	...	Sr.	1	0	...	.....	0	0	.000	...	0	0.0
Robert Artman	G	...	...	So.	1	0	...	.....	0	0	.000	...	0	0.0
...... Mastin	...	...	...	...									..	...
Paul Lohmeyer	...	...	...	So.									..	...
... Dolphi	...	...	...	...									..	...
... Spartz	...	...	...	...									..	...
... Silverman	...	...	...	...									..	...
*Pittsburgh					19	...	..	.....	...	..	.....	...	754	39.7
*Opponents					19	...	..	.....	...	..	.....	...	692	36.4

*Full season.

1941 ARKANSAS

Head Coach—Glen Rose   Final Record—20-3

(Full-season statistics unavailable; individual statistics are for NCAA tourney.)

Player	Pos.	Hgt.	Wgt.	Cl.	G	FG	FGA	Pct.	FT.	FTA	Pct.	Reb.	Pts.	Avg.
John Adams	F	6-4	180	Sr.	2	21	...	.....	6	9	.667	...	48	24.0
R. C. Pitts	G	...	...	Jr.	2	9	...	.....	2	4	.500	...	20	10.0
Gordon Carpenter	F	...	...	So.	2	5	...	.....	3	6	.500	...	13	6.5
John Freiberger	C	...	...	Sr.	2	3	...	.....	6	10	.600	...	12	6.0
Howard Hickey	G	...	...	Sr.	2	2	...	.....	2	5	.400	...	6	3.0
O'Neal Adams	G	...	...	Jr.	2	2	...	.....	2	5	.400	...	6	3.0
Nobel Robbins	G	...	...	...	1	0	...	.....	0	1	.000	...	0	0.0
Clayton Wynne	G	...	...	So.	2	0	...	.....	0	1	.000	...	0	0.0
...... Mitchell	...	...	...	...									..	...
...... Homes	...	...	...	...									..	...
...... Reyenga	...	...	...	...									..	...
...... McCormick	...	...	...	...									..	...
*Arkansas					23	...	..	.....	...	..	.....	...	1184	51.5
*Opponents					23	...	..	.....	...	..	.....	...	830	36.1

*Full season.

(John Adams led the Southwest Conference in scoring with 206 points in 12 games for a 17.2 average.)

1941 FINAL FOUR

Semifinals
At Madison, Wis.

Wisconsin	fg	ft	fta	pf	tp
Kotz	3	4	4	1	10
Scott	0	0	0	0	0
Epperson	2	3	4	0	7
Englund	2	7	8	4	11
Schrage	0	0	0	0	0
Timmerman	0	0	1	0	0
Strain	2	0	2	3	4
Alwin	0	0	0	0	0
Rehm	1	2	2	0	4
Scheiwe	0	0	0	0	0
Totals	10	16	21	8	36

Pittsburgh	fg	ft	fta	pf	tp
Straloski	6	0	1	4	12
Swacus	0	0	0	0	0
Egan	0	0	0	0	0
Kocheran	1	2	2	0	4
Port	1	2	3	4	4
Paffrath	1	1	1	1	3
Milanovich	2	0	0	3	4
Ziolkowski	0	0	0	2	0
Artman	0	0	0	1	0
Klein	0	0	0	1	0
Malarkey	1	1	1	3	3
Totals	12	6	8	18	30

Halftime: Pittsburgh 18-14. Officials: Boyle and Chest.

At Kansas City

Washington State	fg	ft	fta	pf	tp
Gentry	4	1	2	2	9
Butts	5	1	1	1	11
Gilberg	3	0	3	4	6
Zimmerman	0	0	0	2	0
Lindeman	4	6	9	2	14
Gebert	5	2	2	1	12
Sundquist	2	2	2	2	6
Hunt	1	0	0	3	2
Adkkins	0	0	0	0	0
Hooper	2	0	0	4	4
Totals	26	12	19	21	64

Arkansas	fg	ft	fta	pf	tp
J. Adams	10	2	5	1	22
Carpenter	2	1	3	2	5
Freiberger	1	3	5	3	5
Pitts	5	2	4	2	12
Robbins	0	0	1	3	0
Hickey	1	1	2	2	3
Wynne	0	0	1	2	0
O. Adams	2	2	2	3	6
Totals	21	11	23	18	53

Halftime: Washington State 37-25. Technical foul: Carpenter. Officials: Herigstad and O'Sullivan.

Championship
March 29
At Kansas City

Wisconsin	fg	ft	fta	pf	tp
Epperson	2	0	0	3	4
Schrage	0	0	0	1	0
Kotz	5	3	3	2	12
Englund	5	3	4	2	13
Timmerman	1	0	0	1	2
Rehm	2	0	1	2	4
Strain	0	2	2	1	2
Alwin	1	0	0	0	2
Totals	16	7	10	12	39

Washington State	fg	ft	fta	pf	tp
Gentry	0	1	2	1	1
Gilberg	1	0	2	1	2
Butts	1	1	1	1	3
Lindeman	0	3	4	1	3
Zimmerman	0	0	0	0	0
Gebert	10	1	2	1	21
Hunt	0	0	0	0	0
Sundquist	2	0	1	3	4
Hooper	0	0	0	0	0
Totals	14	6	12	8	34

Halftime: Wisconsin 21-17. Officials: Haarlow and Cameron.

1942 Stanford Wins The Big One

The top five players for the 1942 Stanford Indians of Coach Everett Dean (right) were (left to right) Bill Cowden, Howie Dallmar, Ed Voss, Jim Pollard and Don Burness.

Of all the players and teams for whom the NCAA Tournament was realized too late, none had greater cause for disappointment than Hank Luisetti and Stanford.

It was Luisetti, a Stanford All-America, who revolutionized the game in December 1936 when he introduced his running one-handed shot to the East Coast in a game against Long Island University at Madison Square Garden. Although Stanford was selected the best team in the country (by the Helms Athletic Foundation, among others), the Luisetti-era Indians never had the opportunity to play for a true national championship.

Starting in the days of the center jump after each basket, Luisetti helped drag the sport into a new era with his shooting, ballhandling, quickness and ability to hang in midair. It wasn't until the arrival of the giants a decade later that anyone had an effect on basketball as did Luisetti, who finished his collegiate career in 1938. Contemporaries said he was 20 years ahead of his time. He was at least one year early in terms of the NCAA Tournament.

Luisetti led Stanford to three consecutive Pacific Coast Conference championships and to a 46-5 record in his final two seasons. But it wasn't until the year after his graduation that the first NCAA Tournament was staged. Ironically, the first NCAA titlist was an Oregon team whom Luisetti's Stanford club had beaten in his last college game.

Although Luisetti would never get the chance to compete in the national event, Stanford would. But only once. It happened in 1942, when the Indians won a best-of-three playoff series with Oregon State for the conference championship. They were selected to compete in the Western playoffs at Kansas City, along with Rice, Kansas and a Colorado team that had lost only once, and then by a single point in its next-to-last regular-season game.

Stanford was a big team, with all its starting players 6-foot-3 or taller. Yet the Indians, utilizing the one-handed shot that Luisetti had popularized, liked to run. Their acknowledged star was Jim Pollard, who later would become a professional standout with the Minneapolis Lakers.

Remarkably, three Stanford starters—co-captains Don Burness and Bill Cowden and sophomore Howie Dallmar—had attended the same high school in San Francisco. It wasn't by some master plan they were attending the same college in nearby Palo Alto.

"We were lucky," Dallmar said, "and so was the coach."

The coach was Everett Dean, who had been Indiana's first All-America player as well as a successful coach at his alma mater before heading west. Dean had inherited an excellent pool of local talent at Stanford. Pollard hailed from Oakland and center Ed Voss from nearby Piedmont. In fact, the Indians' first eight players all were from the San Francisco Bay Area.

With Burness troubled by an ankle injury, the scoring load in the Western playoffs fell heavily on Pollard. He responded with a spectacular 26-point performance in a 53-47 victory over Rice and a 17-point effort in Stanford's 46-35 triumph over Colorado, which had edged Kansas, 46-44. Since the national championship game was scheduled to be held in the same Municipal Auditorium the following week, the Indians remained in Kansas City, accepting invitations to lunch at local country clubs and to visit defense plants.

A proctor had accompanied the team on the train and some players chose to take examinations while they were in the Midwest.

Stanford's opponent had been decided in the Eastern playoffs at the Tulane gymnasium in New Orleans. It was there that Dartmouth, which had to defeat Princeton in a special playoff for the Eastern Intercollegiate League title to qualify for the tournament, topped Penn State, 44-39, and ripped Kentucky, 47-28. Kentucky had scored an upset of its own in an opening-round game by beating Big Ten Conference champion Illinois, 46-44.

The result of the jousting was a championship matchup that, for the first time, pitted teams from the most distant sections of the nation. It also ensured a contest between schools with the same nickname, Indians. Additionally, Dartmouth Coach Ozzie Cowles had played under Dean during the older man's first year in coaching at Carleton College in Minnesota.

Although Stanford, 26-4 at this juncture, was considered the favorite on the basis of its overall size and speed, its chances were jeopardized when Pollard was stricken with the flu the day before the

Jim Pollard, the leading scorer for the 1942 Stanford Indians, was forced to the sideline for the championship game by a flu bug.

title game. In a weakened condition and suffering from high temperature, all he could do for his teammates was sit on the bench in civilian clothes and cheer.

Because of the manpower shortage, Burness dressed for the first time in the tournament and hobbled onto the court for the opening tip. But his presence was mostly symbolic and he was replaced without scoring a point, leaving the California team without two regulars for the most important game of the season.

The situation would have stopped a lesser team. It did not stop Stanford. Jack Dana had performed well in Burness' absence during the Western com-

Hank Luisetti, the Stanford star who revolutionized basketball with his running one-handed shot, regrettably predated the NCAA Tournament.

petition and he did even better in the title game. And Stanford received additional help from substitute Freddie Linari.

Dartmouth's offense was built around center Jim Olsen and 6-foot forward George Munroe, the smallest starter in the game. Olsen was neutralized by Stanford's superior size, but Munroe gave the West Coast Indians fits with his shooting. It was his one-hander that accounted for the game's first basket. Dana matched it, then Munroe scored again.

After Dallmar tied the score at 4-4, Munroe led Dartmouth on an 8-2 run as it opened a 12-6 lead. A field goal by Voss and a fast-break basket by Cowden cut the deficit to two points and the teams traded baskets until the final minutes of the first half. It was then that Dallmar drove for the tying basket. Dana's layup in the waning seconds of the half boosted Stanford into its first lead, 24-22.

The score was tied at 26-26 four minutes into the second half when the 6-4 Dallmar dribbled the length of the court for a basket. Then Linari, who had played sparingly in both games of the Western playoffs, scored his first two points of the tournament. It lit a spark and Stanford raced ahead. Despite the absence of Pollard and Burness, the Pacific entry won comfortably, 53-38.

Dana, who had scored seven points against Colorado in the Western final, doubled that total against Dartmouth. Linari added three baskets for six points. Voss contributed 13 points. But the high scorer in the game was Dallmar, who had 15 points and played an outstanding floor game.

Dallmar was pleasantly surprised when he was presented with the outstanding-player honor.

"If Pollard hadn't been sick," Dallmar said, "he would have won it." Perhaps. And if Luisetti had been allowed to compete, perhaps he would have earned the award.

But it didn't work out that way. Luisetti never got to play in the NCAA Tournament and Pollard never got to play in the championship game. Dallmar got to do both and he responded with a great performance, one that grew in significance over the years.

For never again in the first 49 years of the NCAA Tournament did a Stanford team receive an invitation. Not under Dean, who coached through 1951. Not under his successor, Robert Burnett, who lasted three seasons. Not under Dallmar, who returned to his alma mater and coached the Indians for 21 years. And not under any of Dallmar's successors.

Dallmar, who played professional basketball with the Philadelphia Warriors and then coached Pennsylvania in the collegiate ranks, guided Stanford to 264 victories. His tenure, unfortunately, corresponded roughly with that of John Wooden of conference rival UCLA.

"We had teams when I was coaching that certainly deserved to be in the NCAA," he said, "but in those days only one team per conference could go, and we were all playing for second place behind UCLA. I feel sorry for those players from those teams who never got the chance."

Only one Stanford team ever made it. It remains the lone school to win the national title in its only NCAA Tournament appearance.

1942 Tournament Results	
First Round	**Semifinals**
Dartmouth 44, Penn State 39	Dartmouth 47, Kentucky 28
Kentucky 46, Illinois 44	Stanford 46, Colorado 35
Stanford 53, Rice 47	**Championship**
Colorado 46, Kansas 44	Stanford 53, Dartmouth 38
Regional Third Place	
Penn State 41, Illinois 34	
Kansas 55, Rice 53	

STATISTICS

1942 STANFORD

Head Coach—Everett Dean   Final Record—28-4

(Full-season statistics unavailable; individual statistics are for Pacific Coast Conference playoff and NCAA Tournament.)

Player	Pos.	Hgt.	Wgt.	Cl.	G	FG	FGA	Pct.	FT.	FTA	Pct.	Reb.	Pts.	Avg.
Jim Pollard	F	6-5	185	Jr.	5	36	...	...	8	14	.571	...	80	16.0
Ed Voss	C	6-6	215	Jr.	6	25	...	...	14	20	.700	...	64	10.7
Howie Dallmar	G	6-4	200	So.	6	16	...	...	9	11	.818	...	41	6.8
Bill Cowden	G	6-4	195	Sr.	6	12	...	...	12	22	.545	...	36	6.0
Jack Dana	F	6-4	187	Jr.	6	17	...	...	2	7	.286	...	36	6.0
Freddie Linari	F	5-9	147	Jr.	5	4	...	...	0	0	.000	...	8	1.6
Don Burness	F	6-3	190	Sr.	3	0	...	...	1	1	1.000	...	1	0.3
Fred Oliver	G	6-3	184	So.	3	0	...	...	0	0	.000	...	0	0.0
John Eikelman	C	6-3	190	So.	3	0	...	...	0	0	.000	...	0	0.0
Morris Madden	C	6-3	184	So.	2	0	...	...	0	0	.000	...	0	0.0
Leo McCaffrey	G	6-2	190	Jr.	6	0	...	...	0	0	.000	...	0	0.0
*Stanford					32	...	...	...	...	...	...	...	1273	39.8
*Opponents					32	...	...	...	...	...	...	...	1105	34.5

*Full season.

Other members of squad: Bill Hooper, G. 6-0, 160, So.; Robert Halstead, G, 6-4, 171, So.; Thomas Fuller, F, 6-2, 190, Jr.; John Leddy, 6-2, 175, So.; Richard McDonough, C, 6-2; 178, So.; Robert Wreisner, 6-4, 195, So.; Arthur Dee, Harold Getz, Jeremy Lamb, Ross Meyer, Richard Middleton, Charles Smith, Richard West and Paul Wilson.

1942 DARTMOUTH

Head Coach—Osborne (Ozzie) Cowles   Final Record—22-4

Player	Pos.	Hgt.	Wgt.	Cl.	G	FG	FGA	Pct.	FT.	FTA	Pct.	Reb.	Pts.	Avg.
George Munroe	F	6-0	160	Jr.	25	152	...	...	71	87	.816	...	375	15.0
Jim Olsen	C	...	...	Jr.	26	151	...	...	62	92	.674	...	364	14.0
Robert Myers	F	...	...	So.	26	103	...	...	40	62	.645	...	246	9.5
Charles Pearson	G	...	...	Sr.	26	42	...	...	39	53	.736	...	123	4.7
Stanley Skaug	G	...	...	Jr.	26	50	...	...	18	30	.600	...	118	4.5
Connor Shaw Jr.	F-C	...	...	Jr.	22	22	...	...	7	14	.500	...	51	2.3
William Parmer	G	...	...	Sr.	26	25	...	...	9	17	.529	...	59	2.3
Gordon McKernan	F	...	...	So.	16	6	...	...	10	11	.909	...	22	1.4
George Galbraith Jr.	F	...	...	So.	12	5	...	...	4	8	.500	...	14	1.2
James Briggs	G	...	...	So.	21	7	...	...	4	9	.444	...	18	0.9
Henry Pogue	F	...	...	Sr.	18	2	...	...	2	5	.400	...	6	0.3
Robert Ehringer	G	...	...	Jr.	9	0	...	...	0	1	.000	...	0	0.0
Others													13	
Dartmouth					26	...	...	...	...	...	...	...	1409	54.2
Opponents					26	...	...	...	...	...	...	...	1114	42.8

1942 COLORADO

Head Coach—Forrest (Frosty) Cox   Final Record—16-2

(Full-season statistics unavailable; individual statistics are for NCAA tourney.)

Player	Pos.	Hgt.	Wgt.	Cl.	G	FG	FGA	Pct.	FT.	FTA	Pct.	Reb.	Pts.	Avg.
Leason McCloud	F	6-1	...	Sr.	2	9	...	...	4	6	.667	..	22	11.0
Bob Doll	C	6-5	...	Sr.	2	5	...	...	7	7	1.000	..	17	8.5
George Hamburg	G	6-3	...	Sr.	2	7	...	...	3	6	.500	..	17	8.5
Bob Kirchner	F	6-3	...	Jr.	2	5	...	...	1	1	1.000	..	11	5.5
Don Putman	G-F	5-10	...	So.	2	3	...	...	0	0	.000	..	6	3.0
Horace Huggins	C-F	6-4	...	So.	2	2	...	...	1	1	1.000	..	5	2.5
Heath Nuckolls	F-G	5-11	...	...	2	1	...	...	1	2	.500	..	3	1.5
Barney Oldham	G	5-8	...	Jr.	...	...	...	...	...	...	...	..	...	...
Lee Robbins	F	6-2	...	So.	...	...	...	...	...	...	...	..	...	...
Jack Stirling	F	6-0	...	...	...	...	...	...	...	...	...	..	...	...
Bill Milliken	F	6-2	...	...	...	...	...	...	...	...	...	..	...	...
Lloyd Norman	F	...	...	...	...	...	...	...	...	...	...	..	...	...
Paaul Schmidt	G	6-1	...	Sr.	...	...	...	...	...	...	...	..	...	...
Reed Hanson	F	6-2	...	Jr.	...	...	...	...	...	...	...	..	...	...
Martin Trotsky	G	5-10	...	Sr.	...	...	...	...	...	...	...	..	...	...
*Colorado					18	...	...	...	...	...	...	..	935	51.9
*Opponents					18	...	...	...	...	...	...	..	683	37.9

*Full season.

1942 KENTUCKY

Head Coach—Adolph Rupp   Final Record—19-6

Player	Pos.	Hgt.	Wgt.	Cl.	G	FG	FGA	Pct.	FT.	FTA	Pct.	Reb.	Pts.	Avg.
Marvin Akers	G	6-2	190	Jr.	25	87	..	...	17	...	...	...	191	7.6
Mel Brewer	C	6-5	194	Jr.	25	69	...	...	37	...	...	...	175	7.0
Milt Ticco	F	6-2½	190	Jr.	25	57	...	...	14	...	...	...	128	5.1
Ken England	G	6-1	180	Jr.	24	39	...	...	39	...	...	...	117	4.9
Ermal Allen	F	5-11	160	Sr.	25	49	...	...	24	...	...	...	122	4.9
Carl Staker	G	6-2½	193	Jr.	25	38	...	...	35	...	...	...	111	4.4
Jim King	C	6-3	180	Sr.	25	32	...	...	31	...	...	...	95	3.8
Waller White	F	6-1	160	Sr.	25	37	...	...	18	...	...	...	92	3.7
Vincent Splane	G	6-1	180	So.	11	13	...	...	13	...	...	...	39	3.5
Frank Etscorn	F	6-1	178	Jr.	5	6	...	...	0	...	...	...	12	2.4
Adrian Back	G	6-0	167	So.	12	9	...	...	4	...	...	...	22	1.8
Jim Mathewson	G	6-2	170	Jr.	2	2	...	...	0	...	...	...	4	2.0
Ed Lander	C	6-3	185	So.	9	7	...	...	2	...	...	...	16	1.8
Lloyd Ramsey	F	6-2	177	Jr.	18	6	...	...	14	...	...	...	26	1.4
Louis Robertson	G	5-11	165	So.	2	1	...	...	0	...	...	...	2	1.0
Bruce Boehler	G	5-11	170	So.	18	4	...	...	1	...	...	...	9	0.5
Kentucky					25	456	...	...	249	...	...	...	1161	46.4
Opponents					25	...	...	...	...	...	...	...	928	37.1

1942 FINAL FOUR

Semifinals
At New Orleans

Dartmouth	fg	ft	fta	pf	tp
Myers	4	1	2	2	9
Pogue	0	0	0	0	0
Munroe	9	2	4	2	20
Briggs	0	0	0	0	0
Olsen	5	1	3	2	11
Shaw	1	0	0	0	2
Pearson	0	3	3	1	3
Parmer	0	0	1	2	0
Skaug	1	0	1	4	2
McKernan	0	0	0	0	0
Totals	20	7	14	13	47

Kentucky	fg	ft	fta	pf	tp
White	0	0	0	2	0
Ramsey	0	0	0	0	0
Allen	2	2	4	2	6
Ticco	0	1	1	1	1
Brewer	1	2	4	1	4
King	1	2	2	0	4
Staker	0	0	0	4	0
England	1	0	0	1	2
Akers	5	1	2	3	11
Totals	10	8	13	14	28

Halftime: Dartmouth 23-13. Officials: Snyder and Adams.

At Kansas City

Stanford	fg	ft	fta	pf	tp
Dana	3	1	2	1	7
Pollard	8	1	1	2	17
Madden	0	0	0	0	0
Voss	4	2	5	3	10
Linari	0	0	0	0	0
Eikelman	0	0	0	1	0
Cowden	2	3	5	2	7
McCaffrey	0	0	0	0	0
Dallmar	2	1	1	0	5
Oliver	0	0	0	0	0
Totals	19	8	14	9	46

Colorado	fg	ft	fta	pf	tp
McCloud	1	1	2	2	3
Huggins	0	0	0	0	0
Nuckolls	0	0	1	3	0
Putman	3	0	0	1	6
Doll	3	5	5	3	11
Hamburg	3	2	2	2	8
Kirchner	3	1	1	0	7
Totals	13	9	11	11	35

Halftime: Stanford 22-15. Officials: Curtis and House.

Championship
March 28
At Kansas City

Stanford	fg	ft	fta	pf	tp
Dana	7	0	0	0	14
Eikelman	0	0	0	0	0
Burness	0	0	0	0	0
Linari	3	0	0	0	6
Voss	6	1	1	2	13
Madden	0	0	0	0	0
Cowden	2	1	2	3	5
McCaffrey	0	0	0	0	0
Dallmar	6	3	5	0	15
Oliver	0	0	0	0	0
Totals	24	5	8	5	53

Dartmouth	fg	ft	fta	pf	tp
Myers	4	0	1	1	8
Parmer	1	0	0	0	2
Munroe	5	2	2	1	12
Shaw	0	0	0	0	0
Olsen	4	0	0	0	8
Pogue	0	0	0	0	0
Pearson	2	2	2	3	6
McKernan	0	0	0	0	0
Skaug	1	0	0	2	2
Briggs	0	0	0	0	0
Totals	17	4	5	7	38

Halftime: Stanford 24-22. Officials: Curtis and Adams.

1943 Cowboys Rope An NCAA Title

To those who believed civilization ended at the Hudson River, Wyoming was the basketball equivalent of Buffalo Bill's Wild West Show, which had filled Madison Square Garden decades earlier. Not only did the Wyoming team hail from what New Yorkers considered the American frontier, but its nickname also was the Cowboys. Ned Irish, the brilliant sports promoter, sought only to enhance public perception.

This would be the first NCAA championship game played in New York and Irish worked hard to build the attraction, held on the night following the final of his own successful creation, the National Invitation Tournament. When the Wyoming party arrived in New York fresh from its victory in the Western playoffs at Kansas City, Irish accorded the players a heroes' welcome. He also made certain they were outfitted with ten-gallon hats and wore them around town.

Although they were not strangers to New York, having played several games in the city during a Christmas excursion three months earlier, the Cowboys fit comfortably into the role of foreign dignitaries. In truth, all the regulars except center Milo Komenich were natives of Wyoming and several, including star playmaker Kenny Sailors, had been raised on ranches. They were accustomed to hats and cowboys boots, and if that's what the Easterners wanted to see, that's the picture they would present.

On the court, the Cowboys also offered a style of play different from that practiced in the East. They were more inclined to run. They all shot the ball one-handed. And Sailors even modeled a pioneer version of a jump shot, holding the ball above his head when he launched one from the outside.

Under Coach Everett Shelton, Wyoming had played a rigorous schedule. In addition to competing in the Mountain States Conference, the Cowboys had twice defeated the Phillips 66ers, who went on to win the Amateur Athletic Union national championship. They had won 27 of 29 games before entraining for Kansas City.

There, in the Western playoffs, the Cowboys faced their sternest tests of the season. After rallying to beat Oklahoma, 53-50, in the opening round, Wyoming found itself trailing a resourceful Texas team in the final. The Longhorns, who had scored a dramatic 59-55 victory over Washington in their first game, roared to a 26-13 lead in the first 10 minutes against Wyoming. In that stretch, forward John Hargis personally equaled the Cowboys' point total on the way to a 29-point performance.

Wyoming did cut the deficit to 33-27 by halftime, but Shelton still was upset with his team's play.

"Well, you guys don't really need me around," he told the Cowboys during intermission. "I'll go back to the hotel and start packing. You take care of the game."

It was a psychological spur that had the desired effect. Wyoming overtook Texas seven minutes into the second half, then sealed the 58-54 triumph after Hargis fouled out late in the game. The Cowboys subsequently boarded a New York-bound train for the second time that season.

Their opponent in the national championship game would be Georgetown, which had survived the Eastern playoffs staged at Madison Square Garden. The Hoyas had overwhelmed hometown favorite New York University, 55-36, in the first round and scored an impressive 53-49 victory over DePaul to qualify for the NCAA title game. DePaul, featuring freshman giant George Mikan and concluding its first year under Coach Ray Meyer, had been selected to represent District 4 when Big Ten Conference champion Illinois, whose "Whiz Kids" were the talk of the Midwest, decided to pass up postseason competition.

The Blue Demons made the best of their opportunity, demoralizing an outstanding Dartmouth team, 46-35, and dominating the first half against Georgetown before the team from Washington, D.C., solved the problems caused by DePaul's center. At the time, goaltending was an acceptable, not to mention effective, form of defense.

Although Komenich was one of the better big men in the country, the 6-foot-7 Wyoming pivotman by way of Gary, Ind., was not the distraction that the 6-10 Mikan was. And Georgetown had an effective post player of its own in 6-8 John Mahnken. The Cowboys, however, enjoyed a height advantage at the forward positions, manned by 6-6 Jim Weir and 6-3 Floyd Volker. They also had Sailors, whose ability to control a game was unparalleled.

As decreed by Irish, the Garden's acting president, Wyoming's presence on the court for the NCAA championship game was greeted by a rendi-

The 1943 Cowboys receive their trophy from NCAA President Philip O. Badger (right) after defeating Georgetown. Front row (left to right) are Don Waite, Earl Ray and Jim Reese. Back row (left to right) are Jim Collins, Floyd Volker, Milo Komenich, Coach Everett Shelton, Lew Roney, Kenny Sailors and Jim Weir.

tion of "Ragtime Cowboy Joe." But there were few whoops and hollers for the Cowboys in the first half. The initial 20 minutes were played at a deliberate pace, and Georgetown exercised most of the deliberation.

The Hoyas opened a 13-8 lead as Mahnken and Bill Hassett each scored four points. Wyoming didn't stage one of its patented runs until the latter stages of the first half when, trailing 16-12, it overtook Georgetown on quick baskets by Weir, Volker and Sailors.

Georgetown nosed in front again at the outset of the second half and gained a five-point lead at 31-26 on a corner shot by outstanding guard Danny Kraus and a free throw by Dan Gabbianelli. Only six minutes remained and it appeared the patient

Hoyas were about to score a notable upset. It was then that the Cowboys staged the first of two spurts that overwhelmed Georgetown.

Komenich and reserve Jim Collins scored the key baskets in an 11-0 run. Wyoming pulled into a 31-31 tie in the span of 90 seconds and assumed a 37-31 lead before Bill Feeney converted a pass from Kraus and Lloyd Potolicchio added a free throw for Georgetown. With a three-point lead and two minutes remaining, Wyoming accelerated again.

Sailors put on a dazzling exhibition of dribbling and shooting as the Cowboys scored the final nine points. The 5-11 captain finished with 16 points—he was the only player in the game in double figures—and was accorded outstanding-player honors in the wake of Wyoming's 46-34 triumph.

"Even if he hadn't tallied a point," said the report in the New York Times, "he would have been worth his weight in ration coupons for his all-around value to his team." And ration coupons were the most valuable commodity around in the war years.

The crowd of 13,000-plus was more than double the number of spectators attending the 1942 championship game in Kansas City. And the total audience of 56,876 for the five sessions represented a tournament record. New York and Irish had delivered for the NCAA.

Nor was that the end of the season. Irish had arranged to stage a special game between the champions of the NCAA Tournament and the NIT two nights later for the benefit of the American Red Cross. At a time when the NIT still carried greater prestige in the minds of many basketball officials and fans, it represented a significant step for the NCAA tourney.

A powerful St. John's team had dismissed three opponents in the NIT to stretch its record to 21-2. The Redmen, coached by a famed member of the Original Celtics, Joe Lapchick, were led by 6-9 sophomore Harry Boykoff and captain Fuzzy Levane, the New York area's collegiate player of the year. Wyoming and St. John's met before a huge crowd in the Garden after Georgetown, which finished second in the NCAA Tournament, overwhelmed NIT runner-up Toledo, 54-40.

If anyone wished to express the opinion that it seemed strange for large young men to be playing Cowboys and Redmen in a New York arena, he wouldn't have been heard above the din. The two teams waged a magnificent struggle that the Red-

The 1943 title aspirations of DePaul and freshman giant George Mikan came up short.

men sent into overtime with an eight-point rally in the final two minutes. Actually, Sailors appeared to have won the game for Wyoming with five seconds left, but his basket was disallowed because celebrated official Pat Kennedy had signaled a timeout for St. John's.

Weir scored five of Wyoming's six points in the extra session. St. John's managed only a single free throw and lost, 52-47. And the Red Cross was presented with a check for $30,909.98.

With another memorable conquest added to their victories over the eventual AAU titleholder and success in the NCAA Tournament, the Wyoming Cowboys headed home to a glorious reception. Fire engines greeted the train in Laramie, classes were canceled for three days and the players couldn't pick up a check in a restaurant or barber shop, such was their impact on the sparsely populated state.

Best of all, some newspapers, taking note of the informal state of professional basketball, acclaimed the Cowboys as mythical world champions.

"For some kids from Wyoming," Sailors said, "that was something."

Wyoming Coach Everett Shelton.

1943 Tournament Results	
First Round	**Semifinals**
Georgetown 55, New York U. 36	Georgetown 53, DePaul 49
DePaul 46, Dartmouth 35	Wyoming 58, Texas 54
Texas 59, Washington 55	**Championship**
Wyoming 53, Oklahoma 50	Wyoming 46, Georgetown 34
Regional Third Place	
Dartmouth 51, New York U. 49	
Oklahoma 48, Washington 43	

STATISTICS

1943 WYOMING

Head Coach—Everett Shelton Final Record—31-2

Player	Pos.	Hgt.	Wgt.	Cl.	G	FG	FGA	Pct.	FT	FTA	Pct.	Reb.	Pts.	Avg.
Milo Komenich	C	6-7	212	Jr.	33	257	...	...	37	...	...	...	551	16.7
Kenny Sailors	F	5-11	155	Jr.	33	198	...	...	100	...	...	...	496	15.0
Jim Weir	F	6-6	...	Jr.	33	135	...	...	62	...	...	...	332	10.1
Floyd Volker	F-G	6-3	...	Jr.	33	91	...	...	29	...	...	...	211	6.4
Jimmie Reese	F	6-1	...	So.	23	45	...	...	8	...	...	...	98	4.3
Jim Darden	G	...	...	...	10	13	...	...	10	...	...	...	36	3.6
Lew Roney	G	6-3	...	Jr.	30	30	...	...	20	...	...	...	80	2.7
Jim Collins	G	5-11	...	So.	31	33	...	...	13	...	...	...	79	2.5
Don Waite	G	...	...	Sr.	11	10	...	...	0	...	...	...	20	1.8
Vernon Jensen	G	...	...	...	10	2	...	...	1	...	...	...	5	0.5
Antone Katana	C	...	...	...	24	15	...	...	5	...	...	...	35	1.5
Earl (Shadow) Ray	G	5-11	...	Jr.	19	7	...	...	2	...	...	...	16	0.8
Jack Downey	G	...	...	...	1	0	...	...	0	...	...	...	0	0.0
Kenneth Tallman	F	...	...	...										
Wyoming					33	836	...	...	287	...	...	...	1959	59.4
Opponents					33	507	...	...	288	...	...	...	1302	39.5

1943 GEORGETOWN

Head Coach—Elmer Ripley Final Record—22-5

(Full-season statistics unavailable; individual statistics are for NCAA Tournament and Red Cross benefit game after NCAA Tournament.)

Player	Pos.	Hgt.	Wgt.	Cl.	G	FG	FGA	Pct.	FT	FTA	Pct.	Reb.	Pts.	Avg.
John Mahnken	C	6-8	215	Fr.	4	28	...	...	7	9	.778	..	63	15.8
Bill Hassett	G	5-10	170	So.	4	10	...	...	11	14	.786	..	31	7.8
Danny Kraus	G	6-0	185	So.	4	9	...	...	5	11	.455	..	23	5.8
Lloyd Potolicchio	F	5-11	175	So.	4	9	...	...	3	6	.500	..	21	5.3
Jim Reilly	F	5-6	150	So.	4	8	...	...	4	5	.800	..	20	5.0
Bill Feeney	F	6-3	180	Fr.	4	9	...	...	0	0	.000	..	18	4.5
Dan Gabbianelli	F-G	6-1	185	Jr.	4	6	...	...	3	4	.750	..	15	3.8
.... Duffey	F-G	...	...	...	4	1	...	...	1	1	1.000	..	3	0.8
Henry Hyde	F-C	6-3	180	Fr.	3	1	...	...	0	0	.000	..	2	0.7
Frank Finnerty	F-G	6-1	190	Jr.	2	0	...	...	0	0	.000	..	0	0.0
Andy Kostecka	F	6-3	192	So.	...									
Lane O'Donnell	F	6-4	200	Jr.	...									
Edward Lavin	F	6-2	183	So.	...									
Edward Cannon	F	6-1	165	Fr.	...									
Peter Timpone	F	5-8	155	Fr.	...									
Sylvester Goedde	C	6-8	205	Fr.										
*Georgetown					27	...	...	...	...	...	...	...	1497	55.4
*Opponents					27	...	...	...	...	...	...	...	1159	42.9

*Full season.

(Mahnken led full-season scoring with 415 points in 27 games for 15.4 average.)

1943 TEXAS

Head Coach—H.C. (Bully) Gilstrap Final Record—19-7

(Full-season statistics unavailable; individual statistics are for NCAA tourney.)

Player	Pos.	Hgt.	Wgt.	Cl.	G	FG	FGA	Pct.	FT	FTA	Pct.	Reb.	Pts.	Avg.
John Hargis	F	6-2	180	Jr.	2	21	...	...	17	23	.739	...	59	29.5
V.C. (Buck) Overall	F	...	...	...	2	10	...	...	9	14	.643	...	29	14.5
John Langdon	C	...	...	So.	2	2	...	...	2	3	.667	...	6	3.0
Roy Cox	G	...	...	...	2	3	...	...	0	0	.000	...	6	3.0
Frank Brahaney	G	...	...	...	2	2	...	...	2	3	.667	...	6	3.0
Jack Fitzgerald	G-F	...	...	...	2	2	...	...	0	1	.000	...	4	2.0
Dudley Wright	G	...	...	...	2	1	...	...	1	1	1.000	...	3	1.5
.... Goss	F	...	...	...	1	0	...	...	0	0	.000	...	0	0.0
.... Kent	G	...	...	...	1	0	...	...	0	0	.000	...	0	0.0
Hutch Bass	F	...	...	...										
Curtis Popham	G	...	...	...										
Tom Price	G	...	...	...										
Don Wagner		...	...	...										
.... Bills		...	...	...										
.... Crawford		...	...	...										
*Texas					26	...	...	...	...	...	...	...	1251	48.1
*Opponents					26	...	...	...	...	...	...	...	1113	42.8

*Full Season.

1943 DEPAUL

Head Coach—Ray Meyer Final Record—19-5

Player	Pos.	Hgt.	Wgt.	Cl.	G	FG	FGA	Pct.	FT	FTA	Pct.	Reb.	Pts.	Avg.
George Mikan	C	6-10	225	...	24	...	...	...	...	...	...	...	274	11.4
Jimmy Cominsky	F	...	...	...	24	...	...	...	...	...	...	...	219	9.1
John Jorgenson	F	...	...	...	19	...	...	...	...	...	...	...	129	6.8
Dick Starzck	G	...	...	...	24	...	...	...	...	...	...	...	162	6.8
Mel Frailey	G-F	...	...	...	24	...	...	...	...	...	...	...	134	5.6
Tony Kelly	G	...	...	...	24	...	...	...	...	...	...	...	119	5.0
Frank Wiscons	C	...	...	...	15	...	...	...	...	...	...	...	54	3.6
Dick Triptow	F	...	...	...	18	...	...	...	...	...	...	...	41	2.3
Jim McGowan		...	...	...	4	...	...	...	...	...	...	...	9	2.3
Joe Demkovich		...	...	...	3	...	...	...	...	...	...	...	6	2.0
Cliff Lind		...	...	...	20	...	...	...	...	...	...	...	32	1.6
Bill Domato	F	...	...	...	13	...	...	...	...	...	...	...	15	1.2
Kevin Crowley	G	...	...	...	12	...	...	...	...	...	...	...	9	0.8
Bill Ryan	G	...	...	...	13	...	...	...	...	...	...	...	9	0.7
Gene Rudnick		...	...	...	6	...	...	...	...	...	...	...	4	0.7
Otto Kerber		...	...	...	5	...	...	...	...	...	...	...	2	0.4
*DePaul					24	...	...	...	...	...	...	...	1218	50.8
*Opponents					24	...	...	...	...	...	...	...	945	39.4

1943 FINAL FOUR

Semifinals
At New York

Georgetown	fg	ft	fta	pf	tp
Gabbianelli	3	0	0	1	6
Feeney	0	0	0	0	0
Duffey	0	0	0	0	0
Potolicchio	5	1	3	1	11
Reilly	0	0	0	0	0
Mahnken	8	1	2	4	17
Hyde	1	0	0	2	2
Hassett	2	7	7	0	11
Kraus	1	4	6	3	6
Totals	20	13	18	13	53

DePaul	fg	ft	fta	pf	tp
Jorgenson	6	2	3	2	14
Frailey	0	0	0	0	0
Cominsky	5	1	3	3	11
Mikan	3	5	8	1	11
Starzck	3	1	1	2	7
Kelly	2	2	2	4	6
Ryan	0	0	0	3	0
Totals	19	11	17	15	49

Halftime: DePaul 28-23. Officials: Kennedy and Nucatola.

At Kansas City

Wyoming	fg	ft	fta	pf	tp
Sailors	4	4	6	3	12
Weir	6	1	1	3	13
Waite	0	0	0	1	0
Komenich	8	1	4	2	17
Volker	3	1	3	4	7
Roney	1	2	3	4	4
Collins	2	1	2	2	5
Totals	24	10	19	18	58

Texas	fg	ft	fta	pf	tp
Overall	5	4	7	3	14
Hargis	11	7	11	3	29
Langdon	1	2	3	2	4
Brahaney	1	0	0	3	2
Fitzgerald	1	0	0	4	2
Wright	1	1	1	2	3
Cox	0	0	0	3	0
Totals	20	14	22	20	54

Halftime: Texas 33-27. Officials: O'Sullivan and Leith.

Championship
March 30
At New York

Wyoming	fg	ft	fta	pf	tp
Sailors	6	4	5	2	16
Collins	4	0	0	1	8
Weir	2	1	3	2	5
Waite	0	0	0	0	0
Komenich	4	1	4	2	9
Volker	2	1	2	3	5
Roney	0	1	2	1	1
Reese	1	0	0	0	2
Totals	19	8	16	11	46

Georgetown	fg	ft	fta	pf	tp
Reilly	1	0	0	0	2
Potolicchio	1	2	3	1	4
Gabbianelli	1	2	3	3	4
Hyde	0	0	0	0	0
Mahnken	2	2	3	2	6
Hassett	3	0	3	4	6
Finnerty	0	0	0	0	0
Kraus	2	0	1	3	4
Feeney	4	0	0	1	8
Duffey	0	0	0	0	0
Totals	14	6	13	14	34

Halftime: Wyoming 18-16. Officials: Kennedy and Begovich.

1944 Stubborn Utes Try, Try Again

The opportunistic 1944 Utes of Utah. Back row (left to right) are Wat Misaka, Ray Kingston and Arnie Ferrin. Front row (left to right) are Fred Lewis, Jim Nance, Bob Lewis, Coach Vadal Peterson, Fred Sheffield, Dick Smuin and Herb Wilkinson.

Utah's second chance to participate in the 1944 NCAA Tournament was not an act of charity. Tournament officials were in a bind. Another team was needed, and quickly, to fill out the field for the Western playoffs.

The Utes had said no once to the opportunity, choosing instead to make the long trip to the National Invitation Tournament in New York. The NIT was offering a larger guarantee, and only two Utah players—Fred Sheffield and Arnie Ferrin—had ever set foot in the Big Apple. Accordingly, it was the overwhelming sentiment of the team to visit New York.

Alas, the experience was soured by a 46-38 loss to a strong Kentucky team in the first round. The NCAA Tournament wouldn't get under way for four more days, but already the Utes were talking about basketball in the past tense. Then came the telephone call from Kansas City. Arkansas was

pulling out of the NCAA's Western field because two of its best players had been injured in an automobile accident. Did the Utes want to take Arkansas' place?

Did they ever! The alternatives offered by the coach, Vadal Peterson, were to spend a few days sightseeing and then go home or entrain the following morning for Kansas City and another chance to play basketball.

"Let's go to Kansas City and win the title," Ferrin said. "Then we can return to New York and prove that our loss was a fluke."

For the second consecutive year, the NCAA championship game was scheduled for Madison Square Garden. Utah was gambling that it could continue playing basketball and earn another week in New York. The team set out for Kansas City, a journey that required 2½ days because of erratic train schedules caused by wartime troop movements.

When Utah faced the Missouri Tigers on the night of March 24, it made history without firing a shot. By its mere presence, it became the first team to participate in both the NIT and the NCAA Tournament in the same season.

The 1944 season had been unprecedented in every way for Utah. Because the Mountain States Conference had suspended basketball for the duration of the war, the Utes had to piece together a schedule heavily flavored with service and industrial teams. Because the school's field house had been commandeered by the U.S. Army, the Utes had to practice at a church gym in downtown Salt Lake City. Because so many older students had enlisted or been drafted, the Utes had to rely almost entirely on freshmen and sophomores. The team's average age was 18 years, six months.

None of the youngsters, all of whom were raised within 35 miles of the campus, had been recruited. Ferrin, the freshman high scorer, knocked on Peterson's door for the opportunity to play. A friend of Wat Misaka's saw a notice for tryouts on a bulletin board and advised the little guard, who hadn't considered the possibility. Thrown together in a makeshift home, the local kids did all right. Entering the NIT, the Utes had won 17 of 20 games.

The loss to Kentucky in New York was Utah's first against collegiate opposition. But Utah did not discourage easily, as it proved in the depleted Western playoffs. By beating Missouri, 45-35, and Iowa State, 40-31, the Utes won the right to get back on a train headed to New York. This time they arrived not as anonymous guests from a distant land, but as cult heroes, the team that wouldn't give up, the Blitz Kids.

They got a chance to see New York and New York got a chance to see them. They were quite a sight.

"We were a bunch of towheaded country kids," Misaka said, "except for me."

Misaka was a living, breathing, dashing Japanese-American whose country was at war with the land of his ancestors. On the West Coast, people of similar background were being herded into camps. The athlete representing Utah heard his share of insults during the wartime years.

"I was thankful for the screen between the players and the floor at Utah State," he said. "They got pretty hostile. Overall, it was a lot more difficult for me than for other Americans, but it was a lot easier for me than for other Japanese-Americans."

Among the places visited in New York by the Utes were the Copacabana nightclub, the Empire State Building and the Queen Mary, the ocean liner that had been refitted as a troop ship.

"If I yelled 'banzai' and started running," Misaka asked his teammates, "what do you think would

All-America Arnie Ferrin was the undisputed leader of Utah's 1944 championship team.

happen?" Fortunately, he chose not to find out.

Utah's opponent in the NCAA championship game would be the Dartmouth Indians. Dartmouth, strengthened by the addition of Navy trainees Dick McGuire and Bob Gale (stationed at the Hanover, N.H., college under the wartime V-12 program), had defeated Catholic University and Ohio State to win the Eastern playoffs at Madison Square Garden. Ironically, McGuire had won an award as the outstanding player in the New York area while attending St. John's earlier in the season. Gale had stood out for Cornell.

Without McGuire, St. John's won a second consecutive NIT title in 1944. Now the Redmen awaited the outcome of the Dartmouth-Utah game. The NIT champions again were scheduled to meet the NCAA survivor in a Red Cross benefit at the Garden (such a matchup first occurring the previous year). On the eve of the NCAA final, however, it was announced by the Department of the Navy that Dartmouth would not be permitted to participate in the exhibition. Because of the trainees on the team, Dartmouth had orders to return to New Hampshire immediately after the NCAA title game.

It was a bitter blow to organizers and the Red Cross. It meant Utah, win or lose, would face St. John's, and the consensus was that Dartmouth was too big and too seasoned for the Utes. Thus the Red Cross game would be anticlimactic.

However, there was at least one party who didn't believe Dartmouth was a sure thing. At 6 a.m. on the day of the game, Peterson was awakened in his hotel room by a sharp knock on the door.

"What is it?" asked Peterson, poking his head into the hall.

"Peterson, coach of Utah?" inquired a large figure bundled in an overcoat, his face shielded by a turned-down hat brim.

"Yes," Peterson said.

"What'll it take to arrange for Dartmouth to win by 12 or more tonight?" the figure asked.

Peterson howled in protest and the intruder retreated.

The Utah players had their own ideas about the opportunity.

"I'd hate to play that (Red Cross) game as losers," Ferrin said. But after so many miles on the rails, the Utes weren't planning to lose.

Peterson devised a gambling "pickup" defense to shut off the high-scoring Gale and big Aud Brindley, who had established a tournament record of 13 field goals in the Indians' 60-53 victory over Ohio State. The maneuver enabled Utah to double-team (at least alternately) the Indians' front-line players, leaving an open man somewhere on the floor. Dartmouth rarely found him.

While neither team's offense performed at the expected level, the game was thoroughly competitive. Dartmouth's lead never exceeded three points. Utah never led by more than four. There were seven lead changes in 2½ minutes in the first half, which ended with Dartmouth ahead, 18-17.

A basket by the 5-foot-7 Misaka, whose spirited play had earned a warm reception from the crowd of 14,990, boosted Utah into a four-point lead with four minutes remaining. The Utes ran more than two minutes off the clock before Dartmouth got another chance. McGuire passed to Harry Leggat, a trainee who previously had played for New York University, for a layup, cutting the margin to two.

That basket was answered by Ferrin. Utah again led by four, at 36-32, and now there were 60 seconds left. But Gale tipped in a rebound and then Ev Nordstrom picked up a loose ball and passed to Frank Murphy, who relayed it to McGuire. McGuire's shot dropped in with three seconds on the clock, tying the score at 36-36. For the first time, the NCAA championship would be decided by an overtime period.

Ferrin, on the verge of exhaustion, kept Utah even in the extra period, pushing his point total to 22 with four free throws. As the final seconds ticked off, Herb Wilkinson worked himself loose behind the free-throw circle and arched a one-hander toward the basket. The ball hung on the back of the

Vadal Peterson offered his 1944 Utes a challenge and they responded well.

rim for an instant and then dropped. Utah was a 42-40 winner. Underdogs everywhere cheered.

The defense concocted by Peterson worked so well that Brindley made only five of 24 shots and Gale sank but five of 18. Meanwhile, Ferrin, the 6-4 great-grandson of a pioneer who trudged across the plains with Brigham Young in 1847, carried the offense. He was honored as the competition's outstanding player.

Two nights later, the Utes toppled yet another favorite, beating NIT titlist St. John's, 43-36, before 18,125 spectators. By the end of the game, they had thoroughly won over New York's critical fans. When they boarded the train for the last leg of their adventure three weeks after leaving home, they carried trophies, medals, watches and the respect of the nation.

1944 Tournament Results

First Round
Dartmouth 63, Catholic 38
Ohio State 57, Temple 47
Iowa State 44, Pepperdine 39
Utah 45, Missouri 35

Regional Third Place
Temple 55, Catholic 35
Missouri 61, Pepperdine 46

Semifinals
Dartmouth 60, Ohio State 53
Utah 40, Iowa State 31

Championship
Utah 42, Dartmouth 40 (ot)

STATISTICS

1944 UTAH

Head Coach—Vadal Peterson   **Final Record—22-4**

(Full-season statistics unavailable; statistics shown are for National Invitation Tournament, NCAA Tournament and Red Cross benefit game.)

Player	Pos.	Hgt.	Wgt.	Cl.	G	FG	FGA	Pct.	FT	FTA	Pct.	Reb.	Pts.	Avg.
Arnie Ferrin	F	6-3	165	Fr.	5	28	...	...	14	...	...	...	70	14.0
Herb Wilkinson	G-F	6-4	190	Fr.	5	18	...	...	9	...	...	...	45	9.0
Bob Lewis	G	6-4	...	Fr.	5	13	...	...	5	...	...	...	31	6.2
Wat Misaka	G	5-7	150	Fr.	5	12	...	...	3	...	...	...	27	5.4
Fred Sheffield	C	6-1	160	So.	5	9	...	...	3	...	...	...	21	4.2
Dick Smuin	F-G	6-2	158	Fr.	5	6	...	...	2	...	...	...	14	2.8
James Nance	F	...	...	...	1	0	...	...	0	...	...	...	0	0.0
Fred Lewis	G	...	...	Fr.	1	0	...	...	0	...	...	...	0	0.0
Ray Kingston	G	...	...	...	1	0	...	...	0	...	...	...	0	0.0
. . . . Kastelic	...	...	...	...	...	...	...	...	...	...	...	...	...	...
Mas Tatsuno	...	...	...	...	...	...	...	...	...	...	...	...	...	...
Abram Bywater	...	...	...	...	...	...	...	...	...	...	...	...	...	...
*Utah					26	...	...	...	...	...	...	...	1374	52.8
*Opponents					26	...	...	...	...	...	...	...	918	35.3

*Full season.

1944 DARTMOUTH

Head Coach—Earl Brown   **Final Record—19-2**

Player	Pos.	Hgt.	Wgt.	Cl.	G	FG	FGA	Pct.	FT	FTA	Pct.	Reb.	Pts.	Avg.
Aud Brindley	C	6-4	180	So.	21	145	...	...	50	73	.685	...	340	16.2
Lionel Baxter	F	...	...	M	16	85	...	...	30	43	.698	...	200	12.5
Bob Gale	C-F	6-4	187	M	5	26	...	...	2	2	1.000	...	54	10.8
Thomas Killick	F	...	...	M	13	54	...	...	22	32	.688	...	130	10.0
Dick McGuire	G	6-0	170	M	5	17	...	...	9	10	.900	...	43	8.6
Harry Leggat	F	...	...	M	20	72	...	...	16	21	.762	...	160	8.0
John Monahan	G	...	...	Jr.	17	37	...	...	12	27	.444	...	86	5.1
Joseph Fater	G	...	...	M	16	26	...	...	10	16	.625	...	62	3.9
Joe Vancisin	G	...	...	Sr.	20	24	...	...	9	16	.563	...	57	2.9
Walter Peterson	F	...	...	M	7	6	...	...	4	6	.667	...	16	2.3
Ed Grygiel	F	...	...	M	4	4	...	...	0	0	.000	...	8	2.0
Walter Mercer	G	...	...	M	16	11	...	...	8	12	.667	...	30	1.9
Robert Maxwell	F	...	...	M	5	3	...	...	2	3	.667	...	8	1.6
Paul Campbell	F	...	...	M	13	6	...	...	3	6	.500	...	15	1.2
Vince Goering	G	...	...	M	15	6	...	...	0	2	.000	...	12	0.8
Floyd Wilson	C	...	...	M	8	3	...	...	0	0	.000	...	6	0.8
Eugene Koch	G	...	...	M	7	1	...	...	2	3	.667	...	4	0.6
Richard Kitsmiller	F	...	...	M	7	1	...	...	0	0	.000	...	2	0.3
Frank Murphy	C	...	...	M	12	1	...	...	1	1	1.000	...	3	0.3
Ev Nordstrom	...	...	...	M	3	...	...	...	...	...	.000	...	...	0.0
Dartmouth					21	528	...	...	180	273	.659	...	1236	58.9
Opponents					21	...	...	...	...	...	...	...	903	43.0

M—Military trainee.

1944 IOWA STATE

Head Coach—Louis Menze   **Final Record—14-4**

Player	Pos.	Hgt.	Wgt.	Cl.	G	FG	FGA	Pct.	FT	FTA	Pct.	Reb.	Pts.	Avg.
Price Brookfield	C	6-3	195	M	16	81	...	...	24	31	.774	...	186	11.6
Ray Wehde	F	6-1	165	M	18	52	...	...	35	46	.761	...	139	7.7
Lloyd Kester	G	6-0	175	M	5	15	...	...	8	15	.533	...	38	7.6
Roy Wehde	F	6-1	168	M	18	46	...	...	25	32	.781	...	117	6.5
Lyle Naylor	G	5-9	180	M	7	17	...	...	1	9	.111	...	35	5.0
James Myers	G	5-10	165	M	18	33	...	...	11	15	.733	...	77	4.3
Gene Oulman	G	6-3	185	M	18	27	...	...	16	47	.340	...	70	3.9
William Block	G	6-0	170	M	11	15	...	...	10	18	.556	...	40	3.6
Robert Sauer	G	6-0	190	M	13	9	...	...	21	22	.955	...	39	3.0
Roy Ewoldt	F	6-1	178	Fr.	6	7	...	...	2	3	.667	...	16	2.7
. . . . Chisholm	C	...	...	...	10	3	...	...	1	11	.091	...	7	0.7
. . . . Nelson	F	...	...	...	10	3	...	...	0	8	.000	...	6	0.6
Dick Bliss	G	6-2	200	Sr.	3	0	...	...	1	2	.500	...	1	0.3
Glenn Myatt	G	5-9	178	Fr.	2	0	...	...	0	6	.000	...	0	0.0
Others									0	6	.00			
Iowa State					18	308	...	...	155	265	.585	...	771	42.8
Opponents					18	...	...	...	...	...	...	...	569	31.6

M—Military trainee.

1944 OHIO STATE

Head Coach—Harold Olsen   **Final Record—14-7**

(Complete full-season statistics are unavailable.)

Player	Pos.	Hgt.	Wgt.	Cl.	G	FG	FGA	Pct.	FT	FTA	Pct.	Reb.	Pts.	Avg.
Don Grate	F	6-2	185	So.	21	...	...	...	...	...	...	...	272	13.0
Arnie Risen	C	6-8	185	Fr.	21	...	...	...	...	...	...	...	266	12.7
Bob Bowen	G	6-2	...	So.	21	...	...	...	...	...	...	...	200	9.5
Rodney Caudill	F-C	...	...	...	...	...	...	...	...	...	...	...	...	...
Jack Dugger	F	6-4	210	Jr.	...	...	...	...	...	...	...	...	...	...
Bill Gunton	G-F	...	...	...	...	...	...	...	...	...	...	...	...	...
Paul Huston	G	6-3	185	Fr.	...	...	...	...	...	...	...	...	...	...
Jack Fink	G	...	...	...	...	...	...	...	...	...	...	...	...	...
Ernie Plank	F	...	...	...	...	...	...	...	...	...	...	...	...	...
*Ohio State					21	...	...	...	...	...	...	...	1157	55.1
*Opponents					21	...	...	...	...	...	...	...	1014	48.3

*Full season.

Other members of the squad included Floyd Griffith, Jack Hammett, Jim Wells, Dick McQuade, Dick Davis, Tom Melziva, Oris Burley, Al Updike and Dave Belknap.

1944 FINAL FOUR

Semifinals
At New York

Dartmouth	fg	ft	fta	pf	tp
Gale	3	1	1	2	7
Leggat	5	2	4	2	12
Brindley	13	2	3	3	28
McGuire	4	1	3	1	9
Vancisin	0	0	0	2	0
Monahan	2	0	0	1	4
Totals	27	6	11	11	60

Ohio State	fg	ft	fta	pf	tp
Grate	3	1	2	2	7
Dugger	3	2	6	4	8
Gunton	0	0	0	0	0
Risen	8	5	6	0	21
Caudill	0	0	0	1	0
Bowen	3	0	0	1	6
Fink	0	0	0	0	0
Huston	5	1	1	3	11
Totals	22	9	15	11	53

Halftime: Dartmouth 28-22. Officials: Menton and De-Groot.

At Kansas City

Utah	fg	ft	tp
Ferrin	3	0	6
Smuin	2	1	5
Sheffield	4	1	9
Misaka	4	1	9
Wilkinson	1	2	4
B. Lewis	3	1	7
Totals	17	6	40

Iowa State	fg	ft	tp
Ray Wehde	2	1	5
Block	2	1	5
Roy Wehde	2	0	4
Brookfield	3	0	6
Ewoldt	0	0	0
Oulman	2	1	5
Sauer	0	2	2
Myers	2	0	4
Totals	13	5	31

Halftime: Utah 19-16. Officials: Curtis and Gibbs.

Championship
March 28
At New York

Utah	fg	ft	fta	pf	tp
Ferrin	8	6	7	0	22
Smuin	0	0	0	2	0
Sheffield	1	0	0	1	2
Misaka	2	0	0	1	4
Wilkinson	3	1	4	0	7
B. Lewis	2	3	3	2	7
Totals	16	10	14	6	42

Dartmouth	fg	ft	fta	pf	tp
Gale	5	0	2	1	10
Mercer	0	1	1	3	1
Leggat	4	0	0	1	8
Nordstrom	0	0	0	0	0
Brindley	5	1	1	3	11
McGuire	3	0	1	3	6
Murphy	0	0	0	0	0
Vancisin	2	0	0	3	4
Goering	0	0	0	0	0
Totals	19	2	5	14	40

Halftime: Dartmouth 18-17. Regulation Score: 36-36. Officials: Osborne and Menton.

1945 Oklahoma A&M Begins Reign

Oklahoma A&M's Henry Iba took an organized, systematic approach to the game he coached.

The game that so intrigued Henry Iba was a primitive one. In the Missouri town where he was raised, there was no indoor facility in which to practice basketball. The children of Easton had a blacksmith forge a backboard and a hoop and, during the years of the Great War, they played in a clearing.

Still, something about the sport challenged Iba's intelligence. A 62-14 defeat in high school led Iba to reflect on a systematic approach to basketball and he gained as much knowledge as he could during his career at Westminster College in Fulton, Mo. Given the early stage of basketball's development, however, Iba was obliged to get much of his training on the job.

That first job was at Classen High School in Oklahoma City.

"I had to coach basketball and baseball and teach geology," he said, "and I didn't know one rock from another."

He knew enough about basketball to see that Jack McCracken got the ball in the post. McCracken was a fine passer who kept the ball moving. Iba saw to it that the other players moved as well and thus was born the motion offense.

The young coach took that concept to Maryville Teachers College (later Northwest Missouri State, where McCracken again starred for him) and later to Colorado. In the fall of 1934, at the age of 30, Iba began his long association with Oklahoma A&M, where he coached the Aggies' basketball team for 36 seasons. He already had become a national figure in the sport when he first encountered Bob Kurland.

Kurland was an awkward 7-footer at a time when the description was redundant.

"You used to go to a playground and run away the big boys," Iba said, "because they were clumsy."

But this big boy had been recommended to Iba by his high school coach, who had attended Maryville.

The youngster wanted to study civil engineering, but hometown schools St. Louis University and Washington University had dropped their programs during World War II. The University of Missouri offered a job waiting tables but not the scholarship Kurland needed. Iba said he would take a look, so the high school senior got on a bus and traveled to Stillwater.

Iba still wasn't sure after watching him work out.

Bob Kurland, selected as the top player in both the 1945 and '46 NCAA Tournaments, looks for a pass against North Carolina in the 1946 title game.

"I don't honestly know if you can play college basketball or not," the coach told Kurland. But Iba said he would work with him as long as he attended class and did as he was told. Kurland placed his future in Iba's hands.

Together, they made history.

Using a jump rope to improve his agility, Kurland improved from a freshman reserve to a sophomore regular to a junior star. Iba built his defense around him. That defense was limited mostly to goaltending in Kurland's sophomore season (1944), but the basketball rules committee outlawed the practice before his junior year. Playing defense with his feet instead of just his arms, Kurland became a more complete player and, along with 6-10 George

Mikan of DePaul, a major attraction in the sport.

Iba made certain people got to see the big boy. He took his team to Chicago. He made an annual swing to the East—Buffalo, New York, Philadelphia, Washington—during the holidays. In Kurland's freshman year, the Aggies lost the final game of the trip to George Washington. On the return, the train was almost in Kansas City before Iba spoke.

"At least," someone finally said to the coach, "we made some people in Washington happy."

Iba, having watched his team lose for the third time in the four-game trip, was not amused.

"We've got to stop going around the country making people happy," he replied.

Mostly, the Aggies made people in Oklahoma

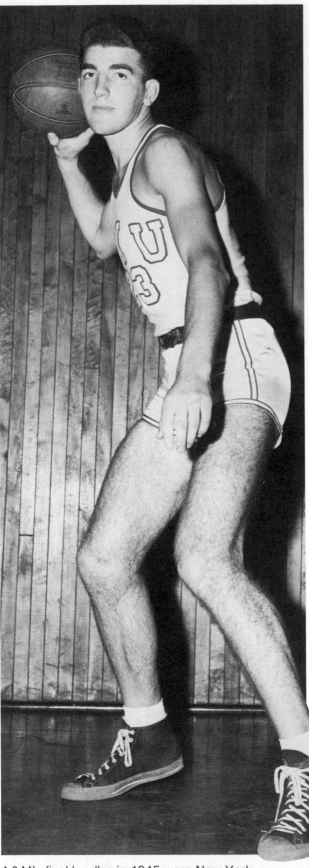

A&M's final hurdles in 1945 were New York University and freshman sensation Dolph Schayes.

happy during Kurland's years in Stillwater. The Aggies were 14-10 and 27-6 in his first two seasons, winning a National Invitation Tournament berth in his sophomore year. At the end of regular-season play in 1945, Oklahoma A&M was 23-4 and bound for the NCAA Tournament for the first time.

The initial postseason stop in '45 was Kansas City, site of the Western playoffs. The Aggies' first opponent was defending national champion Utah. The Utes had been weakened by the absence of Arnie Ferrin and Fred Sheffield, who entered the service after the final game of the regular season. But it's doubtful Utah would have been a match for Oklahoma A&M even with Ferrin, who was the team's tallest player at 6-4.

After breezing past Utah, 62-37, the Aggies met Arkansas for the fourth time that season. They had won two of the previous three encounters against the Razorbacks, both victories coming by nine points. Kurland, who had scored 28 points against Utah, concentrated on rebounding and passing in the Western final. Thus did forward Cecil Hankins score 22 points and guard Doyle Parrack add 16. Arkansas was buried, 68-41.

Those victories earned the Oklahoma A&M Aggies—known a little more than a decade later as the Oklahoma State Cowboys—another train trip to New York for the national championship game in Madison Square Garden. A young New York University team awaited them. Howard Cann's Violets had staged an amazing comeback to defeat Ohio State in the Eastern qualifier, making up a 10-point deficit in the final two minutes of regulation and then outscoring the Buckeyes, 8-3, in overtime for a 70-65 triumph.

Oklahoma A&M had met NYU three months earlier at the Garden, the Aggies coming out 44-41 winners. Since that time, the Violets had added Dolph Schayes, a 6-6 freshman, to the lineup. But the Aggies also had been strengthened. Hankins, a football star at the Oklahoma school, had been practicing for the Cotton Bowl during that first engagement.

The championship contest would present a sharp contrast in styles. NYU was smaller, quicker and blessed with accurate shooters. The Aggies were rangy, slower and more committed to defense. And in Kurland the Aggies had a mature as well as mammoth center. Schayes, the Violets' pivotman, was still two months shy of his 17th birthday.

Although Kurland was no stranger to the Garden, he still marveled at the atmosphere. There were more than 18,000 fans in the stands for the title game.

"There was smoke up to the ceiling," he said. "It was so thick you couldn't see the rafters."

However, Kurland had no trouble seeing the basket. It quickly became apparent that NYU did not have an answer for Kurland. He dominated both ends of the court, even as the Violets used some hot shooting to take a 19-14 lead. The Aggies tightened their defense and pulled ahead, 26-21, by halftime.

Oklahoma A&M pushed the lead to 11 points, 37-26, after six minutes of the second half. Twice the Violets cut the deficit to four points, but that's as close as they came. The final score, 49-45, was a tribute to Iba's sound strategy and Kurland's brilliance.

The big center scored 22 points and limited Schayes to six. Still, he complimented the youngster.

"I wouldn't have liked playing against him when he was a senior," said Kurland, recipient of the outstanding-player award in the NCAA's showcase event.

Three years after he tried out for a scholarship before a doubting coach, Kurland had reached a pinnacle of college basketball. But his season wasn't finished. By virtue of its title, Oklahoma A&M would represent the NCAA in the third and last of the Red Cross benefit games. The opponent would be DePaul, the NIT champion. The Demons' star, of course, was Mikan, the other dominant center in the nation.

It was billed as the "Game of the Century," even though the century wasn't half over. Kurland was the more agile of the two and a better jumper. Mikan was stronger and he wielded his elbows with devastating force. Kurland was more inclined to pass; Mikan, who scored a Garden-record 53 points against Rhode Island in an NIT semifinal, was more likely to shoot. In this showdown, both were inclined to foul.

To the fans who contributed more than $40,000 to the cause, the matchup was a major disappointment. Mikan drew his fifth foul after 14 minutes, leaving the game with a 9-7 edge against Kurland in their personal scoring duel. Kurland finished with 14 points (and four fouls) as the Aggies rallied from a 26-21 halftime deficit to a 52-44 victory.

"I know it was a disappointment to the fans," Kurland said. "They had expected 'the duel' to go on for the full 40 minutes. But I take pride in the victory."

That was one of the lessons he had been taught by Henry Iba, who had picked it up along the way in his on-the-job training.

1945 Tournament Results	
First Round	**Semifinals**
New York U. 59, Tufts 44	New York U. 70, Ohio State 65 (ot)
Ohio State 45, Kentucky 37	Oklahoma A&M 68, Arkansas 41
Arkansas 79, Oregon 76	**Championship**
Oklahoma A&M 62, Utah 37	Oklahoma A&M 49, New York U. 45
Regional Third Place	
Kentucky 66, Tufts 56	
Oregon 69, Utah 66	

Bob Kurland's final '45 hurdle was DePaul's George Mikan in the annual Red Cross game.

STATISTICS

1945 OKLAHOMA A&M

Head Coach—Henry Iba **Final Record—27-4**

Player	Pos.	Hgt.	Wgt.	Cl.	G	FG	FGA	Pct.	FT.	FTA	Pct.	Reb.	Pts.	Avg.
Bob Kurland	C	7-0	215	Jr.	31	214	...	...	101	176	.574	....	529	17.1
Cecil Hankins	F	6-1	175	...	23	127	...	...	53	102	.520	....	307	13.3
Wedlon Kern	F	5-10	145	Jr.	31	114	...	...	77	136	.566	....	305	9.8
Doyle Parrack	G	6-0	165	...	19	62	...	...	20	31	.645	....	144	7.6
J.L. Parks	F	6-0	160	Fr.	31	47	...	...	30	51	.588	....	124	4.0
Blake Williams	G	6-1	188	Fr.	31	52	...	...	14	26	.538	....	118	3.8
Gentry Warren	G	6-1	190	Jr.	10	12	...	...	4	7	.571	....	28	2.8
Jack Lyon	G	5-10	135	Fr.	10	10	...	...	5	9	.556	....	25	2.5
Harry Fenimore	F	5-10	148	Fr.	2	2	...	...	0	0	.000	....	4	2.0
Auddie Hall	G	6-2	192	Fr.	2	2	...	...	0	0	.000	....	4	2.0
John Wylie	G	6-0	165	Fr.	28	20	...	...	10	17	.588	....	50	1.8
Bill Johnson	G	...	...	...	1	3	...	...	2	7	.286	....	8	1.1
Dick Caldwell	..	...	...	...	2	1	...	...	0	0	.000	....	2	1.0
D.W. Jones	G	5-10	145	Fr.	12	4	...	...	3	5	.600	....	11	0.9
Bill York	G	5-9	160	Fr.	8	1	...	...	4	5	.800	....	6	0.8
Joe Halbert	C	6-7	200	Fr.	20	5	...	...	1	1	1.000	....	11	0.6
Carl Alexander	F	6-1	168	Fr.	3	0	...	...	1	2	.500	....	1	0.3
Art Rigg	F	5-11	130	So.	1	0	...	...	0	0	.000	....	0	0.0
Charles Crook	G	6-0	160	Sr.	5	0	...	...	0	0	.000	....	0	0.0
Oklahoma A&M					31	676			325	575	.565		1677	54.1
Opponents					31	368			302	508	.594		1038	33.5

1945 NEW YORK U.

Head Coach—Howard Cann **Final Record—16-8**

(Complete full-season statistics unavailable.)

Player	Pos.	Hgt.	Wgt.	Cl.	G	FG	FGA	Pct.	FT.	FTA	Pct.	Reb.	Pts.	Avg.
Al Grenert	F	6-0	179	Sr.	24	127	...	...	53	...	...	...	307	12.8
Sid Tanenbaum	G	6-0	159	So.	24	121	...	...	60	...	...	...	302	12.6
Dolph Schayes	C	6-6	195	Fr.	11	46	...	...	23	...	...	...	115	10.5
Frank Mangiapane	G	5-11	185	So.	24	..	..	...	..	...	...	...	181	7.5
Marty Goldstein	G-F	5-10	168	So.	..	..	..	...	..	...	...	...	102	...
Frank Benanti	F-C	6-0	186	Fr.	..	..	..	...	..	...	...	...	...	...
Don Forman	F	5-10	150	Fr.	..	..	..	...	..	...	...	...	...	...
Alvin Most	C-F	6-0	165	Fr.	..	..	..	...	..	...	...	...	...	...
Herbert Walsh	C	6-4	200	Fr.	..	..	..	...	..	...	...	...	...	...
Howard Sarath	F	5-11	175	So.	..	..	..	...	..	...	...	...	...	...
Frank Alagia	.	6-0	186	Fr.	..	..	..	...	..	...	...	...	...	...
John Dederian	.	6-0	160	So.	..	..	..	...	..	...	...	...	...	...
Jackie Gordon	.	6-3	170	So.	..	..	..	...	..	...	...	...	...	...
Seymour Kravitz	.	6-4	164	Fr.	..	..	..	...	..	...	...	...	...	...
Burton Monasch	.	5-11	160	Fr.	..	..	..	...	..	...	...	...	...	...
Joe Plentzas	.	5-11	167	Fr.	..	..	..	...	..	...	...	...	...	...
Billy Wells	.	6-0	175	Fr.	..	..	..	...	..	...	...	...	...	...
New York U.					24	..			..	...	...	...	1446	60.3
Opponents					24	..			..	...	...	...	1074	44.8

1945 ARKANSAS

Head Coach—Gene Lambert **Final Record—17-9**

(Complete full-season statistics unavailable.)

Player	Pos.	Hgt.	Wgt.	Cl.	G	FG	FGA	Pct.	FT.	FTA	Pct.	Reb.	Pts.	Avg.
George Kok	C	6-10	190	Fr.	26	187	...	...	65	...	...	...	439	16.9
Mike Schumchyk	F	6-4	200	Jr.	26	78	...	...	56	...	...	...	212	8.2
Bill Flynt	G	6-0	170	Sr.	26	76	...	...	54	...	...	...	206	7.9
Earl Wheeler	G	6-4	215	So.	26	78	...	...	15	...	...	...	171	6.6
Ken Kearns	F	6-3	170	Fr.	26	41	...	...	15	...	...	...	97	3.7
Charles Jolliff	C	6-5	202	So.	..	37	...	...	15	...	...	...	89	...
Frank Schumchyk	G-F	6-0	193	So.	..	18	...	...	8	...	...	...	44	...
Tony Byles	F	5-11	165	Fr.	..	3	...	...	2	...	...	...	8	...
Ocie Richie	F	6-3	195	Jr.	..	..	...	...	..	...	...	...	...	...
Jady Copeland	G	6-1	165	Sr.	..	..	...	...	..	...	...	...	...	...
Mel McGaha	G	6-1	185	So.	..	..	...	...	..	...	...	...	...	...
Arkansas					26	..	...	...	..	...	...	...	1518	58.4
Opponents					26	..	...	...	..	...	...	...	1225	47.1

1945 OHIO STATE

Head Coach—Harold Olsen **Final Record—15-5**

(Complete full-season statistics unavailable.)

Player	Pos.	Hgt.	Wgt.	Cl.	G	FG	FGA	Pct.	FT.	FTA	Pct.	Reb.	Pts.	Avg.
Arnie Risen	C	6-9	185	So.	20	102	...	...	54	...	...	...	258	12.9
Don Grate	F	6-2	185	Jr.	20	95	...	...	46	...	...	...	236	11.8
Rodney Caudill	F	...	...	...	..	...	...	...	..	...	...	...	...	...
Warren Amling	G	5-11	196	So.	..	...	...	...	..	...	...	...	...	...
Jack Dugger	F	6-4	210	Sr.	..	...	...	...	..	...	...	...	...	...
James Sims	F	...	...	Sr.	..	...	...	...	..	...	...	...	...	...
Ray Snyder	F	5-8	...	Jr.	..	...	...	...	..	...	...	...	...	...
Paul Huston	G	6-3	185	So.	..	...	...	...	..	...	...	...	...	...
John Pfeiffer	..	...	...	So.	..	...	...	...	..	...	...	...	...	...
Ohio State					20	...	...	...	..	...	...	...	1073	53.7
Opponents					20	...	...	...	..	...	...	...	859	43.0

1945 FINAL FOUR

Semifinals
At New York

New York U.	fg	ft	fta	pf	tp
Grenert	2	2	5	3	6
Benanti	0	0	0	1	0
Forman	4	2	2	2	10
Schayes	5	4	8	4	14
Walsh	2	2	3	5	6
Most	1	0	1	2	2
Tanenbaum	5	3	3	2	13
Mangiapane	7	3	5	4	17
Goldstein	1	0	0	2	2
Totals	27	16	27	25	70

Ohio State	fg	ft	fta	pf	tp
Grate	2	2	3	4	6
Sims	2	3	4	3	7
Snyder	0	0	0	0	0
Dugger	1	2	5	5	4
Caudill	3	1	1	3	7
Risen	8	10	13	5	26
Huston	2	1	3	5	5
Amling	5	0	2	1	10
Totals	23	19	31	26	65

Halftime: Ohio State 36-34. Regulation score: 62-62. Officials: Boyle and Beiersdorfer.

At Kansas City

Oklahoma A&M	fg	ft	pf	tp
Hankins	8	6	1	22
Kern	3	0	2	6
Kurland	6	3	3	15
Halbert	0	0	1	0
Williams	2	3	2	7
Parks	1	0	1	2
Parrack	7	2	1	16
Wylie	0	0	0	0
Totals	27	14	11	68

Arkansas	fg	ft	pf	tp
Richie	2	0	0	4
Byles	1	0	1	2
M. Schumchyk	1	2	3	4
F. Schumchyk	0	0	1	0
Kearns	1	1	2	3
Kok	4	4	2	12
Jolliff	0	0	3	0
Flynt	5	1	2	11
Copeland	0	1	0	1
Wheeler	2	0	3	4
Totals	16	9	17	41

Halftime: Oklahoma A&M 36-17. Officials: McLarney and Smith.

Championship
March 27
At New York

Oklahoma A&M	fg	ft	fta	pf	tp
Hankins	6	3	6	3	15
Parks	0	0	0	3	0
Kern	3	0	4	3	6
Wylie	0	0	0	0	0
Kurland	10	2	3	3	22
Parrack	2	0	1	3	4
Williams	1	0	1	1	2
Totals	22	5	15	16	49

New York U.	fg	ft	fta	pf	tp
Grenert	5	2	3	3	12
Forman	5	1	2	1	11
Goldstein	0	2	2	2	2
Schayes	2	2	6	2	6
Walsh	0	0	0	2	0
Tanenbaum	2	0	0	2	4
Mangiapane	2	2	4	3	6
Most	1	2	3	2	4
Totals	17	11	20	17	45

Halftime: Oklahoma A&M 26-21. Officials: Curtis and Adams.

1946 Kurland Keeps Aggies at Top

If Bob Kurland didn't eat, drink and breathe basketball at Oklahoma A&M, he did sleep it. That was a direct result of his accommodations on campus. The man never was far from the court on which he developed into a star.

His college career didn't begin that way. As was the case with the majority of freshmen who registered in the fall of 1942, he moved into a dormitory. But it was wartime and when the Army took possession of the building to house trainees, Kurland bunked in a room at the field house.

And that's where he lived, along with two other students, during a significant portion of his days in Stillwater. With the quarters came responsibility for cleaning up after practice and locking the doors. By the time he was a senior, Kurland could joke that he was the only three-time All-America who swept the floor.

As it was, Kurland spent so much time in the field house working to improve himself that it only made sense to spend his nights there. It saved him, he decided, 30 to 40 minutes a day. He could go directly from practice to the shower and from the shower to his room with no wasted motion.

The 7-foot center was determined to wring the most from his ability at a time when others saw no ability at all. In the eyes of many, some of them basketball people, he was a freak.

"They ridiculed him a lot when he first started to play," said Henry Iba, his coach. "It took a strong man to stand up to that."

Kurland stood up to his full height despite the jibes of others. Even Phog Allen, the esteemed coach at Kansas, referred to players Kurland's size as "glandular goons." Kurland held his tongue. But he would show them all, on the court.

He worked on developing his motor skills and then he built up his leg strength and stamina. There wasn't much he could do about his speed.

"He wasn't so good at running," Iba said, "but he had a good mind for competing."

And he progressed each year until he led the Aggies to the national championship as a junior. For those who thought they had seen the best of Kurland, he offered his senior season as silent testimony.

His supporting cast had changed considerably

Bob Kurland was one of the original 7-footers and an Oklahoma A&M Aggie through and through.

A determined Bob Kurland stood up to his full
height despite the jibes of skeptics and opponents.

from 1945. Cecil Hankins and Doyle Parrack had
departed. Among the newcomers was Sam Aubrey,
who had been wounded in Italy during the war and
had returned to school on crutches the previous
spring. Aubrey, a forward, was an all-league selection in the Missouri Valley Conference, which re-
sumed a full schedule in 1946.

Oklahoma A&M went undefeated in conference
play in '46. And Kurland, playing in a deliberate
offense, led the nation in total points. Against St.
Louis, he set an individual major-college scoring
record with 58 points.

Despite its outstanding record, and the presence
of Kurland, the defending champion was not
guaranteed a spot in the NCAA Tournament. Kansas, also included in District 5, had won 19 of 20
games and considered itself deserving of a place.
The selection committee authorized a special playoff for the berth in the NCAA Western competition.

The game was played in Kansas City and it was
no contest, thanks to a big man who resented being
called a glandular goon and was able to do something about it. Kurland scored 28 points in a 49-38
victory over Allen's team. After that, the Western
playoffs were barely challenging. The Aggies routed
Southwest Conference champion Baylor, 44-29, and
Pacific Coast Conference titlist California, 52-35, as
Kurland scored 20 and 29 points, respectively.

In New York, the Eastern playoffs were more
competitive. For the second time in two years, Ohio
State dissipated a sizable lead and was beaten in
overtime in the game that decided the championship representative. A year earlier, New York University had ruined the Buckeyes' plans. This time it
was North Carolina, coached by Lt. Ben Carnevale,
a former NYU player and a Navy V-12 instructor
stationed at Chapel Hill. The Tar Heels won, 60-57.
To reach the Eastern final, in fact, Carnevale's team
had to get by NYU in the first round.

Returning to the Garden in an attempt to win a
second consecutive national championship, Oklahoma A&M had become the most celebrated team
in the country. The Aggies' greatest attraction, of
course, was Kurland.

According to Iba, Kurland had made the very
first dunk in intercollegiate competition. It occurred against Temple in Philadelphia during one
of the Aggies' East Coast swings.

"We never talked about dunking the ball," the
coach said. "This time he just jumped up and did it.
The official took the points away from us."

Of greater concern to basketball legislators had
been Kurland's ability to deflect shots on their
downward arc to the basket. He first attempted to
goaltend in his freshman year against Oklahoma,
which had a fine team that later would be selected
for the NCAA Tournament.

John Dillon's shooting kept North Carolina from getting blown away in the 1946 title game.

"Bruce Drake (the Oklahoma coach) had a fit," Kurland said.

Noting Kurland's increased agility, Iba based his defense on the shot-rejection tactic the following season.

"He'd just pin it up on the boards," Iba said. "Teams had to worry all the time about him tipping it out of there."

Not surprisingly, Oklahoma A&M led the nation in defense in 1944, yielding only 28.8 points per game. In frustration, Drake called on James St. Clair, chairman of the National Basketball Committee, to witness the strategy.

"I think we knocked down only two shots that night," Kurland said. "The damage was mostly psychological."

Nevertheless, in its meeting held in conjunction with the '44 championship game, the committee voted to outlaw the practice of impeding shots on their downward flight. That was all right with Kurland and Iba, who thought goaltending was bad for basketball.

"You could always defeat it with screens or by stepping on the man's feet," Kurland said. "But psychologically it was wrong. It got you out of good practice habits."

Even the new rule couldn't slow Kurland and his team. The Aggies won their national championship without the benefit of goaltending and now they were back in New York to claim another. For the first time in history, the Eastern and Western runners-up were invited to the site to play a consolation game for third place. The result was a tournament record crowd of 18,479.

Kurland rose to the occasion. In 6-6 Horace (Bones) McKinney, North Carolina had a pivotman as quick with his tongue as he was with his feet. McKinney attempted to distract Kurland with his barbs, but the big man had been ridiculed before. The Aggies' star kept his composure and responded with his finest performance in 10 appearances at the Garden.

His hook shots in the early going kept the teams even and, when the Tar Heels concentrated their defense on him, Kurland passed to Weldon Kern for three easy baskets. The Aggies held a 23-17 lead at halftime and extended the margin to 13 points five minutes into the second half. Shortly thereafter, McKinney was charged with his fifth foul and left the game. He had scored only five points.

To North Carolina's credit, it rallied on the hook shots of John Dillon, a 6-3 forward, closing the deficit to 36-33 midway through the second half. But Kurland would not be denied. He scored his team's next seven points as the Aggies opened a 43-34 lead, which the Tar Heels whittled to 43-40 at the final buzzer.

Kurland accounted for nine of Oklahoma A&M's 16 field goals and was awarded a second outstanding-player award for his overall effort. And the Aggies became the first school in tournament history to claim a second championship, consecutively or otherwise.

Iba was particularly pleased for Aubrey, the returning serviceman. As he watched the man walk to center court to receive his championship watch, the coach beamed.

"That," he said, "is the kind of thing you remember."

The accomplishment of the Aggies guaranteed that the team and its star never would be forgotten.

1946 Tournament Results	
First Round	**Semifinals**
Ohio State 46, Harvard 38	North Carolina 60, Ohio State 57
North Carolina 57, New York U. 49	Oklahoma A&M 52, California 35
Oklahoma A&M 44, Baylor 29	**Third Place**
California 50, Colorado 44	Ohio State 63, California 45
Regional Third Place	**Championship**
New York U. 67, Harvard 61	Oklahoma A&M 43, N. Carolina 40
Colorado 59, Baylor 44	

STATISTICS

1946 OKLAHOMA A&M

Head Coach—Henry Iba **Final Record—31-2**

Player	Pos.	Hgt.	Wgt.	Cl.	G	FG	FGA	Pct.	FT.	FTA	Pct.	Reb.	Pts.	Avg.
Bob Kurland	C	7-0	212	Sr.	33	257	...	....	129	223	.578	....	643	19.5
Weldon Kern	F	5-10	145	Jr.	25	71	...	....	64	103	.621	....	206	8.2
J.L. Parks	G	6-0	165	So.	33	70	...	....	47	80	.588	....	187	5.7
Blake Williams	G	6-2	190	So.	33	57	...	....	34	58	.586	....	148	4.5
A.L. Bennett	F	6-2	175	So.	22	34	...	....	15	24	.625	....	83	3.8
Joe Bradley	G	6-2	165	Fr.	30	42	...	....	17	29	.586	....	101	3.4
Sam Aubrey	F	6-4	195	Sr.	33	42	...	....	24	32	.750	....	108	3.3
James Moore	C	6-10	205	Fr.	5	4	...	....	2	4	.500	....	10	2.0
Clarence Parker	G	6-4	180	Fr.	3	3	...	....	0	0	.000	....	6	2.0
Joe Pitts	F	5-10	155	Fr.	25	18	...	....	11	16	.688	....	47	1.9
Gene Bell	G	...	...	...	16	9	...	....	13	14	.929	....	31	1.9
Joe Halbert	C	6-7	210	So.	27	15	...	....	7	12	.583	....	37	1.4
Bill Crowe	F	6-3	165	Sr.	11	6	...	....	2	3	.667	....	14	1.3
Paul Geymann	F	6-1	170	Jr.	21	9	...	....	4	8	.500	....	22	1.0
Martin Loper	F	6 2	200	Fr.	2	1	...	....	0	0	.000	....	2	1.0
Wayne Doles	F	6-0	170	Fr.	8	3	...	....	1	3	.333	....	7	0.9
Larry Hayes	F	6-1	175	Fr.	3	0	...	....	2	2	1.000	....	2	0.7
Ted Hughes	G	6-0	185	Fr.	3	1	...	....	0	0	.000	....	2	0.7
Lou Steinmeier	C	6-5	195	Sr.	12	2	...	....	2	2	1.000	....	6	0.5
Ollie Helderle	F	6-4	185	Fr.	2	0	...	....	1	3	.333	....	1	0.5
Bill Long	F	...	...	...	2	0	...	....	0	0	.000	....	0	0.0
James Stroup	F	6-0	170	Fr.	2	0	...	....	0	0	.000	....	0	0.0
Jack Meredith	C	6-4	180	Fr.	1	0	...	....	0	0	.000	....	0	0.0
Bill Cooper	G	6-2	170	Fr.	1	0	...	....	0	0	.000	....	0	0.0
Don Slocum	C	6-6	165	Fr.	1	0	...	....	0	0	.000	....	0	0.0
Charles Darr	F	6-2	170	Fr.	1	0	...	....	0	0	.000	....	0	0.0
Oklahoma A&M					33	644	...	....	375	616	.609	....	1663	50.4
Opponents					33	358	...	....	342	559	.612	....	1058	32.1

1946 NORTH CAROLINA

Head Coach—Ben Carnevale **Final Record—29-5**

Player	Pos.	Hgt.	Wgt.	Cl.	G	FG	FGA	Pct.	FT.	FTA	Pct.	Reb.	Pts.	Avg.
John Dillon	F	6-3	180	So.	33	178	...	...	96	...	...	...	452	13.7
Jim Jordan	F-G	6-3	180	So.	34	170	...	...	49	...	...	...	389	11.4
Bones McKinney	C	6-6	185	Jr.	19	74	...	...	38	...	...	...	186	9.8
Bob Paxton	F-C	6-2	173	So.	34	106	...	...	62	...	...	...	274	8.1
Don Anderson	G-F	6-1	166	..	29	70	...	...	26	...	...	...	166	5.7
Jim White	G	6-0	160	..	34	54	...	...	32	...	...	...	140	4.1
Taylor Thorne	G-F	5-10	160	..	34	54	...	...	22	...	...	...	130	3.8
Roger Scholbe	F-G	5-11	178	..	18	15	...	...	2	...	...	...	32	1.8
Red Hughes	C-F	6-2	175	..	25	17	...	...	8	...	...	...	42	1.7
Vincent DiLorenzo	G-F	5-11	160	..	14	9	...	...	4	...	...	...	22	1.6
Hall Miles	G-F	5-11	175	..	8	4	...	...	1	...	...	...	9	1.1
Ira Norfolk	F	6-2	180	..	8	4	...	...	0	...	...	...	8	1.0
Buser Stevenson	F-G	6-0	170	..	8	2	...	...	4	...	...	...	8	1.0
.... Fields	G-F	...	...	..	8	2	...	...	2	...	...	...	6	0.8
Max Nathan	G	5-11	155	..	4	0	...	...	3	...	...	...	3	0.8
Jim Hayworth	G	5-11	165	..	19	4	...	...	6	...	...	...	14	0.7
Harold Spurlock	F-G	6-0	180	..	8	2	...	...	1	...	...	...	5	0.6
Michael Fisher	F-G	5-7	150	..	8	0	...	...	1	...	...	...	1	0.1
.... Lewis	G	...	...	..	1	0	...	...	0	...	...	...	0	0.0
.... Chalke	F	...	...	..	1	0	...	...	0	...	...	...	0	0.0
North Carolina					34	765	...	...	357	...	...	...	1887	55.5
Opponents					34	...	...	...	...	...	...	...	1344	39.2

1946 OHIO STATE

Head Coach—Harold Olsen **Final Record—16-5**

Player	Pos.	Hgt.	Wgt.	Cl.	G	FG	FGA	Pct.	FT.	FTA	Pct.	Reb.	Pts.	Avg.
Jack Underman	C	6-6	...	So.	18	90	...	...	49	...	...	...	229	12.7
Robert Bowen	F	6-2	...	Jr.	20	81	...	...	47	...	...	...	209	10.5
Arnie Risen	C	6-9	185	Jr.	6	27	...	...	8	...	...	...	62	10.3
Ray Snyder	G-F	5-8	...	Sr.	21	80	...	...	43	...	...	...	203	9.7
Paul Huston	G	6-3	185	Jr.	21	43	...	...	42	...	...	...	128	6.1
Warren Amling	G	5-11	195	Jr.	20	37	...	...	20	...	...	...	94	4.7
Wayne Wells	F-G	5-10	...	So.	21	32	...	...	9	...	...	...	73	3.5
Clark Elliott	C	6-4	...	Fr.	11	9	...	...	7	...	...	...	25	2.3
James Hall	F	6-1	...	Fr.	1	0	...	...	2	...	...	...	2	2.0
Thomas Watson	C	6-2	...	Fr.	3	2	...	...	0	...	...	...	4	1.3
John Russell	C	6-6	...	Fr.	4	1	...	...	3	...	...	...	5	1.3
Wilbur Johnston	G	6-0	...	Fr.	6	3	...	...	0	...	...	...	6	1.0
Charles Kuhn	G	6-2	...	Fr.	10	3	...	...	3	...	...	...	9	0.9
William Biel	F	5-10	...	Fr.	9	0	...	...	2	...	...	...	2	0.2
John Lovett	F	6-1	...	Jr.	3	0	...	...	0	...	...	...	0	0.0
Charles Goldman	G	5-8	...	Fr.	2	0	...	...	0	...	...	...	0	0.0
.... Genske	..	...	...	...	1	0	...	...	0	...	...	...	0	0.0
David Hackett	G	6-0	...	Fr.	1	0	...	...	0	...	...	...	0	0.0
Robert Merrell	G	6-3	...	Fr.	1	0	...	...	0	...	...	...	0	0.0
Stanley Palmer	G	5-7	...	Jr.	1	0	...	...	0	...	...	...	0	0.0
John Wallin	F	6-0	...	So.	1	0	...	...	0	...	...	...	0	0.0
Ohio State					21	408	...	...	235	...	...	...	1051	50.0
Opponents					21	...	...	...	...	...	...	...	1017	48.4

1946 CALIFORNIA

Head Coach—C.M. (Nibs) Price **Final Record—30-6**

(Complete full-season statistics unavailable.)

Player	Pos.	Hgt.	Wgt.	Cl.	G	FG	FGA	Pct.	FT.	FTA	Pct.	Reb.	Pts.	Avg.
Andy Wolfe	F	6-1	185	So.	34	199	...	...	59	...	...	...	457	13.4
Merv LaFaille	F	...	...	Sr.	36	...	...	...	..	...	...	...	299	8.3
Jim Smith	C	...	...	So.	36	114	...	...	44	...	...	...	272	7.6
Bob Hogeboom	G	...	...	Jr.	36	87	...	...	36	...	...	...	210	5.8
Jim Wray	G	...	...	..	..	57	...	...	29	...	...	...	143	...
George Walker	C	...	...	..	..	18	...	...	23	...	...	...	59	...
Dick Larner	G	...	...	..	..	6	...	...	2	...	...	...	14	...
Les Dean	F-C	...	...	..	..	6	...	...	2	...	...	...	14	...
Cal Riemcke	G	...	...	..	..	1	...	...	1	...	...	...	3	...
Bob Anderson	F	...	...	..	..	..	...	...	..	...	...	...	...	...
Lowell Holcomb	C	...	...	..	..	..	...	...	..	...	...	...	...	...
.... Bower	G	...	...	..	..	..	...	...	..	...	...	...	...	...
Jack Lerond	..	...	...	..	..	..	...	...	..	...	...	...	...	...
Art Mower	..	...	...	..	..	..	...	...	..	...	...	...	...	...
*California					36	..	...	...	..	...	...	...	1647	45.8
*Opponents					36	..	...	...	..	...	...	...	1251	34.8

*Full season.

1946 FINAL FOUR

Semifinals

At New York

North Carolina	fg	ft	fta	pf	tp
Dillon	5	6	13	4	16
Anderson	3	0	1	2	6
Scholbe	0	0	0	1	0
Paxton	4	0	2	3	8
McKinney	4	1	3	5	9
White	2	3	4	4	7
Thorne	1	0	0	1	2
Jordan	4	4	5	3	12
Totals	23	14	28	23	60

Ohio State	fg	ft	fta	pf	tp
Bowen	3	6	6	4	12
Snyder	4	3	7	3	11
Wells	0	0	0	4	0
Underman	8	7	8	4	23
Huston	3	3	6	5	9
Johnston	0	0	0	0	0
Amling	1	0	1	5	2
Totals	19	19	28	25	57

Halftime: Ohio State 20-19. Regulation Score: 54-54. Officials: Nucatola and Orwig.

At Kansas City

Oklahoma A&M	fg	ft	fta	pf	tp
Aubrey	0	0	0	0	0
Bennett	1	2	2	1	4
Kern	2	0	0	1	4
Geymann	0	0	0	0	0
Kurland	12	5	6	3	29
Steinmeier	0	0	0	0	0
Halbert	0	0	0	0	0
Bell	1	2	2	2	4
Bradley	1	1	2	1	3
Williams	1	1	1	0	3
Parks	2	1	1	1	5
Totals	20	12	14	9	52

California	fg	ft	fta	pf	tp
LaFaille	4	2	2	4	10
Wolfe	7	0	1	2	14
Dean	0	0	0	0	0
Smith	0	1	3	3	1
Walker	2	2	3	2	6
Wray	1	0	0	2	2
Larner	0	0	0	0	0
Hogeboom	0	2	3	0	2
Totals	14	7	12	13	35

Halftime: Oklahoma A&M 26-21. Officials: Baker and Curtis.

Championship

March 26

At New York

Oklahoma A&M	fg	ft	fta	pf	tp
Aubrey	0	1	2	1	1
Bennett	3	0	0	4	6
Kern	3	1	3	2	7
Bradley	1	1	2	1	3
Kurland	9	5	9	5	23
Halbert	0	0	0	0	0
Williams	0	2	4	2	2
Bell	0	1	1	1	1
Parks	0	0	0	2	0
Totals	16	11	21	18	43

North Carolina	fg	ft	fta	pf	tp
Dillon	5	6	6	5	16
Anderson	3	2	3	3	8
Paxton	2	0	0	4	4
McKinney	2	1	3	5	5
White	0	1	1	0	1
Thorne	1	0	0	2	2
Jordan	0	4	8	3	4
Totals	13	14	21	22	40

Halftime: Oklahoma A&M 23-17. Officials: Kennedy and Collins.

1947 Holy Cross Beats the Odds

The school was small. The program was an afterthought. The gymnasium was non-existent. That a team from the College of the Holy Cross should find itself in the championship game of the NCAA Tournament was a preposterous notion.

But there was Holy Cross, the product of a happy accident rather than a well-conceived plan, preparing to meet Oklahoma for the national title in New York. In March 1947, the team without a home court had appropriated Madison Square Garden. The mecca of basketball rocked to the Crusaders' locomotive cheer: "Choo-choo-rah-rah!"

Although basketball traced its origins to New England, the region had been left behind in the development of the game. Ol' Doc Naismith would have been thoroughly familiar with the facilities, provided the institutions he visited had bothered to build any. The success of Holy Cross was a triumph of spirit and an act of fantasy.

Instead of rising to basketball prominence, the Crusaders fell into it. Start with Alvin (Doggie) Julian, who was hired from Muhlenberg as an assistant football coach and told that among his duties was the supervision of the school's basketball team. There was no gym on the Worcester, Mass., campus, only an old barn that had been converted for practice use. Nor was there money in the budget for extensive recruiting.

Remarkably, the first class to report to Julian in that barn in the fall of 1945 included several outstanding players from the New York metropolitan area. Gerry Clark, a Holy Cross alumnus and an assistant district attorney in the nation's largest city, took it upon himself to scout Catholic high school players and direct them to Worcester. Among those who accepted an invitation to join the 1,200-member student body was George Kaftan, a 6-foot-3 center with extraordinary leaping ability.

"It never dawned on me that Holy Cross didn't have a gymnasium," Kaftan said. "I just liked the school."

Ironically, the team's first game that season was at Madison Square Garden, against City College of New York. The Beavers had a renowned coach in Nat Holman, years of basketball tradition and the loud support of a Garden crowd.

"Lo and behold," Kaftan said, "we won." In fact, the Crusaders won 12 of 15 games that season and were in contention for a postseason tournament bid that never came.

The presence the next year of service veterans Joe Mullaney and Frank Oftring and the enrollment of another New York schoolboy star, Bob Cousy, built on that foundation. The team still was uncommonly short, but everyone could run and handle the ball. The 1947 Crusaders played a slick brand of give-and-go. Newspapers, in a playful reference to the athletic-club teams of that era, referred to them as the "Fancy Pants A.C."

Holy Cross Coach Alvin (Doggie) Julian was an early proponent of the crying towel.

The 1947 Holy Cross title team. Top row (left to right): Assistant coach Albert Riopel, James Riley, Charles Bollinger, Bobbie McMullen, Charles Graver and manager Frank Dooley. Second row: Bob Curran, Ken Haggerty, Coach Alvin (Doggie) Julian, Joe Mullaney and George Kaftan. Front row: Dermott O'Connell, Bob Cousy, Frank Oftring and Andrew Laska.

Without its own gym, Holy Cross scheduled games at the Boston Garden, where the collegians soon outdrew the professional Celtics of the fledgling Basketball Association of America (later the National Basketball Association). A caravan of cars followed the Crusaders from Worcester, 40 miles away, and all New England rallied behind the team as it defeated one national power after another. After early-season losses to North Carolina State, Duquesne and Wyoming, the Crusaders embarked on a long winning streak, highlighted by a narrow victory over an outstanding Seton Hall team, led by Bobby Wanzer.

In only its second year of top-level competition, Holy Cross was selected to the field of the Eastern playoffs in New York. Other entrants were Big Ten Conference champion Wisconsin, Navy and hometown favorite City College. It marked the first appearance in the NCAA Tournament for all the schools except Wisconsin, which had captured the national championship six years earlier.

On opening night, Mullaney had 18 points (all on field goals) and Kaftan added 15 as the Crusaders handed Navy only its second defeat of the season, 55-47. CCNY struggled for a while against Wisconsin, but the Beavers rallied from a 10-point deficit in the second half to win decisively, 70-56.

Now it would be Holy Cross vs. CCNY at the Garden, and this was where Julian and the Kaftan-led New York brigade—six of the Crusaders' top seven scorers were from the big city and its environs—figured to have special impact.

Natives or not, though, the boys in purple were a distant second in the popular vote on the following night. The vast majority of the 18,000-plus fans roared approval as the Beavers opened fast, rushing to a 10-3 lead. It was nearly eight minutes before the Crusaders made their first field goal but, instead of panicking, they steadily worked their way back into the game and managed to edge in front by halftime.

The second half belonged to Holy Cross in general and to Kaftan in particular. The sophomore finished with 11 field goals and 30 points and dominated the backboards as the Crusaders scored a 60-45 triumph, their 22nd victory in succession. The Crusaders were one step from the top, and New

York was prepared to take out adoption papers.

Meanwhile, in Kansas City, Oklahoma had survived the Western playoffs in perhaps the most thrilling action in tournament history. First, the Sooners subdued favored Oregon State, 56-54. They followed that with a melodramatic 55-54 victory over a Texas team that had lost only once previously. A last-second basket by Ken Pryor—his lone field goal of the game—enabled Oklahoma to prevail over the Longhorns, who had defeated Wyoming in the first round.

The outstanding player in the West had been Gerry Tucker, the Sooners' center. He had returned from the service to lead Oklahoma to the Big Six Conference title and a record of 24-6 entering the NCAA championship game. Basketball fans eagerly awaited his confrontation with Kaftan, the Holy Cross star.

Julian, an excitable type, didn't make much sense as he announced the starting lineup in the dressing room before the final.

"George is going to start," he said. "And Dermie (O'Connell) is going to start. And the Greek (another reference to Kaftan). And Joe Mullaney. And Kaftan."

As nearly as Kaftan and his teammates could figure it, that meant one man was expected to play three positions at once. The Crusaders rolled their eyes as they headed for the floor. The usual starting five went out for the opening tip.

"So you're the young hotshot I've heard so much about," the 25-year-old Tucker said to Kaftan.

"Hang it up, Gerry," Kaftan, 19, replied with a smile. "It's a young man's game."

The two players and teams proceeded to stage a sensational first half. There were eight lead changes and 10 ties as the Sooners and Crusaders battled over every basket. Tucker was particularly formidable, his hook shots accounting for five baskets. It was he who led a seven-point surge in the final minutes of the half for a 31-28 Oklahoma lead.

Holy Cross made two notable changes in the second half. Reserve Bob Curran was assigned the task of guarding Tucker, and the Crusaders began to step up the pace of the game. With an edge in speed and depth, the New Englanders soon took the lead and maintained it. Tucker's only field goal of the half, a hook shot, cut the deficit to four points with three minutes remaining and Pryor's free throw chopped it to 48-45.

But that was as close as the Sooners would come. Holy Cross scored 10 of the last 12 points in the game for a 58-47 conquest. The team without a campus gymnasium reigned over college basketball.

Tucker was the game's high scorer with 22 points, but no other Oklahoma player was in double figures. Kaftan finished with 18 points and was Holy Cross' rebounding star, while O'Connell added 16

George Kaftan's unusual jumping ability was a big factor in Holy Cross' drive to the 1947 NCAA title.

Joe Mullaney (right) was a starter on Doggie Julian's championship team while Bob Cousy (left) was just beginning his illustrious basketball career.

points and Oftring 14 for the Crusaders. Cousy, the freshman substitute who would become the most famous player in school history and a great professional, contributed two free throws.

The implausible championship stimulated college basketball interest throughout New England. And it even resulted in the construction of a practice gym on the Holy Cross campus.

1947 Tournament Results

First Round
Holy Cross 55, Navy 47
CCNY 70, Wisconsin 56
Texas 42, Wyoming 40
Oklahoma 56, Oregon State 54

Regional Third Place
Wisconsin 50, Navy 49
Oregon State 63, Wyoming 46

Semifinals
Holy Cross 60, CCNY 45
Oklahoma 55, Texas 54

Third Place
Texas 54, CCNY 50

Championship
Holy Cross 58, Oklahoma 47

STATISTICS

1947 HOLY CROSS

Head Coach—Alvin (Doggie) Julian   Final Record—27-3

Player	Pos.	Hgt.	Wgt.	Cl.	G	FG	FGA	Pct.	FT	FTA	Pct.	Reb.	Pts.	Avg.
George Kaftan	F-C	6-3	200	So.	28	119	...	...	72	...	...	...	310	11.1
Dermie O'Connell	F	6-0	175	So.	29	116	...	...	28	...	...	...	260	9.0
Bob Cousy	G-F	6-1	170	Fr.	30	91	...	...	45	...	...	...	227	7.6
Ken Haggerty	G	6-0	175	Sr.	29	70	...	...	26	...	...	...	166	5.7
Andy Laska	F-G	5-10	165	Fr.	30	70	...	...	27	...	...	...	167	5.6
Joe Mullaney	G	6-0	155	So.	30	64	...	...	21	...	...	...	149	5.0
Frank Oftring	C-F	6-2	180	Sr.	29	50	...	...	34	...	...	...	134	4.6
Bob Curran	F-C	6-3	195	Jr.	30	45	...	...	43	...	...	...	133	4.4
Charlie Bollinger	C	6-6	220	So.	26	44	...	...	17	...	...	...	105	4.0
Bobbie McMullen	G-F	6-3	180	Fr.	29	43	...	...	24	...	...	...	110	3.8
Dennis O'Shea	G-F	6-1	185	Fr.	2	3	...	...	0	...	...	...	6	3.0
James Sullivan	F				1	1	...	...	0	...	...	...	2	2.0
Jim Riley	F-C	6-3	190	Sr.	17	14	...	...	5	...	...	...	33	1.9
Matt Forman	F-C	6-4	205	Fr.	10	6	...	...	4	...	...	...	16	1.6
Charles Graver	G-F	6-0	185	Fr.	13	3	...	...	2	...	...	...	8	0.6
Dave Mullaney	G	6-2	180	Sr.	1	0	...	...	0	...	...	...	0	0.0
Joseph Collins	G	6-0	175	Fr.	1	0	...	...	0	...	...	...	0	0.0
Holy Cross					30	739	...	...	348	...	...	...	1826	60.9
Opponents					30	494	...	...	371	...	...	...	1359	45.3

1947 OKLAHOMA

Head Coach—Bruce Drake   Final Record—24-7

Player	Pos.	Hgt.	Wgt.	Cl.	G	FG	FGA	Pct.	FT	FTA	Pct.	Reb.	Pts.	Avg.
Gerry Tucker	C	6-4	208	Sr.	31	111	...	...	103	136	.757	...	325	10.5
Paul Courty	F	6-3	187	So.	31	90	...	...	66	107	.617	...	246	7.9
Dick Reich	F	6-3	190	Sr.	31	84	...	...	73	104	.702	...	241	7.8
Allie Paine	G	6-0	166	Sr.	30	58	...	...	57	84	.679	...	173	5.8
Jack Landon	G	6-1	175	So.	31	57	...	...	51	85	.600	...	165	5.3
Bill Waters	G-F	6-5	215	Fr.	29	46	...	...	24	45	.533	...	116	4.0
Ken Pryor	F	5-10	160	So.	29	40	...	...	18	30	.600	...	98	3.4
Harly Day	F	6-1	175	Jr.	21	24	...	...	19	29	.655	...	67	3.2
Paul Merchant	G	6-0	155	Fr	30	23	...	...	19	31	.613	...	65	2.2
Bob Jones	F	6-4	187	So.	21	14	...	...	17	31	.548	...	45	2.1
Jimmy Mitchell	...	6-0	180	So.	10	3	...	...	7	9	.778	...	13	1.3
Wayne Speegle		6-2	150	Fr.	9	2	...	...	2	4	.500	...	6	0.7
Charles Pugsley	...	6-0	170	So.	14	2	...	...	4	13	.308	...	8	0.6
Others												...	108	
Oklahoma					31	...	...	...	...	...	...	...	1676	54.1
Opponents					31	...	...	...	...	...	...	...	1404	45.3

1947 TEXAS

Head Coach—Jack Gray   Final Record—26-2

(Complete full-season statistics are unavailable.)

Player	Pos.	Hgt.	Wgt.	Cl.	G	FG	FGA	Pct.	FT	FTA	Pct.	Reb.	Pts.	Avg.
John Hargis	F	6-2	184	Sr.	28	150	...	...	101	...	...	...	401	14.3
Slater Martin	F	5-10	168	So.	28	108	...	...	39	...	...	...	255	9.1
John Langdon	C	6-7	...	Jr.	28	85	...	...	35	...	...	...	205	7.3
Al Madsen	G	5-10	...	So.	28	56	...	...	90	...	...	...	202	7.2
Tom Hamilton	F	6-3	215	So.	27	32	...	...	42	...	...	...	106	3.3
Dan Wagner	G	5-11	...	So.		...	...	...	...	...	...	...	...	...
Roy Cox	G	5-8	150	Sr.		...	...	...	...	...	...	...	...	...
Vilbry White	G-F	6-1	180	So.		...	...	...	...	...	...	...	...	...
Jack Fitzgerald	...	...	...	Sr.		...	...	...	...	...	...	...	...	...
Philip George	...	...	...	So.		...	...	...	...	...	...	...	...	...
*Texas					28	...	...	...	...	...	...	...	1641	58.6
*Opponents					28	...	...	...	...	...	...	...	1233	44.0

*Full season.

1947 CCNY

Head Coach—Nat Holman   Final Record—17-6

(Complete statistics unavailable.)

Player	Pos.	Hgt.	Wgt.	Cl.	G	FG	FGA	Pct.	FT	FTA	Pct.	Reb.	Pts.	Avg.
Lionel Malamed	G	5-8	175	So.	22	91	...	...	36	...	...	...	218	9.9
Irwin Dambrot	F	6-3	180	Fr.	23	93	...	...	35	...	...	...	221	9.6
Sidney Trubowitz	F	5-10	180	Jr.	23	61	...	...	33	...	...	...	155	6.7
Sonny Jameson	F	6-0	172	So.	23	61	...	...	27	...	...	...	149	6.5
Mason Benson	C	6-5	190	So.	20	49	...	...	26	...	...	...	124	6.2
Hilton Shapiro	F-G	5-11	180	So.	23	53	...	...	27	...	...	...	133	5.8
Everett Finestone	F-G	6-0	175	Jr.	23	41	...	...	43	...	...	...	125	5.4
Joe Galiber	C	6-4	205	Jr.	22	42	...	...	29	...	...	...	113	5.1
Phil Farbman	C-F	6-2	185	Jr.	19	17	...	...	18	...	...	...	52	2.7
Sidney Finger	G	6-0	165	So.	20	20	...	...	4	...	...	...	44	2.2
Paul Malamed	...	5-11	175	So.	9	7	...	...	4	...	...	...	18	2.0
Morris Brickman	F	5-11	175	So.	13	3	...	...	4	...	...	...	10	0.8
Arnold Millman	...	6-2	180	Fr.	7	1	...	...	1	...	...	...	3	0.4
Paul Schmones	G	5-9	159	Sr.		...	...	...	...	...	...	...	...	...
Milton Breenberg	...	6-1	180	Jr.		...	...	...	...	...	...	...	...	...
Isaac Dubrow	...	5-11	187	So.		...	...	...	...	...	...	...	...	...
David Williams	...	5-11	164	Fr.		...	...	...	...	...	...	...	...	...
CCNY					23	...	...	...	...	...	...	...	1452	63.1
Opponents					23	...	...	...	...	...	...	...	1173	51.0

1947 FINAL FOUR

Semifinals
At New York

Holy Cross	fg	ft	fta	pf	tp
Kaftan	11	8	12	2	30
O'Connell	2	1	2	1	5
Oftring	2	3	3	3	7
Mullaney	0	3	5	2	3
Haggerty	2	0	0	3	4
Cousy	2	1	2	3	5
McMullen	1	1	3	2	3
Laska	1	0	0	1	2
Curran	0	1	2	2	1
Totals	21	18	29	19	60

CCNY	fg	ft	fta	pf	tp
Trubowitz	2	0	1	1	4
Dambrot	5	4	7	3	14
Galiber	1	3	5	4	5
Shapiro	2	1	1	3	5
Malamed	1	1	1	2	3
Jameson	1	1	1	5	3
Farbman	0	1	1	1	1
Benson	0	0	0	1	0
Finestone	4	1	2	4	9
Schmones	0	1	1	1	1
Totals	16	13	20	25	45

Halftime: Holy Cross 27-25. Officials: Haarlow and Orwig.

At Kansas City

Oklahoma	fg	ft	tp
Reich	4	3	11
Courty	3	2	8
Pryor	1	0	2
Tucker	6	3	15
Paine	4	0	8
Merchant	0	1	1
Landon	2	2	6
Waters	1	2	4
Totals	21	13	55

Texas	fg	ft	tp
Hargis	3	3	9
Hamilton	0	1	1
Martin	8	2	18
Langdon	3	1	7
Madsen	1	4	6
Cox	1	0	2
Wagner	5	1	11
Totals	21	12	54

Halftime: Texas 29-22. Officials: Leith and Ogden.

Championship
March 25
At New York

Holy Cross	fg	ft	fta	pf	tp
Kaftan	7	4	9	4	18
O'Connell	7	2	4	3	16
Oftring	6	2	3	5	14
Mullaney	0	0	0	2	0
Haggerty	0	0	0	0	0
Laska	0	0	0	0	0
Curran	0	0	1	2	0
Riley	0	0	0	1	0
McMullen	2	4	4	0	8
Cousy	0	2	2	1	2
Bollinger	0	0	0	0	0
Graver	0	0	0	0	0
Totals	22	14	23	18	58

Oklahoma	fg	ft	fta	pf	tp
Reich	3	2	2	3	8
Courty	3	2	3	4	8
Tucker	6	10	12	3	22
Paine	2	2	6	0	6
Landon	1	0	1	4	2
Waters	0	0	0	0	0
Day	0	0	0	0	0
Pryor	0	1	1	2	1
Merchant	0	0	1	0	0
Totals	15	17	21	17	47

Halftime: Oklahoma 31-28. Officials: Andersen and Kennedy.

1948 Adolph Rupp's Fabulous Five

Kentucky's Fabulous Five with Coach Adolph Rupp. Standing (left to right) are Wallace Jones, Alex Groza and Cliff Barker. Seated are Ken Rollins and Ralph Beard.

Basketball was not invented by Adolph Rupp. It only seems that way to citizens of the Commonwealth, which is how Kentuckians refer to their state. More than any other individual, Rupp was responsible for the sport's acquisition of a Southern accent.

When Rupp arrived in Lexington late in the summer of 1930, the popularity of basketball was such that he was required to double as an assistant football coach. Years later, he would tell his players, "I had more sense than to stand out in the wind and rain, so I came indoors."

But basketball always was Rupp's paramount interest. And there was no denying the serendipity of his background.

Raised on a farm near Halstead, Kan., he said he didn't know the story of Dr. James Naismith but he did play the sport, or at least a variation, as a youngster.

"In those days the ball we had out on the farm was just a gunnysack stuffed with rags," he said. "Mother sewed it up and somehow made it round. You couldn't dribble it. Then, in grade school, we got a barrel and used that for a basket. The ball was a little bit better than the one we had on the farm, but not much. We had an old ball, and we'd have to blow it up every day and put a rubber band around it. We had to keep lacing it to keep it from falling apart."

Ironically, upon enrolling at Kansas, Rupp soon found himself in one of Naismith's physical education classes. Rupp learned the origins of basketball from the good doctor's mouth. He also played under Coach Phog Allen, Naismith's foremost protege, on the Jayhawks' 1923 team that went unbeaten against collegiate competition.

Rupp spent five years developing his philosophy of basketball at the high school level before taking the Kentucky job. The Wildcats were 15-3 in his first year and they would do no worse than break even in any of Rupp's 41 seasons in Lexington. He was overly modest about neither his knowledge of the sport nor his ability to impart it.

For a time, Rupp taught a course on the fundamentals of basketball on behalf of the university's physical education department. He enjoyed telling people he was the best professor on campus because everyone who took his course received an "A." The reason all his students excelled, he explained, was that no one could learn basketball from Adolph Rupp without qualifying for such a grade.

It was in the aftermath of World War II that Rupp's Wildcats made their greatest impact. His 1946 team won the National Invitation Tournament and the 1947 Kentucky squad reached the NIT final. That set the stage for the first of his great championship clubs. In 1948 he became the Baron of the Bluegrass, master of all he surveyed, with the rise of the Fabulous Five.

Named by Larry Boeck, a crony of Rupp's who worked for the Louisville Courier-Journal, the team consisted of center Alex Groza, forwards Wallace (Wah Wah) Jones and Cliff Barker and guards Ralph Beard and Ken Rollins. Together, they would attain heights no other college team had ever scaled, reaching the Olympic Games.

Kentucky's remarkable journey started with a regular-season record of 27-2 (the losses were to Temple and Notre Dame) and a fifth consecutive Southeastern Conference postseason tournament title. The first NCAA Tournament stop was New York's Madison Square Garden, where the Wildcats met Columbia in the first round of the Eastern playoffs. Columbia had lost only once in 22 games, and that defeat came in overtime. Jones (21 points), Groza (17) and Beard (15) equaled the scoring total of the entire Columbia team as Kentucky dominated the Lions, 76-53.

The victory boosted the Wildcats into the Eastern final against Holy Cross, the defending national champion. The Crusaders had entered the tournament on the crest of a 19-game winning streak and were a dashing, exciting team sparked by a dynamic sophomore guard named Bob Cousy. The New York youngster scored 23 points against Michigan in the other first-round Eastern game, mystifying the Wolverines with his dribbling and passing in Holy Cross' surprisingly easy 63-45 triumph.

Once again, Kentucky's big three proved virtually unstoppable, particularly the 6-foot-7 Groza. He scored 23 points, eight more than Holy Cross counterpart George Kaftan. The key defensive performance of the night was turned in by Rollins, who shut down Cousy. The Crusaders' sparkplug scored only three points, all on free throws, before Rollins was relieved by Dale Barnstable. The Wildcats won convincingly, 60-52.

Having dethroned the old champion, Kentucky awaited the arrival of Baylor, the unlikely survivor of the Western playoffs at Kansas City. The Bears had rallied from 17 points down to edge Washington, 64-62, and then had overcome a 10-point deficit in defeating Kansas State, 60-52. Baylor's first two victories in tournament history provided the Southwest Conference with its first representative in an NCAA title game.

The New York press made much of the fact that Baylor's floor leader was named Jackie Robinson. Only the previous spring, of course, another Jackie Robinson had broken the color line in major league baseball and earned Rookie of the Year honors in the uniform of the Brooklyn Dodgers. This Robinson was a whiz of a white guard studying for the ministry.

A team of fine ballhandlers, Baylor was even less a physical match for Kentucky than was Holy

The master, Coach Adolph Rupp, with his star pupil, Alex Groza.

Cross. The Bears' center, sophomore Don Heathington, was only 6-3, and there was no forward with the stature of the ruggedly built Jones. Compounding its problems, Baylor seemed intimidated by the Garden and the crowd of 16,174 at the start of the game.

Chances are, Rupp could have thrown the jacket of his famous brown suit on the court and walked off with the championship. Rupp wouldn't dare wear any other color to a game if he planned to win, and the man planned to win every game in which he coached.

"I once wore a blue suit to a game," he explained, "and we got the hell beat out of us. I figured I better go back to brown after that."

It took the Bears five minutes to score their first point, on a free throw. That was after Kentucky had built a 7-0 lead, which it subsequently boosted to 13-1 and 24-7. Baylor did cut a 13-point halftime deficit to nine (44-35) at one stage of the second half while Groza and Jones were resting. Rupp promptly reinserted them and the Wildcats ran away to a 58-42 triumph.

In any other year, that would have been accomplishment enough. But this was an Olympic year and the basketball trials were scheduled to begin within a week after the NCAA championship game. Once again, the Garden provided the backdrop.

The eight-team field included college and Amateur Athletic Union teams. Kentucky and Baylor met again in the semifinals, with the Wildcats once more doing as they pleased in a 77-59 victory. They were finally stopped, 53-49, in the championship game by the AAU champion Phillips Oilers, led by 7-foot Bob Kurland.

So impressive were the Oilers and the Wildcats that the Olympic selectors took the starting fives from each and added one individual from four other teams, including Baylor's Robinson. Bud Browning of the Oilers and Rupp were named coaches for the competition in London.

For players accustomed to huge crowds in the United States, the Olympic competition was a strange experience.

"Some games we had 50 people in the arena," Beard said. "Other games we didn't have that many. Basketball wasn't very popular in Europe then. But it doesn't take away from the gold medal."

The U.S. team won all eight games it played and five Kentucky basketball players were rewarded with another championship. It was an unprecedented postscript to a spectacular season. And it led Rupp to call his Fabulous Five "the greatest (college) basketball team of all time."

Of course, he gave all his players "A" grades. Who do you think taught them so well?

1948 Tournament Results

First Round	Semifinals
Kentucky 76, Columbia 53	Kentucky 60, Holy Cross 52
Holy Cross 63, Michigan 45	Baylor 60, Kansas State 52
Kansas State 58, Wyoming 48	**Third Place**
Baylor 64, Washington 62	Holy Cross 60, Kansas State 54
Regional Third Place	**Championship**
Michigan 66, Columbia 49	Kentucky 58, Baylor 42
Washington 57, Wyoming 47	

STATISTICS

1948 KENTUCKY

Head Coach—Adolph Rupp   Final Record—36-3

(Statistics and record include three games in Olympic Trials [2-1 record] after NCAA Tournament.)

Player	Pos.	Hgt.	Wgt.	Cl.	G	FG	FGA	Pct.	FT.	FTA	Pct.	Reb.	Pts.	Avg.
Alex Groza	C	6-7	220	Jr.	39	200	530	.377	88	140	.629	...	488	12.5
Ralph Beard	G	5-10	175	Jr.	38	194	536	.362	88	149	.591	...	476	12.5
Wallace Jones	F	6-4	225	Jr.	36	133	427	.311	69	103	.670	...	335	9.3
James Line	F	6-2	185	So.	38	107	296	.361	51	62	.823	...	265	7.0
Ken Rollins	G	6-0	175	Sr.	39	95	341	.279	67	92	.728	...	257	6.6
Cliff Barker	F	6-1	185	Jr.	38	98	317	.309	52	93	.559	...	248	6.5
Dale Barnstable	F	6-2	175	So.	38	76	280	.271	24	42	.571	...	176	4.6
Joe Holland	F	6-4	190	Jr.	38	58	207	.280	24	47	.511	...	140	3.7
Jack Parkinson	G	6-0	175	Sr.	29	43	214	.201	10	22	.455	...	96	3.3
Walt Hirsch	F	6-3	180	Fr.	13	16	55	.291	5	9	.556	...	37	2.8
Albert Cummins	G	5-10	160	So.	17	13	37	.351	6	9	.667	...	32	1.9
Jim Jordan	F	6-3	185	So.	30	13	88	.148	18	25	.720	...	44	1.5
Garland Townes	G	6-0	170	Fr.	13	7	22	.318	5	11	.455	...	19	1.5
Roger Day	F	6-3	185	Fr.	11	5	18	.278	7	9	.778	...	17	1.5
Wil Smether	G	6-2	180	Fr.	7	5	10	.500	0	3	.000	...	10	1.4
Robert Henne	G	6-1	165	Fr.	11	5	22	.227	3	7	.429	...	13	1.2
Albert Campbell	C	6-4	200	Sr.	15	6	27	.222	4	7	.571	...	16	1.1
Johnny Stough	G	6-0	170	So.	23	8	38	.211	5	10	.500	...	21	0.9
Kentucky					39	1082	3465	.312	526	840	.626	...	2690	70.0
Opponents					39	....	....	.232				...	1730	44.4

1948 BAYLOR

Head Coach—Bill Henderson   Final Record—24-8

Player	Pos.	Hgt.	Wgt.	Cl.	G	FG	FGA	Pct.	FT.	FTA	Pct.	Reb.	Pts.	Avg.
James (Red) Owens	F	6-3	185	Jr.	32	126			76	111	.685	...	328	10.3
Bill Johnson	G	6-2	175	Jr.	32	122			76	96	.792	...	320	10.0
Don Heathington	C	6-3	180	So.	32	94			112	176	.636	...	300	9.4
Jackie Robinson	G	6-0	165	Jr.	32	100			99	156	.635	...	299	9.3
Bill DeWitt	F	6-3	...	So.	30	64			34	53	.642	...	162	5.4
Odell Preston	C-F	6-3	...	So.	29	42			51	74	.689	...	135	4.7
Bill Hickman	F	6-3	...	So.	10	11			4	12	.333	...	26	2.6
Ralph Pulley	G	6-0	...	Jr.	20	10			8	13	.615	...	28	1.4
Bill Srack	G	5-9	...	So.	..	8			8	14	.571	...	24	...
Charles Devereaux	G	5-10	...		..	7			5	8	.625	...	19	...
Jim Marino	G	5-8	...		..	1			3	4	.750	...	5	...
Clarence McGowan	G	5-11	...		..	0			1	1	1.000	...	1	...
Baylor					32	585			477	718	.664	...	1647	51.5
Opponents					32	547			458	672	.682	...	1552	48.5

1948 HOLY CROSS

Head Coach—Alvin (Doggie) Julian   Final Record—26-4

Player	Pos.	Hgt.	Wgt.	Cl.	G	FG	FGA	Pct.	FT.	FTA	Pct.	Reb.	Pts.	Avg.
Bob Cousy	G	6-1	170	So.	30	207			72	108	.667	...	486	16.2
George Kaftan	C-F	6-3	200	Jr.	30	187			94	158	.595	...	468	15.6
Dermott O'Connell	F	6-0	175	Jr.	30	102			21	52	.404	...	225	7.5
Joe Mullaney	G	6-0	155	Jr.	28	64			25	43	.581	...	153	5.5
Frank Oftring	F-C	6-2	180	So.	30	62			37	55	.673	...	161	5.4
Robert Curran	G	6-3	195	Sr.	30	62			25	41	.610	...	149	5.0
Andrew Laska	G	5-10	165	So.	27	38			22	35	.629	...	98	3.6
Robert McMullan	G	6-3	180	So.	30	42			20	32	.625	...	104	3.5
Charles Bollinger	C	6-6	210	Jr.	14	19			3	6	.500	...	41	2.9
Bert Dolan	F	6-1	175	Sr.	16	15			4	7	.571	...	34	2.1
Matthew Formon	C	6-4	205	So.	29	21			8	23	.348	...	50	1.7
Joseph Collins	F	6-0	175	So.	3	1			2	3	.667	...	4	1.3
James Murphy	G	6-1	190	Jr.	8	5			0	2	.000	...	10	1.3
Charles Graver	G	6-0	185	So.	15	7			3	4	.750	...	17	1.1
Dennis O'Shea	F	6-1	185	So.	9	2			0	2	.000	...	4	0.4
Holy Cross					30	834			336	571	.588	...	2004	66.8
Opponents					30	552			310	517	.600	...	1414	47.1

1948 KANSAS STATE

Head Coach—Jack Gardner   Final Record—22-6

Player	Pos.	Hgt.	Wgt.	Cl.	G	FG	FGA	Pct.	FT.	FTA	Pct.	Reb.	Pts.	Avg.
Howard Shannon	F-G	6-1	170	Jr.	28	109			58	66	.879	...	276	9.9
Rick Harman	F	6-3	190	So.	28	88			86	127	.677	...	262	9.4
Harold Howey	F	6-0	170	Jr.	28	88			69	116	.595	...	245	8.8
Clarence Brannum	C	6-5	210	So.	28	84			61	115	.530	...	229	8.2
Jack Dean	G	6-1	165	Jr.	28	57			58	79	.734	...	172	6.1
Ward Clark	C	6-3	195	So.	28	44			32	43	.744	...	120	4.3
Al Langton	F	5-10	160	So.	28	34			30	53	.566	...	98	3.5
Lloyd Krone	F-G	6-1	185	So.	28	21			19	33	.576	...	61	2.2
Bob Johnson	G	6-0	175	So.	2	2			0	0	.000	...	4	2.0
Dave Weatherby	F	6-4	170	Sr.	21	10			14	18	.778	...	34	1.6
Ken Mahoney	C	6-1	170	So.	16	8			5	9	.556	...	21	1.3
Glen Mitchum	..	...	...		7	1			2	4	.500	...	4	0.6
Jerry Patrick	C-G	6-5	180	Jr.	6	0			3	3	1.000	...	3	0.5
Joe Thornton	G	6-0	180	So.	15	3			1	4	.250	...	7	0.5
Jack Bell	G	6-3	200	So.	3	0			1	1	1.000	...	1	0.3
Bill Thuston	F	6-0	175	So.	13	0			2	4	.500	...	2	0.2
Bob Lewis	F	6-3	175	So.	3	0			0	0	.000	...	0	0.0
Kansas State					28	549			441	675	.653	...	1539	55.0
Opponents					28	....			....		....	...	1281	45.8

1948 FINAL FOUR

Semifinals
At New York

Kentucky	fg	ft	tp
Jones	4	4	12
Barker	2	0	4
Line	0	0	0
Groza	10	3	23
Holland	0	0	0
Beard	6	1	13
Rollins	3	2	8
Barnstable	0	0	0
Totals	25	10	60

Holy Cross	fg	ft	tp
Oftring	4	4	12
McMullan	0	0	0
Cousy	1	3	5
O'Connell	3	3	9
Kaftan	6	3	15
Bollinger	1	0	2
Curran	3	1	7
Formon	0	0	0
Mullaney	0	0	0
Laska	1	0	2
Totals	19	14	52

Halftime: Kentucky 36-28. Officials: Begovich and Osborne.

At Kansas City

Kansas State	fg	ft	pf	tp
Harman	3	6	4	12
Krone	0	2	0	2
Howey	3	3	5	9
Langton	1	1	3	3
Weatherby	0	0	2	0
Brannum	3	1	5	7
Clark	1	3	5	5
Dean	3	2	4	8
Shannon	1	4	1	6
Totals	15	22	29	52

Baylor	fg	ft	pf	tp
Owens	3	2	5	8
Hickman	0	0	2	0
DeWitt	3	0	5	6
Preston	1	3	1	5
Pulley	1	0	0	2
Heathington	3	9	2	15
Johnson	4	5	3	13
Robinson	5	1	4	11
Totals	20	20	22	60

Halftime: Kansas State 32-28. Officials: Curtis and Ogden.

Championship
March 23
At New York

Kentucky	fg	ft	tp
Jones	4	1	9
Barker	2	1	5
Groza	6	2	14
Beard	4	4	12
Rollins	3	3	9
Line	3	1	7
Holland	1	0	2
Barnstable	0	0	0
Totals	23	12	58

Baylor	fg	ft	tp
Owens	2	1	5
DeWitt	3	2	8
Heathington	3	2	8
Johnson	3	4	10
Robinson	3	2	8
Pulley	0	1	1
Hickman	1	0	2
Preston	0	0	0
Srack	0	0	0
Totals	15	12	42

Halftime: Kentucky 29-16. Officials: Haarlow and MacDonald.

1949 Wildcats Strut To Second Title

Kentucky's 1949 championship team. Standing (left to right) are Dale Barnstable, Walter Hirsch, Wallace Jones, Alex Groza, Bob Henne, Roger Day and manager Humzey Yessin. Seated are Coach Adolph Rupp, Jim Line, Cliff Barker, Johnny Stough, Ralph Beard, Joe Hall, Garland Townes and assistant coach Harry Lancaster.

This was the season that the Associated Press introduced its nationwide college basketball poll. And this was a year when the weekly balloting proved superfluous.

From the outset, there was little doubt about the identity of the nation's No. 1 team. It was the defending national champion, the Olympic half-champion, the aspiring folk heroes from Kentucky. Of the Fabulous Five, only Ken Rollins was lost through graduation, and Adolph Rupp had no shortage of replacements.

After an early-season loss to St. Louis, the Wildcats won all their games until falling in the National Invitation Tournament to eventual finalist Loyola of Chicago. They were undefeated in Southeastern Conference play and considered in a class by themselves. The athletic ability of their top three players was a matter of public record.

Alex Groza was the brother of Lou Groza, the standout placekicker and tackle for the Cleveland Browns. Wah Wah Jones, who acquired his nickname from his younger sister's inability to pronounce Wallace, had starred for the Kentucky football team as a two-way end and would earn 11

letters (three in baseball) during his college career. Ralph Beard had been an outstanding halfback in high school and arrived at Lexington with a football scholarship.

"I started the first game," Beard said of his football-playing days at Kentucky, "and I got both my shoulders separated on the same play. I had a hard time brushing my teeth and performing a few other necessities for a while." He decided to concentrate on basketball.

No such calamity befell the 6-foot-4 Jones, a strapping youngster of 225 pounds. He finished his first Kentucky football season under interim Coach Bernie Shively and played three more seasons under the formidable Bear Bryant, whose direction made Rupp's seem gentle by comparison.

"The football players were scared to death of Bryant," Jones said, "and that included the veterans returning from the war who were older than him." Well, almost as old as he was.

Ordinarily, Jones didn't miss a step between the football and basketball seasons.

"The football season would end on a Saturday and basketball would start on a Monday," he said.

In the fall of 1947, behind quarterback George Blanda, Kentucky accepted an invitation to the first and only Great Lakes Bowl, extending its season. Jones was required to play against Villanova in the Cleveland bowl contest before joining the basketball team.

After Jones played his way into basketball shape, there was no stopping the Wildcats as 1948 rolled around. To the relief of Rupp, the next Kentucky football team did not intrude upon the holidays and the 1949 basketball team was able to rely on Jones at the start of the season.

The fourth returning starter, Cliff Barker, was considerably older than his teammates. He had been a flier in World War II and was shot down and detained in a prisoner-of-war camp for more than a year.

After experimenting with the lineup in early games of the '49 season, Rupp achieved the perfect balance by moving the 6-2 Barker from forward to guard and using either Dale Barnstable or Jim Line in the frontcourt.

The maneuver put a devastating combination on the floor, a unit that Rupp was only too happy to display at major facilities around the country. Alumni Gym on the Kentucky campus held only 3,300 fans, and the majority of space was taken by students, effectively freezing out the general public. Wishing to share his Wildcats with basketball fans everywhere and wanting the best return on the dollar for the university, Rupp scheduled games at Freedom Hall in Louisville, Chicago Stadium, Madison Square Garden, Boston Garden and other big-city arenas. The Wildcats became a road show, drawing crowds wherever they went.

It didn't hurt their standing in the Commonwealth. They were renowned from Pikeville in the eastern section to Paducah in the far western part of Kentucky, from Louisville to the smallest mountain hamlet. When the team took a trip out of state or returned home from a big game, a crowd would form at stops along the way. Sometimes, there would be a band.

So it was when the Wildcats left for New York in March 1949 to begin defense of their NCAA championship. They had returned to Lexington immediately after their loss in the NIT (Kentucky had accepted invitations to both tournaments) and practiced as hard as any Rupp team ever had, which was saying something.

"I mean," Rupp said, "we really worked out. I spared no mercy."

The Wildcats boarded the train and rolled past good-luck signs and cheering youngsters all the way to the state line before crossing into West Virginia. They were 29-2 at the time and, even with the loss to Loyola, the overwhelming choice as the top team in

By 1949, the incomparable Adolph Rupp was recognized as the king of college basketball.

the nation. They were about to prove it, or heaven help them.

The first team in Kentucky's path in the Eastern playoffs was Villanova, which boasted a great jump shooter in forward Paul Arizin (who had scored 85 points in a single game that season, albeit against the Naval Air Materiel Center). With Groza and Tony Lavelli of Yale also present, the Eastern competition featured three of the leading scorers in the country. Fans expecting an offensive onslaught were not disappointed.

In the opening game of the Garden doubleheader, Illinois rallied from a six-point deficit with five minutes left to overtake Yale, 71-67, despite Lavelli's 27 points. As fine as that performance was, it suffered in comparison to the individual efforts in the nightcap.

Arizin was superb. He scored 30 points, 19 coming in the second half when he labored under the burden of four fouls. But Groza was not about to

The 30-point effort of Villanova's Paul Arizin was not enough to stop Kentucky's 1949 NCAA title express.

Oklahoma A&M's defensive-minded Bob Harris couldn't contain Alex Groza and Kentucky rolled to a 46-36 title-game victory over the Aggies.

be eclipsed. The Kentucky center also accounted for 30 points—only one below the tournament record set by George Glamack of North Carolina eight years earlier—despite sitting out much of the second half with foul trouble.

For all of Arizin's theatrics, however, the outcome was decided in the first half when Kentucky overcame a 15-10 deficit and used the shooting of Groza and Barker to roll to a 48-37 lead. The defending champion won impressively, thanks in part to 21 points by Line and 18 by Barker. Other than Arizin, only Brooks Ricca (14) scored in double figures for Villanova. The final score, 85-72, set tournament marks for most points by one team and most total points by two teams.

If the Eastern final promised a major struggle, it didn't deliver. Perhaps that's because Kentucky de-

livered too well. Illinois had been ranked No. 4 in the nation, but the Illini were no match for the Wildcats.

With exquisite timing and teamwork, Kentucky overwhelmed Illinois, 76-47. The Wildcats' passing and movement were so sharp that 16 of the team's

31 field goals were layups. Each of the seven Kentucky players had at least one assist, and Jones was credited with five.

Meanwhile, Illinois never got going. Coach Harry Combes used a dozen players in an effort to reverse the momentum, to no avail. With Beard and Barker pressuring the backcourt, the Illinois offense was a shambles. Not one of Combes' players scored in double figures. Groza led all scorers with 27 points. Line had 15 for Kentucky, and Jones and Beard each contributed nine.

As the Wildcats flew to Seattle for the NCAA championship game, it was clear that no more scoring records would be set that season. Oklahoma A&M, the nation's stingiest team, had triumphed in the Western playoffs at Kansas City. In qualifying for their third final in five years, the second-ranked Aggies had squeaked past Wyoming, 40-39, and routed Oregon State, 55-30. Oklahoma A&M center Bob Harris was a standout against the West Coast team, scoring 23 points and dominating the middle.

Aggies Coach Henry Iba, the high priest of defense, believed the 6-7 Harris was the man to contain Groza. He was wrong. In a game played at Washington's Edmundson Pavilion, the first campus site for an NCAA title game since Northwestern played host to the first tournament final in 1939, Groza used superior quickness to beat Harris to the baseline, fouled the defender out of the game early in the second half and scored 25 points in his team's 46-36 victory.

In a major role reversal, the Wildcats broke open a close game in the second half with their defense, holding the Aggies without a field goal for almost 8½ minutes. When Oklahoma A&M made its only run, cutting a 35-23 deficit to 39-32, Groza responded with two baskets to seal the victory. Kentucky thus became the second institution to win consecutive NCAA basketball championships, fittingly at the expense of the first back-to-back champion.

The homecoming featured life-sized posters of the players hung from lamp posts and a 37-unit parade through Lexington.

How good were the Wildcats? Groza, Jones, Beard and Barker moved into the National Basketball Association as a unit the following season and their franchise, the Indianapolis Olympians, finished atop the Western Division. Even at the next level, they remained fabulous.

After Kentucky's 1949 championship campaign, Alex Groza (above), Wallace Jones, Ralph Beard and Cliff Barker teamed with the Indianapolis Olympians of the National Basketball Association.

1949 Tournament Results	
First Round	**Semifinals**
Illinois 71, Yale 67	Kentucky 76, Illinois 47
Kentucky 85, Villanova 72	Oklahoma A&M 55, Oregon St. 30
Oklahoma A&M 40, Wyoming 39	**Third Place**
Oregon State 56, Arkansas 38	Illinois 57, Oregon State 53
Regional Third Place	**Championship**
Villanova 78, Yale 67	Kentucky 46, Oklahoma A&M 36
Arkansas 61, Wyoming 48	

STATISTICS

1949 KENTUCKY

Head Coach—Adolph Rupp **Final Record—32-2**

Player	Pos.	Hgt.	Wgt.	Cl.	G	FG	FGA	Pct.	FT	FTA	Pct.	Reb.	Pts.	Avg.
Alex Groza	C	6-7	220	Sr.	34	259	612	.423	180	248	.726	...	698	20.5
Ralph Beard	G	5-10	176	Sr.	34	144	481	.299	82	115	.713	...	370	10.9
Wallace Jones	F-C	6-4	225	Sr.	32	130	440	.295	49	75	.653	...	309	9.7
Cliff Barker	G-F	6-2	185	Sr.	34	94	315	.298	60	88	.682	...	248	7.3
Dale Barnstable	F-G	6-3	180	Jr.	34	84	309	.272	41	57	.719	...	209	6.1
Jim Line	F	6-2	190	Sr.	32	70	195	.359	43	51	.843	...	183	5.7
Walter Hirsch	F-G	6-4	185	So.	34	67	209	.321	22	32	.688	...	156	4.6
Roger Day	F	6-3	185	So.	19	21	39	.538	9	17	.529	...	51	2.7
Al Bruno	F	6-3	185	So.	9	9	30	.300	2	3	.667	...	20	2.2
Garland Townes	G	6-0	180	So.	16	10	48	.208	11	20	.550	...	31	1.9
Johnny Stough	G	6-0	170	Jr.	25	13	56	.232	12	14	.857	...	38	1.5
Bob Henne	G	6-1	170	So.	9	2	19	.105	3	7	.429	...	7	0.8
Joe B. Hall	G	6-0	165	So.	2	0	3	.000	0	1	.000	...	0	0.0
Kentucky					34	903	2756	.328	514	728	.706	...	2320	68.2
Opponents					34	538	2216	.243	454	756	.601	...	1530	45.0

1949 OKLAHOMA A&M

Head Coach—Henry Iba **Final Record—23-5**

Player	Pos.	Hgt.	Wgt.	Cl.	G	FG	FGA	Pct.	FT	FTA	Pct.	Reb.	Pts.	Avg.
Bob Harris	C	6-7	192	Sr.	28	118	...	....	92	...	....	...	328	11.7
Joe Bradley	F-G	6-2	170	Sr.	28	72	...	....	58	...	....	...	202	7.2
J.L. Parks	G	6-0	175	Sr.	28	52	...	....	83	...	....	...	187	6.7
Vernon Yates	F	6-4	195	Sr.	27	60	...	....	50	...	....	...	170	6.3
Jack Shelton	C	6-6	195	Jr.	27	49	...	....	54	...	....	...	152	5.6
Tom Jaquet	F-G	6-4	180	Jr.	27	26	...	....	35	...	....	...	87	3.2
Gale McArthur	G	6-1	180	So.	28	31	...	....	21	...	....	...	83	3.0
Norman Pilgrim	F	5-10	155	So.	26	13	...	....	13	...	....	...	39	1.5
Keith Smith	G	5-9	150	So.	19	8	...	....	12	...	....	...	28	1.5
Frank Allen	F	6-4	221	So.	8	2	...	....	1	...	....	...	5	0.6
Larry Hayes	F	6-1	170	Jr.	13	2	...	....	2	...	....	...	6	0.5
Bob Seymour	G	6-2	195	So.	..	1	...	....	1	...	....	...	3	...
Jack Hobbs	G	5-10	165	Jr.	..	0	...	....	2	...	....	...	2	...
Carol Bender	G	5-9	180	Jr.	..	0	...	....	0	...	....	...	0	...
Joe Pitts	F	5-10	165	So.	..	0	...	....	0	...	....	...	0	...
Oklahoma A&M					28	434			424			...	1292	46.1
Opponents					28	...			...			....	985	35.2

1949 ILLINOIS

Head Coach—Harry Combes **Final Record—21-4**

Player	Pos.	Hgt.	Wgt.	Cl.	G	FG	FGA	Pct.	FT	FTA	Pct.	Reb.	Pts.	Avg.
Dwight Eddleman	F	6-2	189	Sr.	25	130	449	.290	69	119	.579	...	329	13.2
Bill Erickson	G	6-1	184	Jr.	25	91	272	.335	79	135	.585	...	261	10.4
Wally Osterkorn	F-C	6-4	207	Jr.	25	90	304	.296	81	132	.614	...	261	10.4
Jim Marks	F-G	6-2	177	So.	20	53	167	.317	27	46	.587	...	133	6.7
Fred Green	C	6-7	208	Sr.	25	65	192	.339	24	40	.600	...	154	6.2
Don Sunderlage	G	6-0	180	So.	25	57	184	.310	39	57	.684	...	153	6.1
Burdette Thurlby	G	6-2	190	Jr.	17	36	133	.271	21	37	.568	...	93	5.5
Walt Kersulis	F-C	6-4	197	Jr.	20	43	140	.307	23	36	.639	...	109	5.5
Van Anderson	F-G	6-2	185	Jr.	23	32	123	.260	8	15	.533	...	72	3.1
Dick Foley	G	6-0	165	So.	24	26	80	.325	11	15	.733	...	63	2.6
Ted Beach	F	6-1	165	So.	14	13	43	.302	8	10	.800	...	34	2.4
Roy Gatewood	G	6-2	174	Jr.	9	9	21	.429	4	9	.444	...	22	2.4
Dick Brogren	G	6-1	170	So.	6	4	10	.400	3	3	1.000	...	11	1.8
Benton Odum	F	6-0	175	Jr.	3	1	8	.125	3	6	.500	...	5	1.7
Glen Trugillo	F	5-11	160	So.	9	2	13	.154	2	3	.667	...	6	0.7
Jim Cottrell	G	5-10	167	So.	6	1	6	.167	1	3	.333	...	3	0.5
Bill Boyer	C	6-4	190	So.	2	0	7	.000	0	0	.000	...	0	0.0
Illinois					25	653	2152	.303	403	666	.605	...	1709	68.4
Opponents					25	514	1832	.281	388	584	.664	...	1416	56.6

1949 OREGON STATE

Head Coach—Amory (Slats) Gill **Final Record—24-12**

Player	Pos.	Hgt.	Wgt.	Cl.	G	FG	FGA	Pct.	FT	FTA	Pct.	Reb.	Pts.	Avg.
Cliff Crandall	F-G	6-2	170	Sr.	36	143	397	.360	149	205	.727	...	435	12.1
Alex Petersen	F-C	6-5	186	Sr.	36	80	247	.324	45	67	.672	...	205	5.7
Ray Snyder	F	6-4	192	Jr.	35	66	201	.328	41	59	.695	...	173	4.9
Glen Kinney	F	6-3	192	So.	28	47	139	.338	34	51	.667	...	128	4.6
Dick Ballantyne	G	5-11	175	Jr.	36	47	148	.318	67	100	.670	...	161	4.5
Jim Catterall	G	5-8	159	Jr.	30	48	178	.270	35	51	.686	...	131	4.4
Dan Torrey	G	6-1	178	Jr.	30	47	147	.320	27	41	.659	...	121	4.0
Bill Harper	G	5-11	170	So.	30	43	141	.305	22	38	.579	...	108	3.6
Ed Fleming	C	6-6	197	Jr.	27	27	96	.281	38	57	.667	...	92	3.4
Tom Holman	G	5-10	177	Jr.	31	36	96	.375	21	33	.636	...	93	3.0
Harvey Watt	G	6-4	200	So.	25	29	76	.382	16	48	.333	...	74	3.0
Len Rinearson	F-C	6-4	208	Jr.	35	27	76	.355	23	40	.575	...	77	2.2
Paul Sliper	F-C	6-6	195	Jr.	13	6	28	.214	7	13	.538	...	19	1.5
Rudy Ruppe	G	6-3	180	Sr.	2	1	7	.143	0	0	.000	...	2	1.0
Oregon State					36	647	1977	.327	525	803	.654	....	1819	50.5
Opponents					36	...			...			....	1704	47.3

1949 FINAL FOUR

Semifinals
At New York

Kentucky	fg	ft	pf	tp
Jones	4	1	3	9
Line	6	3	0	15
Groza	10	7	4	27
Beard	4	1	2	9
Barker	3	2	3	8
Hirsch	3	0	1	6
Barnstable	1	0	1	2
Totals	31	14	14	76

Illinois	fg	ft	pf	tp
Eddleman	3	0	1	6
Kersulis	3	3	2	9
Green	3	1	2	7
Osterkorn	2	1	5	5
Erickson	2	1	2	5
Foley	1	1	1	3
Gatewood	3	0	0	6
Marks	1	0	2	2
Cottrell	0	0	1	0
Anderson	0	0	1	0
Beach	1	0	0	2
Sunderlage	0	2	2	2
Totals	19	9	19	47

Halftime: Kentucky 39-22. Officials: Begovich and Gentile.

At Kansas City

Oklahoma A&M	fg	ft	fta	pf	tp
Shelton	3	7	8	3	13
Hobbs	0	0	0	0	0
Yates	0	0	0	0	0
McArthur	0	0	0	2	0
Pilgrim	0	0	0	4	0
Harris	8	7	7	1	23
Bradley	3	1	1	1	7
Jaquet	0	0	0	0	0
Allen	0	0	0	1	0
Parks	2	4	6	2	8
Smith	1	2	2	1	4
Hayes	0	0	0	1	0
Totals	17	21	24	16	55

Oregon State	fg	ft	fta	pf	tp
Petersen	2	0	3	5	4
Catterall	0	1	2	1	1
Sliper	0	0	0	1	0
Fleming	1	0	1	0	2
Snyder	1	0	0	1	2
Watt	0	0	0	1	0
Rinearson	0	0	0	2	0
Crandall	4	3	4	3	11
Harper	1	0	1	2	2
Ballantyne	1	1	1	2	3
Torrey	0	1	1	0	1
Holman	1	2	2	1	4
Totals	11	8	15	18	30

Halftime: Oklahoma A&M 21-11. Officials: Curtis and Ball.

Championship
March 26
At Seattle

Kentucky	fg	ft	pf	tp
Jones	1	1	3	3
Line	2	1	3	5
Groza	9	7	5	25
Beard	1	1	4	3
Barker	1	3	4	5
Barnstable	1	1	1	3
Hirsch	1	0	1	2
Totals	16	14	21	46

Oklahoma A&M	fg	ft	pf	tp
Yates	1	0	1	2
Shelton	3	6	4	12
Harris	3	1	5	7
Bradley	0	3	3	3
Parks	2	3	5	7
Jaquet	0	1	0	1
McArthur	0	2	1	2
Pilgrim	0	2	1	2
Smith	0	0	1	0
Totals	9	18	21	36

Halftime: Kentucky 25-20. Officials: Ogden and Curtis.

1950 CCNY Doubles Its Pleasure

The 1950 double tournament champions from City College of New York enjoyed another kind of celebration during the season, presenting Coach Nat Holman with an anniversary ball in honor of his 30-year association with college basketball.

It was a sound unlike any other that resounded in Madison Square Garden during the post-World War II era, the battle cry of a school and a team destined for one triumphant year on the national stage. The students at City College of New York called it the "allagaroo" cheer.

According to school legend, an allagaroo was either a cross between an alligator and a kangaroo or a corruption of the French phrase "allez guerre" (on to the war). In either case, it was a unique chant for a team intent on completing a unique double, winning the National Invitation Tournament and the NCAA Tournament in the same season.

The Beavers were only one of many college squads that used the Garden as a home base, but as the representatives of a renowned public education system offering free tuition to motivated students, they were special favorites. They were to New York, guard Floyd Layne said, what the Dodgers were to Brooklyn. And their cheer ("allagaroo-garoo-garah, allagaroo-garoo-garah; ee-yah, ee-yah; sis-boom-bah") captivated New York in the early months of 1950.

City College's coach, Nat Holman, was a New York native who had been a star and an innovator with the Original Celtics, the first great barnstorm-

One of the top guns in CCNY's big offensive arsenal was versatile Ed Warner, who displayed a vast assortment of feints from his post position.

ing team. He lectured and wrote books on the sport and was a member of the CCNY faculty. An imperious presence and a fastidious dresser, he was known as nothing less than "Mr. Basketball."

Holman had enjoyed a remarkable stewardship at City, beginning with the 1920 season. Although he continued to play professionally during his first 14 years of coaching and despite the fact the school rarely attracted top athletes, Holman began the 1950 season with a record of 359-127. This team, he predicted, would be his best ever.

Only one senior, 6-foot-4 Irwin Dambrot, was in the starting lineup, but it was a sterling sophomore class that inspired the coach's optimism. Layne, Ed Warner, Al (Fats) Roth and 6-6 Ed Roman constituted a group of exceptionally talented and versatile players. They could play the slick City game the way Holman envisioned it.

Despite their youth, their performance was impressive in the early stage of the season, when the Beavers were ranked as high as seventh in the Associated Press poll. But a second-half slump, during which the Beavers lost to Canisius, Niagara and Syracuse, damaged their reputation and almost cost them a postseason tournament berth. Only by sweeping the so-called "subway series" among metropolitan New York schools did they earn one of the last invitations to the NIT. CCNY was 17-5 and, in the opinion of many observers, headed for an early exit.

The first in a memorable series of upsets occurred against San Francisco, the defending NIT champion. The Beavers' 65-46 victory raised a few eyebrows, but the reaction was nothing like that which greeted an 89-50 rout of Kentucky in the quarterfinals. Kentucky had been ranked third nationally, had won 25 of 29 games and had claimed the NCAA championship the previous two years. Never before had a team coached by Adolph Rupp been so thoroughly embarrassed.

There was nothing at the outset of the game to indicate such a development. Roman, trying to work inside on 7-foot sophomore Bill Spivey, had his first few shots slammed into the nearby seats. So Holman mapped a strategy that sent Roman away from the basket, where his one-hand push shot was on target. Warner, about three inches shorter than Roman but an exceptional pivot player with a vast array of feints, moved into the post. City pushed its fast break into high gear and, with Warner wheeling through the lane for 26 points, roared to an improbable triumph.

A 62-52 victory over a Duquesne team that featured Chuck Cooper not only lifted the Beavers into the NIT final, but also earned them a spot in the upcoming NCAA Tournament. Unable to choose among CCNY, Duquesne and St. John's, the NCAA district selection committee pledged to invite which-

North Carolina State's Sam Ranzino soars over CCNY's Norman Mager (33) and Floyd Layne (3) in a 1950 NCAA semifinal game.

Ohio State and star Dick Schnittker (above) were major hurdles in CCNY's bid to win both the NCAA Tournament and NIT in the same season.

ever of the three advanced furthest in the NIT. When St. John's bowed to Bradley in the other semifinal, City earned the nomination.

First, however, there was the matter of the NIT championship game, pitting an unranked local team against the top-ranked team in the nation. Bradley was a solid favorite on the basis of its 29-3 record and the presence of All-America forward Paul Unruh.

The Braves opened a 29-18 lead, which City narrowed to 30-27 at intermission. The Beavers, with Holman battling a high temperature but on hand for the action, assumed control in the second half and prevailed by the comfortable margin of 69-61 as Dambrot, the captain, scored 23 points. While his players celebrated and students swarmed into the Times Square area, Holman took his 103-degree fever to bed.

He still was ailing when CCNY was honored at a City Hall reception two days later. Mayor William O'Dwyer shook hands with each member of the team, assistant coach Bobby Sand and Athletic Director Sam Winograd and then said, "I congratulate you for making the city of New York so proud."

While the Beavers practiced for their opening game in the NCAA Eastern playoffs, conveniently scheduled for the Garden, Bradley defeated Kansas

in a playoff for the District 5 spot in the Western playoffs at Kansas City.

As they had done during the NIT, the City players continued to attend classes on the upper Manhattan campus once the NCAA Tournament got under way. Layne recalled a class in bacteriology in which a professor awakened him from reverie with a terse observation: "Mr. Layne, the game was played last night. Now look at the slide and tell me what you see."

By then, of course, the Beavers were the toasts of the town and the pride of their coach.

"The team just seemed to arrive in the Kentucky game," said a recuperated Holman as CCNY neared its second major tournament appearance in a week. "I don't think they have been lucky and I don't think they've just been hot. They simply found themselves. And if they stay hale and hearty, I think we can beat anybody and that includes Bradley again."

CCNY and Bradley were the fifth and sixth teams to compete in the NCAA meet and the NIT in the same year. Three teams—most recently Kentucky in 1949—had won the championship of one tournament but been eliminated in the other. City's bid for an unprecedented sweep began against Ohio State, ranked second in the country.

The Buckeyes, led by 6-5 consensus All-America

The late-game efforts of Bradley's Gene Melchiorre almost cost CCNY the title victory it seemed only moments earlier to have well in hand.

Dick Schnittker, started fast and scored repeatedly inside. Utilizing a tight zone defense to clog the middle, Ohio State forced CCNY to rely upon outside shooting in the first half. Fortunately for the Beavers, Layne and senior reserve Norman Mager were able to hit their set shots and the half ended in a 40-40 tie.

After the Beavers went ahead, 43-40, on Warner's three-point play, Holman ordered his players to hold the ball in an attempt to draw Ohio State out of its zone. The Buckeyes didn't budge, and CCNY made no move to score for more than 4½ minutes. Later, though, the Schnittker-led Buckeyes pulled into a 52-49 lead, but set shots by Mager and Layne regained the advantage for CCNY. When Ohio State's Jim Remington missed a shot in the final seconds, City escaped with a 56-55 victory.

Two nights later, the Beavers clinched a spot in the NCAA championship game by turning away fifth-ranked North Carolina State despite a notable

performance by Sam Ranzino. The Wolfpack junior scored 16 of his 24 points in the first 10 minutes of the second half and kept his team in contention before fouling out with 3:30 remaining. N.C. State continued to hang close, but two free throws by Layne and two layups by Warner in the final 1:35 sealed a 78-73 victory.

Meanwhile, Bradley overcame UCLA, 73-59, and struggled past underrated Baylor, 68-66, to win the Western playoffs. The Braves left the following day for New York for another shot at the team that denied them the NIT title. It was a remarkable turn of events.

City was prepared for the rematch. Operating efficiently against Bradley's zone defense, the Beavers assumed a 39-32 halftime lead and increased the margin to 58-47 midway through the second half. The Braves then switched to a pressing man-to-man defense, a stratagem that placed each of the Bradley starters in foul trouble but succeeded in rattling CCNY. Having whittled the deficit to 69-63 in the final minute of play, Bradley got a free throw from Joe Stowell and two quick steals and layups from Gene Melchiorre and, suddenly, the championship was in doubt.

Once again, CCNY lost the ball and Melchiorre drove for the go-ahead basket. But Dambrot picked the ball off his hands as he attempted a shot—Bradley claimed a foul on the play—and looped a long pass downcourt for Mager. The 6-5 Mager had been involved in a nasty collision with the Braves' Aaron Preece near the end of the first half and suffered a five-stitch cut in his forehead. Now, wearing a large bandage, Mager took the pass and scored the final basket in CCNY's thrilling and monumental 71-68 triumph.

Standing on the court moments afterward, Coach Clair Bee of Long Island University noted: "No college team will ever duplicate this fabulous achievement."

It was at once the first and last great shining moment for CCNY basketball. Four prominent City players were indicted in a point-shaving scandal that rocked the sport the following year, the team was ordered to move its games from the Garden to the campus and the level of competition was lowered. What remained was the memory of seven superb NIT/NCAA Tournament games in 2½ weeks and the cry of "allagaroo!"

1950 Tournament Results

First Round	Semifinals
CCNY 56, Ohio State 55	CCNY 78, N. C. State 73
N. C. State 87, Holy Cross 74	Bradley 68, Baylor 66
Baylor 56, Brigham Young 55	**Third Place**
Bradley 73, UCLA 59	N. C. State 53, Baylor 41
Regional Third Place	**Championship**
Ohio State 72, Holy Cross 52	CCNY 71, Bradley 68
BYU 83, UCLA 62	

STATISTICS

1950 CCNY

Head Coach—Nat Holman   **Final Record—24-5**

Player	Pos.	Hgt.	Wgt.	Cl.	G	FG	FGA	Pct.	FT.	FTA	Pct.	Reb.	Pts.	Avg.
Ed Roman	C	6-6	220	So.	29	207	497	.416	61	95	.642	....	475	16.4
Ed Warner	F	6-4	205	So.	29	157	365	.430	115	203	.567	....	429	14.8
Irwin Dambrot	F	6-4	185	Sr.	29	124	334	.371	47	81	.580	....	295	10.2
Floyd Layne	G	6-3	175	So.	29	68	243	.280	63	104	.606	....	199	6.9
Al Roth	G	6-3	200	So.	29	68	236	.288	50	97	.515	....	186	6.4
Herb Cohen	G	6-1	170	So.	24	50	122	.410	30	57	.526	....	130	5.4
Norm Mager	F	6-5	185	Sr.	29	41	116	.353	22	35	.629	....	104	3.6
Ronald Nadell	G	5-11	170	Jr.	19	17	44	.386	13	20	.650	....	47	2.5
Seymour Levy	G	6-1	170	Sr.	6	4	19	.210	4	7	.571	....	12	2.0
Mike Wittlin	G	5-10	165	Sr.	22	16	51	.314	6	10	.600	....	38	1.7
Leroy Watkins	C	6-7	185	Sr.	11	9	18	.500	1	4	.250	....	19	1.7
Joe Galiber	C	6-4	205	Sr.	24	11	46	.239	12	23	.522	....	34	1.4
Arnie Smith	G	6-1	170	Jr.	14	4	22	.182	7	8	.875	....	15	1.1
Larry Meyer	G	5-8	170	So.	8	3	23	.130	2	7	.286	....	8	1.0
Arthur Glass	G	6-1	185	Jr.	9	1	14	.071	0	0	.000	....	2	0.2
CCNY					29	780	2150	.363	433	751	.577	....	1993	68.7
Opponents					29	....	....	....	....	....	....	....	1610	55.5

1950 BRADLEY

Head Coach—Forrest (Forddy) Anderson   **Final Record—32-5**

Player	Pos.	Hgt.	Wgt.	Cl.	G	FG	FGA	Pct.	FT.	FTA	Pct.	Reb.	Pts.	Avg.
Paul Unruh	F-C	6-4	181	Sr.	37	189	480	.394	97	149	.651	...	475	12.8
Gene Melchiorre	F	5-8	175	Jr.	37	153	384	.398	134	202	.663	...	440	11.9
Bill Mann	F	6-1	178	Sr.	37	135	291	.464	82	118	.695	...	352	9.5
Charley Grover	F-G	6-1	175	Jr.	36	127	370	.343	48	76	.632	...	302	8.4
Elmer Behnke	C	6-7	204	Jr.	37	101	261	.387	55	94	.585	...	257	6.9
Aaron Preece	G	6-2	183	Jr.	37	81	196	.413	48	64	.750	...	210	5.7
Fred Schlictman	F	6-1	160	So.	36	66	183	.361	13	31	.419	...	145	4.0
Jim Kelly	C	6-6	180	So.	28	39	118	.331	28	58	.483	...	106	3.8
George Chianakas	G	6-0	181	Jr.	35	55	127	.433	22	42	.524	...	132	3.8
Don Alford	F	5-11	150	Jr.	12	13	43	.302	13	15	.867	...	39	3.3
Joe Stowell	F	5-11	156	Sr.	13	15	27	.556	2	4	.500	...	32	2.5
Dick Mize	G	6-1	175	Jr.	4	3	12	.250	2	4	.500	...	8	2.0
Dave Humerickhouse	G	6-2	194	Sr.	17	13	62	.210	5	15	.333	...	31	1.8
Jack Hills	F-G	5-11	170	So.	9	5	16	.313	2	2	1.000	...	12	1.3
Don Schnake	F	6-1	170	So.	4	2	9	.222	0	3	.000	...	4	1.0
Clarence Christie	F	6-1	160	Jr.	6	2	9	.222	1	1	1.000	...	5	0.8
Deno Melchiorre	F	5-8	175	Jr.	1	0	0	.000	0	0	.000	...	0	0.0
Bradley					37	999	2588	.386	552	878	.629	...	2550	68.9
Opponents					37	783	2442	.321	512	922	.555	...	2078	56.2

1950 NORTH CAROLINA STATE

Head Coach—Ev Case   **Final Record—27-6**

Player	Pos.	Hgt.	Wgt.	Cl.	G	FG	FGA	Pct.	FT.	FTA	Pct.	Reb.	Pts.	Avg.
Sam Ranzino	F	6-1	185	Jr.	33	241	721	.334	142	197	.721	...	624	18.9
Dick Dickey	F	6-1	180	Sr.	33	155	512	.303	150	222	.676	...	460	13.9
Paul Horvath	C	6-6	200	Jr.	33	135	365	.370	95	153	.621	...	365	11.1
Warren Cartier	C	6-4	195	Sr.	32	84	257	.327	39	71	.549	...	207	6.5
Vic Bubas	G	6-2	188	Jr.	33	59	145	.407	63	100	.630	...	181	5.5
Joe Harand	G	6-5	195	Jr.	33	50	163	.307	61	92	.663	...	161	4.9
Bob Cook	C-F	6-4	200	So.	28	26	70	.371	16	28	.571	...	68	2.4
Charlie Stine	F	6-0	175	Sr.	16	10	38	.263	12	18	.667	...	32	2.0
Lee Terrill	G	6-0	180	So.	27	12	54	.222	18	38	.474	...	42	1.6
Pete Jackmowski	G	6-2	195	So.	10	4	9	.444	1	5	.200	...	9	0.9
Joe Stoll	F	6-3	165	So.	9	2	8	.250	3	5	.600	...	7	0.8
Bobby Holt	G	6-3	190	So.	2	0	2	.000	0	0	.000	...	0	0.0
North Carolina St.					33	778	2344	.332	600	929	.646	...	2156	65.3
Opponents					33	631	2291	.275	443	749	.591	...	1705	51.7

1950 BAYLOR

Head Coach—Bill Henderson   **Final Record—14-13**

Player	Pos.	Hgt.	Wgt.	Cl.	G	FG	FGA	Pct.	FT.	FTA	Pct.	Reb.	Pts.	Avg.
Don Heathington	C-F	6-3	180	Sr.	23	96	...	...	111	...	...	...	303	13.2
Odell Preston	C	6-3	...	Sr.	27	73	...	...	73	...	...	...	219	8.1
Bill Srack	G	5-9	...	Sr.	27	86	...	...	44	...	...	...	216	8.0
Bill Hickman	F-C	6-3	...	Sr.	27	89	...	...	32	...	...	...	210	7.8
Bill DeWitt	G-F	6-3	...	Sr.	27	50	...	...	66	...	...	...	166	6.1
Ralph Johnson	F	6-3	190	Sr.	26	41	...	...	25	...	...	...	107	4.1
Gerald Cobb	F	6-0	...	Sr.	21	27	...	...	25	...	...	...	79	3.8
Norman Mullins	F	6-2	175	So.	18	10	...	...	6	...	...	...	26	1.4
Bill Fleetwood	G	6-0	145	So.	20	9	...	...	7	...	...	...	25	1.3
Howard Hovde	G	5-11	165	So.	25	6	...	...	10	...	...	...	22	0.9
Gordon Carrington	G-F	6-0	150	Jr.	..	...	...	...	...	...	...	...	...	...
Others*					..	7	...	...	3	...	...	...	17	...
Baylor					27	494	...	...	402	...	...	...	1390	51.5
Opponents					27	...	...	...	...	...	...	...	1449	53.7

*Includes Carrington.

1950 FINAL FOUR

Semifinals
At New York

CCNY	fg	fga	ft	fta	pf	tp
Dambrot	5	14	3	6	3	13
Warner	5	18	7	11	3	17
Roman	9	17	3	4	5	21
Galiber	0	0	0	0	1	0
Nadell	2	2	0	1	2	4
Roth	2	6	0	0	5	4
Mager	4	11	1	2	5	9
Layne	3	13	4	5	2	10
Cohen	0	0	0	2	0	0
Totals	30	81	18	31	26	78

North Carolina State	fg	fga	ft	fta	pf	tp
Ranzino	9	30	6	9	5	24
Stine	1	2	0	0	0	2
Dickey	7	19	2	6	5	16
Horvath	4	4	6	8	4	14
Bubas	0	2	2	2	4	2
Harand	0	0	2	2	2	2
Cartier	4	8	3	4	5	11
Cook	1	3	0	0	0	2
Totals	26	68	21	31	25	73

Halftime: CCNY 38-37. Officials: Meyer and Boyle.

At Kansas City

Bradley	fg	fga	ft	fta	pf	tp
Mann	4	7	5	8	4	13
Chianakas	1	5	0	0	0	2
Schlictman	0	0	0	0	0	0
G. Melchiorre	4	11	3	3	4	11
Unruh	2	11	3	4	2	7
Behnke	1	7	0	1	0	2
Preece	4	6	4	6	3	12
Kelly	3	7	2	2	2	8
Grover	6	14	1	1	2	13
Totals	25	68	18	25	17	68

Baylor	fg	fga	ft	fta	pf	tp
Hickman	3	7	0	0	3	6
Cobb	3	8	1	2	3	7
Carrington	0	0	0	0	0	0
Heathington	10	20	6	6	5	26
Fleetwood	0	0	0	0	0	0
Preston	4	11	6	7	4	14
Hovde	0	0	0	0	0	0
DeWitt	1	6	2	3	5	4
Johnson	0	2	0	0	0	0
Srack	3	7	3	3	3	9
Totals	24	61	18	21	23	66

Halftime: Bradley 35-32. Officials: Lee and Herigstad.

Championship
March 29
At New York

CCNY	fg	fga	ft	fta	pf	tp
Dambrot	7	14	1	2	0	15
Roman	6	17	0	2	5	12
Warner	4	9	6	14	2	14
Roth	2	7	1	5	2	5
Mager	4	10	6	6	3	14
Galiber	0	0	0	0	1	0
Layne	3	7	5	6	3	11
Nadell	0	0	0	0	1	0
Totals	26	64	19	35	17	71

Bradley	fg	fga	ft	fta	pf	tp
Grover	0	10	2	3	2	2
Schlictman	0	3	0	0	2	0
Unruh	4	9	0	0	5	8
Behnke	3	10	3	4	4	9
Kelly	0	1	0	2	0	0
Mann	2	7	5	5	5	9
Preece	6	11	0	0	5	12
D. Melchiorre	0	0	0	0	0	0
G. Melchiorre	7	16	2	4	4	16
Chianakas	5	7	1	3	4	11
Stowell	0	0	1	0	1	1
Totals	27	74	14	21	32	68

Halftime: CCNY 39-32. Officials: Eisenstein and Gibbs.

1951 Kentucky Is Top Cat Again

The emergence of Frank Ramsey (30) and Cliff Hagan in 1951 helped Kentucky to regain its championship form.

Kentucky's Memorial Coliseum, no small tribute to the university's basketball prosperity, opened its doors in time for the 1951 season. With a seating capacity of 11,500, it was the largest on-campus arena in the South. It also offered additional shelf space for the awards presented annually to Coach Adolph Rupp and his Wildcat teams.

Since his arrival at Kentucky two decades earlier, Rupp had operated out of a bathroom-sized office in cramped Alumni Gym. The entrance was through a door frame that certainly was not constructed with contemporary basketball players in mind.

"If you did not hit your head," Frank Ramsey said, "you were not considered for a scholarship. I went up to visit a friend during my junior year in high school and I stopped to see Coach Rupp. I made sure to stand on my tiptoes and hit my head."

Ramsey, who basically recruited himself, arrived at Kentucky in the company of two other outstanding freshmen, Cliff Hagan and Lou Tsioropoulos. By the time they joined the varsity in their sophomore years, Kentucky's two-year reign (1948, 1949) as national champions had been terminated. It was not another team that performed the dastardly deed; instead, it was the selection committee for District 3. Faced with a choice between two outstanding clubs in March 1950, the selectors picked North Carolina State over Kentucky for the NCAA Tournament berth.

This did not please Rupp, whose Wildcats had won another Southeastern Conference title. Rupp had never been one to feign modesty over his accomplishments, which rankled many basketball people. But that was all right with him. He cared nothing for popularity contests and everything for basketball games.

"I know I have plenty of enemies," he once said, "but I'd rather be the most hated winning coach in the country than the most popular losing one."

So a snubbed Kentucky team went to the National Invitation Tournament in 1950 and was demolished by eventual NIT/NCAA champion City College of New York, a beating that did nothing for the Baron's disposition.

"I want to thank you boys," he told the Wildcats after the 89-50 thrashing, the worst of his coaching career. "You get me elected Coach of the Year (by the New York Basketball Writers Association) and then bring me up here and embarrass the hell out of me."

The negative publicity directed at the NCAA over the Kentucky snub in '50 was at least partially responsible for a new format in the tournament. Effective in 1951, the field would be doubled from eight to 16 teams, with two representatives selected from each district.

Not that Kentucky needed such a favor in 1951.

The 1951 Wildcats were built around 7-foot center Bill Spivey, who led them to a 28-2 regular-season record.

The Wildcats, built around 7-foot center Bill Spivey, won 28 of 30 games before embarking for the NCAA Eastern playoffs, which began in Raleigh, N.C., and continued in New York. Undefeated in league play, their only losses were by one point to St. Louis in the Sugar Bowl Tournament and by four points to Vanderbilt in the SEC postseason tournament. The latter upset might have deprived Kentucky of another chance at the brass ring had not the conference voted that season to nominate the regular-season champion for an NCAA berth (instead of the league tournament titlist, as in previ-

ous years).

Because of the expanded field, a finalist would be required to play four games instead of three. The Wildcats dispatched their first two opponents with a minimum of fuss, beating Louisville at Raleigh and St. John's at Madison Square Garden, but were pushed to the limit in the Eastern final against Illinois at the Garden. It required a superlative effort by Spivey (28 points, 16 rebounds), a clutch second-half performance by Shelby Linville (14 points overall) and a crucial steal by substitute guard C.M. Newton for Kentucky to subdue the Big Ten Conference champion, 76-74.

The victory qualified Rupp's team to meet another band of Wildcats, from Kansas State, in the national title game, staged for the first time in Minneapolis. Kentucky, which had flown to and from conference games that season in small planes prone to sudden fluctuations, boarded a luxurious national carrier in New York for the flight to the Midwest. Ramsey asked an attendant about the strange compartments above the seats. He was told they were sleeping berths.

Although Kentucky had been ranked first in the nation in both wire-service polls (United Press, the forerunner of United Press International, introduced its basketball ratings in the '51 season), Rupp's Wildcats would not be big favorites at Williams Arena on the Minnesota campus. Kansas State had enjoyed an outstanding season under Coach Jack Gardner and appeared to be gaining strength with each game played in the tournament. After edging Arizona in the first round, Kansas State thumped Brigham Young (the newly crowned NIT champion) and then overran Oklahoma A&M, 68-44, in the Western final at Kansas City.

It so happened that Oklahoma A&M was ranked second in the nation when the Aggies were blitzed by Kansas State. Henry Iba, the Aggies' coach, said Kansas State was the best team he had seen all year. He told Rupp, his friend, he didn't think Kentucky could beat the Kansans.

If that assessment didn't concern Rupp, the condition of Hagan did. The 6-4 sophomore, frequently employed as a sixth man, had been a sparkplug of the team. But he was suffering from a head cold, a sore throat and a fever as Kentucky made last-minute preparations for the game.

When the champions of the East gathered for their pregame meeting, Hagan was missing. A search party finally located him in the hotel spa. He greeted his teammates with a mud pack on his face.

Hagan still was in discomfort when the game got under way on the raised court. After a few minutes,

Cliff Hagan, Kentucky's sixth man and sparkplug, struggled against illness as well as Kansas State defenders in the 1951 title game.

Rupp didn't feel much better. Lew Hitch, Kansas State's 6-8 center, was running circles around the uninspired Spivey. After eight minutes, the Wildcats from the plains held a 19-13 lead. Hitch had outscored Spivey, 10-4.

Rupp had been advised by the team doctor not to play Hagan, who was still flushed.

"I told the doctor, 'Hell, he's the right temperature to play,'" the coach recalled later. Almost immediately upon entering the game, Hagan tipped in a missed shot and Kentucky began asserting itself close to the basket.

In the locker room at halftime, with Kentucky trailing 29-27, Rupp lit into his players, Spivey in particular. The coach could be caustic and demanding, but he knew what he was doing at all times. More often than not, the players responded with improved performances.

"He was a tough taskmaster," Hagan said. "And he was a great psychologist. When he attacked someone at halftime or in practice, he got you to play better. You exceeded what you normally would do."

That was the case this time. Spivey was a different player in the second half. And with Hagan helping on the backboards, Kentucky began to dominate Kansas State. The Big Seven Conference champion was further hampered by the loss of Ernie Barrett. The standout guard had injured his left shoulder in the Western final and had to leave the national title game in the early going.

Spivey finished with 22 points and 21 rebounds (Hitch had 13 and nine) in Kentucky's 68-58 triumph. Hagan added 10 points and Ramsey, a 6-3 sophomore guard, had nine (as did junior guard Skip Whitaker). By its victory, Kentucky became the first school to annex three NCAA basketball championships.

The coach acknowledged his center's contribution after the game, which attracted a crowd of 15,348.

"Spivey made the difference after he went to work," Rupp said. "Then we opened up the middle more in the second half, sent the guards driving through and shot more from the outside as well."

It was Iba's contention that Rupp's second-half strategy was nothing more than a delay game, a forerunner of the four-corner offense. And he teased him about it the next day. But Rupp would concede no such thing. Kentucky didn't use delay tactics.

What the Wildcats did mostly was win. Rupp now had won NCAA championships with two groups of players; no one who had played for Kentucky in the 1948 or 1949 title game was on the floor in the '51 final.

"He convinced us we could do things we didn't know we could do," Ramsey said. "We were just

Kansas State Coach Jack Gardner had his Wildcats on a roll by the time they reached the NCAA championship game against Kentucky.

cogs in a wheel. We were country boys, impressed with what we read about other players and teams. He made us believe we were as good as anyone. He told us what he wanted done and we did it."

In 1951, Rupp wanted to win a third NCAA championship because, among other reasons, his team had been denied an opportunity to compete in the tournament the previous year. What Rupp wanted, the not-to-be-denied Wildcats made certain he got.

1951 Tournament Results

First Round
N. C. State 67, Villanova 62
Illinois 79, Columbia 71
St. John's 63, Connecticut 52
Kentucky 79, Louisville 68
Washington 62, Texas A&M 40
Oklahoma A&M 50, Montana St. 46
BYU 68, San Jose St. 61
Kansas State 61, Arizona 59

Second Round
Illinois 84, N. C. State 70
Kentucky 59, St. John's 43
Oklahoma A&M 61, Washington 57
Kansas St. 64, BYU 54

Regional Third Place
St. John's 71, N. C. State 59
Washington 80, BYU 67

Semifinals
Kentucky 76, Illinois 74
Kansas St. 68, Oklahoma A&M 44

Third Place
Illinois 61, Oklahoma A&M 46

Championship
Kentucky 68, Kansas State 58

STATISTICS

1951 KENTUCKY

Head Coach—Adolph Rupp   Final Record—32-2

Player	Pos.	Hgt.	Wgt.	Cl.	G	FG	FGA	Pct.	FT.	FTA	Pct.	Reb.	Pts.	Avg.
Bill Spivey	C	7-0	215	Jr.	33	252	632	.399	131	211	.621	567	635	19.2
Shelby Linville	F	6-5	210	Jr.	34	151	388	.389	53	70	.757	309	355	10.4
Bobby Watson	G	5-10	175	Jr.	34	151	460	.328	51	68	.750	86	353	10.4
Frank Ramsey	G	6-3	180	So.	34	135	413	.327	75	123	.610	434	345	10.1
Cliff Hagan*	F-C	6-4	210	So.	20	69	188	.367	45	61	.738	169	183	9.2
Walt Hirsch**	F	6-3	185	Sr.	30	113	396	.285	48	68	.706	239	274	9.1
Skip Whitaker	G	6-0	175	Jr.	31	64	187	.342	33	55	.600	61	161	5.2
Lou Tsioropoulos	F-C	6-5	195	So.	27	38	122	.311	16	30	.533	130	92	3.4
Dwight Price	F	6-2	175	So.	20	13	47	.277	8	18	.444	43	34	1.7
Roger Layne	C	6-7	185	Sr.	12	6	23	.261	7	11	.636	13	19	1.6
C.M. Newton	G	6-2	190	Jr.	18	8	35	.229	5	11	.454	12	21	1.2
Guy Strong	G	6-0	165	Jr.	10	5	23	.217	0	1	.000	4	10	1.0
Others	..	...	...	...	24	99	.242		10	17	.588	42	58	...
Kentucky					34	1029	3013	.342	482	744	.648	2109	2540	74.7
Opponents					34	656	2422	.271	471	786	.599	1357	1783	52.4

*Became eligible January 26, 1951, when he became a sophomore.
**Ineligible for NCAA Tournament as fourth-year varsity player.

1951 KANSAS STATE

Head Coach—Jack Gardner   Final Record—25-4

Player	Pos.	Hgt.	Wgt.	Cl.	G	FG	FGA	Pct.	FT.	FTA	Pct.	Reb.	Pts.	Avg.
Ernie Barrett	G	6-3	185	Sr.	29	127	307	.414	44	62	.710	167	298	10.3
Jack Stone	F	6-3	190	Jr.	29	112	253	.443	54	93	.581	154	278	9.6
Jim Iverson	G	5-11	170	Jr.	29	95	243	.391	69	90	.767	95	259	8.9
Lew Hitch	C	6-8	205	Sr.	29	96	241	.398	66	104	.635	252	258	8.9
Dick Knostman	F	6-5	205	So.	29	77	212	.363	63	111	.568	206	217	7.5
Ed Head	F	6-0	160	Sr.	26	74	218	.339	33	48	.688	156	181	7.0
Bob Rousey	G	5-11	140	So.	29	79	180	.439	32	54	.593	62	190	6.6
John Gibson	F	6-3	170	Jr.	29	62	149	.416	34	66	.515	153	158	5.4
Dick Peck	F	6-2	180	Jr.	26	22	66	.333	23	32	.719	64	67	2.6
Don Upson	G	5-9	155	Jr.	27	18	69	.261	10	17	.588	33	46	1.7
Glenn Channell	C	6-5	190	Sr.	9	2	6	.333	5	7	.714	11	9	1.0
Dan Schuyler	G	6-2	175	So.	23	9	33	.273	3	10	.300	20	21	0.9
Perk Reitemeier	G	6-0	168	Jr.	11	2	10	.200	6	10	.600	16	10	0.9
Bob Garcia	F	5-8	...	Jr.	9	1	8	.125	0	1	.000	4	2	0.2
Kay Coonrod	F	5-9	160	Jr.	1	0	1	.000	0	2	.000	0	0	0.0
Others	..	...	...	...	1	13	.077		..	...	...	..	2	...
Kansas State					29	777	2009	.387	442	707	.625	1393	1996	68.8
Opponents					29	577	1904	.303	392	627	.625	....	1546	53.3

1951 ILLINOIS

Head Coach—Harry Combes   Final Record—22-5

Player	Pos.	Hgt.	Wgt.	Cl.	G	FG	FGA	Pct.	FT.	FTA	Pct.	Reb.	Pts.	Avg.
Don Sunderlage	G	6-0	180	Sr.	27	150	390	.385	171	218	.784	...	471	17.4
Ted Beach	G-F	6-2	174	Sr.	27	124	333	.372	47	57	.825	...	295	10.9
Rod Fletcher	G	6-4	200	Jr.	27	115	338	.340	60	111	.541	...	290	10.7
Clive Follmer	F-C	6-4	190	So.	27	88	228	.386	64	109	.587	...	240	8.9
Bob Peterson	C	6-8	235	So.	27	85	261	.326	67	120	.558	...	237	8.8
Irv Bemoras	F	6-3	184	So.	27	83	254	.327	49	66	.742	...	215	8.0
Max Baumgardner	C-F	6-6	205	So.	23	29	109	.266	11	20	.550	...	69	3.0
Dick Christiansen	F	6-3	175	Jr.	7	6	13	.462	3	8	.375	...	15	2.1
Dick Ems	F	6-2	185	Jr.	1	1	1	1.000	0	0	.000	...	2	2.0
Mack Follmer	C	6-4	195	Jr.	12	9	37	.243	3	12	.250	...	21	1.8
Jim Bredar	G	5-11	175	So.	20	15	41	.366	4	4	1.000	...	34	1.7
Herb Gerecke	F	6-1	180	Jr.	11	5	21	.238	5	9	.556	...	15	1.4
John Marks	F-C	6-2	185	Sr.	8	4	11	.364	0	2	.000	...	8	1.0
Seymour Gantman	G	5-7	168	Jr.	5	0	3	.000	3	7	.429	...	3	0.6
Jim Schuldt	G	6-1	195	So.	14	1	16	.063	4	4	1.000	...	6	0.4
Illinois					27	715	2056	.348	491	747	.657	...	1921	71.1
Opponents					27	...	...	...	...	...	...	...	1690	62.6

1951 OKLAHOMA A&M

Head Coach—Henry Iba   Final Record—29-6

Player	Pos.	Hgt.	Wgt.	Cl.	G	FG	FGA	Pct.	FT.	FTA	Pct.	Reb.	Pts.	Avg.
Don Johnson	F	6-2	185	Jr.	35	165	478	.345	91	135	.674	233	421	12.0
Gale McArthur	G	6-2	185	Sr.	35	147	422	.348	114	152	.750	143	408	11.7
Norman Pilgrim	F	5-10	165	Sr.	31	91	238	.382	121	151	.801	120	303	9.8
Keith Smith	G	5-10	155	Sr.	34	47	131	.359	68	111	.613	77	162	4.8
Pete Darcey	C	6-8	210	Jr.	34	55	149	.369	51	83	.614	161	161	4.7
Bob Pager	C	6-7	205	Jr.	34	55	136	.404	31	55	.564	105	141	4.1
Bob Seymour	G	6-2	195	Sr.	12	14	30	.467	12	27	.444	69	40	3.3
Gerald Stockton	F	6-5	205	So.	32	34	93	.366	16	28	.571	64	84	2.7
Harold Rogers	F	6-1	175	So.	33	28	84	.333	13	18	.722	42	69	2.1
Glenn Nixon	C	6-8	195	Jr.	17	10	38	.263	6	8	.750	20	26	1.5
John Miller	C-F	6-5	190	Jr.	14	5	20	.250	5	10	.500	29	15	1.1
Kendall Sheets	G	6-2	180	So.	27	8	41	.195	11	22	.500	48	27	1.0
... Amaya			...	..	4	2	5	.400	0	0	.000	3	4	1.0
Dale Roark	G	5-10	165	So.	1	0	2	.000	1	1	1.000	0	1	1.0
Maurice Ward	F	6-2	180	Jr.	12	4	12	.333	0	1	.000	4	8	0.7
Ken Hicks	F	6-1	170	So.	10	2	12	.167	3	10	.300	4	7	0.7
Emmett McAfee	F	6-2	180	Jr.	11	2	8	.250	1	3	.333	4	5	0.5
Joe Pitts	G	5-11	165	Sr.	4	0	4	.000	2	2	1.000	0	2	0.5
Oklahoma A&M					35	669	1903	.352	546	817	.668	1126	1884	53.8
Opponents					35	540	1736	.311	536	820	.654	....	1616	46.2

1951 FINAL FOUR

Semifinals
At New York

Kentucky	fg	fga	ft	fta	rb	pf	tp
Hagan	3	9	2	2	4	5	8
Linville	7	12	0	0	4	4	14
Spivey	11	21	6	10	16	5	28
Watson	5	17	0	0	8	4	10
Ramsey	2	19	1	3	12	2	5
Tsioropoulos	0	2	1	2	1	1	1
Whitaker	4	11	2	4	4	5	10
Newton	0	0	0	0	0	1	0
Totals	32	91	12	21	49	27	76

Illinois	fg	fga	ft	fta	rb	pf	tp
Follmer	2	3	2	5	2	2	6
Bemoras	5	8	2	3	7	2	12
Peterson	3	11	2	5	5	5	8
Fletcher	8	9	5	11	10	0	21
Sunderlage	6	15	8	11	3	2	20
Beach	2	12	3	3	6	1	7
Baumgardner	0	2	0	1	4	0	0
Totals	26	70	22	35	37	16	74

Halftime: Illinois 39-32.

At Kanssas City

Kansas State	fg	fga	ft	fta	rb	pf	tp
Head	4	9	1	1	5	3	9
Gibson	0	0	0	2	3	0	0
Schuyler	2	4	0	1	0	4	4
Stone	5	5	0	0	1	2	10
Peck	0	1	1	1	1	2	1
Hitch	4	11	4	6	8	2	12
Knostman	4	8	3	6	3	0	11
Iverson	3	4	3	3	2	0	9
Rousey	0	1	1	4	0	2	1
Barrett	1	7	3	3	4	4	5
Upson	3	4	0	0	1	2	6
Team					8		
Totals	26	54	16	27	36	18	68

Oklahoma A&M	fg	fga	ft	fta	rb	pf	tp
Johnson	2	10	3	3	5	4	7
McAfee	0	1	0	0	0	3	0
Miller	0	2	0	0	2	3	0
Stockton	0	0	1	1	1	0	1
Ward	1	2	0	0	0	1	2
Darcey	2	5	0	1	1	4	4
Pager	5	10	1	2	2	3	11
Smith	0	0	1	1	1	2	1
Amaya	1	2	0	0	1	0	2
Rogers	2	5	0	0	2	0	4
McArthur	1	11	5	5	2	2	7
Sheets	2	4	1	1	0	1	5
Team					10		
Totals	16	52	12	14	25	25	44

Halftime: Kansas State 37-14.

Championship
March 27
At Minneapolis

Kentucky	fg	fga	ft	fta	rb	pf	tp
Whitaker	4	5	1	1	2	2	9
Linville	2	7	4	8	8	5	8
Spivey	9	29	4	6	21	2	22
Ramsey	4	10	1	3	4	5	9
Watson	3	8	2	4	3	3	8
Hagan	5	6	0	2	4	5	10
Tsioropoulos	1	4	0	0	3	1	2
Newton	0	0	0	0	0	0	0
Totals	28	69	12	24	45	23	68

Kansas State	fg	fga	ft	fta	rb	pf	tp
Head	3	11	2	2	3	2	8
Stone	3	8	6	8	6	2	12
Hitch	6	15	1	1	9	3	13
Barrett	2	12	0	2	3	1	4
Iverson	3	12	1	2	0	3	7
Rousey	2	10	0	0	2	3	4
Gibson	0	2	1	1	5	1	1
Upson	0	1	0	0	2	1	0
Knostman	1	4	1	2	3	1	3
Peck	2	3	0	1	0	0	4
Schuyler	1	2	0	1	1	2	2
Totals	23	80	12	20	30	23	58

Halftime: Kansas State 29-27.

1952 Jayhawks Give Allen His Title

Phog Allen, one of the major forces in the growth and evolution of college basketball, kept the University of Kansas in the sport's spotlight.

In the hierarchy of basketball, a direct line of succession ran from Dr. James Naismith to Forrest C. (Phog) Allen. The latter was the foremost pupil of the sport's inventor. He took a game and turned it into a profession.

Naismith was first and foremost a teacher. It was only as a professor of physical education that he consented to coach the Kansas basketball team. As a student at Kansas, Allen decided that the appeal of the sport went beyond mere recreation. He deter-

mined to devote his life to coaching.

"And so I told Naismith that I was going to be a coach," Allen recalled many years later, "and he said, 'Forrest, you don't coach this game, you just play it.'" It was advice that Allen ignored, much to the greater glory of Kansas.

Allen actually assumed the coaching duties at Kansas from Naismith while attending school on the Lawrence campus in 1908. Before graduation, he added similar positions at the Haskell Institute

Senior forward Bob Kenney was one of the pieces that fit nicely around big center Clyde Lovellette in Kansas' 1952 offense.

(also in Lawrence) and at nearby Baker University and, amazingly, coached all three teams in one season. It wasn't until the 1920 season, after completing seven years as coach at Central Missouri State, that Allen became full-time director of Kansas' basketball program.

His 1922 and 1923 teams, which included a player named Adolph Rupp, were designated as national champions by the Helms Athletic Foundation. He lobbied successfully for the inclusion of basketball in the 1936 Olympic Games. He played a significant role in the creation and development of the NCAA Tournament. He spoke in medical jargon (befitting a graduate of the Kansas City College of Osteopathy), using such words as pronation and supination. And to generations of players he stressed, "Pass at angles, run in curves."

Phog Allen, six years older than the sport itself, was a legendary basketball figure by the time he came to call on Clyde Lovellette in 1948.

Lovellette was a high school star in Terre Haute, Ind., whose outstanding physical characteristic was his height. He was 6 feet, 9 inches tall. Allen thought he could do something with such a gift in the middle of his offense. So did many other coaches, at least 50 by Lovellette's estimate.

In fact, the youngster was surrounded by universities seeking his presence. Indiana, Purdue and Notre Dame all were interested and Lovellette spent time on the Indiana campus in Bloomington, only 80 miles from home. It was assumed by many, including Coach Branch McCracken, that he would enroll at Indiana in the fall.

"My high school coach worked under Branch," Lovellette said. "But Indiana was such a big school. I just didn't think I wanted to get in classes with 50-60 students. I didn't want to be a number."

The Kansas campus was a smaller community. And Allen was a persuasive man. He told Lovellette he was gathering material for a team capable of sweeping the NCAA championship and the Olympic Games in 1952 and he told him he would be the key recruit.

"It was a beautiful idea," Lovellette decided.

Kansas had just endured only its second losing season under Allen, compiling a 9-15 record in '48. The year before, the coach had suffered a head injury in practice and sat out the second half of the season. Now, at the age of 63, Allen was running out of time in which to achieve an elusive national title and just maybe an Olympic conquest as well.

While Lovellette spent his freshman year improving his agility and stamina, the Jayhawks struggled through a .500 season. He reported to the varsity the following fall and immediately became the hub of the Kansas attack, averaging 21.8 points per game overall and 23 in Big Seven Conference play. Kansas finished in a three-way tie for first place with Kansas State and Nebraska, but the Jayhawks lost a playoff for a spot in the NCAA Tournament.

Only a few years earlier, Allen had decried the presence of big men in the sport. But now he was eager to take advantage of the best big man around. He instructed Lovellette to shoot often.

"He is closer to the basket than anyone else on the floor," the coach explained, "so I'd rather see him go for it than anyone else."

And go for it Lovellette did. In his junior season, the player known as "Man Mountain" and "Cumulus Clyde" raised his season scoring average to 22.8 and the Jayhawks won 16 of 24 games. Still, they did no better than tie for second in the conference behind Kansas State, which went all the way to the NCAA championship game.

Allen's team couldn't have been better positioned for the 1952 season. Including Lovellette, four starters returned from the previous year. The Jayhawks were experienced and the bench was deep. Among the reserves was a youngster named Dean Smith, whose grasp of the game was such that he would run the scout team that simulated opponents' tactics in practice.

Other than Lovellette and substitute guard Charlie Hoag, the Kansas players all were native Kansans and hailed from small towns. Their similar backgrounds drew them together.

"We kept the nucleus of our team through all four years," Lovellette said. "We were pretty much a family."

The family won the Big Seven title in 1952, losing only one league game. Lovellette, whose weight soared well above his listed figure of 230 pounds, was a bigger force than ever. He scored 28.6 points per game that season and averaged more than 13 rebounds a contest as the Jayhawks won their last nine league games to clinch the conference championship (Kansas State finished one game behind) and a berth in the NCAA Western Regional.

At the outset of the tournament, which for the first time produced a true Final Four with two separate playoffs held within both the Western and Eastern regionals, Kansas was not the favorite. The balance of power lay in the Eastern portion of the draw. Defending national champion Kentucky, ranked No. 1 in the wire-service polls, headed the field for the Eastern competition scheduled at Raleigh, N.C., and Big Ten Conference titlist Illinois, No. 2 in the ratings, appeared to be the class of the Eastern get-together in Chicago. Few reckoned on St. John's causing much interference.

Although the New York school had been ranked first nationally early in the season, St. John's was humiliated by Kentucky at Lexington, 81-40, in mid-December and largely overlooked thereafter. But the Redmen, stung by La Salle in the quarterfinals of the National Invitation Tournament, rose up in the NCAA Tournament and defeated North Carolina State on its home court in Raleigh, 60-49, and then stunned Kentucky, 64-57, to win their half of the Eastern Regional.

In the latter game, with his Redmen leading by six points at halftime, Coach Frank McGuire began his instructions only to be interrupted by Adolph Rupp's shouting in the adjoining locker room.

"I thought the walls were coming down," McGuire said. "I never did give my halftime talk. We just listened to Rupp screaming at his players."

While the Kentucky team had thought to charter

With big Clyde Lovellette (above) manning the middle, Coach Phog Allen's 1952 Kansas team was in an excellent position to challenge for a national championship.

a flight to Seattle (the Final Four site) in advance of the Eastern Regional, St. John's wasn't quite as prepared.

"Know what I thought of our chances of getting to Seattle?" McGuire said. "I only brought two pair of socks and two pair of drawers. I had to go out and buy underwear."

Meanwhile, Illinois won two games in impressive fashion in Chicago, qualifying to meet St. John's for the Eastern championship and thereby advancing to the first Final Four in NCAA Tournament history. At last, the Western and Eastern crowns and the national title would be decided at the same site.

The flight carrying the St. John's team to the West Coast touched down in Chicago and the Illinois squad boarded.

"I took one look at them," McGuire said of the rangy Illini, "and I thought, 'How can we beat those guys?' "

After struggling past Texas Christian, 68-64, Kansas emphatically won its half of the Western Regional at Kansas City by trouncing St. Louis, 74-55, as Lovellette set a single-game tournament record with 44 points. The Jayhawks would be matched in the Western title game against Santa Clara, which had upset UCLA and Wyoming in Corvallis, Ore.

The national semifinals, consolation game and NCAA title game were staged at Washington's Ed-

Charlie Hoag was one of seven Jayhawks chosen for the United States Olympic team that captured a gold medal in Helsinki, Finland.

mundson Pavilion. The competition provided one final upset in a tournament of surprises. St. John's, led by 6-foot-7 Bob (Zeke) Zawoluk, cut down taller Illinois, featuring 6-9 sophomore center John Kerr, 61-59. In the other semifinal game, Kansas overpowered Santa Clara by the same one-sided margin it had posted in its previous game, 74-55.

So the championship game pitted the country boys against what they perceived as the city slickers.

"It amazed me how fast they talked and the inflection in their voices," Lovellette said. "And I'm sure to them we sounded like hillbillies." But what counted was the manner in which the Jayhawks played.

St. John's had no answer for Lovellette and the Kansas offense. Zawoluk scored 20 points and Jack McMahon added 13, but Lovellette equaled their total by himself. His 33 points represented a championship-game record, and with senior forwards Bob Kenney and Bill Lienhard adding 12 points apiece, the Jayhawks romped to an 80-63 triumph. Big Clyde and his teammates had realized the first of Allen's goals.

Three nights later, Kansas began participation in the eight-team Olympic Trials. The Jayhawks hammered NAIA champion Southwest Missouri State in Kansas City, then defeated NIT titlist La Salle at Madison Square Garden. Had the Jayhawks beaten the AAU champion Peoria Cats in the Garden final, Allen would have been appointed Olympic head coach. But with the score tied at 60-60 in the closing seconds, Lovellette rushed a wide-open shot on a fast break, missed the basket and Peoria converted a long pass into the game-winning field goal.

There was a consolation prize. For his team's second-place finish in the Trials, Allen gained the position of assistant coach. And seven of his players, led by Lovellette, were chosen for the U.S. team that won the gold medal at Helsinki, Finland, with victories in all eight games, including two triumphs over the Soviet Union in the United States' first meetings with the Russians in Olympic basketball competition.

A group of country boys had transformed Allen's beautiful idea into gratifying reality.

1952 Tournament Results

First Round	Regional Championships
Kentucky 82, Penn State 54	St. John's 64, Kentucky 57
St. John's 60, N. C. State 49	Illinois 74, Duquesne 68
Illinois 80, Dayton 61	Kansas 74, St. Louis 55
Duquesne 60, Princeton 49	Santa Clara 56, Wyoming 53
Kansas 68, TCU 64	**Semifinals**
St. Louis 62, New Mexico A&M 53	St. John's 61, Illinois 59
Santa Clara 68, UCLA 59	Kansas 74, Santa Clara 55
Wyoming 54, Oklahoma City 48	**Third Place**
Regional Third Place	Illinois 67, Santa Clara 64
N. C. State 69, Penn St. 60	**Championship**
Dayton 77, Princeton 61	Kansas 80, St. John's 63
TCU 61, New Mexico A&M 44	
Oklahoma City 55, UCLA 53	

STATISTICS

1952 KANSAS

Head Coach—Forrest (Phog) Allen   Final Record—28-3

(Statistics and record include three games in Olympic Trials [2-1 record] after NCAA Tournament.)

Player	Pos.	Hgt.	Wgt.	Cl.	G	FG	FGA	Pct.	FT	FTA	Pct.	Reb.	Pts.	Avg.
Clyde Lovellette	C	6-9	230	Sr.	31	352	742	.474	182	250	.728	410	886	28.6
Bob Kenney	F	6-2	185	Sr.	30	141	392	.360	112	142	.789	115	394	13.1
Bill Hougland	G	6-4	180	Sr.	30	79	202	.391	46	62	.742	168	204	6.8
Dean Kelley	G	5-11	165	Jr.	31	77	194	.397	49	81	.605	101	203	6.5
Bill Lienhard	F	6-5	180	Sr.	29	67	221	.303	35	50	.700	97	169	5.8
Charlie Hoag	F-G	6-2	185	Jr.	21	44	145	.303	22	39	.564	62	110	5.2
John Keller	F-G	6-3	185	Sr.	27	19	49	.388	23	30	.767	73	61	2.3
B.H. Born	C	6-8	195	So.	27	14	46	.304	19	31	.613	33	47	1.7
Bill Heitholt	G-F	6-3	178	Fr.	28	14	59	.237	15	33	.454	53	43	1.5
Dean Smith	G-F	5-10	160	Jr.	19	10	22	.455	8	16	.500	11	28	1.5
Larry Davenport	F	6-2	165	Fr.	22	12	37	.324	7	10	.700	21	31	1.4
Ev Dye	G-F	6-2	155	So.	11	3	16	.188	3	4	.750	4	9	0.8
LaVannes Squires	F	6-0	165	So.	14	5	18	.278	1	2	.500	9	11	0.8
Jerry Alberts	F	6-3	176	Fr.	9	2	6	.333	2	4	.500	5	6	0.7
Wes Johnson	G	6-3	174	So.	13	2	4	.500	3	6	.500	7	7	0.5
Allen Kelley	G-F	5-11	164	So.	9	1	5	.200	0	2	.000	2	2	0.2
Dean Wells	F-G	6-0	170	Sr.	1	0	0	.000	0	0	.000	0	0	0.0
Kansas					31	842	2158	.390	527	762	.692	1171	2211	71.3
Opponents					31	667	2037	.327	473	724	.653	1055	1807	58.3

1952 ST. JOHN'S (N.Y.)

Head Coach—Frank McGuire   Final Record—25-6

(Statistics and record include 71-62 loss to La Salle in Olympic Trials that isn't recognized by the NCAA.)

Player	Pos.	Hgt.	Wgt.	Cl.	G	FG	FGA	Pct.	FT	FTA	Pct.	Reb.	Pts.	Avg.
Bob Zawoluk	C	6-7	215	Sr.	31	204	456	.447	176	231	.762	397	584	18.9
Jack McMahon	F	6-1	180	Sr.	31	161	476	.338	95	167	.569	158	417	13.5
Ron MacGilvray	G	6-1	180	Sr.	31	83	280	.296	87	152	.572	243	253	8.2
Jim Davis	F	6-6	207	So.	31	93	241	.386	38	68	.559	218	224	7.2
Solly Walker	G-F	6-3	194	So.	30	54	216	.250	24	45	.533	115	132	4.4
Dick Duckett	G	6-0	185	Fr.	28	43	129	.333	28	46	.609	71	114	4.1
Jim Coyle	F-G	6-2	179	Fr.	14	22	71	.310	8	18	.444	44	52	3.7
Don Dunn	C	6-7	220	Jr.	19	27	85	.318	10	21	.476	77	64	3.4
Jim Walsh	F	6-5	240	So.	28	28	91	.308	18	34	.529	87	74	2.6
Frank Giancontieri	G	5-10	179	Jr.	27	21	68	.309	9	19	.474	28	51	1.9
Phil Sagona	G	6-0	177	Fr.	20	13	37	.351	6	16	.375	16	32	1.6
Jim McMorrow	G	6-2	197	So.	18	7	32	.219	5	8	.625	18	19	1.1
Carl Peterson	C	6-6	210	So.	9	2	9	.222	1	2	.500	2	5	0.6
Team												204		
St. John's					31	758	2191	.346	505	827	.611	1678	2021	65.2
Opponents					31	630	....	....	494	....	....	....	1754	56.6

1952 ILLINOIS

Head Coach—Harry Combes   Final Record—22-4

Player	Pos.	Hgt.	Wgt.	Cl.	G	FG	FGA	Pct.	FT	FTA	Pct.	Reb.	Pts.	Avg.
John Kerr	C	6-9	205	Jr.	26	143	365	.392	71	124	.573	...	357	13.7
Rod Fletcher	G	6-4	194	Sr.	26	105	366	.287	80	142	.563	...	290	11.2
Irv Bemoras	F	6-3	185	Jr.	26	108	314	.344	69	105	.657	...	285	11.0
Jim Bredar	G	5-11	167	Jr.	26	104	281	.370	52	71	.732	...	260	10.0
Bob Peterson	C	6-7	235	Jr.	26	87	240	.363	77	136	.566	...	251	9.7
Clive Follmer	F	6-4	195	Jr.	26	73	210	.348	91	119	.765	...	237	9.1
Max Hooper	F-G	6-5	200	So.	20	29	122	.238	11	18	.611	...	69	3.5
Herb Gerecke	G-F	6-1	180	So.	20	21	61	.344	17	27	.630	...	59	3.0
Walt Moore	G	6-2	165	Fr.	4	2	7	.286	1	1	1.000	...	5	1.3
Jim Dutcher	F	6-3	185	Fr.	5	2	10	.200	2	7	.286	...	6	1.2
Dick Christiansen	F	6-3	180	Sr.	10	5	16	.313	1	1	1.000	...	11	1.1
Jim Wright	G	6-0	160	So.	12	5	15	.333	2	6	.333	...	12	1.0
Max Baumgardner	C-F	6-6	220	Jr.	7	3	9	.333	0	1	.000	...	6	0.9
Jim Schuldt	G	6-1	190	Jr.	7	1	10	.100	4	5	.800	...	6	0.9
Ed Makovsky	G	6-5	194	Fr.	9	1	12	.083	5	6	.833	...	7	0.8
Mack Follmer	C-F	6-4	200	Sr.	9	0	7	.000	4	9	.444	...	4	0.4
Illinois					26	689	2045	.337	487	778	.626	...	1865	71.7
Opponents					26	...	...	...	...	...	...	...	1599	61.5

1952 SANTA CLARA

Head Coach—Bob Feerick   Final Record—17-12

Player	Pos.	Hgt.	Wgt.	Cl.	G	FG	FGA	Pct.	FT	FTA	Pct.	Reb.	Pts.	Avg.
Jim Young	F	6-3	190	So.	29	127	334	.380	89	127	.701	...	343	11.8
Herb Schoenstein	C	6-5	215	Sr.	29	115	297	.387	67	98	.684	...	297	10.2
Bob Peters	G	6-1	183	Sr.	29	100	289	.346	78	118	.661	...	278	9.6
Kenny Sears	F	6-7	190	Fr.	29	88	222	.396	34	44	.773	...	210	7.2
Dick Soares	F	6-2	175	Jr.	29	73	187	.390	39	56	.696	...	185	6.4
Don Benedetti	G	5-10	170	So.	25	55	180	.306	18	32	.563	...	128	5.1
Dal Brock	G	6-3	185	Jr.	24	39	112	.348	28	44	.636	...	106	4.4
Dick Garibaldi	G	6-4	190	Fr.	29	39	142	.275	32	54	.593	...	110	3.8
Mark Butier	C	6-5	195	Sr.	20	16	49	.327	24	39	.615	...	56	2.8
Gary Gatzert	F	6-3	195	Jr.	21	22	65	.338	12	19	.632	...	56	2.7
Dick Simoni	F	6-4	185	Fr.	16	5	19	.263	1	7	.143	...	11	0.7
Santa Clara					29	679	1896	.358	422	638	.661	...	1780	61.4
Opponents					29	599	1718	.349	487	742	.656	...	1685	58.1

1952 FINAL FOUR

At Seattle

Semifinals

St. John's (N.Y.)	fg	ft	tp
McMahon	3	3	9
Davis	1	0	2
Walsh	2	0	4
Zawoluk	9	6	24
MacGilvray	2	2	6
Duckett	4	3	11
Walker	2	1	5
Totals	23	15	61

Illinois	fg	ft	tp
C. Follmer	4	2	10
Bemoras	1	1	3
Peterson	2	0	4
Kerr	3	2	8
Bredar	7	0	14
Fletcher	5	4	14
Gerecke	3	0	6
Totals	25	9	59

Halftime: St. John's 34-28.

Kansas	fg	ft	tp
Kenney	3	1	7
Lienhard	0	0	0
Hoag	4	2	10
Keller	1	2	4
Lovellette	12	9	33
Born	1	2	4
D. Kelley	4	2	10
Heitholt	2	0	4
Davenport	0	2	2
Totals	27	20	74

Santa Clara	fg	ft	tp
Sears	0	1	1
Young	3	2	8
Garibaldi	1	0	2
Gatzert	1	1	3
Schoenstein	6	1	13
Peters	1	1	3
Brock	3	1	7
Benedetti	1	0	2
Soares	7	2	16
Totals	23	9	55

Halftime: Kansas 38-25.

Championship
March 26

Kansas	fg	fga	ft	fta	rb	pf	tp
Kenney	4	11	4	6	4	2	12
Keller	1	1	0	0	4	2	2
Lovellette	12	25	9	11	17	4	33
Lienhard	5	8	2	2	4	4	12
D. Kelley	2	5	3	6	3	5	7
Hoag	2	6	5	7	4	5	9
Houghland	2	5	1	3	6	2	5
Davenport	0	0	0	0	0	1	0
Heitholt	0	0	0	0	0	0	0
Born	0	0	0	0	1	0	0
A. Kelley	0	0	0	0	1	0	0
Totals	28	61	24	35	43	25	80

St. John's (N.Y.)	fg	fga	ft	fta	rb	pf	tp
McMahon	6	12	1	4	2	4	13
Davis	1	4	2	3	2	4	4
Zawoluk	7	12	6	11	9	5	20
Duckett	2	5	2	2	2	4	6
MacGilvray	3	8	2	5	10	3	8
Walsh	3	6	0	0	4	3	6
Walker	0	2	0	0	2	4	0
McMorrow	1	3	0	0	0	3	2
Sagona	2	2	0	0	0	5	4
Giancontieri	0	0	0	2	1	0	0
Peterson	0	1	0	0	0	0	0
Totals	25	55	13	27	32	35	63

Halftime: Kansas 41-27. Officials: Eisenstein and Ogden.

1953 Little Hoosiers Stand Tall

Indiana basketball coaching wizard Branch McCracken with his starting five (left to right): Charles Kraak, Bob Leonard, Don Schlundt, Dick Farley and Burke Scott.

By all measurements save one, Branch McCracken had enjoyed an enormously successful coaching career at his alma mater. He had won nearly 75 percent of his games at Indiana, struggled through only one losing season (in the aftermath of World War II) and directed the Hoosiers to the championship of the second NCAA Tournament. The only thing missing from his portfolio as the 1953 season approached was a Big Ten Conference basketball title.

Curiously, the Hoosiers had finished second in the conference race on seven occasions in his 11 years. McCracken still was teaching the same style of run-and-gun and his players were executing the fast break as well as any team in the nation, but Indiana consistently was hampered by a lack of size. The coach hadn't been able to recruit the big center so essential in the postwar era.

He thought he had his man in 1948 when Indiana high school star Clyde Lovellette, a 6-foot-9 prospect from Terre Haute, visited the campus and indicated he'd be returning soon with his belongings. Instead, he enrolled at Kansas. McCracken made do with a 6-2 center and Indiana remained competitive but unfulfilled.

Don Schlundt changed that. He was a skinny 6-6 pivotman when McCracken came across him during a trip to South Bend, Ind. The youngster had shot up in his last two years of high school and gave indication of future growth as well. Not willing to take the same chance on this prospect as he did on Lovellette, McCracken suggested that Schlundt enroll in summer school, which he did.

When Schlundt reported for his sophomore season (1953), he stood 6-9. Furthermore, he was able to shoot with either hand and was not reluctant to use his elbows. McCracken had struck it rich. The final piece of the puzzle was fitted into place when

The final pieces to the Indiana championship puzzle were put into place when Coach Branch McCracken signed Don Schlundt (left) and then moved veteran forward Bob Leonard (right) to guard.

the coach moved 6-3 junior Bob Leonard from forward to guard, filling the position vacated by Sam Esposito, who had signed a professional baseball contract.

Leonard was a natural leader and the perfect triggerman for the break. Indiana was a beautifully balanced club with junior forwards Dick Farley, an outstanding defender, and Charles Kraak, a superior rebounder, surrounding Schlundt and sophomore Burke Scott, a fine ballhandler, opposite Leonard. The Hoosiers were young but smooth, in the image of Leonard (who, in fact, answered to "Slick").

Indiana lost two of its first three games, both at the buzzer, in advance of the conference schedule. But the Hoosiers were ready for the Big Ten opener against Michigan. Their 88-60 victory was a glimpse into the future.

Opponents attempted to slow down Indiana, but the Hoosiers would counter with pressure defense and force the pace to their liking. McCracken's team reeled off 13 consecutive victories in conference play before hosting archrival Purdue at home. With the aid of a remarkable 41-point quarter, Indiana demolished the Boilermakers, 113-78.

Defending conference champion Illinois was next

on the schedule. In cramped Huff Gymnasium on the Illinois campus, the Hoosiers mauled the Illini. Indiana led 82-62 at one stage before settling for a 91-79 victory. McCracken finally had his Big Ten championship and was carried off the court on the shoulders of his players.

Even a two-point loss at Minnesota—again at the buzzer—in the next-to-last game of the regular season failed to dent Indiana's confidence. The Hoosiers finished the round-robin Big Ten schedule with a record of 17-1 and survived two difficult games in the Eastern Regional. In their first NCAA Tournament game, the Hoosiers slipped past De-Paul, 82-80. The next evening, Indiana atoned for one of its three last-second defeats by routing Notre Dame, 79-66, as Schlundt established a Chicago Stadium scoring record with 41 points.

Despite its outstanding season, Indiana was not a commanding favorite as the four survivors of Eastern and Western regional play gathered in Kansas City for the Final Four. Many thought Washington, whose 6-7 center Bob Houbregs was the finest practitioner of the hook shot thus far in the modern era, was the team to beat. The Huskies, directed by Tippy Dye, former Ohio State coach, had stormed to a 27-2 regular-season record and advanced easily

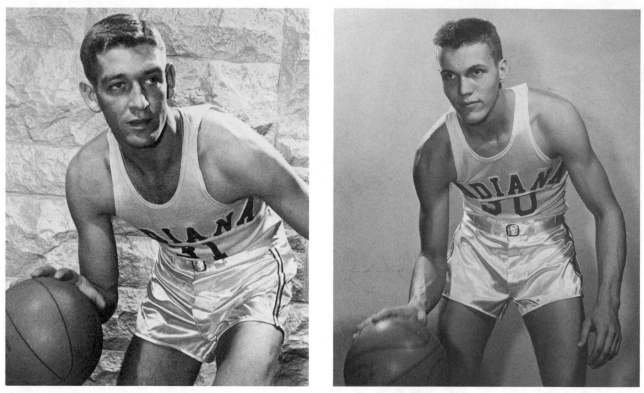

Forward Dick Farley (left) was the defensive weapon Coach Branch McCracken
used against top opposing players and Charles Kraak (right) was recognized as a
superior rebounder.

through their half of the Western Regional bracket at Corvallis, Ore., to gain a berth in Kansas City.

Bob Pettit, an aggressive 6-9 junior, had led once-beaten Louisiana State to victory in its half of the Eastern Regional at Raleigh, N.C. Of the four national semifinalists, in fact, only Kansas was an unexpected visitor. With the graduation of Lovellette and three other starters from the 1952 national championship team, the Jayhawks were expected to struggle. But B.H. Born, a 6-9 junior, proved to be more than adequate as a replacement for Lovellette, and the rest of the starters, none taller than 6-1, transformed Phog Allen's pressure defense into a lethal weapon. Kansas narrowly won the Big Seven Conference title and then overcame Oklahoma City and Oklahoma A&M in the Manhattan, Kan., portion of the Western Regional.

Indiana's Leonard had a hot hand in the semifinals and his long shots opened the middle for Schlundt, who then ripped open LSU's defense. The guard had 22 points and the center 29 in the Hoosiers' 80-67 triumph for the Eastern title. Pettit's 29-point performance simply was not enough against Indiana's superior firepower.

The Hoosiers were feeling pretty good as they trooped out of their dressing room to watch the second game between Washington and Kansas. Their expressions changed in the course of the first half as the Jayhawks' press caused repeated turn-

overs and eventual panic. Leonard thought Kansas was awesome and said so to his backcourt partner, Scott.

"How are we ever going to beat this team?" he wondered.

By the time Kansas had made its 21st and last steal and completed a 79-53 demolition of the Huskies for the Western championship, the Hoosiers were back in their hotel wondering and fretting about the outcome of their season. Clearly, the Jayhawks were playing at the top of their game and would be a difficult opponent, particularly with a crowd composed largely of Kansas rooters.

It was no small irony that Indiana, in its first trip to the title game since 1940, would be facing the same team on the same court as it did 13 years earlier. And the presence of a Phog Allen team served to heighten the drama. McCracken had neither forgotten nor forgiven Lovellette's "defection."

The final was a classic in every sense of the word. Indiana and Kansas met pressure with pressure. Neither team cracked. Kansas held the biggest lead of the game, at 39-33, in the first half while Schlundt was on the bench with three fouls. His return sparked the Hoosiers to an 8-2 run and a 41-41 halftime tie.

Dean Kelley had been particularly effective against Leonard in the first 20 minutes, holding him to one basket. But the Indiana captain became more of a force in the third quarter as the intensity mounted. Late in the period, officials whistled a foul on Born. According to the scorers, it was his fifth. He had fouled out.

But Allen hustled to the scorer's table. The Kansas book, he said, showed Born with only four fouls. The scorers rechecked and determined Allen was correct. McCracken raged along the sidelines.

"Your book shows five personals," the Indiana coach shouted. "Born should be out. We're your guest and you're robbing us."

Born did foul out, but not until midway through the fourth quarter. By then, the strain was showing on both sides. Schlundt and Leonard each had been charged with a technical for questioning an official's call in an indelicate manner. Then, with the Hoosiers clinging to a 68-65 lead—their largest margin—late in the game, Kraak was called for charging, his fifth foul, and angrily slammed the ball. The subsequent technical gave Kansas three free throws and possession of the ball.

Fortunately for Kraak, junior forward Hal Patterson made only one of two free throws after the personal and Al Kelley, Dean's brother and Kansas' No. 2 scorer in the '53 season, failed on the technical. But Dean Kelley's drive succeeded in tying the score at 68-68. There were 65 seconds remaining.

Indiana attempted to work the ball for a final shot but Dean Kelley bumped Leonard, sending him to the foul line with 27 seconds left. He missed the first attempt and Allen called a timeout to make Leonard stew over the failure.

"I had been to the line so much under pressure all season," Leonard said. He took his time, measured the shot and made it. The Hoosiers led, 69-68.

Allen had a play for just such an occasion. It called for the Jayhawks to run precisely 22 seconds off the clock while setting up Al Kelley for a short jump shot. But when the time came, the opening wasn't there. Surrounded by defenders, Kelley passed to Jerry Alberts, a rarely used reserve who had replaced Born, in the corner. Alberts had no choice but to shoot as the clock ran down. It was an off-balance shot from a difficult angle. Still, Leonard tensed. The Hoosiers' only three losses had come amid just such a last-ditch scenario.

"I thought," Leonard said, " 'Please don't let this go through.' "

It did not. Indiana grabbed the rebound. The national championship belonged to the Hoosiers. Although Schlundt had scored 30 points and Kraak 17, Leonard had emerged the hero with his 12th point. In the dressing room, a beaming McCracken told reporters that his captain "had ice water in his veins."

The description was relayed to Leonard.

"If that was ice water," the player said, "it sure felt warm to me." Then he smiled.

Ballhandling duties fell into the capable hands of Burke Scott (above), who combined with Bob Leonard to lead Indiana's fearsome fast break.

1953 Tournament Results

First Round
Notre Dame 72, E. Kentucky 57
DePaul 74, Miami (Ohio) 72
Holy Cross 87, Navy 74
Lebanon Valley 80, Fordham 67
Seattle 88, Idaho State 77
S. Clara 81, Hardin-Simmons 56

Second Round
Notre Dame 69, Pennsylvania 57
Indiana 82, DePaul 80
Holy Cross 79, Wake Forest 71
LSU 89, Lebanon Valley 76
Kansas 73, Oklahoma City 65
Oklahoma St. 71, TCU 54
Washington 92, Seattle 70
Santa Clara 67, Wyoming 52

Regional Third Place
Pennsylvania 90, DePaul 70
Wake Forest 91, Lebanon Valley 71
TCU 58, Oklahoma City 56
Seattle 80, Wyoming 64

Regional Championships
Indiana 79, Notre Dame 66
LSU 81, Holy Cross 73
Kansas 61, Oklahoma State 55
Washington 74, Santa Clara 62

Semifinals
Indiana 80, LSU 67
Kansas 79, Washington 53

Third Place
Washington 88, LSU 69

Championship
Indiana 69, Kansas 68

STATISTICS

1953 INDIANA

Head Coach—Branch McCracken　　　　　　Final Record—23-3

Player	Pos.	Hgt.	Wgt.	Cl.	G	FG	FGA	Pct.	FT	FTA	Pct.	Reb.	Pts.	Avg.
Don Schlundt	C	6-9	210	So.	26	206	477	.432	249	310	.803	...	661	25.4
Bob Leonard	G	6-3	185	Jr.	26	164	503	.326	96	144	.667	...	424	16.3
Dick Farley	F	6-3	183	Jr.	26	94	212	.443	75	108	.694	...	263	10.1
Burke Scott	G	6-1	165	So.	26	76	206	.369	55	85	.647	...	207	8.0
Lou Scott*	C	6-11	227	Jr.	10	28	83	.337	18	28	.643	...	74	7.4
Charles Kraak	F	6-5	180	Jr.	26	63	177	.356	60	102	.588	...	186	7.2
Dick White	F	6-1	170	So.	22	40	128	.313	43	58	.471	...	123	5.6
Paul Poff	G	6-1	181	So.	13	14	45	.311	12	19	.632	...	40	3.1
Phil Byers	G	5-11	165	So.	23	25	72	.347	13	24	.542	...	63	2.7
Jack Wright	F	5-10	168	Jr.	3	2	11	.182	4	4	1.000	...	8	2.7
James DeaKyne	G	6-3	190	Jr.	20	20	87	.230	5	12	.417	...	45	2.3
Goethe Chambers	F	6-2	175	So.	2	1	1	1.000	0	0	.000	...	2	1.0
Ron Taylor	F	6-3	185	Jr.	2	1	2	.500	0	0	.000	...	2	1.0
Don Henry	F	6-2	188	So.	2	0	1	.000	2	4	.500	...	2	1.0
James Schooley	F	6-5	188	Sr.	16	3	14	.214	6	12	.500	...	12	0.8
Indiana					26	737	2019	.365	638	910	.701	...	2112	81.2
Opponents					26	611	2041	.299	586	937	.625	...	1808	69.5

*Ineligible second semester.

1953 KANSAS

Head Coach—Forrest (Phog) Allen　　　　Final Record—19-6

Player	Pos.	Hgt.	Wgt.	Cl.	G	FG	FGA	Pct.	FT	FTA	Pct.	Reb.	Pts.	Avg.
B.H. Born	C	6-9	200	Jr.	25	163	405	.402	148	234	.632	280	474	19.0
Allen Kelley	F-G	5-11	161	Jr.	25	120	298	.403	83	118	.703	115	323	12.9
Dean Kelley	G	5-11	170	Sr.	25	81	236	.343	80	115	.696	76	242	9.7
Hal Patterson	F	6-1	185	Jr.	25	73	176	.415	91	138	.659	168	237	9.5
Gil Reich	G	6-0	187	Jr.	22	62	180	.344	53	75	.707	80	177	8.0
Larry Davenport	F	6-2	172	So.	25	54	135	.400	25	32	.781	45	133	5.3
Bill Heitholt	G	6-3	195	So.	18	16	58	.276	27	40	.675	41	59	3.3
Dean Smith	G	5-10	148	Sr.	25	15	56	.268	19	32	.594	27	49	2.0
Jerry Alberts	F	6-3	181	So.	17	9	35	.257	12	22	.545	18	30	1.8
Eldon Nicholson	C-F	6-6	193	So.	15	10	25	.400	5	11	.455	10	25	1.7
John Anderson	G	6-2	209	So.	19	9	25	.360	6	14	.429	15	24	1.3
LaVannes Squires	F	6-1	170	Jr.	10	4	7	.571	4	6	.667	6	12	1.2
Marvin Deckert	F	6-1	175	Jr.	4	2	3	.667	0	0	.000	3	4	1.0
Wes Whitney	C	6-3	208	Jr.	4	0	1	.000	4	4	1.000	4	4	1.0
Wes Johnson	G	6-3	175	Jr.	2	1	4	.250	0	0	.000	1	2	1.0
Jerry Taylor	G	6-3	186	Jr.	5	0	2	.000	4	4	1.000	2	4	0.8
Ken Buller	F	5-11	180	Sr.	10	1	5	.200	5	16	.313	4	7	0.7
Jack Wolfe	G	5-7	135	So.	6	0	3	.000	4	6	.667	1	4	0.7
Ev Dye	F-G	6-2	150	Jr.	12	1	5	.200	1	3	.333	3	3	0.3
Kansas					25	621	1659	.374	571	870	.656	899	1813	72.5
Opponents					25	491	1392	.353	602	923	.652	867	1584	63.4

1953 WASHINGTON

Head Coach—Tippy Dye　　　　　　Final Record—30-3

Player	Pos.	Hgt.	Wgt.	Cl.	G	FG	FGA	Pct.	FT	FTA	Pct.	Reb.	Pts.	Avg.
Bob Houbregs	C	6-7	210	Sr.	33	325	604	.538	196	264	.742	381	846	25.6
Joe Cipriano	G	5-11	160	Jr.	32	162	459	.353	84	115	.730	97	408	12.8
Mike McCutchen	F	6-1	190	Sr.	33	108	309	.350	107	142	.754	203	323	9.8
Charlie Koon	G	5-11	150	Sr.	33	95	250	.380	66	80	.825	121	256	7.8
Doug McClary	F	6-8	208	Sr.	33	92	263	.350	46	77	.597	346	230	7.0
Dean Parsons	C	6-7	225	So.	33	36	111	.324	84	142	.592	166	156	4.7
Don Tripp	F	6-1	170	Jr.	18	29	124	.234	25	34	.735	59	83	4.6
Larry Ramm	F	6-3	175	So.	9	3	...	....	13	...	....	...	19	2.1
Will Elliott	G	5-10	150	Sr.	25	8	...	....	15	...	....	...	31	1.2
Roland Halle	G	5-11	170	Jr.	14	4	12	.333	5	13	.385	6	13	0.9
Don Apeland	F	6-1	175	So.	15	4	...	....	1	...	....	...	9	0.6
Bill Ward	F	6-4	180	Sr.	15	3	...	....	1	...	....	...	7	0.5
Steve Roake	F	6-1	180	So.	6	0	2	.000	0	0	.000	1	0	0.0
Others						0			4				4	
Washington					33	869	2225	.391	647	919	.704	1429	2385	72.3
Opponents					33	703	2291	.307	543	853	.637	1135	1949	59.1

(Statistics and record include 66-63 and 69-51 victories over Universal Motors not recognized by NCAA.)

1953 LOUISIANA STATE

Head Coach—Harry Rabenhorst　　　　　　Final Record—22-3

(Full statistics for full season are unavailable.)

Player	Pos.	Hgt.	Wgt.	Cl.	G	FG	FGA	Pct.	FT	FTA	Pct.	Reb.	Pts.	Avg.
Bob Pettit	C	6-9	210	Jr.	21	193	394	.490	133	215	.619	263	519	24.7
Norman Magee	G	5-10	155	So.	25	124	...	....	94	...	....	...	342	13.7
Don Belcher	F	6-2	165	So.	25	139	...	....	50	...	....	...	328	13.1
Ned Clark	F	6-4	205	So.	25	98	...	....	51	...	....	...	247	9.9
Benny McArdle	G	5-10	165	Jr.	25	80	...	....	48	...	....	...	208	8.3
Bob Freshley	C-F	6-6	210	Jr.	21	26	...	....	21	...	....	...	73	3.5
Kenny Bridges	F	5-11	150	Sr.	16	8	...	....	8	...	....	...	24	1.5
Don Loughmiller	G	6-0	180	Jr.	9	4	...	....	4	...	....	...	12	1.3
Jim McNeilly	F	6-4	210	So.	9	4	...	....	3	...	....	...	11	1.2
Darrell Schultz	G	5-8	160	Jr.										
Don Sebastian	G	5-10	140	Fr.									...	...
Leslie Jones	F	6-2	160	Fr.									...	...
Bill Lee	C	6-4	170	Fr.									...	...
Charley Roberts	F	6-0	170	Jr.									...	...
LSU					25	703	1783	.394	428			...	1834	73.4
Opponents					25	...	...	....	...			...	1473	58.9

1953 FINAL FOUR

At Kansas City
Semifinals

Indiana	fg	ft	tp
Kraak	2	5	9
Farley	4	2	10
DeaKyne	0	0	0
Schlundt	8	13	29
White	0	3	3
Leonard	9	4	22
Byers	0	0	0
Poff	0	0	0
Scott	2	3	7
Totals	25	30	80

Louisiana State	fg	ft	tp
Belcher	4	2	10
Clark	0	2	2
Freshley	0	1	1
Loughmiller	0	0	0
Pettit	10	9	29
Magee	6	5	17
McArdle	1	1	3
Bridges	1	3	5
Totals	22	23	67

Halftime: Indiana 49-41. Officials: Ogden and Lightner.

Kansas	fg	ft	tp
Patterson	6	5	17
Smith	0	0	0
Alberts	0	0	0
A. Kelley	3	1	7
Davenport	0	2	2
Born	9	7	25
D. Kelley	8	2	18
Heitholt	1	0	2
Reich	3	2	8
Totals	30	19	79

Washington	fg	ft	tp
McCutchen	0	3	3
Halle	0	1	1
McClary	2	2	6
Parsons	0	1	1
Houbregs	8	2	18
Elliott	1	1	3
Cipriano	4	3	11
Apeland	1	0	2
Koon	3	2	8
Totals	19	15	53

Halftime: Kansas 45-34. Officials: Conway and George.

Championship
March 18

Indiana	fg	ft	fta	pf	tp
Kraak	5	7	10	5	17
DeaKyne	0	0	0	1	0
Farley	1	0	0	5	2
Schlundt	11	8	11	3	30
White	1	0	0	2	2
Leonard	5	2	4	2	12
Poff	0	0	0	0	0
Scott	2	2	3	3	6
Byers	0	0	0	1	0
Totals	25	19	28	22	69

Kansas	fg	ft	fta	pf	tp
Patterson	1	7	8	3	9
A. Kelley	7	6	8	3	20
Davenport	0	0	0	0	0
Born	8	10	12	5	26
Smith	0	1	1	1	1
Alberts	0	0	0	1	0
D. Kelley	3	2	4	2	8
Reich	2	0	0	2	4
Totals	21	26	33	17	68

Halftime Score: 41-41. Officials: Lightner and Shaw.

1954 La Salle Gets Rich Quick

It surely was the shortest recruiting trip in history for a celebrated schoolboy athlete. After sampling the campus life at Kentucky and North Carolina State, Tom Gola literally walked downstairs and met the varsity basketball team at La Salle College. The institution's gymnasium was located underneath La Salle High School, where Gola had spent four years.

There was the sense of a small community about the high school and college, both run by the Christian Brothers. Even as a high school student, Gola knew the president of the college. Indeed, it was the president who did the recruiting for La Salle.

Gola liked the tradition at Kentucky, where he was introduced to Wah Wah Jones and Babe Parilli, but Lexington seemed too far away. North Carolina State was big. La Salle was home. Two of Gola's brothers would follow him to the college. They also received scholarships, no small consideration for a family of seven children raised on a policeman's salary.

Although it didn't play any part in his decision, there was an added benefit in attending the Philadelphia commuter school. Because the enrollment at La Salle was below 1,000, Gola would be allowed to play varsity ball in his freshman year. Ken Loeffler, the coach, never doubted that Gola was ready for the big time at the age of 18.

He was that rarest of athletes, a small man in a big man's body. The 6-foot-6 Gola had the quickness and the agility of a guard, yet he was big enough to mix it up inside. He was capable of playing center and forward as well as the backcourt and, best of all, he had a sixth sense about the game. There was nothing flamboyant about his actions, but his anticipation was so acute that he always seemed to be in the right spot.

"I have never seen a youngster with such poise," remarked Loeffler, who had coached at three colleges and in the National Basketball Association before taking the position at La Salle. "Nothing rattles him. He can do everything and do it well."

Furthermore, he did it right away. Gola was in the starting lineup at the outset of his freshman season, 1952, and the Explorers played their way into the prestigious National Invitation Tournament.

When Tom Gola decided to stay home to go to college, La Salle became an instant college basketball power.

Six members of La Salle's 1954 national championship team were (left to right) Charles Greenberg, Bob Maples, Tom Gola, Charlie Singley, Fran O'Malley and Frank Blatcher.

Tom Gola was the most talented member of La Salle's title-winning team, but not the biggest. He shared that honor with John Yodsnukis (left), who is shown posing with Gola and Coach Ken Loeffler.

Gola's performances at Madison Square Garden were a revelation. La Salle, which entered the tournament with a 20-5 record, defeated Seton Hall, St. John's, Duquesne and Dayton en route to the school's first postseason championship, and Gola shared the Most Valuable Player award with a teammate, Norm Grekin.

Loeffler and Gola both thought the 1953 La Salle team, which lost only two games during the regular season, was better. But an injury to Gola hampered the Explorers in the NIT, where they were eliminated in the quarterfinals by St. John's, 75-74. Graduation virtually cleaned house that spring, leaving only Gola and 5-11 guard Frank O'Hara to team with a group of recruits, none of them very big.

La Salle began Gola's junior season with lowered expectations that appeared entirely justified when the Explorers lost three games before New Year's. Two of those defeats, including one in the semifinals of the Holiday Festival, were administered by Niagara. The third occurred in the final of the Kentucky Invitational when Adolph Rupp's Wildcats,

whose uniform Gola had contemplated wearing a few years earlier, thumped La Salle. Both teams would have reason to reflect on that result later in the season.

The Explorers lifted their game after the holidays. They won 14 of their last 15 regular-season contests, losing only to city rival Temple (and that defeat was by a single point). For most of the season, Loeffler's squad anticipated another trip to the NIT, but by season's end the NCAA had other ideas. The organization had expanded the 1954 NCAA Tournament field to 24 teams (it had gone from 16 to 22 the previous year) and authorized an automatic berth for the "champion" of the Middle Atlantic Conference, a loosely aligned collection of East Coast schools of which La Salle was a member.

So, the Explorers, boasting a 21-4 record overall, found themselves headed for Buffalo and a first-round NCAA engagement with a tough Fordham team they had struggled to beat during the regular season, 61-56.

Meanwhile, the Kentucky Wildcats, ranked No. 1

in both wire-service polls in the week preceding the start of the NCAA Tournament, found themselves out in the cold. Although they had won all their games, the Wildcats declined to enter the tournament when their three top players—Cliff Hagan, Frank Ramsey and Lou Tsioropoulos—were barred, under existing NCAA guidelines, from postseason competition because they were attending graduate school. (The three had spent their senior years playing intrasquad games, a result of the NCAA's decision to put the Kentucky program into mothballs for the 1953 season because of major infractions dating to 1948.)

A national championship seemed a long way off for La Salle when Loeffler's squad fell behind Fordham. The Explorers, in fact, trailed by two points in the final seconds when Gola hit Frank O'Malley under the basket with a perfect pass. The 6-3 O'Malley scored just before the buzzer, forcing an overtime in which La Salle triumphed, 76-74.

Gola was outstanding in Eastern Regional games in Philadelphia, sparking the Explorers past North Carolina State and Navy. La Salle, a team Loeffler considered too small to succeed in any postseason tournament, thereby headed for the Final Four—as the favorite. Not only did Kentucky pass on the tournament but Indiana, with the entire starting team that had won the national championship the previous year, had been ousted by Notre Dame in the Eastern bracket at Iowa City, from which unheralded Penn State emerged as the survivor.

There was another major surprise in the Western half of the tournament. Bradley, which had lost 12 games, defeated Oklahoma City in the first round and then, playing in Stillwater, Okla., shocked Colorado and Oklahoma A&M. Bradley scored 71 points against the Aggies on their home court, the most yielded by Henry Iba's defense-oriented team all season.

Bradley's opponent in the national semifinals at Kansas City's Municipal Auditorium was Southern California, which had won a Pacific Coast Conference championship playoff game against Oregon State and upset Santa Clara in Western Regional play in Corvallis, Ore. Between them, the Trojans and the Braves had lost 24 games that season.

The pairing for the Western championship guaranteed that one of the combatants would lose at least one more game. That distinction would go to Southern Cal, by a mere two points. And, after the 74-72 defeat, the Trojans went on to absorb loss No. 14 in the consolation game.

The Eastern title matchup marked the first time two Pennsylvania schools had qualified for the Final Four in the same year. But that was the extent of the competition. La Salle, directed by Penn State graduate Loeffler, was so much better than the Nittany Lions that Gola concentrated on setting up his

Little guard Frank O'Hara was the main ballhandler during La Salle's drive to the 1954 national championship.

teammates. He took only nine shots, scored 19 points and grabbed 17 rebounds. Frank Blatcher also scored 19 for the Explorers, who were 69-54 winners. Blatcher had extra incentive in Kansas City. He had dedicated the event to the memory of his father, who had died on the night the Explorers began tournament play in Buffalo.

Although Gola didn't dominate the Penn State game, it was apparent that his was an extraordinary presence on the court.

"He makes plays a little man should make," said Paul Unruh, the former consensus All-America from Bradley, "and then he turns around and does things only a big man usually does."

Gola not only scored the important basket and came down with the big rebound, but also set the tempo of a game with his ballhandling and passing.

On those rare occasions when Tom Gola had problems scoring, Charlie Singley was the man who would get the ball.

"I have never seen one player control a game by himself as well as Gola does," Loeffler said. It was his opinion, admittedly biased, that Gola was the best-rounded player in basketball, college or pro, present or past.

He certainly was too much for Bradley in the championship game. The gritty Braves managed a 43-42 halftime lead, but La Salle proceeded to go on a 30-14 run in which Gola contributed a three-point play that put the Explorers ahead to stay at 49-47. La Salle had gone to a 2-3 zone at the outset of the second half to protect Gola, who had picked up his fourth foul, and the strategy befuddled the Braves. La Salle wound up winning, 92-76.

Once again, Gola had not monopolized the ball. He scored 19 points, four fewer than teammates Blatcher and Charlie Singley, but led both teams with 19 rebounds in a typically understated performance. Still, despite his selflessness, Gola led all tournament scorers with 114 points and was named the Final Four's outstanding player.

The big-city school with the small-town enrollment had captured the national championship in most implausible fashion, thanks to a practically peerless player. Still, there were skeptics. The final United Press poll ranked Indiana No. 1, Kentucky No. 2 and La Salle No. 11, which seemed reasonable enough considering that the ratings were released nearly two weeks before the NCAA Tournament concluded. The Associated Press, though, conducted its final poll *after* the NCAA final and listed Kentucky No. 1, La Salle No. 2 and upset victim Indiana No. 4.

Down in Lexington, Kentucky's Rupp thought AP's selection of his Wildcats over Gola and company was only fair. Ramsey, one of his stars, pointed to a picture of Loeffler presenting Rupp with the championship trophy from the first Kentucky Invitational the previous December. The Wildcats had just beaten La Salle, 73-60, in the title game.

"In our minds," Ramsey said, "we felt we were good enough (to win the national championship)."

1954 Tournament Results

First Round
La Salle 76, Fordham 74
N. C. St. 75, Geo. Washington 73
Navy 85, Connecticut 80
Notre Dame 80, Loyola (La.) 70
Penn State 62, Toledo 50
Bradley 61, Oklahoma City 55
Idaho State 77, Seattle 75
Santa Clara 73, Texas Tech 64

Second Round
La Salle 88, N. C. State 81
Navy 69, Cornell 67
Penn State 78, LSU 70
Notre Dame 65, Indiana 64
Bradley 76, Colorado 64
Oklahoma A&M 51, Rice 45
Southern Cal 73, Idaho State 59
Santa Clara 73, Colorado A&M 50

Regional Third Place
N. C. State 65, Cornell 54
Indiana 73, LSU 62
Rice 78, Colorado 55
Idaho State 62, Colorado A&M 57

Regional Championships
La Salle 64, Navy 48
Penn State 71, Notre Dame 63
Bradley 71, Oklahoma A&M 57
Southern Cal 66, Santa Clara 65

Semifinals
La Salle 69, Penn State 54
Bradley 74, Southern Cal 72

Third Place
Penn State 70, Southern Cal 61

Championship
La Salle 92, Bradley 76

STATISTICS

1954 LA SALLE

Head Coach—Ken Loeffler   **Final Record—26-4**

Player	Pos.	Hgt.	Wgt.	Cl.	G	FG	FGA	Pct.	FT	FTA	Pct.	Reb.	Pts.	Avg.
Tom Gola	C-G	6-6	207	Jr.	30	252	619	.407	186	254	.732	652	690	23.0
Charles Singley	F	6-3	175	So.	30	125	327	.382	70	107	.654	153	320	10.7
Frank Blatcher	F	6-2	190	So.	27	117	313	.374	48	75	.640	124	282	10.4
Francis O'Hara	G	5-11	155	Sr.	30	102	251	.406	85	120	.708	111	289	9.6
Fran O'Malley	G-F	6-3	177	So.	30	80	232	.345	62	89	.697	139	222	7.4
Bob Maples	C-F	6-5	178	So.	30	80	198	.404	46	83	.554	141	206	6.9
Charles Greenberg	F-G	6-2	170	So.	26	46	148	.311	30	55	.545	78	122	4.7
John Yodsnukis	C	6-6	228	So.	18	34	112	.304	15	24	.625	102	83	4.6
Bob Ames	F	6-3	175	So.	14	9	30	.300	10	13	.769	13	28	2.0
Francis Finegan	G	6-0	170	Jr.	3	1	1	1.000	1	2	.500	1	3	1.0
Fran McMenamin	G	5-11	195	Jr.	4	1	5	.200	1	4	.250	3	3	0.8
Bob Ptak	F	6-5	190	So.	3	1	1	1.000	0	0	.000	2	2	0.7
Manuel Gomez	C	6-5	190	So.	16	2	12	.167	6	13	.462	12	10	0.6
Gary Holmes	F	6-1	160	So.	2	0	1	.000	1	2	.500	1	1	0.5
La Salle					30	850	2250	.378	561	841	.667	1532	2261	75.4
Opponents					30	664	2067	.321	568	877	.648	1359	1896	63.2

1954 BRADLEY

Head Coach—Forrest (Forddy) Anderson   **Final Record—19-13**

Player	Pos.	Hgt.	Wgt.	Cl.	G	FG	FGA	Pct.	FT	FTA	Pct.	Reb.	Pts.	Avg.
Bob Carney	G	6-1	173	Sr.	32	146	401	.364	225	296	.760	223	517	16.2
Dick Estergard	C-F	6-4	196	Sr.	32	137	297	.461	191	249	.767	395	465	14.5
John Kent	G	6-1	185	Jr.	32	170	461	.369	76	133	.571	131	416	13.0
Eddie King	F-G	6-4	190	Jr.	32	84	193	.435	125	158	.791	138	293	9.2
Dick Petersen	F-C	6-5	215	Jr.	30	65	192	.339	59	105	.562	178	189	6.3
Harvey Babetch	F-C	6-2	187	Jr.	31	74	200	.370	42	67	.627	97	190	6.1
Jerry Hansen	F	6-4	186	So.	29	63	172	.366	32	54	.593	83	158	5.4
Lee O'Connell	G	6-2	180	Jr.	28	31	97	.320	28	39	.718	31	90	3.2
Barney Kilcullen	C	6-9	200	Jr.	27	17	78	.218	31	64	.484	102	65	2.4
John Riley	F	6-2	185	Sr.	24	16	70	.229	17	33	.515	33	49	2.0
Jack Gower	F	6-4	185	So.	26	13	53	.245	21	31	.677	42	47	1.8
Ron Johnson	F	6-2	170	Sr.	7	3	7	.429	6	11	.545	4	12	1.7
Don Mathews	F	6-1	192	Sr.	5	2	7	.286	2	4	.500	1	6	1.2
Sam Arbuckle	C	6-3	180	So.	3	1	2	.500	1	1	1.000	2	3	1.0
Charlie Boston	G	5-8	145	So.	10	1	7	.143	4	12	.333	3	6	0.6
Lee Utt	F	6-3	183	So.	21	3	17	.176	5	6	.833	14	11	0.5
Bradley					32	826	2254	.366	865	1263	.685	1477	2517	78.7
Opponents					32	810	2345	.345	704	1083	.650	1228	2324	72.6

1954 PENN STATE

Head Coach—Elmer Gross   **Final Record—18-6**

Player	Pos.	Hgt.	Wgt.	Cl.	G	FG	FGA	Pct.	FT.	FTA	Pct.	Reb.	Pts.	Avg.
Jesse Arnelle	C	6-5	225	Jr.	24	174	...	...	159	227	.700	...	507	21.1
Jack Sherry	F	6-1	185	Jr.	24	92	...	...	95	135	.704	...	279	11.6
Ed Haag	G	6-3	178	Jr.	24	79	...	...	46	60	.767	...	204	8.5
Ron Weidenhammer	F	6-1	165	Jr.	24	77	...	...	28	40	.700	...	182	7.6
Jim Brewer	F	6-1	160	Sr.	24	60	...	...	27	42	.643	...	147	6.1
Jim Blocker	C	6-4	185	Jr.	24	44	...	...	27	48	.563	...	115	4.8
Dave Edwards	F	6-0	170	Jr.	19	20	...	...	16	24	.667	...	56	2.9
Rudy Marisa	C	6-4	180	So.	17	15	...	...	17	25	.680	...	47	2.8
Bob Rohland	G	6-2	195	Jr.	21	18	...	...	21	36	.583	...	57	2.7
Earl Fields	F	6-0	170	So.	18	16	...	...	16	24	.667	...	48	2.7
Chuck Christiansen	G	6-1	180	So.	5	3	...	...	5	10	.500	...	11	2.2
Bob Hoffman	..	5-10	...	...	1	1	...	...	0	0	.000	...	2	2.0
Harry Holm	G	6-4	185	Jr.	4	3	...	...	0	0	.000	...	6	1.5
Joe Malone	G	6-3	175	So.	1	0	...	...	1	2	.500	...	1	1.0
Clarence Watts	F	6-1	170	Jr.	2	0	...	...	0	0	.000	...	0	0.0
Penn State					24	602	...	...	458	673	.681	...	1662	69.3
Opponents					24	488	...	...	529	805	.657	...	1505	62.7

1954 SOUTHERN CALIFORNIA

Head Coach—Forrest Twogood   **Final Record—20-14**

(Statistics and record include 64-59 victory over Universal Plymouths not recognized by NCAA.)

Player	Pos.	Hgt.	Wgt.	Cl.	G	FG	FGA	Pct.	FT.	FTA	Pct.	Reb.	Pts.	Avg.
Roy Irvin	C	6-5	214	Jr.	34	157	433	.363	129	187	.690	266	443	13.0
Dick Welsh	F-G	6-2	165	Jr.	34	104	308	.338	123	198	.621	146	331	9.7
Tony Psaltis	G-F	6-3	201	So.	34	115	330	.348	69	97	.711	177	299	8.8
Chet Carr	F	6-4	191	Jr.	34	102	280	.364	83	130	.638	163	287	8.4
Dick Hammer	G	6-1	171	Sr.	33	76	218	.349	82	113	.726	132	234	7.1
Jack Dunne	F	6-3	180	So.	27	70	208	.337	38	59	.644	123	178	6.6
Ralph Pausig	F	6-2	193	So.	31	53	168	.315	29	45	.644	82	135	4.4
Dick Nagai	G	6-0	158	So.	15	15	30	.500	12	22	.545	11	42	2.8
Jack Findley	F	6-3	194	Jr.	12	11	30	.367	8	12	.667	17	30	2.5
Art Rimdzius	F-C	6-5	207	Jr.	8	3	15	.200	13	20	.650	12	19	2.4
Al Ludecke	C	6-4	190	Jr.	10	6	17	.353	3	9	.333	19	15	1.5
Tom Cooke	C	6-8	208	So.	8	4	10	.400	4	6	.667	8	12	1.5
Pinky Thompson	F	6-2	194	Sr.	17	7	25	.280	9	14	.643	11	23	1.4
Denny White	G	6-2	165	Jr.	3	2	3	.667	0	0	.000	1	4	1.3
Al Luer	G	5-11	185	Jr.	13	6	22	.273	3	9	.333	5	15	1.2
Dave De Groote	C	6-7	210	Jr.	1	0	3	.000	1	1	1.000	4	1	1.0
Hank D'Antonio	G	5-10	165	Jr.	3	1	6	.167	0	0	.000	2	2	0.7
Leroy Kasperski	G	6-2	193	Sr.	2	0	0	.000	0	0	.000	0	0	0.0
Others												29		
USC					34	...	...	...	...	...	...	...	2099	61.7
Opponents					34	...	...	...	...	...	...	...	2080	61.2

1954 FINAL FOUR

At Kansas City
Semifinals

La Salle	fg	ft	tp
Singley	4	2	10
Maples	3	1	7
Blatcher	7	5	19
Gola	5	9	19
O'Malley	3	3	9
O'Hara	2	1	5
Totals	24	21	69

Penn State	fg	ft	tp
Weidenhammer	1	1	3
Haag	2	0	4
Fields	2	1	5
Brewer	3	0	6
Arnelle	5	8	18
Rohland	2	0	4
Blocker	2	0	4
Sherry	1	4	6
Edwards	2	0	4
Totals	20	14	54

Halftime: La Salle 33-22. Officials: Enright and Ball.

Bradley	fg	ft	tp
Petersen	1	3	5
Gower	1	0	2
King	6	5	17
Kilcullen	0	0	0
Estergard	7	7	21
Utt	0	0	0
Carney	6	8	20
O'Connell	0	0	0
Kent	3	1	7
Babetch	1	0	2
Totals	25	24	74

Southern California	fg	ft	tp
Pausig	5	2	12
Carr	1	1	3
Psaltis	2	0	4
Dunne	1	0	2
Irvin	9	5	23
Ludecke	1	0	2
Hammer	2	3	7
Welsh	6	7	19
Totals	27	18	72

Halftime: Southern California 42-36. Officials: Anderson and Dean.

Championship
March 20

La Salle	fg	ft	fta	pf	tp
Singley	8	7	10	4	23
Greenberg	2	1	2	1	5
Maples	2	0	0	4	4
Blatcher	11	1	2	4	23
Gola	7	5	5	5	19
O'Malley	5	1	1	4	11
Yodsnukis	0	0	0	5	0
O'Hara	2	3	4	1	7
Totals	37	18	24	28	92

Bradley	fg	ft	fta	pf	tp
Petersen	4	2	2	2	10
Babetch	0	0	0	0	0
King	3	6	7	4	12
Gower	0	1	2	1	1
Estergard	3	11	12	1	17
Carney	3	11	17	4	17
Utt	0	0	0	1	0
Kent	8	0	2	2	16
Riley	1	1	2	1	3
Totals	22	32	14	16	76

Halftime: Bradley 43-42. Officials: Anderson and Dean.

1955 San Francisco Comes of Age

When Bill Russell and Hal Perry first met at the University of San Francisco, they discovered they had much in common. Not only were the two both black and both Baptist in a predominantly white, Catholic environment, but the school's basketball coach, Phil Woolpert, had seen neither freshman play a game. Furthermore, the scholarship offer from the Jesuit institution was the only one each had received.

The fall of 1952 was not a time of great athletic vitality on the USF campus, which crowned a hilltop near Golden Gate Park. The school had recently dropped its football program and the basketball team, a National Invitation Tournament champion in 1949, had lost more games than it had won in its first two seasons under Woolpert. And the Dons were handicapped by the absence of a campus gymnasium.

Practice was conducted at nearby St. Ignatius High School or at a neighborhood boys club or sometimes at a parish hall. It was to the high school that Russell and Perry had reported the previous spring for what amounted to a one-day audition. Neither youngster knew anything about the university beyond its location—and even that proved elusive to Russell, who got lost attempting to find it.

Russell was a gawky athlete, a 6-foot-7 young man going on 6-9½. He had been a late bloomer at Oakland's McClymonds High School, excelling on defense but serving as little more than a role player on a team of championship caliber. Indeed, Russell scored more than 10 points only once in his scholastic career.

Fortunately for the player and the school, USF alumnus Hal DeJulio was in the stands for a game between McClymonds and Oakland High. He enjoyed scouting area high school games for prospects, and he attended this particular game to assess Truman Bruce, the star of the Oakland team. Russell not only did a fine defensive job on Bruce, but also scored 14 points.

DeJulio recommended Russell to Woolpert, who set up a tryout that Russell almost missed because he got lost.

"When I finally got there," he said, "I was in a daze from frustration and nervousness, which was probably good because it numbed me. I don't remember anything about the workout except that I ran and jumped without the ball a lot."

Afterward, Woolpert was noncommittal. The coach said he would be in touch.

Perry was a small man, just under 5-11. He was a star of his team in Ukiah, north of San Francisco, but the school and the community also were small and the level of competition nothing like that which abounded in the Bay Area. His high school coach wrote to a number of college coaches in Perry's behalf. Only Woolpert responded.

And so the guard, accompanied by his father, made the 125-mile trip to San Francisco to display his skill with a basketball. Woolpert greeted him and introduced him to a USF freshman named K.C. Jones, who proceeded to demonstrate Perry's limitations.

"He reversed everything I tried to do," Perry recalled. "I don't think I got a shot off."

After the workout, Woolpert sat with Perry and his father and patiently listed seven or eight reasons why he would be unable to offer a scholarship. The youngster was not intimidated. In addition to being a five-sport athlete, he was the senior class president as well as the student body president at Ukiah High School. First, Perry rebutted all of Woolpert's arguments and then, standing to his full height, he said, "Before you make this decision, please pray for guidance."

On the way home, Perry's father attempted to console him after his subpar performance.

"It doesn't matter," Perry replied. "I'm still going to get the scholarship."

Two days later, he was offered tuition, room and board if he would attend USF. Russell received a similar invitation in the mail. Those two non-recruits, along with the 6-1 Jones, would form the nucleus of the greatest college team assembled to that time.

But first, while Russell and Perry worked hard to develop their skills on the freshman squad, Woolpert and the Dons struggled through a third successive losing season in 1953. The pressure on the coach mounted the following year when Jones, after one game, suffered a ruptured appendix. He did not return that season. Furthermore, Woolpert and Russell were at odds over the sophomore's attitude, particularly in practice. And the Dons' other starters appeared more interested in individual statistics than winning. The record of 14-7 was an improvement, yet a disappointment.

The Big Two of the 1955 national-champion San Francisco Dons—defensive wizards K.C. Jones (above) and Bill Russell (right), who led USF to a 28-1 record.

It wasn't until the 1955 season that the team pulled together. Now Jones and Russell, who had grown to an intimidating 6-9½, both were in the starting lineup. But the Dons weren't firing on all cylinders. After trouncing Chico State in their season opener, the Dons didn't exactly blitz Loyola of Los Angeles (USF won by nine) and then lost at UCLA. Woolpert's solution was to elevate Perry to the first team. The promotion proved to be a significant step, and not just in terms of on-court success. It also meant that San Francisco would have more black starters than white starters, a most unusual arrangement at the time *anywhere.*

"It was never said, but you knew as a coach that you had to be aware of the quota thing," Woolpert said. The coach gambled that any ensuing criticism among alumni, boosters and the media would be negated by winning. The Dons won immediately.

That very weekend, in a two-game series at the Cow Palace, San Francisco handily defeated Oregon State and the same UCLA team it had stumbled against the previous week. Then the Dons left for the All-College Tournament at Oklahoma City and a test of character. Upon arrival, they were informed that the blacks could not stay at the downtown hotel reserved for the team. A meeting ensued at which every player was granted a chance to speak.

Should the Dons be split, half at a hotel and half on the Oklahoma City University campus? In what he termed his "crowning moment," Perry advised against it.

"We are going to hang together as a team," he said. And that's what USF did. The Dons' entire party stayed at the university.

And after it was over, after USF had won the holiday tournament, the Dons celebrated back at the otherwise empty dorm. "Tonight," Perry said, "is the beginning of the dynasty."

No one was quite sure exactly what that meant, but it sounded good. United as never before, and with Russell's well-timed leaps reshaping the sport,

San Francisco Coach Phil Woolpert had experienced three straight losing seasons before improving to 14-7 in 1954.

San Francisco rolled over all opponents for the remainder of the season, climbing slowly in the national polls. When Kentucky, the early-season leader, was upset twice in January by Georgia Tech, the Dons moved into the No. 1 position to stay.

Still, San Francisco was not an overwhelming favorite as it prepared for its first Final Four. Even the elimination of No. 2-ranked Kentucky by Marquette in Eastern Regional play offered no guarantees. Third-ranked La Salle had devastated competition in its half of the Eastern bracket and boasted the premier player in the country, Tom Gola. Iowa and Colorado rounded out the field, the Hawkeyes accompanying La Salle into the Eastern final and the Buffaloes joining USF in the Western title game.

Of the four national semifinalists, the Dons had survived the greatest scare in the tournament. After rolling over West Texas State and Utah, USF was severely challenged by Pacific Coast Conference champion Oregon State. There were two major differences from the first meeting between the teams back in December, a game the Dons won by 26 points. Swede Halbrook, a 7-3 center, was now in the Beavers' lineup, and the NCAA regional game was scheduled for Oregon State's home court in Corvallis.

Jerry Mullen, USF's forward and captain, was hampered by a sprained ankle in the rematch and

USF did not dominate on the boards in its usual manner. Despite timely shooting by Stan Buchanan, the Dons' other forward, Oregon State had a chance to win at the end of the game, but Ron Robins' shot from the corner hit the back rim. The top-ranked team escaped with a 57-56 victory.

La Salle struggled to beat Iowa in the first semifinal at Kansas City, but San Francisco ended the suspense in the second game by taking a six-point lead in the final three minutes of the first half and then coasting past Colorado, 62-50. Now the NCAA Tournament had the ideal East-West matchup between the defending champion and its primary challenger. While observers speculated on the outcome, Woolpert planned a surprise.

Reasoning that Jones could compensate for a five-inch height differential with his speed and quick hands, he assigned his best defensive player to Gola. Such an alignment also enabled Russell to spend more time near the basket rather than be drawn outside by the smooth La Salle star. It turned out to be a masterful bit of strategy.

Jones, a high school football star and a marvelous athlete, disrupted the Explorers' five-man rotating offense. He limited Gola, a three-time consensus All-America, to 16 points and, displaying some uncharacteristically accurate shooting from long range, scored 24 himself. For all that, Russell was the major difference in the game.

Russell blocked shots time and again, grabbed 25 rebounds and scored 23 points, including 18 in the first half when the Dons broke open the game. Russell played above the rim, steering some of his teammates' errant shots into the basket and tipping in others. USF won its first NCAA championship with consummate ease by the score of 77-63.

An obscure high school athlete three years earlier, Russell was honored as the Final Four's outstanding player. Phog Allen, the Kansas coach who thought he had seen everything in basketball, shook his head at the junior's performance.

"I'm for the 20-foot basket," Allen decided.

1955 Tournament Results

First Round
Marquette 90, Miami (Ohio) 79
Penn State 59, Memphis State 55
La Salle 95, West Virginia 61
Villanova 74, Duke 73
Canisius 73, Williams 60
Bradley 69, Oklahoma City 65
Seattle 80, Idaho State 63
San Fran. 89, West Texas St. 66

Second Round
Marquette 79, Kentucky 71
Iowa 82, Penn State 53
La Salle 73, Princeton 46
Canisius 73, Villanova 71
Bradley 81, SMU 79
Colorado 69, Tulsa 59
Oregon State 83, Seattle 71
San Francisco 78, Utah 59

Regional Third Place
Villanova 64, Princeton 57
Kentucky 84, Penn State 59
Tulsa 68, SMU 67
Utah 108, Seattle 85

Regional Championships
La Salle 99, Canisius 64
Iowa 86, Marquette 81
Colorado 93, Bradley 81
San Francisco 57, Oregon State 56

Semifinals
La Salle 76, Iowa 73
San Francisco 62, Colorado 50

Third Place
Colorado 75, Iowa 54

Championship
San Francisco 77, La Salle 63

STATISTICS

1955 SAN FRANCISCO

Head Coach—Phil Woolpert   **Final Record—28-1**

Player	Pos.	Hgt.	Wgt.	Cl.	G	FG	FGA	Pct.	FT.	FTA	Pct.	Reb.	Pts.	Avg.
Bill Russell	C	6-10	205	Jr.	29	229	423	.541	164	278	.590	594	622	21.4
Jerry Mullen	F	6-5	195	Sr.	27	136	359	.379	94	129	.729	192	366	13.6
K.C. Jones	G	6-1	202	Jr.	29	105	293	.358	97	144	.674	148	307	10.6
Hal Perry	G	5-10	172	Jr.	29	73	196	.372	54	72	.750	55	200	6.9
Stan Buchanan	F	6-3	180	Sr.	29	48	159	.302	54	76	.711	93	150	5.2
Bob Wiebusch	F	6-3	180	Sr.	28	38	118	.322	25	35	.714	60	101	3.6
Rudy Zannini	G	5-7	152	Sr.	27	15	50	.300	21	29	.724	10	51	1.9
Dick Lawless	F	6-3	185	Sr.	26	17	63	.270	12	20	.600	29	46	1.8
Warren Baxter	G	5-8	165	Jr.	19	11	21	.524	12	17	.706	9	34	1.8
Bill Bush	G	6-0	165	Jr.	25	10	30	.333	20	36	.556	25	40	1.6
Steve Balchios	G	6-0	170	So.	8	2	3	.667	4	8	.500	5	8	1.0
Jack King	F	6-3	170	So.	16	4	12	.333	7	10	.700	7	15	0.9
Tom Nelson	F	6-4	195	So.	10	2	8	.250	1	2	.500	5	5	0.5
Gordon Kirby	C	6-4	205	Sr.	20	3	15	.200	1	5	.200	13	7	0.4
Team												81		
San Francisco					29	693	1750	.396	566	861	.657	1326	1952	67.3
Opponents					29	513	1611	.318	489	743	.658	977	1515	52.2

1955 LA SALLE

Head Coach—Ken Loeffler   **Final Record—26-5**

Player	Pos.	Hgt.	Wgt.	Cl.	G	FG	FGA	Pct.	FT.	FTA	Pct.	Reb.	Pts.	Avg.
Tom Gola	C	6-6	210	Sr.	31	274	624	.439	202	267	.757	618	750	24.2
Charles Singley	F	6-3	175	Jr.	31	145	...	...	75	...	...	182	365	11.8
Alonzo Lewis	G	6-3	187	So.	31	127	...	...	98	...	...	228	352	11.4
Frank Blatcher	F-G	6-2	190	Jr.	30	112	...	...	61	...	...	97	285	9.5
Charles Greenberg	G	6-2	175	Jr.	31	111	...	...	26	...	...	113	248	8.0
Bob Maples	F-C	6-5	175	Jr.	30	84	...	...	42	...	...	149	210	7.0
Fran O'Malley	F	6-3	180	Jr.	31	65	...	...	62	...	...	208	192	6.2
Bob Ames	F	6-3	181	Jr.	10	9	...	...	6	...	...	...	24	2.4
Walt Fredricks	C-F	6-6	190	So.	15	14	...	...	2	...	...	48	30	2.0
Bob Kraemer	G	6-3	180	So.	10	3	...	...	6	...	...	7	12	1.2
John Gola	F	6-2	176	So.		...	...	...	...	...	...	...	...	...
Joe Gilson	C	6-4	185	Sr.		...	...	...	...	...	...	...	...	...
Manuel Gomez	C	6-5	190	Jr.		...	...	...	...	...	...	...	...	...
John Yodsnukis	C	6-6	209	Jr.		...	...	...	...	...	...	...	...	...
*Others						...	...	...	...	...	...	35		
La Salle					31	...	...	...	...	...	...	2503		80.7
Opponents					31	...	...	...	...	...	...	1974		63.7

*Includes J. Gola, Gilson, Gomez and Yodsnukis.

1955 COLORADO

Head Coach—H.B. (Bebe) Lee   **Final Record—19-6**

Player	Pos.	Hgt.	Wgt.	Cl.	G	FG	FGA	Pct.	FT.	FTA	Pct.	Reb.	Pts.	Avg.
Burdette Haldorson	C	6-7	207	Sr.	25	182	423	.430	160	211	.758	346	524	21.0
Bob Jeangerard	F	6-3	195	Sr.	25	140	375	.373	119	151	.789	170	399	16.0
Charlie Mock	G	6-0	163	Sr.	25	58	150	.387	80	112	.714	58	196	7.8
Tom Harrold	G	5-11	165	Sr.	24	48	181	.265	75	115	.652	100	171	7.1
Mel Coffman	F	6-3	185	Jr.	24	53	168	.315	32	46	.696	114	138	5.8
Bob Yardley	F	6-3	170	Sr.	21	19	85	.224	37	61	.607	67	75	3.6
Jim Ranglos	G	6-4	190	Jr.	24	27	67	.403	29	39	.744	82	83	3.5
George Hannah	C	6-7	205	Jr.	22	17	65	.262	23	38	.605	62	57	2.6
Dave Mowbray	G	6-1	165	So.	15	13	30	.433	13	24	.542	24	39	2.6
Bill Peterson	G	6-0	168	Jr.	11	5	21	.238	11	12	.917	9	21	1.9
Mick Mansfield	G	6-4	193	So.	23	10	32	.313	21	35	.600	16	41	1.8
Jamie Grant	G	5-10	165	Sr.	8	4	12	.333	4	5	.800	3	12	1.5
Sam Morrison	G	5-8	150	Jr.	7	1	4	.250	7	11	.636	5	9	1.3
Wilbert Walter	F	6-2	192	Sr.	6	2	6	.333	0	2	.000	4	4	0.7
Bob Helzer	F	6-2	190	So.	7	1	11	.091	1	3	.333	7	3	0.4
Team												164		
Colorado					25	580	1630	.356	612	865	.708	1231	1772	70.9
Opponents					25	527	1528	.345	514	764	.673	982	1568	62.7

1955 IOWA

Head Coach—Frank (Bucky) O'Connor   **Final Record—19-7**

Player	Pos.	Hgt.	Wgt.	Cl.	G	FG	FGA	Pct.	FT.	FTA	Pct.	Reb.	Pts.	Avg.
Bill Logan	C	6-6	195	Jr.	26	155	387	.401	103	157	.656	285	413	15.9
Carl Cain	F	6-3	181	Jr.	26	133	333	.399	94	140	.671	244	360	13.8
Bill Seaberg	G	6-0	170	Jr.	26	124	293	.423	92	120	.767	102	340	13.1
Deacon Davis	F	6-2	175	Sr.	26	102	228	.447	67	113	.593	139	271	10.4
Sharm Scheuerman	G	6-2	176	Jr.	26	68	159	.428	77	101	.762	102	213	8.2
Bill Schoof	F	6-6	200	Jr.	24	56	156	.359	38	65	.585	116	150	6.3
Bob George	F-C	6-7	200	Jr.	23	31	71	.437	32	52	.615	63	94	4.1
Roy Johnson	G	6-5	190	Jr.	24	23	104	.221	27	40	.675	54	73	3.0
Les Hawthorne	F	5-8	162	Jr.	22	18	45	.400	16	27	.593	19	52	2.4
Augie Martel	G	5-10	155	So.	19	19	55	.345	5	14	.357	9	43	2.3
Dick Ritter	F	6-6	205	Jr.	11	7	24	.292	4	9	.444	22	18	1.6
Henry Berry	F	6-1	205	Jr.	2	1	1	1.000	1	1	1.000	1	3	1.5
Jerry Ridley	F	6-2	180	Sr.	15	8	37	.216	0	10	.000	19	16	1.1
Frank Sebolt	F	6-3	183	So.	12	5	17	.294	2	8	.250	11	12	1.0
Carter Crookham	F	6-3	175	So.	3	0	6	.000	2	2	1.000	1	2	0.7
Jerry Reichow	G	6-2	196	Jr.	3	1	4	.250	0	4	.000	3	2	0.7
Douglas Duncan	G	6-6	190	Jr.	12	1	18	.056	4	4	1.000	17	6	0.5
John Liston	F	6-4	190	So.	8	0	10	.000	3	5	.600	16	3	0.4
Tom Choules	F	6-3	155	Jr.	3	0	3	.000	0	0	.000	4	0	0.0
Iowa					26	752	1951	.385	567	872	.650	1227	2071	79.7
Opponents					26	630	1850	.341	604	918	.658	992	1864	71.7

1955 FINAL FOUR

At Kansas City
Semifinals

La Salle	fg	ft	tp
O'Malley	1	4	6
Maples	1	2	4
Singley	5	6	16
Blatcher	2	1	5
Gola	8	7	23
Lewis	5	4	14
Greenberg	4	0	8
Totals	26	24	76

Iowa	fg	ft	tp
Davis	1	0	2
Schoof	3	0	6
Cain	8	1	17
Logan	7	6	20
Seaberg	5	5	15
Scheuerman	1	11	13
Totals	25	23	73

Halftime: La Salle 45-36. Officials: Milner and Ogden.

San Francisco	fg	ft	tp
Wiebusch	1	0	2
King	1	2	4
Buchanan	0	6	6
Russell	10	4	24
Jones	3	2	8
Baxter	2	3	7
Bush	0	1	1
Perry	5	0	10
Zannini	0	0	0
Kirby	0	0	0
Totals	22	18	62

Colorado	fg	ft	tp
Jeangerard	1	2	4
Coffman	1	2	4
Ranglos	1	2	4
Yardley	1	2	4
Haldorson	3	3	9
Hannah	2	5	9
Mock	2	0	4
Mansfield	0	4	4
Grant	1	0	2
Peterson	2	2	6
Totals	14	22	50

Halftime: San Francisco 25-19. Officials: Fox and Mohr.

Championship
March 19

San Francisco	fg	ft	fta	pf	tp
Mullen	4	2	5	5	10
Buchanan	3	2	2	1	8
Russell	9	5	7	1	23
Jones	10	4	4	2	24
Perry	1	2	2	4	4
Wiebusch	2	0	0	0	4
Zannini	1	0	0	0	2
Lawless	1	0	0	0	2
Kirby	0	0	0	1	0
Totals	31	15	20	14	77

La Salle	fg	ft	fta	pf	tp
O'Malley	4	2	3	1	10
Singley	8	4	4	1	20
Gola	6	4	5	4	16
Lewis	1	4	9	1	6
Greenberg	1	1	2	4	3
Blatcher	4	0	0	1	8
Maples	0	0	0	0	0
Fredricks	0	0	0	0	0
Totals	24	15	23	12	63

Halftime: San Francisco 35-24.

1956 Dons Win Again As Russell Soars

The 1956 San Francisco starting lineup featured K.C. Jones and Hal Perry at guard, Bill Russell at center and upgraded forwards Carl Boldt (left) and Mike Farmer (right).

Defending a national championship should have been sufficient challenge for any team. But San Francisco, coming off a 28-1 season, was not just any team and the Dons were faced with an additional test as they attempted to repeat in 1956. They were deprived of their captain and floor leader for the NCAA Tournament.

K.C. Jones had been permitted to return for a fifth season because he had missed all but one game of the 1954 season after his emergency appendectomy. But that one game, authorities ruled, rendered him ineligible for postseason competition. One of three returning starters from the 1955 team, Jones had directed USF to a regular-season record of 25-0.

With Jones and Hal Perry operating in the backcourt for a second successive year and Russell flanked by upgraded forwards Mike Farmer and Carl Boldt, the Dons overwhelmed all opposition. Their lowest margin of victory in establishing a college record for consecutive victories was seven points.

"The best college team I've ever seen," declared Joe Lapchick, the respected coach at St. John's. "They play a defense I never saw before."

San Francisco's presence was requested from coast to coast. The Dons—particularly Russell—wowed the critics in New York, sweeping three games in the ECAC Holiday Festival. First, they drubbed La Salle (minus the graduated Gola), 79-62, behind the center's 26 points and 22 rebounds. Then, they battered Holy Cross, 67-51, as Russell rejected a half-dozen shots, outscored All-America Tom Heinsohn, 24-12, and added 22 rebounds. Finally, their defense so thoroughly suffocated UCLA in a 70-53 finale that the big man was required to do nothing more than score 17 points and seize 18 rebounds.

So loose and confident was the team that it appeared to intimidate opponents off the court as well as on. The USF and UCLA teams were staying at the same hotel for the Holiday Festival and the crowded conditions made it necessary for the two groups to eat their pregame meals at the same time in the same room. The Bruins were all business. They ate quietly while meditating on their assignments as directed by Coach John Wooden.

Nearby, well within earshot, the Dons enjoyed themselves, needling each other and even rising one at a time to say a few words on behalf of Coach Phil Woolpert's wedding anniversary. The subject of San Francisco's opponents, notably UCLA star Willie (the Whale) Naulls, did come up.

"Hey, Bill," someone said to Russell, "do you think you could possibly be courteous to the Whale tonight?"

He obviously was not.

A month later, USF posted its 40th straight triumph over two seasons and thereby surpassed the accepted all-time major college record. (Various other streaks were adjusted above 40 in a later-year rewriting of the record books, but USF would tack on another 15 consecutive victories in the '56 season and five more in its first post-Russell season.) No. 40 came across the bay at Berkeley as the Dons overcame a slowdown ordered by Pete Newell, Woolpert's former college teammate at Loyola of Los Angeles and his predecessor at San Francisco. The final score was 33-24.

Jones' final college game, against St. Mary's, attracted a sellout crowd to Kezar Pavilion. Woolpert pulled all three prominent seniors—Jones, Russell and Perry—midway through the second half with the Dons comfortably in front and then everyone stood around through a tumultuous five-minute ovation.

"I could feel the chills down my back," the coach said.

The only question left to be answered was whether San Francisco—without Jones—would be vulnerable in the NCAA Tournament, which for the first time would crown regional champions from four distinct geographic areas (the Far West, West, Midwest and East, designations that would undergo modifications as early as the next season and in later years as well). The Dons' first opponent in the Far West Regional was UCLA, the last team to defeat USF but a badly beaten victim in the clubs' previous meeting.

"UCLA can whip San Francisco without Jones on the floor," volunteered Tippy Dye, the Washington coach.

If UCLA's Wooden felt that way, he certainly chose to suppress his feelings.

"We have improved a great deal," he said, "and perhaps the loss of K.C. Jones will hurt them. However, they've still got Russell and he's the ball club."

His impact on his team and the sport was incalculable. In his first visit to Woolpert's office, Russell had informed the coach that he intended to become an All-America. As farfetched as that may have seemed at the time, he had done better. Russell was altering time-honored concepts of the game, leading basketball into a new order.

His desire to improve and to win was remarkable. He spent hours working in an otherwise empty gym with assistant coach Ross Giudice. He spent hours talking defensive strategy with Jones. He spent hours playing one-on-one with Perry, a quick little man. "If you can catch the flea," Perry told him, "you can catch the elephant."

Russell had caught everybody and everything, including the brass ring. All that remained was the opportunity to play for the first undefeated champions in NCAA Tournament history. He would be surrounded by Perry, Boldt, Farmer and Gene

San Francisco star Bill Russell (right) receives an award from professional great George Mikan after the Dons' 1956 title-winning campaign.

Brown, a sophomore guard who was a better outside shot than Jones but not in his class as a defender.

Coach Dudey Moore of Duquesne had called Brown "the best substitute in the country," and he lived up to that billing against UCLA. He scored a team-high 23 points, complementing Russell's 21 in San Francisco's 72-61 triumph. He scored 18 more in the following game, Russell added 27 and the Dons romped over Utah, 92-77. The senior center had 45 rebounds in the two games.

The rest of the field in the Final Four, staged at Evanston, Ill., for the first time since the initial NCAA championship was held there in 1939, consisted of Temple from the East, Iowa from the Midwest and Southern Methodist from the West. Patten Gymnasium had been replaced by a new field house, McGaw Hall, on the Northwestern campus and 10,600 fans, almost double the figure that attended the inaugural event, saw Iowa stop Temple, 83-76. What followed was a dismemberment of an SMU team that had won 25 of 27 previous games.

Perry, chosen captain for the tournament, and Brown hit consistently from outside and the 6-foot-7 Farmer, left open whenever the Mustangs tried to cover Russell with two men, scored as he pleased. The Dons took a 40-19 lead en route to an 86-68 victory that pleased everyone but Russell. He didn't think he played well, despite the fact he backed Farmer's 26-point effort with 17 points of his own.

Nevertheless, USF once again had qualified for the championship game. Iowa, the Big Ten Conference champion, was a resourceful team and wasted no time in exploiting a weakness in the Dons' defense to open a 15-4 lead. The Hawkeyes positioned

Bill Logan, a 6-7 center, at the free-throw line. When Russell moved out to guard him, star forward Carl (Sugar) Cain slipped in behind him, took a lob pass and scored.

"We didn't have a forward quick enough to stay with him (Cain)," Perry said. So Woolpert called a timeout, removed Boldt and shifted Brown from guard to forward. Warren Baxter, a 5-8 reserve, came in at guard.

The Dons responded to the situation at both ends of the court and pushed into the lead at 24-23. By halftime, they held a 38-33 advantage and then drained the mystery from the game in the second half. USF prevailed, 83-71.

Fittingly, Russell was immense in his final game for San Francisco. One of four Dons in double figures, he scored 26 points, grabbed 27 rebounds and intimidated Logan—a 36-point scorer in the semifinals—into a 12-point performance from distant spots on the floor. The outstanding-player award was denied the Dons' pivotman only because Temple's Hal Lear used the consolation game as a stage for the greatest scoring performance in tournament history, 48 points. Lear hadn't done badly in the Owls' semifinal game, either, netting 32 points against Iowa.

In stretching its record for consecutive victories to 55, USF completed a 29-0 season and became the third school to win back-to-back championships. Of the three men primarily responsible for two years of dominance, only Russell and Perry were in uniform for the '56 Final Four. Jones had watched from the bench in civilian clothes.

But when the trophy presentation was made, Perry coaxed Jones to the center of the court.

"I wanted to show my respect for the man," Perry said. And the two captains, regular-season and postseason, accepted the award.

The best group of players never recruited had capped the most successful season in college basketball history.

1956 Tournament Results

First Round

Connecticut 84, Manhattan 75
Temple 74, Holy Cross 72
Dartmouth 61, West Virginia 59
Canisius 79, N. C. St. 78 (4 ot)
Wayne State 72, DePaul 63
Morehead State 107, Marshall 92
Seattle 68, Idaho State 66
SMU 68, Texas Tech 67
Oklahoma City 97, Memphis St. 81

Second Round

Iowa 97, Morehead State 83
Temple 65, Connecticut 59
Kentucky 84, Wayne State 64
Canisius 66, Dartmouth 58
San Francisco 72, UCLA 61
Utah 81, Seattle 72
SMU 89, Houston 74
Oklahoma City 97, Kansas St. 93

Regional Third Place

Morehead State 95, Wayne State 84
Dartmouth 85, Connecticut 64
UCLA 94, Seattle 70
Kansas State 89, Houston 70

Regional Championships

Temple 60, Canisius 58
Iowa 89, Kentucky 77
San Francisco 92, Utah 77
SMU 84, Oklahoma City 63

Semifinals

Iowa 83, Temple 76
San Francisco 86, SMU 68

Third Place

Temple 90, SMU 81

Championship

San Francisco 83, Iowa 71

STATISTICS

1956 SAN FRANCISCO

Head Coach—Phil Woolpert **Final Record—29-0**

Player	Pos.	Hgt.	Wgt.	Cl.	G	FG	FGA	Pct.	FT.	FTA	Pct.	Reb.	Pts.	Avg.
Bill Russell	C	6-10	215	Sr.	29	246	480	.513	105	212	.495	609	597	20.6
K.C. Jones*	G	6-1	205	Sr.	25	76	208	.365	93	142	.655	130	245	9.8
Hal Perry	G	5-10	160	Sr.	29	107	293	.365	51	70	.729	57	265	9.1
Carl Boldt	F	6-4	190	Jr.	28	94	288	.326	54	69	.783	140	242	8.6
Mike Farmer	F	6-7	210	So.	28	101	272	.371	34	62	.548	218	236	8.4
Gene Brown	G	6-2	170	So.	29	78	207	.377	50	78	.641	127	206	7.1
Bill Mallen	F	6-3	230	So.	11	19	48	.396	8	15	.533	38	46	4.2
Mike Preaseau	F	6-5	191	So.	29	45	123	.366	28	46	.609	91	118	4.1
Warren Baxter	G	5-8	171	Sr.	26	22	73	.301	14	21	.667	18	58	2.2
Harold Payne	G	5-11	160	So.	15	6	17	.353	3	5	.600	2	15	1.0
John Koljian	F	6-3	190	So.	11	4	12	.333	3	7	.429	11	11	1.0
Bill Bush	G	6-0	170	So.	22	5	24	.208	10	16	.625	17	20	0.9
Jack King	F	6-3	170	Jr.	22	6	37	.162	6	13	.462	21	18	0.8
Tom Nelson	C	6-4	192	Jr.	19	3	15	.200	3	5	.600	13	9	0.5
Steve Balchios	G	6-0	162	Jr.	13	3	5	.600	0	0	.000	3	6	0.5
Vince Boyle	C	6-5	190	So.	10	0	0	.000	1	5	.200	4	1	0.1
Team												74		
San Francisco					29	815	2102	.388	463	766	.604	1573	2093	72.2
Opponents					29	509	1599	.318	496	742	.688	1069	1514	52.2

*Ineligible for NCAA Tournament as fifth-year player.

1956 IOWA

Head Coach—Frank (Bucky) O'Connor **Final Record—20-6**

Player	Pos.	Hgt.	Wgt.	Cl.	G	FG	FGA	Pct.	FT.	FTA	Pct.	Reb.	Pts.	Avg.
Bill Logan	C	6-7	200	Sr.	26	175	420	.417	110	179	.615	268	460	17.7
Carl Cain	F	6-3	185	Sr.	26	165	403	.409	81	112	.723	257	411	15.8
Bill Seaberg	G	6-0	175	Sr.	26	126	331	.381	110	141	.780	126	362	13.9
Bill Schoof	F	6-6	210	Sr.	26	92	255	.361	96	128	.750	199	280	10.8
Sharm Scheuerman	G	6-2	178	Sr.	23	70	159	.440	93	123	.756	108	233	10.1
Bob George	C	6-7	200	Sr.	23	33	104	.317	21	44	.477	94	87	3.8
Tom Payne	F	6-6	207	So.	18	20	71	.282	14	33	.424	63	54	3.0
Augie Martel	G	5-10	160	Jr.	22	22	54	.407	5	10	.500	17	49	2.2
Jim McConnell	G	6-2	170	So.	15	8	31	.258	3	8	.375	11	19	1.3
Gregg Schroeder	F	6-3	185	So.	7	2	5	.400	5	6	.833	6	9	1.3
Carter Crookham	F	6-3	175	Jr.	3	2	5	.400	0	0	.000	5	4	1.3
Les Hawthorne	G	5-8	160	Sr.	18	4	31	.129	14	20	.700	11	22	1.2
Frank Seebolt	F	6-3	185	Jr.	16	8	20	.400	2	11	.182	21	18	1.1
Norman Paul	F	6-4	185	So.	11	4	12	.333	3	7	.429	9	11	1.0
Gene Pitts	C	6-7	196	So.	4	0	2	.000	1	2	.500	1	1	0.3
Iowa					26	731	1903	.384	558	824	.677	1196	2020	77.7
Opponents					26	679	1852	.367	460	763	.603	1151	1818	69.9

1956 TEMPLE

Head Coach—Harry Litwack **Final Record—27-4**

Player	Pos.	Hgt.	Wgt.	Cl.	G	FG	FGA	Pct.	FT.	FTA	Pct.	Reb.	Pts.	Avg.
Hal Lear	G	5-11	168	Sr.	31	278	570	.488	189	241	.784	109	745	24.0
Guy Rodgers	G	6-1	180	So.	31	243	552	.440	87	155	.561	186	573	18.5
Fred Cohen	C	6-6	210	Sr.	31	97	224	.433	60	91	.659	308	254	8.2
Hal Reinfeld	F	6-2	185	Sr.	31	96	277	.347	54	77	.701	217	246	7.9
Jay Norman	F	6-3	196	So.	31	74	223	.332	69	119	.580	299	217	7.0
Tink Van Patton	C	6-8	235	So.	28	48	137	.350	19	39	.487	206	115	4.1
Dan Fleming	F	6-5	210	So.	18	28	86	.326	10	16	.625	94	66	3.7
Leon Smith	F	6-2	195	Sr.	10	13	26	.500	8	21	.381	23	34	3.4
Barry Goldstein	G	6-0	165	So.	22	25	62	.403	19	32	.594	21	69	3.1
Bernie Osherow	G	6-0	170	Jr.	11	7	22	.318	16	20	.800	7	30	2.7
Bill Smith	F	6-4	170	Jr.	21	21	73	.288	7	12	.583	54	49	2.3
Mel Brodsky	F	6-1	180	So.	16	12	26	.462	5	9	.556	19	29	1.8
John Granozio	F	6-2	190	Jr.	15	4	16	.250	0	2	.000	9	8	0.5
Temple					31	946	2294	.412	543	834	.651	1552	2435	78.5
Opponents					31	712	2090	.341	610	921	.662	1353	2034	65.6

1956 SOUTHERN METHODIST

Head Coach—E.O. (Doc) Hayes **Final Record—26-4**

(Record and statistics include 88-77 victory over All-Air Force team in game not included in NCAA records.)

Player	Pos.	Hgt.	Wgt.	Cl.	G	FG	FGA	Pct.	FT.	FTA	Pct.	Reb.	Pts.	Avg.
Jim Krebs	C	6-8	225	Jr.	30	228	532	.429	118	156	.756	299	574	19.1
Bobby Mills	G	6-0	180	Jr.	30	116	274	.423	158	203	.778	67	390	13.0
Joel Krog	F	6-3	195	Sr.	30	135	338	.399	90	117	.769	275	360	12.0
Larry Showalter	F-G	6-3	190	Sr.	30	125	291	.430	79	95	.832	104	329	11.0
Ron Morris	G	6-1	180	Sr.	30	91	196	.464	123	151	.815	122	305	10.2
Rick Herrscher	F-G	6-3	185	So.	29	48	131	.366	71	91	.780	79	167	5.8
Tom Miller	C	6-6	195	Sr.	26	39	71	.549	47	69	.681	60	125	4.8
Bob McGregor	C	6-5	190	Jr.	20	15	25	.600	2	7	.286	12	32	1.6
Bill Eldridge	G	5-10	155	So.	15	8	20	.400	8	12	.667	8	24	1.6
Carl Scharffenberger	F	6-4	195	So.	15	8	15	.533	6	14	.429	14	22	1.5
Herschel O'Kelley	F	6-1	185	So.	..	6	18	.333	7	11	.636	13	19	...
Pepper Lee	G	5-11	165	Sr.	..	4	13	.307	3	6	.500	2	11	...
Others	..	..			1	6	.167	3	7	.429		5	...	
Team												81		
SMU					30	824	1930	.427	715	939	.761	1202	*2365	78.8
Opponents					30	766	2087	.367	500	760	.658	1134	2032	67.7

*Includes two points made by opponents.

1956 FINAL FOUR

At Evanston, Ill.
Semifinals

Iowa	fg	ft	tp
Cain	8	4	20
Schoof	5	8	18
Logan	13	10	36
Seaberg	1	0	2
Scheuerman	1	2	4
Martel	1	1	3
Totals	29	25	83

Temple	fg	ft	tp
Reinfeld	1	0	2
Norman	1	0	2
Fleming	2	0	4
Cohen	3	0	6
Van Patton	1	0	2
Rodgers	12	4	28
Lear	15	2	32
Totals	35	6	76

Halftime: Iowa 39-36.

San Francisco	fg	ft	tp
Boldt	3	1	7
Farmer	11	4	26
Preaseau	1	0	2
King	0	0	0
Russell	8	1	17
Perry	6	2	14
Brown	5	2	12
Baxter	4	0	8
Totals	38	10	86

Southern Methodist	fg	ft	tp
Showalter	4	0	8
Krog	3	0	6
McGregor	1	1	3
Krebs	10	4	24
Miller	1	0	2
Mills	1	9	11
Morris	4	2	10
Herrscher	1	2	4
Totals	25	18	68

Halftime: San Francisco 44-32.

Championship
March 24

San Francisco	fg	ft	fta	pf	tp
Boldt	7	2	2	4	16
Farmer	0	0	0	2	0
Preaseau	3	1	2	3	7
Russell	11	4	5	2	26
Nelson	0	0	0	0	0
Perry	6	2	2	2	14
Brown	6	4	4	0	16
Baxter	2	0	0	0	4
Totals	35	13	15	13	83

Iowa	fg	ft	fta	pf	tp
Cain	7	3	4	1	17
Schoof	5	4	4	3	14
Logan	5	2	2	3	12
George	0	0	0	0	0
Scheuerman	4	3	4	2	11
Seaberg	5	7	10	1	17
Martel	0	0	0	0	0
McConnell	0	0	0	0	0
Totals	26	19	24	10	71

Halftime: San Francisco 38-33.

1957 North Carolina Stops Goliath

North Carolina Coach Frank McGuire (right) poses with three of his 1956 stars (left to right): Lennie Rosenbluth, Joe Quigg and Jerry Vayda. Rosenbluth and Quigg went on to help the Tar Heels to the 1957 national championship.

The mismatch was deliberate. There wasn't anyone on the North Carolina team capable of looking Wilt Chamberlain in the eye without standing on a ladder, so Tar Heels Coach Frank McGuire decided to challenge the 7-foot center's pride instead of his muscle. It resulted in perhaps the single-most unforgettable sight in Final Four history.

This was only the start of the evening but it set the tone for the most fascinating, most compelling and most bizarre championship game in the annals of the NCAA Tournament. If Carolina couldn't stand up to Chamberlain and his Kansas teammates physically, the Tar Heels would attack them psychologically. After mulling the consequences of playing against the most overpowering individual in college basketball, McGuire decided to send out Tommy Kearns to jump center.

Kearns, it so happened, was the shortest Carolina starter, 5-11 in his sneakers.

"I told him if he jumped high enough," McGuire said, "he might reach Wilt's stomach. You're not going to get the tap anyway, so why waste a big man? Wilt looked freakish standing there, so far above our man."

That was precisely the idea, to embarrass the sophomore who had led the nation in intimidation in his first varsity season. Such was the force of Chamberlain's presence that Kansas, 24-2 entering the title game, was favored to win the championship even though Carolina was undefeated in 31 games, was ranked No. 1 and was better manned at every position but one. Where Chamberlain was concerned, one against five seemed to be pretty good odds.

Only the previous night, after the East Regional champion Tar Heels survived in three overtimes against Mideast titlist Michigan State, Midwest winner Kansas had demolished Far West survivor San Francisco, 80-56. Granted, the defending NCAA champion Dons were without Bill Russell, yet the scope of the beating administered to a sound defensive team was awesome to behold. The Jayhawks had lost only twice all season, dropping road games at Iowa State and Oklahoma State, and had won earlier NCAA Tournament games against Southern Methodist (in overtime) and Oklahoma City.

The circumstances in this game favored Kansas. Not only had Carolina encountered nothing like Chamberlain all season, but the game was scheduled for the Municipal Auditorium in Kansas City, a short drive from the Lawrence campus. For all Dick Harp's agonizing over living up to the great expectations of Chamberlain's arrival, the former aide to Phog Allen seemed to have one hand on the championship trophy in his first season as a major-college head coach.

In speaking to his team, McGuire deliberately fed the growing Chamberlain legend.

"I said he was so good," McGuire recalled, "maybe we better not show up. I said he might stuff some of them through the basket with the ball. I said we didn't have a chance unless our entire team defensed him at all times, and he'd still probably beat us so bad it would be embarrassing to go home.

"Of course, I was kidding them, and they knew it, but it was psyching them up and loosening them up at the same time. Like, hey, let's not take this seriously, it's only a game. But they were gung-ho."

All McGuire's starters were New York City-area kids, personally recruited by the dapper, silver-tongued coach who had directed St. John's to the title game against, ironically, Kansas five years earlier. The steady parade of metropolitan standouts to Carolina became known as McGuire's "underground railroad." The joke was that they had built a Southern terminus of the New York subway system in Chapel Hill, N.C.

Regardless of what uniform they wore, the Tar Heels had inbred New York cockiness.

"We're a chilly club," Kearns said of the Tar Heels, who seemingly would have been emotionally drained after their 74-70 escape against Michigan State in a game in which Carolina's Lennie Rosenbluth scored 29 points overall and converted two third-overtime steals into field goals. "We play it chilly all the time. I mean, we just keep cool. Chamberlain won't give us the jitters like he did to all those (other) clubs."

But just in case, McGuire selected Kearns for the opening tip against Kansas. It was a comic masterstroke that ridiculed the Jayhawks' major asset and brought smiles to his own players. "Hey, McGuire," yelled one amazed fan, "you giving up already?" Not a chance.

"That tipoff took the edge away from Kansas," decided Rosenbluth, the 6-5 consensus All-America who finished the season with a 28-point scoring average. As it developed, Kansas was almost as concerned with Rosenbluth as Carolina was with Chamberlain. The Jayhawks opened in a box-and-one defense, with four players in a zone and one shadowing Rosenbluth. It was a mistake.

After Rosenbluth scored the first two points of the game on free throws, Carolina center Joe Quigg stepped to the corner, hoping to draw Chamberlain outside. Chamberlain stayed close to the basket, so Quigg, a 6-9 junior and the weakest outside shot on the team, popped in a one-hander. He did so again the next time he touched the ball and Pete Brennan's basket and free throw boosted the Tar Heels to a 9-2 lead.

The game was almost five minutes old and Chamberlain had scarcely touched the ball. McGuire had instructed Quigg to front the big man, preventing easy passes into the post, while the forwards attempted to seal Chamberlain from the basket. Finally, at 4:48 of the first half, Chamberlain scored.

But Carolina worked the ball for open shots against the zone and kept making them. In fact, the Tar Heels hit their first seven field-goal attempts, widening the gap to 19-7. Finally, Harp called a timeout, scrapped the box-and-one and ordered Kansas to play man-to-man.

That was fine with McGuire. Now when Quigg went to the corner, Chamberlain moved with him, freeing the inside for the resourceful Rosenbluth. With his shifty moves and wide assortment of soft shots, he took control in the final minutes of the half. He missed only two field-goal tries in the first 20 minutes, scored 14 points and helped Carolina to a 29-22 lead.

The Tar Heels had been successful on 64.7 percent of their floor shots in the first half, while Kansas made a dismal 27.3 percent of its attempts.

"Don't panic," Harp told his team. "Play your game. We'll catch them."

Harp had been a co-captain of Kansas' 1940 tournament finalist and an eight-year assistant to the legendary Allen. It was Allen who had won the nationwide recruiting battle for Chamberlain, but he was prevented from coaching him because he had reached the

A young Wilt Chamberlain displays some of his skills during a summer basketball camp.

Kansas center Wilt Chamberlain dominated the college basketball scene in
1956-57 and carried the Jayhawks to the championship game.

mandatory retirement age of 70. The old man
didn't do any favors for his successor when he predicted, "We could win the championship with Wilt,
two sorority girls and two Phi Beta Kappas."

The Jayhawks were having trouble enough win-
ning the championship with sophomore forward
Ron Loneski and seniors Gene Elstun, Maurice
King and John Parker alongside Chamberlain. But

Harp reckoned that Carolina wouldn't continue to
shoot 64 percent in the second half. He was correct.

The Jayhawks closed the deficit within four minutes. Then they inched ahead. The game remained
close as both teams waited and waited for an opening. Carolina's hopes appeared to evaporate when
Rosenbluth fouled out with 1:45 remaining and
Kansas in front, 46-43. Elstun, a 6-3 forward, went

Dick Harp had the enviable task of coaching the Chamberlain-led Jayhawks, who seemed to have one hand on the championship trophy.

to the free-throw line and missed. A Quigg field goal cut the deficit to one point and, after Loneski threw away an inbounds pass, Kearns was fouled and made the free throw. The score after the regulation 40 minutes was 46-46.

Carolina scored first in the overtime, on a driving basket by Bob Young, Rosenbluth's replacement. Chamberlain matched the basket with a spinning jump shot. Then the Tar Heels tried to hold for a last shot, but Brennan was tied up by Loneski. Kansas gained possession, but Loneski missed the chance at victory.

Neither team scored in a cautiously played second overtime. Kearns suddenly shocked the crowd at the outset of the third extra period, hitting a basket and two free throws for a 52-48 Carolina lead. Chamberlain then took a pass inside, scored with the Tar Heels draped over him and made the foul shot to complete a three-point play. One of two free throws by King retied the score.

Again, Carolina played for the final shot with little success. Parker, a 6-foot guard, flicked the ball

away from Quigg and passed to Elstun, who was knocked down by Kearns. Referee Gene Conway signaled a deliberate foul. Two shots for Kansas. Elstun made only one.

Thirty-one seconds remained. Kearns drove the lane and attempted to spin around Chamberlain. The giant swatted it away but Quigg, trailing on the play, grabbed the ball, went up for the shot and drew a foul. He would have two chances. Quigg had dreamed of winning a big game at the end.

"Only in my dream," he recalled later, "it was a jump shot with no time left."

In this case, the clock was stuck on six seconds. "Follow through," assistant coach Buck Freeman told Quigg on the sidelines, "and end up on your toes." Quigg finished on his toes both times—the foul shots sent the Tar Heels ahead, 54-53—and Carolina finished on top when Quigg batted away a long, high pass intended for Chamberlain.

The longest game in championship history ended at 12:14 a.m., Carolina time. For the second time in two nights, the Tar Heels had gone three overtimes to win. They had completed an implausible, undefeated season with their fifth tournament victory. (Carolina's pre-Final Four triumphs had come against Yale, Canisius and Syracuse.)

Chamberlain slumped on a stool in the Kansas dressing room. He had scored a game-high 23 points and accounted for half of his team's rebounds, but one man had not been enough.

"We lost," Chamberlain said. "That's all, we lost."

It was a loss that presaged a career of great individual accomplishment and collective disappointment. He was outdone this time because Carolina had four players in double figures and more help on the backboards, where the Tar Heels outrebounded Kansas, 42-28.

"We had the better team," said McGuire who, as fate would have it, was Chamberlain's coach when he scored 100 points in a National Basketball Association game five years later. "We played him, not Kansas. We beat Kansas, not him."

1957 Tournament Results	
First Round	**Regional Third Place**
Syracuse 82, Connecticut 76	Canisius 82, Lafayette 76
Canisius 64, West Virginia 56	Notre Dame 86, Pittsburgh 85
North Carolina 90, Yale 74	SMU 78, St. Louis 68
Pittsburgh 86, Morehead State 85	Brigham Young 65, Idaho State 54
Notre Dame 89, Miami (Ohio) 77	**Regional Championships**
Okla. City 76, Loyola (La.) 55	North Carolina 67, Syracuse 58
Idaho St. 68, Hardin-Simmons 57	Michigan State 80, Kentucky 68
Second Round	Kansas 81, Oklahoma City 61
Syracuse 75, Lafayette 71	San Francisco 50, California 46
North Carolina 87, Canisius 75	**Semifinals**
Kentucky 98, Pittsburgh 92	N. Carolina 74, Mich. St. 70 (3 ot)
Michigan State 85, Notre Dame 83	Kansas 80, San Francisco 56
Kansas 73, SMU 65 (ot)	**Third Place**
Oklahoma City 75, St. Louis 66	San Francisco 67, Michigan St. 60
San Francisco 66, Idaho State 51	**Championship**
California 86, BYU 59	N. Carolina 54, Kansas 53 (3 ot)

STATISTICS

1957 NORTH CAROLINA

Head Coach—Frank McGuire   **Final Record—32-0**

Player	Pos.	Hgt.	Wgt.	Cl.	G	FG	FGA	Pct.	FT	FTA	Pct.	Reb.	Pts.	Avg.
Lennie Rosenbluth	F	6-5	195	Sr.	32	305	631	.483	285	376	.758	280	895	28.0
Pete Brennan	F	6-6	190	Jr.	32	143	363	.394	185	262	.706	332	471	14.7
Tommy Kearns	G	5-11	188	Jr.	32	138	318	.434	135	190	.711	100	411	12.8
Joe Quigg	C	6-9	205	Jr.	31	111	256	.434	97	135	.719	268	319	10.3
Bob Cunningham	G	6-4	190	Jr.	32	88	224	.393	55	92	.598	214	231	7.2
Tony Radovich	G	6-2	192	Sr.	16	21	40	.525	20	26	.769	29	62	3.9
Bill Hathaway	C	6-11	240	So.	15	16	48	.333	10	24	.417	75	42	2.8
Stan Groll	G	6-0	182	So.	12	10	27	.370	5	9	.556	18	25	2.1
Bob Young	C	6-6	200	Jr.	15	11	43	.256	7	13	.538	32	29	1.9
Ken Rosemond	G	5-9	150	Jr.	15	6	15	.400	5	9	.556	9	17	1.1
Danny Lotz	F	6-7	198	So.	24	7	20	.350	9	23	.391	39	23	1.0
Gehrmann Holland	F	6-3	200	So.	12	4	8	.500	0	1	.000	6	8	0.7
Roy Searcy	F	6-4	185	Jr.	11	0	3	.000	4	5	.800	11	4	0.4
Team												82		
North Carolina					32	860	1996	.431	817	1165	.701	1495	2537	79.3
Opponents					32	720	2043	.352	658	956	.688	1151	2098	65.6

1957 KANSAS

Head Coach—Dick Harp   **Final Record—24-3**

Player	Pos.	Hgt.	Wgt.	Cl.	G	FG	FGA	Pct.	FT	FTA	Pct.	Reb.	Pts.	Avg.
Wilt Chamberlain	C	7-0	214	So.	27	275	588	.468	250	399	.627	510	800	29.6
Gene Elstun	F	6-3	175	Sr.	26	110	259	.425	73	112	.652	189	293	11.3
Maurice King	G	6-2	190	Sr.	27	101	278	.363	61	88	.693	122	263	9.7
Ron Loneski	F	6-3	210	So.	17	51	155	.329	61	87	.701	115	163	9.6
John Parker	G	6-0	173	Sr.	27	60	132	.455	28	39	.718	53	148	5.5
Ron Johnston	F	6-1	180	Sr.	12	17	50	.340	17	25	.680	41	51	4.3
Lew Johnson	C-F	6-6	198	Sr.	26	31	102	.304	15	29	.517	101	77	3.0
Bob Billings	G	5-11	173	So.	22	10	34	.294	28	35	.800	19	48	2.2
John Cleland	G	6-3	170	Jr.	6	4	5	.800	4	5	.800	4	12	2.0
Larry Kelley	G	5-11	155	So.	1	1	2	.500	0	0	.000	2	2	2.0
Eddie Dater	G	6-2	195	Sr.	15	11	29	.379	2	2	1.000	10	24	1.6
Harry Jett	F	6-3	166	So.	8	3	10	.300	4	4	1.000	4	10	1.3
Blaine Hollinger	G	5-10	159	So.	18	8	26	.308	5	12	.417	14	21	1.2
Monte Johnson	F	6-5	168	So.	11	4	19	.211	4	5	.800	16	12	1.1
Lee Green	F	6-5	190	So.	10	5	12	.417	0	2	.000	14	10	1.0
Gary Thompson	F	6-4	207	Jr.	7	3	5	.600	1	4	.250	10	7	1.0
Lynn Kindred	G	6-2	156	So.	16	1	14	.071	2	5	.400	14	4	0.3
Joe Ensley	G	6-1	167	So.	1	0	0	.000	0	0	.000	2	0	0.0
Team												59		
Kansas					27	695	1720	.404	555	853	.651	1299	1945	72.0
Opponents					27	586	1688	.347	411	648	.634	949	1583	58.6

1957 SAN FRANCISCO

Head Coach—Phil Woolpert   **Final Record—22-6**

Player	Pos.	Hgt.	Wgt.	Cl.	G	FG	FGA	Pct.	FT	FTA	Pct.	Reb.	Pts.	Avg.
Gene Brown	G	6-2	175	Jr.	22	121	317	.382	91	139	.655	125	333	15.1
Mike Farmer	F-C	6-7	215	Jr.	28	127	339	.375	83	107	.776	267	337	12.0
Art Day	C	6-9	200	So.	27	114	329	.347	94	142	.662	270	322	11.9
Al Dunbar	G	5-11	155	Jr.	28	60	164	.366	86	118	.729	110	206	7.4
Mike Preseau	F	6-5	185	Jr.	26	62	166	.373	55	68	.809	118	179	6.9
Dave Lillevand	G	5-11	160	So.	27	31	116	.267	46	71	.648	56	108	4.0
Bill Mallen	F	6-3	230	Jr.	24	29	83	.349	22	29	.759	62	80	3.3
Charles Russell	F	6-4	198	Jr.	22	16	68	.235	7	19	.368	40	39	1.8
John Koljian	F	6-3	195	Jr.	16	7	31	.226	14	21	.667	11	28	1.8
Jack King	F	6-3	175	Sr.	19	5	26	.192	6	10	.600	8	16	0.8
Ron Mancasola	G	5-7	147	Jr.	14	3	14	.214	1	2	.500	6	7	0.5
Bob Radovich	F	6-3	180	So.	14	2	16	.125	0	1	.000	9	4	0.3
Others						40	104	.385	16	31	.516	81	96	
Team												71		
San Francisco					28	617	1773	.348	521	758	.687	1234	1755	62.7
Opponents					28	527	1527	.345	500	774	.646	1237	1554	55.5

1957 MICHIGAN STATE

Head Coach—Forrest (Forddy) Anderson   **Final Record—16-10**

Player	Pos.	Hgt.	Wgt.	Cl.	G	FG	FGA	Pct.	FT	FTA	Pct.	Reb.	Pts.	Avg.
Jack Quiggle	G	6-3	190	Jr.	25	142	355	.400	100	140	.714	139	384	15.4
Larry Hedden	F	6-5	185	Jr.	26	147	385	.382	78	122	.639	202	372	14.3
George Ferguson	F	6-3	190	Sr.	26	137	320	.428	69	97	.711	152	343	13.2
John Green	C	6-5	215	So.	18	96	247	.389	46	81	.568	262	238	13.2
Bob Anderegg	F-G	6-3	195	So.	26	75	227	.330	73	127	.575	130	223	8.6
Chuck Bencie	C-F	6-6	195	Jr.	24	54	168	.321	24	37	.649	87	132	5.5
Pat Wilson	G	6-0	186	So.	26	41	110	.373	28	43	.651	72	110	4.2
Dave Scott	G	6-2	150	So.	24	34	78	.436	25	46	.543	43	93	3.9
Tom Markovich	F	6-3	195	So.	9	2	6	.333	6	8	.750	6	10	1.1
Harry Lux	G	5-10	150	Sr.	15	4	17	.235	6	13	.462	13	14	0.9
Tom Rand	G	6-2	175	So.	10	2	13	.154	2	2	1.000	9	6	0.6
Jim Stouffer	F	6-0	165	So.	4	0	2	.000	2	2	1.000	0	2	0.5
Gary Siegmeier	C	6-5	180	So.	4	1	2	.500	0	0	.000	1	2	0.5
Larry Jennings	G	6-5	195	So.	2	0	0	.000	0	0	.000	0	0	0.0
John Russell	F	6-1	155.	So.	1	0	0	.000	0	0	.000	0	0	0.0
Team												65		
Michigan State					26	735	1930	.381	459	718	.639	1181	1929	74.2
Opponents					26	658	1776	.370	507	711	.713	991	1823	70.1

1957 FINAL FOUR

At Kansas City
Semifinals

North Carolina	fg	fga	ft	fta	rb	pf	tp
Rosenbluth	11	42	7	9	3	1	29
Cunningham	9	18	3	5	12	5	21
Brennan	6	16	2	4	17	5	14
Kearns	1	8	4	5	6	4	6
Quigg	0	1	2	3	4	5	2
Lotz	0	1	0	0	4	1	0
Young	1	3	0	1	2	1	2
Searcy	0	0	0	0	1	0	0
Team					5		
Totals	28	89	18	27	54	22	74

Michigan State	fg	fga	ft	fta	rb	pf	tp
Quiggle	6	21	8	10	10	1	20
Green	4	12	3	6	19	2	11
Ferguson	4	8	2	3	1	5	10
Hedden	4	20	6	7	15	5	14
Wilson	0	3	2	5	1	1	2
Anderegg	2	7	3	6	3	2	7
Bencie	1	6	0	0	2	1	2
Scott	2	3	0	2	3	1	4
Team					7		
Totals	23	80	24	36	65	18	70

Halftime Score: 29-29. Regulation Score: 58-58. First Overtime: 64-64. Second Overtime: 66-66. Officials: Ogden and Lightner.

Kansas	fg	fga	ft	fta	rb	pf	tp
M. King	6	8	1	1	4	1	13
Elstun	8	12	0	0	6	3	16
Chamberlain	12	22	8	11	11	0	32
Parker	1	1	0	0	3	0	2
Loneski	2	6	3	4	7	3	7
L. Johnson	1	3	0	0	8	0	2
Billings	0	1	0	0	0	0	0
Hollinger	1	1	0	1	0	0	2
Dater	1	1	0	0	2	1	2
Green	1	1	0	0	2	1	2
Kindred	0	0	0	2	2	0	0
M. Johnson	1	1	0	0	0	0	2
Team					1		
Totals	34	57	12	19	44	10	80

San Francisco	fg	fga	ft	fta	rb	pf	tp
Day	3	14	3	8	7	2	9
Dunbar	2	8	0	0	4	1	4
Brown	5	14	0	0	2	2	10
Farmer	6	15	2	2	4	2	14
Preseau	5	8	2	2	2	2	12
Mallen	0	2	0	0	1	1	0
Lillevand	1	3	0	0	0	0	2
Koljian	0	1	3	4	0	0	3
J. King	0	3	0	0	0	1	0
Russell	0	0	0	0	1	0	0
Radanovich	0	1	0	0	0	0	0
Mancasola	1	2	0	0	0	1	2
Team					4		
Totals	23	71	10	16	25	13	56

Halftime: Kansas 38-34. Officials: Conway and Anderson.

Championship
March 23

North Carolina	fg	fga	ft	fta	rb	pf	tp
Rosenbluth	8	15	4	4	5	5	20
Cunningham	0	3	0	1	5	4	0
Brennan	4	8	3	7	11	3	11
Kearns	4	8	3	7	1	4	11
Quigg	4	10	2	3	9	4	10
Lotz	0	0	0	0	2	0	0
Young	1	1	0	0	3	1	2
Team					6		
Totals	21	45	12	22	42	21	54

Kansas	fg	fga	ft	fta	rb	pf	tp
Chamberlain	6	13	11	16	14	3	23
King	3	12	5	6	4	4	11
Elstun	4	12	3	6	4	0	11
Parker	2	4	0	0	0	4	4
Loneski	0	5	2	3	3	2	2
L. Johnson	0	1	2	2	0	1	2
Billings	0	0	0	0	0	2	0
Team					3		
Totals	15	47	23	33	28	14	53

Halftime: North Carolina 29-22. Regulation Score: 46-46. First Overtime: 48-48. Second Overtime: 48-48. Officials: Conway and Anderson.

1958 Rupp's 'Cats Fiddle Away

Forward John Crigler (32, here fouling Seattle's Jerry Frizzell) helped Kentucky in the 1958 title game by getting Chieftains star Elgin Baylor in foul trouble.

Kentucky forward Johnny Cox snatches the ball away from Seattle guard Francis Saunders during the Wildcats' 84-72 championship-game victory.

Adolph Rupp not only coached them, he named them. The players who represented Kentucky in the 1958 season were far from the Baron's finest but, collectively, they ranked among his favorite teams. Their achievement exceeded all expectations.

The coach had little reason to believe this group would be the one to restore Kentucky to the throne of college basketball, to earn the Wildcats another championship that he felt had been unfairly denied the school. These players weren't particularly big or talented, they had contributed to a disappointing finish the previous year and then they opened the new season by losing three of their first seven games.

"We've got fiddlers, that's all," Rupp decided. "They're pretty good fiddlers. Be all right entertaining at a barn dance. But I tell you, you need a violinist to play in Carnegie Hall. We don't have any violinists."

Thus was born the legend of the "Fiddlin' Five." It was a team without a dominant player, a major star. Not only would no Kentucky player win consensus All-America recognition after the season, but the Wildcats didn't even place a man on the All-Southeastern Conference first team.

Kentucky compensated for its shortcomings with balance, its ability to run Rupp's intricate offensive patterns with precision and an uncanny knack for winning tight games. Even in claiming the conference title and an automatic berth in the NCAA Tournament, however, the Wildcats did not appear a formidable contender for the national championship. Their overall pre-tournament record of 19-6 was subpar for a team coached by Rupp.

Working in Kentucky's favor was a schedule that granted the Wildcats a home-state advantage throughout the NCAA meet. In fact, the Mideast Regional was being staged at the Memorial Coliseum on Kentucky's Lexington campus for the second consecutive year. And Freedom Hall in Louisville would host the Final Four in 1958.

The Wildcats, featuring four seniors and a junior, were at their best in the regional, blowing past Miami of Ohio, 94-70, and Notre Dame, 89-56. And

Chieftains guard Charley Brown (45) scored 17 points but was unable to keep Kentucky from winning its fourth national championship.

while they were having their way, many top teams suffered stunning upsets. West Virginia, No. 1 in both wire-service polls, was a first-round loser to Manhattan in the East Regional. Cincinnati, ranked second, was beaten by Kansas State in the Midwest semifinals and San Francisco, rated third in one poll and fourth in the other, was toppled by Seattle in a Far West semifinal.

Suddenly, a path to the top had been cleared. And Rupp wanted nothing so much as he did a fourth championship. He still was steaming over NCAA sanctions that forced Kentucky to cancel its 1953 season. The Wildcats, playing with a vengeance the next season, won all 25 games but declined to participate in the NCAA Tournament because their three best players were graduate students and thereby ineligible for postseason competition. The 1954 national tournament was won by

a La Salle team that Kentucky had defeated by 13 points during the season.

All of this preyed on Rupp's mind. Again and again he had vowed, "I will not retire until Kentucky wins another NCAA championship." Now, surprisingly, he had the opportunity. At the age of 56, Rupp was taking his fiddlers to Louisville for the big dance.

The other three national semifinalists were Temple, Kansas State and Seattle. Of the Final Four teams, Temple was the quickest, Kansas State the tallest and Seattle the possessor of the most extraordinary player, Elgin Baylor. If Kentucky had any edge, it was in teamwork.

Although the Wildcats had handed East Regional winner Temple one of its two regular-season defeats, the Kentucky triumph in December was anything but decisive. It required, among other things, three overtimes and a half-court shot by Vern Hatton. And that game had been played on Kentucky's home floor.

Once again Kentucky and Temple were matched up, and once again they played an enthralling contest. Sparked by Guy Rodgers, the brilliant guard, Temple held a 60-59 lead with 23 seconds remaining. During a timeout, Rupp told the Wildcats to place the ball in Hatton's hands. The 6-foot-3 senior guard promptly drove the lane, ducked underneath traffic around the basket and dropped in a layup. Temple had time to reverse matters, but sophomore Bill (Pickles) Kennedy couldn't connect with a Rodgers pass and Kentucky hung on to win, 61-60.

With 6-8 Bob Boozer, 6-9 Jack Parr and 6-8 Wally Frank on the front line, Kansas State was the most imposing team in Louisville. Parr had been particularly effective in the regular season against Wilt Chamberlain, helping Coach Tex Winter's team supplant Kansas as the Big Eight Conference champion. But Kansas State's trio was no match for the smooth and powerful Baylor, who led Seattle to a 73-51 romp in the other semifinal.

Baylor had been unstoppable during the season. He averaged more than 30 points per game in the Chieftains' free-lance attack. The 6-6 youngster from Washington, D.C., who had taken a football scholarship at the College of Idaho and then transferred to Seattle after proving himself in basketball, had a bewildering series of fakes and, in apparent defiance of gravity, was able to hang in the air long after defenders returned to earth.

There was considerable doubt in Rupp's mind that Kentucky could contain Baylor. His strategy was to attack Baylor at the defensive end and force him into foul trouble. To that end, he was aided by John Castellani, the young Seattle coach.

Rupp had expected Baylor to draw the defensive assignment on 6-7 center Ed Beck, who didn't look to score but was content to rebound and play defense. For that reason, Rupp and assistant Harry Lancaster had planned to have Beck drive to the basket around set screens. But Castellani chose to send Baylor—who was playing with injured ribs— against John Crigler, a quick 6-3 forward. During an early timeout, Crigler was instructed to drive the baseline whenever possible.

As a result, while Baylor hurt the Wildcats on offense, the Seattle star had his hands full with Crigler on defense. The Chieftains raced to a 29-18 lead, but Baylor was charged with three fouls in the first 10 minutes. Determined to keep him in the game, Castellani switched to a zone defense, with Baylor on the back line, and slowed the tempo on offense. The outside shooting of Hatton and forward Johnny Cox brought Kentucky back, cutting the deficit to 39-36 at halftime.

"Baylor had those three fouls," Castellani said, "and with his rib injury we had to slow it down to protect him. My object was to go to the locker room with a lead and only three fouls on Baylor."

The strategy succeeded in that regard. And Seattle pushed the lead to 44-38 in the first 3½ minutes of the second half. It was then that Baylor drew his fourth foul, curtailing his natural aggressiveness for the rest of the game. Kentucky seized the initiative.

Cox, a 6-4 junior, led the charge. Exploiting the Chieftains' zone, he scored 16 of his 24 points in the final 15 minutes. It was his long jump shot that tied the score at 56-56. The Wildcats finally grabbed the lead at 61-60 on a hook shot by reserve Don Mills, who entered the game when Beck got into foul difficulty attempting to handle Baylor. Cox followed Mills' basket with another jump shot and Kentucky, thanks to an 8-0 run, was en route to victory and the unlikeliest of its four championships.

The gallant 25-point effort by Baylor was not sufficient against Kentucky's superior team play. Seattle's consensus All-America was accorded outstanding-player honors, but Hatton led all scorers in the title game with 30 points as Kentucky wound up an 84-72 winner. Rupp preened after the trophy presentation.

"These were just a bunch of ugly ducklings," he said. "Not one of them made the all-conferenece team. And I didn't get a single vote for 'coach of the year,' so I know it wasn't overcoaching. Frankly, I didn't think we'd get this far."

The fiddlers got as far as any team in Rupp's tenure and they presented him with what would be his final national championship. For that reason or perhaps because they squeezed so much out of their abilities, they remained special to him until the day he died in 1977.

"This team played the best, as a unit, of any of the championship teams I've coached," he said that night in Louisville, "each player making up for the particular weaknesses that the others had."

The 1958 Wildcats made such beautiful music together that no one missed the violinist.

1958 Tournament Results

First Round
Dartmouth 75, Connecticut 64
Manhattan 89, West Virginia 84
Maryland 86, Boston College 63
Miami (Ohio) 82, Pittsburgh 77
Notre Dame 94, Tenn. Tech 61
Oklahoma St. 59, Loyola (La.) 42
Idaho State 72, Arizona State 68
Seattle 88, Wyoming 51

Second Round
Dartmouth 79, Manhattan 62
Temple 71, Maryland 67
Notre Dame 94, Indiana 87
Kentucky 94, Miami (Ohio) 70
Oklahoma State 65, Arkansas 40
Kansas St. 83, Cincinnati 80 (ot)
California 54, Idaho State 43
Seattle 69, San Francisco 67

Regional Third Place
Maryland 59, Manhattan 55
Indiana 98, Miami (Ohio) 91
Cincinnati 97, Arkansas 62
San Francisco 57, Idaho State 51

Regional Championships
Temple 69, Dartmouth 50
Kentucky 89, Notre Dame 56
Kansas State 69, Oklahoma St. 57
Seattle 66, California 62 (ot)

Semifinals
Kentucky 61, Temple 60
Seattle 73, Kansas State 51

Third Place
Temple 67, Kansas State 57

Championship
Kentucky 84, Seattle 72

STATISTICS

1958 KENTUCKY

Head Coach—Adolph Rupp　　　　　　Final Record—23-6

Player	Pos.	Hgt.	Wgt.	Cl.	G	FG	FGA	Pct.	FT.	FTA	Pct.	Reb.	Pts.	Avg.
Vernon Hatton	G	6-3	188	Sr.	29	192	458	.419	112	144	.778	144	496	17.1
Johnny Cox	F	6-4	185	Jr.	29	173	471	.367	86	115	.748	365	432	14.9
John Crigler	F	6-3	180	Sr.	28	162	400	.405	58	82	.707	278	382	13.6
Adrian Smith	G	6-0	178	Sr.	29	118	318	.371	124	162	.765	101	360	12.4
Ed Beck	C	6-7	188	Sr.	29	62	219	.283	39	54	.722	337	163	5.6
Earl Adkins	G	6-4	180	Sr.	19	39	86	.453	23	31	.742	29	101	5.3
Don Mills	C	6-7	190	So.	20	25	99	.253	20	32	.625	99	70	3.5
Phil Johnson	F-C	6-6	190	Jr.	22	30	98	.306	15	29	.517	126	75	3.4
Lowell Hughes	G	6-0	175	So.	7	7	19	.368	9	10	.900	7	23	3.3
Bill Cassady	G	6-2	191	Sr.	14	15	35	.429	4	6	.667	10	34	2.4
Lincoln Collinsworth	G	6-3	185	Sr.	15	6	19	.316	10	13	.769	17	22	1.5
Harold Ross	G	6-2	180	Sr.	3	1	2	.500	2	2	1.000	1	4	1.3
Dick Howe	C-F	6-5	208	Jr.	4	1	5	.200	0	0	.000	8	2	0.5
Bill Smith	F	6-5	203	Sr.	5	1	4	.250	0	0	.000	9	2	0.4
Team												31		
Kentucky					29	832	2233	.373	502	680	.738	1562	2166	74.7
Opponents					29	690	1945	.355	437	635	.688	1227	1817	62.7

1958 SEATTLE

Head Coach—John Castellani　　　　　Final Record—24-7

Player	Pos.	Hgt.	Wgt.	Cl.	G	FG	FGA	Pct.	FT.	FTA	Pct.	Reb.	Pts.	Avg.
Elgin Baylor	C	6-6	225	Jr.	29	353	697	.506	237	308	.769	559	943	32.5
Charley Brown	G	6-2	180	Jr.	29	124	287	.432	64	99	.646	211	312	10.8
Jerry Frizzell	F	6-4	190	Jr.	29	106	206	.515	59	86	.686	128	271	9.3
Don Ogorek	F	6-4	200	So.	29	104	239	.435	62	92	.674	183	270	9.3
Jim Harney	G	5-10	170	Sr.	27	84	187	.449	15	23	.652	33	183	6.8
Francis Saunders	G	6-2	175	Jr.	27	69	141	.489	15	26	.577	78	153	5.7
Don Piasecki	G	6-2	190	So.	28	43	95	.453	14	23	.609	51	100	3.6
Thornton Humphries	C	6-7	180	Jr.	21	24	71	.338	10	32	.313	78	58	2.8
Jude Petrie	F	6-6	220	So.	15	10	24	.417	1	7	.143	31	21	1.4
John Stepan	C	6-6	215	So.	13	8	18	.444	2	5	.400	23	18	1.4
John Kootnekoff	G	6-2	190	So.	19	10	31	.323	1	5	.200	11	21	1.1
Bill Wall	F	6-2	200	Jr.	14	3	15	.200	1	6	.167	14	7	0.5
Bob Siewarga	G	5-10	170	So.	5	0	0	.000	0	2	.000	0	0	0.0
Seattle					29	938	2011	.466	481	714	.674	1400	2357	81.3
Opponents					29	758	2069	.366	471	743	.634	980	1987	68.5

1958 TEMPLE

Head Coach—Harry Litwack　　　　　Final Record—27-3

Player	Pos.	Hgt.	Wgt.	Cl.	G	FG	FGA	Pct.	FT.	FTA	Pct.	Reb.	Pts.	Avg.
Guy Rodgers	G	6-0	180	Sr.	30	249	564	.441	105	171	.614	199	603	20.1
Bill Kennedy	G	5-11	170	Sr.	30	146	332	.440	112	133	.842	98	404	13.5
Jay Norman	F	6-3	190	Sr.	29	150	377	.398	77	127	.606	346	377	13.0
Mel Brodsky	F	6-2	180	Sr.	29	134	311	.431	47	61	.770	218	315	10.9
Tink Van Patton	C	6-8	225	Sr.	30	82	198	.414	35	56	.625	314	199	6.6
Dan Fleming	F	6-6	210	Sr.	30	59	133	.444	33	48	.688	130	151	5.0
Ophie Franklin	F	6-4	170	Jr.	24	17	51	.333	17	37	.459	60	51	2.1
Erv Abrams	F	6-6	190	So.	12	8	16	.500	2	4	.500	10	18	1.5
Joe Goldenberg	G	5-7	155	Jr.	19	9	30	.300	9	15	.600	10	27	1.4
Pete Goss	C	6-2	215	Jr.	17	8	23	.348	6	16	.375	23	22	1.3
Jack Peepe	G	6-2	202	Jr.	19	10	32	.313	1	3	.333	21	21	1.1
Cliff Crispin	G	6-0	183	So.	7	2	5	.400	1	2	.500	5	5	0.7
Gerry Lipson	G	6-0	190	So.	7	0	7	.000	4	6	.667	9	4	0.6
Al Staines	...	...	...	...	1	0	1	.000	0	0	.000	2	0	0.0
Temple					30	874	2080	.420	449	679	.661	1445	2197	73.2
Opponents					30	628	1937	.324	496	769	.645	1109	1752	58.4

1958 KANSAS STATE

Head Coach—Tex Winter　　　　　　Final Record—22-5

Player	Pos.	Hgt.	Wgt.	Cl.	G	FG	FGA	Pct.	FT.	FTA	Pct.	Reb.	Pts.	Avg.
Bob Boozer	F	6-8	214	Jr.	27	195	441	.442	154	215	.716	281	544	20.1
Jack Parr	C	6-9	212	Sr.	25	125	386	.324	89	142	.627	259	339	13.6
Wally Frank	F-C	6-8	212	So.	27	88	184	.478	55	79	.696	135	231	8.6
Roy DeWitz	G	6-3	184	Sr.	27	71	227	.313	74	100	.740	149	216	8.0
Hayden Abbott	F	6-3	186	Sr.	26	84	233	.361	31	58	.534	132	199	7.7
Don Matuszak	G	6-0	183	Jr.	27	69	147	.469	54	81	.667	99	192	7.1
Larry Fischer	F	6-4	190	Jr.	13	13	23	.565	10	17	.588	15	36	2.8
Glen Long	F	6-4	189	So.	13	10	30	.333	10	19	.526	29	30	2.3
Jim Holwerda	G	6-0	160	Jr.	20	15	40	.375	3	8	.375	12	33	1.7
Steve Douglas	G	6-4	183	So.	11	3	13	.231	10	14	.714	14	16	1.5
Don Richards	G	6-1	160	Sr.	7	3	20	.150	4	9	.444	7	10	1.4
Sonny Ballard	G	6-0	150	So.	11	5	18	.278	4	8	.500	7	14	1.3
Bill Laude	F	6-4	190	So.	6	3	3	1.000	2	4	.500	5	8	1.3
Bill Guthridge	G	5-9	147	So.	6	3	4	.750	0	2	.000	4	6	1.0
Howie Rice	C	6-7	202	So.	3	0	1	.000	1	2	.500	0	1	0.3
Others					2	1	4	.250	3	4	.750	2	5	
Team												89		
Kansas State					27	688	1774	.388	504	762	.661	1239	1880	69.6
Opponents					27	602	1696	.355	457	720	.635	1037	1661	61.5

1958 FINAL FOUR

At Louisville, Ky.
Semifinals

Kentucky	fg	fga	ft	fta	rb	pf	tp
Crigler	3	11	0	2	9	4	6
Cox	6	17	10	11	13	4	22
Collinsworth	0	0	0	0	1	0	0
Beck	3	9	2	2	15	2	8
Hatton	5	16	3	4	2	3	13
Smith	2	10	8	9	5	3	12
Team					5		
Totals	19	63	23	28	49	17	61

Temple	fg	fga	ft	fta	rb	pf	tp
Norman	7	17	2	3	6	3	16
Brodsky	2	5	0	2	14	2	4
Van Patton	1	1	1	2	3	4	3
Fleming	3	7	3	6	5	1	9
Rodgers	9	24	4	6	5	4	22
Kennedy	3	7	0	1	3	4	6
Team					5		
Totals	25	61	10	20	41	18	60

Halftime: 31-31. Officials: Morrow and Mercer.

Seattle	fg	fga	ft	fta	rb	pf	tp
Ogorek	3	9	1	2	4	4	7
Frizzell	2	4	6	7	2	2	10
Petrie	0	0	0	0	0	0	0
Baylor	9	21	5	7	22	3	23
Humphries	0	0	0	0	0	0	0
Harney	0	4	0	0	2	1	0
Brown	5	6	4	5	13	2	14
Saunders	5	11	2	3	8	1	12
Piasecki	1	1	3	4	0	1	5
Kootnekoff	1	1	0	0	0	0	2
Team					5		
Totals	26	57	21	28	56	14	73

Kansas State	fg	fga	ft	fta	rb	pf	tp
Boozer	6	15	3	5	4	4	15
Frank	6	12	3	4	7	4	15
Abbott	0	4	0	0	2	1	0
Long	2	6	0	1	4	2	4
Fischer	0	1	0	0	0	1	0
Parr	2	11	0	1	8	1	4
Matuszak	3	8	1	3	7	1	7
DeWitz	2	7	2	3	0	2	6
Holwerda	0	2	0	0	1	2	0
Team					1		
Totals	21	66	9	17	34	18	51

Halftime: Seattle 37-32. Officials: Conway and Mihalik.

Championship
March 22

Kentucky	fg	fga	ft	fta	rb	pf	tp
Cox	10	23	4	4	16	3	24
Crigler	5	12	4	7	14	4	14
Beck	0	1	0	1	3	4	0
Mills	4	9	1	4	5	3	9
Hatton	9	20	12	15	3	3	30
Smith	2	8	3	5	6	4	7
Team					8		
Totals	30	73	24	36	55	21	84

Seattle	fg	fga	ft	fta	rb	pf	tp
Frizzell	4	6	8	11	5	3	16
Ogorek	4	7	2	2	11	5	10
Baylor	9	32	7	9	19	4	25
Harney	2	5	0	1	1	4	4
Brown	6	17	5	7	5	5	17
Saunders	0	2	0	0	2	3	0
Piasecki	0	0	0	0	0	0	0
Team					3		
Totals	25	69	22	30	46	21	72

Halftime: Seattle 39-36.

1959 | Mysterious Cal Takes the Cake

California Coach Pete Newell shares the championship trophy and a big smile with (left to right) Bob Dalton, Al Buch and Bernie Simpson.

In Oscar Robertson and Jerry West, the two finest amateur basketball players on earth, the 1959 Final Four had sufficient star quality. In addition to the superstar-led Cincinnati and West Virginia teams, it also had something dear to every promoter's heart, a hometown team, this one representing the University of Louisville. Last and least in terms of advance publicity was California, the mystery guest from the West.

These were the survivors of a particularly formless NCAA Tournament in which Kansas State and Kentucky, ranked first and second in the nation, were eliminated by Cincinnati and Louisville, respectively. North Carolina and Michigan State were

other favored teams that fell short of the national semifinals, scheduled for Freedom Hall. Before the start of the weekend activities, it was clear only that the new champion would be something of a surprise.

Ironically, West Virginia and Cincinnati had been expected to contend for the ultimate honor the previous year when they lost a total of three games between them during the regular season. Although they weren't quite so powerful in the 1959 season, the Mountaineers and Bearcats still had the two players acknowledged as the finest in the land. If West wasn't better than Robertson, he was better than any other mortal. The latter obviously belonged in some higher league.

For the second consecutive season, the 6-foot-5 Robertson had led the nation in scoring. He averaged 32.6 points per game after posting a 35.1 mark as a sophomore and was adept at every phase of the game—dribbling, passing and rebounding, as well as shooting.

"There's never been one like him," decided Joe Lapchick, the St. John's coach who had been associated with basketball for nearly half a century.

Perhaps the only proper comparison of Robertson and West was to note that West was two inches shorter. The West Virginia standout was a remarkably complete player. Besides possessing outstanding shooting range, West was the Mountaineers' finest defender and their leading rebounder.

"If you sat down to build the perfect 6-foot, 3-inch basketball player," said his coach, Fred Schaus, "you'd come up with Jerry West."

West himself conceded the edge to the player known as the Big O.

"If I were a coach," West said, "I'd take Robertson. He's a better passer and a better dribbler. He has bigger hands and his ballhandling is superior. He has quicker reactions. He's unbelievable."

But that's what basketball people were calling West after his one-man show in the East Regional. Against St. Joseph's, he accounted for 36 points and 15 rebounds and almost single-handedly rallied the Mountaineers from an 18-point deficit in the final 13 minutes. In the regional final, another close game, he responded with 33 points and 17 rebounds in an 86-82 victory over Boston University.

Meanwhile, in the Midwest Regional, Robertson showcased a talent other than scoring when top-ranked Kansas State ganged up on him. He foiled the double team with his passing and was credited with 13 assists as well as 24 points in Cincinnati's stunning 85-75 triumph.

The draw made it possible, even likely, that the two stars—only juniors—would oppose each other for the first time in the NCAA title game. West Virginia did its part against Mideast titlist Louisville, battering the Cardinals, 94-79. West gave an awesome performance. He scored 27 points in the first half and contented himself with passing for much of the second half. He finished with 38 points and 15 rebounds. "We didn't play a better game all year," he said.

But the great showdown between the two future Olympians and professional stars never materialized. California, the Far West Regional kingpin, was the culprit. The anonymous team from Berkeley that placed defense ahead of individual glory thoroughly baffled high-powered Cincinnati in the other national semifinal.

The confusion started just seconds before the opening tap when Cal's Bob Dalton, a 6-3 senior

California center Darrall Imhoff goes high for a shot over a West Virginia defender in the 1959 championship game.

forward who had been given the assignment of his life, extended his hand to the great Robertson. "My name's Dalton," he said in feigned innocence. "What's yours?"

If the Bears were largely unknown outside the West Coast, they didn't seem to mind. They were supremely confident in their ability to function as a unit. And if the Associated Press didn't rank that unit in the Top 10 despite its 21-4 regular-season record (United Press International listed Cal in the ninth spot), the Golden Bears were convinced no team—and certainly no individual—in Louisville could beat them. After all, they had been prepared by Pete Newell.

Newell was an intense 43-year-old who had coached successfully at San Francisco and Michigan State before taking on the challenge at Berkeley. The Bears had made but one appearance in the NCAA Tournament before Newell's arrival four seasons earlier. Now Cal was back for its third successive year, corresponding with its third consecutive Pacific Coast Conference championship.

The Golden Bears' strength was in their system and conditioning. Newell had his players run the back hills of Berkeley once a day in the preseason. It readied them for the full-court press he would employ throughout a game against a difficult opponent. The Bears also participated in extensive drills, including one in which they were required to simulate defensive movement while holding one hand above their heads. The period of time ranged from five minutes in the beginning to nearly half an hour. "Absolute torture," Dalton called it.

California was a small team other than at center, where 6-10 junior Darrall Imhoff had made tremendous strides. He reported to Berkeley with few credentials and little mobility. Under Newell, he had developed into an efficient player with good quickness and a soft touch. Imhoff didn't score a lot of points, but sizable production wasn't necessary. The Bears won by stopping the other team from scoring. In 1959, they yielded only 51 points per game.

Now all they had to do was stop Oscar Robertson, who had scored 56 points in a game twice the previous year. Since Robertson liked to back his way toward the baseline, Newell devised a strategy to force him to spin toward the middle of the floor, where the weak-side guard would rush to help out. Dalton, who entered school on a football scholarship and played behind quarterback Joe Kapp before an injury in his freshman year convinced him to stick to basketball, used his speed to combat the Big O. Additionally, Imhoff blocked a couple of his penetrations and senior guard Denny Fitzpatrick registered a few steals.

While Cincinnati managed a 33-29 halftime lead and expanded that edge to 36-29, the game was deadlocked at 54-54 when Imhoff rejected a Robertson jump shot. Then the Bears' pivotman scored a basket of his own. Cal never again surrendered the lead and won, 64-58, limiting the premier player to 19 points. So effective was the Bears' defense that Cincinnati attempted only 56 shots, compared with 73 for the winners.

There wasn't much time to savor that one, however. On the next night, the Bears had to contend with West, who could score from outside and inside with equal facility. Newell chose to make him shoot from the outside, as far from the basket as possible.

The strategy appeared vulnerable at the outset as West Virginia, forced into a control game, patiently shot its way to a 23-13 advantage. But Cal took its time, ran its patterns, applied relentless pressure and soon pulled even. By halftime, the Bears held a 39-33 lead.

Second-half turnovers dropped the Mountaineers further back until they trailed by 13 at 57-44 about midway through the period. West, who had drawn his fourth foul, was sitting on the bench at the time. Schaus sent his star back into the game and ordered a full-court press, a taste of Cal's own strategy.

Amazingly, the normally imperturbable Bears began to lose the ball and their composure. As Newell chewed on his towel for relief, West Virginia edged closer and closer as the noise in the arena rose and the drama built. The Mountaineers' opponent no longer was Cal, it was the clock.

Once again, Imhoff made the big basket. With his team holding a 69-68 lead, he followed a rebound of his own miss and pushed the Bears ahead by three points with 15 seconds left. Willie Akers scored an uncontested basket for the Mountaineers eight seconds later and that's the way it ended, 71-70 in favor of the no-names from Berkeley.

As usual, Cal had won with balance. Four players scored in double figures, led by Fitzpatrick with 20 points and Dalton with 15. As pleased as the Bears were to win, the finish left them shaken.

"What happened out there?" the Cal players asked each other. They had been taught to be analytical; accordingly, before they could fully appreciate the enormity of their accomplishment, they had some questions to answer in their own minds.

For West, the experience was empty. He had finished with 28 points, 11 rebounds, outstanding-player honors and a hole in the pit of his stomach. He fought back tears as he watched Al Buch, the Cal captain, accept the championship trophy.

"I wasn't too proud to cry," West said later. "What good are the fancy records and the high honors if you lose the championship by one point? I wouldn't want to play badly in any game or any tournament, but I'd rather have just played fair and had Imhoff or Oscar get the records and have my team get the title."

The smooth and always exciting Oscar Robertson was the big man in Cincinnati's potent offense.

West Virginia reached the Final Four thanks largely to the amazing talents of Jerry West.

1959 Tournament Results

First Round
West Virginia 82, Dartmouth 68
Boston U. 60, Connecticut 58
Navy 76, North Carolina 63
Louisville 77, E. Kentucky 63
Marquette 89, Bowling Green 71
DePaul 57, Portland 56
Idaho State 62, New Mexico St. 61

Second Round
W. Virginia 95, St. Jos. (Pa.) 92
Boston University 62, Navy 55
Louisville 76, Kentucky 61
Michigan State 74, Marquette 69
Kansas State 102, DePaul 70
Cincinnati 77, Texas Christian 73
St. Mary's (Cal.) 80, Idaho St. 71
California 71, Utah 53

Regional Third Place
Kentucky 98, Marquette 69
Navy 70, St. Joseph's (Pa.) 56
Texas Christian 71, DePaul 65
Idaho State 71, Utah 65

Regional Championships
West Virginia 86, Boston U. 82
Louisville 88, Michigan State 81
Cincinnati 85, Kansas State 75
California 66, St. Mary's (Cal.) 46

Semifinals
West Virginia 94, Louisville 79
California 64, Cincinnati 58

Third Place
Cincinnati 98, Louisville 85

Championship
California 71, West Virginia 70

STATISTICS

1959 CALIFORNIA

Head Coach—Pete Newell   **Final Record—25-4**

Player	Pos.	Hgt.	Wgt.	Cl.	G	FG	FGA	Pct.	FT.	FTA	Pct.	Reb.	Pts.	Avg.
Denny Fitzpatrick	G	6-0	160	Sr.	29	152	333	.456	82	96	.854	81	386	13.3
Darrall Imhoff	C	6-10	205	Jr.	29	134	316	.424	61	114	.535	318	329	11.3
Al Buch	G	6-2	190	Sr.	29	102	285	.358	62	96	.646	82	266	9.2
Bill McClintock	F	6-3	215	So.	28	79	190	.416	60	107	.561	205	218	7.8
Bob Dalton	F	6-3	175	Sr.	29	76	207	.367	59	89	.663	132	211	7.3
Jack Grout	F	6-5	190	Sr.	28	65	140	.464	23	36	.639	103	153	5.5
Dick Doughty	C	6-8	210	Jr.	29	41	97	.423	18	31	.581	76	100	3.4
Jim Langley	F	6-3½	184	Sr.	27	32	75	.427	6	18	.333	40	70	2.6
Bernie Simpson	G	6-0	172	Sr.	28	18	61	.295	22	32	.688	35	58	2.1
Dave Stafford	F	6-3	175	So.	8	4	14	.286	4	5	.800	7	12	1.5
Tandy Gillis	F	6-5½	190	Jr.	12	8	14	.571	0	0	.000	13	16	1.3
Earl Shultz	G	6-4	185	So.	17	6	20	.300	7	13	.538	8	19	1.1
Stan Morrison	F-C	6-7	195	So.	3	1	5	.200	1	1	1.000	3	3	1.0
Jerry Mann	G	6-2	172	Jr.	19	2	14	.143	9	12	.750	6	13	0.7
Bob Wendell	G	6-0	165	So.	5	0	1	.000	0	1	.000	3	0	0.0
Ned Averbuck	F	6-4	195	So.	2	0	0	.000	0	1	.000	0	0	0.0
Wally Torkells	F	6-4	195	Jr.	1	0	0	.000	0	1	.000	1	0	0.0
Ed Pearson	G	6-0	165	So.	1	0	0	.000	0	0	.000	0	0	0.0
Witto McCullough	G	5-11	155	So.	1	0	1	.000	0	0	.000	0	0	0.0
Team												194		
California					29	720	1773	.406	414	653	.634	1307	1854	63.9
Opponents					29	524	1484	.353	432	672	.643	1163	1480	51.0

1959 WEST VIRGINIA

Head Coach—Fred Schaus   **Final Record—29-5**

Player	Pos.	Hgt.	Wgt.	Cl.	G	FG	FGA	Pct.	FT.	FTA	Pct.	Reb.	Pts.	Avg.
Jerry West	F	6-3	175	Jr.	34	340	656	.518	223	320	.697	419	903	26.6
Bob Smith	G	6-4	185	Sr.	34	165	408	.404	100	140	.714	180	430	12.6
Bucky Bolyard	G	5-11	185	Sr.	34	135	281	.480	74	104	.712	105	344	10.1
Willie Akers	F	6-5	195	Jr.	34	93	236	.394	67	96	.698	245	253	7.4
Jim Ritchie	F	6-5	185	So.	34	84	187	.449	77	121	.636	169	245	7.2
Bob Clousson	C	6-6	200	Sr.	34	85	188	.452	72	108	.667	190	242	7.1
Lee Patrone	G	6-1	185	So.	31	74	162	.457	44	69	.638	70	192	6.2
Ronnie Retton	G	5-7	160	Sr.	33	43	100	.430	45	61	.738	47	131	4.0
Joe Posch	C	6-7	205	So.	28	23	60	.383	22	25	.880	77	68	2.4
Butch Goode	G	6-2	185	Jr.	15	16	28	.571	3	11	.273	19	35	2.3
Nick Visnic	G	6-0	165	So.	13	10	25	.400	4	10	.400	13	24	1.8
Jay Jacobs	G	5-9	160	Jr.	5	2	2	1.000	1	2	.500	0	5	1.0
Howie Schertzinger	F	6-4	190	Sr.	14	4	17	.235	2	5	.400	25	10	0.7
Jim Warren	G	6-2	170	Jr.	5	1	4	.250	0	0	.000	1	2	0.4
Bob Davis	C	6-4	215	So.	6	0	1	.000	0	0	.000	3	0	0.0
Team												247		
West Virginia					34	1075	2355	.456	734	1072	.685	1810	2884	84.8
Opponents					34	901	2302	.391	660	959	.688	1508	2462	72.4

1959 CINCINNATI

Head Coach—George Smith   **Final Record—26-4**

Player	Pos.	Hgt.	Wgt.	Cl.	G	FG	FGA	Pct.	FT.	FTA	Pct.	Reb.	Pts.	Avg.
Oscar Robertson	F	6-5	197	Jr.	30	331	650	.509	316	398	.794	489	978	32.6
Ralph Davis	G	6-4	180	Jr.	30	214	474	.451	37	62	.597	81	465	15.5
Mike Mendenhall	G	6-4	180	Sr.	26	137	267	.513	78	113	.690	83	352	13.5
Dave Tenwick	C	6-6	196	Sr.	30	105	271	.387	65	97	.670	222	275	9.2
Bob Wiesenhahn	F	6-4	212	So.	29	76	158	.481	29	47	.617	185	181	6.2
Mel Landfried	C	6-7	210	So.	22	19	41	.463	19	34	.559	98	57	2.6
Bill Whitaker	G	6-1	166	Sr.	19	20	41	.488	8	18	.444	14	48	2.5
Carl Bouldin	G	6-1	165	So.	29	30	67	.448	7	14	.500	26	67	2.3
Larry Willey	C-F	6-6	205	Jr.	25	23	43	.535	9	21	.429	71	55	2.2
Ron Dykes	F	6-4	204	Jr.	10	4	15	.267	3	6	.500	11	11	1.1
Rod Nall	F	6-4	185	Sr.	22	8	24	.333	6	9	.667	33	22	1.0
John Bryant	F	6-3	170	So.	13	2	10	.200	2	5	.400	5	6	0.5
Dick Cetrone	G	6-2	171	Sr.	7	1	1	1.000	0	3	.000	4	2	0.3
Dick Taylor	C	6-7	185	So.	4	0	0	.000	0	0	.000	1	0	0.0
Team												209		
Cincinnati					30	970	2062	.470	579	827	.700	1532	2519	84.0
Opponents					30	794	2060	.385	493	733	.673	1314	2081	69.4

1959 LOUISVILLE

Head Coach—Peck Hickman   **Final Record—19-12**

Player	Pos.	Hgt.	Wgt.	Cl.	G	FG	FGA	Pct.	FT.	FTA	Pct.	Reb.	Pts.	Avg.
John Turner	F	6-5	200	So.	31	184	454	.405	66	102	.647	300	434	14.0
Don Goldstein	F	6-5	185	Sr.	31	156	400	.390	115	153	.752	342	427	13.8
Fred Sawyer	C	6-11	235	So.	31	124	323	.384	114	198	.576	358	362	11.7
Roger Tieman	G	6-0	170	Jr.	31	119	337	.353	46	66	.697	63	284	9.2
Harold Andrews	G	6-2	180	Sr.	27	92	244	.377	54	79	.684	86	238	8.8
Ron Rubenstein*	G	6-1	180	So.	13	32	80	.400	23	39	.590	24	87	6.7
Howard Stacey	G	6-2	185	So.	28	51	143	.357	38	56	.679	42	140	5.0
Buddy Leathers	G	6-2	185	So.	22	32	72	.444	16	25	.640	40	80	3.6
Joe Kitchen	F	6-5	190	Jr.	28	36	97	.371	28	39	.718	81	100	3.6
Alex Mantel	F	6-2	175	Sr.	15	14	49	.286	6	11	.545	10	34	2.3
Bryan Hall	G	6-2	180	So.	2	1	1	1.000	2	2	1.000	0	4	2.0
Gerry Watkins	F	6-5	195	So.	6	4	15	.267	0	0	.000	7	8	1.3
Bill Geiling	C	6-7	195	Sr.	17	6	25	.240	5	11	.455	24	17	1.0
Harley Andrews	G	6-2	180	So.	10	1	21	.048	8	8	1.000	4	10	1.0
George Burnette	C	6-5	195	So.	2	0	3	.000	2	2	1.000	3	2	1.0
Team												312		
Louisville					31	852	2264	.376	523	791	.661	1696	2227	71.8
Opponents					31	729	2002	.364	620	934	.664	1570	2078	67.0

*Ineligible second semester.

1959 FINAL FOUR

At Louisville, Ky.
Semifinals

California	fg	fga	ft	fta	rb	pf	tp
McClintock	2	11	2	4	11	1	6
Dalton	2	4	3	4	7	5	7
Imhoff	10	25	2	5	16	4	22
Fitzpatrick	2	9	0	0	3	4	4
Buch	7	15	4	6	6	2	18
Grout	2	7	1	2	2	1	5
Simpson	1	2	0	0	3	0	2
Team					8		
Totals	26	73	12	21	56	17	64

Cincinnati	fg	fga	ft	fta	rb	pf	tp
Robertson	5	16	9	11	19	4	19
Wiesenhahn	5	11	0	0	3	1	10
Tenwick	2	6	1	1	4	1	5
Davis	6	15	1	2	2	2	13
Whitaker	4	7	0	2	3	3	8
Landfried	0	1	3	5	4	3	3
Bouldin	0	0	0	1	0	1	0
Team					7		
Totals	22	56	14	22	42	15	58

Halftime: Cincinnati 33-29. Officials: Mihalik and Bell.

West Virginia	fg	fga	ft	fta	rb	pf	tp
West	12	21	14	20	15	3	38
Akers	2	5	1	2	8	5	5
Clousson	5	5	2	2	4	4	12
Smith	5	9	2	4	5	0	12
Bolyard	4	10	5	7	3	1	13
Ritchie	2	6	0	2	5	1	4
Patrone	1	4	0	0	1	0	2
Retton	3	4	0	0	0	1	6
Schertzinger	0	0	0	0	0	0	0
Posch	1	2	0	0	0	0	2
Goode	0	0	0	0	0	0	0
Visnic	0	0	0	0	0	0	0
Team					8		
Totals	35	66	24	37	49	15	94

Louisville	fg	fga	ft	fta	rb	pf	tp
Goldstein	6	10	9	9	9	4	21
Turner	8	16	2	5	7	4	18
Sawyer	2	6	3	4	2	5	7
Tieman	1	7	1	1	0	0	3
Andrews	9	15	1	1	2	3	19
Kitchen	3	7	0	0	5	4	6
Leathers	2	8	1	1	3	3	5
Geiling	0	0	0	0	0	1	0
Stacey	0	0	0	0	2	1	0
Team					7		
Totals	31	69	17	21	37	25	79

Halftime: West Virginia 48-32.

Championship
March 21

West Virginia	fg	fga	ft	fta	rb	pf	tp
West	10	21	8	12	11	4	28
Akers	5	8	0	1	6	0	10
Clousson	4	7	2	3	4	4	10
Smith	2	5	1	1	2	3	5
Bolyard	1	4	4	4	3	4	6
Retton	0	0	2	2	0	0	2
Ritchie	1	4	2	2	4	0	4
Patrone	2	6	1	2	4	1	5
Team					7		
Totals	25	55	20	27	41	16	70

California	fg	fga	ft	fta	rb	pf	tp
McClintock	4	13	0	1	10	1	8
Dalton	6	11	3	4	2	4	15
Imhoff	4	13	2	2	9	3	10
Buch	0	4	2	2	3	2	2
Fitzpatrick	8	13	4	7	2	1	20
Simpson	0	1	0	0	2	2	0
Grout	4	5	2	2	3	1	10
Doughty	3	6	0	0	1	3	6
Team					7		
Totals	29	66	13	18	38	18	71

Halftime: California 39-33.

1960 Buckeyes Roll Behind Lucas

They formed the best and the brightest recruiting class in Ohio State basketball history. As freshmen, they routinely scored 100 points or more in a restricted schedule, and twice they defeated the varsity in closed scrimmages. It was by no means unusual for thousands to stream out of St. John Arena after the preliminary game even as the varsity was about to take on a Big Ten Conference opponent.

Foremost among the newcomers was Jerry Lucas, a 6-foot-8 center who had led Middletown High School to two Ohio championships. His team's only loss in three years was a one-point decision to Columbus North in his final game. Such was his good fortune, however, that he made the acquaintance of a Columbus North cheerleader who would later become his wife.

In addition to being an excellent shooter, Lucas was a skilled passer and superb rebounder particularly adept at starting the fast break. He rarely shot when it wasn't for the good of the team, was unfailingly polite and had been a straight-A student in high school.

His priorities were such that he sought and received an academic scholarship rather than a basketball grant. Lucas said he chose Ohio State because it was the only major school to stress education in its recruiting pitch.

"All the others talked only about basketball," he said.

The youngster had a photographic mind that enabled him to commit anything that interested him to memory. Lucas could recount how many telephone poles there were to a mile on the highway, how many steps he had to climb in the dormitory and each classroom building and all the cards that had been played in a hand. He could recite a long list of numbers, forward and backward.

"About the only time he did study," said John Havlicek, his roommate, "was the night before an exam. Then he'd stay up all night and wind up with a great mark." In his freshman year, in the College of Commerce, Lucas took 50 percent more than the normal workload and averaged just below a straight A.

Lucas would have been the centerpiece of whatever program he joined. But he was only one of several all-stars in his class at Ohio State. Havlicek, a scholastic football talent, was a 6-5 forward who excelled on defense. Mel Nowell was a 6-2 guard with extraordinary offensive gifts. Gary Gearhart and Bob Knight both had been exceptional scorers in high school.

It didn't take Coach Fred Taylor long to realize the future did not lie with the nucleus of the 1959 Ohio State team, his first varsity squad. That year he installed an offense to take advantage of Lucas' abilities, even though he wouldn't be available until the following season.

"We put in the whole kit and caboodle," the coach conceded later. "The boys learned the offense just the way we were going to play it with Lucas in 1960."

Lucas was an instant starter in his sophomore year, and Nowell also earned a starting berth alongside junior Larry Siegfried in the backcourt. Although Havlicek didn't start his first varsity game, he replaced an injured player in that contest and remained in the lineup thereafter. The fifth starter was forward Joe Roberts, a senior.

After early-season losses at Utah and Kentucky, the Buckeyes tore through the Big Ten. They compiled a 13-1 conference record, losing only to Indiana (a team they had edged earlier in the season). The league title meant an automatic berth in the 1960 NCAA Tournament. It was the school's first NCAA appearance since 1950 when, with Fred Taylor at center, Ohio State was defeated by eventual champion City College of New York by a single point.

"We immediately developed almost total communication on the floor," Havlicek said. "Our basketball intellects meshed perfectly. We never had to call a play. The offense was geared on keys and movement. You never saw us running down the floor holding up two or three fingers, or heard us calling out plays."

Lucas threw the outlet pass as well as anyone in basketball and the Buckeyes were able to overwhelm many of their opponents with the fast break. They moved the ball without excessive dribbling and rarely took a bad-percentage shot. In fact, Lucas led the nation in 1960 with 63.7 percent field-goal accuracy.

Ohio State was ranked third nationally preceding the NCAA Tournament, trailing only Oscar Robertson's Cincinnati team and defending national champion California. (The Bearcats were ranked No. 1 by the Associated Press, while Cal headed the

Ohio State Coach Fred Taylor (holding trophy) whoops it up with the rest of the
Buckeyes after the 1960 national championship game.

United Press International poll.) There was little
suspense in any of the four regionals. The Buckeyes
battered Western Kentucky, 98-79, and Georgia
Tech, 86-69, in the Mideast to qualify for the Final
Four in San Francisco. Cincinnati and California
also won handily in the Midwest and Far West, respectively. The three top clubs were joined by New
York University, surprise conqueror of West Virginia and Duke in the East Regional.

NYU was no match for Ohio State in the first
national semifinal at the Cow Palace. The Violets
were nervous at the outset and never did find their
composure. They bowed, 76-54, in a game that impressed few in the audience.

Cincinnati and California staged a significantly
better contest in the second game. The Bearcats, expecting to reverse their semifinal loss to Cal the previous year, opened a 20-11 lead midway through the
first half. But the Golden Bears seized the advantage
before halftime and held on in the second half. Two
baskets by Earl Shultz following Bearcat errors in
the closing two minutes sealed the 77-69 victory and
thwarted Robertson in his final attempt to play for
an NCAA titlist. The Big O had to settle for a third
consecutive scoring title as a memento of his last
collegiate season.

The final attraction pitted the national leaders in
offense and defense. Ohio State averaged 90.4 points

Buckeyes guard Larry Siegfried contributes two points toward Ohio State's 75-55 conquest of California in the 1960 championship game in San Francisco.

that season, while California yielded only 49.5 points per game. Playing just across the Bay from Berkeley and appearing in the NCAA championship game for a second consecutive year, the Golden Bears were favored.

California had lost three starters from the 1959 title team, but 6-10 center Darrall Imhoff had developed into a consensus All-America, 6-4 junior Bill McClintock was a fine rebounder and the entire team exercised the self-restraint demanded by Pete Newell. There appeared to be no team in America better suited to combat Ohio State than California, which had won 28 of 29 games. The Buckeyes were 24-3.

Such was Newell's reputation for defense that Taylor had sought his advice the previous summer.

"My team last year had the worst defensive record in Ohio State's history," Taylor said of a club

that yielded 122 points in one game and more than 90 points in four others. "I had to do something, and Pete's the best in the business at this. I asked him to help me and he did. He showed me everything. He confirmed some of my ideas and he gave me the courage to try things I was afraid were too radical. Last year, our boys couldn't have caught Marilyn Monroe in a phone booth."

So smooth and efficient was the Buckeyes' offense that Ohio State rarely was credited with good defense. But on the night of the championship game, the Buckeyes played superbly at both ends of the court. In the first half, they took 19 shots and hit a remarkable 16. Lucas missed one of six, Havlicek two of four and the other three starters—Roberts, Nowell and Siegfried—made a combined nine of nine.

Just as impressively, the Buckeyes held California

California's Tandy Gillis appears to have the edge but Ohio State's John Havlicek (blocked by Gillis) gets the rebound in the 1960 title game.

Ohio State guard Mel Nowell looks for a path to get past forward Tandy Gillis (32) and guard Bob Wendell (23) of the Bears.

to a shooting mark below 30 percent. Imhoff, who had scored 25 points in the victory over Cincinnati, was shackled by Lucas inside. The score at halftime was 37-19.

California fans were accustomed to their team falling behind, although not by this margin. Still, the Bears' press was a potent weapon and Newell unleashed it at the start of the second half. The defending champions did cut into the deficit, outscoring Ohio State 10-5 and suggesting the possibility of a memorable comeback. But no sooner had the hope been raised than it was crushed by the Buckeyes.

There was an open man or two on the floor and Ohio State began to exploit the situation. The mismatches enabled the Buckeyes to roll up a 20-point lead. Taylor began sending in reserves with five minutes left. All five regulars scored in double figures, topped by Lucas' 16 points, and the starters sank 75 percent of their floor shots (27 of 36).

California never was able to run its offense, to display the patience for which it was famous. Imhoff scored only eight points, and none of the Bears had more than 11.

"I used many of Pete's ideas," said Taylor after the Buckeyes' 75-55 triumph. "And they paid off for us tonight."

The defeat marked the last game as California coach for Newell, who was retiring to become the school's athletic director. But he did have the satisfaction that summer of coaching the U.S. Olympic team to a gold medal in Rome. The stars of that team included Lucas and Robertson.

1960 Tournament Results	
First Round	**Regional Third Place**
Duke 84, Princeton 60	W. Virginia 106, St. Jos. (Pa.) 100
West Virginia 94, Navy 86	Western Kentucky 97, Ohio 87
New York U. 78, Connecticut 59	Utah 89, Santa Clara 81
Ohio 74, Notre Dame 66	DePaul 67, Texas 61
W. Kentucky 107, Miami (Fla.) 84	**Regional Championships**
California 71, Idaho State 44	New York University 74, Duke 59
Oregon 68, New Mexico State 60	Ohio State 86, Georgia Tech 69
Utah 80, Southern Cal 73	Cincinnati 82, Kansas 71
DePaul 69, Air Force 63	California 70, Oregon 49
Second Round	**Semifinals**
Duke 58, St. Joseph's (Pa.) 56	Ohio State 76, New York U. 54
New York U. 82, West Virginia 81	California 77, Cincinnati 69
Georgia Tech 57, Ohio 54	**Third Place**
Ohio St. 98, W. Kentucky 79	Cincinnati 95, New York U. 71
Kansas 90, Texas 81	**Championship**
Cincinnati 99, DePaul 59	Ohio State 75, California 55
California 69, Santa Clara 49	
Oregon 65, Utah 54	

STATISTICS

1960 OHIO STATE

Head Coach—Fred Taylor | **Final Record—25-3**

Player	Pos.	Hgt.	Wgt.	Cl.	G	FG	FGA	Pct.	FT	FTA	Pct.	Reb.	Pts.	Avg.
Jerry Lucas	C	6-8	220	So.	27	283	444	.637	144	187	.770	442	710	26.3
Larry Siegfried	G	6-4	195	Jr.	28	145	311	.466	81	108	.750	107	371	13.3
Mel Nowell	G	6-2	174	So.	28	156	330	.473	56	73	.767	72	368	13.1
John Havlicek	F	6-5	196	So.	28	144	312	.462	53	74	.716	205	341	12.2
Joe Roberts	F	6-6	214	Sr.	28	135	281	.480	38	56	.679	194	308	11.0
Richard Furry	F	6-7	208	Sr.	28	61	134	.455	20	33	.606	92	142	5.1
Robert Knight	F	6-4	186	So.	21	30	74	.405	17	27	.630	42	77	3.7
Howard Nourse	C	6-7	183	Sr.	17	24	47	.511	5	5	1.000	46	53	3.1
Gary Gearhart	G	6-2	167	So.	19	21	52	.404	7	16	.438	22	49	2.6
Richie Hoyt	G	6-4	194	Jr.	23	22	52	.423	14	18	.778	19	58	2.5
David Barker	G	6-2	174	Sr.	16	11	27	.407	1	6	.167	13	23	1.4
John Cedargren	F	6-5	183	Sr.	13	7	12	.583	2	5	.400	14	16	1.2
James Allen	G	5-9	164	Jr.	7	1	9	.111	5	6	.833	2	7	1.0
Nelson Miller	G	6-3	187	So.	6	2	5	.400	1	3	.333	4	5	0.8
J. T. Landes	G	5-11	165	So.	6	2	8	.250	0	0	.000	1	4	0.7
Gary Milliken	G	5-11	171	Jr.	2	0	3	.000	0	0	.000	1	0	0.0
Team												139		
Ohio State					28	1044	2101	.497	444	619	.717	1415	2532	90.4
Opponents					28	753	1941	.388	447	645	.693	1032	1953	69.8

1960 CALIFORNIA

Head Coach—Pete Newell | **Final Record—28-2**

Player	Pos.	Hgt.	Wgt.	Cl.	G	FG	FGA	Pct.	FT	FTA	Pct.	Reb.	Pts.	Avg.
Darrall Imhoff	C	6-10	220	Sr.	30	154	346	.445	102	162	.630	371	410	13.7
Bill McClintock	F	6-4	215	Jr.	30	138	309	.447	83	136	.610	289	359	12.0
Tandy Gillis	F	6-6	190	Jr.	30	128	308	.416	33	47	.702	134	289	9.6
Earl Shultz	G	6-4	185	Jr.	30	105	232	.453	72	113	.637	110	282	9.4
Dick Doughty	C	6-8	210	Sr.	28	53	117	.453	50	75	.667	109	156	5.6
Bob Wendell	G	5-8	155	Jr.	30	49	183	.268	48	87	.552	83	146	4.9
Dave Stafford	F	6-3	180	Jr.	30	28	98	.286	56	90	.622	60	112	3.7
Jerry Mann	G	6-2	175	Sr.	29	33	91	.363	21	33	.636	34	87	3.0
John Wible	G	5-10	170	So.	8	4	8	.500	2	2	1.000	0	10	1.3
Stan Morrison	F-C	6-7	200	Jr.	21	7	23	.304	6	15	.400	32	20	1.0
Bill Alexander	G	6-1	175	Jr.	9	1	1	1.000	5	7	.714	1	7	0.8
Wally Torkells	F	6-4	205	Sr.	4	1	1	1.000	0	0	.000	3	2	0.5
Ed Pearson	G	6-0	165	Jr.	21	3	15	.200	3	5	.600	10	9	0.4
Ed Donahue	C	6-5	190	So.	5	1	5	.200	0	0	.000	1	2	0.4
Ned Averbuck	F	6-4	210	Jr.	13	0	3	.000	2	5	.400	6	2	0.2
Jim Butenschoen	G	6-2	170	Sr.	1	0	1	.000	0	0	.000	0	0	0.0
Neal Satre	F	6-3	180	So.	1	0	0	.000	0	0	.000	0	0	0.0
Team												162		
California					30	705	1741	.405	483	777	.622	1405	1893	63.1
Opponents					30	519	1423	.365	448	687	.652	1069	1486	49.5

1960 CINCINNATI

Head Coach—George Smith | **Final Record—28-2**

Player	Pos.	Hgt.	Wgt.	Cl.	G	FG	FGA	Pct.	FT	FTA	Pct.	Reb.	Pts.	Avg.
Oscar Robertson	F	6-5	198	Sr.	30	369	701	.526	273	361	.756	424	1011	33.7
Ralph Davis	G	6-4	180	Sr.	30	182	364	.500	46	70	.657	60	410	13.7
Paul Hogue	C	6-9	240	So.	30	152	264	.576	63	130	.485	331	367	12.2
Larry Willey	F	6-6	210	So.	30	98	157	.624	46	71	.648	145	242	8.1
Bob Wiesenhahn	F	6-4	215	Jr.	23	70	157	.446	32	50	.640	156	172	7.5
Carl Bouldin	G	6-1	166	Jr.	30	72	160	.450	31	48	.646	54	175	5.8
Sandy Pomerantz	F	6-6	195	So.	26	37	74	.500	20	34	.588	48	94	3.6
Tom Sizer	G	6-2	175	So.	27	22	57	.386	9	17	.529	24	53	2.0
Mel Landfried	C	6-8	215	Jr.	12	8	21	.381	5	10	.500	30	21	1.8
Jim Calhoun	G	6-0	175	So.	19	15	35	.429	3	9	.333	16	33	1.7
John Bryant	G	6-3	170	Jr.	22	6	18	.333	3	5	.600	16	15	0.7
Ron Reis	C	6-10	230	So.	10	2	9	.222	1	6	.167	7	5	0.5
Fred Dierking	F	6-6	210	So.	14	2	8	.250	0	5	.000	26	4	0.3
Team												185		
Cincinnati					30	1035	2025	.511	532	816	.652	1522	2602	86.7
Opponents					30	738	1924	.384	466	693	.672	1165	1942	64.7

1960 NEW YORK U.

Head Coach—Lou Rossini | **Final Record—22-5**

Player	Pos.	Hgt.	Wgt.	Cl.	G	FG	FGA	Pct.	FT	FTA	Pct.	Reb.	Pts.	Avg.
Tom Sanders	C	6-6	205	Sr.	27	211	408	.517	155	231	.671	411	577	21.4
Ray Paprocky	G	6-1	175	So.	26	108	286	.378	134	181	.740	87	350	13.5
Russ Cunningham	G	5-8	160	Jr.	27	114	289	.394	73	117	.624	56	301	11.1
Al Barden	F	6-5	205	Jr.	27	119	300	.397	53	90	.589	236	291	10.8
Al Filardi	F	6-5	215	So.	27	54	121	.446	35	54	.648	135	143	5.3
Jim Reiss	F	6-1	190	Jr.	26	38	120	.317	26	37	.703	89	102	3.9
Art Loche	G	6-0	175	Jr.	27	30	68	.441	39	47	.830	26	99	3.7
Mike DiNapoli	F	6-3	215	Jr.	19	28	65	.431	6	11	.545	48	62	3.3
Bob Bigelow	G	5-9	150	Jr.	8	3	10	.300	4	4	1.000	2	10	1.3
Richard Keith	F	6-4	175	Sr.	10	4	22	.182	2	3	.667	11	10	1.0
Leo Murphy	C	6-9	220	Sr.	17	7	31	.226	2	4	.500	33	16	0.9
Bob Regan	G	6-0	170	Sr.	11	5	15	.333	1	3	.333	3	11	0.9
Bill McBain	F	6-4	185	So.	6	0	0	.000	5	6	.833	1	5	0.8
Bernie Mlodinoff	G	6-0	185	So.	15	2	8	.250	7	8	.875	3	11	0.7
Team												160		
NYU					27	723	1743	.415	542	796	.681	1301	1988	73.6
Opponents					27	659	1627	.405	436	681	.640	1185	1754	65.0

1960 FINAL FOUR

At San Francisco
Semifinals

California	fg	fga	ft	fta	rb	pf	tp
McClintock	5	12	8	10	10	3	18
Gillis	5	10	3	3	4	4	13
Imhoff	10	21	5	5	11	4	25
Shultz	4	7	3	5	3	1	11
Wendell	0	4	4	7	3	2	4
Stafford	1	4	2	2	0	2	4
Doughty	1	3	0	0	2	1	2
Team					10		
Totals	26	61	25	32	43	17	77

Cincinnati	fg	fga	ft	fta	rb	pf	tp
Robertson	4	16	10	12	10	4	18
Willey	4	9	1	2	4	4	9
Hogue	5	9	4	6	11	5	14
Davis	4	8	2	2	2	1	10
Bouldin	4	7	0	0	4	4	8
Sizer	0	0	0	1	1	0	0
Wiesenhahn	5	8	0	0	9	3	10
Bryant	0	1	0	0	1	3	0
Pomerantz	0	0	0	0	0	0	0
Team					2		
Totals	26	58	17	23	40	24	69

Halftime: California 34-30.

Ohio State	fg	fga	ft	fta	rb	pf	tp
Nowell	3	8	0	0	0	4	6
Gearhart	1	3	1	1	1	3	3
Havlicek	2	8	2	2	10	0	6
Cedargren	1	1	0	0	1	0	2
Lucas	9	15	1	1	13	2	19
Furry	4	7	2	3	7	2	10
Hoyt	0	0	2	2	0	0	2
Roberts	3	6	1	2	7	0	7
Barker	1	1	0	0	0	0	2
Siegfried	7	11	5	5	3	3	19
Knight	0	0	0	0	1	0	0
Nourse	0	0	0	0	0	0	0
Team					5		
Totals	31	60	14	16	48	14	76

New York Univ.	fg	fga	ft	fta	rb	pf	tp
DiNapoli	0	0	0	0	1	0	0
Paprocky	4	17	1	2	0	3	9
Cunningham	4	14	6	8	3	2	14
Loche	0	3	1	1	0	0	1
Murphy	1	1	0	0	0	2	2
Barden	2	11	4	4	8	2	8
Sanders	4	13	0	3	22	2	8
Reiss	0	0	0	0	1	1	0
Keith	0	1	0	0	0	0	0
Filardi	6	12	0	1	6	3	12
Regan	0	1	0	0	0	1	0
Mlodinoff	0	1	0	0	0	0	0
Team					3		
Totals	21	74	12	20	44	14	54

Halftime: Ohio State 37-28.

Championship
March 19

Ohio State	fg	fga	ft	fta	rb	pf	tp
Havlicek	4	8	4	5	6	2	12
Roberts	5	6	0	1	5	1	10
Lucas	7	9	2	2	10	2	16
Nowell	6	7	3	3	4	2	15
Siegfried	5	6	3	6	1	2	13
Gearhart	0	1	0	0	1	0	0
Cedargren	0	0	1	2	1	1	1
Furry	2	4	0	0	3	1	4
Hoyt	0	1	0	0	0	0	0
Barker	0	0	0	0	0	0	0
Knight	0	1	0	0	0	1	0
Nourse	2	3	0	0	3	1	4
Team					1		
Totals	31	46	13	19	35	13	75

California	fg	fga	ft	fta	rb	pf	tp
McClintock	4	15	2	3	3	3	10
Gillis	4	9	0	0	1	1	8
Imhoff	3	9	2	2	5	2	8
Wendell	0	6	4	4	0	2	4
Shultz	2	8	2	2	4	4	6
Mann	3	5	1	1	0	0	7
Doughty	4	5	3	3	6	1	11
Stafford	0	1	1	2	0	1	1
Morrison	0	0	0	0	1	1	0
Averbuck	0	0	0	1	1	0	0
Pearson	0	0	0	0	0	0	0
Alexander	0	0	0	0	0	0	0
Team					7		
Totals	20	59	15	18	28	15	55

Halftime: Ohio State 37-19.

1961 The Best Team in Ohio

The basketball euphoria in Ohio did not extend all the way to the state's southwestern corner. While Ohio State fans reveled in the 1960 national championship and eagerly anticipated two more seasons with Jerry Lucas, there was a genuine sense of loss at the University of Cincinnati. It was felt, among other places, at the box office.

Not only had the great Oscar Robertson graduated, but he also had signed with the Cincinnati Royals of the National Basketball Association. This left the university's program with a twofold problem: It had to replace a superstar, and it had to face up to constant comparison with a legend. Many fans decided to take their business crosstown to the Big O's new home, the Cincinnati Gardens.

Even George Smith, the man who had coached Robertson, abandoned the Bearcats' basketball team. He decided this was the perfect time to assume the position of athletic director at the university. Ed Jucker, his longtime assistant, inherited a team with talent but with no great expectations.

"My main concern," Jucker said, "is to make the games close. And for us to stay close, we have to change our style." And so, from a high-scoring, free-wheeling outfit that was as entertaining as any college aggregation in the country, Cincinnati evolved into a cautious, defense-oriented team whose approach to basketball did little to attract fans. At least in the early going.

In fact, in the first month of the season, the Bearcats' average home attendance was down by thousands compared with the Robertson-era crowds. It didn't help that Cincinnati lost three of its first eight games, including wipeouts to Missouri Valley Conference rivals St. Louis (17-point margin) and Bradley (19 points). At least one player suggested to Jucker that it might be better to let the team run.

But the coach was convinced that a pressing defense and a ball-control offense would succeed with this team, while past tactics would fail.

"None of you can be an Oscar Robertson," Jucker told the players, "but with all five working together, maybe we can do as much." Jucker had yet to envision a trip to the Final Four. With Cincinnati suffering losses in its first two league games,

the coach's goal was to make a good showing in the Missouri Valley race.

The victory the Bearcats needed to foster a belief

John Havlicek (5) was part of the Ohio State machine that chewed up Kentucky in a regional final encounter.

The victory the Bearcats needed to foster a belief in the system and in themselves occurred against non-conference rival Dayton. Staging an impressive rally, Cincinnati beat the Flyers by 10 points. The team embraced Jucker's style. As the victories started to come with regularity, the fans returned.

Meanwhile, up in Columbus, the Buckeyes were proving themselves to be every bit as good as imagined. Their fast break was beautiful to behold, they had exquisite offensive balance and Jerry Lucas, their star, was utterly selfless. The question was not whether they were the best team in the nation but whether they were the best team of all time. Ohio State sailed undefeated through the Big Ten Conference schedule and arrived at the Mideast Regional in Louisville's Freedom Hall with a record of 24-0.

There, it received a real scare from hometown Louisville. Triple-teaming Lucas and daring the other Buckeyes to beat them, the Cardinals led by five points with three minutes remaining. Ohio State rallied to tie, and John Havlicek's long jump shot finally provided the Buckeyes with the winning margin in a 56-55 escape.

"I was guarded so tightly," said Lucas, who was limited to nine points, "I felt like I was in jail."

He broke out the following night, making 14 of 18 shots from the field, scoring 33 points and collecting 30 rebounds against Kentucky. The 87-74 romp by Ohio State convinced Kentucky Coach Adolph Rupp.

"That team," the Baron said, "is truly great. They're going all the way."

So it appeared. And while Cincinnati raised a few eyebrows by polishing off Texas Tech and fourth-ranked Kansas State in the Midwest Regional, increasing its winning streak to 20 games, it still was regarded as nothing more than a potential victim for the Buckeyes. Far West Regional titlist Utah and East champion St. Joseph's joined the two Ohio schools in Kansas City for the Final Four.

As expected, Ohio State conducted a clinic against St. Joseph's, crushing Jack Ramsay's well-coached team, 95-69. In the other semifinal, Cincinnati hounded Utah's high-scoring center, Billy (The Hill) McGill, and won convincingly, 82-67. While McGill managed 25 points, he made only 11 of 31 field-goal attempts.

There was no doubt the Bearcats could take one exceptional player out of his game, but what could they do against such a complete team as Ohio State? The Kansas City newspapers weren't optimistic. One even joked that the Bearcats could not be found in their rooms because they had checked out of town. Given little chance to win, Jucker said his team felt pressured by expectations that "we would

be the victims of another blowout."

Fred Taylor, the Ohio State coach, was taking nothing for granted. The scouting report he delivered to his team noted Cincinnati's great strength on the backboards. Especially notable was the work of 6-foot-9 center Paul Hogue and forward Bob Wiesenhahn, whose 215 pounds appeared to have been sculpted. The Bearcats did not have a strong bench and were particularly thin at center. Taylor

Cincinnati center Paul Hogue (22) reaches for a rebound in front of Ohio State big man Jerry Lucas.

underlined Hogue's name and said, "Make him foul."

In his pregame instructions, Jucker told his team to concentrate on the first 20 minutes.

"If we can stay in the game for the first half," he

said, "we can beat them." He also wanted the Bearcats to send a fourth man to the boards, to stop the Ohio State fast break before it could get started. He didn't want the Buckeyes running under any circumstance.

As it happened, both teams spent a lot of time sitting in the Municipal Auditorium. The consolation game between St. Joseph's and Utah went on and on and on. It wasn't until the fourth overtime that St. Joseph's secured a 127-120 victory, no triumph for the kind of defense Jucker preached.

Regardless of the long wait, the Bearcats remained calm and confident. Without a great scorer, they had developed into a team whose offense was spread among all five starters. Tom Thacker, the lithe 6-2 forward, was the most creative of the Cincinnati players, point guard Tony Yates the most steady and Carl Bouldin the best outside shooter. Given the presence of Hogue—a tree trunk with glasses—and Wiesenhahn, the Bearcats had been outrebounded only once all season.

The game unfolded exactly as Jucker had planned. Cincinnati's superior rebounding denied Ohio State many fast-break opportunities. As well as Lucas was shooting, the Bearcats' defense had forced him from the low post, where his whirling moves were most effective. Neither team conceded a basket in the first half, which ended with the Buckeyes clinging to a 39-38 lead.

Cincinnati had not been blown out and the tempo of the game was in its favor. But Ohio State had induced Hogue to foul three times. Jucker thought about sitting his pivotman down at the start of the second half, but he didn't dare risk changing the momentum. He stayed with Hogue, and the big man finished the game with the same three fouls.

Ohio State had concentrated on stopping Hogue in the first half and succeeded by dropping guard Larry Siegfried, the Buckeyes' captain, back inside. Bouldin took advantage of that tactic to make five consecutive shots in the second half and Cincinnati grabbed a six-point lead. Slowed to a shot-a-minute pace, Ohio State came back to edge five points ahead at 58-53. The Bearcats clawed back to tie the score, 59-59, and even seized the lead on Thacker's short jump shot. But a driving layup by a brash Ohio State junior reserve named Bob Knight made it 61-61 with 1:41 to play, and that was the score when regulation play ended.

It was fast approaching midnight when Cincinnati took its final, slow steps to the title that had eluded the Bearcats during the Robertson era. The Bearcats began the overtime with two free throws by Hogue and steadily pulled away to a stunning

Ohio State's John Havlicek goes up for a jump shot over Cincinnati's Tom Thacker.

Ohio State's Larry Siegfried clutches the second-place trophy and fights back the tears.

70-65 victory. In the final 25 minutes, they had held one of college basketball's most dynamic offenses to 26 points.

Lucas finished as the game's high scorer with 27 points, but he was ably assisted only by Siegfried, who had 14. The Buckeyes' stronger bench resulted in a scoring edge of only 4-0.

By contrast, Hogue was the only Cincinnati starter not to score in double figures—and he had nine points.

Although Lucas was honored as the Final Four's outstanding player for the second consecutive year, the Bearcats had won just as Jucker had pledged, as a team. They celebrated together while Siegfried, the huge second-place trophy clutched to his chest, placed a towel over his head and cried.

1961 Tournament Results

First Round
Princeton 84, George Wash. 67
St. Bonaventure 86, Rhode Isl. 76
Wake Forest 97, St. John's 74
Louisville 76, Ohio 70
Morehead State 71, Xavier 66
Houston 77, Marquette 61
Arizona State 72, Seattle 70
Southern Cal 81, Oregon 79

Second Round
*St. Jos. (Pa.) 72, Princeton 67
Wake Forest 78, St. Bon. 73
Ohio State 56, Louisville 55
Kentucky 71, Morehead State 64
Cincinnati 78, Texas Tech 55
Kansas State 75, Houston 64
Utah 91, Loyola (Cal.) 75
Arizona St. 86, Southern Cal 71

Regional Third Place
St. Bonaventure 85, Princeton 67
Louisville 83, Morehead State 61
Loyola (Cal.) 69, Southern Cal 67
Texas Tech 69, Houston 67

Regional Championships
*St. Jos. (Pa.) 96, Wake F'r'st 86
Ohio State 87, Kentucky 74
Cincinnati 69, Kansas State 64
Utah 88, Arizona State 80

Semifinals
Ohio St. 95, *St. Joseph's (Pa.) 69
Cincinnati 82, Utah 67

Third Place
*St. Jos. (Pa) 127, Utah 120 (4ot)

Championship
Cincinnati 70, Ohio State 65 (ot)

*St. Joseph's participation in 1961 tournament voided.

STATISTICS

1961 CINCINNATI

Head Coach—Ed Jucker   Final Record—27-3

Player	Pos.	Hgt.	Wgt.	Cl.	G	FG	FGA	Pct.	FT	FTA	Pct.	Reb.	Pts.	Avg.
Bob Wiesenhahn	F	6-4	215	Sr.	30	206	428	.481	101	149	.678	299	513	17.1
Paul Hogue	C	6-9	235	Jr.	30	208	391	.532	87	168	.518	374	503	16.8
Tom Thacker	F	6-2	170	So.	30	139	351	.396	91	133	.684	284	369	12.3
Carl Bouldin	G	6-1	174	Sr.	30	140	327	.428	72	90	.800	85	352	11.7
Sandy Pomerantz	F	6-6	205	Jr.	2	6	10	.600	3	4	.750	7	15	7.5
Tony Yates	G	6-0	175	So.	30	84	173	.486	53	88	.602	106	221	7.4
Dale Heidotting	F-C	6-8	190	So.	26	39	91	.429	15	23	.652	96	93	3.6
Fred Dierking	F-C	6-6	210	Jr.	25	29	60	.483	7	15	.467	55	65	2.6
Jim Calhoun	G	6-0	175	Jr.	17	14	37	.378	7	13	.538	9	35	2.1
Tom Sizer	G	6-2	180	Jr.	24	18	48	.375	12	16	.750	23	48	2.0
Larry Shingleton	G	5-10	158	So.	20	7	24	.292	4	10	.400	11	18	0.9
Mark Altenau	F	6-3	195	So.	18	6	14	.429	4	9	.444	11	16	0.9
Ron Reis	C	6-10	240	Jr.	11	1	7	.143	1	4	.250	6	3	0.3
Frank Turner	F	6-7	191	So.	3	0	1	.000	0	0	.000	0	0	0.0
Team												187		
Cincinnati					30	897	1962	.457	457	722	.633	1553	2251	75.0
Opponents					30	693	1844	.376	437	662	.660	1153	1823	60.8

1961 OHIO STATE

Head Coach—Fred Taylor   Final Record—27-1

Player	Pos.	Hgt.	Wgt.	Cl.	G	FG	FGA	Pct.	FT	FTA	Pct.	Reb.	Pts.	Avg.
Jerry Lucas	C	6-8	224	Jr.	27	256	411	.623	159	208	.764	470	671	24.9
Larry Siegfried	G	6-4	192	Sr.	28	151	314	.481	123	143	.860	141	425	15.2
John Havlicek	F	6-5	192	Jr.	28	173	321	.539	61	87	.701	244	407	14.5
Mel Nowell	G	6-2	166	Jr.	28	155	317	.489	70	90	.778	80	380	13.6
Richie Hoyt	F	6-4	191	So.	28	60	140	.429	33	43	.767	80	153	5.5
Robert Knight	F	6-4	180	Jr.	28	54	136	.397	15	26	.577	77	123	4.4
Gary Gearhart	G	6-2	170	Jr.	24	25	66	.379	17	26	.654	24	67	2.8
Richard Reasbeck	G	6-0	171	So.	20	22	45	.489	6	11	.545	24	50	2.5
Douglas McDonald	F	6-5	191	So.	22	18	43	.419	4	12	.333	48	40	1.8
Kenneth Lee	C	6-5	174	So.	20	9	38	.237	9	10	.900	45	27	1.4
J. T. Landes	G	5-11	168	Jr.	13	6	17	.353	3	5	.600	8	15	1.2
Donald Furry	C	6-2	185	Jr.	3	1	2	.333	1	2	.500	2	3	1.0
Nelson Miller	F	6-3	187	Jr.	16	6	20	.300	1	2	.500	14	13	0.8
James Allen	G	5-9	170	Sr.	7	1	5	.200	2	4	.500	1	4	0.6
Raymond Apple	F	6-3	184	Sr.	8	1	6	.167	1	2	.500	4	3	0.4
John Noble	F	6-4	176	So.	6	1	3	.333	0	0	.000	3	2	0.3
Gary Milliken	G	5-11	168	Sr.	4	0	2	.000	0	0	.000	1	0	0.0
Team												152		
Ohio State					28	939	1886	.498	505	671	.753	1418	2383	85.1
Opponents					28	690	1895	.364	460	691	.666	1053	1840	65.7

1961 ST. JOSEPH'S (PA.)

Head Coach—Jack Ramsay   Final Record—25-5

Player	Pos.	Hgt.	Wgt.	Cl.	G	FG	FGA	Pct.	FT	FTA	Pct.	Reb.	Pts.	Avg.
Jack Egan	F	6-6	215	Sr.	29	247	600	.412	142	200	.710	348	636	21.9
Billy Hoy	G	6-0	165	So.	29	133	361	.368	82	121	.678	139	348	12.0
Jim Lynam	G	5-8	160	So.	30	110	260	.423	118	143	.825	71	338	11.3
Vince Kempton	C	6-8	225	Sr.	30	136	277	.491	64	84	.762	306	336	11.2
Tom Wynne	F	6-5	225	So.	30	109	304	.359	60	93	.645	190	278	9.3
Frank Majewski	F	6-3	200	Jr.	30	99	248	.399	66	93	.710	200	264	8.8
Bob Gormley	G-F	6-0	180	Jr.	22	36	75	.480	10	18	.556	23	82	3.7
Harry Booth	G	5-9	160	Jr.	30	24	95	.316	33	45	.733	44	93	3.1
Paul Westhead	G	6-2	175	Jr.	16	12	30	.400	7	13	.538	17	31	1.9
Bob Dickey	F-G	6-3	190	Jr.	21	11	34	.324	1	5	.200	45	23	1.1
Dan Bugey	F-G	6-3	180	Jr.	11	3	16	.188	1	1	1.000	11	6	0.5
St. Joseph's					30	926	2300	.403	583	816	.714	1394	2435	81.2
Opponents					30	804	1959	.410	550	791	.695	1266	2158	71.9

Team Rebounds (both teams)—337.

1961 UTAH

Head Coach—Jack Gardner   Final Record—23-8

Player	Pos.	Hgt.	Wgt.	Cl.	G	FG	FGA	Pct.	FT	FTA	Pct.	Reb.	Pts.	Avg.
Billy McGill	C	6-9	200	Jr.	31	342	649	.527	178	249	.715	430	862	27.8
Jim Rhead	F	6-4	205	Sr.	31	164	331	.495	92	138	.667	321	420	13.5
Rich Ruffell	F	6-3	190	So.	31	157	313	.502	57	86	.663	182	371	12.0
Joe Morton	G	6-0	175	Sr.	31	130	269	.483	70	110	.636	88	330	10.6
Ed Rowe	G	6-2	165	Jr.	31	61	136	.449	17	22	.773	73	139	4.5
Joe Aufderheide	F	6-5	204	Jr.	31	52	112	.464	32	45	.711	113	136	4.4
Bo Crain	F-G	6-2	170	So.	31	55	113	.487	25	39	.641	111	135	4.4
Jim Thomas	C-F	6-5	200	Sr.	23	24	82	.293	28	38	.737	62	76	3.3
Bob Cozby	F-G	6-1	177	So.	18	6	11	.545	12	18	.667	21	24	1.3
Barry Epstein	G	6-1	185	Sr.	12	5	19	.263	6	17	.353	11	16	1.3
Neil Jenson	G	5-9	140	So.	15	6	16	.375	2	3	.667	5	14	0.9
Mel Yergensen	G	6-0	172	So.	9	4	9	.444	0	1	.000	5	8	0.9
Jerry Peterson	F	6-4	195	So.	9	1	8	.125	3	5	.600	7	5	0.6
Team												163	*2	
Utah					31	1007	2068	.487	522	771	.677	1592	2538	81.9
Opponents					31	840	2187	.384	498	779	.639	1346	2178	70.3

*Scored by opponent.

1961 FINAL FOUR

At Kansas City
Semifinals

Cincinnati

	fg	fga	ft	fta	rb	pf	tp
Wiesenhahn	5	7	4	6	5	4	14
Thacker	1	7	5	6	6	3	7
Hogue	9	16	0	4	14	4	18
Bouldin	7	14	7	8	3	0	21
Yates	4	6	5	7	5	2	13
Heidotting	3	8	1	1	6	1	7
Sizer	1	1	0	0	0	0	2
Dierking	0	0	0	0	1	1	0
Altenau	0	0	0	0	0	0	0
Shingleton	0	0	0	0	0	0	0
Calhoun	0	0	0	0	0	0	0
Team					5		
Totals	30	59	22	32	45	15	82

Utah

	fg	fga	ft	fta	rb	pf	tp
Ruffell	6	11	2	2	5	4	14
Rhead	2	5	4	6	10	4	8
McGill	11	31	3	4	8	4	25
Morton	3	9	1	1	1	4	7
Rowe	1	3	0	0	1	2	2
Crain	2	5	0	1	5	4	4
Aufderheide	2	3	2	2	3	1	6
Cozby	0	0	0	0	0	0	0
Thomas	0	0	1	2	0	0	1
Jenson	0	0	0	0	0	0	0
Team					6		
Totals	27	67	13	18	39	23	67

Halftime: Cincinnati 35-20. Officials: Wertz and Fox.

Ohio State

	fg	fga	ft	fta	rb	pf	tp
Nowell	7	11	1	1	0	2	15
Havlicek	5	6	1	2	9	2	11
Lucas	10	11	9	10	13	2	29
Hoyt	2	6	0	1	3	4	4
Siegfried	8	11	5	7	9	4	21
Knight	2	5	1	2	3	2	5
McDonald	1	4	0	0	2	1	2
Gearhart	0	2	2	2	1	2	2
Reasbeck	0	1	0	1	1	1	0
Lee	1	1	0	0	2	0	2
Miller	0	0	0	0	0	0	0
Landes	2	2	0	0	0	1	4
Team					9		
Totals	38	60	19	25	50	20	95

St. Joseph's, Pa.

	fg	fga	ft	fta	rb	pf	tp
Lynam	2	5	3	4	0	0	7
Hoy	6	17	1	1	2	2	13
Majewski	4	12	5	7	4	1	13
Egan	3	15	2	3	5	2	8
Kempton	5	9	8	8	8	3	18
Wynne	1	9	2	2	4	4	4
Booth	0	3	2	2	2	3	2
Gormley	1	5	2	2	1	3	4
Westhead	0	1	0	1	2	0	0
Bugey	0	0	0	0	1	1	0
Dickey	0	0	0	0	0	0	0
Team					9		
Totals	22	76	25	30	35	18	69

Halftime: Ohio State 45-28. Officials: Glennon and Filiberti.

Championship
March 25

Cincinnati

	fg	fga	ft	fta	rb	pf	tp
Wiesenhahn	8	15	1	1	9	3	17
Thacker	7	21	1	4	7	0	15
Hogue	3	8	3	6	7	3	9
Yates	4	8	5	5	2	3	13
Bouldin	7	12	2	3	4	4	16
Sizer	0	0	0	0	1	0	0
Heidotting	0	0	0	0	0	0	0
Team					6		
Totals	29	64	12	19	36	13	70

Ohio State

	fg	fga	ft	fta	rb	pf	tp
Havlicek	1	5	2	2	4	2	4
Hoyt	3	5	1	1	3	7	7
Lucas	10	17	7	7	12	4	27
Nowell	3	9	3	3	3	1	9
Siegfried	6	10	2	3	3	2	14
Knight	1	3	0	1	1	4	2
Gearhart	1	1	0	0	0	1	2
Team					8		
Totals	25	50	15	16	32	14	65

Halftime: Ohio State 39-38. Regulation Score: 61-61. Officials: Fox and Filiberti.

1962 Bearcats Prove Their Point

At Cincinnati, satisfaction was a temporary condition. Although the Bearcats had won the 1961 national championship, they hadn't convinced skeptics that they were the best team in their own state. To many Ohio State supporters and to some members of the media, Cincinnati's great triumph was a fluke.

Such talk goaded the Bearcats as they prepared to defend their title. They had proven something to themselves and their fans in '61. Now they faced the challenge of proving their worth to the outside world.

A nucleus of outstanding players returned to both finalists of the '61 NCAA Tournament. Paul Hogue, Tony Yates and Tom Thacker reported to Coach Ed Jucker at Cincinnati. Ohio State Coach Fred Taylor had the services of consensus All-America Jerry Lucas, John Havlicek and Mel

Cincinnati Coach Ed Jucker gets a triumphant ride after his Bearcats had defeated in-state rival Ohio State to win their second straight national championship.

Nowell for another season. There was every reason to believe the two teams had not seen the last of each other.

The new faces at Cincinnati included 6-foot-8 George Wilson, a terrific leaper whose presence enabled Jucker to shift the 6-2 Thacker to the backcourt, and 6-5 Ron Bonham. The latter had been a celebrated high school star in Indiana, where his jump shot was regarded as an automatic two points. Their availability significantly raised the athletic skill of the Bearcats, although they needed some time to absorb Jucker's highly disciplined system.

It didn't take long, however, for even the offense-minded Bonham to fall into line.

"He (Jucker) gives us three weeks of defense before we're allowed a shot in scrimmage," the sophomore forward said. "Even a lousy defensive player like me learned something."

By the midway point of the regular season, the Bearcats had lost only two games—the first by one point, the second by two points in overtime. Applying Jucker's lessons as diligently as it had the previous season, Cincinnati soon appeared equal—if not superior—to the team that had surprised the nation in '61. Still, in the minds of many, the Bearcats continued to suffer by comparison with Ohio State.

Up in Columbus, the Buckeyes were playing as well as they ever had in the Lucas era. With the addition of a strong, versatile sixth man in 6-8 Gary Bradds, Ohio State rolled to 22 consecutive victories and its smallest winning margin was eight points. Even a late-season loss at Wisconsin, after the Buckeyes had clinched the Big Ten Conference championship, failed to loosen Ohio State's grip on the No. 1 ranking.

Of course, a victory over the Buckeyes was cause for great rejoicing in Madison. More than 13,000 fans spilled out of the stands and applauded with such vigor that an amused Lucas picked up several timepieces from the arena floor.

"People clapped so hard," Havlicek reported, "that their watches flew off."

If there was any doubt about the pecking order in Ohio, it was erased at a banquet in Columbus, the state capital as well as site of the state university. There, Gov. Michael DiSalle proclaimed Ohio State the No. 1 team in the country. Although this did not differ from the opinions expressed in the weekly wire-service polls, it was not well-received in Cincinnati, a sizable city that would have its say in the forthcoming election. There are those who contend the sentiment may have contributed to the man losing his job.

Yet, the Buckeyes did sail into the NCAA Tournament as the favorites. In many minds, they were the uncrowned champions. And their performance in the Mideast Regional at Iowa City did nothing to discourage such an assessment. When Western Kentucky tied Lucas into knots with double- and triple-teaming, Bradds provided a spark with 10 points and seven rebounds and the Buckeyes romped, 93-73. On the following night, Havlicek throttled Kentucky scoring ace Cotton Nash and Lucas scored 25 points in the first half and 33 overall in a 74-64 triumph.

Cincinnati didn't experience any difficulty working through the Midwest Regional at Manhattan, Kan. The Bearcats' problem was qualifying for the regional. Led by Chet (the Jet) Walker, an outstanding Bradley team had tied Cincinnati for the Missouri Valley Conference title, forcing a one-game playoff at Evansville, Ind., for the league's automatic NCAA Tournament berth.

Ohio State star Jerry Lucas (11) gets his layup blocked by Cincinnati center Paul Hogue.

If the playoff proved anything, it was that Cincinnati's defense was as tight as ever. The Bearcats slowly turned the screws on Bradley, which had been averaging 80.6 points per game, and prevailed 61-46. They yielded the same paltry point total in regional victories over Creighton and Colorado. The scores were 66-46 and 73-46, respectively.

Clearly, an all-Ohio final loomed as the teams arrived in Louisville for the Final Four. Ohio State was a sizable favorite over Atlantic Coast Conference representative Wake Forest, and Cincinnati appeared too stingy and strong for the exciting-but-small UCLA Bruins. Even the UCLA coach, in his first national semifinals in 14 years at the school, conceded as much.

"I don't think we can beat Cincinnati at its slow-down game," John Wooden said, "and I don't think we can beat them at our fast one, either."

It appeared Wooden was understating his team's plight at the outset of the game. Grabbing every loose ball and scoring on every possession, Cincinnati gained an 18-4 advantage. The Bearcats were not in the habit of squandering leads but UCLA, a nine-time loser during the regular season, kept its poise and forced a halftime tie on the shot-making of forward Gary Cunningham and guard John Green and the leadership of sophomore Walt Hazzard.

Furthermore, the Far West Regional champion Bruins hung with the Bearcats throughout the second half. Only Hogue was playing to his potential for Cincinnati, and UCLA was getting a remarkable team effort. The teams were deadlocked at 70-70 and the Bruins were holding for a last shot in the final two minutes.

"I was afraid," admitted the imperturbable Yates, the Air Force veteran and walk-on who set the tone for the defending national champions.

A whistle with 1:34 remaining reversed the momentum of the game. Hazzard was assessed an offensive foul—Wooden later said the charging call was "questionable"—and the ball was turned over to Cincinnati. The Bearcats ran down the clock and called a timeout with 10 seconds left. Jucker instructed his team to get the ball to Hogue, who had scored Cincinnati's last 14 points and 36 in all. But Hogue was covered down low and Thacker, unable to penetrate, took a long jump shot. It fell, and so did UCLA, 72-70.

There was no mystery about the other semifinal. Ohio State had demoralized Wake Forest by 22 points on the Demon Deacons' home court early in the season and the Deacons weren't a match for the Buckeyes the second time, either. Havlicek harassed

burly Len Chappell, Wake Forest's 6-8 consensus All-America, into errant shots and the Buckeyes took a 46-34 halftime lead en route to an 84-68 victory over the East Regional titlist.

However, Ohio State paid a price in the game. With about 6½ minutes left, Lucas jumped for a rebound, brushed the leg of Wake Forest's 6-11 Bob Woollard and landed awkwardly. He fell to the floor and had to be helped off the court after wrenching his left knee.

Now the long-awaited rematch of college basketball's heavyweights had a sub-plot. It was articulated by Lucas'

Cincinnati's Tom Thacker gets his shot blocked by Ohio State's Gary Bradds.

Cincinnati's Tom Thacker grabs a loose ball as an Ohio State player tumbles over his back.

wife, Treva, who sent a message into the Ohio State dressing room after the game.

"Will he be able to play tomorrow?" she asked on behalf of everyone in Freedom Hall, not to mention millions of television viewers.

"Will the sun come up in the East?" Lucas replied.

It did. And Lucas, his left leg encased in tape, did appear at center court for the opening tap the next night. He was not the same player who had dominated games for three seasons. But Hogue had something to do with that. The big Cincinnati center had become a force at both ends of the court and he was determined to show everyone that he was Lucas' equal.

Indeed, this was the chance for all the Bearcats to prove they were better than their more-publicized rivals.

"We were nervous before the first (championship) game," Yates said. "But this time, we were totally confident going in. We felt we had superior talent up and down the line."

They also had superior strategy. Hampered by his knee injury and matched against the aggressive Hogue, Lucas needed all the rebounding help he could get from Havlicek. But Havlicek was assigned to guard Cincinnati's best shooter, Bonham, as Jucker suspected he would be. So the Bearcats' coach instructed Bonham to remain on the perimeter, effectively keeping Havlicek away from the backboards.

"We sort of stood there and held hands at mid-court," Havlicek said, "while the others played four-on-four."

Havlicek had 11 points and Bonham 10, effectively negating the other's efforts. But Cincinnati's other four players were far superior. Lucas was limited to 11 points and it was Bradds, the sophomore reserve, who led the Buckeyes in scoring with 15. Meanwhile, Hogue gave a towering performance with 22 points and 19 rebounds and Thacker added 21 points. The Bearcats boosted a 37-29 halftime lead to 18 and won easily and convincingly, 71-59.

The point had been remade. Public opinion—and a governor's vote—to the contrary, Cincinnati once again was the nation's best team.

"We really proved it this time," Yates said. "You don't repeat flukes."

1962 Tournament Results

First Round
Wake Forest 92, Yale 82
New York U. 70, Massachusetts 50
Villanova 90, West Virginia 75
Butler 56, Bowling Green 55
Western Kentucky 90, Detroit 81
Texas Tech 68, Air Force 66
Creighton 87, Memphis State 83
Oregon State 69, Seattle 65
Utah State 78, Arizona State 73

Second Round
Wake Forest 96, St. Jos. (Pa.) 85
Villanova 79, New York U. 76
Kentucky 81, Butler 60
Ohio State 93, W. Kentucky 73
Colorado 67, Texas Tech 60
Cincinnati 66, Creighton 46
Oregon State 69, Pepperdine 67
UCLA 73, Utah State 62

Regional Third Place
New York U. 94, St. Jos. (Pa.) 85
Butler 87, Western Kentucky 86
Creighton 63, Texas Tech 61
Pepperdine 75, Utah State 71

Regional Championships
Wake Forest 79, Villanova 69
Ohio State 74, Kentucky 64
Cincinnati 73, Colorado 46
UCLA 88, Oregon State 69

Semifinals
Ohio State 84, Wake Forest 68
Cincinnati 72, UCLA 70

Third Place
Wake Forest 82, UCLA 80

Championship
Cincinnati 71, Ohio State 59

STATISTICS

1962 CINCINNATI

Head Coach—Ed Jucker　　　　**Final Record—29-2**

Player	Pos.	Hgt.	Wgt.	Cl.	G	FG	FGA	Pct.	FT.	FTA	Pct.	Reb.	Pts.	Avg.
Paul Hogue	C	6-9	235	Sr.	31	211	424	.498	99	175	.566	383	521	16.8
Ron Bonham	F	6-5	200	So.	31	174	382	.455	95	125	.760	156	443	14.3
Tom Thacker	G-F	6-2	170	Jr.	31	134	331	.405	74	121	.612	266	342	11.0
George Wilson	F-C	6-8	210	So.	31	109	216	.505	67	101	.663	248	285	9.2
Tony Yates	G	6-1	175	Jr.	31	97	253	.383	61	91	.670	94	255	8.2
Fred Dierking	F	6-6	210	Sr.	28	42	97	.433	30	51	.588	81	114	4.1
Larry Shingleton	G	5-10	158	Jr.	25	42	101	.416	14	25	.560	34	98	3.9
Dale Heidotting	F	6-8	195	Jr.	22	24	47	.511	20	35	.571	50	68	3.1
Tom Sizer	G	6-2	180	Sr.	25	26	57	.456	15	24	.625	33	67	2.7
Jim Calhoun	G	6-0	175	Sr.	18	14	38	.368	2	3	.667	7	30	1.7
Bill Abernethy	F	6-5	200	So.	3	1	4	.250	0	0	.000	2	2	0.7
Ron Reis	C	6-10	235	Sr.	15	3	10	.300	2	4	.500	2	8	0.5
Larry Elasser	G	6-2	185	So.	10	2	7	.286	1	4	.250	5	5	0.5
Team												175		
Cincinnati					31	879	1967	.447	480	759	.632	1536	2238	72.2
Opponents					31	663	1799	.369	381	556	.685	1142	1707	55.1

1962 OHIO STATE

Head Coach—Fred Taylor　　　　**Final Record—26-2**

Player	Pos.	Hgt.	Wgt.	Cl.	G	FG	FGA	Pct.	FT.	FTA	Pct.	Reb.	Pts.	Avg.
Jerry Lucas	C	6-8	223	Sr.	28	237	388	.611	135	169	.799	499	609	21.8
John Havlicek	F	6-5	205	Sr.	28	196	377	.520	83	109	.761	271	475	17.0
Mel Nowell	G	6-2	174	Sr.	28	140	358	.391	72	92	.783	80	352	12.6
Richard Reasbeck	G	6-0	178	Jr.	27	97	218	.445	19	29	.655	63	213	7.9
Douglas McDonald	F	6-5	203	Jr.	28	92	180	.511	34	53	.642	99	218	7.8
Gary Bradds	C	6-8	207	So.	27	50	72	.694	23	40	.575	72	123	4.6
Gary Gearhart	G	6-2	172	Sr.	19	32	86	.372	21	36	.583	40	85	4.5
James Doughty	F	6-4	211	Jr.	26	39	92	.424	23	31	.742	61	101	3.9
Robert Knight	F	6-4	191	Sr.	25	35	89	.393	9	11	.818	38	79	3.2
Richard Taylor	G	6-4	193	So.	23	9	24	.375	10	15	.667	12	28	1.2
Donald Flatt	G	6-4	205	So.	24	9	28	.321	8	16	.500	18	26	1.1
Gene Lane	F	6-8	209	So.	18	8	23	.348	2	4	.500	16	18	1.0
Donald Furry	F	6-3	198	Sr.	2	1	1	1.000	0	1	.000	0	2	1.0
LeRoy Frazier	G	6-5	167	So.	21	7	24	.292	1	5	.200	11	15	0.7
John Noble	C	6-4	190	Jr.	5	0	0	.000	0	0	.000	2	0	0.0
Donald DeVoe	F	6-5	183	So.	5	0	1	.000	0	0	.000	1	0	0.0
Team												108		
Ohio State					28	952	1961	.485	440	611	.720	1391	2344	83.7
Opponents					28	706	1848	.382	443	622	.712	971	1855	66.3

1962 WAKE FOREST

Head Coach—Horace (Bones) McKinney　　　　**Final Record—22-9**

Player	Pos.	Hgt.	Wgt.	Cl.	G	FG	FGA	Pct.	FT.	FTA	Pct.	Reb.	Pts.	Avg.
Len Chappell	C	6-8	240	Sr.	31	327	597	.548	278	383	.726	470	932	30.1
Billy Packer	G	5-9	180	Sr.	31	180	372	.484	77	97	.794	71	437	14.1
Dave Wiedeman	G	5-11	165	Jr.	31	153	359	.426	57	78	.731	143	363	11.7
Bob Woollard	C	6-11	222	Jr.	31	98	196	.500	57	79	.722	228	253	8.2
Frank Christie	F	6-4	185	So.	31	86	210	.410	52	77	.675	159	224	7.2
Tommy McCoy	F	6-3	175	Sr.	30	43	97	.443	24	34	.706	59	110	3.7
Bill Hull	F	6-6	220	Sr.	23	24	52	.462	14	31	.452	87	62	2.7
Richard Carmichael	F	6-5	195	So.	25	23	75	.307	15	25	.600	44	61	2.4
Butch Hassell	G	5-11	175	So.	27	17	42	.405	3	7	.429	13	37	1.4
Al Koehler	G	6-2	185	Jr.	19	8	25	.320	11	16	.688	19	27	1.4
Ted Zawacki	F	6-4	185	Jr.	9	1	2	.500	9	15	.600	4	11	1.2
Brad Brooks	F	6-7	200	So.	13	2	8	.250	2	3	.667	7	6	0.5
Trask Buxton	..	......	......	......	4	0	1	.000	0	0	.000	0	0	0.0
Team												154		
Wake Forest					31	962	2036	.472	599	845	.709	1458	2523	81.4
Opponents					31	876	2026	.432	552	780	.708	1240	2304	74.3

1962 UCLA

Head Coach—John Wooden　　　　**Final Record—18-11**

Player	Pos.	Hgt.	Wgt.	Cl.	G	FG	FGA	Pct.	FT.	FTA	Pct.	Reb.	Pts.	Avg.
John Green	G	6-2	198	Sr.	29	179	459	.390	201	262	.767	185	559	19.3
Gary Cunningham	F	6-6	190	Sr.	29	151	351	.430	86	104	.827	201	388	13.4
Walt Hazzard	G	6-2	180	So.	28	134	338	.396	102	143	.713	163	370	13.2
Pete Blackman	F	6-5	188	Sr.	29	123	245	.502	88	113	.779	163	334	11.5
Fred Slaughter	C	6-5	230	So.	28	88	196	.449	40	78	.513	268	216	7.7
Dave Waxman	F-C	6-6	210	Jr.	28	50	132	.379	32	49	.653	114	132	4.7
Kim Stewart	F-C	6-4	205	So.	28	26	57	.456	21	33	.636	82	73	2.6
Bill Hicks	G	6-2	180	Sr.	21	18	45	.400	2	6	.333	23	38	1.8
Jim Rosvall	G	6-3	172	So.	17	11	34	.324	2	3	.667	17	24	1.4
Mike Huggins	G	5-10½	162	So.	4	2	3	.667	1	3	.333	2	5	1.3
Larry Gower	G	5-11	165	So.	11	3	10	.300	6	8	.750	7	12	1.1
Jim Milhorn	G	5-10	145	Jr.	21	6	31	.194	5	10	.500	9	17	0.8
Rich Gugat	F	6-2	185	So.	14	4	11	.364	1	3	.333	9	9	0.6
Team												208		
UCLA					29	795	1912	.416	587	815	.720	1451	2177	75.1
Opponents					29	787	1997	.394	444	663	.670	1295	2018	69.6

1962 FINAL FOUR

At Louisville, Ky.
Semifinals

Wake Forest	fg	fga	ft	fta	rb	pf	tp
Chappell	10	24	7	11	18	5	27
Christie	0	2	1	1	4	2	1
Woollard	1	3	1	2	3	2	3
Wiedeman	5	16	3	6	8	0	13
Packer	8	14	1	2	5	3	17
Hull	0	2	0	0	2	2	0
McCoy	0	1	2	2	1	1	2
Carmichael	0	0	0	0	1	1	0
Hassell	1	2	0	0	0	0	2
Zawacki	0	0	1	3	0	0	1
Koehler	0	1	0	0	0	0	0
Brooks	0	1	2	2	1	1	2
Totals	25	66	18	29	43	17	68

Ohio State	fg	fga	ft	fta	rb	pf	tp
Havlicek	9	19	7	9	16	3	25
McDonald	5	10	1	2	5	3	11
Lucas	8	16	3	4	16	1	19
Nowell	2	11	0	0	2	4	4
Reasbeck	5	7	0	0	3	4	10
Gearhart	2	5	0	0	0	4	4
Doughty	2	4	4	4	5	1	8
Bradds	0	0	0	1	4	3	0
Knight	0	2	0	0	2	3	0
Flatt	0	0	1	2	0	0	1
Taylor	0	0	0	0	0	1	0
Frazier	1	1	0	0	0	0	2
Totals	34	75	16	22	53	24	84

Halftime: Ohio State 46-34.

UCLA	fg	fga	ft	fta	rb	pf	tp
Blackman	2	3	0	0	2	5	4
Cunningham	8	14	3	3	9	2	19
Slaughter	1	4	0	0	7	5	2
Green	9	16	9	11	7	1	27
Hazzard	5	10	2	3	6	2	12
Waxman	2	3	2	3	3	1	6
Stewart	0	0	0	0	1	2	0
Totals	27	50	16	20	35	18	70

Cincinnati	fg	fga	ft	fta	rb	pf	tp
Bonham	8	14	3	6	2	4	19
Wilson	1	6	1	2	4	1	3
Hogue	12	18	12	17	19	3	36
Thacker	1	7	0	0	4	3	2
Yates	4	10	2	3	3	3	10
Sizer	1	3	0	0	1	3	2
Totals	27· 58	18	24	28	33	17	72

Halftime Score: 37-37.

Championship
March 24

Ohio State	fg	fga	ft	fta	rb	pf	tp
Havlicek	5	14	1	2	9	1	11
McDonald	0	1	3	3	1	2	3
Lucas	5	17	1	2	16	3	11
Reasbeck	4	6	0	0	4	8	8
Nowell	4	16	1	1	6	2	9
Doughty	0	1	0	0	2	2	0
Gearhart	1	4	0	0	4	3	2
Bradds	5	7	5	6	4	2	15
Totals	24	66	11	14	42	19	59

Cincinnati	fg	fga	ft	fta	rb	pf	tp
Bonham	3	12	4	4	6	3	10
Wilson	1	6	4	4	11	2	6
Hogue	11	18	0	2	19	2	22
Thacker	6	14	9	11	6	2	21
Yates	4	8	4	7	1	1	12
Sizer	0	0	0	0	0	0	0
Totals	25	58	21	28	43	10	71

Halftime: Cincinnati 37-29.

1963 Loyola Races Into Spotlight

Loyola couldn't go anywhere without toting its city along with it. The designation "of Chicago" was necessary baggage if people were to differentiate the university from Loyola of the South (in New Orleans) and Loyola of Los Angeles. Both those smaller Jesuit schools were NCAA Tournament participants before the Chicago institution gladly accepted its first invitation in 1963.

Loyola's entrance into the tournament was the initial step of a journey with historic implications in both basketball and social justice. The civil-rights movement was gaining momentum in the United States and the Ramblers, with four black starters, found themselves in the vanguard. Loyola had ventured into the South in the 1962 and 1963 seasons, and its players had been forced to stay in separate hotels in New Orleans and had been denied service in Houston. The Ramblers' coach, George Ireland, had raised a ruckus about the inequities, which focused attention not only on segregation, but also on

the basketball program he had built.

There was much about the program to admire. For the second consecutive season, adhering to Ireland's philosophy that "the object of the game is to put the ball in the basket," Loyola had led the nation in scoring. A third-place finish in the 1962 National Invitation Tournament had provided the impetus for a truly remarkable year in which the Ramblers lost only two games and 6-foot-2 star Jerry Harkness, a former track man who didn't play organized basketball until his senior year of high school, had been chosen a consensus All-America.

But there was so much more involved, including one meeting notable for its contribution to race relations. A staggering 111-42 rout of Tennessee Tech in the first round of the NCAA Tournament sent Loyola to the Mideast Regional semifinals at East Lansing, Mich. The opposition was scheduled to be Southeastern Conference champion Mississippi

Loyola Coach George Ireland celebrates with his victorious Ramblers.

State.

In the past, the Bulldogs had bypassed the tournament because they might be required to play against teams with black players. Only the previous year, in fact, Mississippi State had turned down an invitation after compiling a 24-1 record and earning a No. 4 national ranking. But in 1963, Coach Babe McCarthy and his players chose to ignore the wishes of state authorities. They slipped surreptitiously out of Starkville before possibly being served with a court order blocking the trip.

Oh, they would be playing against blacks, all right. By March, Loyola's fame had spread clear into Mississippi.

"I'm happy my boys could come," McCarthy said upon his arrival at East Lansing, "just to see a team like Loyola play." As it developed, Mississippi State didn't travel that distance and risk the wrath of politicians and citizens just

Cincinnati's Tony Yates drives toward the basket as Loyola's Jerry Harkness gives chase.

to watch. The methodical Bulldogs slowed the pace to their liking, took a 7-0 lead and limited explosive Loyola to 26 points in the first half. The Ramblers nevertheless led by seven points at intermission and pulled out a 61-51 victory, but this was one contest in which the outcome seemed secondary to the fact the game was played at all.

When Harkness, the Loyola captain, shook hands with Mississippi State captain Joe Dan Gold before the game, flashbulbs popped throughout the field house.

"I couldn't imagine what was going on," Harkness said. To him and his teammates, it was just another game en route to the Final Four, one the Ramblers were hard-pressed to win. It was only later that Harkness was struck by the consequence of the moment.

Mississippi State stayed another night and defeated Bowling Green, 65-60, in the Mideast consolation game for its first NCAA Tournament victory. Following that game, Loyola dismantled Big Ten Conference co-champion Illinois, 79-64, to earn a ticket to the Final Four in Louisville. The season was getting more interesting with every game.

The field at Freedom Hall was made up of the Associated Press' three top-ranked teams—in order, Cincinnati, Duke and Loyola—and one interloper. Oregon State, which had overwhelmed fourth-ranked Arizona State in the Far West Regional final, was an item of extreme curiosity. In Mel Counts, the Beavers featured a 7-foot center with a fine outside shot. Their floor leader, Terry Baker, had won the Heisman Trophy three months earlier as the country's outstanding college football player.

Oregon State's opponent in the national semifinals would be Cincinnati, which had given little cause for the public to believe it would not become the first school to win three consecutive NCAA basketball titles. Although Paul Hogue had graduated, the Midwest Regional champion Bearcats had enjoyed another phenomenal season, losing only to Wichita State (by one point) in 26 games. They led the nation in defense, yielding 52.9 points per game during the 1963 season.

In Hogue's absence, Coach Ed Jucker had moved George Wilson into the pivot, shifted 6-2 Tom Thacker from guard to forward (where he had played as a sophomore two seasons earlier) and inserted unselfish Larry Shingleton into the backcourt. Tony Yates and Ron Bonham were back at their guard and forward slots. What the Bearcats lost in rebounding strength, they appeared to gain in defensive quickness and ballhandling.

So overpowering did Cincinnati appear that on one occasion, a 70-40 thrashing of a sound St. Louis team, Jucker apologized to the Billikens' athletic director. "I'm sorry we had to be so good," he said.

There wasn't much question that offense would prevail in the Loyola-Duke semifinal. The East Regional-winning Blue Devils were a tall team that used the fast break at every opportunity and boasted the wire services' Player of the Year in senior Art Heyman. However, Heyman shot poorly against Loyola and the Ramblers ran wild, 94-75. As impressive as that was, it didn't sway impartial observers, not after Cincinnati dismissed Oregon State, 80-46.

The title-game matchup of the leading offensive and defensive teams in the country suggested a classic. Of course, the same kind of pairing had occurred in 1960, when Ohio State rolled to a 20-point victory over California.

Loyola, which had faced all kinds of pressure during a memorable season, seemed on the brink of a nervous breakdown in the first 20 minutes of the 1963 NCAA championship game. The Ramblers missed 13 of their first 14 shots, fell behind 19-9 and

saw Harkness fail to make a field goal in the first half, which ended with Cincinnati on top, 29-21.

Harkness, the cool New Yorker, was shaken.

"I didn't want to be embarrassed," said Harkness, reflecting on the fact that family and friends were watching the game that marked Loyola's only appearance on national television all season. "I was thinking, 'Don't let them kill us.' "

Cincinnati did go for the kill at the outset of the second half. With Bonham popping from the corners, the Bearcats boosted their lead to 45-30. There were 12 minutes remaining.

The team with the steely composure suddenly and inexplicably lost its grip on the game. Cincinnati began making turnovers against the frantic Loyola press. Wilson picked up his fourth foul and was replaced for a four-minute stretch by Dale Heidotting, the only reserve on either team to play. The Bearcats began misfiring from the free-throw line. And, gradually, the lead dwindled—to 48-39, 48-43

Little Loyola guard John Egan looks for a shot during the 1963 title game against Cincinnati.

and, with 2:42 left, 50-48. Yates and Thacker, as well as Wilson, had four fouls. The Cincinnati delay game was malfunctioning.

"Our execution down the stretch wasn't as good as it had been," Yates acknowledged.

Loyola's Les Hunter cut the deficit to one at 53-52 by tipping in a Harkness shot, and Harkness immediately fouled Shingleton to stop the clock with 12 seconds left. Shingleton made the first free throw, but his second attempt rolled off the rim. Hunter rebounded, flipped an outlet pass to Ron Miller and Miller got the ball into the hands of Harkness.

Much later, when they looked at game films, the Ramblers would needle Miller about running with the ball—not just walking with it. But everyone in Freedom Hall—the officiating team included—was caught up in the drama of Loyola's magnificent comeback. Harkness shot the ball from instinct. Five seconds were left on the clock.

"I don't think I felt anything," Harkness said. "When I shot, I normally had a touch for it. But this time I never felt it. It was almost like somebody guided it for me."

The shot was true, and Cincinnati didn't react quickly enough to call a timeout that would have set up a last-second shot. An overtime would be required to break the 54-54 tie.

Harkness scored first for Loyola in the extra session, and the teams traded baskets until it was 58-58. The Ramblers, trying to play for one shot, were forced into a jump-ball situation when guard John Egan, attempting to latch on to a poor pass, was tied up by Shingleton. Loyola, though, regained possession when Egan tipped the ball to Miller.

Once more, the Ramblers went to Harkness. He dribbled around looking for an opening, but he couldn't shake Bonham. With the clock running down, Harkness went up for his shot. Bonham brushed the ball.

"I felt I was losing it," Harkness said. "I grabbed it again. Then I saw Les out of the corner of my eye."

He passed to Hunter, who took the jump shot from the left side of the lane. The ball bounced over the rim, directly into the hands of Vic Rouse, Loyola's other big man who was undefended to the right of the basket.

"I didn't tip it," Rouse said. "I grabbed it tight, jumped up and laid it in. I'd missed a couple like that and I wanted to be so sure. Oh, my, it felt good."

The basket, coming with one second left, lifted Loyola to an improbable victory and dethroned a Cincinnati team that felt it couldn't be beaten. The Ramblers, who averaged nearly 92 points per game that season, needed an overtime to get to 60 but still won. While missing 61 of 84 field-goal attempts, Loyola had committed only three turnovers com-

Cincinnati's Ron Bonham drives around Loyola's Vic Rouse during the Ramblers' title-clinching victory.

pared with 16 for Cincinnati.

"Our game plan worked for us 99 out of 100 times," Cincinnati's Yates said after Loyola's 60-58 triumph. "On this night, it didn't."

And the championship belonged to Loyola of Chicago, the 100-1 shot.

1963 Tournament Results

First Round
New York U. 93, Pittsburgh 83
West Virginia 77, Connecticut 71
St. Joseph's (Pa.) 82, Princeton 81
Bowling Green 77, Notre Dame 72
Loyola (Ill.) 111, Tenn. Tech 42
Oklahoma City 70, Colorado St. 67
Texas 65, Texas Western 47
Arizona State 79, Utah State 75
Oregon State 70, Seattle 66

Second Round
Duke 81, New York University 76
St. Jos. (Pa.) 97, W. Virginia 88
Illinois 70, Bowling Green 67
Loyola (Ill.) 61, Mississippi St. 51
Colorado 78, Oklahoma City 72
Cincinnati 73, Texas 68
Arizona State 93, UCLA 79
Oregon St. 65, San Francisco 61

Regional Third Place
Miss. St. 65, Bowling Green 60
West Virginia 83, New York U. 73
Texas 90, Oklahoma City 83
San Francisco 76, UCLA 75

Regional Championships
Duke 73, St. Joseph's (Pa.) 59
Loyola (Ill.) 79, Illinois 64
Cincinnati 67, Colorado 60
Oregon St. 83, Arizona State 65

Semifinals
Loyola (Ill.) 94, Duke 75
Cincinnati 80, Oregon State 46

Third Place
Duke 85, Oregon State 63

Championship
Loyola (Ill.) 60, Cincinnati 58 (ot)

STATISTICS

1963 LOYOLA OF CHICAGO

Head Coach—George Ireland   **Final Record—29-2**

Player	Pos.	Hgt.	Wgt.	Cl.	G	FG	FGA	Pct.	FT	FTA	Pct.	Reb.	Pts.	Avg.
Jerry Harkness	F	6-2	175	Sr.	31	244	484	.504	174	240	.725	236	662	21.4
Leslie Hunter	C	6-7	212	Jr.	31	206	389	.530	114	156	.731	354	526	17.0
John Egan	G	5-10	175	Jr.	31	140	388	.361	146	185	.789	111	426	13.7
Vic Rouse	F	6-6	210	Jr.	31	169	418	.404	81	111	.730	375	419	13.5
Ron Miller	G	6-2	190	Jr.	31	170	419	.406	71	102	.696	166	411	13.3
Billy Smith*	F-C	6-5	197	So.	20	54	115	.470	46	75	.613	109	154	7.7
Pablo Robertson*	G	5-9	142	So.	17	39	94	.415	8	13	.615	49	86	5.1
Earl Johnson**	F	6-4	203	So.	15	16	42	.381	14	21	.667	53	46	3.1
Jim Reardon	F	6-4	215	Sr.	14	9	28	.321	13	16	.813	30	31	2.2
Dan Connaughton	G	6-1	182	So.	17	14	33	.424	5	8	.625	19	33	1.9
Chuck Wood	F-G	6-3	175	Jr.	17	11	28	.393	10	14	.714	33	32	1.9
Rich Rochelle	C	6-9	249	Jr.	14	9	25	.360	3	8	.375	20	21	1.5
Team												235		
Loyola					31	1081	2463	.439	685	949	.722	1790	2847	91.8
Opponents					31	838	2089	.401	434	664	.654	1335	2110	68.1

*Ineligible second semester. **Withdrew from school during second semester.

1963 CINCINNATI

Head Coach—Ed Jucker   **Final Record—26-2**

Player	Pos.	Hgt.	Wgt.	Cl.	G	FG	FGA	Pct.	FT	FTA	Pct.	Reb.	Pts.	Avg.
Ron Bonham	F	6-5	200	Jr.	28	208	449	.463	173	194	.892	178	589	21.0
Tom Thacker	F	6-2	170	Sr.	28	169	357	.473	103	155	.665	281	441	15.8
George Wilson	C	6-8	210	Jr.	28	160	299	.535	101	170	.594	314	421	15.0
Tony Yates	G	6-1	175	Sr.	28	90	222	.405	33	62	.532	115	213	7.6
Larry Shingleton	G	5-10	160	Sr.	28	43	115	.374	18	29	.621	46	104	3.7
Dale Heidotting	F-C	6-8	195	Sr.	21	20	37	.541	11	17	.647	47	51	2.4
Ken Cunningham	G	5-11	165	So.	17	10	23	.435	13	19	.684	9	33	1.9
Larry Elsasser	G	6-2	185	Jr.	14	11	22	.500	4	8	.500	9	26	1.9
Fritz Meyer	G	5-10	150	So.	18	11	23	.478	7	15	.467	12	29	1.6
Bill Abernethy	F	6-5	200	Jr.	11	7	17	.412	3	4	.750	11	17	1.5
Gene Smith	F	6-6	210	So.	21	11	31	.355	7	17	.412	42	29	1.4
Team												149	2	
Cincinnati					28	740	1595	.464	473	690	.686	1213	1955	69.8
Opponents					28	595	1567	.380	290	449	.646	990	1480	52.9

1963 DUKE

Head Coach—Vic Bubas   **Final Record—27-3**

Player	Pos.	Hgt.	Wgt.	Cl.	G	FG	FGA	Pct.	FT	FTA	Pct.	Reb.	Pts.	Avg.
Art Heyman	F	6-5	205	Sr.	30	265	586	.452	217	314	.691	324	747	24.9
Jeff Mullins	F	6-4	185	Jr.	30	256	466	.549	96	131	.733	241	608	20.3
Jay Buckley	C	6-10	215	Jr.	30	130	217	.599	76	145	.524	298	336	11.2
Fred Schmidt	G	6-3	190	Sr.	29	104	198	.525	32	38	.842	53	240	8.3
Buzzy Harrison	G	6-3	180	Jr.	27	73	148	.493	21	33	.636	103	167	6.2
Hack Tison	C	6-10	205	So.	30	61	112	.545	25	41	.610	133	147	4.9
Denny Ferguson	G	6-0	170	So.	25	42	78	.538	13	15	.867	36	97	3.9
Ron Herbster	G	6-2	178	So.	30	30	66	.455	24	31	.774	33	84	2.8
Brent Kitching	F	6-6	215	So.	17	10	22	.455	14	18	.778	8	34	2.0
Ray Cox	G	6-0	165	Jr.	13	4	8	.500	4	8	.500	8	12	0.9
Bob Jamieson	F	6-5	205	Jr.	12	5	6	.833	1	3	.333	11	11	0.9
Scott Williamson	F	6-5	210	Jr.	11	3	8	.375	4	4	1.000	10	10	0.9
Fred Cox	C	6-5	205	Jr.	2	0	0	.000	1	2	.500	1	1	0.5
Ted Mann Jr.	F	6-5	197	So.	12	1	11	.091	0	1	.000	10	2	0.2
Team												199		
Duke					30	984	1926	.511	528	784	.673	1468	2496	83.2
Opponents					30	819	2037	.402	431	611	.705	1127	2069	70.0

1963 OREGON STATE

Head Coach—Amory (Slats) Gill   **Final Record—22-9**

Player	Pos.	Hgt.	Wgt.	Cl.	G	FG	FGA	Pct.	FT	FTA	Pct.	Reb.	Pts.	Avg.
Mel Counts	C	7-0	228	Jr.	31	253	574	.441	155	189	.820	485	661	21.3
Terry Baker	G	6-3	196	Sr.	25	120	280	.429	94	127	.740	71	334	13.4
Steve Pauly	F	6-4	200	Sr.	31	121	289	.419	42	69	.609	188	284	9.2
Frank Peters	G	6-2	195	So.	31	114	296	.385	55	75	.733	145	283	9.1
Jim Jarvis	G	6-0	160	So.	31	76	233	.326	39	54	.722	94	191	6.2
Jim Kraus	F	6-7	180	So.	26	36	87	.414	33	42	.786	117	105	4.0
Tim Campbell	C	6-6	196	Sr.	17	15	37	.405	11	18	.611	34	41	2.4
Gary Rossi	G	6-1	175	Sr.	29	21	58	.362	14	19	.737	22	56	1.9
Rex Benner	F	6-3	185	Jr.	21	12	27	.444	0	1	.000	23	24	1.1
Dave Hayward	G	5-10	170	Sr.	21	10	29	.345	3	6	.500	16	23	1.1
Ray Torgerson	F	6-4	197	Jr.	26	11	25	.440	0	8	.000	27	22	0.8
Grant Harter	C	6-11	230	Jr.	3	0	5	.000	0	0	.000	3	0	0.0
Team												191		
Oregon State					31	789	1940	.407	446	608	.738	1416	2024	65.3
Opponents					31	688	1834	.375	499	794	.628	1297	1875	60.4

1963 FINAL FOUR

At Louisville, Ky.
Semifinals

Cincinnati	fg	fga	ft	fta	rb	pf	tp
Bonham	3	12	8	9	5	3	14
Thacker	5	8	4	8	11	5	20
Wilson	8	9	8	12	13	2	24
Yates	5	9	2	3	5	1	12
Shingleton	1	2	0	0	2	1	2
Heidotting	0	0	1	2	1	1	1
Cunningham	2	3	0	0	0	1	4
Meyer	1	1	1	2	1	1	3
Smith	1	3	0	2	1	1	2
Elsasser	1	2	0	1	1	0	2
Abernethy	1	2	0	0	3	0	2
Totals	28	51	24	39	44	14	80

Oregon State	fg	fga	ft	fta	rb	pf	tp
Pauly	2	8	0	1	3	5	4
Kraus	1	6	1	1	3	3	3
Counts	8	14	4	4	9	5	20
Peters	1	5	2	4	4	4	4
Baker	0	9	0	1	2	0	0
Jarvis	1	6	3	4	0	3	5
Rossi	1	3	0	0	1	2	2
Campbell	0	2	1	1	2	2	1
Torgerson	1	2	0	0	0	0	2
Hayward	0	2	1	1	2	3	1
Benner	2	2	0	0	1	0	4
Totals	17	59	12	15	26	26	46

Halftime: Cincinnati 30-27.

Loyola of Chicago	fg	fga	ft	fta	rb	pf	tp
Harkness	7	18	6	9	11	3	20
Rouse	6	12	1	2	6	4	13
Hunter	11	20	7	9	18	3	29
Egan	4	9	6	7	3	2	14
Miller	8	11	2	2	5	4	18
Wood	0	1	0	0	3	0	0
Rochelle	0	0	0	0	0	0	0
Reardon	0	0	0	0	0	0	0
Cannaughton	0	0	0	0	0	0	0
Team					5		
Totals	36	71	22	29	51	16	94

Duke	fg	fga	ft	fta	rb	pf	tp
Heyman	11	30	7	9	12	5	29
Mullins	10	20	1	3	9	4	21
Buckley	4	10	2	4	13	3	10
Schmidt	0	2	0	0	2	3	0
Harrison	0	3	2	3	3	0	2
Herbster	0	2	0	0	0	1	0
Ferguson	1	2	0	0	0	1	2
Jamieson	0	0	0	0	0	0	0
Cox	0	0	0	0	0	0	0
Mann	0	1	0	0	0	0	0
Tison	5	12	1	3	8	3	11
Team					5		
Totals	31	82	13	22	52	21	75

Halftime: Loyola 44-31.

Championship
March 23

Loyola of Chicago	fg	fga	ft	fta	rb	pf	tp
Harkness	5	18	4	8	6	4	14
Rouse	6	22	3	4	12	4	15
Hunter	6	22	4	11	3	16
Egan	3	8	3	5	3	3	9
Miller	3	14	0	0	2	3	6
Team					11		
Totals	23	84	14	21	45	17	60

Cincinnati	fg	fga	ft	fta	rb	pf	tp
Bonham	8	16	6	6	4	3	22
Thacker	5	12	3	4	15	4	13
Wilson	4	8	2	3	13	4	10
Yates	4	6	1	4	8	4	9
Shingleton	1	3	2	3	4	0	4
Heidotting	0	0	0	0	1	2	0
Team					7		
Totals	22	45	14	20	52	17	58

Halftime: Cincinnati 29-21. Regulation Score: 54-54.

1964 The Rise Of UCLA

Little did UCLA Coach John Wooden realize that his team's 1964 championship was just the beginning of a long reign atop the college basketball world.

UCLA guard Walt Hazzard battles Duke's Jeff Mullins for a loose ball during action in the 1964 NCAA championship game.

It was a high school defense, one that John Wooden had used successfully at South Bend (Ind.) Central in the years prior to World War II. It was designed to chop an opponent down to size, to counteract superior height and strength with quickness and agility. It was the weapon that would lift UCLA to basketball pre-eminence.

For the longest time, Wooden didn't think the defense would stand up to major-college competition. It wasn't until the 1964 season, when he found himself with a 6-foot-5 center and some mischievous elves, that he dared to experiment with it. Before long, he was convinced that the 2-2-1 zone press was not only viable, but also a natural extension of the Bruins' available talent.

He had two superb guards in consensus All-America Walt Hazzard, a creative passer, and Gail Goodrich, a marvelous shooter. The undersized center, Fred Slaughter, had been a track star in high school. Jack Hirsch, a 6-3 forward, was a skilled defender. And the key man, 6-5 Keith Erickson, was a volleyball player of Olympic stature.

Erickson made it all work. He was the ideal safety man, an astonishing leaper and graceful runner who was unsurpassed at picking off the long passes that the point men invariably forced with their aggressive traps.

"When we do it properly," Wooden said, "our press sets a tempo for the whole game, and when we get the other team falling into our tempo, we have gained a big advantage."

Bolstered by two sophomores—Kenny Washington and Doug McIntosh, who were adept at coming off the bench—UCLA became an unstoppable whirlwind. The Bruins suggested what was to come in December when they routed Michigan, a preseason powerhouse, in the Los Angeles Classic by the stunning score of 98-80. For the first time since Wooden, a schoolboy and college legend in Indiana, arrived on the West Coast, UCLA gained national recognition.

What frustrated opponents, especially burly ones like Michigan, was the team's apparent fragility. The guards did the majority of the scoring and the press could be ineffective for long stretches of a game. But when it ensnared a team, the effect was so sudden and startling that the outcome could be determined in about two minutes. It had the impact of an explosion.

The Bruins believed in the zone press because it never had failed them. They qualified for the Final Four with their 27th and 28th victories of the season, over Seattle and San Francisco in the West Regional. They arrived in Kansas City as the only undefeated team in the country.

Still, there were at least two reasons to believe UCLA would not join the 1956 San Francisco Dons and the 1957 North Carolina Tar Heels as the only unbeaten champions in NCAA Tournament history. Those reasons were Michigan and Duke, the

The big guns in UCLA's decisive victory over Duke were guard Gail Goodrich (left), who scored 27 points, and reserve forward Kenny Washington (right), who hit 11 of 16 shots and finished with 26 points.

second- and third-ranked schools in the nation. Michigan, the Big Ten Conference co-champion with Ohio State, was uncommonly strong and Duke, pride of the Atlantic Coast Conference, was uncommonly tall. Duke's supporters said the Blue Devils had improved tremendously since being ravaged by Michigan early in the season, just as Michigan's boosters said the Wolverines had experienced an uncharacteristically bad night against UCLA.

In UCLA's favor was a schedule that pitted Duke against Michigan in one game while the Bruins tangled with surprising semifinalist Kansas State. As a result, UCLA would be required to beat only one of the bigger teams in order to win its first NCAA title. That was fine with Wooden.

"I have been asked," the coach said, "whether I'd like taller boys. Goodness gracious sakes alive!"

The latter was about as strong an expression as Wooden allowed himself in public. He didn't drink, didn't smoke and didn't believe in appealing to his players' emotions. As far as Westerners could ascertain, his only vices in life were the fast break and the zone press.

Besides, Wooden didn't really recruit these people—at least not in the contemporary sense. Hazzard had starred at Wilt Chamberlain's old high

school in Philadelphia but came to UCLA via a junior college in Southern California. Erickson, another junior college recruit, was more skilled at swatting volleyballs than basketballs when he became a Bruin. Hirsch's father implored him to attend UCLA. Goodrich was a high school runt in whom no other major programs expressed interest until the end of his senior season. Washington was a shy youngster from South Carolina who was recommended to Wooden by Hazzard, against whom he had played on a Philadelphia playground one summer. Hazzard, however, told the coach that Washington was 6-5 and weighed 230 pounds.

"Bless his heart," said Washington, who turned up in Westwood a lot closer to 6-3 and 175 pounds. "He didn't have to do it."

Of the first seven players, only Slaughter had been a blue-chip recruit. And his role was limited mostly to screening and rebounding because not even UCLA was about to entrust its offense to a 6-5 center. The Bruins placed Slaughter in a high post, enabling the smaller men to exploit their quickness by driving the lane and the baseline.

What pushed UCLA seemingly beyond its physical limitations were its teamwork and poise. The teamwork was the result of efficient and taxing

The Bruins' Keith Erickson got in first-half foul trouble and wasn't a big factor in the '64 title game.

practices in an old, stuffy gymnasium on the Westwood campus. (The Bruins played their home games several miles away at the Los Angeles Sports Arena.) The poise probably was a reflection of the coach, who actually watched games from a seated position, his legs crossed and a rolled-up program in his hand. Although Wooden had a reputation for quietly flaying officials, he resembled a stern headmaster observing his students at play. He prepared his players well for a game and disliked calling timeouts to remind them of what they already should have known.

Both the teamwork and the poise were evident in Municipal Auditorium, where the Bruins, three-point victors over Kansas State during the regular season, trailed the Wildcats, 75-70, with 7:28 remaining in the game that would decide the Western title. Suddenly, it happened. Just about the time that four Bruin cheerleaders arrived at the game—their plane had been delayed by bad weather—UCLA reversed the game's momentum. Perhaps spurred by the pompon girls' conspicuous appearance, the Bruins scored 11 consecutive points in less than three minutes and hung on for a 90-84 victory. Erickson led UCLA with 28 points.

"Lately," Wooden said, "we have not been going well, but somehow we keep our poise and get out of the jams we get ourselves into. Now we have to do it one more time."

They would have to do it against Duke, which played a marvelous game against Michigan. The Blue Devils' two 6-10 frontcourt players, Jay Buckley and Hack Tison, held their own against the intimidating Bill Buntin and Oliver Darden. In addition, the backcourt shot well and star forward Jeff Mullins provided a sure hand, all of which contributed to Duke's 91-80 victory. Only 31 points by

sophomore sensation Cazzie Russell, who was playing on a swollen ankle, kept the Wolverines in contention.

The big question concerning Duke was its ability to handle the press. The early notices from the championship game were good. The Blue Devils were able to pass over it and take advantage of the mismatches downcourt often enough to assume a 30-27 lead with 7:14 left in the first half. And then, in a breathtaking two minutes and 34 seconds, their challenge was over. UCLA ran off 16 unanswered points for a 43-30 margin and never again was threatened.

Goodrich, finding his touch for the first time in the tournament, led the Bruins with 27 points in the 98-83 triumph. Hazzard scored only 11 points and fouled out with more than six minutes to play, but his superb floor leadership earned him the outstanding-player award. At least as significant was the work of the two sophomore reserves. The lithe Washington, who had taken a 2,400-mile bus ride to California to play for UCLA, sight unseen, relieved the foul-plagued Erickson in the first half. He took 16 shots from the field, hit 11 and finished with 26 points and a team-high 12 rebounds. McIntosh, filling in for Slaughter, had eight points and 11 rebounds.

Despite its considerable size advantage, Duke was outrebounded, 43-35. And the press harassed the Blue Devils into 29 turnovers. There wasn't much doubt about UCLA's quality. The little team from the West Coast could play.

The Bruins were 30-0. They were college basketball's finest. They were champions.

"I am immensely proud of you," Wooden told his players. "You're really the best. You've proved it. Now, don't let it change you. You are champions and you must act like champions. You met some people going up to the top. You will meet the same people going down."

In 1964, not even John Wooden could imagine how long UCLA would remain at or near the top.

1964 Tournament Results	
First Round	**Regional Third Place**
Villanova 77, Providence 66	Villanova 74, Princeton 62
Connecticut 53, Temple 48	Loyola (Ill.) 100, Kentucky 91
Princeton 86, Virginia Military 60	Texas Western 63, Creighton 52
Ohio 71, Louisville 69	Seattle 88, Utah State 78
Loyola (Ill.) 101, Murray St. 91	**Regional Championships**
Creighton 89, Oklahoma City 78	Duke 101, Connecticut 54
Texas Western 68, Texas A&M 62	Michigan 69, Ohio 57
Seattle 61, Oregon State 57	Kansas State 94, Wichita State 86
Utah State 92, Arizona State 90	UCLA 76, San Francisco 72
Second Round	**Semifinals**
Duke 87, Villanova 73	Duke 91, Michigan 80
Connecticut 52, Princeton 50	UCLA 90, Kansas State 84
Ohio 85, Kentucky 69	**Third Place**
Michigan 84, Loyola (Ill.) 80	Michigan 100, Kansas State 90
Wichita State 84, Creighton 68	**Championship**
Kansas State 64, Texas Western 60	UCLA 98, Duke 83
UCLA 95, Seattle 90	
San Francisco 64, Utah State 58	

STATISTICS

1964 UCLA

Head Coach—John Wooden   **Final Record—30-0**

Player	Pos.	Hgt.	Wgt.	Cl.	G	FG	FGA	Pct.	FT.	FTA	Pct.	Reb.	Pts.	Avg.
Gail Goodrich	G	6-1	160	Jr.	30	243	530	.458	160	225	.711	156	646	21.5
Walt Hazzard	G	6-2	188	Sr.	30	204	458	.445	150	209	.718	142	558	18.6
Jack Hirsch	F	6-3	190	Sr.	30	160	303	.528	101	152	.664	227	421	14.0
Keith Erickson	F	6-5	181	Jr.	30	127	315	.403	66	106	.623	272	320	10.7
Fred Slaughter	C	6-5	230	Sr.	30	103	221	.466	30	62	.484	242	236	7.9
Kenny Washington	F-G	6-3	177	So.	30	71	155	.458	42	67	.627	126	184	6.1
Steve Brucker	F	6-4	201	So.	1	2	4	.500	0	1	.000	2	4	4.0
Doug McIntosh	C	6-6	196	So.	30	40	77	.519	28	56	.500	131	108	3.6
Kim Stewart	F	6-5	220	Sr.	23	22	56	.393	7	15	.467	45	51	2.2
Rich Levin	F	6-4	190	Jr.	19	16	43	.372	6	12	.500	12	38	2.0
Kent Graham	F	6-3	174	Jr.	1	1	2	.500	0	0	.000	1	2	2.0
Mike Huggins	G	5-11	165	So.	23	13	34	.382	11	23	.478	22	37	1.6
Chuck Darrow	G	5-11	183	So.	23	11	29	.379	14	24	.583	27	36	1.6
Vaughn Hoffman	C	6-7	223	So.	21	10	21	.476	5	10	.500	27	25	1.2
Team												238		
UCLA					30	1023	2248	.455	620	962	.644	1670	2666	88.9
Opponents					30	798	2080	.384	506	783	.646	1428	2102	70.1

1964 DUKE

Head Coach—Vic Bubas   **Final Record—26-5**

Player	Pos.	Hgt.	Wgt.	Cl.	G	FG	FGA	Pct.	FT.	FTA	Pct.	Reb.	Pts.	Avg.
Jeff Mullins	F	6-4	190	Sr.	31	300	613	.489	150	183	.820	276	750	24.2
Jay Buckley	C	6-10	223	Sr.	31	160	271	.590	109	166	.657	278	429	13.8
Hack Tison	C	6-10	202	Jr.	30	130	260	.500	93	136	.684	229	353	11.8
Buzzy Harrison	G	6-3	190	Sr.	31	112	247	.453	44	61	.721	79	268	8.6
Jack Marin	F	6-6	200	So.	31	97	219	.443	50	65	.769	146	244	7.9
Steve Vacendak	G	6-1	189	So.	30	61	167	.365	42	58	.724	77	164	5.5
Denny Ferguson	G	6-0	176	Jr.	31	77	181	.425	8	15	.533	50	162	5.2
Brent Kitching	F	6-7	210	Jr.	27	42	97	.433	19	27	.704	42	103	3.8
Ron Herbster	G	6-2	176	Jr.	30	28	56	.500	20	37	.541	27	76	2.5
Phil Allen	F	6-4	195	So.	5	6	7	.857	0	0	.000	4	12	2.4
Frank Harscher	G	6-3	177	So.	15	8	21	.381	7	8	.875	5	23	1.5
Ted Mann Jr.	F	6-5	205	Jr.	17	5	19	.263	8	14	.571	19	18	1.1
Ray Cox	G	6-0	168	Sr.	9	2	4	.500	1	1	1.000	7	5	0.6
Terry Murray	F	6-5	197	So.	1	0	1	.000	0	0	.000	2	0	0.0
Team												185		
Duke					31	1028	2163	.475	551	771	.715	1426	2607	84.1
Opponents					31	872	2009	.434	399	612	.652	1279	2143	69.1

1964 MICHIGAN

Head Coach—Dave Strack   **Final Record—23-5**

Player	Pos.	Hgt.	Wgt.	Cl.	G	FG	FGA	Pct.	FT.	FTA	Pct.	Reb.	Pts.	Avg.
Cazzie Russell	G	6-5	218	So.	27	260	507	.513	150	178	.843	244	670	24.8
Bill Buntin	C	6-7	230	Jr.	27	238	481	.495	151	192	.786	338	627	23.2
Oliver Darden	F	6-7	220	So.	28	125	253	.494	34	63	.540	260	284	10.1
Larry Tregoning	F	6-5	195	Jr.	27	115	260	.442	29	46	.630	200	259	9.6
Bob Cantrell	G	5-10	165	Sr.	27	85	179	.475	28	40	.700	55	198	7.3
Jim Myers	F	6-8	210	Jr.	25	65	174	.374	9	20	.450	99	139	5.6
George Pomey	F	6-4	196	Jr.	27	49	101	.485	23	37	.622	56	121	4.5
Doug Herner	G	5-10	160	Sr.	25	18	53	.340	18	26	.692	18	54	2.2
Bill Yearby	F	6-3	220	So.	1	1	3	.333	0	0	.000	3	2	2.0
John Clawson	G	6-4	200	So.	17	10	27	.370	6	13	.462	15	26	1.5
John Thompson	G	6-0	165	So.	14	6	21	.286	7	10	.700	8	19	1.4
Charles Adams	G	6-2	190	Jr.	3	2	3	.667	0	1	.000	1	4	1.3
Tom Ludwig	G	5-11	168	Jr.	13	3	10	.300	6	7	.857	3	12	0.9
Doug Greenwold	G	6-6	210	Sr.	10	2	8	.250	1	3	.333	10	5	0.5
Van Tillotson	G	6-5	204	So.	1	0	0	.000	0	0	.000	1	0	0.0
Dan Brown	G	6-5	200	So.	5	0	4	.000	0	0	.000	6	0	0.0
Team												160		
Michigan					28	979	2084	.470	462	636	.726	1477	2420	86.4
Opponents					28	831	1999	.416	448	643	.697	1167	2110	75.4

1964 KANSAS STATE

Head Coach—Tex Winter   **Final Record—22-7**

Player	Pos.	Hgt.	Wgt.	Cl.	G	FG	FGA	Pct.	FT.	FTA	Pct.	Reb.	Pts.	Avg.
Willie Murrell	F	6-6	190	Sr.	29	251	536	.468	146	192	.760	321	648	22.3
Roger Suttner	C	7-0	197	Sr.	29	138	295	.468	97	169	.574	243	373	12.9
Max Moss	G	6-0	176	Sr.	28	104	272	.382	47	74	.635	129	255	9.1
Jeff Simons	F	6-5	181	Jr.	28	105	230	.457	31	45	.689	142	241	8.6
Sammy Robinson	G	6-0	163	So.	29	102	220	.464	36	57	.632	143	240	8.3
Dave Nelson	F	6-5	186	Sr.	24	51	116	.440	25	36	.694	71	127	5.3
Ron Paradis	G	6-2	165	So.	23	53	126	.421	13	18	.722	23	119	5.2
Gary Williams	F-C	6-7	185	So.	22	35	82	.427	16	47	.340	82	86	3.9
Bob McConnell	G	6-0	188	So.	11	10	25	.400	6	8	.750	11	26	2.4
Joe Gottfrid	F-C	6-5	200	Sr.	23	15	39	.385	14	23	.609	48	44	1.9
Lou Poma	F	6-4	195	Jr.	15	6	23	.261	10	10	1.000	15	22	1.5
Dick Barnard	G	6-1	173	So.	11	5	20	.250	1	4	.250	9	11	1.0
Jim Hoffman	F	6-6	185	So.	5	2	6	.333	0	0	.000	3	4	0.8
Tom Haas	G	6-0	175	So.	4	1	2	.250	0	0	.000	3	2	0.5
Larry Berger	F	6-5	210	So.	2	0	0	.000	0	0	.000	0	0	0.0
Team												188		
Kansas State					29	878	1992	.441	442	683	.647	1431	2198	75.8
Opponents					29	764	1935	.395	466	689	.676	1318	1994	68.8

1964 FINAL FOUR

At Kansas City

Semifinals

UCLA	fg	fga	ft	fta	rb	pf	tp
Goodrich	7	18	0	0	6	3	14
Slaughter	2	6	0	0	5	4	4
Hazzard	7	10	5	7	7	2	19
Hirsch	2	11	0	0	1	4	4
Erickson	10	21	8	9	10	2	28
McIntosh	3	5	2	3	10	3	8
Washington	5	11	3	4	6	1	13
Totals	36	82	18	23	45	19	90

Kansas State	fg	fga	ft	fta	rb	pf	tp
Moss	3	9	1	1	5	3	7
Robinson	2	7	0	1	5	4	4
Simons	10	17	4	6	7	3	24
Suttner	3	9	0	5	10	2	6
Murrell	13	22	3	5	13	3	29
Paradis	5	9	0	0	1	0	10
Williams	1	1	2	3	1	2	4
Nelson	0	1	0	0	0	1	0
Gottfrid	0	0	0	0	0	1	0
Barnard	0	1	0	0	0	0	0
Totals	37	76	10	21	42	19	84

Halftime: UCLA 43-41. Officials: Mihalik and Honzo.

Duke	fg	fga	ft	fta	rb	pf	tp
Ferguson	6	11	0	1	0	0	12
Buckley	11	16	3	5	14	4	25
Tison	3	10	6	10	13	4	12
Harrison	6	15	2	3	2	2	14
Mullins	8	19	5	6	8	1	21
Marin	1	2	0	0	2	1	2
Vacendak	2	5	1	2	2	1	5
Herbster	0	0	0	0	0	0	0
Totals	37	78	17	27	41	13	91

Michigan	fg	fga	ft	fta	rb	pf	tp
Buntin	8	18	3	3	9	5	19
Cantrell	6	10	0	0	4	2	12
Russell	13	19	5	6	8	5	31
Tregoning	3	11	2	2	6	4	8
Darden	2	6	1	1	9	5	5
Myers	2	5	0	0	5	2	4
Pomey	0	1	1	2	0	0	1
Herner	0	1	0	0	0	0	0
Totals	34	71	12	14	41	23	80

Halftime: Duke 48-39. Officials: Fouts and Glennon.

Championship
March 21

UCLA	fg	fga	ft	fta	rb	pf	tp
Goodrich	9	18	9	9	3	1	27
Slaughter	0	1	0	0	1	0	0
Hazzard	4	10	3	5	3	5	11
Hirsch	5	9	3	5	6	3	13
Erickson	2	7	4	5	5	3	8
McIntosh	4	9	0	0	11	2	8
Washington	11	16	4	4	12	4	26
Darrow	0	1	3	4	1	2	3
Stewart	0	1	0	0	1	0	0
Huggins	0	1	0	1	1	2	0
Hoffman	1	2	0	0	0	0	2
Levin	0	1	0	0	0	0	0
Totals	36	76	26	32	43	25	98

Duke	fg	fga	ft	fta	rb	pf	tp
Ferguson	2	6	0	1	1	3	4
Buckley	5	8	8	12	9	4	18
Tison	3	8	1	1	1	2	7
Harrison	1	1	0	0	1	2	2
Mullins	9	21	4	4	5	2	22
Marin	8	16	0	1	10	3	16
Vacendak	2	7	3	3	6	4	7
Herbster	1	4	0	0	2	0	2
Kitching	1	1	0	0	1	0	2
Mann	0	0	3	4	2	1	3
Harscher	0	0	0	0	0	0	0
Cox	0	0	0	0	0	0	0
Totals	32	72	19	28	35	24	83

Halftime: UCLA 50-38. Officials: Mihalik and Glennon.

1965 Bruins Sneak In Back Door

Though the UCLA Bruins were coming off an undefeated season, so much media attention was directed elsewhere in 1965 that the defending national champions were overlooked, if not forgotten, as they moved steadily toward another Final Four.

The public's preoccupation with UCLA began to wane after the Bruins lost their first game of the year, 110-83, at Illinois. A loss to another Big Ten Conference team (Iowa) several weeks later seemed to confirm that UCLA was back among the mortal. But the Bruins' departure from center stage wasn't as much a reflection on their fall from grace as it was a tribute to the rise of a star in the East and a program in the Midwest. The clash of those two forces in the semifinal round of a holiday tournament in New York colored the entire season. No one who was there would ever forget the night Bill Bradley took on mighty Michigan and almost won.

The game was played December 30, 1964, in the ECAC Holiday Festival at Madison Square Garden. Bradley, a 6-foot-5 forward, had been a consensus All-America selection as a junior, but his Princeton team appeared hopelessly young (three sophomores among the first six players) and barely a cut above its Ivy League competition. Michigan was ranked first in the nation and, in 6-5 junior guard Cazzie Russell, possessed the most celebrated player in the country.

Bradley grew into a legend that night. Before fouling out with 4:37 remaining he scored 41 points, gathered nine rebounds, added four assists and limited his opponent to one point. More significantly, he provided the Tigers with a shocking 75-63 lead.

"I never thought one man could control a game like that," Michigan Coach Dave Strack said in admiration.

The true value of his presence, however, was underscored by his absence. With Bradley on the bench, Princeton collapsed. The Wolverines roared from behind to tie the score in the final minute and to prevail, 80-78, on a jump shot by Russell with three seconds left. Because of the remarkable nature of that game, both Princeton and Michigan spent the rest of the season in the spotlight.

Few people outside New York would remember that Michigan lost the championship game of the Holiday Festival to St. John's by a single point. After the loss, the Wolverines promptly launched a 13-game winning streak that was halted in their reg-

High-scoring guard Gail Goodrich returned in 1965 to spearhead UCLA's drive for a second straight NCAA championship.

ular-season finale at Ohio State. Russell was the star shooter, but the Big Ten champions squashed opponents with a brutal inside game featuring 6-7, 235-pound center Bill Buntin and 6-7, 220-pound forward Oliver Darden. The smallest starter on the team of big shoulders was George Pomey, a 6-4, 196-pound guard.

Although Princeton was not a physically impressive team, Coach Bill van Breda Kolff's Tigers were lifted to unprecedented heights by Bradley. He was that rare individual who made everyone around him play to his maximum potential and perhaps beyond. Part of the fascination with Bradley was, of course, his intelligence. At an elite school, he was among the more elite students. He already had been designated a Rhodes scholar and planned to pass up professional basketball, at least temporarily, to attend Oxford University.

Despite his academic bent, Bradley practiced basketball with an almost religious fervor. He wasn't particularly fast or strong, and he didn't jump all that well. But through diligent work, he had become a great shooter and developed a total comprehension of the game. With Bradley as the focal point, Princeton won the Ivy League title and an automatic berth in the NCAA Tournament.

Returning to the tournament for the fourth consecutive year was defending champion UCLA, which again was using the zone press. After seeing how well the defense worked for the Bruins, teams throughout the country began using versions of the press, with varying results. Even Michigan's lumberjacks had opted for a half-court zone press, as much to get their own offense in gear as to harass opponents.

"All I am asked about is the UCLA press," Strack said. "But anybody can press. To make it work, you need the personnel. The UCLA press is mostly the UCLA players."

The players were not the same in 1965 and neither was the press. Fred Slaughter had been replaced in the pivot and on the front line of the press by junior Doug McIntosh. Junior Fred Goss had moved into Walt Hazzard's backcourt spot, and sophomore Edgar Lacey had taken the place of forward Jack Hirsch. Returning to the starting lineup were guard Gail Goodrich and forward Keith Erickson. The Bruins still were short and quick, but the synchronization was not as fine as it had been in 1964 and teams were better prepared for the press this time.

Still, UCLA unquestionably played the defense better than any of its imitators. Coach John Wooden was concerned enough about scouts taking notes that he called off the zone press in his team's final two regular-season games, both against Southern California. Without the pressure defense, the Bruins struggled to win both games.

Another UCLA returnee was forward Kenny Washington, who specialized in high-scoring championship games.

"I just didn't want to give anyone the opportunity to personally analyze the press," he said.

UCLA began defense of its title as the second-ranked team in the nation. No. 1-ranked Michigan was the tournament favorite, an honor it did nothing to dispel in winning the Mideast Regional. In the West, the Bruins routed Brigham Young but had to rally to beat San Francisco. Wichita State survived underwhelming competition in the Midwest.

But the regional that drew the greatest interest was the East, where Princeton came of age. After squeezing past Penn State and handling North Carolina State with surprising ease, the Tigers were matched against Providence. The Friars, featuring Jimmy Walker, were ranked fourth in the nation, had lost only one game and were heavy favorites. They never had a chance.

Bradley made 14 of 20 field-goal attempts as well as all 13 free throws for 41 points. He also had 10 rebounds and nine assists and precipitated the 109-69 rout of an outstanding team. His indelible per-

Doug McIntosh, shown grabbing a rebound against Duke in the 1964
championship game, returned in '65 and took over the pivot position.

formance earned Princeton its first trip to the Final
Four and made possible a rematch with Michigan.

"I'll just tell them," said Wolverines assistant
Tom Jorgensen, who was scouting the Tigers, "that
he's the greatest that ever lived because they won't
believe anything else."

By then, the other Tigers not only believed in
Bradley but in themselves. All of them—center
Robby Brown, point guard Gary Walters and reserve center Ed Hummer (all sophomores) as well as
guard Don Rodenbach and forward Bob Haarlow
(both juniors)—played magnificently against Providence. The entire team made 68.3 percent of its
field-goal tries and, in one 12-minute stretch, connected on all 14 shots from the field.

The Tigers, who had been haunted by their Holiday Festival defeat all season, were pleased to have
another shot at the Wolverines.

"We have been thinking of only one thing since
December 30," Bradley said. "We have been thinking about beating Michigan."

The semifinal encounter at the Portland Memorial Coliseum, however, did not live up to the expectations of Princeton or the general public. Bradley
was charged with his fourth foul early in the second
half, forcing Princeton into an unfamiliar zone that
Michigan shredded. The Tigers stayed reasonably
close until Bradley fouled out with five minutes remaining, then were overrun, 93-76. UCLA met only
limited resistance from outmanned Wichita State,
which relied upon, of all things, a full-court press.
The Bruins won as they pleased, 108-89.

That set up the long-awaited final between the
bulls and the bears. But first, the crowd in the Oregon city was granted an unusual treat. Bradley, appearing in his last college game, set a Final Four
record with 58 points (on 22-of-29 shooting from
the field, 14-of-15 from the free-throw line) in
Princeton's 118-82 demolition of Wichita State. His
was such a captivating finale that referee Bob Korte
sought out Bradley afterward and said, "... that
was the greatest exhibition I ever saw. It was a pleasure to watch, and I wanted to thank you."

Yet, all Bradley's artistry did was decide third
place in the tournament. Goodrich didn't top the
performance, but he came close, and unlike Bradley
he was rewarded with a championship. The littlest
Bruin regular dazzled the Wolverines and set a
scoring record for a title game with 42 points.

Goodrich was 6-1 and slender with a boyish face

The amazing talents of two of college basketball's premier players, Princeton's Bill Bradley (left) and Michigan's Cazzie Russell (right), were on display in 1965 when the NCAA field was trimmed to four.

that, according to one observer, would not have been out of place underneath a beanie and a propeller. He had assumed a larger role for UCLA as the season progressed, scoring a school-record 40 points against BYU and then 30 against San Francisco in the team's West Regional victories. Against Michigan, darting around the massive Wolverines, the consensus All-America was uncanny.

For the second straight year, the Bruins also got another lift from forward Kenny Washington. The sixth man hit seven of nine attempts from the floor and was the team's second-leading scorer with 17 points. He had scored a career-high 26 points in UCLA's title-winning triumph over Duke a year earlier.

"I guess if we can just make it to the finals," Wooden mused, "Washington will take care of us."

Despite the tremendous efforts by Goodrich and Washington, UCLA's emphatic 91-80 triumph would not have been possible without the press. Michigan started fast and held a 20-13 lead barely seven minutes into the game. Furthermore, a leg injury had sidelined Erickson, UCLA's co-captain and floor leader, forcing the young Lacey to play the vital safety position in the press.

It didn't matter. As had happened to so many opponents in the last two years, the Wolverines suddenly became unglued. They couldn't get the ball across midcourt. Their passes were tipped or intercepted. The Bruins pulled even midway through the first half and then inched ahead for good. They won the game, for all intents and purposes, with a 12-1 run in the final four minutes of the first half, taking a 47-34 lead that proved insurmountable. The Bruins were up by 20 when Wooden slowed down the offense in the second half. He sat back and watched his players draw fouls and sink free throw after free throw down the stretch.

Finesse had triumphed over muscle. The Bruins were national champions for the second year in a row. And as long as Wooden coached, UCLA never again would be overlooked.

1965 Tournament Results	
First Round	**Regional Third Place**
Princeton 60, Penn State 58	N. C. State 103, St. Jos. (Pa.) 81
St. Joseph's (Pa.) 67, Conn. 61	Dayton 75, DePaul 69
Providence 91, West Virginia 67	SMU 89, Houston 87
DePaul 99, Eastern Kentucky 52	Oklahoma City 112, BYU 102
Dayton 66, Ohio 65	**Regional Championships**
Houston 99, Notre Dame 98	Princeton 109, Providence 69
Okla. City 70, Colorado St. 68	Michigan 87, Vanderbilt 85
Second Round	Wichita State 54, Oklahoma St. 46
Princeton 66, N. C. State 48	UCLA 101, San Francisco 93
Prov. 81, St. Jos. (Pa.) 73 (ot)	**Semifinals**
Vanderbilt 83, DePaul 78 (ot)	Michigan 93, Princeton 76
Michigan 98, Dayton 71	UCLA 108, Wichita St. 89
Wichita St. 86, SMU 81	**Third Place**
Oklahoma St. 75, Houston 60	Princeton 118, Wichita State 82
UCLA 100, BYU 76	**Championship**
San Francisco 91, Okla. City 67	UCLA 91, Michigan 80

STATISTICS

1965 UCLA

Head Coach—John Wooden   **Final Record—28-2**

Player	Pos.	Hgt.	Wgt.	Cl.	G	FG	FGA	Pct.	FT.	FTA	Pct.	Reb.	Pts.	Avg.
Gail Goodrich	G	6-1	170	Sr.	30	277	528	.525	190	265	.717	158	744	24.8
Keith Erickson	F	6-5	185	Sr.	29	147	332	.443	79	109	.725	255	373	12.9
Fred Goss	G	6-1	185	Jr.	30	157	355	.442	51	70	.729	99	365	12.2
Edgar Lacey	F	6-6	191	So.	30	135	288	.469	77	133	.579	305	347	11.6
Kenny Washington	F	6-3	180	Jr.	30	99	233	.425	79	121	.653	151	277	9.2
Mike Lynn	C	6-7	215	So.	30	79	157	.503	43	74	.581	152	201	6.7
Doug McIntosh	C	6-6	200	Jr.	30	69	161	.429	56	76	.737	168	194	6.5
John Lyons	G	6-0	165	So.	17	7	18	.389	10	15	.667	9	24	1.4
John Galbraith	G	6-2	180	So.	18	9	23	.391	1	6	.167	10	19	1.1
Brice Chambers	G	6-1	200	Jr.	21	10	24	.417	0	5	.000	13	20	1.0
Vaughn Hoffman	C	6-7	220	Jr.	20	7	19	.368	3	10	.300	26	17	0.9
Bill Winkelholz	F	6-8	190	So.	11	3	14	.214	0	1	.000	14	6	0.5
Mike Serafin	G	6-3	170	So.	7	1	3	.333	0	1	.000	1	2	0.3
Rich Levin	F	6-4	195	Sr.	8	0	7	.000	0	0	.000	3	0	0.0
Team												195		
UCLA					30	1000	2162	.463	589	886	.665	1559	2589	86.3
Opponents					30	830	2005	.414	480	734	.654	1332	2140	71.3

1965 MICHIGAN

Head Coach—Dave Strack   **Final Record—24-4**

Player	Pos.	Hgt.	Wgt.	Cl.	G	FG	FGA	Pct.	FT.	FTA	Pct.	Reb.	Pts.	Avg.
Cazzie Russell	G	6-5	218	Jr.	27	271	558	.486	152	186	.817	213	694	25.7
Bill Buntin	C	6-7	235	Sr.	28	221	454	.487	122	159	.767	323	564	20.1
Oliver Darden	F	6-7	220	Jr.	28	152	322	.472	59	95	.621	246	363	13.0
Larry Tregoning	F	6-5	195	Sr.	28	133	292	.455	44	63	.698	211	310	11.1
George Pomey	G	6-4	196	Sr.	28	86	194	.443	37	56	.661	104	209	7.5
John Thompson	G	6-0	165	Jr.	25	52	119	.437	18	25	.720	29	122	4.9
Craig Dill	C	6-10	210	So.	21	32	66	.485	30	42	.714	53	94	4.5
Jim Myers	C	6-8	210	Jr.	27	44	140	.314	14	23	.609	117	102	3.8
John Clawson	G	6-4	200	Jr.	18	22	48	.458	6	11	.545	24	50	2.8
Tom Ludwig	G	5-11	168	Sr.	14	5	17	.294	4	4	1.000	7	14	1.0
Van Tillotson	F	6-5	204	Jr.	4	0	1	.000	2	5	.400	4	2	0.5
Dan Brown	G	6-5	210	Jr.	8	1	7	.143	1	3	.333	8	3	0.4
Dennis Bankey	G	6-1	170	So.	13	0	6	.000	5	6	.833	5	5	0.4
Charles Adams	G				3	0	1	.000	0	0	.000	0	0	0.0
Team												177		
Michigan					28	1019	2225	.458	494	678	.729	1521	2532	90.4
Oponents					28	876	1976	.443	448	649	.690	1174	2200	78.6

1965 PRINCETON

Head Coach—Bill van Breda Kolff   **Final Record—23-6**

Player	Pos.	Hgt.	Wgt.	Cl.	G	FG	FGA	Pct.	FT.	FTA	Pct.	Reb.	Pts.	Avg.
Bill Bradley	F	6-5	205	Sr.	29	306	574	.533	273	308	.886	342	885	30.5
Bob Haarlow	F	6-2	190	Jr.	29	117	238	.492	45	72	.625	114	279	9.6
Ed Hummer	C	6-6	190	So.	29	88	176	.500	67	95	.705	178	243	8.4
Don Rodenbach	G	6-2	175	Jr.	29	103	235	.438	28	36	.778	86	234	8.1
Gary Walters	G	5-10	160	So.	29	90	212	.425	35	44	.795	73	215	7.4
Robby Brown	C	6-9	200	So.	28	71	156	.455	41	63	.651	195	183	6.5
Ken Shank	C	6-6	200	Sr.	12	18	27	.667	3	6	.500	20	39	3.3
Bill Koch	F	6-3	195	So.	20	23	56	.411	9	28	.321	56	55	2.8
Al Adler	F	6-3	180	So.	19	21	51	.412	3	4	.750	33	45	2.4
Chris Chimera	G	6-0	160	So.	17	13	30	.433	10	18	.556	14	36	2.1
Bill Kingston	G	5-10	155	Sr.	23	11	23	.478	25	35	.714	14	47	2.0
Don Roth	G	6-1	200	Sr.	21	14	30	.467	4	12	.333	34	32	1.5
Don Niemann	C	6-6	200	Sr.	16	6	23	.261	2	10	.200	16	14	0.9
Larry Lucchino	G	5-10	160	So.	4	1	4	.250	0	0	.000	1	2	0.5
Team												156	2	
Princeton					29	883	1835	.481	545	731	.746	1332	2311	79.7
Opponents					29	700	1855	.377	552	786	.702	1167	1952	67.3

1965 WICHITA STATE

Head Coach—Gary Thompson   **Final Record—21-9**

Player	Pos.	Hgt.	Wgt.	Cl.	G	FG	FGA	Pct.	FT.	FTA	Pct.	Reb.	Pts.	Avg.
Dave Stallworth*	F	6-7	200	Sr.	16	153	275	.556	94	139	.676	194	400	25.0
Kelly Pete	G	6-1	180	Jr.	30	194	396	.490	130	173	.751	211	518	17.3
Jamie Thompson	F	6-3	190	So.	24	112	224	.491	76	93	.817	125	300	12.5
Nate Bowman**	C	6-10	215	Sr.	14	71	138	.514	32	56	.571	121	174	12.4
Dave Leach	C-F	6-5	210	Sr.	30	160	344	.465	49	80	.613	159	369	12.3
Vernon Smith	F	6-4	190	Sr.	30	96	207	.464	58	75	.773	131	250	8.3
John Criss	G	5-10	165	Jr.	28	81	195	.415	28	30	.933	57	190	6.8
Melvin Reed	F	6-5	190	So.	27	41	99	.414	31	51	.608	78	113	4.2
Gerald Davis	C	6-9	185	Jr.	24	27	78	.346	16	32	.500	58	70	2.9
Larry Nosich	C	6-7	200	Sr.	21	12	23	.522	7	18	.389	22	31	1.5
Bob Powers**	C	6-8	225	So.	2	1	1	1.000	0	0	.000	0	2	1.0
Gerald Reimond	C	6-8	210	Sr.	5	0	2	.000	1	1	1.000	5	1	0.2
Manny Zafiros	G	5-11	150	Sr.	4	0	3	.000	0	0	.000	0	0	0.0
Al Trope	F	6-7	190	So.	2	0	2	.000	0	0	.000	0	0	0.0
Team												148		
Wichita State					30	948	1987	.477	522	748	.698	1309	2418	80.6
Opponents					30	890	1957	.455	446	711	.627	1288	2226	74.2

*Completed eligibility after 16 games. **Ineligible second semester.

1965 FINAL FOUR

At Portland, Ore.

Semifinals

Michigan

	fg	fga	ft	fta	rb	pf	tp
Tregoning	6	9	1	1	10	2	13
Darden	6	13	1	3	9	3	13
Buntin	7	13	8	10	14	4	22
Russell	10	21	8	9	10	0	28
Pomey	2	8	2	2	3	4	6
Myers	1	4	0	0	4	1	2
Thompson	0	1	2	2	0	0	2
Dill	0	0	3	4	1	2	3
Ludwig	0	0	0	0	0	1	0
Clawson	2	2	0	1	1	0	4
Totals	34	71	25	32	52	17	93

Princeton

	fg	fga	ft	fta	rb	pf	tp
Bradley	12	25	5	7	5	2	29
Haarlow	4	10	1	4	3	1	9
Brown	2	6	0	0	3	5	4
Walters	5	10	1	2	3	1	11
Rodenbach	2	5	2	2	1	3	6
Hummer	4	10	4	5	9	4	12
Koch	1	4	1	2	4	1	3
Kingston	0	1	2	2	2	1	2
Totals	30	71	16	22	32	21	76

Halftime: Michigan 40-36. Officials: Korte and Magnuson.

Wichita State

	fg	fga	ft	fta	rb	pf	tp
Smith	4	11	0	1	2	3	8
Thompson	13	19	10	11	6	2	36
Leach	6	14	0	1	10	3	12
Pete	6	11	5	5	6	5	17
Criss	4	13	0	0	4	4	8
Reed	2	3	1	1	4	4	5
Davis	1	2	0	0	1	0	2
Trope	0	1	0	0	0	0	0
Nosich	0	0	1	3	0	0	1
Reimond	0	1	0	0	1	0	0
Team					4		
Totals	36	75	17	22	38	21	89

UCLA

	fg	fga	ft	fta	rb	pf	tp
Lacey	9	13	6	10	13	2	24
Erickson	1	6	0	0	5	2	2
McIntosh	4	5	3	4	4	2	11
Goodrich	11	21	6	8	5	2	28
Goss	8	13	3	3	9	2	19
Washington	4	13	2	4	7	1	10
Lynn	5	9	0	0	8	1	10
Chambers	0	5	0	0	2	1	0
Lyons	2	3	0	0	1	2	4
Levin	0	1	0	0	1	1	0
Galbraith	0	0	0	0	1	0	0
Hoffman	0	0	0	0	0	0	0
Team					5		
Totals	44	89	20	29	60	17	108

Halftime: UCLA 65-38. Officials: Mihalik and Honzo.

Championship
March 20

UCLA

	fg	fga	ft	fta	rb	pf	tp
Erickson	1	1	1	2	1	1	3
Lacey	5	7	1	2	7	3	11
McIntosh	1	2	1	2	0	2	3
Goodrich	12	22	18	20	4	4	42
Goss	4	12	0	0	3	1	8
Washington	7	9	3	4	5	2	17
Lynn	2	3	1	2	6	1	5
Lyons	0	0	0	0	0	1	0
Galbraith	0	0	0	0	0	0	0
Hoffman	1	1	0	0	1	0	2
Levin	0	1	0	0	1	0	0
Chambers	0	0	0	1	0	0	0
Team					6		
Totals	33	58	25	33	34	15	91

Michigan

	fg	fga	ft	fta	rb	pf	tp
Darden	8	10	1	1	4	5	17
Pomey	2	5	0	0	2	2	4
Buntin	6	14	2	4	6	5	14
Russell	10	16	8	10	5	2	28
Tregoning	2	7	1	1	5	5	5
Myers	0	4	0	0	3	2	0
Brown	0	0	0	0	0	0	0
Ludwig	1	2	0	0	0	0	2
Thompson	0	0	0	0	0	0	0
Bankey	0	0	0	0	0	0	0
Clawson	3	4	0	0	0	2	6
Dill	1	2	2	2	1	1	4
Team					7		
Totals	33	64	14	18	33	24	80

Halftime: UCLA 47-34. Officials: Mihalik and Honzo.

1966 Texas Western Stuns Kentucky

Kentucky Coach Adolph Rupp (left) was in the twilight of his legendary career when he tried to spark his Wildcats to victory in 1966. Don Haskins (right) had his Texas Western team on the verge of a major upset.

The contrast was as stark as black and white. At a time when race relations had become a major national issue, it escaped nobody's attention that the NCAA championship game between Kentucky and Texas Western pitted an all-white aggregation against five black starters. That one team represented the basketball mainstream and the other was a virtual unknown served to heighten the differences between the opponents.

Top-ranked Kentucky was in pursuit of its fifth championship under Coach Adolph Rupp, and the smart money said that only Duke among the other Final Four qualifiers would be able to stop the Wildcats from achieving their goal. After all, the traditionally strong Blue Devils were ranked second in the nation and were making their third trip to the national semifinals in four years.

It's true that Texas Western (now Texas-El Paso) was ranked third in both wire-service polls, but the Miners appeared to be interlopers on the national scene. Theirs was not a well-known program, and for good reason. In amassing a 23-1 record during the regular season, the Miners had not beaten a single Top 10 team. As an independent, they could boast of no conference championship. And in the Miners' only two previous trips to the NCAA Tournament, they had been eliminated before the regional finals.

Nor did they have a transcendent star. The Miners were a collection of quick inner-city dunk artists from New York, Detroit, Houston and Gary, Ind., whose presence suggested a schoolyard game

David Lattin (42) and forward Willie Cager helped Texas Western control the boards and Kentucky's Wildcats in the 1966 championship game.

was about to break out at any moment. The impression of many was that they had to be uncoachable, if not incorrigible. It was a decidedly false impression.

Despite their talent for running and jumping, the Miners were dedicated almost fanatically to defense. Don Haskins, their strong-willed coach, would have it no other way. He had played under the legendary Henry Iba at Oklahoma A&M and had carried his coach's values of hard work and discipline with him to El Paso. Practices at Texas Western were strenuous, to say the least.

"Every day after practice," said Bobby Joe Hill, the Miners' floor leader, "I wanted to shoot him."

But the hard work paid off for the Miners. After being hounded relentlessly in practice, they inflict-

ed more of the same on opponents. "My God," Haskins said, "could they do that."

The Miners were accorded little respect at the start of the tournament. Their schedule had not been difficult—Eastern New Mexico, Pan American and South Dakota were among the victims—and they appeared to be regressing when they lost their final game, by two points, to Seattle.

"Best thing that ever happened to us," said Hill, who sensed his team was growing complacent.

Texas Western proved its mettle in the Midwest Regional. After routing Oklahoma City, the Miners clawed past a strong Cincinnati team, 78-76, in overtime and then overcame a favored Kansas team featuring JoJo White and 6-foot-11 Walt Wesley, 81-80, in double overtime.

David (Big Daddy) Lattin, Texas Western's bruising 6-7 center, had difficulty defending the huge Wesley in the latter game. Hill, a cocky 5-10 guard, said he would take care of the big man.

"Every time Wesley put the ball on the floor," Lattin said, "Bobby Joe would grab it away."

Still, two victories by a total of three points weren't enough to convince people that the Miners were of championship caliber. Duke had overpowered St. Joseph's and Syracuse in the East Regional, and Kentucky had been even more impressive in beating Dayton and then Michigan (putting an end to consensus All-America Cazzie Russell's brilliant college career) in the Mideast. These two, both all-white teams, appeared to be the class of the Final Four.

Their semifinal game strengthened that conviction. With its finest shooter, guard Bob Verga, weakened by illness and unable to contribute much more than spirit, Duke put up a tremendous struggle. And Kentucky, with its own sick-bed case in forward Larry Conley, received maximum effort and prevailed, 83-79, to win the Eastern championship. In the Western battle, the Miners had a relatively easy time subduing Utah, 85-78, despite 38 points by Jerry Chambers, the tournament's high scorer and outstanding player.

The Wildcats had been dubbed "Rupp's Runts" because, like UCLA's first championship team, they didn't have a starter taller than 6-5. But they were quick, shot well and displayed exceptional teamwork. Rupp seemed inordinately fond of them and they of him. It was the public perception that this might be his last hurrah in the championship spotlight.

Haskins, meanwhile, was enjoying his first hurrah.

"Mr. Rupp is 64 and he made it a lot of times," the Miners' burly 36-year-old coach said the day before the title game at Cole Field House on the Maryland campus. "But it's probably going to be just once in a lifetime for me."

Little Willie Worsley got a surprise start for Texas Western and later took an active part in the traditional rim-stripping ceremonies (left). Their hopes dashed, Kentucky cheerleaders (right) console each other.

Kentucky opened in a zone, which was what Haskins expected. He had one little surprise for the Wildcats, electing to start 5-6 Willie Worsley in place of 6-8 Nevil Shed and employ a three-guard offense to counteract Kentucky's speed. With Lattin and 6-5 Harry Flournoy in the game, he wasn't concerned about rebounding. The addition of Worsley to Hill and 6-1 Orsten Artis in the backcourt would enable Texas Western to better control the pace of the game. The three guards all would play 40 minutes.

In the Kentucky dressing room, Rupp asked, "Who's captain tonight?" Conley said the honor belonged to high-scoring forward Pat Riley, who would be celebrating a birthday the next day. "All right then," Rupp said, "let's have a birthday present for him."

But there would be no present. Almost from the start, it was clear that the Miners were quicker and fresher than the Wildcats and that their defense had been badly underrated. The game turned on a sequence near the midpoint of the first half. With his team leading, 10-9, Hill stole the ball from guard Tommy Kron, dribbled half the length of the court and made a layup. Seconds later, guard Louie Dampier, Kentucky's brightest star, brought the ball to the midcourt line and tried to maneuver around Hill. He failed. Hill picked off the dribble and went all the way for another uncontested layup.

Kentucky never fully recovered from those affronts, as well as thunderous dunks by Lattin and Willie Cager, an aptly named reserve forward. Still, they hung in on the shooting of Dampier and Riley, who scored 19 points each. After whittling Texas Western's lead down to three points (34-31) at the half, Kentucky pulled to within one point on three occasions, the last (46-45) with 12:26 to play. Moments later, with the Miners up by two, the Wildcats had three consecutive shots to tie—and missed them all. As time slipped away, they had no choice

Bobby Joe Hill, pictured in a semifinal game against Utah's Rich Tate, was Texas Western's offensive catalyst and floor leader.

but to foul. And Texas Western was tremendous from the free-throw line, making 28 of 34 attempts. Kentucky, meanwhile, shot only 13 free throws, sinking 11. Though the Wildcats made five more baskets than the Miners, they couldn't compensate for the free-throw disparity. Two foul shots by Cager gave the Miners their biggest advantage of the game, 68-57, and they went on to win, 72-65.

Hill, the junior with the fast hands, finished with a game-high 20 points. He was the only Texas Western player selected to the all-tournament team. Even in victory, the Miners were largely anonymous.

For his part, the coach felt humble. "I'm just a young punk," Haskins said. "It was a thrill playing against Mr. Rupp, let alone beating him."

Even John Wooden was impressed by Texas Western's poise.

"To take a bunch of seemingly undisciplined kids and do what Don Haskins did," the UCLA coach marveled, "is one of the most remarkable coaching jobs I've seen."

But Haskins didn't think it was so remarkable, perhaps because he never considered his players undisciplined. Nor did he think there was anything special about starting five black players. (None of Texas Western's five white athletes played against Kentucky.)

"It wasn't the first black team we played with," he said. "And it wasn't the first black team in the country. There were others.

"I never thought a thing about it, but after we won the title with five black guys, everybody made a big deal out of it. You play your five best guys."

Nevertheless, the game became a racial topic that stirred the nation. Haskins said he received thousands of pieces of hate mail, most of it from the South, and not all of it from whites. The blacks who wrote accused him of exploitation. So he took it from both sides.

"There was a time," he said, "when I almost wished we hadn't won."

But Texas Western's victory had a positive effect on college basketball. Shortly thereafter, Rupp began recruiting black players and big-time programs throughout the South changed their unwritten policies. A barrier had fallen, quietly, thanks to a small group of young men and a demanding coach from an unheralded school in west Texas.

1966 Tournament Results

First Round
St. Jos. (Pa.) 65, Providence 48
Davidson 95, Rhode Island 65
Dayton 58, Miami (Ohio) 51
W. Kentucky 105, Loyola (Ill.) 86
Texas Western 89, Okla. City 74
Houston 82, Colorado State 76

Second Round
Duke 76, St. Joseph's (Pa.) 74
Syracuse 94, Davidson 78
Kentucky 86, Dayton 79
Michigan 80, Western Kentucky 79
Tex. W'tern 78, Cincinnati 76 (ot)
Kansas 76, SMU 70
Oregon State 63, Houston 60
Utah 83, Pacific 74

Regional Third Place
St. Joseph's (Pa.) 92, Davidson 76
Western Kentucky 82, Dayton 68
SMU 89, Cincinnati 84
Houston 102, Pacific 91

Regional Championships
Duke 91, Syracuse 81
Kentucky 84, Michigan 77
Tex. Western 81, Kansas 80 (2 ot)
Utah 70, Oregon State 64

Semifinals
Kentucky 83, Duke 79
Texas Western 85, Utah 78

Third Place
Duke 79, Utah 77

Championship
Texas Western 72, Kentucky 65

STATISTICS

1966 TEXAS WESTERN

Head Coach—Don Haskins   Final Record—28-1

Player	Pos.	Hgt.	Wgt.	Cl.	G	FG	FGA	Pct.	FT.	FTA	Pct.	Reb.	Pts.	Avg.
Bobby Joe Hill	G	5-10	170	Jr.	28	161	392	.411	97	159	.610	85	419	15.0
David Lattin	C	6-7	240	So.	29	148	299	.495	111	158	.703	248	407	14.0
Orsten Artis	G	6-1	175	Sr.	28	141	300	.470	72	83	.867	98	354	12.6
Nevil Shed	F-C	6-8	185	Jr.	29	116	235	.494	74	98	.755	229	306	10.6
Harry Flournoy	F	6-5	190	Sr.	29	96	192	.500	48	74	.649	309	240	8.3
Willie Worsley	G	5-6	165	So.	29	81	201	.403	69	96	.719	66	231	8.0
Willie Cager	F	6-5	170	So.	27	55	134	.410	68	100	.680	108	178	6.6
Louis Baudoin	F	6-7	203	Jr.	16	17	44	.386	1	5	.200	20	35	2.2
Jerry Armstrong	F	6-4	200	Sr.	24	12	43	.279	21	24	.875	33	45	1.9
David Palacio	G	6-2	180	So.	15	6	24	.250	2	5	.400	8	14	0.9
Dick Myers	F	6-4	185	Jr.	14	4	12	.333	4	8	.500	9	12	0.9
Togo Railey	G	6-0	175	Jr.	4	0	0	.000	1	2	.500	0	1	0.3
Others						9	23	.391	0	0	.000	11	18	—
Team												206		
Texas Western					29	846	1899	.445	568	812	.700	1430	2260	77.9
Opponents					29	647	1614	.401	523	739	.708	1050	1817	62.7

1966 KENTUCKY

Head Coach—Adolph Rupp   Final Record—27-2

Player	Pos.	Hgt.	Wgt.	Cl.	G	FG	FGA	Pct.	FT.	FTA	Pct.	Reb.	Pts.	Avg.
Pat Riley	F	6-3	205	Jr.	29	265	514	.516	107	153	.699	259	637	22.0
Louie Dampier	G	6-0	167	Jr.	29	249	482	.517	114	137	.832	144	612	21.1
Thad Jaracz	C	6-5	230	So.	29	164	328	.500	55	92	.598	218	383	13.2
Larry Conley	F	6-3	172	Sr.	29	128	273	.469	77	97	.794	162	333	11.5
Tommy Kron	G	6-5	202	Sr.	29	120	249	.482	57	67	.851	240	297	10.2
Cliff Berger	C	6-8	225	So.	25	27	63	.429	30	39	.769	86	84	3.4
Bob Tallent	G	6-1	179	So.	18	22	56	.393	10	15	.667	19	54	3.0
Steve Clevenger	G	6-0	185	So.	11	8	16	.500	8	12	.667	5	24	2.2
Brad Bounds	C-F	6-5	207	Jr.	12	11	29	.379	3	5	.600	18	25	2.1
Jim LeMaster	G	6-2	188	So.	19	7	25	.280	13	17	.765	12	27	1.4
Tommy Porter	F	6-3	188	So.	14	7	15	.467	4	4	1.000	13	18	1.3
Gene Stewart	F	6-2	187	Jr.	6	3	4	.750	2	3	.667	9	8	1.3
Bob Windsor	F	6-4	230	Jr.	2	1	7	.143	0	0	.000	3	2	1.0
Gary Gamble	F	6-4	185	So.	17	5	17	.294	5	7	.714	18	15	0.9
Larry Lentz	C	6-8	217	Sr.	6	0	1	.000	0	0	.000	5	0	0.0
Team												157		
Kentucky					29	1017	2079	.489	485	648	.748	1368	2519	86.9
Opponents					29	770	1916	.402	488	690	.707	1205	2028	69.9

1966 DUKE

Head Coach—Vic Bubas   Final Record—26-4

Player	Pos.	Hgt.	Wgt.	Cl.	G	FG	FGA	Pct.	FT.	FTA	Pct.	Reb.	Pts.	Avg.
Jack Marin	F	6-6	200	Sr.	30	221	451	.490	116	148	.784	292	558	18.6
Bob Verga	G	6-0	180	Jr.	28	216	441	.490	87	119	.731	113	519	18.5
Mike Lewis	C	6-7	225	So.	30	161	271	.595	84	112	.750	139	406	13.5
Steve Vacendak	G	6-1	190	Sr.	29	152	354	.429	80	108	.741	117	384	13.2
Bob Riedy	F	6-6	212	Jr.	29	105	228	.461	61	89	.685	224	271	9.3
Warren Chapman	C	6-8	220	So.	27	56	99	.566	37	58	.638	104	149	5.5
Joe Kennedy	F	6-6	210	So.	10	11	29	.379	9	11	.818	27	31	3.1
Ron Wendelin	G	6-1	185	So.	28	33	73	.452	10	20	.500	28	76	2.7
Tim Kolodziej	F	6-5	205	So.	6	5	7	.714	5	6	.833	4	15	2.5
Jim Liccardo	F	6-5	190	Sr.	24	23	55	.418	7	11	.636	40	53	2.2
Phil Allen	F	6-4	185	So.	10	5	11	.455	3	5	.600	8	13	1.3
Bill Zimmer	G	6-0	185	Sr.	3	0	3	.000	2	3	.667	2	2	0.7
Tony Barone	G	5-8	145	So.	9	1	3	.333	1	1	1.000	5	3	0.3
Stuart McKaig	G	6-1	175	Jr.	11	1	11	.091	1	4	.250	4	3	0.3
Dick Warren	G	5-11	150	So.	3	0	3	.000	1	2	.500	3	1	0.2
Team												187		
Duke					30	990	2039	.486	504	697	.723	1297	2484	82.8
Opponents					30	837	1972	.424	473	694	.682	1108	2147	71.6

1966 UTAH

Head Coach—Jack Gardner   Final Record—23-8

Player	Pos.	Hgt.	Wgt.	Cl.	G	FG	FGA	Pct.	FT.	FTA	Pct.	Reb.	Pts.	Avg.
Jerry Chambers	F-C	6-4	180	Sr.	31	343	614	.559	206	252	.817	360	892	28.8
George Fisher	F-C	6-7	215	Sr.	25	129	271	.476	70	108	.648	231	328	13.1
Rich Tate	G	5-11	175	Sr.	30	127	303	.419	113	161	.702	92	367	12.2
Mervin Jackson	G-F	6-2	170	So.	31	147	310	.474	39	60	.650	181	333	10.7
Lyndon MacKay	F-C	6-6	200	So.	31	138	293	.471	44	66	.667	221	320	10.3
Jeff Ockel	C	6-7	225	So.	31	76	183	.415	66	83	.795	193	218	7.0
Eugene Lake	G	6-1	185	So.	29	61	154	.396	21	28	.750	34	143	4.9
Leonard Black	F	6-3	180	Sr.	27	51	104	.490	19	30	.633	64	121	4.5
Joe Day	G	6-0	180	Sr.	24	44	83	.530	13	18	.722	7	101	4.2
Ron Cunningham	F-C	6-5	195	So.	25	40	92	.435	26	39	.667	115	106	4.2
Kent Stepan	G	5-11	170	Jr.	2	2	7	.286	1	2	.500	2	5	2.5
Bill Ivey	C	6-8	220	Jr.	12	4	13	.308	2	5	.400	17	10	0.8
Gene Rodgers	F	6-5	215	So.	12	4	20	.200	2	2	1.000	13	10	0.8
Team												192		
Utah					31	1166	2447	.477	622	854	.728	1722	2954	95.3
Opponents					31	977	2393	.408	504	728	.692	1431	2458	79.3

1966 FINAL FOUR

At College Park, Md.
Semifinals

Duke	fg	fga	ft	fta	rb	pf	tp
Marin	11	18	7	10	7	2	29
Riedy	2	7	2	2	8	3	6
Lewis	9	13	3	3	6	3	21
Verga	2	7	0	0	3	1	4
Vacendak	7	16	3	3	3	5	17
Wendelin	1	4	0	1	2	4	2
Liccardo	0	1	0	0	0	0	0
Barone	0	0	0	0	0	1	0
Team					7		
Totals	32	66	15	19	36	19	79

Kentucky	fg	fga	ft	fta	rb	pf	tp
Conley	3	5	4	4	1	0	10
Riley	8	17	3	4	8	5	19
Jaracz	3	5	2	3	4	5	8
Dampier	11	20	1	2	4	3	23
Kron	5	13	2	2	10	1	12
Tallent	1	2	2	2	1	0	4
Berger	1	4	5	6	5	1	7
Gamble	0	0	0	1	0	1	0
Team					8		
Totals	32	66	19	24	41	16	83

Halftime: Duke 42-41. Officials: Honzo and Jenkins.

Texas Western	fg	fga	ft	fta	rb	pf	tp
Hill	5	20	8	10	11	4	18
Artis	10	20	2	3	5	2	22
Shed	2	3	5	6	3	3	9
Lattin	5	7	1	1	4	5	11
Flournoy	3	6	2	2	9	5	8
Cager	2	5	1	1	0	3	5
Worsley	5	8	2	3	5	3	12
Armstrong	0	2	0	1	3	2	0
Totals	32	71	21	27	40	27	85

Utah	fg	fga	ft	fta	rb	pf	tp
Tate	0	4	1	3	2	5	1
Jackson	3	9	2	2	2	1	8
Mackay	4	10	6	9	7	2	14
Ockel	1	1	3	3	9	5	5
Chambers	14	31	10	12	17	3	38
Black	3	8	2	4	2	3	8
Lake	1	1	0	0	0	0	2
Day	1	2	0	0	0	0	2
Totals	27	66	24	33	39	20	78

Halftime: Texas Western 42-39. Officials: Bussenius and Wirtz.

Championship
March 19

Kentucky	fg	fga	ft	fta	rb	pf	tp
Dampier	7	18	5	5	9	4	19
Kron	3	6	0	0	7	2	6
Conley	4	9	2	2	8	5	10
Riley	8	22	3	4	4	4	19
Jaracz	3	8	1	2	5	5	7
Berger	2	3	0	0	0	4	4
Gamble	0	0	0	0	0	1	0
LeMaster	0	1	0	0	0	1	0
Tallent	0	3	0	0	0	1	0
Totals	27	70	11	13	33	23	65

Texas Western	fg	fga	ft	fta	rb	pf	tp
Hill	7	17	6	9	3	3	20
Artis	5	13	5	5	8	1	15
Shed	1	1	1	1	3	3	3
Lattin	5	10	6	6	9	4	16
Cager	1	3	6	7	6	3	8
Flournoy	1	1	0	0	2	0	2
Worsley	2	4	4	6	4	0	8
Totals	22	49	28	34	35	12	72

Halftime: Texas Western 34-31. Officials: Honzo and Jenkins.

1967 The Beginning Of a Legend

The first of several key meetings between UCLA's Lew Alcindor (33) and Houston's Elvin Hayes occurred in a 1967 semifinal contest won by the Bruins.

On May 4, 1965, Ferdinand Lewis Alcindor Jr. stood in a high school gymnasium in New York City and announced at an unprecedented news conference that he had decided to attend college on the West Coast. As of that moment—12:33 p.m., to be exact—basketball fans conceded three national championships to the UCLA Bruins.

No previous player, not even Wilt Chamberlain or Oscar Robertson, had attracted as much attention while in high school as Lew Alcindor. The graduate of Power Memorial Academy was not only a full inch taller than 7 feet, but also quick, lithe, graceful and polished. He was a skilled passer and rebounder as well as an excellent shooter. His potential and UCLA's ambition both seemed limitless.

If anyone still needed convincing, Alcindor gave a startling demonstration in his first game in Westwood. Playing for the freshman team against the varsity, which included several veterans of the two previous NCAA championship teams, Alcindor scored 31 points and grabbed 21 rebounds in a 75-60 victory. That performance only whetted appetites when the varsity struggled through an 18-8 season while the freshman team went undefeated.

Finally, on December 3, 1966, it was time to unveil the big man. In his first varsity game, Alcindor scored a school-record 56 points in a devastating victory over rival Southern California. A few weeks later, USC Coach Bob Boyd ordered a stall and the Trojans managed to frustrate the Bruins long enough to force an overtime before bowing, 40-35.

A stall was the only hope many teams had of beating the Bruins. Run with UCLA and risk being embarrassed; hold the ball and make a travesty of the game. Most opponents attempted to keep up with the Bruins' pace, but none succeeded. And those that tried to control the tempo merely prompted UCLA Coach John Wooden to pronounce himself in favor of a shot clock similar to that employed by the pros.

By no means was Alcindor the Bruins' only weapon. Wooden was blessed with a superb backcourt consisting of swift Mike Warren and dynamic leaper Lucius Allen, a spectacular corner shooter in Lynn Shackelford and a hard-working defender in Ken Heitz. What concerned coaches around the country most was that five of UCLA's first six players were sophomores. The 1967 Bruins had nary a senior, but Warren, a junior who directed the offense, offered all the experienced leadership UCLA needed.

Other than the contest against Southern Cal and another slowdown game at Oregon, the Bruins romped through the regular season, winning all 26 games. Then they demolished Wyoming and Pacific in the West Regional and arrived at the Final Four

Dayton, unable to match up physically with Lew Alcindor, crowded the middle and tried to make life miserable for the Bruins' big man.

as the overwhelming favorite. They were matched against Houston in one semifinal while North Carolina played upstart Dayton in the other.

For UCLA and Houston, it would be the first of three games in two years, a mini-rivalry that would catapult college basketball into an era of tremendous growth. The Cougars, making their first appearance in a Final Four, were led by 6-8 consensus All-America forward Elvin Hayes. He was accompanied on the front line by 6-8 Don Kruse and 6-7 Melvin Bell. The guard who ran the offense, Don Chaney, was a sturdy 6-5. No team in the nation could match Houston's physical strength.

For that reason and a history of weak outside

Guards Lucius Allen (shown scoring against Dayton, left) and Mike Warren
(right) were the leaders of the UCLA team that featured a young, but dominant,
Lew Alcindor.

shooting, Coach Guy Lewis decided to take the basketball directly at Alcindor. Maybe the Cougars could muscle him. Perhaps they could force him into foul trouble. As it developed, they were able to do neither.

Alcindor wasn't charged with his first foul until the 33rd minute. Houston got no easy follow-up baskets. Still, the Cougars made a game of it for about eight minutes. They passed over the UCLA press, played intelligently and limited Alcindor to one basket in taking a 19-18 lead.

At that point, Shackelford buried a jump shot, the Bruins' press forced a steal and Alcindor scored on a slam dunk (a shot that would be outlawed the next season, presumably to give Big Lew's opponents a chance against him). Before Houston could react, UCLA had jumped ahead, 28-19. It was never close thereafter. The Bruins won, 73-58.

Publicly, Hayes was critical of the young center. "He's not aggressive enough on the boards, particularly on offense," the Houston star said. "Defensively, he just stands around. He's not at all, you know, all they really put him up to be."

If Hayes' comments disturbed Alcindor, he didn't let it affect their relationship. They visited the next afternoon, discussing music and basketball. Hayes would be playing that night in the consolation game against North Carolina. Alcindor would be back in the spotlight, playing for the national championship against Dayton.

The Flyers had surprised even themselves in qualifying for the final. Unranked all season, they had followed upsets in the Mideast Regional by stunning North Carolina, 76-62, behind forward Don May's 34 points and 17 rebounds. But Dayton was a small team and had little hope of matching up against Alcindor.

Don Donoher, the young Dayton coach, concocted a defense in which 6-6 sophomore Dan Sadlier was given primary responsibility for the UCLA center, with considerable help provided by his teammates. In crowding the middle, however, the other Flyers left gaps that were fully exploited by the Bruins. Alcindor had been taught to hit the open man and had outstanding court vision.

Rather than challenge the rigged defense, Alcindor passed off, allowing Allen, Warren and Shackelford all to score in double figures while he tallied 20 points, nine below his season average.

"We play team," he said. "You don't play one man. You lose playing one man."

Nevertheless, Alcindor's mere presence was pivotal. Some writers even went so far as to refer to the Bruins as "LewCLA" and to dateline their Final Four stories "LEW-isville" rather than Louisville, Ky. Indeed, Alcindor was the focal point of the

Bruins' defense, which was primarily responsible for their third national title in four years. Dayton went more than five minutes before scoring and fell behind early, 20-4. May, whose offense had carried the Flyers throughout the NCAA Tournament, was hounded into distraction by Heitz, a skinny honors student who played with glasses. May made only three of 12 field-goal attempts in the first half, when the outcome was determined.

"May is just a terrific player," Heitz said. "He's so strong and he knows how to use his strength. I knew that he was trying to get inside on me, but I could tell all along that he wouldn't take me in as far as he would normally like to because Lew would be there."

Alcindor was credited with four blocked shots, all in the first half. They made a lasting impression on the Flyers, who subsequently altered enough attempts to ruin their shooting percentage and any chance they had against UCLA. The final score of 79-64 was a gesture of mercy on Wooden's part. The Bruins led, 70-46, when the coach removed Alcindor and Warren with 5:17 remaining. The gap was 74-47 when Allen, the last starter in the lineup, went to the bench.

This was an entirely new situation for Wooden and UCLA. Yes, they had won two previous national titles, but with little teams that were praised for playing clever and exciting basketball. Suddenly, the Bruins were big, bad bullies.

Ironically, the player who felt the wrath of the crowd of 18,892 the most was Heitz, the most unlikely looking enforcer imaginable. May, who finished with a game-high 21 points, had fallen to the floor hard early in the game from an accidental blow and Heitz became the target of everyone in Freedom Hall who wanted to see a close game, which was everyone who did not attend or was not employed by UCLA.

"We're not very popular, are we?" Heitz decided.

The Bruins were not. They made it look so easy. "You know," Heitz said, "we're even starting to feel hurt. We are not a bully team at all. You practically have to smash Lew in the mouth before he gets tough.

"Oh well, I'm learning to understand these things. I used to root for all the underdogs myself. Now I'm a big fan of Green Bay and Muhammad Ali. I guess we all have to stick together."

As far as the nation was concerned, this was the beginning of a dynasty. Only a sophomore, Alcindor already was further advanced than any big man in the history of college basketball. The thought of what he might do in his next two seasons boggled the mind.

Even his coach, conservative by nature, called his prodigy awesome. "At times," Wooden conceded, "he frightens me."

Dayton's Don May (21), who almost single-handedly dismantled North Carolina in a semifinal victory, was held in check by UCLA defensive specialist Ken Heitz.

1967 Tournament Results	
First Round	**Regional Third Place**
Princeton 68, West Virginia 57	Princeton 78, St. John's 58
St. John's 57, Temple 53	Indiana 51, Tennessee 44
Boston College 48, Connecticut 42	Kansas 70, Louisville 68
Dayton 69, W. Kentucky 67 (ot)	Texas Western 69, Wyoming 67
Virginia Tech 82, Toledo 76	**Regional Championships**
Houston 59, New Mexico State 58	N. Carolina 96, Boston College 80
Texas Western 62, Seattle 54	Dayton 71, Virginia Tech 66 (ot)
Second Round	Houston 83, SMU 75
N. Carolina 78, Princeton 70 (ot)	UCLA 80, Pacific 64
Boston College 63, St. John's 62	**Semifinals**
Dayton 53, Tennessee 52	Dayton 76, North Carolina 62
Virginia Tech 79, Indiana 70	UCLA 73, Houston 58
Houston 66, Kansas 53	**Third Place**
SMU 83, Louisville 81	Houston 84, North Carolina 62
Pacific 72, Texas Western 63	**Championship**
UCLA 109, Wyoming 60	UCLA 79, Dayton 64

STATISTICS

1967 UCLA

Head Coach—John Wooden   Final Record—30-0

Player	Pos.	Hgt.	Wgt.	Cl.	G	FG	FGA	Pct.	FT	FTA	Pct.	Reb.	Pts.	Avg.
Lew Alcindor	C	7-1	230	So.	30	346	519	.667	178	274	.650	466	870	29.0
Lucius Allen	G	6-2	180	So.	30	187	390	.479	92	129	.713	175	466	15.5
Mike Warren	G	5-10	160	Jr.	30	144	310	.465	94	124	.758	134	382	12.7
Lynn Shackelford	F	6-5	190	So.	30	143	298	.480	55	67	.821	177	341	11.4
Ken Heitz	F	6-3	180	So.	30	78	154	.506	27	45	.600	95	183	6.1
Bill Sweek	F-G	6-3	192	So.	30	58	121	.479	26	46	.565	85	142	4.7
Jim Nielsen	C-F	6-7	205	So.	27	54	104	.519	15	33	.455	91	123	4.6
Don Saffer	G	6-1	170	Jr.	27	32	71	.451	13	24	.542	22	77	2.9
Gene Sutherland	G	6-1	175	Jr.	20	15	33	.455	7	12	.583	15	37	1.9
Neville Saner	F-C	6-6	212	Jr.	24	12	39	.308	10	15	.667	46	34	1.4
Joe Chrisman	F	6-3	185	Jr.	19	8	25	.320	4	11	.364	28	20	1.1
Dick Lynn	F	6-2	177	So.	9	4	13	.308	2	21	.095	7	10	1.1
Kent Taylor	F	6-2	180	So.	4	1	5	.200	0	0	.000	1	2	0.5
Team												153		
UCLA					30	1082	2082	.520	523	801	.653	1495	2687	89.6
Opponents					30	779	1989	.392	352	570	.618	1196	1910	63.7

1967 DAYTON

Head Coach—Don Donoher   Final Record—25-6

Player	Pos.	Hgt.	Wgt.	Cl.	G	FG	FGA	Pct.	FT	FTA	Pct.	Reb.	Pts.	Avg.
Don May	F	6-4	210	Jr.	31	258	543	.475	173	213	.812	519	689	22.2
Bob Hooper	G	6-0	160	Jr.	31	140	286	.490	82	102	.804	122	362	11.7
Rudy Waterman	G	6-1	160	Jr.	29	132	291	.454	60	93	.645	89	324	11.2
Glinder Torain	F	6-6	189	Jr.	29	119	285	.418	61	84	.726	174	299	10.3
Gene Klaus	G	6-0	160	Sr.	31	107	214	.500	72	93	.774	65	286	9.2
Dan Sadlier	F	6-6	201	So.	29	95	180	.528	37	60	.617	152	227	7.8
Dan Obrovac	C	6-10	215	So.	29	68	147	.463	42	84	.500	185	178	6.1
Ned Sharpenter	C	6-7	220	So.	15	20	40	.500	9	23	.391	50	49	3.3
Jim Wannemacher	F	6-6	200	Sr.	20	19	51	.373	12	18	.667	31	50	2.5
Rich Fox	F	6-4	198	Jr.	11	9	16	.563	6	10	.600	12	24	2.2
Tom Heckman	G	6-1	160	So.	19	9	21	.429	6	10	.600	3	24	1.3
Dennis Papp	G	6-3	190	Sr.	7	3	7	.429	1	2	.500	2	7	1.0
John Samanich	F	6-7	190	Sr.	6	3	8	.375	0	1	.000	7	6	1.0
Dave Inderrieden	G	5-11	165	Sr.	7	0	2	.000	1	4	.250	4	1	0.1
John Rohm	C	6-6	205	Jr.	1	0	0	.000	0	0	.000	0	0	0.0
Team												129		
Dayton					31	982	2091	.470	562	797	.705	1544	2526	81.5
Opponents					31	855	2063	.414	462	711	.650	1257	2172	70.1

1967 HOUSTON

Head Coach—Guy Lewis   Final Record—27-4

Player	Pos.	Hgt.	Wgt.	Cl.	G	FG	FGA	Pct.	FT	FTA	Pct.	Reb.	Pts.	Avg.
Elvin Hayes	F	6-8	235	Jr.	31	373	750	.497	135	227	.595	488	881	28.4
Don Chaney	G	6-5	210	So.	31	197	448	.440	80	116	.690	160	474	15.3
Melvin Bell	F	6-7	235	So.	31	160	332	.482	78	131	.595	282	398	12.8
Gary Grider	G	6-1	175	Sr.	31	92	202	.455	68	98	.694	96	252	8.1
Leary Lentz	C-F	6-6	210	Sr.	31	100	230	.435	45	71	.634	250	245	7.9
Don Kruse	C	6-8	235	Sr.	31	67	174	.385	38	53	.717	131	172	5.5
Ken Spain	C	6-9	230	So.	31	69	135	.511	28	49	.571	137	166	5.4
Andrew Benson	F	6-7	220	Sr.	19	21	38	.553	4	10	.400	32	46	2.4
Theodis Lee	F-G	6-7	200	So.	23	20	57	.351	10	18	.556	31	50	2.2
Niemer Hamood	G	6-0	170	So.	23	14	40	.350	7	13	.538	5	35	1.5
David Starks	G	5-10	170	Jr.	11	4	10	.400	6	6	1.000	7	14	1.3
Vernon Lewis	G	5-11	170	Jr.	29	9	40	.225	8	17	.471	13	26	0.9
Elliott McVey	G	5-10	180	Jr.	7	2	3	.667	2	4	.500	5	6	0.9
Team												225		
Houston					31	1128	2459	.459	509	813	.626	1862	2765	89.2
Opponents					31	898	2283	.393	461	665	.693	1589	2257	72.5

1967 NORTH CAROLINA

Head Coach—Dean Smith   Final Record—26-6

Player	Pos.	Hgt.	Wgt.	Cl.	G	FG	FGA	Pct.	FT	FTA	Pct.	Reb.	Pts.	Avg.
Larry Miller	F	6-3	210	Jr.	32	278	553	.503	144	218	.661	299	700	21.9
Bob Lewis	F	6-3	180	Sr.	32	212	472	.449	167	211	.791	176	591	18.5
Rusty Clark	C	6-10	228	So.	32	181	328	.552	85	123	.691	330	447	14.0
Dick Grubar	G	6-3	190	So.	32	103	209	.493	88	141	.624	94	294	9.2
Bill Bunting	C	6-8	195	So.	32	96	212	.453	55	86	.640	179	247	7.7
Tom Gauntlett	G	6-4	190	Sr.	29	53	145	.366	14	23	.609	57	120	4.1
Joe Brown	F	6-5	195	So.	26	31	83	.373	10	20	.500	63	72	2.8
Gerald Tuttle	G	6-0	160	So.	30	25	53	.472	23	39	.590	14	73	2.4
Ralph Fletcher	F	6-5	190	Jr.	17	14	37	.378	1	9	.111	27	29	1.7
Mark Mirken	F	6-6	225	Sr.	14	9	27	.333	5	6	.833	32	23	1.6
Jim Bostick	G	6-3	185	So.	14	8	19	.421	2	5	.400	8	18	1.3
Jim Frye	F	6-5	180	Jr.	5	2	6	.333	0	1	.000	4	4	0.8
Donnie Moe	G	6-2	170	Jr.	17	4	10	.400	4	12	.333	9	12	0.7
Team												213		
North Carolina					32	1016	2154	.472	598	894	.669	1505	2630	82.2
Opponents					32	873	2094	.417	531	772	.688	1392	2277	71.2

1967 FINAL FOUR

At Louisville, Ky.
Semifinals

UCLA

	fg	fga	ft	fta	rb	pf	tp
Heitz	0	0	1	1	0	1	1
Shackelford	11	19	0	1	8	1	22
Alcindor	6	11	7	13	20	1	19
Allen	6	15	5	5	9	2	17
Warren	4	10	6	7	9	0	14
Nielsen	0	3	0	0	3	5	0
Sweek	0	4	0	0	1	2	0
Saffer	0	0	0	0	0	0	0
Team					1		
Totals	27	62	19	27	51	12	73

Houston

	fg	fga	ft	fta	rb	pf	tp
Hayes	12	31	1	2	24	4	25
Bell	3	11	4	7	11	4	10
Kruse	2	5	1	1	0	2	5
Grider	2	7	0	0	2	2	4
Chaney	3	11	0	2	4	4	6
Lentz	1	2	0	3	4	1	2
Spain	1	5	0	4	4	2	2
Lewis	0	0	0	1	0	1	0
Lee	2	3	0	0	1	0	4
Team					1		
Totals	26	75	6	16	51	20	58

Halftime: UCLA 39-28.

Dayton

	fg	fga	ft	fta	rb	pf	tp
May	16	22	2	6	17	2	34
Sadlier	4	7	0	1	0	0	8
Obrovac	0	0	0	0	1	1	0
Klaus	3	6	9	10	8	4	15
Hooper	1	7	3	4	4	1	5
Torain	4	14	6	8	11	5	14
Wannemacher	0	0	0	2	0	0	0
Waterman	0	0	0	0	0	0	0
Team					5		
Totals	28	56	20	31	46	13	76

North Carolina

	fg	fga	ft	fta	rb	pf	tp
Miller	6	18	1	1	13	4	13
Bunting	1	3	1	1	5	4	3
Clark	8	14	3	5	11	4	19
Lewis	5	18	1	1	3	3	11
Grubar	2	7	3	3	2	4	7
Gauntlett	1	4	0	0	3	0	2
Brown	0	3	0	0	0	0	0
Tuttle	3	5	1	1	1	3	7
Team					5		
Totals	26	72	10	12	43	22	62

Halftime: Dayton 29-23.

Championship
March 25

UCLA

	fg	fga	ft	fta	rb	pf	tp
Heitz	2	7	0	0	6	2	4
Shackelford	5	10	0	2	3	1	10
Alcindor	8	12	4	11	18	0	20
Allen	7	15	5	8	9	2	19
Warren	8	16	1	1	7	1	17
Nielsen	0	1	0	1	1	3	0
Sweek	1	1	0	0	0	1	2
Saffer	2	5	0	0	4	1	4
Saner	1	1	0	0	2	2	2
Chrisman	0	0	1	2	1	2	1
Sutherland	0	0	0	0	0	0	0
Lynn	0	1	0	0	0	0	0
Team					2		
Totals	34	69	11	25	54	15	79

Dayton

	fg	fga	ft	fta	rb	pf	tp
May	9	23	3	4	17	4	21
Sadlier	2	5	1	2	7	5	5
Obrovac	0	2	0	0	2	1	0
Klaus	4	7	0	0	0	1	8
Hooper	2	7	2	4	5	2	6
Torain	3	14	0	0	4	3	6
Waterman	4	11	2	3	1	3	10
Sharpenter	2	5	4	5	5	1	8
Samanich	0	2	0	0	2	0	0
Beckman	0	0	0	0	0	0	0
Inderrieden	0	0	0	0	0	0	0
Wannemacher	0	0	0	0	0	0	0
Team					8		
Totals	26	76	12	18	51	20	64

Halftime UCLA 38-20.

1968 The Bruins Get Revenge

The story of college basketball in 1968 was a tale of two games, two teams and one court. With nothing less than a No. 1 ranking and the national championship at stake, UCLA and Houston conducted perhaps the most memorable home-and-home series in the sport's history. Remarkably, the two games, staged half a continent apart, were played on the same floor.

The first meeting, in Houston, opened the sport to new vistas. The second encounter, at the Final Four in Los Angeles, then demonstrated nothing really had changed. If the former suggested that even the Bruins of Lew Alcindor were not invincible, the latter proved just how extraordinary was their defeat.

Even before the unbeaten teams walked to the center jump circle on the night of January 20, it was apparent that they were participants in an event of historic significance. Every seat in the mammoth Astrodome plus some 4,000 standing-room positions had been sold, a total of 52,693 paid admissions. In addition, a network of more than 150 television stations in 49 states had been hastily assembled to bring the game to millions of households. The setting was spectacular if bizarre.

Located smack in the middle of the world's first enclosed baseball-football stadium was a portable court on loan from the Los Angeles Sports Arena, which was scheduled to host the NCAA Tournament semifinal and championship games in March. Arena officials had agreed to provide the court free of charge, although it cost $10,000 to convert the Astrodome for basketball, a process that required trucking 225 floor panels from and to the West Coast. The court was surrounded by strips of AstroTurf and sat in isolated splendor, more than 100 feet from the nearest seats.

What seared the game into the nation's consciousness, of course, was the result. Houston's 71-69 upset was as colossal as the facility in which it occurred. UCLA had won 47 consecutive games, including all 43 it had played since Alcindor joined the varsity, and appeared as unbeatable as any team

Lew Alcindor (33) controlled the opening tip of a 1968 semifinal game against Houston's Elvin Hayes and dominated his counterpart the rest of the way.

in NCAA annals. Furthermore, the Cougars edged the Bruins not by playing a slowdown game, but by taking it to Alcindor.

Granted, Alcindor was not at his best for the meeting. Only the week before, the consensus All-America had suffered a scratched eyeball against California. He sat out the next two games and wore an eye patch for the better part of the week. He appeared distracted by the scene and affected by the lighting, making only four of 18 field-goal attempts in the grips of Houston's 1-3-1 zone.

But UCLA did not lose the game. The Cougars won it, thanks to a magnificent performance by 6-foot-9 senior Elvin Hayes. The consensus All-America scored 29 points in the first half and 10 more in the second—including the deciding free throws with 28 seconds left—grabbed 15 rebounds, blocked eight shots and even managed four assists. The sound of 50,000 fans chanting "E, E, E" created an unprecedented sensation.

The victory was Houston's 18th in succession since a loss to UCLA in the 1967 national semifinals, and it boosted the Cougars from second place in the wire-service polls to first.

"I hope they come back to L.A. undefeated," Bruins guard Lucius Allen said. "That would be very nice."

Houston did just that, routing Loyola of Chicago, Louisville and Texas Christian in the Midwest Regional to carry a 31-0 record, as well as the No. 1 ranking, into the Final Four. As for the Bruins, they quickly rebounded from their first defeat and won the remainder of their games, dismissing stubborn New Mexico State and Santa Clara in the West Regional. UCLA and Houston were bracketed for a rematch in the semifinals at the Sports Arena, whose court had been returned from the Astrodome and was back in its normal setting. Only now it was the Final Floor.

As had been the case the previous year in Louisville, North Carolina won the East Regional and an underdog team from Ohio, in this case Ohio State, was representing the Mideast. But the attention in Los Angeles focused almost exclusively on the UCLA-Houston game. The Cougars were treated like the sudden celebrities they were, visiting movie sets, appearing on TV shows and resting their heads in a Beverly Hills hostelry.

Never at a loss for words, Hayes said this was the rubber match of the series and he didn't want to hear another word about Alcindor's eye injury.

"Last year, when they beat us in the tournament, I didn't make excuses," he said. "All I said was that

After making short work of Houston and Elvin Hayes in a semifinal contest, Lew Alcindor, shown rebounding over North Carolina's Charlie Scott (33), dominated the Tar Heels in the title game.

Houston Coach Guy Lewis, who had guided his Cougars to a major upset of UCLA in the regular season, watched in consternation as the Bruins got revenge.

he had beaten me but I wasn't going to believe he was better than me until I had one more look. Well, I had one more look and I won. We won. I guess this will settle it, best two out of three."

Hayes, already selected Player of the Year for his performance in the regular season, had been at his best in the tournament, averaging 41 points per game in three contests. But this was a UCLA team that had been stung for the first time in two years. The result was an almost perfect game by an almost perfect team.

Start with the defense, because that's what the Bruins did. At the suggestion of assistant coach Jerry Norman, Coach John Wooden instructed forward Lynn Shackelford to shadow Hayes while the other four players aligned themselves in a diamond-shaped zone. Guard Mike Warren was stationed at the top of the key, Allen and forward Mike Lynn on the wings and Alcindor under the basket. Hayes, growing more and more discouraged by Shackelford's relentless pressure as the game wore on, was virtually eliminated from the Houston offense. He finished with only three field goals in 10 attempts and a total of 10 points.

UCLA also stepped up its full-court press, creating easy baskets. And unlike that night in the Astrodome, the outside shooting was sure. The Bruins used a 21-5 run midway through the first half to bolt ahead, 41-24, and a timeout by Cougars Coach Guy Lewis failed to slow the momentum. The lead was 22 at the half, then 28, 35 and, at its peak, 44 (95-51). Only massive substitutions held the final score to 101-69.

"That's the greatest exhibition of basketball I've ever seen," Lewis conceded.

The victory was so complete that Alcindor shared scoring honors with Allen and Lynn. Each player had 19 points. Big Lew added 18 rebounds and keyed a defense that limited the Cougars to 28.2 percent field-goal shooting.

"Our mental attitude wasn't right," said Houston forward Theodis Lee, who was two of 15 from the field.

The Bruins, who sent the hometown crowd of 15,742 into a frenzy, had no such problem.

"We haven't really said anything publicly," Warren said after the Bruins qualified to meet North Carolina in the championship game, "but we're a vindictive team. We've been looking forward to this game for a long time."

They had but one day to look forward to the Tar Heels, who had beaten Ohio State, 80-66, in the other semifinal game. That wouldn't be a problem.

"We're not looking past North Carolina," insisted Warren, a senior whose greatest fame would come years later on "Hill Street Blues," a TV show in which he portrayed Officer Bobby Hill. "We'll run them back down South, too."

Even if the Bruins weren't looking past the Tar Heels, their supporters certainly were. Supremely confident that the victory over Houston locked up a second straight title, the fans didn't even fill the Sports Arena. A crowd of 14,438 attended the championship game.

Tar Heels Coach Dean Smith had hoped to slow the tempo of the game with his spread offense, the four corners, and to take only high-percentage shots. But the presence of Alcindor in the middle ruined the strategy. He rejected at least seven shots and altered countless others, and the Tar Heels made an unacceptable 34.9 percent of their field-goal tries. Alcindor was equally devastating on offense, scoring a game-high 34 points against Carolina's ineffective man-to-man in a decisive 78-55 triumph. The 23-point spread was the largest in championship-game history.

UCLA's total domination of the Tar Heels and Cougars led to the selection of four Bruins—Alcindor, Allen, Warren and Shackelford—for the all-tournament team along with Carolina's Larry Miller, a consensus All-America forward. Alcindor, of course, reigned as the outstanding player for the second time in two years. He was, Smith decided, "the greatest player who ever played the game."

And he had one more year of eligibility left—one more year in which to do something no player or group of classmates had ever done before.

"Our next goal," said Allen, speaking for himself and his fellow Bruins of the class of 1969, "is a third NCAA title next year."

Said Wooden: "It's difficult to do, very difficult. Look back through the history of the NCAA. Isn't it difficult?"

Difficult, yes. Impossible, no.

The smile, the finger and the sign say it all as Lew Alcindor enjoys his second straight championship celebration.

1968 Tournament Results

First Round
St. Bonaventure 102, Bos. Col. 93
Columbia 83, La Salle 69
Davidson 79, St. John's 70
Marquette 72, Bowling Green 71
East Tenn. St. 79, Florida St. 69
Houston 94, Loyola (Ill.) 76
New Mexico St. 68, Weber State 57

Second Round
N. Carolina 91, St. Bonaventure 72
Davidson 61, Columbia 59 (ot)
Kentucky 107, Marquette 89
Ohio State 79, East Tenn. St. 72
Houston 91, Louisville 75
Texas Christian 77, Kansas St. 72
UCLA 58, New Mexico State 49
Santa Clara 86, New Mexico 73

Regional Third Place
Columbia 95, St. Bonaventure 75
Marquette 69, East Tenn. St. 57
Louisville 93, Kansas State 63
New Mexico St. 62, New Mexico 58

Regional Championships
North Carolina 70, Davidson 66
Ohio State 82, Kentucky 81
Houston 103, Texas Christian 68
UCLA 87, Santa Clara 66

Semifinals
North Carolina 80, Ohio State 66
UCLA 101, Houston 69

Third Place
Ohio State 89, Houston 85

Championship
UCLA 78, North Carolina 55

STATISTICS

1968 UCLA

Head Coach—John Wooden **Final Record—29-1**

Player	Pos.	Hgt.	Wgt.	Cl.	G	FG	FGA	Pct.	FT.	FTA	Pct.	Reb.	Pts.	Avg.
Lew Alcindor	C	7-2	230	Jr.	28	294	480	.613	146	237	.616	461	734	26.2
Lucius Allen	G	6-2	178	Jr.	30	186	403	.462	80	118	.678	181	452	15.1
Mike Warren	G	5-11	155	Sr.	30	152	353	.431	58	76	.763	111	362	12.1
Edgar Lacey	F	6-6	190	Sr.	14	72	125	.576	22	32	.688	110	166	11.9
Lynn Shackelford	F	6-5	192	Jr.	30	146	293	.498	28	33	.848	151	320	10.7
Mike Lynn	F	6-7	205	Sr.	30	128	280	.457	54	79	.684	156	310	10.3
Ken Heitz	G	6-3	181	Jr.	27	59	118	.500	26	35	.743	62	144	5.3
Jim Nielsen	F	6-7	205	Jr.	30	58	117	.496	23	35	.657	99	139	4.6
Bill Sweek	G	6-3	186	Jr.	27	40	85	.471	17	26	.654	32	97	3.6
Gene Sutherland	G	6-1	177	Sr.	27	10	24	.417	23	26	.885	15	43	1.6
Neville Saner	C	6-6	212	Sr.	24	16	43	.372	3	5	.600	38	35	1.5
Team												187		
UCLA					30	1161	2321	.500	480	702	.684	1603	2802	93.4
Opponents					30	781	2029	.385	453	688	.658	1238	2015	67.2

1968 NORTH CAROLINA

Head Coach—Dean Smith **Final Record—28-4**

Player	Pos.	Hgt.	Wgt.	Cl.	G	FG	FGA	Pct.	FT.	FTA	Pct.	Reb.	Pts.	Avg.
Larry Miller	F	6-4	215	Sr.	32	268	545	.492	181	256	.707	258	717	22.4
Charlie Scott	G	6-5	178	So.	32	234	490	.478	94	141	.667	191	562	17.6
Rusty Clark	C	6-10	225	Jr.	31	187	393	.476	115	168	.685	341	489	15.8
Dick Grubar	G	6-4	185	Jr.	32	97	227	.427	64	90	.711	97	258	8.1
Bill Bunting	F	6-9	189	Jr.	31	85	199	.427	75	110	.682	186	245	7.9
Joe Brown	F	6-5	201	Jr.	32	82	196	.418	37	63	.587	132	201	6.3
Eddie Fogler	G	5-11	160	So.	32	26	81	.321	17	26	.654	34	69	2.2
Ralph Fletcher	F	6-6	205	Jr.	23	10	28	.357	21	27	.778	30	41	1.8
Gerald Tuttle	G	5-11	160	Jr.	29	18	47	.383	14	23	.609	20	50	1.7
Jim Frye	F	6-5	175	Jr.	13	7	16	.438	5	7	.714	6	19	1.5
Jim Delany	G	5-11	165	So.	17	11	29	.379	1	3	.333	5	23	1.4
Gra Whitehead	F	6-4	185	So.	12	2	5	.400	0	0	.000	1	4	0.3
Ricky Webb	F	6-4	175	So.	7	1	5	.200	0	2	.000	2	2	0.3
Team												208		
North Carolina					32	1028	2261	.455	624	916	.681	1511	2680	83.8
Opponents					32	912	2052	.444	492	708	.695	1370	2316	72.4

1968 OHIO STATE

Head Coach—Fred Taylor **Final Record—21-8**

Player	Pos.	Hgt.	Wgt.	Cl.	G	FG	FGA	Pct.	FT.	FTA	Pct.	Reb.	Pts.	Avg.
Bill Hosket	F	6-7	228	Sr.	29	228	422	.540	128	190	.674	332	584	20.1
Steve Howell	F	6-5	232	Jr.	29	217	428	.507	73	98	.745	157	507	17.5
Dave Sorenson	C	6-7	214	So.	29	196	329	.596	82	115	.713	289	474	16.3
Denny Meadors	G	6-0	176	Jr.	29	94	230	.409	82	112	.732	98	270	9.3
Jody Finney	G	6-3	180	So.	23	61	128	.477	32	46	.696	66	154	6.7
Mike Swain	G	6-4	206	Sr.	23	34	81	.420	24	37	.649	56	92	4.0
Ed Smith	F	6-5	215	So.	26	35	97	.361	15	46	.326	93	85	3.3
Bruce Schnabel	G	6-0	174	Jr.	23	25	48	.521	16	22	.727	14	66	2.9
Jim Geddes	G	6-1	177	So.	21	23	56	.411	12	27	.444	40	58	2.8
Gary McDavid	F	6-0	177	Jr.	2	2	2	1.000	0	0	.000	1	4	2.0
Dan Andreas	F	6-3	208	So.	22	18	47	.383	6	11	.545	39	42	1.9
Tom Spies	G	6-2	168	So.	7	4	11	.364	4	7	.571	5	12	1.7
Craig Barclay	G	6-3	186	So.	19	8	27	.296	12	18	.667	8	28	1.5
Steve Barnard	C	6-7	200	Jr.	9	3	9	.333	2	3	.667	14	8	0.9
Ted Bauer	C	6-7	196	Sr.	3	1	2	.500	0	0	.000	0	2	0.7
Others	.	.....	.....	..		0	4	.000	0	3	.000	4	0	0.0
Team												164		
Ohio State					29	949	1921	.494	488	735	.664	1380	2386	82.3
Opponents					29	821	2035	.403	493	731	.674	1157	2135	73.6

1968 HOUSTON

Head Coach—Guy Lewis **Final Record—31-2**

Player	Pos.	Hgt.	Wgt.	Cl.	G	FG	FGA	Pct.	FT.	FTA	Pct.	Reb.	Pts.	Avg.
Elvin Hayes	F	6-9	235	Sr.	33	519	945	.549	176	285	.618	624	1214	36.8
Ken Spain	C	6-9	230	Jr.	33	191	406	.470	92	157	.586	422	474	14.4
Theodis Lee	F	6-7	210	Jr.	33	203	466	.436	54	99	.545	260	460	13.9
Don Chaney	G	6-5	210	Sr.	33	189	431	.439	50	84	.595	191	428	13.0
George Reynolds	G	6-4	205	Jr.	28	106	197	.538	68	93	.731	136	280	10.0
Tom Gribben	F-G	6-2	180	So.	30	38	116	.328	22	33	.667	70	98	3.3
Niemer Hamood	G	6-0	170	Jr.	25	31	65	.477	17	22	.773	17	79	3.2
Carlos Bell	C-F	6-5	220	Jr.	23	27	53	.509	17	24	.708	50	71	3.1
Vern Lewis	G	5-11	170	Sr.	33	35	91	.385	23	38	.605	34	93	2.8
Larry Cooper	F	6-6	210	So.	18	11	22	.500	3	10	.300	20	25	1.4
Kent Taylor	G	6-2	180	So.	8	1	8	.125	0	2	.000	6	2	0.3
Billy Bane	G	6-2	188	Jr.	11	1	9	.111	0	3	.000	9	2	0.2
Team												215		
Houston					33	1352	2809	.481	522	850	.614	2074	3226	97.8
Opponents					33	943	2449	.385	497	699	.711	1418	2383	72.2

1968 FINAL FOUR

At Los Angeles
Semifinals

Ohio State	fg	fga	ft	fta	rb	pf	tp
Howell	6	17	1	2	3	2	13
Hosket	4	11	6	9	9	5	14
Sorenson	5	17	1	3	11	3	11
Schnabel	0	1	0	0	2	1	0
Meadors	3	13	2	2	3	3	8
Finney	8	13	0	2	4	2	16
Smith	2	6	0	0	5	1	4
Andreas	0	0	0	0	0	0	0
Barclay	0	1	0	0	0	0	0
Geddes	0	0	0	0	1	1	0
Team					11		
Totals	28	79	10	18	49	18	66

North Carolina	fg	fga	ft	fta	rb	pf	tp
Miller	10	23	0	1	6	2	20
Bunting	4	7	9	10	12	2	17
Clark	7	9	1	1	11	4	15
Scott	6	16	1	4	5	3	13
Grubar	4	9	3	3	6	0	11
Fogler	1	2	0	0	0	1	2
Brown	0	4	0	0	4	2	0
Tuttle	1	1	0	1	0	0	2
Team					10		
Totals	33	71	14	20	54	14	80

Halftime: North Carolina 34-27. Officials: Bussenius and Jenkins.

Houston	fg	fga	ft	fta	rb	pf	tp
Lee	2	15	0	4	4	4	4
Hayes	3	10	4	7	5	4	10
Spain	4	12	7	10	13	1	15
Chaney	5	13	5	7	7	2	15
Lewis	2	8	2	2	5	0	6
Hamood	3	5	4	6	0	2	10
Gribben	0	5	0	1	5	1	0
Bell	3	8	3	4	5	0	9
Taylor	0	0	0	0	0	0	0
Cooper	0	2	0	0	1	0	0
Team					9		
Totals	22	78	25	37	54	14	69

UCLA	fg	fga	ft	fta	rb	pf	tp
Shackelford	6	10	5	5	3	4	17
Lynn	8	10	3	8	4	4	19
Alcindor	7	14	5	6	18	3	19
Warren	7	18	0	0	5	3	14
Allen	9	18	1	2	9	1	19
Nielsen	2	3	0	0	1	4	4
Heitz	3	6	1	1	1	1	7
Sweek	1	1	0	0	0	2	2
Sutherland	0	1	0	0	0	1	0
Saner	0	2	0	0	1	2	0
Team					11		
Totals	43	83	15	18	57	23	101

Halftime: UCLA 53-31. Officials: Honzo and Fouty.

Championship
March 23

UCLA	fg	fga	ft	fta	rb	pf	tp
Shackelford	3	5	0	1	2	0	6
Lynn	1	7	5	7	6	3	7
Alcindor	15	21	4	4	16	3	34
Warren	3	7	1	1	3	2	7
Allen	3	7	5	7	5	0	11
Nielsen	1	1	0	0	1	1	2
Heitz	3	6	1	1	2	3	7
Sutherland	1	2	0	0	2	1	2
Sweek	0	1	0	0	0	1	0
Saner	1	3	0	0	2	2	2
Team							
Totals	31	60	16	21	48	16	78

North Carolina	fg	fga	ft	fta	rb	pf	tp
Miller	5	13	4	6	6	3	14
Bunting	1	3	1	2	2	5	3
Clark	4	12	1	3	8	3	9
Scott	6	17	0	1	3	3	12
Grubar	2	5	1	2	0	2	5
Fogler	1	4	2	2	0	0	4
Brown	2	5	2	2	5	1	6
Tuttle	0	0	0	0	0	0	0
Frye	1	2	0	1	1	0	2
Whitehead	0	0	0	0	0	0	0
Delany	0	1	0	0	0	0	0
Fletcher	0	1	0	0	0	0	0
Team					10		
Totals	22	63	11	19	35	17	55

Halftime: UCLA 32-22. Officials: Honzo and Fouty.

1969 Three and Counting . . .

Three was the magic number as a happy group of UCLA Bruins celebrated an unprecedented third straight national title.

There seemed to be only one fitting conclusion to the Lew Alcindor era at UCLA. Before the center of attention became the focus of a bidding war between the pro leagues, it was all but written in the stars that he lead the Bruins to a third consecutive national championship. To his everlasting credit, what others promised, Alcindor delivered.

But his was not a senior season without incident. Alcindor had felt the need to defend himself against published charges of racism and criticism of his school and country. He had joined other prominent black athletes in boycotting the 1968 Olympic Games, a decision that generated quite a bit of hate mail, and an article by a former UCLA student charged Alcindor with espousing racial separatism.

For those reasons or perhaps for the absence of challenging competition, UCLA's play throughout the regular season did not approach the level achieved in the NCAA Tournament the previous

spring. Indeed, Alcindor's last scheduled game ended in disappointment. Employing a delay game, archrival Southern California squeezed out a 46-44 upset at Pauley Pavilion—the Bruins' first loss ever on the court they had called home for four years. It marked UCLA's first defeat after 41 victories and, since it followed by one night a shaky double-overtime victory over the Trojans at the Los Angeles Sports Arena, caused more than a little consternation.

Still, the Bruins unquestionably were the team to beat in the NCAA Tournament. They even had the advantage of hosting the West Regional at Pauley Pavilion. They didn't really need that edge, but it gave Alcindor two more chances to strut his stuff in front of the home folks and gave the students and fans two more chances to say goodbye.

The victims were New Mexico State and Santa Clara. They never had a chance. After handling the

The Bruins' top gun, as usual, was Lew Alcindor, who is pictured here in a post-championship-game scene with his father.

Aggies, 53-38, UCLA opened the throttle and demolished a Santa Clara team that had lost only once all season and was ranked among the top four teams in the national wire-service polls. The game was so one-sided that the Broncos were behind 7-0 before they managed to push the ball over the midcourt line. They didn't manage a shot for the first 3½ minutes and trailed by 11-0 and then 18-2 before the game was eight minutes old.

These Bruins were perceived to have a weakness in the backcourt—Mike Warren had graduated and Lucius Allen was an academic casualty—but Santa Clara never got a chance to probe. John Wooden unleashed his famous zone press, which he had used to harass opponents in 1964 and 1965 but had used sparingly during the Alcindor era.

"The press tore us apart," Santa Clara Coach Dick Garibaldi said. "And then their shooting blasted us completely out. We never got to play the game we prepared for."

Alcindor, who was flanked up front by a good pair of sophomores, Curtis Rowe and Sidney Wicks, was replaced with just under eight minutes remaining and UCLA on its way to a 90-52 rout. The ovation was so deafening that Wooden motioned for him to stand and acknowledge the cheers. He pulled up teammate Ken Heitz and the two seniors stood and waved their index fingers to the crowd.

"We finally played our game," Wooden said afterward.

If that thought was disturbing to the other teams in the Final Four—Drake, Purdue and old standby North Carolina—they weren't about to admit it. Dolph Pulliam, Drake's outstanding defender, warned that his team deserved respect after its triumph in the Midwest Regional.

"If (the Bruins) don't give it to us," he said, "they'd better look out. I can't think of a better way of getting our 13th straight (victory) than by beating UCLA."

It seemed a farfetched notion. But the Bulldogs, champions of the Missouri Valley Conference, certainly were not intimidated by UCLA's reputation. Using a hyperactive man-to-man defense that sometimes left Alcindor to 6-foot-5 Al Williams, Drake dogged the Bruins throughout the game, and only guard John Vallely's hot shooting in the second half enabled the defending champions to open an 83-74 lead in the final two minutes.

But even then, UCLA's victory was not secure. Drake ran off eight consecutive points to cut the deficit to one with nine seconds left and was one turnover away from a staggering upset when Bruins forward Lynn Shackelford was fouled just before the final buzzer. He made two free throws, raising the final margin to a harrowing 85-82.

"I feel," Wooden said, "like I've had a reprieve."

Despite the support from its avid followers and
cheerleaders, Purdue was easy pickings for
the overpowering Bruins.

High-scoring Purdue star Rick Mount (10)
was held in check by unsung UCLA defensive
specialist Ken Heitz (22).

Purdue, featuring deadeye jump shooter Rick
Mount, qualified for the other berth in the title
game by dismantling a tall, accomplished North
Carolina team. Although it ranked as only a mild
upset, there was nothing modest about the score,
92-65. Mount, the second-leading scorer in the nation and a consensus All-America, scored 36 points
and the Tar Heels contributed 26 turnovers.

Now that UCLA was 40 minutes away from an
unprecedented third consecutive national championship, it didn't seem possible the Bruins would
be denied. They were not. Nor were they threatened
as they had been in the semifinal. Purdue, which
had opened its season by losing to UCLA, 94-82,
would close it in similar fashion. The Boilermakers'
man-to-man defense caused no problems for Alcindor, and the most dominant player of his time
burned them for 37 points in 36 minutes. He added
20 rebounds in a ho-hum 92-72 victory.

In the final game of his collegiate career, Alcin-

dor had to share the spotlight with Heitz. Although
the bespectacled senior didn't score a point, his defense on Mount was a key to victory. It recalled his
effort against Don May of Dayton in the championship game two years earlier on the same court in
Louisville's Freedom Hall.

Mount, who was averaging 33.5 points per game
entering the contest, led his team in scoring with 28
points but missed 24 of 36 field-goal attempts, and
the majority of his baskets came in the second half
after the decision had been settled.

"I feel that every point Mount scored under his
average before the game was decided," Wooden
said, "should be counted for Kenny."

It was a nice moment for Heitz, whose three-year
career had been something less than one long joy-
ride. The depth of talent at UCLA was such that he
had to sit for long stretches of time.

"There were just so many of us, all the time, every
year," he reflected. "The only thing to aim for was

not so much winning—we would win—but playing. If you had a good game, you got playing time the next game. There were disappointments. I didn't get much time last season, but that's personal."

Even Shackelford, who got more playing time in three years than any of Alcindor's classmates, had mixed emotions about the experience. A lot of it, he said, "has been boring, sitting on the bench or even playing when the other team was obviously weaker. From the start, everybody said we would win three championships. That has taken a lot out of the actual accomplishment. I think it's one reason for our businesslike manner on the court. We were only doing what we'd been expected to do.

"I'm glad we won the first year, though. Now we'll have three, and a long time from now I can look back and hold that over all the teams to come along. 'What have they done?' I'll say. 'Have they done what we did?' "

When the third successive championship was a reality, the first reaction of many was relief.

"The yoke is removed now," said guard Bill Sweek, a reserve for all three seasons. "Let them try to match us."

In the course of his varsity career, Alcindor had faced many obstacles. A rule had been passed to stop college players—specifically him—from dunking, he had been poked in the eye, hometown New York fans had booed him during a two-game engagement at Madison Square Garden and he had struggled with the decision to become a Muslim, which later would precipitate changing his name to Kareem Abdul-Jabbar. As Wilt Chamberlain had noted years earlier, "Nobody loves Goliath." But Alcindor had persevered and done everything required—even demanded—of him.

"I'll just say it feels nice," said Alcindor, who was named the Final Four's outstanding player an unprecedented third time. "Everything was up in my throat all week. I could see ahead to the end, but there was apprehension and fear. Fear of losing. I don't know why, but it was there. Before the other two tournaments it didn't feel this way. This one did. But, wow, today after I came to the bench, I was yelling. Wow, I was excited. We just had to bring this thing down in front again where it belongs."

He and his teammates had produced under the most severe pressure. Perhaps Wooden, whose security measures to shield his players from the media were considered excessive by many, felt it most of all.

"It was not as easy an era as it might have seemed to outsiders," the coach said. "But it's been a tremendous era, I think.

"I've heard it said that any coach would have won championships with Lewis. That might be true, it really might. But they'll never know. I do."

UCLA's only real test of the 1969 tournament came in the semifinals from an inspired Drake team that lost by three points.

1969 Tournament Results

First Round
Duquesne 74, St. Joseph's (Pa.) 52
Davidson 75, Villanova 61
St. John's 72, Princeton 63
Marquette 82, Murray State 62
Miami (Ohio) 63, Notre Dame 60
Texas A&M 81, Trinity (Tex.) 66
Colorado State 52, Dayton 50
New Mexico St. 74, BYU 62
Weber State 75, Seattle 73

Second Round
North Carolina 79, Duquesne 78
Davidson 79, St. John's 69
Marquette 81, Kentucky 74
Purdue 91, Miami (Ohio) 71
Drake 81, Texas A&M 63
Colorado State 64, Colorado 56
UCLA 53, New Mexico State 38
Santa Clara 63, Weber State 59

Regional Third Place
Duquesne 75, St. John's 72
Kentucky 72, Miami (Ohio) 71
Colorado 97, Texas A&M 82
Weber State 58, New Mexico St. 56

Regional Championships
North Carolina 87, Davidson 85
Purdue 75, Marquette 73 (ot)
Drake 84, Colorado State 77
UCLA 90, Santa Clara 52

Semifinals
Purdue 92, North Carolina 65
UCLA 85, Drake 82

Third Place
Drake 104, North Carolina 84

Championship
UCLA 92, Purdue 72

STATISTICS

1969 UCLA

Head Coach—John Wooden   Final Record—29-1

Player	Pos.	Hgt.	Wgt.	Cl.	G	FG	FGA	Pct.	FT.	FTA	Pct.	Reb.	Pts.	Avg.
Lew Alcindor	C	7-1	235	Sr.	30	303	477	.635	115	188	.612	440	721	24.0
Curtis Rowe	F	6-6	216	So.	30	144	287	.502	99	146	.678	237	387	12.9
John Vallely	G	6-2	177	Jr.	28	116	234	.496	77	102	.755	91	309	11.0
Sidney Wicks	F	6-8	220	So.	30	84	193	.435	58	100	.580	153	226	7.5
Lynn Shackelford	F	6-5	190	Sr.	30	94	203	.463	22	44	.500	121	210	7.0
Ken Heitz	G	6-3	180	Sr.	30	84	180	.467	26	38	.684	69	194	6.5
Bill Sweek	G	6-3	188	Sr.	30	80	158	.506	30	48	.625	66	190	6.3
Steve Patterson	C	6-9	221	So.	29	58	110	.527	30	40	.750	112	146	5.0
Don Saffer	G	6-1	170	Sr.	8	13	25	.520	3	5	.600	4	29	3.6
Terry Schofield	G	6-3	186	So.	24	27	65	.415	11	18	.611	39	65	2.7
John Ecker	F	6-6	188	So.	20	12	24	.500	8	12	.667	24	32	1.6
Bill Seibert	F	6-6	175	So.	15	6	23	.261	5	7	.714	12	17	1.1
George Farmer	F	6-4	215	So.	6	2	3	.667	2	2	1.000	1	6	1.0
Lee Walczuk	G	6-0	175	So.	10	3	17	.176	0	0	.000	6	6	0.6
Jim Nielsen	F	6-7	204	Sr.	3	1	2	.500	0	0	.000	1	2	0.7
Team												137		
UCLA					30	1027	2001	.513	486	750	.648	1513	2540	84.7
Opponents					30	758	2026	.374	399	591	.675	1141	1915	63.8

1969 PURDUE

Head Coach—George King   Final Record—23-5

Player	Pos.	Hgt.	Wgt.	Cl.	G	FG	FGA	Pct.	FT.	FTA	Pct.	Reb.	Pts.	Avg.
Rick Mount	G	6-4	180	Jr.	28	366	710	.515	200	236	.847	90	932	33.3
Herman Gilliam	F	6-3	195	Sr.	24	144	306	.471	90	105	.857	204	378	15.8
Bill Keller	G	5-10	185	Sr.	27	135	290	.465	88	98	.898	123	358	13.3
George Faerber	F	6-5	215	So.	28	101	163	.620	51	71	.718	196	253	9.0
Larry Weatherford	F-G	6-2	170	So.	28	75	171	.439	36	45	.800	60	186	6.6
Chuck Bavis	C	7-0	235	Jr.	24	56	118	.475	21	28	.750	108	133	5.5
Jerry Johnson	C	6-10	215	Jr.	27	53	116	.457	24	48	.500	124	130	4.8
Tyrone Bedford	F	6-5	210	Jr.	26	40	94	.426	16	26	.615	121	96	3.7
Frank Kaufman	C	6-8	190	So.	24	24	41	.585	19	30	.633	49	67	2.8
Ralph Taylor	F	6-2	195	Sr.	22	14	25	.560	15	19	.789	35	43	2.0
Ted Reasoner	C	6-6	210	Sr.	17	7	26	.269	7	16	.438	27	21	1.2
Steve Longfellow	G	5-10	165	So.	11	2	14	.143	2	5	.400	5	6	0.5
Glenn Young	G	6-3	170	Jr.	...	...	...	...	...	...	...	...	...	...
Team												227		
Purdue					28	1017	2074	.490	569	727	.783	1369	2603	93.0
Opponents					28	815	1967	.414	586	837	.700	1254	2216	79.1

1969 DRAKE

Head Coach—Maurice John   Final Record—26-5

Player	Pos.	Hgt.	Wgt.	Cl.	G	FG	FGA	Pct.	FT.	FTA	Pct.	Reb.	Pts.	Avg.
Willie McCarter	G	6-3	170	Sr.	31	272	610	.446	89	112	.795	116	633	20.4
Willie Wise	F	6-5	200	Sr.	30	170	326	.521	98	155	.632	343	438	14.6
Dolph Pulliam	G	6-4	205	Sr.	31	158	345	.458	96	146	.658	240	412	13.3
Don Draper	G	5-11	160	Sr.	31	174	389	.447	30	42	.714	75	378	12.2
Al Williams	F	6-5	195	Jr.	31	107	220	.486	65	88	.739	226	279	9.0
Gary Zeller	G	6-2	185	Jr.	31	68	173	.393	59	86	.686	51	195	6.3
Rick Wanamaker	C	6-8	200	Jr.	28	45	84	.536	32	42	.762	95	122	4.4
Garry Odom	C	6-8	230	Sr.	30	45	82	.549	23	43	.535	134	113	3.8
Ron Gwin	G	6-2	180	Sr.	25	18	33	.545	17	27	.630	34	53	2.1
Al Sakys	G	6-0	170	So.	7	4	9	.444	5	6	.833	2	13	1.9
Larry Sharp	C	6-9	220	Sr.	17	7	15	.467	13	19	.684	20	27	1.6
Dale Teeter	F	6-4	175	Jr.	13	7	12	.583	1	1	1.000	8	15	1.2
Jim Nordrum	F	6-7	190	So.	2	1	2	.500	0	0	.000	0	2	1.0
Jim O'Dea	C	6-8	220	Sr.	7	1	4	.250	1	2	.500	7	3	0.4
Bob Mast	G	5-10	165	Sr.	11	2	4	.500	0	3	.000	4	4	0.4
Dave Wicklund	G	6-0	150	So.	2	0	1	.000	0	0	.000	0	0	0.0
Team												191		
Drake					31	1079	2309	.467	529	772	.685	1546	2687	86.7
Opponents					31	858	2010	.427	599	854	.701	1339	2315	74.7

1969 NORTH CAROLINA

Head Coach—Dean Smith   Final Record—27-5

Player	Pos.	Hgt.	Wgt.	Cl.	G	FG	FGA	Pct.	FT.	FTA	Pct.	Reb.	Pts.	Avg.
Charlie Scott	*F	6-5	178	Jr.	32	290	577	.503	134	191	.702	226	714	22.3
Bill Bunting	F	6-8	193	Sr.	32	217	363	.598	143	173	.827	247	577	18.0
Rusty Clark	F	6-10	225	Sr.	28	145	282	.514	113	157	.720	258	403	14.4
Dick Grubar	B	6-4	185	Sr.	28	142	286	.497	80	106	.755	94	364	13.0
Lee Dedmon	B	6-10	195	So.	32	109	237	.460	59	97	.608	221	277	8.7
Eddie Fogler	B	5-11	160	Jr.	32	69	180	.383	26	42	.619	52	164	5.1
Joe Brown	F	6-5	201	Sr.	31	54	120	.450	21	38	.553	85	129	4.2
Jim Delany	B	5-11	165	Jr.	30	19	53	.358	40	50	.800	15	78	2.6
Dave Chadwick	F	6-7	200	So.	20	17	35	.486	7	10	.700	32	41	2.1
Gerald Tuttle	B	5-11	160	Sr.	32	21	52	.404	12	16	.750	19	54	1.7
Dale Gipple	B	6-0	170	So.	20	6	24	.250	10	13	.769	13	22	1.1
Richard Tuttle	B	6-0	160	So.	15	3	5	.600	7	9	.778	4	13	0.9
Don Eggleston	F	6-8	225	So.	18	1	8	.125	3	7	.429	15	5	0.3
Ricky Webb	F-B	6-4	175	Jr.	13	1	6	.167	1	3	.333	8	3	0.2
Team												179		
North Carolina					32	1094	2228	.491	656	912	.719	1468	2844	88.9
Opponents					32	937	2076	.451	547	781	.700	1295	2421	75.7

*Positions listed as frontcourt and backcourt.

1969 FINAL FOUR
At Louisville, Ky.
Semifinals

North Carolina	fg	fga	ft	fta	rb	pf	tp
Bunting	7	13	5	7	7	2	19
Scott	6	19	4	6	6	3	16
Clark	7	9	6	10	9	2	20
Fogler	1	4	0	0	2	2	2
G. Tuttle	2	4	0	1	3	4	4
Delany	0	2	0	0	1	4	0
Dedmon	0	0	1	1	4	2	0
Brown	1	4	0	0	1	0	2
Gipple	0	3	0	0	1	0	0
Chadwick	1	2	0	0	2	0	2
R. Tuttle	0	1	0	0	0	0	0
Eggleston	0	0	0	0	0	0	0
Team					1		
Totals	25	62	15	25	37	18	65

Purdue	fg	fga	ft	fta	rb	pf	tp
Gilliam	3	11	0	0	8	0	6
Faerber	3	3	2	2	9	3	8
Johnson	2	5	1	3	5	4	5
Mount	14	28	8	9	4	0	36
Keller	9	19	2	3	5	3	20
Kaufman	0	1	2	3	6	4	2
Weatherford	3	6	1	1	2	1	7
Bedford	3	3	0	0	5	4	6
Taylor	1	1	0	1	3	0	2
Longfellow	0	1	0	0	2	0	0
Reasoner	0	0	0	0	0	1	0
Young	0	0	0	0	0	0	0
Team					2		
Totals	38	78	16	22	51	20	92

Halftime: Purdue 53-30. Officials: Overby and Brown.

Drake	fg	fga	ft	fta	rb	pf	tp
Pulliam	4	4	4	5	5	4	12
Williams	0	1	0	0	1	4	0
Wise	5	7	3	4	16	3	13
McCarter	10	27	4	4	1	3	24
Draper	5	13	2	2	1	2	12
Odom	0	2	0	1	2	4	0
Wanamaker	4	7	1	1	7	4	9
Zeller	4	12	4	6	3	3	12
Gwin	0	0	0	1	1	3	0
Team					4		
Totals	32	83	18	24	41	30	82

UCLA	fg	fga	ft	fta	rb	pf	tp
Shackelford	2	5	2	3	2	4	6
Rowe	6	9	2	2	13	2	14
Alcindor	8	14	9	16	21	3	25
Heitz	3	6	1	3	1	5	7
Vallely	9	11	11	14	6	5	29
Wicks	0	2	0	0	1	1	0
Sweek	0	0	0	0	0	1	0
Patterson	0	0	2	2	0	0	2
Schofield	0	3	2	4	0	0	2
Team					4		
Totals	28	50	29	44	48	21	85

Halftime: UCLA 44-43. Officials: Fouty and DiTomasso.

Championship
March 22

UCLA	fg	fga	ft	fta	rb	pf	tp
Shackelford	3	8	5	8	9	3	11
Rowe	4	10	4	4	12	2	12
Alcindor	15	20	7	9	20	2	37
Heitz	0	3	0	1	3	4	0
Vallely	4	9	7	10	4	3	15
Sweek	3	3	0	1	1	3	6
Wicks	0	1	3	6	4	1	3
Schofield	1	2	0	0	0	0	2
Patterson	1	1	2	2	2	0	4
Seibert	0	0	0	0	1	0	0
Farmer	0	0	0	0	1	0	0
Ecker	1	1	0	0	0	0	2
Team					5		
Totals	32	58	28	41	61	19	92

Purdue	fg	fga	ft	fta	rb	pf	tp
Gilliam	2	14	3	3	11	2	7
Faerber	1	2	0	3	5	5	2
Johnson	4	9	3	4	9	2	11
Mount	12	36	4	5	1	3	28
Keller	4	17	3	4	4	5	11
Kaufman	0	0	2	5	5	2	2
Bedford	3	8	1	3	8	3	7
Weatherford	1	5	2	2	1	3	4
Reasoner	0	1	0	1	2	3	0
Taylor	0	0	0	0	0	2	0
Team					5		
Totals	27	92	18	24	48	30	72

Halftime: UCLA 50-41. Officials: DiTomasso and Brown.

1970 Alcindorless UCLA Rolls On

The size and strength advantage belonged to Jacksonville and 7-foot-2 Artis Gilmore (left), but UCLA and Sidney Wicks (right) neutralized the big man and the Bruins captured their fourth straight national championship.

Point guard Henry Bibby directed a fast-moving UCLA offense that had to change its style with the departure of big man Lew Alcindor.

After three years of hitching themselves to Lew Alcindor's star, UCLA's Bruins were in the strange position of looking up at college basketball's big man and finding him wearing an opponent's uniform. With each passing game, it appeared that the tower of power in the 1970 NCAA Tournament was Jacksonville's Artis Gilmore.

That the Bruins had returned to the Final Four in the season after Alcindor's graduation was extremely gratifying to the players left behind. Four starters on the 1970 team had played in the shadow of the great center, and their roles in the most recent championship had been minimized by Alcindor's presence. In many respects it was his triumph, not theirs.

"I remember our 1969 championship," senior guard John Vallely said, "and a lot of guys didn't feel anything about it because they didn't think they had contributed. And they hadn't; it was all so easy. But now everyone is helping each other a lot more—not just saying 'too damn bad' if another guy makes a mistake—and if we win again, they're all going to have contributed."

As usual, there was no shortage of talent in Westwood. The difference this season was that UCLA would need all of it, acting in unison, to compensate for the loss of perhaps the most dominant collegiate player in history. The Bruins would have to work not only harder, but also together.

That is precisely what they did. Blessed with two superb forwards in 6-foot-8 Sidney Wicks and 6-6 Curtis Rowe, an underrated center in 6-9 Steve Patterson, a fine shooter in Vallely and a dynamic point guard in sophomore Henry Bibby, John Wooden went back to his pre-Alcindor playbook. UCLA set up in a high-post offense, ran the fast break whenever it was available and revived the devastating zone press. The result was another hugely successful regular season in which the Bruins played with great verve and won all but two games.

The team's spirit, according to Patterson, was far superior to that exhibited in 1969.

"This wasn't because of Lew," the junior said. "He wasn't a detriment; there will never be a better team player than Lew. But we were all too concerned with points and playing time, not with winning. We would win. The main thing was contending with each other to get into games. We're so much more together this year."

Even Wooden appeared to be enjoying himself more. The pressure of having to win was lifted. The excitement of formulating strategy was restored.

"Now I feel like I have something to do," the coach said. "I feel more alive. It's been a long time."

Of course, it had seemed even longer to other championship hopefuls. Although UCLA still was winning with regularity on the West Coast, the absence of Alcindor made the Bruins appear vulnerable. Several clubs were eager to meet UCLA in the NCAA Tournament and bring the Bruins down a notch or two because, for a change, the big man was on their side.

Burly Bob Lanier, a 6-11 consensus All-America and a tremendous offensive force, had led St. Bonaventure to a 22-1 regular-season record. Kentucky, led by 6-9 consensus All-America Dan Issel, had lost only once and climbed to the top of the national rankings. At 6-10, Sam Lacey made New Mexico State (23-2) a dangerous opponent. And then there was Jacksonville (23-1), which had risen from basketball obscurity largely on the muscular shoulders of the 7-2 Gilmore.

Jacksonville even boasted a second 7-footer, Pembrook Burrows, and the two of them were too much for Issel and Kentucky in a rousing Mideast Regional final showdown won by the Dolphins, 106-100. Incredibly, in three regional contests, Jacksonville averaged 106.3 points per game. Although the Dolphins' defense was limited almost exclusively to Gilmore's shot-blocking, they had good outside shooters in 6-5 Rex Morgan and 5-10 Vaughn Wedeking to complement the big men inside and form a high-powered offense. Together, the dynamic duo of Gilmore and Morgan was known as "Batman and Robin."

St. Bonaventure also qualified for the Final Four, but the Bonnies arrived at College Park, Md., without their most formidable weapon. In the course of a 97-74 rout of Villanova in the East Regional final, Lanier had been clipped accidentally by Chris Ford and fallen heavily to the floor. The center limped to the bench.

"I can't move," he told Coach Larry Weise. The injury was diagnosed as a torn medial collateral ligament, which required surgery.

Without Lanier, the Bonnies were at Jacksonville's mercy in an uninspired semifinal at Maryland's Cole Field House. Gilmore tallied 29 points and four other Jacksonville players scored in double figures to lead the Dolphins to a 91-83 triumph.

In the other semifinal, UCLA's front line was much too quick for that of New Mexico State, which got good performances from guards Jimmy Collins (28 points) and Charlie Criss (19) but not from Lacey (eight points). The Bruins coasted to a 93-77 victory after previous romps over Long Beach State and Utah State in the West Regional. The stage was set for a championship matchup of great contrast.

This game would bring together the most celebrated basketball program in the nation and one of the most surprising, a tradition vs. a happening. It would pair an esteemed and conservative older coach (Wooden) and a young man (Joe Williams), whose reputation to date was based mostly on a flashy wardrobe. And it would pit a team that had claimed three consecutive national titles with a giant but now had no one taller than 6-9 against a team that featured two 7-footers as well as 6-10 reserve forward Rod McIntyre.

The Bruins certainly were not awed by the task. "Steve, you ever have any practice against a 7-footer?" Wooden publicly asked Patterson after practice the day before the game. Patterson, who knew the joy of scrimmaging against Alcindor every day during his sophomore season, smiled.

It was assumed that Patterson would be assigned to defend Gilmore, but Wooden informed Wicks just before the game that he was the lucky individual. Wicks was UCLA's finest shot-blocker and, judging by his facial expression on the court, its fiercest competitor. A natural comedian away from the arena, Wicks received as much attention for his game face as his talent.

Steve Patterson (32) was an underrated 6-foot-9 center who went about his business with a quiet precision.

Even Wicks wasn't prepared for the tactic. "I thought I was going to guard anybody but him (Gilmore)," he said.

And in the first few minutes, he might as well have been guarding the press table. Wooden had instructed Wicks to play on Gilmore's inside shoulder while the other Bruins pressured the passers, but the Jacksonville center scored three quick baskets, Wicks picked up two quick fouls and the Dolphins opened a 14-6 lead.

During a timeout, the coach adjusted, moving Wicks behind Gilmore and asking his other players to drop back on the big man.

"If Gilmore did get it inside," Wooden reasoned, "it would be in close quarters and difficult for him to get the shot. With men all around you with their hands up, it's just not that easy."

What happened shortly after the timeout changed the momentum of the game. Gilmore took a pass, turned for a short jump shot and had it slammed back into his chest by Wicks. Having delivered the message, the UCLA forward pumped his fist in momentary triumph. Although six inches shorter than Gilmore, Wicks used his leaping ability and exquisite timing to reject Gilmore's shots five times in the course of the afternoon. The big man became flustered.

"I tried to make him get the ball six or seven feet from the basket," Wicks said, "and I'd back off him. Then I had room to jump between him and the hoop."

With Gilmore under control, the Bruins started to battle back. They scored nine straight points late in the first half to move ahead and went to the locker room with a 41-36 halftime lead.

"We knew the first couple of minutes of the second half would determine the outcome," Patterson said. "They were down by five and could catch us, or we could move out by 10."

Gilmore's first five shots of the second half failed to drop and UCLA did indeed move out as Wicks' hot hand put his team up by 11. The UCLA lead was 16 when Gilmore, who had endured one 16½-minute stretch without a basket, fouled out with less than two minutes remaining. He finished with only nine baskets in 29 attempts and 16 rebounds, compared with 18 rebounds by Wicks, who was named the Final Four's outstanding player.

The Bruins won decisively, 80-69. They had seized another championship—this time without Big Lew.

"Every time somebody mentioned the three in a row, they'd say Lew did it," said Rowe, who led UCLA's balanced scoring with 19 points. "Now we just proved that four other men from that team could play basketball with the best of them."

It was apparent that if the great UCLA dynasty was the work of one man, that man was not Alcindor. It was John Wooden.

Senior guard John Vallely was the purest shooter in UCLA's 1970 lineup.

1970 Tournament Results

First Round
St. Bonaventure 85, Davidson 72
Niagara 79, Pennsylvania 69
Villanova 77, Temple 69
Notre Dame 112, Ohio 82
Jacksonville 109, W. Kentucky 96
Houston 71, Dayton 64
New Mexico State 101, Rice 77
Long Beach St. 92, Weber State 73
Utah State 91, Texas-El Paso 81

Second Round
St. Bonaventure 80, N. C. State 68
Villanova 98, Niagara 73
Kentucky 109, Notre Dame 99
Jacksonville 104, Iowa 103
Drake 92, Houston 87
New Mexico State 70, Kansas St. 66
UCLA 88, Long Beach State 65
Utah State 69, Santa Clara 68

Regional Third Place
North Carolina St. 108, Niagara 88
Iowa 121, Notre Dame 106
Kansas State 107, Houston 98
Santa Clara 89, Long Beach St. 86

Regional Championships
St. Bonaventure 97, Villanova 74
Jacksonville 106, Kentucky 100
New Mexico State 87, Drake 78
UCLA 101, Utah State 79

Semifinals
Jacks'nv'lle 91, St. Bonaventure 83
UCLA 93, New Mexico State 77

Third Place
New Mex. St. 79, St. Bon'v'nt're 73

Championship
UCLA 80, Jacksonville 69

STATISTICS

1970 UCLA

Head Coach—John Wooden **Final Record—28-2**

Player	Pos.	Hgt.	Wgt.	Cl.	G	FG	FGA	Pct.	FT.	FTA	Pct.	Reb.	Pts.	Avg.
Sidney Wicks	F	6-8	220	Jr.	30	221	415	.533	117	185	.632	357	559	18.6
John Vallely	G	6-2	177	Sr.	30	192	395	.486	106	147	.721	111	490	16.3
Henry Bibby	G	6-1	180	So.	30	189	377	.501	90	108	.833	105	468	15.6
Curtis Rowe	F	6-6	216	Jr.	30	168	303	.554	123	192	.641	260	459	15.3
Steve Patterson	C	6-9	230	Jr.	30	166	335	.496	43	58	.741	300	375	12.5
John Ecker	F	6-6	188	Jr.	30	40	80	.500	24	31	.774	74	104	3.5
Kenny Booker	F-G	6-3	182	Jr.	28	31	69	.449	24	37	.649	42	86	3.1
Terry Schofield	G	6-3	186	Jr.	29	30	76	.395	17	20	.850	23	77	2.7
Andy Hill	G	6-1	173	So.	24	11	38	.289	20	28	.714	15	42	1.8
Jon Chapman	C	6-6	201	So.	20	11	32	.344	13	15	.867	33	35	1.8
Rick Betchley	G	6-5	190	So.	23	12	26	.462	10	16	.625	15	34	1.5
Bill Seibert	F	6-6	175	Jr.	21	12	38	.316	6	15	.400	34	30	1.4
Team												150		
UCLA					30	1083	2184	.496	593	852	.696	1519	2759	92.0
Opponents					30	906	2156	.420	391	554	.706	1229	2203	73.4

1970 JACKSONVILLE

Head Coach—Joe Williams **Final Record—27-2**

Player	Pos.	Hgt.	Wgt.	Cl.	G	FG	FGA	Pct.	FT.	FTA	Pct.	Reb.	Pts.	Avg.
Artis Gilmore	C	7-2	235	Jr.	28	307	529	.580	128	202	.634	621	742	26.5
Rex Morgan	G	6-5	190	Sr.	28	190	372	.511	129	176	.733	179	509	18.2
Vaughn Wedeking	G	5-10	165	Jr.	28	172	326	.528	39	53	.736	52	383	13.7
Pembrook Burrows	C	7-0	240	Jr.	27	124	199	.623	44	77	.571	198	292	10.8
Greg Nelson	F	6-6	205	Jr.	28	109	212	.514	80	107	.748	176	298	10.6
Chip Dublin	G	6-0	180	Jr.	28	78	175	.446	76	98	.776	90	232	8.3
Rod McIntyre	F	6-10	235	Sr.	22	59	127	.465	26	42	.619	87	144	6.5
Mike Blevins	F	6-5	190	Jr.	26	32	90	.356	24	43	.558	34	88	3.4
Rusty Baldwin	G	5-10	170	So.	26	23	46	.500	15	23	.652	9	61	2.3
Don Hawkins	F	6-5	180	Sr.	14	11	32	.344	8	11	.727	9	30	2.1
Curtis Kruer	G	6-5	170	So.	13	8	17	.471	4	6	.667	5	20	1.5
Ken Selke	C	6-7	180	Sr.	12	5	12	.417	2	4	.500	15	12	1.0
Team												86		
Jacksonville					28	1118	2137	.523	575	842	.683	1561	2811	100.4
Opponents					28	848	2038	.416	502	717	.700	1130	2198	78.5

(Forfeit victory not included in individual statistics.)

1970 NEW MEXICO STATE

Head Coach—Lou Henson **Final Record—27-3**

Player	Pos.	Hgt.	Wgt.	Cl.	G	FG	FGA	Pct.	FT.	FTA	Pct.	Reb.	Pts.	Avg.
Jimmy Collins	G	6-2	175	Sr.	31	322	628	.513	111	138	.804	143	755	24.4
Sam Lacey	C	6-10	235	Sr.	31	231	499	.463	88	138	.638	493	550	17.7
Jeff Smith	F	6-8	225	Jr.	31	152	276	.551	94	153	.614	257	398	12.8
Charlie Criss	G	5-8	170	Sr.	24	109	274	.398	82	112	.732	54	300	12.5
Chito Reyes	F	6-6	205	Jr.	31	110	237	.464	35	47	.745	144	255	8.2
Roy Neal	F	6-5	190	So.	31	61	144	.424	48	81	.593	160	170	5.5
John Burgess	F	6-5	195	Sr.	31	60	157	.382	27	47	.574	169	147	4.7
Milton Horne	G	6-1	165	So.	31	42	103	.408	51	74	.689	56	135	4.4
Bill Moore	G	6-3	182	So.	29	26	65	.400	7	13	.538	38	59	2.0
Lonnie Lefevre	C	6-8	250	So.	19	11	27	.407	3	7	.429	36	25	1.3
Tom McCarthy	G	6-1	180	So.	16	0	8	.000	5	6	.833	4	5	0.3
Rudy Franco	F	6-5	200	Sr.	19	1	5	.200	1	1	1.000	6	3	0.2
Team												153		
New Mexico State					31	1125	2423	.464	552	817	.667	1713	2802	90.4
Opponents					31	919	2149	.428	472	699	.675	1310	2310	74.5

1970 ST. BONAVENTURE

Head Coach—Larry Weise **Final Record—25-3**

Player	Pos.	Hgt.	Wgt.	Cl.	G	FG	FGA	Pct.	FT.	FTA	Pct.	Reb.	Pts.	Avg.
Bob Lanier	C	6-11	275	Sr.	26	308	549	.561	141	194	.727	416	757	29.1
Matt Gantt	F-C	6-5	200	So.	28	191	416	.459	45	86	.523	272	427	15.3
Greg Gary	F	6-3	180	Jr.	28	133	277	.480	57	92	.620	227	323	11.5
Paul Hoffman	G	6-1	185	So.	28	125	254	.492	57	90	.633	134	307	11.0
Billy Kalbaugh	G	6-1	185	So.	28	100	202	.495	31	37	.838	70	231	8.3
Mike Kull	G	6-1	190	Sr.	26	63	142	.444	13	19	.684	45	139	5.3
Vic Thomas	G	6-2	175	So.	21	33	74	.446	15	24	.625	26	81	3.9
Tom Baldwin	F	6-5	205	So.	22	33	65	.508	8	19	.421	31	74	3.4
Paul Grys	G	6-0	205	Jr.	20	22	45	.489	9	13	.692	19	53	2.7
Gene Fahey	F	6-1	170	Jr.	16	12	31	.387	12	16	.750	13	36	2.3
Dale Tepas	G	6-1	205	Jr.	15	10	31	.323	5	6	.833	10	25	1.7
Pete Wisniowski	F	6-1	205	Sr.	16	5	15	.333	10	12	.833	9	20	1.3
Team												15		
St. Bonaventure					28	1035	2101	.493	403	608	.663	1287	2473	88.3
Opponents					28	731	1865	.392	383	567	.675	917	1845	65.8

1970 FINAL FOUR

At College Park, Md.
Semifinals

Jacksonville	fg	fga	ft	fta	rb	pf	tp
Wedeking	7	15	1	1	6	4	15
Morgan	6	15	5	6	5	3	17
Burrows	2	4	1	1	4	4	5
McIntyre	0	3	0	0	3	1	0
Gilmore	9	14	11	15	21	2	29
Dublin	1	3	9	9	2	2	11
Nelson	1	7	10	12	7	3	12
Blevins	1	1	0	0	0	1	2
R. Baldwin	0	1	0	1	0	1	0
Team					4		
Totals	27	63	37	45	52	21	91

St. Bonaventure	fg	fga	ft	fta	rb	pf	tp
Kalbaugh	5	8	2	2	4	3	12
Hoffman	4	14	2	4	6	3	10
Gary	2	7	5	8	13	5	9
T. Baldwin	2	10	1	2	4	5	5
Gantt	8	17	0	0	8	5	16
Kull	4	7	0	0	0	5	8
Thomas	7	17	1	2	4	3	15
Grys	1	5	2	2	1	2	4
Tepas	0	0	2	2	1	0	2
Fahey	1	1	0	0	0	1	2
Team					6		
Totals	34	86	15	22	47	32	83

Halftime: Jacksonville 42-34. Officials: Scott and Marich.

UCLA	fg	fga	ft	fta	rb	pf	tp
Rowe	4	7	7	11	15	0	15
Patterson	5	9	2	2	6	3	12
Wicks	10	12	2	5	16	3	22
Vallely	7	19	9	10	4	3	23
Bibby	8	13	3	3	2	5	19
Booker	0	1	0	0	0	2	0
Betchley	0	0	0	0	0	0	0
Schofield	0	0	0	0	0	1	0
Ecker	0	0	0	0	0	0	0
Seibert	0	1	0	0	1	0	0
Hill	0	0	0	1	0	1	0
Chapman	1	1	0	0	1	0	2
Team					0		
Totals	35	63	23	32	45	18	93

New Mexico State	fg	fga	ft	fta	rb	pf	tp
Criss	6	16	7	9	2	5	19
Collins	13	23	2	3	0	3	28
Burgess	1	6	0	0	2	2	2
Smith	4	11	2	3	7	5	10
Lacey	3	9	2	3	16	3	8
Reyes	1	6	0	0	4	2	2
Neal	2	4	0	0	6	2	4
Horne	0	4	2	2	1	2	2
Moore	1	1	0	0	1	0	2
Lefevre	0	0	0	0	1	0	0
Franco	0	0	0	0	0	0	0
McCarthy	0	0	0	0	0	0	0
Team					5		
Totals	31	80	15	20	45	24	77

Halftime: UCLA 48-41. Officials: White and Wirtz.

Championship
March 21

Jacksonville	fg	fga	ft	fta	rb	pf	tp
Wedeking	6	11	0	0	2	2	12
Blevins	1	2	1	2	0	1	3
Morgan	5	11	0	0	4	5	10
Burrows	6	9	0	0	6	1	12
Gilmore	9	29	1	1	16	5	19
Nelson	3	9	2	2	5	1	8
Dublin	0	5	2	2	1	4	2
R. Baldwin	0	0	0	0	0	0	0
McIntyre	1	3	0	0	3	4	2
Hawkins	0	1	1	1	1	1	1
Selke	0	0	0	0	0	0	0
Team					2		
Totals	31	80	7	8	40	24	69

UCLA	fg	fga	ft	fta	rb	pf	tp
Rowe	7	15	5	5	8	4	19
Patterson	8	15	1	4	11	0	17
Wicks	5	9	7	10	18	3	17
Vallely	5	10	5	7	7	2	15
Bibby	2	11	4	4	1	8	8
Booker	0	0	2	3	0	0	2
Seibert	0	1	0	0	1	1	0
Ecker	1	1	0	0	0	0	2
Betchley	0	0	0	0	0	0	0
Chapman	0	1	0	0	1	0	0
Hill	0	0	0	1	0	0	0
Schofield	0	0	0	0	0	0	0
Team					3		
Totals	28	63	24	35	53	12	80

Halftime: UCLA 41-36. Officials: Scott and Wirtz.

1971 Ho Hum! UCLA Is No. 1

UCLA Coach John Wooden holds the 1971 NCAA trophy as forwards Sidney Wicks (35) and Curtis Rowe, wearing the traditional net, look on.

College basketball had gotten a glimpse of the future when UCLA and Houston played a regular-season game in the Astrodome. Three years later, the sport officially embraced the new order. The NCAA scheduled the 1971 Final Four in the massive Houston stadium with the plexiglass roof and seating for thousands more customers than any basketball arena in the nation.

It clearly wasn't a matter of aesthetics. "Playing in large arenas is for one reason only," UCLA Coach John Wooden said.

The reason was evident in the gate receipts. A record crowd of 52,693 attended the historic duel between the Bruins' Lew Alcindor and Houston's Elvin Hayes in 1968.

The attendance record would not be threatened in 1971. Tournament officials decided to move the basketball floor closer to one end rather than place it in the middle of the Astrodome, as had been done in 1968, thus eliminating thousands of the more distant seats. And the defeat of hometown Houston in the Midwest Regional didn't help.

Still, interest in college basketball had grown to a level that made it worthwhile—and profitable—to hold the Final Four under a monstrous dome. Indeed, the crowd of 31,428 at the national semifinals dwarfed the largest previous gathering for an NCAA Tournament event.

If there was a price for such a financial windfall, it was the strangeness of the setting. The court was raised four feet above the floor so that the players might better be viewed by spectators at ground level. That arrangement, however, left precious little space between the sidelines and potential calamity.

"Here's my first prediction," Western Kentucky Coach John Oldham said at his team's first practice session. "Clarence Glover goes over the side."

Glover, a 6-foot-8 forward/center, was one of the Hilltoppers' two prime players, a rebounding marvel and an all-out competitor.

"I'll go after the ball," said guard Rex Bailey, Glover's teammate. "I may not want to, but when you're playing for the national championship, you don't hold back. Of course, I'll land on somebody's head."

Another bizarre feature was the presence of an 80-foot camera crane above one end of the court. It was a sight to jar the memory of someone who remembered the old gymnasiums where the sport had taken its first significant steps—someone like John Wooden, Purdue University, class of '32. Wooden and UCLA would provide the constant in this festival of change.

Somehow, the Bruins' presence in the 1971 Final Four offered reassurance that God still was in his heaven and that the world below was not completely out of kilter. The Bruins had been hard-pressed throughout the season, rallying to win several games in the final minutes. They had been taken to the wire by Long Beach State in the West Regional final before pulling out a 57-55 triumph. But here they were again, ranked No. 1 in the country and with only a single blemish on their record.

Two of the teams expected to challenge UCLA in the Astrodome had fallen. Both Marquette and Pennsylvania had concluded their regular seasons with undefeated marks, but Marquette was nipped by Ohio State in the Mideast Regional, which eventually was won by Western Kentucky. And Penn was embarrassed, 90-47, in the East Regional final by a Villanova team it had beaten earlier in the year.

Kansas, the Midwest Regional favorite, advanced to the national semifinals, but not without some nervous moments. The Jayhawks won their two games by a total of three points, earning the right to be ground down by UCLA, 68-60, in the semifinals.

Much of the conversation in Houston centered on the war for players being waged by the upstart American Basketball Association and the established National Basketball Association. Newsmen had reported seeing ABA contracts signed by 7-foot consensus All-America center Jim McDaniels of Western Kentucky and Villanova star forward Howard Porter. As a result, the NCAA had asked for and received signed affidavits from the two players to the effect that they were still amateurs before allowing them to compete.

Both men played with professional assurance in their semifinal matchup. McDaniels scored at will, but his lackadaisical defense against 6-7 Hank Sie-

Henry Bibby directed the UCLA offense and put the finishing touches on the Bruins' 68-62 championship-game victory over Villanova.

miontkowski, who scored a game-high 31 points and grabbed 15 rebounds, was a major factor in the Hilltoppers' defeat. Meanwhile, the 6-8 Porter scored 22 points and added 16 rebounds in Villanova's 92-89 double-overtime victory.

UCLA's Steve Patterson was a pro prospect who could have skipped the 1971 season after being redshirted for the '68 campaign. But the 6-9 center turned down two professional offers to return for his senior year.

"I know I'm not a famous entity," he said, "but I might have been infamous if I had left and UCLA lost a national championship because of that."

At the moment, Patterson's assessment of his value to the team appeared to be unjustifiably high. He had suffered through an erratic season in which he made barely 40 percent of his field-goal attempts and averaged 12.4 points per game. He also had been benched for most of one conference game and had scored a paltry six points against Kansas in the semifinal game.

"I was nearly always in the teens in scoring and rebounding," he said, "so the Kansas game was very disheartening."

Center Steve Patterson took Coach John Wooden's accusations to heart and produced a career performance in his final college game.

The pro draft, he admitted, was on his mind. He could not ignore the pressure of trying to impress NBA and ABA scouts.

"Coach Wooden accused the seniors of thinking too much about our pro contracts," Patterson said, "and we probably were. I know I was pressing too hard."

He had dinner with his parents the night before his last college game and decided to play not for future riches, but for fun. Patterson was as relaxed as anyone on the court in the finale, and that was fortunate. Both of the Bruins' forwards—Sidney Wicks and Curtis Rowe, the team's top two scorers —were shut down by Villanova's zone defense, so UCLA needed a career performance from Patterson. That's what he produced.

Despite the fact that Villanova already had lost six games that season, the Wildcats gave the Bruins their most closely contested championship game ever. Largely responsible for keeping the game tight was Wooden's decision to stall after his team took a 45-37 halftime lead. The last thing anyone expected was to see the Bruins holding the ball.

Many assumed it was Wooden's intention to force the Wildcats out of their zone defense, to play man-to-man. And it was. But the coach later conceded that he had something else in mind, too.

"I wanted the rules committee to see the argument for a shot clock," he said. "There had been some farcical games recently with teams just standing around. I held the ball to make a point."

Whatever the reason for Wooden's strategy, Villanova did emerge from its zone. And UCLA found itself seriously challenged. After trailing by as many as 12 points in the second half, the Wildcats cut the deficit to four, 58-54, with 5:09 remaining.

"I think the slowdown made our players scrap all the more and thus helped us get back into the game," Villanova Coach Jack Kraft said.

Twice in the final minutes, jump shots by Porter closed the deficit to three. On each occasion, however, UCLA answered. The victory was not secured until Patterson's layup, aided by a goaltending call, boosted the lead to 66-60 with 38 seconds left. Patterson finished as the game's high scorer with 29 points.

While guard Henry Bibby was putting the finishing touches (a pair of free throws) on UCLA's 68-62 triumph and its fifth consecutive national championship, Wicks leaned over the side of the court and shook Wooden's hand.

"Coach," the consensus All-America forward said, "you're really something." The Wizard beamed.

It had been a most unusual Final Four, and not only because of the Astrodome's vast dimensions. During UCLA's semifinal victory over Kansas, Wooden had clashed openly with assistant Denny Crum on a matter of substitutions and strategy. Although this did not drive a wedge between the master and his former pupil, Crum left Westwood shortly thereafter. He was ready to run his own program, and Louisville presented an excellent opportunity.

In addition, the outstanding-player award was presented to Porter, who had 25 points and eight rebounds in Villanova's losing effort. While it was not unprecedented for a player from a vanquished team to be so honored, the ceremony was mocked when the Pittsburgh Condors of the ABA announced that they had signed Porter to a contract prior to the Final Four. Porter subsequently was declared ineligible by the NCAA and his award deleted from the tournament honor roll.

A similar fate befell McDaniels, who had been selected to the all-tournament team. As a result of those players' participation in the tournament, both Villanova and Western Kentucky, a victor in the consolation game, relinquished their claims to second and third place, respectively. The 1971 Final Four remains the only one in which the identities of two teams and the outstanding player are denoted as "vacated."

Howard Porter signed a pro contract before the 1971 tournament and cost Villanova its second-place finish.

Western Kentucky lost its third-place finish when it was revealed that 7-foot center Jim McDaniels had signed a pro contract.

1971 Tournament Results

First Round
Pennsylvania 70, Duquesne 65
*Villanova 93, St. Jos. (Pa.) 75
Fordham 105, Furman 74
*W. Kentucky 74, Jacksonville 72
Marquette 62, Miami (Ohio) 47
Notre Dame 102, TCU 94
Houston 72, New Mexico State 69
BYU 91, Utah State 82
*Long Beach St. 77, Weber St. 66

Second Round
Pennsylvania 79, S. Carolina 64
*Villanova 85, Fordham 75
*W. Kentucky 107, Kentucky 83
Ohio State 60, Marquette 59
Drake 79, Notre Dame 72 (ot)
Kansas 78, Houston 77
UCLA 91, BYU 73
*Long Beach St. 78, Pacific 65

Regional Third Place
Fordham 100, South Carolina 90
Marquette 91, Kentucky 74
Houston 119, Notre Dame 106
Pacific 84, BYU 81

Regional Championships
*Villanova 90, Pennsylvania 47
*W. Kentucky 81, Ohio St. 78 (ot)
Kansas 73, Drake 71
UCLA 57, *Long Beach St. 55

Semifinals
*Villanova 92, *W. Ky. 89 (2 ot)
UCLA 68, Kansas 60

Third Place
*W. Kentucky 77, Kansas 75

Championship
UCLA 68, *Villanova 62

*Villanova's, Western Kentucky's and Long Beach State's participation in 1971 tournament voided.

STATISTICS

1971 UCLA

Head Coach—John Wooden　　　　Final Record—29-1

Player	Pos.	Hgt.	Wgt.	Cl.	G	FG	FGA	Pct.	FT.	FTA	Pct.	Reb.	Pts.	Avg.
Sidney Wicks	F	6-8	230	Sr.	30	244	466	.524	150	227	.661	384	638	21.3
Curtis Rowe	F	6-7	225	Sr.	30	207	396	.523	111	177	.627	299	525	17.5
Steve Patterson	C	6-9	217	Sr.	30	166	395	.420	57	92	.620	294	389	13.0
Henry Bibby	G	6-1	180	Jr.	30	137	364	.376	81	97	.835	105	355	11.8
Terry Schofield	G	6-3	195	Sr.	30	82	190	.432	23	41	.561	72	187	6.2
Kenny Booker	G	6-4	185	Sr.	30	71	161	.441	24	50	.480	79	166	5.5
Larry Farmer	F	6-5	195	So.	22	33	82	.402	13	27	.481	81	79	3.6
John Ecker	F	6-6	190	Sr.	26	21	48	.438	30	34	.882	51	72	2.8
Rick Betchley	G	6-5	190	Jr.	20	14	26	.538	7	15	.467	13	35	1.8
Larry Hollyfield	G	6-5	205	So.	11	9	33	.273	1	4	.250	8	19	1.7
Andy Hill	G	6-1	177	Jr.	19	7	16	.438	17	20	.850	4	31	1.6
Jon Chapman	C	6-6	200	Jr.	18	4	20	.200	0	6	.000	23	8	0.4
Team												161		
UCLA					30	995	2197	.453	514	790	.651	1574	2504	83.5
Opponents					30	849	2001	.424	357	520	.687	1212	2055	68.5

1971 VILLANOVA

Head Coach—Jack Kraft　　　　Final Record—27-7

Player	Pos.	Hgt.	Wgt.	Cl.	G	FG	FGA	Pct.	FT.	FTA	Pct.	Reb.	Pts.	Avg.
Howard Porter	F	6-8	215	Sr.	34	336	634	.530	127	171	.743	503	799	23.5
Hank Siemiontkowski	C	6-7	230	Jr.	34	223	464	.481	91	113	.805	308	537	15.8
Chris Ford	G	6-5	190	Jr.	34	180	400	.450	108	176	.614	200	468	13.8
Tom Ingelsby	G	6-3	175	So.	34	169	362	.467	114	156	.731	129	452	13.3
Clarence Smith	F	6-5	210	Sr.	34	183	384	.477	76	118	.644	266	442	13.0
Ed Hastings	G	6-2	165	So.	6	6	14	.429	9	13	.692	4	21	3.5
Joe McDowell	F	6-4	195	Jr.	31	38	99	.384	15	24	.625	72	91	2.9
Bob Gohl	G	6-0	165	Jr.	25	24	49	.490	13	21	.619	23	61	2.4
John Fox	G	6-2	180	Sr.	28	18	52	.346	11	13	.846	18	47	1.7
Mike Daly	G	6-1	175	Jr.	21	10	20	.500	4	5	.800	12	24	1.1
Team												145		
Villanova					34	1187	2478	.479	568	810	.701	1677	2942	86.5
Opponents					34	1006	2447	.411	468	674	.694	1489	2480	72.9

1971 WESTERN KENTUCKY

Head Coach—John Oldham　　　　Final Record—24-6

Player	Pos.	Hgt.	Wgt.	Cl.	G	FG	FGA	Pct.	FT.	FTA	Pct.	Reb.	Pts.	Avg.
Jim McDaniels	C	7-0	220	Sr.	30	357	684	.522	164	221	.742	454	878	29.3
Jerry Dunn	F	6-5	205	Jr.	30	182	443	.411	98	151	.649	260	462	15.4
Jim Rose	G	6-3	180	Jr.	30	195	446	.437	72	100	.720	145	462	15.4
Clarence Glover	F-C	6-8	210	Sr.	30	99	283	.350	53	90	.589	326	251	8.4
Rex Bailey	G	6-2	175	Jr.	29	82	208	.394	25	43	.581	71	189	6.5
Terry Davis	G	6-2	180	Jr.	18	31	69	.449	9	10	.900	22	71	3.9
Chuck Witt	F-C	6-5	182	So.	27	33	70	.471	9	18	.500	53	75	2.8
Gary Sundmacker	G	6-4	175	Jr.	27	29	63	.460	15	36	.417	64	73	2.7
Danny Johnson	G	6-1	175	Jr.	21	20	48	.417	15	22	.682	21	55	2.6
Ray Kleykamp	G	6-3	180	So.	13	15	39	.385	4	4	1.000	17	34	2.6
Steve Eaton	G	6-3	185	Jr.	12	10	23	.435	7	15	.467	14	27	2.3
Dennis Fox	G	6-0	180	So.	3	1	1	1.000	3	3	1.000	1	5	1.7
Don Waldron	F	6-3	185	So.	7	4	10	.400	2	2	1.000	8	10	1.4
Jeff Eckel	G	6-0	180	Jr.	3	0	5	.000	0	1	.000	2	0	0.0
Tony Duke	F	6-2	175	So.	2	0	0	.000	0	0	.000	1	0	0.0
Team												175		
Western Kentucky					30	1058	2392	.442	476	716	.665	1634	2592	86.4
Opponents					30	890	2157	.413	494	744	.664	1457	2274	75.8

1971 KANSAS

Head Coach—Ted Owens　　　　Final Record—27-3

Player	Pos.	Hgt.	Wgt.	Cl.	G	FG	FGA	Pct.	FT.	FTA	Pct.	Reb.	Pts.	Avg.
Dave Robisch	F	6-10	235	Sr.	30	215	511	.421	146	233	.627	302	576	19.2
Bud Stallworth	G	6-5	190	Jr.	30	215	470	.457	77	119	.647	198	507	16.9
Roger Brown	C	6-10	225	Sr.	29	131	278	.471	64	114	.561	322	326	11.2
Pierre Russell	F	6-4	200	Sr.	30	119	301	.395	71	98	.724	234	309	10.3
Aubrey Nash	G	6-1	195	Jr.	29	80	203	.394	32	73	.438	79	192	6.6
Mark Williams	G	5-11	165	So.	26	49	120	.408	37	45	.822	24	135	5.2
Randy Canfield	C	6-9	235	So.	16	29	57	.509	15	25	.600	56	73	4.6
Bob Kivisto	G	6-1	180	Jr.	30	32	80	.400	49	91	.538	47	113	3.8
Greg Douglas	F	6-8	220	Sr.	19	21	62	.339	10	13	.769	45	52	2.7
Mark Mathews	F	6-2	175	Jr.	21	7	13	.538	6	8	.750	13	20	1.0
Jerry House	F	6-6	175	So.	15	7	12	.583	0	1	.000	9	14	0.9
Neal Mask	F	6-7	200	Jr.	15	5	15	.333	1	4	.250	11	11	0.7
Team												203		
Kansas					30	910	2122	.429	508	824	.617	1543	2328	77.6
Opponents					30	687	1767	.389	565	798	.708	1298	1939	64.6

1971 FINAL FOUR

At Houston
Semifinals

Western Kentucky	fg	fga	ft	fta	rb	pf	tp
Glover	5	15	2	4	20	4	12
Dunn	11	33	3	6	8	5	25
McDaniels	10	24	2	4	17	5	22
Rose	8	21	2	3	8	2	18
Bailey	5	11	2	3	8	1	12
Witt	0	1	0	0	3	0	0
Sundmacker	0	0	0	0	0	1	0
Team					8		
Totals	39	105	11	20	69	21	89

Villanova	fg	fga	ft	fta	rb	pf	tp
Smith	5	14	3	6	11	1	13
Porter	10	20	2	3	16	4	22
Siemiontkowski	11	20	9	10	15	5	31
Ingelsby	5	10	4	7	4	1	14
Ford	3	6	2	2	1	4	8
McDowell	2	3	0	3	3	1	4
Team					4		
Totals	36	73	20	31	54	16	92

Halftime: Western Kentucky 38-35. Regulation Score: 74-74. First Overtime: 85-85. Officials: Bain and Brown.

Kansas	fg	fga	ft	fta	rb	pf	tp
Robisch	7	19	3	6	6	3	17
Russell	5	12	2	4	4	4	12
Brown	3	8	1	3	9	4	7
Stallworth	5	10	2	4	5	5	12
Nash	3	9	1	2	3	1	7
Kivisto	1	1	1	4	1	2	3
Canfield	0	0	0	0	0	1	0
Williams	0	1	2	2	0	2	2
Mathews	0	0	0	0	0	0	0
Douglas	0	0	0	0	1	0	0
Team					3		
Totals	24	60	12	23	32	22	60

UCLA	fg	fga	ft	fta	rb	pf	tp
Rowe	7	10	2	4	15	2	16
Wicks	5	9	11	13	8	2	21
Patterson	3	11	0	0	6	2	6
Bibby	6	9	6	6	4	3	18
Booker	1	2	1	2	5	3	3
Schofield	1	3	0	1	0	3	2
Farmer	0	2	0	1	2	1	0
Betchley	0	0	0	1	0	0	0
Ecker	0	1	2	2	1	0	2
Hill	0	0	0	0	0	0	0
Chapman	0	0	0	0	1	2	0
Team					5		
Totals	23	47	22	30	47	18	68

Halftime: UCLA 32-25. Officials: White and Honzo.

Championship
March 27

Villanova	fg	fga	ft	fta	rb	pf	tp
Smith	4	1	1	1	2	4	9
Porter	10	21	5	6	8	1	25
Siemiontkowski	9	16	1	2	8	3	19
Ingelsby	3	9	1	1	4	2	7
Ford	0	4	2	3	5	4	2
McDowell	0	1	0	0	2	0	0
Fox	0	0	0	0	0	0	0
Team					4		
Totals	26	62	10	13	31	14	62

UCLA	fg	fga	ft	fta	rb	pf	tp
Rowe	2	3	4	5	8	0	8
Wicks	3	7	1	1	9	2	7
Patterson	13	18	3	5	8	1	29
Bibby	6	12	5	5	2	1	17
Booker	0	0	0	0	0	0	0
Schofield	3	9	0	0	1	4	6
Betchley	0	0	1	2	1	1	1
Team					5		
Totals	27	49	14	18	34	9	68

Halftime: UCLA 45-37. Officials: Bain and Brown.

1972 The Walton Era Begins

Florida State's determined Seminoles literally surrounded UCLA big man Bill Walton, but couldn't derail the Bruin express.

This was the second coming, nothing less. Opponents that had lived through the era of Lew Alcindor cursed their fate as they looked upon Bill Walton. Once again, the dominant team had enlisted a dominant player.

Walton stretched 6 feet, 11 inches from the soles of his feet to the top of his curly red hair. He had huge hands, a take-charge attitude and a rare gift for the game. The arrival of Walton, the standout of a remarkable recruiting class, moved UCLA from the category of team to beat to that of unbeatable team.

Those who were relieved to see four starters from the 1971 champions graduate were appalled when they saw the replacements. In addition to Walton, two other sophomores stepped directly into prime roles. Keith Wilkes was a smooth, versatile forward with a fine shooting touch. Greg Lee was a 6-4 point guard whose ability to direct an offense freed 6-1 senior Henry Bibby, the only returning starter, to concentrate on his jump shot. Larry Farmer, a 6-5 junior who had played behind Sidney Wicks and Curtis Rowe the previous season, claimed the other starting position.

While the team's inexperience gave opponents some hope, they were distressed by the realization that these Bruins would be around for three years. Besides, while Coach John Wooden was pointing

Florida State's front line was anchored by a pair of towering ball hawks: Reggie Royals (25) and Lawrence McCray (44).

out how many mistakes his youngsters were making, they were trouncing some pretty good teams. Unlike the Alcindor group that appeared to play with almost professional detachment, the Walton Gang approached the task like a band of religious zealots.

The result was a succession of routs. This UCLA team didn't just win, it plundered. A prime example was a game against a solid Ohio State team in the final of the Bruin Classic at Pauley Pavilion. The Buckeyes had been a regional finalist in the NCAA Tournament the previous season, had won seven of their first eight games and were ranked sixth in one wire-service poll. But UCLA assumed an impressive 32-10 lead en route to a 79-53 triumph.

That was the norm, not the exception. Walton was an outstanding scorer, but he preferred to expend his energy on rebounding, passing and coaching the revived zone press from his safety position. While he didn't have Alcindor's grace as a shooter, he was a greater force on the backboards, and his crisp, quick outlet passes keyed many a fast break. Walton's style of play created a situation in which the maximum number of players shared in the glory. He cringed at the attention focused on him.

"It hurts me when people talk as if I'm the only player on the team," he said. "I wish reporters wouldn't ask me anything personally at all. I would like to see them get the whole team together to talk. I don't like to be singled out as an individual because we don't play as individuals, we play as a team."

When it came to basketball, Walton preferred to express himself on the court. He was shielded from the media by Wooden, much as the coach had done for Alcindor five years earlier, but he was outspoken among teammates and in the general college community. It would develop that he had opinions about almost everything but the sport that brought him fame.

In sweeping all 26 opponents in the regular season, UCLA was threatened only once. That was at Oregon State, where the Beavers came within six points of the Bruins, 78-72. UCLA's average margin of victory entering the NCAA Tournament was a staggering 32.2 points per game, well beyond the previous record of 27.2 established by the 1954 Kentucky team.

As if UCLA needed another edge in its quest for a sixth consecutive NCAA championship, the Final Four was scheduled for the Los Angeles Sports Arena. In addition, the team voted most likely to challenge the Bruins in the tournament, Marquette, was undone by the decision of 6-11 consensus All-America center Jim Chones, the oldest child in a poor family, to sign a professional contract late in the season. Though the Warriors were undefeated at the time of the defection, Chones had the blessing of his coach, Al McGuire, who said, "I've looked in his refrigerator."

Marquette was eliminated in the semifinal round of the Mideast Regional by Kentucky. For Adolph Rupp, it was his 875th and final victory as a college coach. He had reached the mandatory retirement age of 70. Two days later, he suffered his 190th defeat when upstart Florida State eliminated the Wildcats, 73-54.

Second-ranked North Carolina overpowered third-ranked Pennsylvania to win the East Regional. Louisville held off Kansas State in the Midwest. Meanwhile, UCLA breezed through the West Regional at Provo, Utah, crushing Weber State, 90-58, and grinding down a fine Long Beach State team, 73-57.

Lending the national semifinals a neat little twist was the pairing of UCLA and Louisville, which pitted teacher against student, Wooden vs. Denny Crum. The latter had sat on the Bruins' bench at the Final Four only the year before. In his first season as a head coach, Crum had led the Cardinals to their first Final Four appearance in 13 years.

"We are pleased to play a team led by one of our own, proud that Dennis Crum has taken his team this far, and we expect a difficult game," Wooden said diplomatically.

Crum smiled. "I don't think Mr. Wooden will give me anything," he said.

What Mr. Wooden and the Bruins gave Crum and his team was a headache. Despite double- and occasional triple-teaming, Walton did as he pleased. He hit 11 of 13 field-goal attempts, added 11 of 12 from the free-throw line and complemented his 33 points with 21 rebounds and six blocked shots. The Bruins romped, 96-77, as 10 UCLA players scored.

To the surprise of many, Florida State defeated North Carolina and consensus All-America Bob McAdoo, 79-75, in the other semifinal. By qualifying for their first championship game, the Seminoles added a touch of controversy to the event. They had just regained tournament eligibility after serving three years of NCAA probation for recruiting violations. Many coaches were not pleased to see Florida State in the spotlight.

One said so publicly. His name was Bill Wall of MacMurray (Ill.) College, and he happened to be president of the National Association of Basketball Coaches.

"I resent the fact that they're here," he said at a press conference, "and a lot of other coaches do, too. Our coaches are amazed, disgusted and disillusioned at this. Their coach was caught with his fingers in the till not once, but twice."

While Seminoles Coach Hugh Durham charged that Wall was ignorant of the facts and Florida State President Stanley Marshall announced that the university was considering legal action, Wooden

Florida State was able to remain within striking distance because of the long-range shooting of guard Ron King.

said he regretted the fuss on the eve of the season finale.

"I'm sorry about this," he told Durham. "I want you to know we don't feel the same way (as Wall)."

The Seminoles began the game as if they had something to prove. After two misses, they canned their next seven field-goal attempts to open a 21-14 lead. It marked the first time all season that UCLA had trailed by as many as seven points. The magic moment, however, did not last.

The Seminoles tried to contain Walton by having 6-10 Reggie Royals help 6-11 Lawrence McCray.

That tactic, however, left Wilkes open in the high post, and he shot and scored. Bibby, like Walton a consensus All-America, popped open in the corners. He shot and scored. Guard Tommy Curtis, another of those sensational sophomores, came off the bench. He shot and scored, his 12-footer staking the Bruins to a 27-25 lead.

Six minutes into the game, McCray had to take a seat with three fouls and UCLA poured it on. By halftime, Bibby had 16 points, Walton had 15, Wilkes had 13 and the Bruins held a 50-39 advantage. It was up to 16 points (67-51) with 12:18 left in the second half.

Less than a minute later, Walton was charged with his fourth foul and sat down. In his absence, reserve center Swen Nater was victimized by McCray, and Seminoles guard Ron King found the target repeatedly with his corner jumper.

Florida State cut the deficit to seven on four occasions while Walton was on the bench. Walton re-entered the game with about five minutes remaining, at which point Wooden ordered a delay game.

Three times in the next three minutes the Seminoles gained possession with a chance to force the issue, but each time they committed a turnover. Finally, Wilkes scored an uncontested layup, giving him 23 points for the game, to boost the UCLA lead to nine, 81-72, in the final minute. Two baskets by forward Ron Harris reduced the final deficit to 81-76—the Bruins' smallest margin of victory all year.

Although the Seminoles did not treat the close score as a moral victory, the Bruins seemed to regard it as a moral defeat.

"I'm really embarrassed," said Walton, who finished with 24 points, 20 rebounds and the outstanding-player award. "I can't believe how bad I played. I'd have to say it was one of my worst games. We should have beat these guys with ease. I guess I should be happy that we won, but in all honesty, I'm not."

In all honesty, only Curtis seemed overjoyed. He had good reason. He had contributed eight points and six assists against a team from his hometown. In his hands he held one of the nets and his championship watch.

"It will be something to show the people back in Tallahassee," he said.

The rest of the Bruins were rather unimpressed with their championship and undefeated season. "It gets to be old after a while," sighed Bibby, a senior who had his third title in as many seasons.

Indeed, it already was getting old for Walton, who was unaccustomed to an open dressing room and prying reporters. Reluctantly, he proceeded to an interview session that he was requested to attend. He answered a few questions disdainfully, grew hostile over others and finally stalked off, mumbling, "I've answered enough questions."

Clearly, Walton was a different breed of basketball player. Just as clearly, every other college team was in a familiar position, looking up at UCLA.

UCLA guard Tommy Curtis contributed eight points and six assists against the Seminoles, his hometown team.

1972 Tournament Results

First Round
South Carolina 53, Temple 51
Villanova 85, East Carolina 70
Pennsylvania 76, Providence 60
Marquette 73, Ohio 49
Florida State 83, E. Kentucky 81
*SW Louisiana 112, Marshall 101
Texas 85, Houston 74
Weber State 91, Hawaii 64
*Long Beach St. 95, BYU 90 (ot)

Second Round
N. Carolina 92, South Carolina 69
Pennsylvania 78, Villanova 67
Kentucky 85, Marquette 69
Florida State 70, *Minnesota 56
Louisville 88, *SW Louisiana 84
Kansas State 66, Texas 55
UCLA 90, Weber State 58
*Long Beach St. 75, San Fran. 55

Regional Third Place
South Carolina 90, Villanova 78
*Minnesota 77, Marquette 72
*SW Louisiana 100, Texas 70
San Francisco 74, Weber State 64

Regional Championships
N. Carolina 73, Pennsylvania 59
Florida State 73, Kentucky 54
Louisville 72, Kansas State 65
UCLA 73, *Long Beach State 57

Semifinals
Florida State 79, N. Carolina 75
UCLA 96, Louisville 77

Third Place
N. Carolina 105, Louisville 91

Championship
UCLA 81, Florida State 76

*SW Louisiana's, Long Beach State's and Minnesota's participation in 1972 tournament voided.

STATISTICS

1972 UCLA

Head Coach—John Wooden   **Final Record—30-0**

Player	Pos.	Hgt.	Wgt.	Cl.	G	FG	FGA	Pct.	FT.	FTA	Pct.	Reb.	Pts.	Avg.
Bill Walton	C	6-11	210	So.	30	238	372	.640	157	223	.704	466	633	21.1
Henry Bibby	G	6-1	185	Sr.	30	183	407	.450	104	129	.806	106	470	15.7
Keith Wilkes	F	6-6	174	So.	30	171	322	.531	64	92	.696	245	406	13.5
Larry Farmer	F	6-5	195	Jr.	30	141	309	.456	39	71	.549	164	321	10.7
Greg Lee	G	6-4	195	So.	29	98	199	.492	56	68	.824	57	252	8.7
Larry Hollyfield	F	6-5	210	Jr.	30	95	185	.514	28	43	.651	98	218	7.3
Swen Nater	C	6-11	238	Jr.	29	83	155	.535	28	46	.609	139	194	6.7
Tommy Curtis	G	5-10	175	So.	30	55	126	.437	14	22	.636	63	124	4.1
Andy Hill	G	6-0	175	Sr.	26	16	45	.356	39	55	.709	20	71	2.7
Vince Carson	F	6-6	190	So.	28	26	65	.400	16	24	.667	72	68	2.4
Jon Chapman	F	6-6	210	Sr.	28	20	43	.465	6	12	.500	45	46	1.6
Gary Franklin	F	6-5	185	So.	26	14	34	.412	7	16	.438	26	35	1.3
Team												2	146	
UCLA					30	1140	2262	.504	558	803	.695	1647	2838	94.6
Opponents					30	766	2003	.382	396	578	.685	1140	1928	64.3

1972 FLORIDA STATE

Head Coach—Hugh Durham   **Final Record—27-6***

Player	Pos.	Hgt.	Wgt.	Cl.	G	FG	FGA	Pct.	FT.	FTA	Pct.	Reb.	Pts.	Avg.
Ron King	G	6-4	185	Jr.	32	239	558	.428	95	126	.754	192	573	17.9
Reggie Royals	F	6-10	200	Jr.	32	196	415	.472	109	159	.686	351	501	15.7
Rowland Garrett	F	6-6	212	Sr.	32	169	352	.480	80	109	.734	253	418	13.1
Lawrence McCray	C	6-11	210	So.	32	166	300	.554	52	89	.584	263	384	12.0
Ron Harris	F	6-4	195	Sr.	32	104	232	.448	50	74	.676	161	258	8.1
Greg Samuel	G	5-8	150	Sr.	30	71	152	.467	55	74	.743	50	197	6.6
Otto Petty	G	5-7	150	Sr.	31	66	149	.443	72	101	.713	63	204	6.6
Otis Cole	G	6-2	175	So.	32	68	150	.453	35	47	.745	59	171	5.3
Larry Gay	F	6-5	195	Jr.	22	28	52	.538	10	16	.625	42	66	3.0
John Amick	F	6-7	195	So.	11	3	10	.300	3	3	1.000	5	9	0.8
Jim Calkin	G	6-4	190	So.	3	0	0	.000	0	1	.000	1	0	0.0
Artie Fryer	F	6-5	195	So.	2	0	1	.000	0	1	.000	1	0	0.0
Bill Wright	C	6-7	200	So.	2	0	1	.000	0	0	.000	2	0	0.0
Team												165		
Florida State					32	1110	2372	.468	561	800	.701	1608	2781	86.9
Opponents					32	904	2153	.420	478	722	.662	1386	2286	71.4

*Record includes forfeit loss not included in individual statistics.

1972 NORTH CAROLINA

Head Coach—Dean Smith   **Final Record—29-5**

Player	Pos.	Hgt.	Wgt.	Cl.	G	FG	FGA	Pct.	FT.	FTA	Pct.	Reb.	Pts.	Avg.
Bob McAdoo	C	6-9	210	Jr.	31	243	471	.516	118	167	.707	312	604	19.5
Dennis Wuycik	F	6-6	215	Sr.	31	189	310	.610	181	212	.854	176	559	18.0
George Karl	G	6-2	183	Jr.	29	125	241	.519	89	113	.788	72	339	11.7
Bill Chamberlain	F	6-6	185	Sr.	30	134	266	.504	60	83	.723	169	328	10.9
Bobby Jones	F	6-8	205	So.	31	127	190	.668	62	95	.653	195	316	10.2
Kim Huband	F	6-5	181	Sr.	31	60	122	.492	53	57	.930	57	173	5.6
Steve Previs	G	6-3	183	Sr.	31	56	135	.415	51	80	.638	83	163	5.3
Donn Johnston	C	6-8	206	Jr.	31	35	66	.530	8	17	.471	48	78	2.5
Bill Chambers	F	6-4	190	Sr.	29	19	40	.474	31	43	.721	23	69	2.4
John O'Donnell	F	6-6	190	So.	24	18	40	.450	14	27	.519	26	50	2.1
Craig Corson	C	6-9	219	Sr.	29	14	32	.438	15	23	.652	59	43	1.5
Ray Hite	G	5-10	173	So.	29	7	23	.304	18	24	.750	18	32	1.1
Roger Jamison	G	5-11	160	Jr.	5	2	8	.250	0	1	.000	0	4	0.8
Darrel Elston	F-G	6-3	196	So.	13	2	10	.200	0	0	.000	7	4	0.3
Team												133		
North Carolina					31	1031	1954	.528	700	942	.743	1378	2762	89.1
Opponents					31	808	1918	.421	597	853	.700	1153	2213	71.4

1972 LOUISVILLE

Head Coach—Denny Crum   **Final Record—26-5**

Player	Pos.	Hgt.	Wgt.	Cl.	G	FG	FGA	Pct.	FT.	FTA	Pct.	Reb.	Pts.	Avg.
Jim Price	G	6-3	195	Sr.	31	244	493	.495	164	198	.828	122	652	21.0
Ron Thomas	F	6-5	210	Sr.	31	191	347	.550	103	172	.599	420	485	15.6
Mike Lawhon	F	6-5	202	Sr.	31	140	307	.456	106	131	.809	136	386	12.4
Henry Bacon	F	6-4	210	Sr.	31	140	310	.452	54	93	.581	152	334	10.7
Al Vilichek	C	6-10	210	Sr.	31	127	268	.474	39	62	.629	244	293	9.4
Bill Bunton	F	6-7	215	So.	30	53	121	.411	15	24	.625	136	121	4.0
Larry Carter	G	6-0	180	Sr.	31	59	147	.401	7	14	.500	16	125	4.0
Ron Stallings	F	6-4	200	Sr.	21	28	65	.431	13	26	.500	40	69	3.2
Ken Bradley	F	6-6	225	Jr.	24	30	60	.500	16	23	.696	53	76	3.1
Tim Cooper	G	6-0	175	So.	19	16	32	.500	15	20	.750	3	47	2.4
Paul Pry	F	6-5	210	Sr.	15	6	9	.667	4	5	.800	6	16	1.1
Joe Meiman	G	6-2	185	Jr.	17	5	18	.278	0	1	.000	11	10	0.5
Rick Miles	C	6-7	197	Jr.	1	0	1	.000	0	0	.000	1	0	0.0
Larry Loehle	F-G	6-4	195	So.	1	0	0	.000	0	0	.000	0	0	0.0
Team												40		
Louisville					31	1039	2186	.475	536	769	.697	1380	2614	84.3
Opponents					31	883	2090	.422	492	730	.674	1445	2258	72.4

1972 FINAL FOUR

At Los Angeles
Semifinals

North Carolina	fg	fga	ft	fta	rb	pf	tp
Jones	4	8	1	1	9	3	9
Wuycik	7	16	6	6	6	4	20
McAdoo	10	19	4	5	15	5	24
Previs	1	5	3	6	3	4	5
Karl	5	14	1	3	6	3	11
Huband	0	1	0	0	2	2	0
Chamberlain	2	5	2	3	10	4	6
Johnston	0	1	0	0	1	0	0
Chambers	0	1	0	1	0	1	0
Team					1		
Totals	29	70	17	25	52	27	75

Florida State	fg	fga	ft	fta	rb	pf	tp
Garrett	4	8	3	7	5	4	11
King	6	17	10	10	5	1	22
Royals	6	8	6	7	10	5	18
McCray	3	6	3	6	9	3	9
Samuel	2	4	1	4	1	0	5
Harris	1	6	2	2	4	2	4
Petty	3	5	4	7	1	5	10
Gay	0	1	0	0	0	0	0
Team					6		
Totals	25	55	29	43	41	20	79

Halftime: Florida State 45-32. Officials: Scott and Brown.

Louisville	fg	fga	ft	fta	rb	pf	tp
Lawhon	0	7	1	2	3	3	1
Thomas	2	4	0	0	3	5	4
Vilcheck	3	6	0	0	1	5	6
Price	11	23	8	9	5	3	30
Bacon	5	11	5	7	4	0	15
Carter	4	8	0	0	2	0	8
Bunton	1	5	1	1	4	1	3
Bradley	1	3	0	0	2	1	2
Stallings	1	2	0	1	1	2	2
Cooper	0	1	2	2	1	1	2
Pry	2	3	0	0	1	1	4
Meiman	0	1	0	0	1	0	0
Team					4		
Totals	30	74	17	22	32	22	77

UCLA	fg	fga	ft	fta	rb	pf	tp
Wilkes	5	11	2	2	6	0	12
Farmer	6	12	3	5	4	2	15
Walton	11	13	11	12	21	2	33
Lee	3	6	4	6	4	1	10
Bibby	1	5	0	0	3	5	2
Curtis	4	5	0	0	2	2	8
Hollyfield	3	6	0	0	4	1	6
Carson	1	1	0	0	0	1	2
Nater	0	0	2	4	1	1	2
Hill	1	1	4	4	0	1	6
Chapman	0	0	0	1	1	0	0
Franklin	0	1	0	0	2	0	0
Team					3		
Totals	35	61	26	34	51	16	96

Halftime: UCLA 39-31. Officials: Hernjack and Copeland.

Championship
March 25

Florida State	fg	fga	ft	fta	rb	pf	tp
Garrett	1	9	1	1	5	1	3
King	12	20	3	3	6	1	27
Royals	5	7	5	6	10	5	15
McCray	3	6	2	5	6	4	8
Samuel	3	10	0	0	1	1	6
Harris	7	13	2	3	6	1	16
Petty	0	0	1	1	0	1	1
Cole	0	2	0	0	2	1	0
Team					6		
Totals	31	67	14	19	42	15	76

UCLA	fg	fga	ft	fta	rb	pf	tp
Wilkes	11	16	1	2	10	4	23
Farmer	2	6	0	0	6	2	4
Walton	9	17	6	11	20	4	24
Lee	0	0	0	0	2	0	0
Bibby	8	17	2	3	3	2	18
Curtis	4	14	0	1	4	1	8
Hollyfield	1	6	0	0	2	2	2
Nater	1	2	0	1	1	0	2
Team					2		
Totals	36	78	9	18	50	15	81

Halftime: UCLA 50-39. Officials: Brown and Scott.

1973 Bill Walton's Showcase

UCLA big man Bill Walton was awesome, dominating every phase of the Bruins' 1973 championship-game victory over Memphis State.

Many who considered the UCLA teams built around Lew Alcindor to be the most formidable in college basketball history suddenly were having second thoughts. The reason was another UCLA aggregation that revolved around another consensus All-America center, Bill Walton. This team appeared unbeatable—and had the record to prove it.

The mark for consecutive victories had been established by San Francisco, beginning in the Bill Russell era and continuing five games into the first season after his departure. The Dons had won 60 games in succession and no team since, not even Alcindor's Bruins, had seriously threatened it. Until now.

This UCLA team would get the opportunity to equal and perhaps surpass the record at midseason on the road against two noteworthy opponents. First up was Loyola of Chicago, which had hosted San Francisco when the Dons won their 60th consecutive game in 1956. Two days later, UCLA was scheduled to play Notre Dame, the last team to beat the Bruins two years earlier at South Bend, Ind.

Without a struggle, UCLA tied the record by beating Loyola, 87-73, and increased it to 61 by routing Notre Dame, 82-63. The streak continued as the Bruins advanced to the NCAA Tournament, which a team coached by John Wooden had won the previous six years. No one, Wooden included, expressed reservations about a seventh consecutive title.

"There are two leagues in college basketball," New Mexico Coach Norm Ellenberger noted as the quartet of national finalists gathered in St. Louis, "and one contains only UCLA."

Dave Gavitt, whose Providence team qualified for the Final Four by winning the East Regional, recalled receiving a number of letters before the Friars met the Bruins in the regular season.

"One letter listed 22 different things a rival coach should know about UCLA," said Gavitt, whose team suffered a 101-77 thrashing in becoming the Bruins' 59th consecutive victim, "and all of them were terrifying."

To the credit of Indiana, UCLA's semifinal opponent at the St. Louis Arena, it was not terrified. The Hoosiers, who won the Mideast Regional in only their second season under Coach Bob Knight, even had the effrontery to take an 18-13 lead in the early minutes of the game. It was just the sort of slap in the face the Bruins needed.

Between that moment and the end of the first half, UCLA outscored Indiana, 27-4, including a run of 18 unanswered points. The Bruins eventually pushed the lead to 46-24 and then 54-34 before suddenly losing inspiration in the second half.

"It takes some of the intensity out of the game when you're up by 20 points," senior guard Larry Hollyfield said. "They made a run at us and caught us napping."

Indeed, the Hoosiers scored 17 consecutive points, awakening UCLA and the crowd in the process. Wooden was concerned enough to rush Walton back into the game after he had rested him with four personal fouls for two minutes. Starting forwards Keith Wilkes (a consensus All-America) and Larry Farmer also were in foul trouble, and the Bruins needed to assert themselves in the frontcourt.

Walton did just that. He drew a fourth foul on Indiana star Steve Downing and, shortly thereafter, a fifth. Though the Hoosiers edged within 57-55 with 5:51 left, the Bruins sped away in the final minutes for a 70-59 victory.

"I think part of it was Walton," Indiana forward John Ritter said, "and part of it was that we had come back so far, so fast, that we just exhausted ourselves."

In the other semifinal, it appeared that Providence was about to earn itself a rematch against UCLA when the Friars were victimized by a costly injury. With consensus All-America point guard Ernie DiGregorio popping long jump shots and throwing dazzling passes from all angles, Providence raced to a 24-16 lead over Memphis State, the Midwest Regional winner. But then Marvin Barnes, the Friars' 6-8 center, went up for a rebound and took his team's hopes with him to the floor.

Barnes had to leave the game with a dislocated right kneecap, surrendering the backboards to Memphis State's outstanding frontcourt tandem of Larry Kenon and Ronnie Robinson. Still, the Friars hung on. Spurred by DiGregorio, forward Fran Costello and guard Kevin Stacom, they took a 49-40 advantage into the second half and, after being overtaken at 57-55, opened a 69-62 lead midway through the final period.

In time, however, the smaller team was worn down. DiGregorio's shooting touch deserted him and the Tigers forged ahead a second time. With his team trailing, 80-75, Barnes got the permission of the team doctor to play and all but begged Gavitt for one more chance. He returned to the game with 5:51 left and Providence did cut the deficit to 85-84 before yielding, 98-85.

"We did it in the second half when it counted," said Larry Finch, the Memphis State guard whose 21 points complemented the 24 by Robinson and 28 by Kenon. "Everybody keeps asking me how much losing Barnes meant to Providence. All I know is that we don't think that way. We were down with him in there and without him in there, and we came back playing the basketball we've played all year."

Still, the overpowering impression of the afternoon was expressed by DiGregorio. "With Marvin, we win," said the game's high scorer (32 points).

UCLA Coach John Wooden gives Bill Walton a pat on the head near the end of the Bruins' 87-66 title-game triumph.

UCLA forward Keith Wilkes (above) was smooth as silk and a nice complement to the rugged, dominating Bill Walton.

Memphis State's Larry Kenon did everything he could to keep the Tigers in contention during the '73 championship game.

UCLA's Larry Farmer battles Indiana's Steve Downing in a 1973 semifinal game.

"It's as simple as that."

Oddly enough, the Friars wouldn't even have been playing Memphis State if not for a change in the tournament format that year. Ever since the first tournament in 1939, the final had paired an Eastern team against one from the West. But in 1973, the NCAA began a system of rotating regional matchups in the Final Four. The alignment in the first season under the new system pitted East vs. Midwest in one semifinal pairing of regional champs and Mideast vs. West in the other. As a result, Providence played Memphis State in the semifinals rather than the Mideast titlist (in this case, Indiana), which previously had met the East champion for the right to advance to the championship game.

All of this probably was irrelevant in 1973 because any team hoping to win the national title ultimately would have to answer to UCLA. The Bruins might not have been overwhelming against Indiana, but they were the class of college basketball.

"That's an awesome team," Indiana's Ritter said. "You know the Yankees were awesome like that a few years back. Even if we'd beaten them, they'd still be the best."

The Bruins had one more game in which to prove they were the best in 1973, if not the best of all time, and they made the most of it. Before 19,301 fans, they walloped an outstanding Memphis State team, thanks in large measure to the greatest individual performance in championship-game history.

Walton dominated the contest from start to finish. He made 21 of his 22 field-goal attempts and added two free throws for 44 points, a championship-game record. He also had 13 rebounds in UCLA's 87-66 triumph.

"That was the best performance I've ever seen," Tigers Coach Gene Bartow said. "Ever."

Memphis State was able to draw close and remain competitive only when Walton was in foul trouble. His first 22 points paced the Bruins to a 37-30 lead after 15:30 of the first half. A few seconds later he drew his third personal foul and took a seat on the bench. The Tigers took the opportunity to create a 39-39 halftime tie. Thirty of Memphis State's 39 points were credited to Finch and Kenon.

The Tigers edged in front, 41-39, at the start of the second half, but that represented their final lead. Walton scored three consecutive baskets, two on lob passes from guard Greg Lee, and UCLA built a 57-47 advantage. Even when Walton committed his fourth foul and backed off slightly with the Tigers down by six (61-55), Memphis State could not catch up. The Bruins pushed the lead to 73-62 and went to their delay game with 5:42 remaining. Even though Walton was forced to the sidelines with a sprained ankle three minutes later, Memphis State was helpless to prevent UCLA's 75th consecutive victory and its seventh NCAA title in succession.

Despite the fact that he had enjoyed an extraordinary game in the national spotlight, Walton declined interviews. Beset by questions about lucrative professional offers and his involvement in peace protests on the UCLA campus, the junior wanted only to be left alone. With the season officially over, he decided he had to answer to no one.

"I'm not talking because the season is over," Walton told one reporter. "You don't see me frowning. You see how I'm happy we won and that it's over. But it's just that I'm no longer number 32 on the basketball court. I can be Joe Walton now if I want to be. And I'm not talking because I don't want to."

What he had demonstrated on the court, of course, was enough to ensure him a prominent place in basketball history. It even moved Wooden, a man of modest words, to conclude what many had suspected. "I'd have to say this is my best team ever," the coach said.

1973 Tournament Results

First Round	Regional Third Place
Syracuse 83, Furman 82	Syracuse 69, Pennsylvania 68
Pennsylvania 62, St. John's 61	S. Carolina 90, *SW Louisiana 85
Providence 89, St. Jos. (Pa.) 76	Marquette 88, *Austin Peay 73
South Carolina 78, Texas Tech 70	*Long Beach St. 84, Arizona St. 80
*SW Louisiana 102, Houston 89	**Regional Championships**
Marquette 77, Miami (Ohio) 62	Providence 103, Maryland 89
*Austin Peay 77, Jacksonville 75	Memphis State 92, Kansas State 72
*Long Beach St. 88, Weber St. 75	Indiana 72, Kentucky 65
Arizona St. 103, Oklahoma City 78	UCLA 54, San Francisco 39
Second Round	**Semifinals**
Maryland 91, Syracuse 75	Memphis State 98, Providence 85
Providence 87, Pennsylvania 65	UCLA 70, Indiana 59
Memphis St. 90, S. Carolina 76	**Third Place**
Kansas St. 66, *SW Louisiana 63	Indiana 97, Providence 79
Indiana 75, Marquette 69	**Championship**
Ky. 106, *Austin Peay 100 (ot)	UCLA 87, Memphis State 66
San Fran. 77, *Long Beach St. 67	
UCLA 98, Arizona State 81	

*SW Louisiana's, Long Beach State's and Austin Peay's participation in 1973 tournament voided.

STATISTICS

1973 UCLA

Head Coach—John Wooden   **Final Record—30-0**

Player	Pos.	Hgt.	Wgt.	Cl.	G	FG	FGA	Pct.	FT	FTA	Pct.	Reb.	Pts.	Avg.
Bill Walton	C	6-11	220	Jr.	30	277	426	.650	58	102	.569	506	612	20.4
Keith Wilkes	F	6-6	180	Jr.	30	200	381	.525	43	66	.652	220	443	14.8
Larry Farmer	F	6-5	215	Sr.	30	160	313	.511	47	67	.701	150	367	12.2
Larry Hollyfield	G	6-4	215	Sr.	30	146	313	.466	29	59	.492	88	321	10.7
Tommy Curtis	G	5-11	170	Jr.	24	64	125	.512	26	39	.667	41	154	6.4
Dave Meyers	F	6-7	205	So.	28	52	109	.477	34	45	.756	82	138	4.9
Greg Lee	G	6-4	191	Jr.	30	44	93	.473	49	62	.790	38	137	4.6
Swen Nater	C	6-11	230	Sr.	29	39	85	.459	15	23	.652	95	93	3.2
Pete Trgovich	G-F	6-5	175	So.	25	34	89	.382	10	25	.400	43	78	3.1
Vince Carson	F	6-5	195	Jr.	26	18	35	.514	8	17	.471	58	44	1.7
Gary Franklin	F	6-4	187	Jr.	24	16	33	.485	6	12	.500	31	38	1.6
Casey Corliss	G	6-6	197	Fr.	2	0	0	.000	2	2	1.000	0	2	1.0
Bob Webb	G	6-2	160	Jr.	21	4	27	.148	5	6	.833	4	13	0.6
Ralph Drollinger	C	7-0	210	Fr.	2	0	1	.000	0	0	.000	1	0	0.0
Team												112		
UCLA					30	1054	2030	.519	332	525	.632	1469	2440	81.3
Opponents					30	794	2006	.396	214	315	.679	1014	1802	60.1

1973 MEMPHIS STATE

Head Coach—Gene Bartow   **Final Record—24-6**

Player	Pos.	Hgt.	Wgt.	Cl.	G	FG	FGA	Pct.	FT	FTA	Pct.	Reb.	Pts.	Avg.
Larry Finch	G	6-2	185	Sr.	30	256	575	.445	209	250	.836	40	721	24.0
Larry Kenon	F	6-9	200	Jr.	30	273	520	.525	57	100	.570	501	603	20.1
Ronnie Robinson	C	6-8	220	Sr.	29	166	313	.530	60	98	.612	325	392	13.5
Wes Westfall	F	6-8	205	Jr.	30	76	150	.507	21	41	.512	159	173	5.8
Billy Buford	F	6-7	210	Jr.	29	73	148	.493	16	29	.552	105	162	5.6
Bill Cook	G	6-5	195	Fr.	25	50	117	.427	36	43	.837	19	136	5.4
Ken Andrews	F	6-6	200	Jr.	20	41	91	.451	8	14	.571	56	90	4.5
Shannon Kennedy	G	6-3	165	So.	2	4	5	.800	0	0	.000	1	8	4.0
Ed Wilson	F-C	6-6	220	Fr.	1	2	2	1.000	0	2	.000	4	4	4.0
Bill Laurie	G	5-10	160	Jr.	30	43	100	.430	32	40	.800	52	118	3.9
Clarence Jones	G-F	6-6	185	Fr.	17	20	58	.345	3	7	.429	29	43	2.5
Doug McKinney	G	6-0	180	Sr.	23	15	36	.417	18	26	.692	10	48	2.1
Jerry Tetzlaff	G	6-4	200	Sr.	10	5	15	.333	7	14	.500	6	17	1.7
John Tunstall	F	6-7	190	Fr.	6	4	12	.333	2	2	1.000	5	10	1.7
John Washington	C	6-10	207	Fr.	2	0	2	.000	3	4	.750	3	3	1.5
Jim Liss	G	6-2	175	So.	14	9	31	.290	2	9	.222	6	20	1.4
Larry Trosper	F	6-6	190	So.	9	1	4	.250	4	6	.667	6	6	0.7
Team												170		
Memphis State					30	1038	2179	.476	478	685	.698	1497	2554	85.1
Opponents					30	932	2097	.444	394	594	.663	1216	2258	75.3

1973 INDIANA

Head Coach—Bob Knight   **Final Record—22-6**

Player	Pos.	Hgt.	Wgt.	Cl.	G	FG	FGA	Pct.	FT	FTA	Pct.	Reb.	Pts.	Avg.
Steve Downing	C	6-8	231	Sr.	28	246	473	.520	71	128	.555	296	563	20.1
John Ritter	F	6-5	193	Sr.	28	147	294	.500	117	134	.873	123	411	14.7
Quinn Buckner	G	6-2	198	Fr.	28	130	318	.409	41	69	.594	134	301	10.8
John Laskowski	G	6-5	182	So.	28	108	220	.491	71	88	.807	133	287	10.3
Steve Green	F	6-7	218	So.	28	116	249	.466	50	65	.769	130	282	10.1
Jim Crews	G	6-4	193	So.	28	65	132	.492	17	25	.680	58	147	5.3
John Kamstra	G	6-1	165	So.	13	21	42	.500	9	15	.600	18	51	3.9
Tom Abernethy	F	6-6	206	Fr.	18	18	48	.375	4	7	.571	46	40	2.2
Craig Morris	G	6-4	185	Fr.	11	7	10	.700	5	9	.555	4	19	1.7
Trent Smock	F	6-5	217	Fr.	16	10	23	.435	2	4	.500	19	22	1.4
Jerry Memering	F	6-7	218	Sr.	14	7	11	.636	4	6	.667	4	18	1.3
Don Noort	F	6-8	225	Fr.	12	5	14	.357	5	8	.625	18	15	1.3
Steve Ahlfeld	G	6-0	180	So.	14	3	11	.273	7	10	.700	6	13	0.9
Frank Wilson	G	6-3	192	Sr.	13	6	20	.300	0	1	.000	11	12	0.9
Doug Allen	F	6-5	222	So.	10	1	6	.167	0	0	.000	5	2	0.2
Bootsie White	G	5-8	176	Sr.	4	0	0	.000	0	1	.000	0	0	0.0
Team											1	179		
Indiana					28	890	1871	.476	403	571	.706	1184	2183	78.0
Opponents					28	821	1861	.441	313	471	.665	1158	1955	69.8

1973 PROVIDENCE

Head Coach—Dave Gavitt   **Final Record—27-4**

Player	Pos.	Hgt.	Wgt.	Cl.	G	FG	FGA	Pct.	FT	FTA	Pct.	Reb.	Pts.	Avg.
Ernie DiGregorio	G	6-0	170	Sr.	31	348	728	.478	65	81	.802	99	761	24.5
Marvin Barnes	C	6-8	210	Jr.	30	237	436	.544	75	109	.688	571	549	18.3
Kevin Stacom	G	6-4	185	Jr.	31	238	431	.552	75	87	.862	121	551	17.8
Fran Costello	F	6-8	215	Jr.	31	115	230	.500	52	80	.650	149	282	9.1
Nehru King	F	6-4	185	Sr.	29	108	192	.563	36	44	.818	112	252	8.7
Charles Crawford	F	6-5	200	Sr.	31	70	140	.500	32	46	.696	187	172	5.5
Ron Norwood	G	6-3	180	Fr.	14	15	33	.455	7	9	.778	14	37	2.6
Al Baker	C	6-6	220	Jr.	25	20	45	.444	22	34	.647	62	62	2.5
Rick Dunphy	F	6-5	185	Fr.	21	16	36	.444	19	33	.576	23	51	2.4
Dave Modest	G	5-9	165	Fr.	10	8	16	.500	2	4	.500	4	18	1.8
Mark McAndrew	F	6-4	185	Fr.	15	8	18	.444	3	5	.600	17	19	1.3
Gary Bello	G	5-9	155	So.	23	9	30	.300	6	9	.667	11	24	1.0
Tom Walters	G	6-0	170	Jr.	2	0	2	.000	2	2	1.000	3	2	1.0
Team												115		
Providence					31	1192	2337	.510	396	543	.729	1488	2780	89.7
Opponents					31	1022	2416	.423	324	493	.657	1361	2368	76.4

1973 FINAL FOUR

At St. Louis
Semifinals

Memphis State	fg	fga	ft	fta	rb	pf	tp
Buford	3	7	0	0	3	2	6
Kenon	14	27	0	4	22	1	28
Robinson	11	17	2	3	16	2	24
Laurie	1	3	2	1	4	3	4
Finch	7	16	7	9	6	4	21
Cook	3	6	2	3	1	2	8
Westfall	2	3	3	4	2	0	7
Jones	0	1	0	0	0	0	0
Team					3		
Totals	41	80	16	26	54	15	98

Providence	fg	fga	ft	fta	rb	pf	tp
Crawford	5	12	0	0	15	3	10
Costello	5	5	1	1	8	5	11
Barnes	5	7	2	3	3	4	12
DiGregorio	15	36	2	2	2	4	32
Stacom	6	15	3	3	5	5	15
King	2	6	0	0	1	1	4
Baker	0	0	0	0	1	0	0
Dunphy	0	1	1	2	1	0	1
Bello	0	0	0	0	0	0	0
Team					3		
Totals	38	82	9	11	39	22	85

Halftime: Providence 49-40. Officials: Ditty and White.

UCLA	fg	fga	ft	fta	rb	pf	tp
Wilkes	5	10	3	4	6	3	13
Farmer	3	6	1	2	3	4	7
Walton	7	12	0	0	17	4	14
Lee	0	1	0	0	0	0	0
Hollyfield	5	6	0	0	2	1	10
Curtis	9	15	4	7	2	2	22
Meyers	2	3	0	0	5	1	4
Nater	0	0	0	0	0	1	0
Team					3		
Totals	31	53	8	13	38	16	70

Indiana	fg	fga	ft	fta	rb	pf	tp
Buckner	3	10	0	1	5	2	6
Crews	4	10	0	0	2	3	8
Downing	12	20	2	4	5	5	26
Green	1	7	0	0	5	2	2
Ritter	6	10	1	1	2	3	13
Laskowski	1	8	0	0	4	0	2
Abernethy	0	1	0	0	1	1	0
Smock	0	0	0	0	0	0	0
Noort	0	0	0	0	1	0	0
Wilson	0	0	0	0	0	0	0
Morris	0	0	0	0	0	0	0
Ahlfield	0	0	0	0	0	0	0
Allen	1	1	0	0	0	0	2
Memering	0	0	0	0	0	0	0
Team					4		
Totals	28	67	3	6	29	16	59

Halftime: UCLA 40-22. Officials: Shosid and Howell.

Championship
March 26

UCLA	fg	fga	ft	fta	rb	pf	tp
Wilkes	8	14	0	0	7	2	16
Farmer	1	4	0	0	2	2	2
Walton	21	22	2	5	13	4	44
Lee	1	1	3	3	3	2	5
Hollyfield	4	7	0	0	3	4	8
Curtis	1	4	2	2	3	1	4
Meyers	2	7	0	0	3	1	4
Nater	1	1	0	0	3	2	2
Franklin	1	2	0	1	1	0	2
Carson	0	0	0	0	0	0	0
Webb	0	0	0	0	0	0	0
Team					2		
Totals	40	62	7	11	40	18	87

Memphis State	fg	fga	ft	fta	rb	pf	tp
Buford	3	7	1	2	3	1	7
Kenon	8	16	4	4	8	3	20
Robinson	3	6	0	1	7	4	6
Laurie	0	1	0	0	0	0	0
Finch	9	21	11	13	1	2	29
Westfall	0	1	0	0	0	5	0
Cook	1	4	2	2	0	1	4
McKinney	0	0	0	0	0	0	0
Jones	0	0	0	0	1	0	0
Tetzlaff	0	0	0	2	0	1	0
Liss	0	0	0	0	0	0	0
Andrews	0	0	0	0	0	0	0
Team					2		
Totals	24	57	18	24	21	17	66

Halftime Score: 39-39. Officials: Howell and Shosid.

1974 The UCLA Streak Ends

North Carolinians packed the Greensboro Coliseum in anticipation of N.C. State snapping UCLA's national championship streak at seven in a semifinal game.

The myth of invincibility had died slowly in the final 3½ minutes of a game against Notre Dame in South Bend, Ind., where John Wooden had coached a high school team four decades earlier. Riding the crest of an unprecedented 88-game winning streak, Wooden's UCLA Bruins failed to hold an 11-point lead and were defeated by the Fighting Irish, 71-70.

Ironically, the Bruins had won at Notre Dame to break San Francisco's NCAA record for consecutive victories (60) a year earlier. Moreover, UCLA's long winning streak had begun after an 89-82 loss at Notre Dame in 1971. But on January 19, 1974, the Irish inflicted the first varsity loss on the collection of players known as the Walton Gang.

Bill Walton, the consensus All-America center and star of the team, appeared bemused by the result. The 6-foot-11 senior left the Notre Dame Athletic and Convocation Center humming the "Notre Dame Victory March," which had been played loudly and incessantly throughout the latter stages of the stunning upset. Nor did the Bruins appear terribly distraught when they lost consecutive Pacific-8 Conference games at Oregon State and Oregon four weeks later. Oh, it was a bit of a shock, but

they recovered in time to win their last five regular-season games and their eighth straight Pac-8 title.

Even though the Bruins had fallen behind North Carolina State in the national rankings, they were supremely confident entering the NCAA Tournament. Their three losses represented their highest season total since 1966, when UCLA was 18-8, but winning seven consecutive national championships in the interim had fostered an understandable degree of complacency.

After a first-round bye, UCLA needed three overtimes to squeeze by Dayton. The Bruins then overwhelmed San Francisco, 83-60, in the West Regional final to proceed to the Final Four, where only N.C. State was conceded a reasonable chance of dethroning UCLA. But the Bruins weren't worried. After all, they had smashed the Wolfpack, 84-66, in a nationally televised game earlier that season in St. Louis.

That loss was the only one suffered by N.C. State in the regular season. In fact, it represented the Wolfpack's lone defeat in two seasons. A year earlier, Norm Sloan's team had gone 27-0 but had been denied a berth in the NCAA Tournament because

Both N.C. State and UCLA had their big guns primed when the teams met in the NCAA Tournament. High-flying David Thompson (left) was the Wolfpack's offensive answer to UCLA big man Bill Walton (right).

of recruiting violations.

In the eyes of N.C. State's players, students and supporters, the December meeting on a neutral court would settle the 1973 championship. It did. The Bruins won handily as consensus All-America forward David Thompson, a 6-4 Wolfpack star whose 42-inch vertical leap propelled him to heights heretofore unknown, was grounded by UCLA's consensus All-America forward, Keith Wilkes. Wilkes not only limited Thompson to 17 points, but also scored 27 himself.

Though disappointed by the result, N.C. State did not suffer a competitive hangover from the thrashing. The Wolfpack emerged undefeated from a taxing Atlantic Coast Conference schedule, then scored a dramatic 103-100 overtime victory over Maryland for the ACC Tournament title and a spot in the NCAA East Regional, where Providence and Pittsburgh were defeated easily.

College basketball fans were eager to watch a UCLA-N.C. State rematch for the national title, but the Final Four pairings pitted West against East in one semifinal, meaning that the nation's top two teams would meet a game earlier than hoped. The rematch, however, differed from the first encounter in one important respect: The site of the championship, the Greensboro (N.C.) Coliseum, was just 70 miles up the road from the N.C. State campus.

Not that the talent-laden Wolfpack needed it, but N.C. State clearly benefited from some fortuitous scheduling. The ACC Tournament was held in Greensboro and the East Regional semifinals and final were played in Raleigh, N.C. Now, Sloan's team had an opportunity to win the national title without playing an NCAA Tournament game outside its home state.

"I want North Carolina State to remember that we beat them by 18 on a neutral court," Wooden said as he prepared his team. "I want them to think about who has the psychological advantage."

The Wolfpack contended that it had been too anxious in that first game and that it had gained experience over the course of the season and now was playing at maximum efficiency.

"We're more versatile than UCLA," Sloan said. "We have something left to prove. And we still have Thompson. I like the odds."

With all the interest focused on the UCLA-N.C. State matchup, scant attention was paid to the other two semifinalists. Marquette and Kansas had struggled to win the Mideast and Midwest regionals, respectively, but their meeting provoked mostly yawns in North Carolina. Kansas Coach Ted Owens jokingly referred to the first semifinal as the "preliminary" game. And after his Marquette team, which he personally rated only seventh best in the country, had scored a humdrum 64-51 victory over the Jayhawks, Warriors Coach Al McGuire decided not to waste either his or the media's time.

"We'll answer a few questions," he said, "and then you guys can go watch the championship game."

The long and short of North Carolina State's high-powered offense consisted of 7-foot-4 center Tom Burleson (above) and 5-7 playmaker Monte Towe (right), who created problems for UCLA's backcourt.

Certainly, the game that followed belonged in a championship setting. UCLA never led by more than two points and N.C. State never led by more than five in the first half, which ended, fittingly, in a 35-35 tie as Bruins forward Dave Meyers sank a 29-foot desperation jump shot at the buzzer. Thompson was every bit the force he hadn't been in St. Louis, while 7-4 senior Tom Burleson was conceding little to Walton. And Monte Towe, a 5-7 whippet of a guard, was creating havoc in UCLA's erratic backcourt.

Still, the Bruins surged ahead in the second half. They scored 14 of the first 17 points after intermission to open a 49-38 lead. An 8-2 Wolfpack run reduced the deficit to 51-46, but then UCLA scored the next six points to go up by 11 a second time at 57-46. Only 10:56 remained on the clock.

Although they had a chance to put away the Wolfpack then and there, the Bruins responded with turnovers. Walton was whistled for traveling. Backcourt leader Greg Lee and Meyers forced passes. Senior Tommy Curtis took questionable shots. Wilkes, who was hounded into a five-for-17 shooting performance, couldn't steady the team.

N.C. State closed the gap to one at 57-56 and again at 61-60. Suddenly, there was Thompson elevating himself above the crowd, taking a lob pass from forward Tim Stoddard, slamming the ball through the hoop and drawing a foul. His three-point play pushed the Wolfpack into the lead, 63-61. UCLA rallied to tie at 65-65 with a little more than two minutes remaining.

The Bruins worked more than a minute off the clock before Walton rolled to his left and attempted a hook shot.

"Down at the end, all they could do was go to Wilkes or Walton," Wolfpack guard Moe Rivers said. "And we had them covered." Walton's shot rolled off the rim and Burleson rebounded.

N.C. State had a final chance. With Burleson and Thompson blanketed, the ball went to Stoddard in the corner. His jump shot missed. Lee's shot at the buzzer also missed for the Bruins, forcing an overtime.

The extra session was played in slow motion. After Lee matched a basket by Burleson, the Wolfpack killed most of the final three minutes setting up a last shot. But Burleson's potential game-winner was off-target, so with the score still tied, 67-67, a second overtime was necessary.

UCLA appeared to be the fresher team at the start of the extra five-minute period. Walton and Wilkes combined for the first seven points, opening a 74-67 UCLA lead.

"The thought went through my head that we had two opportunities to win this game," Towe recalled. "And when we were seven points down, I thought maybe this was their turn."

Curtis obviously thought so. The cocky UCLA guard took the occasion to wave his right index finger at the pro-Wolfpack crowd with 3:27 left. Moments later, he answered two free throws by Towe with one of his own. It would be the last point his team would score until it was too late. Turnovers by Curtis, Lee and Walton enabled N.C. State to gain control. The Wolfpack edged in front, 76-75, on a bank shot by Thompson, and his two free throws with 34 seconds left made it 78-75 and gave him a team-high 28 points. Towe's two foul shots clinched the 80-77 victory.

The sentiment in the UCLA locker room was that the Bruins had beaten themselves.

"There's nobody better than us," Lee said. "We're better than that team. You think they don't know that? We helped them. We got careless with the ball. We made the mistakes."

At least one N.C. State player was inclined to agree. "Once it got down close," Rivers said, "they seemed to choke."

No matter what the cause, N.C. State had succeeded in handing UCLA its first NCAA Tournament loss in 39 games—a stretch that began after successive losses in the 1963 tournament—and in toppling what everyone but Wooden called a dynasty. Still, the Wolfpack had yet to fulfill its goal. Shortly after the Walton era officially ended with UCLA's 78-61 consolation victory over Kansas, the Wolfpack won its first national championship with a convincing if uninspired 76-64 victory over Marquette.

In the finale, N.C. State had considerable help from McGuire. The rival coach earned two technical fouls late in the first half, helping to transform a 28-27 Marquette lead into a 37-28 deficit. Including the two technical-foul shots converted by Thompson, the Wolfpack scored 10 unanswered points in a 53-second span to take charge of the game.

"We never got back on our feet after that," Warriors center Maurice Lucas said.

McGuire took the blame. "I cost us the game," he said. Still, he didn't want to detract from the Wolfpack's performance or talent.

"The simple truth of the matter," McGuire said, "is that State is a better team. If we played them 10 times, we might win three, we might win two. We might not even win one."

When it mattered most, N.C. State was triumphant. The Wolfpack led 39-30 at halftime, stretched its margin to 19 five minutes into the second half and won handily. And college basketball finally had a new champion after seven years of domination by UCLA.

Once the UCLA title streak was broken, N.C. State turned its attention to Marquette and talented big man Maurice Lucas (above).

1974 Tournament Results

First Round
Providence 84, Pennsylvania 69
Pitts. 54, St. Joseph's (Pa.) 42
Furman 75, South Carolina 67
New Mexico 73, Idaho State 65
Dayton 88, Los Angeles State 80
Notre Dame 108, Austin Peay 66
Marquette 85, Ohio 59
Oral Roberts 86, Syracuse 82 (ot)
Creighton 77, Texas 61

Second Round
N. C. State 92, Providence 78
Pittsburgh 81, Furman 78
San Francisco 64, New Mexico 61
UCLA 111, Dayton 100 (3 ot)
Michigan 77, Notre Dame 68
Marquette 69, Vanderbilt 61
Oral Roberts 96, Louisville 93
Kansas 55, Creighton 54

Regional Third Place
Providence 95, Furman 83
New Mexico 66, Dayton 61
Notre Dame 118, Vanderbilt 88
Creighton 80, Louisville 71

Regional Championships
N. C. State 100, Pittsburgh 72
UCLA 83, San Francisco 60
Marquette 72, Michigan 70
Kansas 93, Oral Roberts 90 (ot)

Semifinals
N. C. State 80, UCLA 77 (2 ot)
Marquette 64, Kansas 51

Third Place
UCLA 78, Kansas 61

Championship
N. C. State 76, Marquette 64

STATISTICS

1974 NORTH CAROLINA STATE

Head Coach—Norm Sloan **Final Record—30-1**

Player	Pos.	Hgt.	Wgt.	Cl.	G	FG	FGA	Pct.	FT.	FTA	Pct.	Reb.	Pts.	Avg.
David Thompson	F	6-4	195	Jr.	31	325	594	.547	155	208	.745	245	805	26.0
Tom Burleson	C	7-4	235	Sr.	31	228	442	.516	106	162	.654	377	562	18.1
Monte Towe	G	5-7	145	Jr.	31	168	325	.517	60	74	.811	67	396	12.8
Moe Rivers	G	6-1	165	Jr.	30	155	320	.484	53	81	.654	86	363	12.1
Phil Spence	F	6-8	215	So.	30	74	149	.497	32	52	.615	188	180	6.0
Tim Stoddard	F	6-7	225	Jr.	31	74	178	.416	23	33	.697	141	171	5.5
Steve Nuce	F	6-8	210	Sr.	28	51	110	.464	22	28	.786	89	124	4.4
Mark Moeller	G	6-3	175	Jr.	30	30	69	.435	21	23	.913	36	81	2.7
Greg Hawkins	F	6-5	185	Sr.	25	23	49	.469	25	34	.735	36	71	2.8
Dwight Johnson	G	6-0	160	So.	19	9	18	.500	11	18	.611	14	29	1.5
Bill Lake	C	6-11	190	Fr.	14	6	16	.375	3	5	.600	11	15	1.1
Steve Smith	F	6-10	210	So.	8	3	4	.750	1	2	.500	5	7	0.9
Ken Gehring	F	6-9	203	Fr.	8	2	6	.333	1	2	.500	4	5	0.6
Mike Buurma	C	6-10	220	Fr.	13	3	14	.214	1	2	.500	7	7	0.5
Craig Kuszmaul	G	6-5	181	Jr.	18	3	8	.375	2	5	.400	6	8	0.4
Bruce Dayhuff	G	6-2	175	Fr.	16	2	14	.143	3	4	.750	6	7	0.4
Jerry Hunt	F	6-5	200	So.	5	1	3	.333	0	0	.000	1	2	0.4
Team												134		
North Carolina State					31	1157	2319	.499	519	733	.708	1452	2833	91.4
Opponents					31	957	2198	.435	403	608	.663	1249	2317	74.7

1974 MARQUETTE

Head Coach—Al McGuire **Final Record—26-5**

Player	Pos.	Hgt.	Wgt.	Cl.	G	FG	FGA	Pct.	FT.	FTA	Pct.	Reb.	Pts.	Avg.
Maurice Lucas	C	6-9	205	Jr.	31	211	429	.492	69	94	.734	328	491	15.8
Bo Ellis	F	6-9	190	Fr.	31	167	312	.535	44	61	.721	264	378	12.2
Earl Tatum	F	6-5	170	So.	31	136	293	.464	40	67	.597	158	312	10.1
Marcus Washington	G	6-1	160	Sr.	31	130	352	.369	40	60	.667	100	300	9.7
Lloyd Walton	G	6-0	160	So.	31	119	282	.422	54	69	.783	79	292	9.4
Rick Campbell	F	6-5	190	Jr.	31	55	123	.447	17	30	.567	69	127	4.1
Ed Daniels	G	6-3	190	Sr.	31	44	97	.454	16	20	.800	36	104	3.4
Jerry Homan	C-F	6-7	205	Jr.	31	37	97	.381	17	21	.810	65	91	2.9
Dave Delsman	G	5-10	160	Jr.	30	27	82	.329	20	28	.714	25	74	2.5
Barry Brennan	G	5-10	150	So.	11	2	4	.500	7	8	.875	2	11	1.0
John Bryant	F	6-7	190	Fr.	15	2	7	.286	4	6	.667	10	8	0.5
Paul Vollmer	F	6-4	180	Jr.	11	1	4	.250	1	4	.250	7	3	0.3
Greg Johnson	F	6-5	175	So.	7	1	6	.167	0	1	.000	5	2	0.3
Team												120		
Marquette					31	932	2088	.446	329	469	.701	1268	2193	70.7
Opponents					31	721	1704	.423	415	582	.713	1067	1857	59.9

1974 UCLA

Head Coach—John Wooden **Final Record—26-4**

Player	Pos.	Hgt.	Wgt.	Cl.	G	FG	FGA	Pct.	FT.	FTA	Pct.	Reb.	Pts.	Avg.
Bill Walton	C	6-11	220	Sr.	27	232	349	.665	58	100	.580	398	522	19.3
Keith Wilkes	F	6-7	180	Sr.	30	209	426	.491	82	94	.872	198	500	16.7
Dave Meyers	F	6-7	205	Jr.	30	144	295	.488	54	77	.701	171	342	11.4
Tommy Curtis	G	5-11	170	Sr.	30	88	199	.442	27	33	.818	49	203	6.8
Marques Johnson	F	6-5	212	Fr.	27	83	131	.634	28	38	.737	90	194	7.2
Pete Trgovich	G-F	6-5	175	Jr.	29	85	188	.452	24	29	.828	53	194	6.7
Ralph Drollinger	C	7-1	210	So.	21	44	91	.484	21	31	.677	102	109	5.2
Richard Washington	C-F	6-9	220	Fr.	24	41	80	.513	17	34	.500	66	99	4.1
Greg Lee	G	6-3	191	Sr.	30	44	111	.396	29	37	.784	41	117	4.0
Andre McCarter	G	6-2	174	So.	23	37	92	.402	15	25	.600	30	89	3.9
Jim Spillane	G	5-10	150	Fr.	9	9	21	.429	4	7	.571	3	22	2.4
Bob Webb	G	6-1	160	Sr.	12	12	32	.375	2	3	.667	4	26	2.2
Gary Franklin	F	6-4	187	Jr.	19	14	37	.378	5	9	.556	22	33	1.7
Wilbert Olinde	F	6-6	198	Fr.	6	5	7	.714	0	0	.000	7	10	1.7
Gavin Smith	G	6-4	185	Fr.	7	4	9	.444	1	2	.500	5	9	1.3
Casey Corliss	F-G	6-6	197	So.	1	0	2	.500	1	2	.500	1	1	1.0
Team												112		
UCLA					30	1051	2070	.508	368	521	.706	1352	2470	82.3
Opponents					30	791	1911	.414	300	422	.711	1030	1882	62.7

1974 KANSAS

Head Coach—Ted Owens **Final Record—23-7**

Player	Pos.	Hgt.	Wgt.	Cl.	G	FG	FGA	Pct.	FT.	FTA	Pct.	Reb.	Pts.	Avg.
Danny Knight	C	6-10	220	Jr.	30	157	332	.473	58	94	.617	213	372	12.4
Roger Morningstar	F	6-6	200	Jr.	28	152	339	.448	40	52	.769	154	344	12.3
Dale Greenlee	G	6-2	170	Jr.	29	150	302	.497	43	48	.896	123	343	11.8
Norman Cook	F	6-8	210	Fr.	30	144	291	.495	53	80	.663	196	341	11.4
Rick Suttle	C	6-10	200	Jr.	30	142	287	.495	56	77	.727	160	340	11.3
Tom Kivisto	G	6-2	180	Sr.	30	92	210	.438	44	62	.710	92	228	7.6
Tommie Smith	F	6-5	205	Jr.	24	69	166	.416	8	17	.471	116	146	6.1
Dave Taynor	G	6-4	185	Sr.	9	18	35	.516	12	13	.923	10	48	5.3
Nino Samuel	F	6-5	215	So.	9	11	37	.297	18	23	.783	34	40	4.4
Donnie Von Moore	F	6-9	200	Fr.	13	12	35	.343	2	5	.400	23	26	2.0
Reuben Shelton	G	6-4	190	Fr.	7	4	11	.364	0	0	.000	2	8	1.1
Paul Werner	G	6-0	175	Fr.	1	0	0	.000	1	2	.500	0	1	1.0
Jack Hollis	G	6-5	190	Fr.	5	1	3	.333	2	2	1.000	1	4	0.8
Bob Emery	F	6-6	210	Fr.	4	1	2	.500	0	0	.000	2	2	0.5
Chris Barnthouse	G	6-4	180	Fr.	2	0	0	.000	0	0	.000	1	0	0.0
Dwight Haley	F	6-4	190	Jr.	1	0	1	.000	0	0	.000	0	0	0.0
Team												182		
Kansas					30	953	2051	.465	337	475	.709	1309	2243	74.8
Opponents					30	822	1889	.435	387	561	.690	968	2031	67.7

1974 FINAL FOUR

At Greensboro, N.C.
Semifinals

UCLA	fg	fga	ft	fta	rb	pf	tp
Meyers	6	9	0	1	8	4	12
Wilkes	5	17	5	5	7	5	15
B. Walton	13	21	3	3	18	2	29
Curtis	4	8	3	4	5	5	11
Lee	4	11	0	0	4	2	8
M. Johnson	0	3	0	0	0	0	0
McCarter	1	2	0	0	0	0	2
Team					2		
Totals	33	71	11	13	44	18	77

North Carolina St.	fg	fga	ft	fta	rb	pf	tp
Stoddard	4	11	1	2	9	5	9
Thompson	12	25	4	6	10	3	28
Burleson	9	20	2	6	14	4	20
Rivers	3	8	1	2	2	3	7
Towe	4	10	4	4	2	4	12
Spence	2	3	0	0	5	4	4
Hawkins	0	0	0	0	0	0	0
Team					2		
Totals	34	77	12	20	44	19	80

Halftime Score: 35-35. Regulation Score: 65-65. First Overtime: 67-67. Officials: Weiler and Galvan.

Kansas	fg	fga	ft	fta	rb	pf	tp
Cook	1	3	2	4	5	5	4
Morningstar	5	13	0	0	5	4	10
Knight	0	5	0	0	5	4	0
Greenlee	3	7	0	0	3	4	6
Kivisto	2	7	2	5	2	4	6
Suttle	8	13	3	4	9	2	19
Smith	3	4	0	0	4	3	6
Team					4		
Totals	22	52	7	13	37	25	51

Marquette	fg	fga	ft	fta	rb	pf	tp
Ellis	2	9	1	2	10	3	5
Tatum	5	11	4	6	3	3	14
Lucas	7	11	4	4	14	2	18
L. Walton	2	7	3	4	1	4	7
Washington	5	12	6	11	3	4	16
Daniels	2	0	0	0	0	1	0
Campbell	0	1	0	0	1	0	0
Homan	1	2	0	0	2	2	2
Delsman	0	1	2	2	0	1	2
Brennan	0	0	0	0	0	0	0
Bryant	0	0	0	0	0	0	0
Vollmer	0	0	0	0	0	0	0
G. Johnson	0	0	0	0	0	0	0
Team					6		
Totals	22	56	20	29	38	20	64

Halftime: Kansas 24-23. Officials: Brown and Howell.

Championship
March 25

Marquette	fg	fga	ft	fta	rb	pf	tp
Ellis	6	16	0	0	11	5	12
Tatum	2	7	0	0	3	4	4
Lucas	7	13	7	9	13	4	21
L. Walton	4	10	0	0	2	2	8
Washington	3	13	5	8	4	3	11
Delsman	0	0	0	0	0	2	0
Daniels	1	3	1	2	0	3	3
Campbell	2	3	0	0	1	3	4
Homan	0	4	1	2	6	2	1
Brennan	0	0	0	0	0	1	0
Team					3		
Totals	25	69	14	21	43	29	64

North Carolina St.	fg	fga	ft	fta	rb	pf	tp
Stoddard	3	4	2	2	7	5	8
Thompson	7	12	7	8	7	3	21
Burleson	6	9	2	6	11	4	14
Rivers	4	9	6	9	2	2	14
Towe	5	10	6	7	3	1	16
Spence	1	2	1	2	3	2	3
Moeller	0	0	0	0	0	0	0
Team					1		
Totals	26	46	24	34	34	17	76

Halftime: North Carolina State 39-30. Officials: Howell and Brown.

1975 UCLA Wins One For the Wizard

With a short, cryptic announcement in the UCLA dressing room, John Wooden signaled the end of a remarkable era. Moments after the Bruins had reached the NCAA championship game for the 10th time in 12 years, the coach who had built the greatest dynasty in college basketball history told his players the next game would be his last. He did so with characteristic understatement and an economy of words.

"I think he had it all planned out," senior guard Pete Trgovich said. "I think he was planning to announce it if we got to the final. Everything was quiet in here when he spoke. He said: 'I'm bowing out. I don't want to, but I have to.' I don't know what he meant by that. He didn't say too much else. His voice was kind of cracking."

The disclosure came in the aftermath of a taxing and thrilling 75-74 overtime victory in the national semifinals against Louisville at the San Diego Sports Arena. The announcement gave a good but not exceptional UCLA team additional motivation after some difficult games in the NCAA Tournament, which had an enlarged bracket with 32 teams, seven more than the year before. In addition, the tournament was opened up to more than one representative from the same conference for the first time ever.

The Bruins, however, did not need one of the NCAA's extra invitations because they won their ninth straight Pacific-8 Conference title in 1975. Nor was Wooden seeking an edge in the championship game by telling his players that it would be his swan song.

"I don't want to use this to hype up my ball players," he said. "I don't believe in that."

Wooden traditionally shunned emotional ploys. In his 27 years at UCLA, he had maintained his distance from his players and cultivated an image as one who was successful because of thoughtful planning and a sensible approach to the sport. He coached not on his feet or from his knees, but from a seat on the bench, always second from the end nearest the scorer's table, where he crossed his legs, rolled up his program and directed his team with the air of a man studying a knotty problem in quantum physics.

"The coach shies away from people who are jumping up and down," said consensus All-America forward Dave Meyers, the UCLA captain.

A happy UCLA squad whoops it up in the background as a smiling John Wooden (basketball in lap) enjoys his final, triumphant moment as the team's coach.

According to the coach, the timing of the announcement was forced by the imminent revelation of his retirement plans in Los Angeles newspapers. Beyond the issue of his health, he declined to comment on his reasons for stepping down at 64.

Wooden had suffered a mild heart attack two years earlier and had been advised by many people to retire.

"I haven't been sick," he said, "but lately I haven't been feeling as well as usual. Over the years, I've never had trouble sleeping, except, of course, after games, but I couldn't even do that as a player. But the last two weeks I couldn't sleep at all. I've been worried, concerned about my physical well-being, worried about my team and other things."

His team had given him cause for concern. The Bruins had been taken into overtime by Michigan in the first round of the tournament two weeks earlier and had been pressed to defeat Montana in the West Regional semifinals. Their 89-75 triumph over Arizona State in the regional final was convincing, but they hadn't so much beaten Louisville as survived in one of the finest games in the annals of the Final Four.

Louisville, which was coached by Denny Crum, a former player and assistant under Wooden, opened a 65-61 lead with 1:06 remaining on two free throws by guard Phillip Bond. But 6-foot-9 sophomore Richard Washington made two foul shots and classmate Marques Johnson stole an inbounds pass, then followed a missed shot for a 65-65 tie. Junior guard Andre McCarter had a chance to win the game for UCLA in regulation but missed a driving layup. A last-second jump shot from the corner by Louisville's Junior Bridgeman was off-target, forcing an extra period.

UCLA fell behind, 72-69, in overtime as forward Allen Murphy scored the Cardinals' first seven points. Johnson and Louisville forward Wesley Cox traded baskets and then Meyers sank both free throws in a one-and-one foul situation to cut the deficit to 74-73 with 57 seconds left. The Cardinals went to a four-corner offense, trying to protect the ball and draw a foul. Reserve Terry Howard, a ball-handling specialist and free-throw marksman, worked the clock, dribbling around the middle of the floor.

Howard was the last man the Bruins wanted to foul, but at the 20-second mark they had no alternative. Guard Jim Spillane reached in and Howard, a senior who had not missed a free throw in 28 attempts that season, went to the line. He picked a terrible time to miss his first. The ball spun around the rim and out, Washington grabbed the rebound and UCLA called a timeout. Assistant coach Gary Cunningham diagramed a play while Wooden stood by his side, watching and listening.

The play worked just as planned. The Bruins passed the ball around until Washington freed himself for a short jump shot from the right side of the lane. It caught only net, boosting UCLA into the lead with three seconds remaining. Murphy, who led all scorers with 33 points, fumbled the inbounds

It was power vs. power when Kentucky's Kevin Grevey and UCLA's Dave Meyers fought for this title-game rebound.

pass for Louisville, assuring Wooden of a grand finale.

Kentucky, the Bruins' opponent in the championship game, was a physical team with a massive front line and impressive depth. The Wildcats had upset previously undefeated Indiana in the Mideast Regional final before trouncing Syracuse, 95-79, in the national semifinals. Kentucky's victory over the undermanned Orangemen had resembled an execution, and not a neat one, either.

"We have great momentum at the present time," Wildcats Coach Joe B. Hall said. "I don't think Coach Wooden's resignation will have any negative effect on our team psychologically. What it does to his team, I can't say."

Wooden wasn't about to appeal to hysteria. A man who was as proud of his self-control as he was of his record didn't want the last game of his coaching career to sound like a personal crusade. He had no intention of asking his players to win one for the Wizard.

Wooden addressed them briefly before the game.

"He just said, 'Good luck, fellows,' " McCarter recalled. "It was like he was stepping out of it and just leaving it up to us. But he had us prepared. And I feel his retirement was a great motivation factor even though he stressed winning it for ourselves."

Key members of UCLA's talented front line were 6-foot-9 sophomore Richard Washington (left) and 6-6 sophomore Marques Johnson (right, shooting over Kentucky's Rick Robey).

What the Bruins did, without benefit of a pep talk, was accomplish as much as any UCLA team of the past, as much as any team can be expected to do. The Bruins defeated Kentucky, 92-85, and presented their coach with a crowning achievement, his 10th NCAA title.

"I played my heart out for Coach Wooden," said Meyers, the team's intense leader. "It meant that much to me. He deserves to go out a winner."

For their part, the Wildcats didn't concede readily. They went to their inside muscle game immediately and then forward Kevin Grevey, their finest outside shooter, sparked Kentucky to a 17-12 lead. UCLA roared back to take a 43-40 advantage at halftime, then pushed the lead to 66-56 after eight minutes of the second half.

It was at that stage that Grevey, the game's high scorer with 34 points, rediscovered his touch. He scored two three-point plays and the lead melted until, with 6:49 remaining, it was down to one, 76-75. The critical moment was at hand.

UCLA worked to set up Meyers from the top of the key, but as the Bruin forward went up to shoot, Grevey appeared in his path. Meyers landed on Grevey, both men went sprawling and the UCLA player was whistled for the foul, his fourth.

"I was very upset," Meyers said, "because I felt he

went underneath me as I went up."

Meyers' display of anger—he screamed and pounded the floor in disgust—drew a technical foul, giving Grevey the opportunity to shoot a one-and-one and then a technical. The Wildcats also would gain possession. If everything went smoothly, Kentucky would have five points and a four-point lead.

Instead, the Wildcats got none. Grevey missed both the front end of the one-and-one and the technical. Kentucky then committed a turnover. The game was lost then and there.

The Wildcats climbed within one point when 6-9 Bob Guyette hit a 13-foot shot to make it 78-77 with 5:14 on the clock, but they were never closer than three points thereafter. McCarter clinched the victory by driving the lane and scoring on a layup for a 90-85 lead with 40 seconds left. Washington, who earned the outstanding-player award after leading UCLA in scoring in both Final Four games, provided the Bruins' last two points on a pair of free throws.

UCLA had used only six men to combat perhaps the strongest team in the country, but those six (including backup center Ralph Drollinger) were magnificent. At the end, they bounded off the court, thrusting their fists in the air in acknowledgment of

There was sentiment around the San Diego Sports Arena in 1975 that Louisville was the top basketball team in the country, but UCLA dispelled that notion in a tough overtime victory. The Cardinals' Wesley Cox grabs a rebound (below) in that hard-fought semifinal contest.

their conquest. Wooden trailed quietly behind, holding a basketball in his hands.

"I suppose anyone would like to go out with a victory," he said, his face almost devoid of expression. "The fact that the victory was for the national championship doesn't lessen the pleasure."

The realization of what had transpired didn't seem to sink in until after he had spoken to his players, newsmen and well-wishers. It happened about 45 minutes after the game in the corridor leading to the UCLA dressing room, where he encountered Nell Wooden, his wife of 42 years. John Wooden, who had stared clear-eyed through those spectacles that lent him the appearance of a Mid western schoolmaster, silently cried. And the two embraced for what seemed like an eternity.

1975 Tournament Results

First Round

Syracuse 87, La Salle 83 (ot)
N. Carolina 93, New Mexico St. 69
Boston College 82, Furman 76
Kansas St. 69, Pennsylvania 62
Cent. Michigan 77, Georgetown 75
Kentucky 76, Marquette 54
Indiana 78, Texas-El Paso 53
Oregon St. 78, Middle Tenn. St. 67
Cincinnati 87, Texas A&M 79
Louisville 91, Rutgers 78
Maryland 83, Creighton 79
Notre Dame 77, Kansas 71
Arizona State 97, Alabama 94
Nev.-L.V. 90, San Diego St. 80
UCLA 103, Michigan 91 (ot)
Montana 69, Utah State 63

Louisville 78, Cincinnati 63
Maryland 83, Notre Dame 71
Arizona St. 84, Nev.-Las Vegas 81
UCLA 67, Montana 64

Regional Third Place

N. Carolina 110, Boston College 90
Central Michigan 88, Oregon St. 87
Cincinnati 95, Notre Dame 87 (ot)
Nevada-Las Vegas 75, Montana 67

Regional Championships

Syracuse 95, Kansas State 87 (ot)
Kentucky 92, Indiana 90
Louisville 96, Maryland 82
UCLA 89, Arizona State 75

Semifinals

Kentucky 95, Syracuse 79
UCLA 75, Louisville 74 (ot)

Second Round

Syracuse 78, North Carolina 76
Kansas St. 74, Boston College 65
Kentucky 90, Central Michigan 73
Indiana 81, Oregon State 71

Third Place

Louisville 96, Syracuse 88

Championship

UCLA 92, Kentucky 85

STATISTICS

1975 UCLA

Head Coach—John Wooden   **Final Record—28-3**

Player	Pos.	Hgt.	Wgt.	Cl.	G	FG	FGA	Pct.	FT.	FTA	Pct.	Reb.	Pts.	Avg.
Dave Meyers	F	6-8	220	Sr.	31	230	475	.484	106	144	.736	244	566	18.3
Richard Washington	C-F	6-9	213	So.	31	204	354	.576	84	116	.724	242	492	15.9
Marques Johnson	F	6-6	211	So.	29	138	254	.543	59	86	.686	205	335	11.6
Pete Trgovich	G	6-4	173	Sr.	31	134	311	.431	48	75	.640	102	316	10.2
Ralph Drollinger	C	7-1	215	Jr.	31	109	205	.532	56	85	.659	229	274	8.8
Andre McCarter	G	6-3	177	Jr.	31	78	217	.359	62	85	.729	72	218	7.0
Jim Spillane	G	5-11	149	So.	29	57	144	.396	16	21	.762	34	130	4.5
Gavin Smith	G	6-5	186	So.	17	25	59	.424	10	15	.667	18	60	3.5
Brett Vroman	C	6-11	206	Fr.	13	13	34	.382	19	26	.731	34	45	3.5
Wilbert Olinde	F	6-6	202	So.	22	27	57	.474	14	25	.560	43	68	3.1
Casey Corliss	F	6-6	199	So.	21	24	46	.522	17	20	.850	27	65	3.1
Marvin Thomas	F	6-5	165	Fr.	8	8	21	.381	3	4	.750	7	19	2.4
Ray Townsend	G	6-1	158	Fr.	20	16	39	.410	6	9	.667	13	38	1.9
Team												147		
UCLA					31	1063	2217	.479	500	711	.703	1417	2626	84.7
Opponents					31	934	2149	.435	370	546	.678	1290	2238	72.2

1975 KENTUCKY

Head Coach—Joe B. Hall   **Final Record—26-5**

Player	Pos.	Hgt.	Wgt.	Cl.	G	FG	FGA	Pct.	FT.	FTA	Pct.	Reb.	Pts.	Avg.
Kevin Grevey	F	6-5	205	Sr.	31	303	592	.512	124	157	.790	199	730	23.5
Jimmy Dan Conner	G	6-4	200	Sr.	31	171	338	.506	42	69	.609	101	384	12.4
Rick Robey	C	6-10	242	Fr.	31	135	248	.544	51	63	.810	214	321	10.4
Jack Givens	F	6-4	200	Fr.	31	126	255	.494	40	54	.741	152	292	9.4
Mike Flynn	G	6-3	190	Sr.	31	109	232	.470	62	84	.738	120	280	9.0
Bob Guyette	C-F	6-9	236	Sr.	31	107	216	.495	53	76	.697	209	267	8.6
Mike Phillips	C	6-10	245	Fr.	31	108	212	.509	26	47	.553	136	242	7.8
Larry Johnson	G	6-2	195	So.	31	57	137	.416	18	35	.514	67	132	4.3
James Lee	F	6-5	220	Fr.	25	27	52	.519	20	32	.625	47	74	3.0
G. J. Smith	F	6-7	190	Sr.	18	17	42	.405	0	0	.000	21	34	1.9
Dan Hall	C	6-10	225	Fr.	17	15	23	.652	0	3	.000	29	30	1.8
Reggie Warford	G	6-1	170	Jr.	14	4	16	.250	8	10	.800	7	16	1.1
Joey Holland	G	6-2	165	So.	8	2	5	.400	5	6	.833	7	9	1.1
Jerry Hale	G	6-1	180	Sr.	23	6	14	.429	11	21	.524	13	23	1.0
Merion Haskins	F	6-4	200	So.	26	10	30	.333	4	7	.571	25	24	0.9
Team												95		
Kentucky					31	1197	2412	.496	464	664	.699	1442	2858	92.2
Opponents					31	925	2096	.441	584	828	.705	1274	2434	78.5

1975 LOUISVILLE

Head Coach—Denny Crum   **Final Record—28-3**

Player	Pos.	Hgt.	Wgt.	Cl.	G	FG	FGA	Pct.	FT.	FTA	Pct.	Reb.	Pts.	Avg.
Allen Murphy	F	6-4	190	Sr.	31	208	444	.468	91	112	.813	136	507	16.4
Junior Bridgeman	G-F	6-5	205	Sr.	31	187	356	.525	127	156	.814	230	501	16.2
Wesley Cox	F	6-5	200	So.	30	133	281	.473	66	102	.647	208	332	11.1
Phillip Bond	G	6-2	175	So.	31	111	209	.531	68	81	.840	80	290	9.4
Ricky Gallon	C	6-10	225	Fr.	31	101	190	.532	47	72	.653	150	249	8.0
Bill Bunton	C	6-8	225	Sr.	31	97	182	.533	38	62	.613	238	232	7.5
Danny Brown	G	6-4	170	So.	31	59	125	.472	32	41	.780	40	150	4.8
Rick Wilson	G	6-4	205	Fr.	27	38	73	.521	17	24	.708	49	93	3.4
Ike Whitfield	F	6-8	210	Sr.	27	36	83	.434	11	13	.846	59	83	3.1
Terry Howard	G	6-1	180	Sr.	29	10	27	.370	28	29	.966	10	48	1.7
Billy Harmon	G	6-3	185	So.	19	5	16	.313	12	21	.571	22	22	1.2
Stanley Bunton	F-C	6-7	190	So.	12	3	14	.214	6	9	.667	10	12	1.0
Team & Dead Ball												183		
Louisville					31	988	2000	.494	543	722	.752	1415	2519	81.3
Opponents					31	910	2132	.427	366	535	.684	1180	2186	70.5

1975 SYRACUSE

Head Coach—Roy Danforth   **Final Record—23-9**

Player	Pos.	Hgt.	Wgt.	Cl.	G	FG	FGA	Pct.	FT.	FTA	Pct.	Reb.	Pts.	Avg.
Rudy Hackett	F	6-9	210	Sr.	32	280	482	.581	149	217	.687	407	709	22.2
Jim Lee	G	6-2	160	Sr.	32	226	464	.487	98	114	.860	99	550	17.2
Chris Sease	F	6-4	185	Jr.	32	172	316	.544	43	60	.717	227	387	12.1
Jim Williams	G	5-10	165	So.	30	99	228	.434	29	54	.537	47	227	7.6
Kevin King	F	6-4	175	Jr.	32	93	198	.470	40	68	.588	88	226	7.1
Ross Kindel	G	6-2	185	Fr.	25	54	131	.421	25	34	.735	36	133	5.3
Earnie Seibert	C	6-9	230	So.	31	58	141	.411	22	36	.611	144	138	4.5
Larry Kelley	G	6-0	160	So.	18	26	71	.366	2	6	.333	12	54	3.0
Bill DeMarle	F	6-5	205	Jr.	6	7	15	.467	3	4	.750	10	17	2.8
Steve Shaw	F	6-4	185	Sr.	28	27	66	.409	19	34	.559	56	73	2.6
Bob Parker	F-C	6-9	220	So.	26	21	50	.420	9	22	.409	49	51	2.0
Mark Meadors	F	6-5	190	Jr.	12	9	21	.429	2	4	.500	12	20	1.7
Larry Arrington	G	6-2	205	So.	12	8	23	.348	4	6	.667	3	20	1.7
Don Degner	F	6-4	195	Sr.	4	2	7	.286	0	1	.000	4	4	1.0
Marty Byrnes	F	6-5	205	Fr.	19	6	15	.400	6	12	.500	26	18	0.9
Kevin James	G	6-3	180	Fr.	1	0	0	.000	0	0	.000	0	0	0.0
Team												185		
Syracuse					32	1088	2228	.488	451	672	.671	1405	2627	82.1
Opponents					32	971	2148	.452	429	659	.651	1363	2371	74.1

1975 FINAL FOUR
At San Diego
Semifinals

Syracuse	fg	fga	ft	fta	rb	pf	tp
Hackett	4	6	6	9	5	5	14
Sease	7	11	4	4	10	4	18
Seibert	2	3	0	2	6	5	4
Lee	10	17	3	3	3	4	23
Williams	2	9	0	1	2	5	4
King	2	8	1	3	5	1	5
Kindel	1	3	1	2	1	1	3
Shaw	0	0	0	0	2	2	0
Parker	2	3	4	7	2	3	8
Byrnes	0	1	0	1	1	0	0
Kelley	0	1	0	0	0	0	0
Meadors	0	0	0	0	1	0	0
Team					2		
Totals	30	61	19	32	40	30	79

Kentucky	fg	fga	ft	fta	rb	pf	tp
Grevey	5	13	4	5	3	5	14
Guyette	2	3	3	4	6	3	7
Robey	3	8	3	7	11	4	9
Conner	5	9	2	4	5	4	12
Flynn	4	9	3	5	3	4	11
Givens	10	20	4	8	11	2	24
L. Johnson	2	4	0	0	1	3	4
Phillips	5	6	0	2	4	4	10
Lee	1	4	0	1	2	1	2
Haskins	0	0	2	2	1	0	2
Hale	0	1	0	0	3	0	0
Hall	0	0	0	0	1	1	0
Warford	0	0	0	0	0	0	0
Smith	0	1	0	0	0	0	0
Team					6		
Totals	37	78	21	38	57	31	95

Halftime: Kentucky 44-32. Officials: Soriano and Galvan.

Louisville	fg	fga	ft	fta	rb	pf	tp
Murphy	14	28	5	7	2	2	33
Cox	5	8	4	11	16	2	14
Bunton	3	4	1	2	7	2	7
Bridgeman	4	15	4	4	15	4	12
Bond	2	6	2	2	3	1	6
Whitfield	0	0	0	0	1	1	0
Gallon	0	3	0	0	2	2	0
Brown	1	1	0	0	1	0	2
Wilson	0	0	0	0	0	0	0
Howard	0	0	0	1	0	0	0
Team					2		
Totals	29	65	16	27	49	14	74

UCLA	fg	fga	ft	fta	rb	pf	tp
Meyers	6	16	4	6	7	3	16
M. Johnson	5	10	0	0	11	2	10
Washington	11	19	4	6	8	4	26
Trgovich	6	12	0	0	2	5	12
McCarter	3	12	0	0	2	2	6
Drollinger	1	2	1	2	4	5	3
Olinde	0	0	0	0	0	0	0
Spillane	1	2	0	0	1	1	2
Team					1		
Totals	33	73	9	14	36	22	75

Halftime: Louisville 37-33. Regulation Score: 65-65. Officials: Wortman and Nichols.

Championship
March 31

UCLA	fg	fga	ft	fta	rb	pf	tp
Meyers	9	18	6	7	11	4	24
M. Johnson	3	9	0	1	7	2	6
Washington	12	23	4	5	12	4	28
Trgovich	7	16	2	4	5	4	16
McCarter	3	6	2	3	2	1	8
Drollinger	4	6	2	5	13	4	10
Team					5		
Totals	38	78	16	25	55	19	92

Kentucky	fg	fga	ft	fta	rb	pf	tp
Grevey	13	30	8	10	5	4	34
Guyette	7	11	2	2	7	3	16
Robey	1	3	0	0	9	5	2
Conner	4	12	1	2	5	1	9
Flynn	3	9	4	5	3	4	10
Givens	3	10	2	3	6	3	8
L. Johnson	0	3	0	0	3	3	0
Phillips	1	7	2	3	6	4	4
Hall	1	1	0	0	1	0	2
Lee	0	0	0	0	0	1	0
Team					4		
Totals	33	86	19	25	49	28	85

Halftime: ULCA 43-40. Officials: Nichols and Wortman.

1976 A Perfect Ending

A triumphant Indiana trio of (left to right) Coach Bob Knight, forward Scott May and guard Quinn Buckner share the postgame joys of a national championship.

There was only one college basketball team against which to measure Indiana, and that was the one in Bob Knight's mind. The team he envisioned was hard-working, unselfish and perfect in every way. The team he brought to the 1976 Final Four occasionally missed a free throw.

The mistake in assessing the Hoosiers was to compare them to their peers, the other top teams in the nation. Knight, Indiana's coach, did not make that mistake. Michigan, Alabama, Marquette, UCLA— they were all the same. They were just opponents, and imperfect ones at that. The standards set by Knight were beyond the capabilities of those teams.

After Indiana defeated powerful St. John's, Alabama and Marquette in the Mideast Regional to raise its record to 30-0, Knight said the identity of the next opponent did not concern him.

"Will we be able to play as well as we can? That's what concerns me in every game," he said. "I don't know that you ever do, but you keep trying."

No team tried harder than the Hoosiers. They were driven not only by their coach's demanding expectations, but also by the memory of a painful defeat in the final game of the Mideast Regional the previous year. After winning the first 31 games of their 1975 season, the Hoosiers were stopped by a huge and powerful Kentucky team, 92-90. Indiana began the 1976 season with the goal of winning the NCAA championship in Philadelphia, which had been selected as the Final Four site in recognition of the U.S. Bicentennial.

Knight had created a team not of individuals, but of components. It was a team whose ego had been sacrificed for the sake of a mission. The coach demanded perfection from his players. Perfection, of course, was impossible, but they gave him the next best thing: Consistency. The Hoosiers' consistency was almost eerie in its execution.

Indiana's efficiency chilled UCLA in one of the semifinals at the Spectrum. The Bruins were the defending national champions, but they were returning without the Wizard, Coach John Wooden. Still, Gene Bartow had marshaled UCLA's considerable talent and guided it to a return engagement against Indiana, which had humbled the Bruins, 84-64, at the start of the season.

The Bruins were confident of winning the rematch because they had improved so much in the course of the season. Alas, Indiana had done likewise. The Hoosiers brushed aside the Bruins, 65-51, with barely a flicker of emotion.

"They're very mechanical," Marques Johnson, UCLA's flamboyant forward, said after the game. "I'm not saying that in a derogatory sense. It's a compliment, but they're almost mechanical."

Indeed, during those moments when it functioned at its highest level, Indiana appeared to be a machine—a collection of 10 interchangeable legs and arms setting picks, trapping ballhandlers, whirling closer and closer to the basket for the best percentage shot available. Whenever forward Scott May and 6-foot-11 center Kent Benson—the Hoosiers' consensus All-Americas—misfired, another teammate was ready to take over.

Such were the circumstances against UCLA. When Benson drew his second foul barely 90 seconds into the game while attempting to guard 6-10 consensus All-America Richard Washington, unheralded forward Tom Abernethy was handed the assignment. Not only did he force the Bruins' primary offensive threat out to the perimeter, but he also scored 14 points and grabbed six rebounds. Other unlikely heroes included 6-7 guard/forward Bobby Wilkerson, who had an astonishing 19 rebounds and seven assists, and reserve guard Jim Crews, who ran Indiana's delay game flawlessly over the final seven minutes of play.

To Abernethy, one of four senior starters, it was nothing out of the ordinary. The Hoosiers took little for granted.

"If you ever think you're infallible," he said, "that's when you're going to stumble. I don't think there's anything special about this team that makes us win. We just play hard."

Indiana's opponent in the championship game knew all about the Hoosiers' work ethic. Michigan, a second-place finisher in the Big Ten Conference, overran previously undefeated Rutgers, 86-70, in the other semifinal. For the first time in history, the NCAA title would be contested by two teams representing the same conference.

The familiarity of the opposition unleashed the

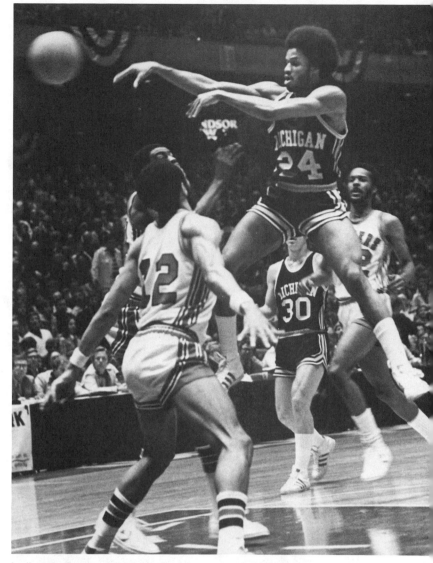

Indiana's first order of business was to stop the breakneck fast break directed by Michigan guard Rickey Green (24).

practical joker in Knight. It occurred to him that a congratulatory message might be forthcoming from that noted Michigan alumnus, Gerald Ford, after the Wolverines' victory over Rutgers. Knight preyed upon that belief. He placed a call to Michigan Coach Johnny Orr, whom he considered a friend, and introduced himself as the President.

"John said, 'Really?'" Knight recalled the next day. "But then I overplayed my hand."

By halftime of the championship game, President Ford might have been tempted to pick up a phone. Michigan, with swift Rickey Green running a breathtaking fast break, rushed to a 35-29 lead. Indiana's bid to become the seventh team in history to complete the season and the NCAA Tournament undefeated was in jeopardy.

Furthermore, the Hoosiers would be without Wilkerson, their standout defensive player, for the second half. Early in the game, the senior had stepped in the path of Wayman Britt as the Michigan forward drove for the basket with the game tied, 4-4. Britt scored and in his follow-through struck Wilkerson with an elbow in the vicinity of the left temple.

Wilkerson collapsed. He lay on the court for almost 10 minutes as doctors attempted to revive him. When those efforts failed, he was placed on a stretcher and wheeled into the Indiana locker room. He was accompanied by two physicians.

Just before the end of the first half, Wilkerson was led from the locker room down a corridor 100 feet to a door marked "UCLA," the empty locker room that had been reserved for Indiana's 31st victim. His legs were wobbly but his eyes were open, and he held a towel to the left side of his head.

With Wilkerson effectively hidden down the hall, the other Indiana players carried on because that's what they had been taught to do. May and guard Quinn Buckner, the senior captain, spoke in the locker room. Then Knight walk-

ed in, his tie loosened, his plaid jacket draped over his shoulder.

"Coach Knight," Buckner said, "always gets the last word."

The coach demanded 20 minutes of the best basketball Indiana could deliver, and that's what he got. It didn't matter that Wilkerson, a two-year starter, was being wheeled to an ambulance that would deliver him to Temple University Hospital on the other side of town.

"Once you're in the flow of the game," Abernethy said, "you can't worry

Kent Benson, the big man behind Indiana's romp to an undefeated season, tells the world that Indiana is No. 1 (left). Scott May and Quinn Buckner share their victorious enthusiasm with a leaping hug (right).

about other things. I didn't think it was that bad, so maybe it didn't hit me as hard. . . . I was just thinking about the game, about what we had to do."

What the Hoosiers had to do was to nullify Green's sprints. They accomplished that by scoring nearly every time they had the ball. During a 14-minute stretch that began less than three minutes into the half, the Hoosiers scored on virtually every possession. In the process, Indiana went from four points down (37-33) to 14 points up (73-59).

"There's just something that happens," May said. "Maybe I'll get a bucket and that'll get us going. Or maybe Benny (Kent Benson) will get a tough rebound that'll get us going. Or maybe Quinn will make a great pass."

It was all of the above against Michigan. May, Benson and Buckner combined for 36 of Indiana's

first 38 points in the second half. May, shooting over the Wolverines' zone, finished the game with 26 points, one more than Benson managed from inside. Buckner totaled 16 points.

Meanwhile, sophomore Jim Wisman did a remarkable job directing the offense in Wilkerson's absence, leading the Hoosiers with six assists. Any hopes of a Michigan comeback were dimmed when 6-7 freshman Phil Hubbard fouled out with 7:27 to play and then Britt fouled out 2½ minutes later.

The result was an 86-68 triumph, an undefeated season, a championship. Knight replaced Buckner with 44 seconds left and the two men hugged. With 12 seconds to play, May and Benson were removed and all 17,540 fans—even the Michigan supporters —stood and applauded. May hopped into Buckner's arms and they shouted above the din, "Four years, man!"

Wilkerson, who had worked three years for that goal after being ineligible as a freshman, heard the news in a hospital bed several miles away. The messenger was a medical technician, Corlie Stills.

"He didn't ask for the score," Stills said. "I just thought he'd like to know. He was in a daze. He could understand, I think, but there was not much of a reaction."

The 21-year-old basketball player, still in his Indiana uniform, lay in the emergency room undergoing an examination by a neurosurgeon.

"He was knocked unconscious," said Dr. Joseph Torg, the team physician for the Philadelphia 76ers. "He sustained a moderate concussion. He does not appear to be in any danger. He is being admitted for observation."

His eyes closed, the player was wheeled upstairs. Knight came to visit after midnight. The Indiana party flew home without him the next day.

Wilkerson remained in the hospital for an additional 24 hours before being released. Of all the Indiana players, he was the one who never forgot the night and never remembered the game.

Indiana's Kent Benson goes high for a rebound over UCLA's Richard Washington (31) during action in a Final Four semifinal game.

1976 Tournament Results

First Round
DePaul 69, Virginia 60
Virginia Military 81, Tennessee 75
Rutgers 54, Princeton 53
Connecticut 80, Hofstra 78 (ot)
Michigan 74, Wichita State 73
Notre Dame 79, Cincinnati 78
Missouri 69, Washington 67
Texas Tech 69, Syracuse 56
Alabama 79, North Carolina 64
Indiana 90, St. John's 70
Marquette 79, W. Kentucky 60
W. Mich. 77, Virginia Tech 67 (ot)
Pepperdine 87, Memphis State 77
UCLA 74, San Diego State 64
Arizona 83, Georgetown 76
Nev.-Las Vegas 103, Boise St. 78

Second Round
Virginia Military 71, DePaul 66
Rutgers 93, Connecticut 79

Missouri 86, Texas Tech 75
Michigan 80, Notre Dame 76
Indiana 74, Alabama 69
Marquette 62, W. Michigan 57
UCLA 70, Pepperdine 61
Ariz. 114, Nev.-Las Vegas 109 (ot)

Regional Championships
Rutgers 91, Virginia Military 75
Michigan 95, Missouri 88
Indiana 65, Marquette 56
UCLA 82, Arizona 66

Semifinals
Michigan 86, Rutgers 70
Indiana 65, UCLA 51

Third Place
UCLA 106, Rutgers 92

Championship
Indiana 86, Michigan 68

STATISTICS

1976 INDIANA

Head Coach—Bob Knight   Final Record—32-0

Player	Pos.	Hgt.	Wgt.	Cl.	G	FG	FGA	Pct.	FT	FTA	Pct.	Reb.	Pts.	Avg.
Scott May	F	6-7	218	Sr.	32	308	584	.527	136	174	.782	245	752	23.5
Kent Benson	C	6-11	245	Jr.	32	237	410	.578	80	117	.684	282	554	17.3
Tom Abernethy	F	6-7	220	Sr.	32	133	237	.561	55	74	.743	169	321	10.0
Quinn Buckner	G	6-3	203	Sr.	32	123	279	.441	40	82	.488	91	286	8.9
Bobby Wilkerson	G-F	6-7	200	Sr.	32	111	225	.493	29	46	.630	156	251	7.8
Wayne Radford	G-F	6-3	194	So.	30	49	87	.563	42	59	.712	64	140	4.7
Jim Crews	G	6-5	195	Sr.	31	36	77	.468	30	35	.857	23	102	3.3
Jim Wisman	G	6-2	175	So.	26	22	60	.367	21	29	.724	21	65	2.5
Rich Valavicius	F	6-5	215	Fr.	28	29	60	.483	10	16	.625	49	68	2.4
Bob Bender	G	6-3	178	Fr.	17	13	23	.565	9	12	.750	13	35	2.1
Mark Haymore	F-C	6-8	220	So.	13	11	27	.407	2	7	.286	28	24	1.8
Jim Roberson	F-C	6-9	185	Fr.	12	7	12	.583	5	6	.833	16	19	1.6
Scott Eells	F	6-9	185	Fr.	12	4	13	.308	3	4	.750	9	11	0.9
Team										1		158		
Indiana					32	1083	2094	.517	462	662	.698	1324	2628	82.1
Opponents					32	837	1921	.436	400	572	.699	1143	2074	64.8

1976 MICHIGAN

Head Coach—Johnny Orr   Final Record—25-7

Player	Pos.	Hgt.	Wgt.	Cl.	G	FG	FGA	Pct.	FT	FTA	Pct.	Reb.	Pts.	Avg.
Rickey Green	G	6-2	170	Jr.	32	266	542	.491	106	135	.785	117	638	19.9
Phil Hubbard	C	6-7	195	Fr.	32	208	381	.546	66	113	.584	352	482	15.1
John Robinson	F	6-6	205	Jr.	32	173	302	.573	102	123	.829	262	448	14.0
Wayman Britt	F	6-2	185	Sr.	32	153	326	.469	42	54	.778	135	348	10.9
Steve Grote	G	6-2	195	Jr.	32	134	265	.506	69	95	.726	96	337	10.5
Dave Baxter	G	6-2	155	So.	32	80	164	.488	46	56	.821	45	206	6.4
Joel Thompson	F	6-8	190	So.	28	42	86	.488	10	17	.588	63	94	3.4
Alan Hardy	F	6-6	190	Fr.	29	41	83	.494	10	19	.526	44	92	3.2
Tom Bergen	C	6-9	195	So.	29	24	43	.558	15	17	.882	35	63	2.2
Tom Staton	G	6-3	185	Fr.	22	14	34	.412	6	10	.600	13	34	1.5
Bobby Jones	F	6-6	190	Fr.	5	2	2	1.000	1	2	.500	0	5	1.0
Lloyd Schinnerer	G	6-2	170	Sr.	11	1	3	.333	4	6	.667	4	6	0.5
Len Lillard	C	6-7	215	So.	5	0	0	.000	0	0	.000	3	0	0.0
Team												170		
Michigan					32	1138	2231	.510	477	647	.737	1339	2753	86.0
Opponents					32	1005	2132	.471	446	635	.702	1240	2456	76.8

(Team totals include dead-ball rebounds.)

1976 UCLA

Head Coach—Gene Bartow   Final Record—27-5

Player	Pos.	Hgt.	Wgt.	Cl.	G	FG	FGA	Pct.	FT	FTA	Pct.	Reb.	Pts.	Avg.
Richard Washington	F-C	6-10	226	Jr.	32	276	538	.513	92	125	.736	274	644	20.1
Marques Johnson	F	6-6	215	Jr.	32	223	413	.540	106	140	.757	301	552	17.3
Andre McCarter	G	6-3	175	Sr.	32	126	271	.465	38	51	.745	64	290	9.1
Raymond Townsend	G	6-2	160	So.	32	112	219	.511	29	42	.690	68	253	7.9
Ralph Drollinger	C	7-2	230	Sr.	32	101	188	.537	40	63	.635	214	242	7.6
Gavin Smith	F	6-6	189	Jr.	30	64	174	.460	19	23	.826	55	179	6.0
David Greenwood	C	6-10	217	Fr.	31	62	122	.508	28	35	.800	114	152	4.9
Brad Holland	G	6-2	180	Fr.	24	45	92	.489	17	23	.739	19	107	4.5
Jim Spillane	G	5-11	149	Fr.	30	46	99	.465	19	25	.760	29	111	3.7
Brett Vroman	C	6-11	210	So.	22	15	31	.484	12	19	.632	36	42	1.9
Wilbert Olinde	F	6-7	205	Jr.	26	19	40	.475	4	8	.500	37	42	1.6
Roy Hamilton	G	6-2	168	Fr.	21	6	28	.214	13	27	.481	12	25	1.2
Chris Lippert	F	6-5	178	Fr.	5	1	5	.200	4	4	1.000	1	6	1.2
Team												160		
UCLA					32	1112	2220	.501	421	585	.720	1384	2645	82.7
Opponents					32	963	2149	.448	400	557	.718	1234	2326	72.7

1976 RUTGERS

Head Coach—Tom Young   Final Record—31-2

Player	Pos.	Hgt.	Wgt.	Cl.	G	FG	FGA	Pct.	FT	FTA	Pct.	Reb.	Pts.	Avg.
Phil Sellers	F	6-5	200	Sr.	33	243	543	.448	148	203	.729	337	634	19.2
Mike Dabney	G	6-4	180	Sr.	33	272	573	.475	85	111	.766	148	629	19.1
Ed Jordan	G	6-1	170	Jr.	33	187	397	.471	90	113	.796	102	464	14.1
Hollis Copeland	F	6-6	180	So.	33	197	392	.503	32	63	.508	220	426	12.9
Abdel Anderson	C-F	6-7	185	Jr.	33	112	218	.514	86	114	.754	144	310	9.4
James Bailey	C	6-9	195	Fr.	33	121	240	.504	40	68	.588	233	282	8.5
Steve Hefele	G-F	6-5	190	So.	32	51	115	.443	16	41	.390	83	118	3.7
Jeff Kleinbaum	G-F	6-2	190	Sr.	27	29	61	.475	16	35	.457	25	74	2.7
Bruce Scherer	C	6-7	200	Sr.	13	12	29	.414	4	5	.800	23	28	2.2
Mark Conlin	G	6-2	175	Jr.	32	25	43	.581	18	25	.720	26	68	2.1
Mike Palko	C	6-7	200	Jr.	22	17	33	.515	7	14	.500	62	41	1.9
Stan Nance	G	6-3	170	So.	14	6	25	.240	4	9	.444	10	16	1.1
Team												166		
Rutgers					33	1272	2669	.477	546	801	.682	1579	3090	93.6
Opponents					33	1013	2282	.444	511	726	.704	1356	2537	76.9

1976 FINAL FOUR

At Philadelphia
Semifinals

Michigan	fg	fga	ft	fta	rb	pf	tp
Britt	5	9	1	1	5	4	11
Robinson	8	13	4	5	16	2	20
Hubbard	8	13	0	3	13	4	16
Green	7	16	2	2	6	4	16
Grote	4	13	6	6	4	4	14
Baxter	2	5	1	2	3	0	5
Staton	1	1	2	2	0	1	4
Bergen	0	0	0	0	0	0	0
Thompson	0	0	0	0	0	0	0
Schinnerer	0	0	0	0	0	1	0
Hardy	0	0	0	0	0	0	0
Jones	0	0	0	0	0	0	0
Lillard	0	0	0	0	0	0	0
Team					3		
Totals	35	70	16	21	50	20	86

Rutgers	fg	fga	ft	fta	rb	pf	tp
Sellers	5	13	1	3	8	4	11
Copeland	7	12	1	1	5	3	15
Bailey	1	3	4	6	6	0	6
Jordan	6	20	4	4	4	0	16
Dabney	5	17	0	1	5	4	10
Anderson	3	8	0	1	6	3	6
Conlin	2	2	0	0	1	2	4
Hefele	1	1	0	0	1	2	2
Team					2		
Totals	30	76	10	16	38	22	70

Halftime: Michigan 46-29. Officials: Wortman and Fouty.

UCLA	fg	fga	ft	fta	rb	pf	tp
Washington	6	15	3	4	8	3	15
Johnson	6	10	0	1	6	2	12
Greenwood	2	5	1	2	10	2	5
Townsend	2	10	0	0	3	1	4
McCarter	2	9	0	0	4	5	4
Drollinger	0	3	2	2	1	3	2
Holland	0	2	0	0	0	0	0
Spillane	0	2	0	0	1	0	0
Smith	3	4	0	0	0	3	6
Hamilton	0	1	1	2	0	0	1
Vroman	0	0	0	0	1	2	0
Lippert	0	0	2	2	0	0	2
Olinde	0	0	0	0	0	0	0
Team					3		
Totals	21	61	9	13	37	21	51

Indiana	fg	fga	ft	fta	rb	pf	tp
Abernethy	7	8	0	1	6	3	14
May	5	16	4	6	4	2	14
Benson	6	15	4	6	9	4	16
Wilkerson	1	5	3	4	19	3	5
Buckner	6	14	0	1	3	3	12
Crews	1	1	2	3	3	0	4
Team					1		
Totals	26	59	13	21	45	15	65

Halftime: Indiana 34-26. Officials: Brown and Bain.

Championship
March 29

Michigan	fg	fga	ft	fta	rb	pf	tp
Britt	5	6	1	1	3	5	11
Robinson	4	8	0	1	6	2	8
Hubbard	4	8	2	2	11	5	10
Green	7	16	4	5	6	3	18
Grote	4	9	4	6	1	4	12
Bergen	0	1	0	0	0	1	0
Staton	2	5	3	4	2	3	7
Baxter	0	2	0	0	0	2	0
Thompson	0	0	0	0	0	0	0
Hardy	1	2	0	0	2	0	2
Team					1		
Totals	27	57	14	19	32	25	68

Indiana	fg	fga	ft	fta	rb	pf	tp
Abernethy	4	8	3	3	4	2	11
May	10	17	6	6	8	4	26
Benson	11	20	3	5	9	3	25
Wilkerson	0	1	0	0	0	1	0
Buckner	5	10	6	9	8	4	16
Radford	0	1	0	0	1	0	0
Crews	0	1	2	2	1	1	2
Wisman	0	1	2	3	1	4	2
Valavicius	0	1	0	0	0	0	0
Haymore	1	1	0	0	1	0	2
Bender	0	0	0	0	0	0	0
Team					3		
Totals	32	61	22	28	36	19	86

Halftime: Michigan 35-29. Officials: Wortman and Brown.

1977 McGuire Gets Fond Farewell

Butch Lee made eye contact with Bo Ellis and motioned toward the Marquette bench. There, in the waning seconds of the NCAA championship game, a most remarkable scene was unfolding, one that Lee didn't want Ellis or any of his teammates on the court to miss.

Al McGuire, the fast-talking, street-smart coach who had bounced through life with a quip on his lips, had been rendered speechless. What's more, he was holding his head in his hands and sobbing.

The man's background, intelligence and understanding of human nature had prepared him for almost anything. His definition of the ideal education, McGuire once said, was four years of college supplemented by a stint tending bar and another driving a cab. That was his ticket to the arena. The experience had prepared him for good times and bad, for uptown and down, for joy and sorrow. It had prepared him well.

But it had not prepared him for this. This was not a moment to which an Al McGuire should rightfully aspire. This was a moment for those few men descended from Olympus, the kind who were called heroes and were admired from afar. McGuire didn't fit that mold. He was too human, a mixture of wise man and fool, clown and tragedian, a pro and, yes, a con.

"Normally," he said, "alley fighters, street fighters like me don't end up in lace."

So what happened in Atlanta was the one thing for which McGuire was totally unprepared. His career as a college basketball coach was ending the way these things do in cheap novels and children's classics. McGuire was a detective-story kind of guy—tough, cynical and fiercely proud of his ability to control a situation. And suddenly, there he sat, unable to control himself.

McGuire was driven to tears when the realization struck that Marquette was about to win the national title in his final game as a coach. And the tears embarrassed him. Too many people—16,086 at the Omni, millions more watching on television—were witnesses to his private emotions. While his players danced and celebrated their 67-59 triumph over

Al McGuire's long-awaited moment in the sun came, ironically, in his final game as Marquette's basketball coach.

North Carolina, McGuire slipped through the crowd and into the team's dressing room.

There, holding a towel to his eyes, his body shaking with the immensity of the moment, he paced back and forth, back and forth. For the longest time, not a word was spoken.

"I'm not ashamed to cry," he finally said. "It's just that I don't like to do it in front of people."

It was a side of McGuire few outside his immediate family had been privileged to see. But it was a spontaneous reaction to a stunning turn of events. Marquette had lost seven games in the 1977 season, and there was some doubt whether the Warriors would be invited to the NCAA

Tournament. Once in, they appeared to be a likely candidate for an early exit. If they were determined to give McGuire a going-away present, surely they wouldn't have lost to Wichita State at home on the day the coach was honored by the university.

McGuire undoubtedly had coached other Marquette teams that seemed more goal-oriented, better suited to take the prize. Only three teams in his previous 12 seasons at the Milwaukee school had lost as many as seven games. Yet, this team was ready for the NCAA Tournament. It gathered momentum with victories over Cincinnati, Kansas State and Wake Forest in the Midwest Regional and then edged North Carolina-Charlotte, conqueror of top-ranked Michigan in the Mideast Regional final, in the national semifinals, 51-49.

That game wasn't decided until the final three

The top guns in Marquette's offensive arsenal were sparkplug guard Butch Lee (15) and big man Bo Ellis, who enjoyed his post-championship-game celebration from a different perspective.

seconds. A floor-length pass by Lee skipped off Ellis' fingertips, eluded the grasp of the 49ers' Cedric (Cornbread) Maxwell and plopped into the grasp of Marquette's Jerome Whitehead. The 6-foot-10 junior center, the son of a minister, whirled, took one step toward the basket and laid it in as the buzzer sounded. The points were his 20th and 21st of the game.

Meanwhile, North Carolina had outlasted Nevada-Las Vegas, the highest-scoring team in the country, 84-83, in the other semifinal. The Tar Heels' four-corner offense had undone the Rebels, spreading their soft defense so thin it enabled Mike O'Koren to slip undetected along the baseline, take passes from slick playmaker Phil Ford and score a series of uncontested layups. The freshman forward sank 14 of 19 shots from the field and had 31 points.

North Carolina, the team with the pedigree, was favored in the final. That distinction probably had more to do with the reputations of the coaches than the talent on the floor. Dean Smith was acknowledged as one of the game's finest innovators and motivators, a man whose presence at a clinic would draw a crowd of his peers. He was an organizer who planned meticulously.

And McGuire? "My ability," he had said the day before the game, "is in putting people in the stands."

Yes, he was an entertainer. But he didn't just roll the balls on the court at practice. He taught defense, the same tough defense he had played against the likes of Bob Cousy during a short-lived pro career. On offense, he preached the kind of patience he rarely exhibited himself. He coached, he once said, by the seat of his pants, reacting instinctively to the spur of the moment. His instincts sometimes betrayed him, such as in the 1974 championship game when he was hit with two technical fouls, effectively sabotaging Marquette's chances against North Carolina State.

The colorful McGuire was fire to Smith's ice. Nevertheless, the two men were friends. When Jim Boylan decided to transfer from Assumption College, a Division II school in Massachusetts, to a big-time program, he thought of North Carolina. Smith told the youngster he didn't accept transfers but suggested that he look into Marquette, and he recommended Boylan to McGuire. In 1977, Boylan was a starter alongside Lee in the Warriors' backcourt.

It was Boylan, in fact, who proved to be one of the deciding factors in the game with his tremendous defense on Ford, a consensus All-America who was playing with a damaged elbow and scored only six points. Boylan also scored 14 points, the same number as Ellis, and only five fewer than Lee, who received the Final Four outstanding-player award. So inspired were the Warriors that Ellis, the

One of the main cogs in North Carolina's well-balanced offensive machine was Mike O'Koren, who is shown driving for two points over Marquette's Bill Neary.

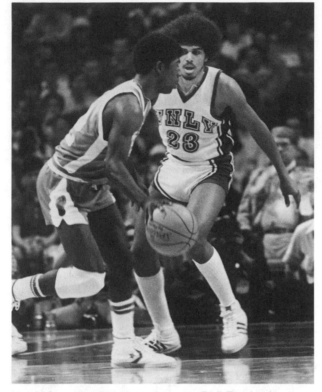

North Carolina's ballhandler was Phil Ford, who was matched against Nevada-Las Vegas' talented Reggie Theus (23) in a semifinal game.

senior captain, and Whitehead played much of the evening above the rim. And Lee displayed the form he exhibited the previous summer while almost single-handedly sparking Puerto Rico to the brink of an upset against the Smith-coached U.S. Olympic team.

With Marquette orchestrating the offense and dictating the tempo, the Warriors took a 39-27 half-time lead. Carolina made its run at the start of the second half, tying for the first time in the half at 41-41 on forward Walter Davis' 14-foot jump shot. The Tar Heels then assumed a temporary lead, 45-43, on guard Tom Zaliagiris' steal and layup with 13:48 left. McGuire had done a few minutes of what he called his "psycho act" as Carolina crept back into the game, but once the Tar Heels pulled even, he became calm. Marquette needed the coach, and the coach was alert.

Forward Bernard Toone retied the game at 45-45 with a 16-foot basket for the Warriors. Twelve minutes, 45 seconds remained. Smith gave the signal for the four corners.

"Everybody gets psyched out by it," Boylan said. "I was dreading it."

But the Carolina coach played directly into McGuire's hands. The Tar Heels lost the momentum as Ford dribbled around for the better part of two minutes. Marquette moved out of its zone to challenge, but as soon as Ford looked to set up a basket underneath, Ellis and Whitehead dropped back to the baseline. It happened a second time and a third time. Finally, with 9:48 showing, forward Bruce Buckley drove for a layup. He missed.

Marquette came up with the ball and McGuire came off the bench. He wanted his own delay game. More than a minute later, with Ford reaching for the steal, Boylan reversed his direction and drove for the go-ahead basket. McGuire ordered more of the same.

The Warriors stayed with the delay to the end, and it worked gloriously. Marquette never trailed the rest of the way. Carolina sent Boylan, Ellis and guard Gary Rosenberger to the foul line time and again in an effort to catch up, but they kept making free throws. Marquette made its last 12 attempts and 23 of 25 overall in the 67-59 victory.

"We played a chess game there for a while," McGuire recalled. "I hope it was enjoyable. I know I enjoyed it."

But the magnitude of an NCAA championship left McGuire shaken on the bench in the final minute and sent him rushing to a sanctuary while celebrants flooded the court. After regaining his composure, he returned to the arena floor for the ceremonies. The Marquette students were chanting "Al's last hurrah, Al's last hurrah" as he made his re-entrance. By this time he was smiling broadly, with satisfaction and a measure of disbelief. Ellis walked over to McGuire and draped a souvenir net around the coach's neck. No words were needed.

At 48, McGuire was leaving at the pinnacle of his profession. His final thoughts, he said, were of "all the wet socks and jocks, all the PAL (Police Athletic League) and CYO (Catholic Youth Organization) games, all the old gyms, all the fights when we were young, when I was obnoxious." He smiled. "The wildness of it all," McGuire marveled.

And so it ended with the wildest of possible endings. "This time," he said, "the numbers came up right."

And there would be no next time.

1977 Tournament Results	
First Round	North Carolina 79, Notre Dame 77
Virginia Military 73, Duquesne 66	Idaho State 76, UCLA 75
Kentucky 72, Princeton 58	Nevada-Las Vegas 88, Utah 83
Notre Dame 90, Hofstra 83	Michigan 86, Detroit 81
North Carolina 69, Purdue 66	N. Caro.-Charlotte 81, Syracuse 59
UCLA 87, Louisville 79	Marquette 67, Kansas State 66
Idaho State 83, Long Beach St. 72	Wake Forest 86, S. Illinois 81
Utah 72, St. John's 68	**Regional Championships**
Nev.-Las Vegas 121, San Fran. 95	North Carolina 79, Kentucky 72
Michigan 92, Holy Cross 81	Nevada-Las Vegas 107, Idaho St. 90
Detroit 93, Middle Tennessee St. 76	N. Caro.-Charlotte 75, Michigan 68
N.C.-Charlotte 91, C. Mich. 86 (ot)	Marquette 82, Wake Forest 68
Syracuse 93, Tennessee 88 (ot)	**Semifinals**
Marquette 66, Cincinnati 51	Marquette 51, N. C.-Charlotte 49
Kansas State 87, Providence 80	N. Carolina 84, Nev.-Las Vegas 83
Wake Forest 86, Arkansas 80	**Third Place**
Southern Illinois 81, Arizona 77	Nev.-L.V. 106, N.C.-Charlotte 94
Second Round	**Championship**
Kentucky 93, Virginia Military 78	Marquette 67, North Carolina 59

STATISTICS

1977 MARQUETTE

Head Coach—Al McGuire   **Final Record—25-7**

Player	Pos.	Hgt.	Wgt.	Cl.	G	FG	FGA	Pct.	FT.	FTA	Pct.	Reb.	Pts.	Avg.
Butch Lee	G	6-1	180	Jr.	32	239	501	.477	150	172	.872	121	628	19.6
Bo Ellis	F	6-9	195	Sr.	32	192	379	.507	115	153	.752	266	499	15.6
Jerome Whitehead	C	6-10	215	Jr.	32	150	290	.517	36	62	.581	262	336	10.5
Gary Rosenberger	G	6-0	155	Jr.	32	97	206	.471	38	50	.760	44	232	7.3
Jim Boylan	G	6-2	175	Jr.	32	89	195	.456	47	51	.922	88	225	7.0
Ullice Payne	F-G	6-6	195	Jr.	21	40	82	.488	14	15	.933	55	94	4.5
Bernard Toone	F	6-9	210	So.	32	57	139	.410	27	38	.711	69	141	4.4
Bill Neary	F	6-5	185	Sr.	32	22	67	.328	10	13	.769	88	54	1.7
Jim Dudley	F	6-6	190	So.	17	10	24	.417	6	10	.600	29	26	1.5
Robert Byrd	F	6-6	180	Fr.	12	4	14	.286	1	4	.250	8	9	0.8
Mark Lavin	G	6-0	155	Fr.	9	2	6	.333	1	2	.500	4	5	0.6
Craig Butrym	C	7-0	205	Sr.	13	3	13	.231	1	3	.333	15	7	0.5
Team												121		
Marquette					32	905	1916	.472	446	573	.778	1170	2256	70.5
Opponents					32	770	1786	.431	360	509	.707	1032	1900	59.4

1977 NORTH CAROLINA

Head Coach—Dean Smith   **Final Record—28-5**

Player	Pos.	Hgt.	Wgt.	Cl.	G	FG	FGA	Pct.	FT.	FTA	Pct.	Reb.	Pts.	Avg.
Phil Ford	G	6-2	171	Jr.	33	230	431	.534	157	184	.853	63	617	18.7
Walter Davis	F	6-6	190	Sr.	32	203	351	.578	91	117	.778	183	497	15.5
Tommy LaGarde	C	6-10	234	Sr.	20	108	182	.593	86	110	.782	147	302	15.1
Mike O'Koren	F	6-7	198	Fr.	33	172	298	.577	114	157	.726	217	458	13.9
John Kuester	G	6-3	174	Sr.	33	125	242	.517	71	87	.816	73	321	9.7
Tom Zaliagiris	G	6-5	190	Jr.	33	52	86	.605	21	38	.553	38	125	3.8
Rich Yonakor	C	6-10	205	Fr.	32	45	91	.495	27	37	.730	79	117	3.7
Steve Krafcisin	C	6-9	219	Fr.	29	29	58	.500	25	35	.714	43	83	2.9
Bruce Buckley	F	6-9	210	Sr.	33	30	79	.380	33	52	.635	76	93	2.8
Jeff Wolf	C	6-10	205	Fr.	23	15	28	.536	8	19	.421	32	38	1.7
John Virgil	G	6-5	175	Fr.	24	12	25	.480	7	11	.636	10	31	1.3
Dudley Bradley	F	6-5	195	So.	33	17	48	.354	2	9	.222	39	36	1.1
Randy Wiel	F	6-4	189	So.	16	6	13	.462	0	4	.000	10	12	0.8
Ged Doughton	G	6-1	168	So.	23	5	12	.417	7	10	.700	8	17	0.7
Dave Colescott	G	6-1	167	Fr.	18	3	10	.300	2	3	.667	6	8	0.4
Woody Coley	F	6-7	190	Sr.	26	2	7	.286	0	0	.000	6	4	0.2
Team												94		
North Carolina					33	1054	1961	.537	651	873	.746	1124	2759	83.6
Opponents					33	978	2050	.477	440	626	.703	1078	2396	72.6

1977 NEVADA-LAS VEGAS

Head Coach—Jerry Tarkanian   **Final Record—29-3**

Player	Pos.	Hgt.	Wgt.	Cl.	G	FG	FGA	Pct.	FT.	FTA	Pct.	Reb.	Pts.	Avg.
Eddie Owens	F	6-7	210	Sr.	32	284	546	.520	131	158	.829	178	699	21.8
Sam Smith	F	6-4	201	Sr.	29	185	359	.515	60	73	.822	88	430	14.8
Glen Gondrezick	G	6-6	216	Sr.	32	188	374	.503	91	124	.734	347	467	14.6
Reggie Theus	G	6-7	200	So.	32	178	358	.497	108	132	.818	145	464	14.5
Robert Smith	G	5-11	165	Sr.	32	155	318	.487	98	106	.925	79	408	12.8
Lewis Brown	C	6-11	225	Sr.	31	134	292	.459	49	69	.710	253	317	10.2
Tony Smith	G	6-1	166	So.	31	123	276	.446	33	45	.733	42	279	9.0
Larry Moffett	C	6-9	204	Jr.	32	116	214	.542	25	54	.463	293	257	8.0
Dale Thompson	..	....	....	..	2	2	2	1.000	0	0	.000	2	4	2.0
Pepper Bartlett	..	....	....	..	1	1	1	1.000	0	0	.000	0	2	2.0
Mike Milke	G	6-4	175	Jr.	20	15	36	.417	2	8	.250	15	32	1.6
John Rodriguez	F	6-5	188	So.	14	10	13	.769	3	5	.600	16	23	1.6
Gary Wagner	G	6-3	180	Jr.	16	11	22	.500	2	8	.250	14	24	1.5
Matt Porter	G	6-5	199	Jr.	18	5	27	.185	8	11	.727	17	18	1.0
Tom Schuberth	G	5-9	158	Fr.	8	1	2	.500	0	0	.000	3	2	0.3
Team												152		
Nevada-Las Vegas					32	1408	2840	.496	610	793	.769	1644	3426	107.1
Opponents					32	1105	2301	.480	596	869	.686	1440	2806	87.7

1977 NORTH CAROLINA-CHARLOTTE

Head Coach—Lee Rose   **Final Record—30-5**

Player	Pos.	Hgt.	Wgt.	Cl.	G	FG	FGA	Pct.	FT.	FTA	Pct.	Reb.	Pts.	Avg.
Cedric (Cornbread) Maxwell	C	6-8	202	Sr.	31	244	381	.640	202	263	.768	376	690	22.3
Lew Massey	F	6-4	202	Jr.	29	246	468	.526	79	105	.752	197	571	19.7
Chad Kinch	G	6-4	186	Fr.	33	218	444	.491	72	87	.828	124	508	15.4
Kevin King	F	6-7	200	So.	33	156	302	.517	55	72	.764	165	367	11.1
Melvin Watkins	G	6-4	204	Sr.	31	130	263	.494	39	57	.684	116	299	9.6
Jeff Gruber	G	6-0	155	Jr.	33	73	146	.500	40	47	.851	29	186	5.6
Phil Scott	F	6-6	170	Fr.	27	29	61	.475	27	45	.600	76	85	3.1
Mike Hester	F	6-7	190	Fr.	27	35	72	.486	15	28	.536	60	85	3.1
Henry Caldwell	F	6-2	180	Sr.	3	3	10	.300	0	0	.000	6	6	2.0
Greg Spain	C	6-8	200	Jr.	1	1	1	1.000	0	0	.000	1	2	2.0
Todd Crowley	G	6-4	170	Fr.	15	8	19	.421	9	11	.818	10	25	1.7
Ken Angel	F	6-8	201	Sr.	19	8	20	.400	5	11	.455	20	21	1.1
Jerry Winston	G	5-9	150	So.	10	4	13	.308	2	2	1.000	3	10	1.0
Lee Whifield	G	6-1	160	Fr.	28	7	20	.350	4	12	.333	13	18	0.6
Team												141		
North Carolina-Charlotte					33	1162	2220	.523	549	740	.742	1337	2873	87.1
Opponents					33	1047	2332	.449	317	475	.667	1218	2411	73.1

1977 FINAL FOUR

At Atlanta
Semifinals

North Carolina	fg	fga	ft	fta	rb	pf	tp
Davis	7	7	5	6	5	3	19
O'Koren	14	19	3	5	8	1	31
Yonakor	5	7	1	4	9	0	11
Ford	4	10	4	5	6	2	12
Kuester	2	5	5	7	6	0	9
Zaliagiris	0	1	0	0	0	0	0
Krafcisin	0	0	0	1	2	1	0
Buckley	1	5	0	0	2	3	2
Bradley	0	1	0	0	1	0	0
Wolf	0	1	0	0	1	0	0
Colescott	0	0	0	0	1	0	0
Team					1		
Totals	33	56	18	28	41	11	84

Nevada-Las Vegas	fg	fga	ft	fta	rb	pf	tp
Owens	7	15	0	0	2	4	14
Gondrezick	4	8	0	5	4	8	
Moffett	6	9	1	2	9	5	13
R. Smith	4	11	0	1	1	1	8
S. Smith	10	18	0	0	2	1	20
T. Smith	6	8	0	2	1	3	12
Theus	4	11	0	5	4	8	
Brown	0	0	0	0	1	0	0
Team					3		
Totals	41	80	1	5	29	22	83

Halftime: Nevada-Las Vegas 49-43. Officials: Brown and Copeland.

N.C.-Charlotte	fg	fga	ft	fta	rb	pf	tp
Massey	7	13	0	0	8	1	14
King	2	7	0	0	5	2	4
Maxwell	5	6	7	9	12	2	17
Kinch	1	7	2	2	4	2	4
Watkins	2	4	2	3	0	5	6
Gruber	2	6	0	0	0	0	4
Scott	0	0	0	0	0	0	0
Team					1		
Totals	19	43	11	14	30	12	49

Marquette	fg	fga	ft	fta	rb	pf	tp
Ellis	2	8	0	0	5	4	4
Neary	0	1	0	2	3	0	
Whitehead	10	16	1	2	16	1	21
Lee	5	18	1	1	3	3	11
Boylan	4	9	0	0	3	2	8
Toone	2	6	2	2	1	3	6
Rosenberger	0	0	1	2	1	0	1
Team					3		
Totals	23	58	5	7	33	16	51

Halftime: Marquette 25-22. Officials: Fouty and Galvan.

Championship
March 28

North Carolina	fg	fga	ft	fta	rb	pf	tp
Davis	6	13	8	10	8	4	20
O'Koren	6	10	2	4	11	5	14
Yonakor	3	5	0	0	4	0	6
Ford	3	10	0	0	2	3	6
Kuester	2	6	1	2	0	5	5
Krafcisin	1	1	0	0	0	0	2
Zaliagiris	2	3	0	0	0	3	4
Bradley	1	1	0	0	0	2	2
Buckley	0	1	0	0	2	1	0
Wolf	0	1	0	0	1	0	0
Colescott	0	0	0	0	0	0	0
Coley	0	0	0	0	0	0	0
Doughton	0	0	0	0	0	0	0
Virgil	0	0	0	0	1	0	0
Team					2		
Totals	24	51	11	16	28	24	59

Marquette	fg	fga	ft	fta	rb	pf	tp
Ellis	5	9	4	5	9	4	14
Neary	0	2	0	0	1	0	0
Whitehead	2	8	4	4	11	2	8
Lee	6	14	7	7	3	1	19
Boylan	5	7	4	4	4	3	14
Rosenberger	1	1	4	4	1	1	6
Toone	3	6	0	1	0	1	6
Team					2		
Totals	22	47	23	25	29	13	67

. Halftime: Marquette 39-27. Officials: Galvan and Copeland.

1978 Kentucky Is All Business

Kentucky's man of the hour was sweet-shooting senior forward Jack Givens (21), who took charge of the championship game and riddled Duke's zone defense for 41 points.

The 1978 national title was sweet vindication for Kentucky Coach Joe B. Hall, who believed he was on the basketball hot seat.

They filed onto the dais with the demeanor of condemned men sitting down to a last supper. These were college students on the verge of achieving a dream, but they represented the University of Kentucky and wore the label like a yoke around their necks. The Wildcats labored under the greatest of expectations.

As successful as they had been throughout the 1978 season—29 victories in 31 games—there remained one more contest to play and win. The NCAA title had escaped them three years earlier in John Wooden's coaching finale at UCLA, and no one involved in the Kentucky program would forget that the day before another championship game. They would not, could not, settle for anything less than the grand prize.

"That's what we're in business for," Wildcats Coach Joe B. Hall said.

Yes, it was a business at Kentucky, pure and simple. No code words to disguise the all-out effort and commitment. No talk of fun and games. No fooling around. And so when the Kentucky players followed the Duke players into the ballroom of a St.

Louis hotel for a press conference, they were stone-faced.

"You have to dedicate yourself to winning," senior forward/center Rick Robey said. "To be successful, you can't enjoy it during the grind."

The contrast between Kentucky and Duke could not have been more pronounced. The Blue Devils were a collection of young players—Coach Bill Foster started two freshmen, two sophomores and a junior—who were out having the time of their lives.

"I haven't had this much fun playing basketball since the sixth grade," freshman forward Kenny Dennard said after Duke outlasted Notre Dame, 90-86, in one of the Final Four semifinal games.

"If you're not having fun, you shouldn't be playing the game," said junior guard Jim Spanarkel, the acknowledged leader of the team.

To the Blue Devils, everything they had accomplished on the road to St. Louis—an Atlantic Coast Conference Tournament title and the East Regional championship—was cause for celebration. The philosophy at Kentucky was that the achievement of only one objective was worthy of a demonstration.

"During the season," Robey said, "you can't celebrate if you want to win."

If that bit of wisdom had been passed on by the coach, understand that it did not originate with Hall. He merely was the caretaker of a tradition that would not be satisfied with second best. It had started with Adolph Rupp, the Baron of the Bluegrass, who had died the previous December. Rupp's teams had won four NCAA titles and dominated Southern basketball. He hadn't coached in six years or guided a team to the national championship game since 1966, but that didn't matter. He was the man who had built the program and created the fanaticism.

"At Kentucky," Hall said, "you're competing more against the past than against other teams."

A 64-59 victory over Arkansas in the national semifinals wasn't about to quiet his critics. Had Kentucky lost its first game of the NCAA Tournament to Florida State—a game the Wildcats salvaged only after Hall had benched Robey, senior forward Jack Givens and junior guard Truman Claytor—the coach said he expected to be fired. And that would have been after his team had gone 25-2 in the regular season. Reaching the Final Four may have made his job safe for another year, but Hall could find temporary relief from his detractors only with a victory over Duke.

In his office, Hall kept a thick folder that he called his "hate file." It was a collection of letters and twisted Christmas cards that offered advice on how he should spend the rest of his life—and they didn't mean coaching basketball. Rupp's mail had always been screened by his personal secretary, who made sure that the discouraging words never were

heard by the coach. Hall, however, discontinued that practice.

"I needed to toughen myself," he said.

Nor did he spare his players that hard-bitten approach to the sport. Hall contended that nothing but a tough team would survive at Kentucky, so he tongue-lashed the Wildcats until they could take anything emotionally and mentally. Meanwhile, he drilled them so they could stand up to any team physically.

"There's been a lot of days when you just want to fall out, to have it end," Givens said. "But I think the hard work and the pressure make a better man out of you. It prepares you for life."

Of all the Kentucky players, Givens had been the target of Hall's harshest blasts. He was not only an upperclassman, but also the team's designated shooter and scorer, a gazelle among the elephants. But he had this habit, the coach decided, of disappearing at key moments of the most important games.

That alleged tendency enraged Hall. At Alabama the previous season, Hall had called Givens "gutless" in front of his teammates at halftime. Givens responded with an 18-point second half and the

Kentucky big man Rick Robey (53) contributed 20 points and some sterling defense to the Wildcats' championship-game victory.

Truman Claytor (22) and Mike Phillips (55) sandwich Duke's Mike Gminski (left photo), but still lose the rebound to the Blue Devils' big man. Rick Robey wears the traditional victory net (right) during Kentucky's postgame celebration.

Wildcats won, 87-85. But later that season against Tennessee, when a victory would have given the Wildcats the Southeastern Conference title and the opportunity to host an NCAA regional on their home court, Givens went up for open jump shots late in the game and passed backward. As a senior, Givens had done much the same thing in his team's loss at Louisiana State, Hall thought, and that time the coach had ripped him publicly.

"He uses that type of thing to work on your head," Robey said. "When you're the shooter, when you're the guy who can hit the open shot, he's going to put that kind of pressure on you. He wanted Jack and I, in pressure situations, to want the ball. Want it bad."

Givens said he never took the criticism personally. And that was fortunate for Hall and Kentucky because in the NCAA championship game at the Checkerdome, Givens would be the man on the spot. Duke played a 2-3 zone defense and attempted to stretch it from the baseline, where the 6-foot-10 Robey and the massive Mike Phillips stood like twin towers, to the backcourt, manned by Kyle Macy and Claytor.

"Hank Iba once told me," said Hall, invoking a legend other than Rupp's, "that when you stretch a zone that far, the middle has to be weak."

The middle was open for Givens. Wide open. Whenever the Duke guards crowded Macy or Claytor, the 6-4 forward would bolt toward the free-

throw area, take a pass and launch a jump shot. Mike Gminski, the Blue Devils' 6-11 sophomore center, was reluctant to challenge Givens because he was concerned with Robey and Phillips underneath the basket.

"I kept thinking that Gminski would come out and get me," Givens said, "but he didn't. So I kept shooting them."

He shot 12 times in the first 20 minutes and sank nine. Givens scored Kentucky's last 16 points of the half for a total of 23 and the Wildcats went to the locker room with a 45-38 lead.

Duke cut the deficit to three points three times in the first two minutes of the second half. But a long shot by Claytor, two free throws by Macy following a technical foul against Foster and Robey's dunk on a nifty pass from Macy raised the margin to nine and effectively ended the suspense. Givens continued to find open areas in the Blue Devils' zone and fire away. He scored from the baseline, he scored from the side, he scored driving the lane and he scored twice on offensive rebounds. He had nine more field goals in the second half and finished the game and his college career with 41 points.

It didn't matter that Duke received balanced scoring from freshman Gene Banks (22 points), Spanarkel (21) and Gminski (20). In fact, it didn't matter what the Blue Devils did at the offensive end. They couldn't handle the outside-inside combination of Givens, whose selection as the Final Four's

Two of the 1978 tournament's top players, Notre Dame's Kelly Tripucka (left) and Arkansas' Sidney Moncrief (right), were relegated to secondary roles after their teams lost semifinal games.

outstanding player was almost unanimous, and Robey (20 points). The Blue Devils made a belated effort to close the gap when Hall gave several of his reserves some playing time, cutting the Kentucky lead to 92-88 with 12 seconds left. But forward James Lee eliminated any doubt about the outcome with a resounding dunk four seconds before the final buzzer. The pressure imposed by the program and by Hall reaped a 94-88 victory and a championship.

But even the coach seemed to question the cost of such an achievement. While he stood near the Kentucky bench, awaiting the call to accept the championship trophy after the game, Hall said, "I pushed them so hard for four years, I hope it was worth it."

Later, he denied there was any special significance to the statement.

"This is what it's all about," he said. "It's a lifelong ambition for a coach. And it's immortalization for those players in Kentucky."

Immortalization. And for winning a basketball game. What an awesome thought. No wonder there was so little time and opportunity to smile. Yes, after the great victory, everyone celebrated and decided it had been worth the effort. The Wildcats had beaten five good teams under the greatest pressure of their lives, perhaps because of Hall's approach.

"I'm like a big, mean parent," the coach said. "I stay on them. No one knows how much guff they've taken from me. But I love every last one of them. All this talk about fun . . . no one gets to the Final Four without hard work."

Just then, Hall spotted reserve guard Jay Shidler dressing nearby. "Did you have fun, Jay?" the coach called out.

Shidler looked up and smiled broadly. "Yeah, coach," he said. "We won, didn't we?" And Joe B. Hall smiled back.

1978 Tournament Results

First Round

Michigan State 77, Providence 63
W. Kentucky 87, Syracuse 86 (ot)
Miami (O.) 84, Marquette 81 (ot)
Kentucky 85, Florida State 76
UCLA 83, Kansas 76
Arkansas 73, Weber State 52
San Francisco 68, N. Carolina 64
Fullerton State 90, New Mexico 85
Duke 63, Rhode Island 62
Penn 92, St. Bonaventure 83
Indiana 63, Furman 62
Villanova 103, La Salle 97
Utah 86, Missouri 79 (2 ot)
Notre Dame 100, Houston 77
DePaul 80, Creighton 78
Louisville 76, St. John's 68

Second Round

Michigan St. 90, W. Kentucky 69
Kentucky 91, Miami (Ohio) 69
Arkansas 74, UCLA 70
Fullerton St. 75, San Francisco 72
Duke 84, Pennsylvania 80
Villanova 61, Indiana 60
Notre Dame 69, Utah 56
DePaul 90, Louisville 89 (2 ot)

Regional Championships

Kentucky 52, Michigan State 49
Arkansas 61, Fullerton State 58
Duke 90, Villanova 72
Notre Dame 84, DePaul 64

Semifinals

Kentucky 64, Arkansas 59
Duke 90, Notre Dame 86

Third Place

Arkansas 71, Notre Dame 69

Championship

Kentucky 94, Duke 88

STATISTICS

1978 KENTUCKY

Head Coach—Joe B. Hall   **Final Record—30-2**

Player	Pos.	Hgt.	Wgt.	Cl.	G	FG	FGA	Pct.	FT.	FTA	Pct.	Reb.	Pts.	Avg.
Jack Givens	F	6-4	205	Sr.	32	238	430	.553	102	134	.761	217	578	18.1
Rick Robey	F-C	6-10	225	Sr.	32	263	167	.635	126	175	.720	261	460	14.4
Kyle Macy	G	6-3	180	So.	32	143	267	.536	115	129	.891	76	401	12.5
James Lee	F	6-5	230	Sr.	32	136	239	.569	78	105	.743	165	350	10.9
Mike Phillips	C	6-10	235	Sr.	31	125	210	.595	66	87	.759	145	316	10.2
Truman Claytor	G	6-1	178	Jr.	32	90	193	.466	41	53	.774	28	221	6.9
Jay Shidler	G	6-1	185	So.	29	42	102	.412	23	27	.852	23	107	3.7
Chuck Aleksinas	C	6-10	250	Fr.	27	37	65	.569	25	36	.694	60	99	3.7
LaVon Williams	F	6-6	205	So.	31	21	56	.375	17	28	.607	63	59	1.9
Fred Cowan	F	6-8	190	Fr.	19	15	30	.500	6	9	.667	17	36	1.9
Dwane Casey	G	6-2	195	Jr.	26	13	34	.382	6	10	.600	17	32	1.2
Tim Stephens	G	6-3	180	So.	19	8	24	.333	6	7	.857	11	22	1.2
Scott Courts	F-C	6-10	230	Fr.	13	4	6	.667	2	6	.333	11	10	0.8
Chris Gettelfinger	G	6-2	185	Fr.	9	1	3	.333	0	2	.000	1	2	0.2
Team												76		
Kentucky					32	1040	1922	.541	613	808	.759	1171	2693	84.2
Opponents					32	878	1889	.465	478	718	.666	1000	2234	69.8

1978 DUKE

Head Coach—Bill Foster   **Final Record—27-7**

Player	Pos.	Hgt.	Wgt.	Cl.	G	FG	FGA	Pct.	FT.	FTA	Pct.	Reb.	Pts.	Avg.
Jim Spanarkel	G	6-5	190	Jr.	34	244	460	.530	220	255	.863	116	708	20.8
Mike Gminski	C	6-11	245	So.	32	246	450	.547	148	176	.841	319	640	20.0
Gene Banks	F	6-7	205	Fr.	34	238	451	.528	105	146	.719	292	581	17.1
Kenny Dennard	F	6-7	200	Fr.	34	140	254	.551	51	76	.671	215	331	9.7
John Harrell	G	6-0	170	So.	34	68	140	.486	38	46	.826	34	174	5.1
Bob Bender	G	6-2	175	So.	22	41	84	.488	31	42	.738	32	113	5.1
Cameron Hall	F	6-9	215	So.	7	9	16	.563	6	7	.857	11	24	3.4
Steve Gray	G	6-2	180	Jr.	25	32	69	.464	18	21	.857	18	82	3.3
Scott Goetsch	F-C	6-9	215	Jr.	32	41	66	.621	12	19	.632	69	94	2.9
Jim Suddath	F	6-6	185	Fr.	31	30	62	.484	18	25	.720	49	78	2.5
Harold Morrison	F	6-7	200	Jr.	22	16	40	.400	13	17	.765	32	45	2.0
Bruce Bell	G	6-0	165	Sr.	21	10	25	.400	5	10	.500	12	25	1.2
Rob Ilardy	G	6-3	170	Jr.	13	8	14	.571	0	1	.000	8	16	1.2
Team												88		
Duke					34	1123	2131	.527	665	841	.791	1295	2911	85.6
Opponents					34	1047	2236	.468	434	634	.685	1129	2528	74.4

1978 ARKANSAS

Head Coach—Eddie Sutton   **Final Record—32-4**

Player	Pos.	Hgt.	Wgt.	Cl.	G	FG	FGA	Pct.	FT.	FTA	Pct.	Reb.	Pts.	Avg.
Ron Brewer	G	6-4	180	Sr.	36	258	486	.531	131	157	.834	112	647	18.0
Sidney Moncrief	G	6-4	185	Jr.	36	209	354	.590	203	256	.793	278	621	17.3
Marvin Delph	F	6-4	180	Sr.	35	253	452	.560	82	94	.872	199	588	16.8
Steve Schall	C	6-11	220	Jr.	36	151	269	.561	46	67	.687	193	348	9.7
Jim Counce	F	6-7	200	Sr.	36	55	100	.550	44	66	.667	152	154	4.3
Ulysses Reed	G	6-2	160	Fr.	31	27	48	.563	31	45	.689	37	85	2.7
James Crockett	C	6-9	215	Fr.	22	22	50	.440	10	28	.357	17	54	2.5
Steve Bates	C	6-10	225	Fr.	15	10	17	.588	13	15	.867	8	33	2.2
Michael Watley	G	6-4	170	Fr.	27	26	57	.456	6	14	.429	24	58	2.1
Chris Bennett	G	6-5	190	So.	27	21	45	.467	13	21	.619	24	55	2.0
Alan Zahn	F	6-7	195	So.	25	22	51	.431	5	12	.416	48	49	2.0
Mike Young	G	6-4	175	Fr.	16	6	13	.462	1	6	.167	13	13	0.8
Andre Tarver	G	6-3	185	Fr.	3	0	1	.000	0	0	.000	0	0	0.0
Team												127		
Arkansas					36	1060	1943	.546	585	781	.749	1232	2705	75.1
Opponents					36	942	2195	.429	334	486	.687	1109	2220	61.7

1978 NOTRE DAME

Head Coach—Digger Phelps   **Final Record—23-8**

Player	Pos.	Hgt.	Wgt.	Cl.	G	FG	FGA	Pct.	FT.	FTA	Pct.	Reb.	Pts.	Avg.
Dave Batton	F-C	6-9	235	Sr.	31	188	332	.566	59	79	.747	210	435	14.0
Don Williams	G	6-3	180	Sr.	30	165	337	.490	69	91	.758	48	399	13.3
Kelly Tripucka	F-G	6-7	210	Fr.	31	141	247	.571	80	108	.741	161	362	11.7
Rich Branning	G	6-3	160	So.	30	129	277	.466	71	97	.732	55	329	11.0
Bill Laimbeer	C	6-11	250	So.	29	97	175	.554	42	62	.677	190	236	8.1
Bruce Flowers	F-C	6-8	210	Jr.	31	86	179	.480	41	64	.641	149	213	6.9
Tracy Jackson	G-F	6-5	205	Fr.	28	66	120	.550	26	40	.650	91	158	5.6
Orlando Woolridge	F-C	6-9	195	Fr.	24	41	78	.526	16	33	.485	51	98	4.1
Bill Hanzlik	G-F	6-7	185	So.	30	40	78	.513	30	38	.789	57	110	3.7
Stan Wilcox	G	6-3	175	Fr.	29	30	61	.492	12	18	.667	23	72	2.5
Gilbert Salinas	F-C	6-11	185	Fr.	17	14	33	.424	14	19	.737	28	42	2.5
Jeff Carpenter	G	6-0	165	Sr.	26	13	35	.371	5	12	.417	15	31	1.2
Randy Haefner	F	6-6	205	Sr.	17	6	17	.353	2	4	.500	1	14	0.8
Tim Healy	G	6-1	170	Sr.	12	1	5	.200	0	1	.000	3	2	0.2
Team												105		
Notre Dame					31	1017	1974	.515	467	666	.701	1187	2501	80.7
Opponents					31	840	1883	.446	431	591	.729	993	2111	68.1

1978 FINAL FOUR

At St. Louis
Semifinals

Arkansas	fg	fga	ft	fta	rb	pf	tp
Counce	2	2	2	3	2	4	6
Delph	5	13	5	6	8	3	15
Schall	3	5	0	0	3	5	6
Brewer	5	12	6	8	5	2	16
Moncrief	5	11	3	7	5	3	13
Zahn	1	1	1	2	2	3	3
Reed	0	0	0	0	0	2	0
Team					1		
Totals	21	44	17	26	26	22	59

Kentucky	fg	fga	ft	fta	rb	pf	tp
Givens	10	16	3	4	9	2	23
Robey	3	6	2	2	8	2	8
Phillips	1	6	3	4	2	4	5
Macy	2	8	3	4	3	4	7
Claytor	1	2	0	1	0	4	2
Shidler	3	5	0	0	4	4	6
Lee	4	8	5	5	8	4	13
Casey	0	0	0	0	0	0	0
Stephens	0	0	0	0	0	0	0
Cowan	0	0	0	0	0	1	0
Williams	0	0	0	0	0	1	0
Team					0		
Totals	24	51	16	20	32	26	64

Halftime: Kentucky 32-30. Officials: Howell and Bain.

Duke	fg	fga	ft	fta	rb	pf	tp
Banks	8	15	6	7	12	1	22
Dennard	2	3	3	5	7	5	7
Gminski	13	17	3	4	5	2	29
Harrell	0	2	6	6	2	2	6
Spanarkel	4	11	12	12	4	1	20
Bender	0	1	2	3	2	2	2
Goetsch	1	1	0	0	0	2	2
Suddath	1	3	0	0	0	2	2
Team					2		
Totals	29	53	32	37	34	15	90

Notre Dame	fg	fga	ft	fta	rb	pf	tp
Tripucka	5	17	2	2	9	3	12
Batton	3	6	4	4	2	1	10
Flowers	5	8	0	0	6	3	10
Branning	4	10	0	0	1	3	8
Williams	8	15	0	1	2	2	16
Laimbeer	1	5	5	6	10	5	7
Hanzlik	3	8	2	2	6	5	8
Jackson	5	6	1	2	0	4	11
Wilcox	2	2	0	0	0	0	4
Team					1		
Totals	36	77	14	17	37	26	86

Halftime: 43-29. Officials: Kelley and Clymer.

Championship
March 27

Duke	fg	fga	ft	fta	rb	pf	tp
Banks	6	12	10	12	8	2	22
Dennard	5	7	0	0	8	5	10
Gminski	6	16	8	8	12	3	20
Harrell	2	2	0	0	0	3	4
Spanarkel	8	16	5	6	2	4	21
Suddath	1	3	2	3	2	1	4
Bender	1	2	5	5	1	3	7
Goetsch	0	1	0	0	1	1	0
Team					1		
Totals	29	59	30	34	35	22	88

Kentucky	fg	fga	ft	fta	rb	pf	tp
Givens	18	27	5	8	8	4	41
Robey	8	11	4	6	11	2	20
Phillips	1	4	2	2	5	4	4
Macy	3	3	3	4	0	1	9
Claytor	3	5	2	4	0	2	8
Lee	4	8	0	0	4	4	8
Shidler	1	5	0	1	1	3	2
Aleksinas	0	0	0	0	1	0	0
Williams	1	3	0	0	4	2	2
Cowan	0	2	0	0	2	1	0
Stephens	0	0	0	0	0	0	0
Courts	0	0	0	0	0	0	0
Gettelfinger	0	0	0	0	0	0	0
Casey	0	0	0	0	1	0	0
Team					0		
Totals	39	68	16	25	32	26	94

Halftime: Kentucky 45-38. Officials: Bain and Clymer.

1979 A Magical Performance

As professionals, the two men would share the glory of the next decade. They would become great rivals, leaders of the National Basketball Association's dominant teams, catalysts in the growth of the game. In time, Larry Bird and Earvin (Magic) Johnson would be recognized as titans of their sport.

In view of their lifetime achievements, perhaps a historical marker should be struck and mounted on the wall of the Special Events Center on the Utah campus in Salt Lake City. Such a plaque would be suitable recognition of the first meeting of these men on a basketball court. Even at the time, the early spring of 1979, it was acknowledged that the individual matchup was a special occasion over and above the NCAA championship contested by Bird's

High-scoring Indiana State forward Larry Bird (left) and Michigan State guard Earvin (Magic) Johnson brought their immense talents to the same court for the first time in 1979, when their teams met for the national championship.

Indiana State Sycamores and Johnson's Michigan State Spartans.

Bird and Johnson were not only the two finest players in college basketball, but also versatile athletes with an intuitive understanding of the sport. Bird was a 6-9 senior forward/center and Johnson a 6-8 sophomore guard, yet both passed the ball with dexterity matching that of the best little men. Both players were proudest of their passing, a skill that separated them from their peers and immediate predecessors.

"A lot of guys can find the open man by driving in and throwing the ball out," Michigan State Coach Jud Heathcote said. "But few can find the open man in the basket area, can thread the needle like the Birdman and the Magicman. What you must realize is that the pass is more important than the basket."

Bird and Johnson had demonstrated their mastery of this lost art in the national semifinals. Johnson had led the Spartans in scoring with 29 points in a 101-67 rout of Pennsylvania, but he really mesmerized the crowd with his 10 assists—some on the fast break, some on beautifully conceived lob passes to forward Greg Kelser, some just out of this world. And while Indiana State needed all of Bird's 35 points to turn back determined DePaul, 76-74, it was his passing that captivated the fans. Among his nine assists was a lefthanded, behind-the-neck pass to 6-8 Alex Gilbert while driving across the lane.

"One of the greatest passes I've ever seen," Heathcote called it.

Perhaps it was fitting that they would rise to such prominence in the same year. So similar were their abilities, despite their differences in position and personality, that Johnson was given the task of imitating Bird in practice for the benefit of the Spartans' matchup zone defense. He considered it a compliment.

"I'm a fan of Larry Bird," he said. "You've got to be a fan of his if you like basketball."

The admiration was mutual.

"He's such a good player," Bird said of Johnson. "He's so young, a sophomore, but he already plays like he's a graduate."

Their appreciation of each other's talents was shared by the pros. Bird had been selected in the first round of the NBA draft by the Boston Celtics the previous spring even though he had a year of college eligibility remaining and planned to use it. And Johnson was sufficiently polished that he would be chosen by the Los Angeles Lakers as the first pick of the entire 1979 pro draft the following summer.

High-flying Greg Kelser (32), alias Special K, was the biggest beneficiary of Magic Johnson's passing and ballhandling wizardry.

When all was said and done, Indiana State star Larry Bird was reduced to burying his face in a towel while his talented counterpart, Magic Johnson, was celebrating his team's hard-earned national championship.

But before they moved into the upper tax brackets, the two consensus All-Americas had one final game to play for the teams they had carried to their initial appearances in an NCAA title game. Only once had Michigan State qualified for the Final Four before Johnson, a hometown youngster, enrolled at the school in East Lansing. And Indiana State, which had spent much of its history competing at the small-college level, had no greater claim to basketball fame before the emergence of Bird than the signing of John Wooden to his first college coaching contract. Sycamore fans might still be talking about that in Terre Haute if a homesick Bird hadn't left Indiana after 3½ weeks. To the self-described "hick from French Lick," the Bloomington campus was too big, the adjustment in life style too great. The small-town environment at Indiana State was more comfortable for the country boy.

Of course, Bird would have been surrounded by outstanding players at Indiana. But at Indiana State, he took average players and made them better. Remarkably, the Sycamores had won all 33 of their games that season before encountering Michigan State. So commanding was Bird's presence that

in one game, Bradley Coach Dick Versace assigned two of his players to shadow him wherever he went. Bird went to a corner of the court, folded his arms and watched his teammates, playing four-on-three, win by 19 points.

Even in the course of Michigan State's semifinal destruction of Penn, the Spartans' cheering section chanted: "We want Bird. We want Bird." To which the Indiana State students replied: "You'll get the Bird. You'll get the Bird." Indeed, his mystique was so great that it didn't seem excessive when Sycamore fans turned up on the night of the final wearing buttons proclaiming, "The State Bird of Indiana is Larry."

Johnson was no less central to Michigan State's success, even though he had a better supporting cast. There was the high-flying Kelser, burly center Jay Vincent and a wispy guard, Terry Donnelly, who could shoot holes in a zone. The Spartans (25-6 entering the NCAA final) had been overpowering late in the season and throughout the NCAA Tournament, culminating with a 50-17 first-half explosion over Penn, which had upset North Carolina, Syracuse and St. John's to win the East Regional.

Michigan State Coach Jud Heathcote clutches the trophy that officially made his Spartans champions of the college basketball world.

And they had that matchup zone that had befuddled opponents. Michigan State was not the only college team to employ it, but because of the Spartans' unusual combination of size and quickness, Heathcote's team played it better than anyone else —as Larry Bird was about to discover.

It was clear from the outset of the championship game that Bird was not going to duplicate his performance against DePaul, which had watched while he made 16 of 19 field-goal attempts. As Bird commented later, "I was hitting so good, I felt sorry for the other team." But the Spartans refused to let Bird get started. There was a man in his face whenever he touched the ball, two when he began to dribble and no open passing lane to the baseline.

"He was getting frustrated," Vincent said. "I

never saw him so far off. He shot two shots *over* the basket."

When Indiana State fell behind in the first half, Bird tried to bring the Sycamores back himself, as he had done so often in the past. But five times he shot and hit nothing. Absolutely nothing. At half-time he had only four baskets in 11 tries and his team trailed, 37-28. It would get worse.

The first five minutes of the second half belonged to Donnelly, whom Indiana State was leaving open in an attempt to contain Johnson. Quickly sensing the double team, Magic got the ball to Donnelly, who hit four consecutive long jump shots, swelling Michigan State's lead to 50-34. It might have turned into a rout then and there if not for Bird's efforts.

His shots still weren't falling—he would finish the game with seven-of-21 shooting from the floor and 19 points—but that didn't detract from other parts of his game. He was leading both teams in rebounding and his defense against Kelser was superb. Bird had four steals in the first half alone, including an above-the-rim interception of Johnson's first lob pass. Then, during a two-minute stretch of the second half, he drew Kelser's fourth personal foul on a charging call, forced forward Mike Brkovich into a turnover with a quick defensive move at midcourt and intercepted an inbounds pass, only to step on the line as he

whirled to pass to a teammate.

Bird kept working and slowly the Sycamores pulled themselves back into the game. With the Spartans' lead cut to six points with 10:10 remaining, Heathcote instructed Johnson to take charge of the game. He did just that, scoring seven of his game-high 24 points in the next five minutes. Magic hit one free throw, then a seven-foot jumper and finally delivered the key play of the game.

Working from a semi-delay, Johnson shook defender Brad Miley with a fake, took a return pass from Kelser and slammed the ball in just as Indiana State's Bob Heaton attempted to slide in front of him for a charge. Heaton, a step late, was whistled for undercutting, a two-shot foul. Johnson made both free throws to complete a four-point play and boost the Michigan State lead to 61-50 with 5:06 remaining. The rest of the game was a parade to the free-throw line, and the Spartans capped their 75-64 victory with a perfect lead pass from Johnson to Kelser for an emphatic slam dunk.

If a couple of Bird's teammates had been hot, Indiana State might have been able to complete an undefeated season. But the Sycamores combined for a .422 shooting percentage.

"We just had a bad shooting game, both from the field and the free-throw line," said Bill Hodges, the Sycamores' first-year coach. "That was the whole difference."

No Indiana State player took the loss harder than Bird. Only the previous day he had shrugged off the possibility of defeat by saying winning or losing the championship game would make no difference because he was going to sign a big professional contract either way. But his actions betrayed his true feelings. At the final buzzer, he walked to the Sycamores' bench, put a towel to his eyes and cried.

Before taking on the Indiana State challenge, Magic Johnson displayed his talents in a lopsided semifinal victory over Pennsylvania.

1979 Tournament Results

First Round	
St. John's 75, Temple 70	Indiana State 86, Virginia Tech 69
Penn 73, Iona 69	Oklahoma 90, Texas 76
Lamar 95, Detroit 87	**Regional Semifinals**
Tennessee 97, Eastern Kentucky 81	St. John's 67, Rutgers 65
Southern Cal 86, Utah St. 67	Penn 84, Syracuse 76
Pepperdine 92, Utah 88 (ot)	Michigan State 87, Louisiana St. 71
Weber St. 81, N. Mexico St. 78 (ot)	Notre Dame 79, Toledo 71
Virginia Tech 70, Jacksonville 53	DePaul 62, Marquette 56
Second Round	UCLA 99, San Francisco 81
St. John's 80, Duke 78	Arkansas 73, Louisville 62
Rutgers 64, Georgetown 58	Indiana State 93, Oklahoma 72
Penn 72, North Carolina 71	**Regional Championships**
Syracuse 89, Connecticut 81	Penn 64, St. John's 62
Michigan State 95, Lamar 64	Michigan State 80, Notre Dame 68
LSU 71, Appalachian St. 57	DePaul 95, UCLA 91
Notre Dame 73, Tennessee 67	Indiana State 73, Arkansas 71
Toledo 74, Iowa 72	**Semifinals**
DePaul 89, Southern Cal 78	Michigan State 101, Penn 67
Marquette 73, Pacific 48	Indiana State 76, DePaul 74
UCLA 76, Pepperdine 71	**Third Place**
San Francisco 86, BYU 63	DePaul 96, Penn 93
Arkansas 74, Weber State 63	**Championship**
Louisville 69, South Alabama 66	Michigan State 75, Indiana State 64

STATISTICS

1979 MICHIGAN STATE

Head Coach—Jud Heathcote   Final Record—26-6

Player	Pos.	Hgt.	Wgt.	Cl.	G	FG	FGA	Pct.	FT	FTA	Pct.	Reb.	Pts.	Avg.
Greg Kelser	F	6-7	190	Sr.	32	246	451	.545	110	164	.671	278	602	18.8
Earvin (Magic) Johnson	G	6-8	207	So.	32	173	370	.468	202	240	.842	234	548	17.1
Jay Vincent	C	6-8	228	So.	31	170	343	.496	54	93	.581	161	394	12.7
Ron Charles	F	6-7	190	Jr.	32	115	173	.665	51	82	.622	162	281	8.8
Mike Brkovich	F	6-4	183	So.	32	85	167	.509	53	66	.803	56	223	7.0
Terry Donnelly	G	6-2	159	Jr.	32	83	155	.535	46	61	.754	50	212	6.6
Gerald Busby	F	6-4	168	Fr.	13	12	26	.462	6	8	.750	12	30	2.3
Rob Gonzalez	F	6-7	218	Fr.	28	18	31	.581	12	15	.800	27	48	1.7
Greg Lloyd	G	6-1	166	Jr.	19	8	16	.500	11	16	.688	10	27	1.4
Mike Longaker	G	6-1	182	Jr.	19	9	14	.643	8	12	.667	6	26	1.4
Rick Kaye	F	6-7	201	So.	16	8	11	.727	4	9	.444	10	20	1.3
Don Brkovich	F	6-6	183	Fr.	11	3	5	.600	1	4	.250	6	7	0.6
Gerald Gilkie	F	6-5	182	So.	5	1	4	.250	1	3	.333	4	3	0.6
Jaimie Huffman	G	6-3	173	So.	7	1	3	.333	0	2	.000	5	2	0.3
Team												93		
Michigan State					32	932	1769	.527	559	775	.721	1186	2423	75.7
Opponents					32	830	1912	.434	343	510	.673	1116	2003	62.6

(Team totals include dead-ball rebounds.)

1979 INDIANA STATE

Head Coach—Bill Hodges   Final Record—33-1

Player	Pos.	Hgt.	Wgt.	Cl.	G	FG	FGA	Pct.	FT	FTA	Pct.	Reb.	Pts.	Avg.
Larry Bird	F-C	6-9	215	Sr.	34	376	707	.532	221	266	.831	505	973	28.6
Carl Nicks	G	6-2	186	Jr.	34	267	576	.464	122	183	.667	118	656	19.3
Alex Gilbert	C-F	6-8	184	Jr.	34	154	311	.495	20	79	.253	207	328	9.6
Bob Heaton	G-F	6-5	192	Jr.	34	99	188	.527	50	64	.781	112	248	7.3
Leroy Staley	F	6-5	193	Sr.	34	83	174	.477	72	112	.643	118	238	7.0
Brad Miley	F	6-8	194	Jr.	34	74	118	.627	46	90	.511	203	194	5.7
Steve Reed	G	6-3	166	So.	34	68	141	.482	34	48	.708	63	170	5.0
Scott Turner	F	6-6	193	Fr.	18	16	28	.571	6	9	.667	20	38	2.1
Tom Crowder	F	6-5	197	Sr.	19	15	29	.517	6	13	.462	25	36	1.9
Rich Nemcek	G-F	6-6	182	Jr.	24	17	41	.415	6	13	.462	24	40	1.7
Bob Ritter	G	6-3	189	Jr.	15	7	22	.318	1	2	.500	8	15	1.0
Eric Curry	C-F	6-9	180	Jr.	17	6	20	.300	0	2	.000	19	12	0.7
Rod McNelly	G	6-2	173	Fr.	16	1	6	.167	2	9	.222	5	4	0.3
Team												123		
Indiana State					34	1183	2361	.501	586	890	.658	1639	2952	86.8
Opponents					34	1050	2328	.451	376	546	.689	1297	2476	72.8

(Team totals include dead-ball rebounds.)

1979 DePAUL

Head Coach—Ray Meyer   Final Record—26-6

Player	Pos.	Hgt.	Wgt.	Cl.	G	FG	FGA	Pct.	FT	FTA	Pct.	Reb.	Pts.	Avg.
Mark Aguirre	F	6-7	225	Fr.	32	302	581	.520	163	213	.765	244	767	24.0
Curtis Watkins	F	6-6	190	Sr.	32	210	354	.593	125	144	.868	259	545	17.0
Gary Garland	G	6-5	185	Sr.	32	237	532	.445	69	84	.821	180	543	17.0
Clyde Bradshaw	G	6-0	170	So.	32	136	313	.435	79	111	.712	125	351	11.0
James Mitchem	C-F	6-9	215	Jr.	32	115	269	.428	35	58	.603	186	265	8.3
Dennis McGuire	F	6-7	195	So.	13	17	30	.567	17	22	.773	17	51	3.9
Scott Feiereisel	G	6-2	185	Jr.	7	5	11	.455	7	9	.778	2	17	2.4
Dennis Moore	G	6-1	175	So.	11	9	17	.529	7	9	.778	8	25	2.3
Bill Madey	C-F	6-8	220	Jr.	25	15	30	.500	6	12	.500	50	36	1.4
Chris Nikitas	G	6-2	190	Fr.	15	8	12	.667	5	9	.556	8	21	1.4
Tom Barr	G-F	6-6	200	So.	9	3	11	.273	4	5	.800	15	10	1.1
Sam Manella	F	6-5	220	Fr.	7	4	9	.444	0	0	.000	8	8	1.1
Team												65		
DePaul					32	1061	2169	.489	517	676	.765	1167	2639	82.5
Opponents					32	1037	2117	.490	318	469	.678	1173	2392	74.8

1979 PENNSYLVANIA

Head Coach—Bob Weinhauer   Final Record—25-7

Player	Pos.	Hgt.	Wgt.	Cl.	G	FG	FGA	Pct.	FT	FTA	Pct.	Reb.	Pts.	Avg.
Tony Price	F	6-7	205	Sr.	32	244	465	.524	145	194	.747	279	633	19.8
Tim Smith	F-G	6-5	190	Sr.	32	175	363	.482	78	91	.857	205	428	13.4
Matt White	C	6-10	215	Sr.	32	157	248	.633	61	88	.693	239	375	11.7
James Salters	G	5-11	150	Jr.	32	118	238	.496	62	76	.816	32	298	9.3
Bobby Willis	G	6-2	180	Sr.	31	117	269	.418	49	75	.653	66	283	9.1
Ken Hall	G	6-2	195	So.	31	48	94	.511	47	58	.810	26	143	4.6
Vincent Ross	F	6-8	185	Fr.	28	31	81	.383	18	34	.529	100	80	2.9
Angelo Reynolds	G	6-2	180	Fr.	21	29	61	.475	3	5	.600	8	61	2.9
Ted Flick	F	6-7	185	So.	14	9	30	.300	9	11	.818	16	27	1.9
Tom Leifsen	F	6-9	215	Fr.	27	14	29	.483	12	22	.545	41	40	1.5
Ed Kuhl	F	6-5	195	Sr.	19	9	30	.300	9	12	.750	10	27	1.4
David Jackson	G	6-3	180	Fr.	20	5	20	.250	10	20	.500	11	20	1.0
Tom Condon	C	6-9	210	So.	17	2	11	.182	8	11	.727	16	12	0.7
Team												103		
Pennsylvania					32	958	1950	.491	511	697	.733	1152	2427	75.8
Opponents					32	869	1812	.480	541	737	.734	1034	2279	71.2

1979 FINAL FOUR

At Salt Lake City
Semifinals

Pennsylvania	fg	fga	ft	fta	rb	pf	tp
Price	7	18	4	4	7	5	18
Smith	0	6	0	0	5	0	0
White	5	12	3	4	11	4	13
Salters	1	5	0	0	1	2	2
Willis	4	13	1	3	6	2	9
Ross	2	6	0	0	6	3	4
Hall	3	8	0	1	2	1	6
Reynolds	1	3	0	0	0	3	2
Leifsen	0	1	1	2	4	1	1
Flick	0	6	6	6	2	3	6
Jackson	1	2	4	4	1	0	6
Kuhl	0	2	0	0	0	5	0
Condon	0	0	0	0	2	2	0
Team					2		
Totals	24	82	19	24	44	31	67

Michigan State	fg	fga	ft	fta	rb	pf	tp
M. Brkovich	6	10	0	0	1	4	12
Kelser	12	19	4	6	9	2	28
Charles	2	2	0	0	6	4	4
Donnelly	3	5	0	0	3	0	6
Johnson	9	10	11	12	10	2	29
Vincent	0	1	3	4	1	2	3
Gonzalez	1	5	0	0	3	2	2
Longaker	2	2	0	0	2	0	4
Lloyd	0	2	6	7	0	1	6
Kaye	2	2	1	3	2	1	5
Huffman	0	0	0	1	2	2	0
Gilkie	0	1	0	0	1	1	0
D. Brkovich	1	1	0	1	1	1	2
Team					3		
Totals	38	60	25	34	44	22	101

Halftime: Michigan State 50-17. Officials: Buckiewicz, Weiler and Silvester.

DePaul	fg	fga	ft	fta	rb	pf	tp
Watkins	8	11	0	0	2	4	16
Aguirre	9	18	1	2	5	3	19
Mitchem	6	11	0	0	5	4	12
Bradshaw	4	8	0	0	3	1	8
Garland	9	18	1	3	4	2	19
Team					2		
Totals	36	66	2	5	21	14	74

Indiana State	fg	fga	ft	fta	rb	pf	tp
Miley	2	2	0	0	3	1	4
Gilbert	6	7	0	1	5	2	12
Bird	16	19	3	4	16	3	35
Nicks	4	13	2	2	1	3	10
Reed	3	5	0	0	2	0	6
Heaton	3	6	0	0	3	4	6
Staley	1	4	1	2	2	3	3
Team					2		
Totals	35	56	6	9	34	14	76

Halftime: Indiana State 45-42. Officials: Muncy, Nichols and Wirtz.

Championship
March 26

Michigan State	fg	fga	ft	fta	rb	pf	tp
M. Brkovich	1	2	3	7	4	1	5
Kelser	7	13	5	6	8	4	19
Charles	3	3	1	2	7	5	7
Donnelly	5	5	5	6	4	2	15
Johnson	8	15	8	10	7	3	24
Vincent	2	5	1	2	2	4	5
Gonzalez	0	0	0	0	0	0	0
Longaker	0	0	0	0	0	0	0
Team					2		
Totals	26	43	23	33	34	19	75

Indiana State	fg	fga	ft	fta	rb	pf	tp
Miley	0	0	0	1	3	1	0
Gilbert	2	3	0	4	4	4	4
Bird	7	21	5	8	13	3	19
Nicks	7	14	3	6	2	5	17
Reed	4	9	0	0	0	4	8
Heaton	4	14	2	2	6	2	10
Staley	2	2	0	1	3	2	4
Nemcek	1	1	0	0	0	3	2
Team					3		
Totals	27	64	10	22	34	24	64

Halftime: Michigan State 37-28. Officials: Nichols, Muncy and Wirtz.

1980 The Cardinals Fly High

He was a legend before he graduated from high school. Not only was Darrell Griffith regarded as the finest prep player in America in the winter of 1976, but he also was said to be one of the best ever, in a league with the young Oscar Robertson and Jerry West. The 6-foot-4 leaper from Male High School in Louisville, Ky., was the subject of national magazine articles, an intense recruiting battle and considerable speculation.

There even was talk that he would bypass college entirely and report directly to the American Basketball Association, which just happened to have a franchise in town. But in late May, with the ABA on its way out of business, Griffith called a press conference to announce his intention of enrolling at the local university. He had big plans.

"I hope," he said that afternoon, Louisville Coach Denny Crum standing by his side, "to win several national championships."

Such great expectations were shared by his teammates, Louisville students and fans. As a result, the hometown hero endured a frustrating three years. The Cardinals won no less than 21 games in each season and Griffith treated his admirers to some spectacular performances, but Louisville failed to reach the Final Four, let alone capture an NCAA title. The 1980 season, which marked the expansion of the NCAA Tournament field to 48 teams (eight more than in 1979 and 16 more than in 1978), would be his last opportunity.

For that reason, Griffith spent hour after hour in the gym during the summer. No one had to teach him how to jump, which he did better than any

Darrell Griffith was the man of the hour after leading Louisville to the 1980 college basketball championship.

Darrell Griffith, with a little help from his friends, cuts the final threads of net after Louisville's title-game victory.

The bright-eyed Louisville fan (left) seemed more confident of victory than
Cardinals Coach Denny Crum during the waning moments of the Cardinals' 59-54
victory over UCLA.

collegian since David Thompson arrived at North Carolina State, or to shoot. But his game lacked the intensity and consistency that were necessary to boost the Cardinals to the top. It wasn't until his senior year that Griffith delivered on his promise, doing so with astonishing virtuosity.

The 1980 Cardinals were the youngest Louisville team in a decade. Crum started a freshman, three sophomores and one senior. But that senior was unrelenting, and Louisville reached the Final Four in Indianapolis with a record of 31-3 and the mantle of favorite.

Iowa, the Cardinals' semifinal opponent, boasted a wonderful guard of its own in Ronnie Lester. The senior had sparked the Hawkeyes through the East Regional, where they made a stunning second-half comeback to beat Georgetown in the final, but he had spent a good part of the season resting a wounded knee. That knee finally gave out after barely 12 minutes of play against Louisville. Lester scored Iowa's first 10 points as the Hawkeyes fell behind, 12-10, but about five minutes later he was

helped to the bench and then to the locker room, from which he failed to return. That was bad news for his teammates, whose dreadful shooting was clear evidence of their Final Four jitters.

Meanwhile, Griffith was hoisting rainbow jumpers over the Hawkeye defense and hitting with monotonous regularity. He attempted 12 field goals in the first half and made eight. Still, Iowa played tenaciously and, less than four minutes into the second half, cut the Louisville lead to two points.

Time for Griffith to take charge. He scored baskets. He drew defenders to him and then whipped passes to Derek Smith, Wiley Brown and Rodney McCray underneath. He handled the ball flawlessly. And the Cardinals pulled away to an 80-72 victory. Griffith, the driving force behind the "Doctors of Dunk," totaled 34 points, six assists, three steals, two blocked shots and at least one astonished opponent.

"I've played against a lot of guys who can jump," said Bob Hansen, one of several Hawkeyes who attempted to guard Griffith. "But they came down."

Ironically, the only team now standing in the way of Louisville's first NCAA title was the UCLA Bruins, who had denied the Cardinals on the occasion of their previous Final Four appearance.

There had been even greater consternation in Westwood than in Louisville during the intervening years. Two coaches, Gene Bartow and Gary Cunningham, had succumbed to the pressure of trying to replace John Wooden. It fell to Larry Brown, a rookie college coach who had done time in the pros, to return UCLA to the championship game.

The Bruins arrived on the strength of a 67-62 semifinal victory over a Purdue team that had the home-state advantage in Market Square Arena. Brown's team advanced to the title game despite a lineup that was even more youthful than Louisville's. Four of the top seven Bruins were freshmen, including two starters (guards Rod Foster and Michael Holton) and the first two men off the bench (forward Cliff Pruitt and guard Darren Daye). A

One of the biggest obstacles Louisville had to overcome was high-scoring Kiki Vandeweghe, who was held to 14 title-game points.

sophomore, 6-6 Mike Sanders, was UCLA's starting pivotman.

Kiki Vandeweghe, the only prominent senior, filled the same role for the Bruins as Griffith did for the Cardinals. The 6-8 forward was both his team's high scorer and its stabilizing factor.

Also like Griffith, Vandeweghe was a hometown boy who grew up minutes away from his eventual college campus. In fact, his father, Dr. Ernie Vandeweghe, was the Bruins' team physician as well as a former basketball player of some note. He had been an All-America at Colgate and later played for the New York Knicks while attending medical school. There was considerable talent on the other side of the family as well. Mel Hutchins, his mother's brother, had been an All-America at Brigham Young before advancing to the National Basketball Association.

While Vandeweghe may have been blessed with the genes for the sport, he lacked seasoning when it came time to choose a college, and he had to sell himself to the major college of his choice, unlike Griffith. Vandeweghe had been a national age-group champion swimmer at 10 and 12 before an early case of burnout convinced him his future lay on land. He didn't start working at basketball until the ninth grade.

"Basketball is one of the few things that did not come easily to me," he said. "Since I'm the type of person who does not enjoy not doing things well, I worked at it."

And worked and worked. He played in four or five summer leagues, trying to make up for lost time. He succeeded in making himself into a nice player as a high school senior. Not a great player. Not a fully developed player. But a nice player.

Utah expressed interest. And BYU offered a scholarship. But young Vandeweghe wanted to attend UCLA, which was so close to his home he could and did walk to Pauley Pavilion.

It wasn't until Vandeweghe had starred in several postseason all-star games and was ready to announce his decision that Bartow made contact. Kiki got the last scholarship to UCLA. He may have been the least advanced member of the freshman class, but in four years no one improved more than Vandeweghe. He went from being a quiet role player to a leader of a team otherwise dominated by freshmen.

And his game flowered in the NCAA Tournament. Vandeweghe was at his best against Purdue in the semifinals, scoring 24 points in a performance that featured nine-for-12 shooting from the field and included three resounding dunks in the face of 7-1 consensus All-America Joe Barry Carroll. Though the Bruins already had lost nine games that season—more than any UCLA team since 1963—Kiki and his youthful teammates gave Brown an excellent chance to become the first rookie college coach to win the national title.

The championship game was anything but a classic. These may have been the quickest teams ever to meet in an NCAA final, and they appeared at times to be caught up in a two-legged version of the Indy 500. UCLA would race in one direction, then chase Louisville the other way, neither remembering to take the basketball along for the ride. Speed was all that seemed to matter.

"I'd be running," said sophomore guard Jerry Eaves, one of Louisville's sports cars, "and I'd turn around and five UCLA players would pass me. Then UCLA would run and five of us would pass them."

All of which left two flustered teams on the court —and three officials blowing whistles, signaling the other way. By halftime, when UCLA held a 28-26 lead, the Bruins and Cardinals had combined for 16 turnovers, 11 steals and 18 fouls. The second half didn't look much better than the first. The totals then were 17 turnovers, seven steals and 20 fouls.

"It's funny," Eaves said. "I looked at the two teams and really thought there was going to be a lot of points scored."

There weren't. Louisville managed only 59 points, but that was sufficient for victory. High-powered UCLA scored but 54.

The contest remained close through most of the second half, but UCLA took a five-point lead with 6:28 remaining. The key play that shifted the momentum back to Louisville was a great defensive effort by Eaves and Brown, a 6-8 sophomore. As Vandeweghe drove for a dunk and a potential six-point lead with about four minutes to play, the two Cardinals caused Vandeweghe's off-balance shot to bounce off the rim. Brown collected the rebound, and Eaves' 16-foot jump shot with 3:26 left brought Louisville back within two, 54-52.

Another anxious moment came when Smith, a 6-6 sophomore forward, went to the free-throw line in a one-and-one situation with Louisville clinging to a 56-54 lead in the final minute. At that point, Crum remembered Terry Howard's critical miss in San Diego five years earlier.

"Thoughts of the '75 game flashed through my mind," the coach said. "I thought: 'Let's not let it happen again. Let's make the free throws.'"

Smith made both. Louisville had its championship.

Fittingly, it was Griffith's 18-foot jumper that broke a 54-54 tie and proved to be the winning basket. The consensus All-America was the only Louisville player in double figures, finishing the night with 23 points and the knowledge that he had fulfilled his mission. Griffith hadn't won several championships, but he had won one, and that was one more than Louisville had ever won before.

Louisville forward/center Wiley Brown goes up for a jump shot despite the effort of UCLA defender James Wilkes.

1980 Tournament Results

First Round
Villanova 77, Marquette 59
Iowa 86, Vir. Commonwealth 72
*Iona 84, Holy Cross 78
Tennessee 80, Furman 69
Alcorn State 70, South Alabama 62
Missouri 61, San Jose State 51
Texas A&M 55, Bradley 53
Kansas State 71, Arkansas 53
Florida State 94, Toledo 91
Penn 62, Washington St. 55
Purdue 90, La Salle 82
Virginia Tech 89, W. Kentucky 85
UCLA 87, Old Dominion 74
Arizona St. 99, *Loyola (Calif.) 71
Clemson 76, Utah State 73
Lamar 87, Weber State 86

Second Round
Syracuse 97, Villanova 83
Iowa 77, N.C. State 64
Georgetown 74, *Iona 71
Maryland 86, Tennessee 75
LSU 98, Alcorn State 88
Missouri 87, Notre Dame 84
Texas A&M 78, N. Caro. 61 (2 ot)
Louisville 71, Kansas St. 69 (ot)
Kentucky 97, Florida State 78
Duke 52, Penn 42

Purdue 87, St. John's (N.Y.) 72
Indiana 68, Virginia Tech 59
UCLA 77, DePaul 71
Ohio State 89, Arizona State 75
Clemson 71, BYU 66
Lamar 81, Oregon State 77

Regional Semifinals
Iowa 88, Syracuse 77
Georgetown 74, Maryland 68
LSU 68, Missouri 63
Louisville 66, Texas A&M 55 (ot)
Duke 55, Kentucky 54
Purdue 76, Indiana 69
UCLA 72, Ohio State 68
Clemson 74, Lamar 66

Regional Finals
Iowa 81, Georgetown 80
Louisville 86, LSU 66
Purdue 68, Duke 60
UCLA 85, Clemson 74

Semifinals
Louisville 80, Iowa 72
UCLA 67, Purdue 62

Third Place
Purdue 75, Iowa 58

Championship
Louisville 59, UCLA 54

*Iona's and Loyola's participation in 1980 tournament voided.

STATISTICS

1980 LOUISVILLE

Head Coach—Denny Crum   Final Record—33-3

Player	Pos.	Hgt.	Wgt.	Cl.	G	FG	FGA	Pct.	FT	FTA	Pct.	Reb.	Pts.	Avg.
Darrell Griffith	G	6-4	190	Sr.	36	349	631	.553	127	178	.713	174	825	22.9
Derek Smith	F	6-6	205	So.	36	213	372	.573	105	150	.700	299	531	14.8
Wiley Brown	F-C	6-8	220	So.	36	151	291	.519	72	118	.610	201	374	10.4
Rodney McCray	F-C	6-7	220	Fr.	36	107	197	.543	66	102	.647	269	280	7.8
Jerry Eaves	G	6-4	180	So.	34	92	179	.514	78	117	.667	61	262	7.7
Poncho Wright	G-F	6-5	195	So.	36	99	220	.450	35	48	.729	89	233	6.5
Scooter McCray	F-C	6-8	185	So.	3	5	11	.454	4	6	.667	11	14	4.7
Roger Burkman	G	6-5	175	Jr.	36	38	93	.409	66	94	.702	60	142	3.9
Daryl Cleveland	F	6-7	190	Jr.	14	7	21	.333	13	19	.684	12	27	1.9
Tony Branch	G	6-0	175	Sr.	25	11	29	.379	19	21	.905	3	41	1.6
Greg Deuser	G	6-0	170	So.	22	9	25	.360	15	22	.682	11	33	1.5
Marty Pulliam	C	6-9	225	So.	12	1	4	.250	4	4	1.000	4	6	0.5
Steve Clark	G	6-5	175	Fr.	6	1	5	.200	0	1	.000	3	2	0.3
Team												170		
Louisville					36	1083	2078	.521	604	880	.686	1367	2770	76.9
Opponents					36	967	2092	.462	467	658	.710	1220	2401	66.7

1980 UCLA

Head Coach—Larry Brown   Final Record—22-10

Player	Pos.	Hgt.	Wgt.	Cl.	G	FG	FGA	Pct.	FT	FTA	Pct.	Reb.	Pts.	Avg.
Kiki Vandeweghe	F	6-8	220	Sr.	32	234	420	.557	155	196	.791	216	623	19.5
Rod Foster	G	6-1	159	Fr.	32	144	263	.548	80	95	.842	59	368	11.5
Mike Sanders	C-F	6-6	205	So.	32	142	248	.573	76	96	.792	190	360	11.3
James Wilkes	F	6-7	205	Sr.	32	111	221	.502	60	91	.659	153	282	8.8
Cliff Pruitt	F	6-7	185	Fr.	31	69	153	.451	55	78	.705	94	193	6.2
Michael Holton	G	6-3	182	Fr.	32	55	105	.524	54	73	.740	78	164	5.1
Darren Daye	G	6-7	195	Fr.	32	59	103	.573	43	76	.566	60	161	5.0
Gig Sims	C	6-9	202	Sr.	20	37	69	.536	18	32	.563	63	92	4.6
Darrell Allums	C	6-9	225	Sr.	30	49	98	.500	25	48	.521	105	123	4.1
Tyren Naulls	G	6-3	206	So.	20	31	69	.449	14	25	.560	26	76	3.8
Tony Anderson	F	6-4	195	So.	27	28	56	.500	27	36	.750	45	83	3.1
Randy Arrillage	G	6-1	165	Fr.	7	5	8	.625	7	10	.700	1	17	2.4
Chris Lippert	G-F	6-5	189	Sr.	7	4	16	.250	4	8	.500	7	12	1.7
Team												97		
UCLA					32	968	1828	.530	618	864	.715	1193	2554	79.8
Opponents					32	880	1984	.444	465	652	.713	1012	2225	69.5

1980 PURDUE

Head Coach—Lee Rose   Final Record—23-10

Player	Pos.	Hgt.	Wgt.	Cl.	G	FG	FGA	Pct.	FT	FTA	Pct.	Reb.	Pts.	Avg.
Joe Barry Carroll	C	7-1	245	Sr.	33	301	558	.539	134	203	.660	302	736	22.3
Keith Edmonson	G	6-5	195	So.	33	172	333	.517	99	126	.786	136	443	13.4
Drake Morris	F	6-5	195	Jr.	33	137	286	.479	92	127	.724	154	366	11.1
Arnette Hallman	F	6-7	205	Sr.	32	124	283	.438	33	65	.508	190	281	8.8
Mike Scearce	F	6-7	210	So.	32	69	180	.383	36	48	.750	99	174	5.4
Brian Walker	G	6-2	185	Jr.	33	43	104	.413	37	59	.627	83	123	3.7
Kevin Stallings	G	6-5	200	So.	33	30	63	.476	11	20	.550	21	71	2.2
Steve Walker	F	6-5	210	Sr.	33	24	48	.500	20	30	.667	69	68	2.1
Ted Benson	C	6-10	225	Fr.	32	10	25	.400	28	39	.718	27	48	1.5
Roosevelt Barnes	G	6-2	195	Jr.	24	5	24	.208	4	6	.667	23	14	0.6
Jon Kitchel	F	6-5	195	So.	20	4	9	.444	2	6	.333	8	10	0.5
John Anthrop	G	5-11	175	Sr.	10	1	1	1.000	2	4	.500	3	4	0.4
Lee Cummings	G	6-2	180	So.	8	1	5	.200	0	1	.000	1	2	0.3
Team												185		
Purdue					33	921	1919	.480	498	734	.678	1301	2340	70.9
Opponents					33	832	1939	.429	425	603	.705	1218	2089	63.3

1980 IOWA

Head Coach—Lute Olson   Final Record—23-10

Player	Pos.	Hgt.	Wgt.	Cl.	G	FG	FGA	Pct.	FT	FTA	Pct.	Reb.	Pts.	Avg.
Ronnie Lester	G	6-2	175	Sr.	17	86	185	.465	80	100	.800	29	252	14.8
Kenny Arnold	G	6-2	185	So.	33	171	363	.471	102	136	.750	114	444	13.5
Steve Krafcisin	C	6-10	230	Jr.	33	155	289	.536	95	142	.669	211	405	12.3
Kevin Boyle	F	6-6	195	So.	33	163	318	.513	62	88	.705	205	388	11.8
Vince Brookins	F	6-5	205	Jr.	32	147	294	.500	57	72	.792	148	351	11.0
Steve Waite	C	6-10	225	Jr.	33	103	203	.507	59	92	.641	194	265	8.0
Bob Hansen	G	6-5	190	Fr.	33	71	167	.425	43	73	.589	67	185	5.6
Mark Gannon	F	6-6	215	Fr.	13	29	63	.460	15	20	.750	50	73	5.6
Randy Norton	G	6-10	170	So.	2	0	0	.000	4	6	.667	0	4	2.0
Greg Boyle	G	6-2	180	Jr.	3	1	3	.333	2	4	.500	1	4	1.3
Mike Henry	F	6-9	205	Jr.	20	10	17	.588	4	7	.571	14	24	1.2
Jon Darsee	F	6-5	195	So.	12	4	9	.444	0	0	.000	8	8	0.7
Mike Heller	F	6-8	215	Fr.	14	2	7	.286	0	0	.000	8	4	0.3
Tom Grogan	G	6-3	179	Fr.	7	0	0	.000	2	4	.500	2	2	0.3
Mike Arens	G	6-4	180	Sr.	7	0	4	.000	0	0	.000	1	0	0.0
Team												163		
Iowa					33	942	1922	.490	525	744	.706	1215	2409	73.0
Opponents					33	885	1885	.469	394	559	.705	1149	2164	65.6

1980 FINAL FOUR

At Indianapolis
Semifinals

Iowa	fg	fga	ft	fta	rb	pf	tp
Brookins	6	18	2	2	6	5	14
Boyle	0	8	0	0	7	2	0
Krafcisin	4	5	4	4	3	5	12
Lester	4	4	2	2	1	2	10
Arnold	9	17	2	2	3	1	20
Waite	4	6	1	1	2	5	9
Hansen	2	8	3	4	4	2	7
Gannon	0	0	0	0	0	0	0
Henry	0	0	0	0	0	1	0
Team					0		
Totals	29	66	14	15	26	23	72

Louisville	fg	fga	ft	fta	rb	pf	tp
Brown	1	3	0	2	5	4	2
Smith	3	7	7	8	8	2	13
McCray	5	7	4	4	9	2	14
Eaves	2	4	4	5	4	1	8
Griffith	14	21	6	8	5	1	34
Wright	1	2	0	0	3	1	2
Burkman	2	3	3	4	2	3	7
Branch	0	0	0	0	0	0	0
Deuser	0	0	0	0	0	0	0
Cleveland	0	0	0	0	0	0	0
Pulliam	0	0	0	0	0	0	0
Team					0		
Totals	28	47	24	31	36	14	80

Halftime: Louisville 34-29. Officials: Turner, Lembo and Nichols.

Purdue	fg	fga	ft	fta	rb	pf	tp
Morris	5	14	2	2	6	2	12
Hallman	1	7	0	0	7	4	2
Carroll	8	14	1	4	8	3	17
Edmonson	9	16	5	6	3	3	23
B. Walker	1	3	4	5	1	4	6
Stallings	0	0	0	0	0	0	0
Scearce	0	2	0	0	3	0	0
Barnes	1	1	0	0	0	1	2
S. Walker	0	1	0	0	1	4	0
Team					3		
Totals	25	58	12	17	32	21	62

UCLA	fg	fga	ft	fta	rb	pf	tp
Wilkes	2	2	0	0	1	5	4
Vandeweghe	9	12	6	6	5	1	24
Sanders	3	7	6	6	6	2	12
Foster	4	7	1	2	3	5	9
Holton	1	3	2	2	1	1	4
Allums	0	0	0	0	4	3	0
Daye	1	5	4	5	3	2	6
Sims	0	3	0	0	1	0	0
Pruitt	3	7	2	2	1	1	8
Team					3		
Totals	23	46	21	25	30	21	67

Halftime: UCLA 33-25. Officials: Rhodes, Herrold and Weiler.

Championship
March 24

UCLA	fg	fga	ft	fta	rb	pf	tp
Wilkes	1	4	0	0	6	3	2
Vandeweghe	4	9	6	6	7	3	14
Sanders	4	10	2	4	6	4	10
Foster	6	15	4	4	1	3	16
Holton	1	3	2	2	2	2	4
Pruitt	2	8	2	2	6	2	6
Daye	1	3	0	0	1	1	2
Allums	0	0	0	0	2	0	0
Anderson	0	0	0	0	0	0	0
Team					3		
Totals	19	52	16	18	34	18	54

Louisville	fg	fga	ft	fta	rb	pf	tp
Brown	4	12	0	2	7	3	8
Smith	3	9	3	4	2	9	9
McCray	2	4	3	4	11	4	7
Eaves	4	7	0	2	3	3	8
Griffith	9	16	5	8	2	3	23
Burkman	0	1	0	0	1	4	0
Wright	2	4	0	0	4	1	4
Branch	0	0	0	0	0	0	0
Team					3		
Totals	24	53	11	20	36	20	59

Halftime: UCLA 28-26. Officials: Weiler, Lembo and Nichols.

1981 Indiana's Show Goes On

Indiana's physical and spiritual leaders, Isiah Thomas and Coach Bob Knight, were in top form while guiding the Hoosiers to a 63-50 championship-game victory over North Carolina.

The show almost didn't go on. And even after it did, there were those who thought it shouldn't have. Such was the state of the union on the evening of March 30, 1981.

At the time Indiana and North Carolina were scheduled to meet in the national championship game at the Spectrum in Philadelphia, the nation was experiencing a trauma. President Ronald Reagan lay in a Washington, D.C., hospital with gunshot wounds suffered in an assassination attempt that afternoon. The President's press secretary, a Secret Service officer and a Washington policeman also had been struck down.

The NCAA Tournament committee was charged with deciding whether to proceed with the game. If the answer was yes, then NBC, which had covered the aftermath of the attempted assassination to the exclusion of other programming, had to decide whether to telecast it. In Los Angeles, the annual Academy Awards show already had been postponed for 24 hours.

Had the game been postponed, NBC might not have been in position to clear air time. In addition, the Philadelphia 76ers were scheduled to host a National Basketball Association playoff game at the Spectrum the following night. The committee authorized the start of the consolation game between Virginia and Louisiana State while awaiting further word on the President's condition.

It wasn't until Dr. Dennis O'Leary, dean of clinical affairs at George Washington University Hospital, announced that surgery on the President had been successful and he was out of danger that the decision to proceed with the title game finally was rendered. The coaches, Bob Knight of Indiana and Dean Smith of North Carolina, then informed their players, who had been awaiting word in their respective locker rooms. NBC News concluded its live

reporting from the capital at 8:15 p.m., and the network switched to basketball.

The announcers working the game had reservations about the decision and were permitted to express them on the air.

"I had hoped the game would be postponed 24 hours," play-by-play announcer Dick Enberg said.

Al McGuire, the colorful analyst and former Marquette coach whose team had won the championship game four years earlier, was subdued.

"I would have preferred not to go on," he said, "but this is my job."

A moment of silent prayer was inserted in the program, and the national anthem, ordinarily played before the telecast, this time was aired nationally.

Although North Carolina had defeated Indiana, 65-56, on its home court three months earlier and had a superior record, the Tar Heels were decided underdogs. They had finished three games behind Virginia in the Atlantic Coast Conference but had won the ACC Tournament and advanced through the West Regional to the Final Four. Then in the national semifinals, the Tar Heels overcame 7-foot-4 Ralph Sampson and the Cavaliers for the first time in three tries that season, 78-65, with the help of Al Wood's marvelous 39-point performance.

Still, North Carolina's accomplishments paled alongside those of Indiana. After a slow start, the

Sam Perkins (41) and his North Carolina teammates had their moments in the 1981 championship game, but couldn't stay with Indiana. Tar Heel Al Wood (right) gives Isiah Thomas a congratulatory hug.

A big Southern contingent left disappointed when Louisiana State was dismantled by Indiana in a semifinal contest.

Hoosiers rallied to win the Big Ten Conference title on the final day of the season, devastated Maryland by 35 points in a triumphant march through the Mideast Regional and then dismantled a 31-3 LSU team, 67-49, to reach the final.

The Hoosiers were tough and aggressive on defense, in the mold of the best Knight teams and of the coach himself. The day before the championship game, while Reagan still was safe in the White House and the mood of the tournament was upbeat, the Indiana coach had recounted the tale of meeting an abusive LSU fan in the team's hotel after Saturday's semifinal and depositing him in a nearby garbage can. He spread out the Sunday papers before him and read the story aloud, glowing with satisfaction.

The Hoosiers appeared to be outmanned up front, where North Carolina had three big men who could soar and score in forwards Wood and James Worthy and 6-9 freshman center Sam Perkins. But Indiana, which had won the only previous NCAA championship game played in Philadelphia, in the Bicentennial year of 1976, had Isiah Thomas at point guard, and his presence on the floor was something to behold.

Thomas was only a sophomore, and when he smiled, he appeared even younger than his 19 years. Looks, however, were deceptive in Thomas' case. After helping to lead a U.S. team coached by Knight to a gold medal in the 1979 Pan American Games—when he had yet to set foot inside a college classroom—he was acknowledged as something of a child prodigy, and the seniors at Indiana looked to him to make the big play.

His choice of Indiana surprised some because Knight was such a demanding coach and was perceived as someone who would limit Thomas' creativity. But Thomas wanted to improve, to invest his game with structure.

"If I wanted to be an individual," Thomas said, "I could have gone to the 'Y' and played by myself. I don't have to hide myself in the system."

Instead, the system was modified somewhat to accommodate the skills of the 6-1 youngster with the sweet face. It paid off with consecutive Big Ten titles and Indiana's first trip to the Final Four since 1976. A sign in the Indiana student section said it succinctly: "A child shall lead them."

That wasn't necessarily clear at the start of the championship game. Carolina jumped to an 8-2 lead, and after Indiana tied the score at 8-8, the Tar Heels went on an 8-0 run. Less than five minutes into the game, starting forward Ted Kitchel was on the bench with three fouls and the Hoosiers were being repelled by Carolina's zone defense.

With Kitchel on the bench, the addition of reserve guard Jim Thomas to the lineup enabled Indiana to put a quicker defensive player on Wood. The Carolina star finished with a team-high 18 points, but that was less than half his output against Virginia.

Jim Thomas' presence also pushed Randy Wittman, the Hoosiers' 6-6 guard and best outside shooter, to the corner, where the zone was most vulnerable. Indiana was trailing, 20-14, when Wittman took his first shot from the baseline. Just like that, it was 20-16. A minute later, he tied the score at 20-20 with a second corner jumper. Wittman scored again 35 seconds later to create a 22-22 tie.

Isiah Thomas knew exactly what he wanted to do as the half wound down with the Hoosiers trailing, 26-25. He passed the ball to Wittman, once again free in the corner, and the junior did not hesitate. He had been shooting that shot all half. In fact, he had been shooting that shot all the way back to grade school and always, in his mind, for the Hoosiers.

"I'm just one of those guys who loves to shoot," Wittman said. "I've always been that way. When I was little, we always had a basket in the back. I shot all my free time. I have no great quickness. I'm not a great ballhandler, like Isiah. But I can shoot."

And he did. His 18-footer from the right baseline dropped cleanly through the net with one second on the clock and Indiana had its first lead of the game, 27-26. The uphill struggle from the eight-point deficit was over.

"The most important shot of the whole game," Thomas called it.

If it was, it was only because of Isiah's work in the second half. The consensus All-America started by stealing the ball after the Tar Heels controlled

the opening tip and driving for a layup. Then he fed 6-10 Landon Turner for a layup. A second steal and layup preceded a 16-foot jump shot. Isiah followed with another layup and then a 14-foot jumper from the circle. In less than seven minutes, the sophomore scored 10 points and helped to push the Indiana lead to 43-34.

"Isiah went to work on us," marveled Smith, a losing coach in an NCAA final for the third time. "He really broke it open."

Thomas scored 19 of his 23 points and accounted for four steals in the second half. Indiana won convincingly, 63-50. And the star of the show, not unexpectedly, turned out to be Thomas.

"Don't you all realize," said Ray Tolbert, Indiana's 6-9 forward/center who had a game-high 11 rebounds, "that Isiah already is a pro?"

In ability, certainly. In actuality, that transformation would take place the following season when Thomas left school after two years to run the Detroit Pistons' backcourt.

Meanwhile, the country had been treated to a stylish performance and an exciting show on a night of great anxiety. During the game, an announcement of the President's improved condition was made at the Spectrum. And late in the telecast, a news update provided a smile of relief for the NBC staff and those watching at home.

Reporting from Washington for NBC News, John Palmer quoted a message that the President had scribbled on a pad of paper in his hospital room shortly after awaking from surgery.

"All in all," Reagan had written, borrowing W.C. Fields' celebrated comic line, "I'd rather be in Philadelphia."

1981 Tournament Results

First Round
Lamar 71, Missouri 67
Arkansas 73, Mercer 67
Wichita St. 95, Southern U. 70
Kansas 69, Mississippi 66
St. Joseph's (Pa.) 59, C'ghton 57
Boston College 93, Ball State 90
Maryland 81, Tenn.-Chattanooga 69
Ala.-Birm. 93, W. Kentucky 68
Kansas State 64, San Francisco 60
Wyoming 78, Howard 43
Northeastern 55, Fresno State 53
Pittsburgh 70, Idaho 69
Villanova 90, Houston 72
Va. Commonwealth 85, LIU 69
BYU 60, Princeton 51
James Madison 61, Georgetown 55

Second Round
LSU 100, Lamar 78
Arkansas 74, Louisville 73
Wichita State 60, Iowa 56
Kansas 88, Arizona State 71
St. Joseph's (Pa.) 49, DePaul 48
Boston College 67, Wake Forest 64
Indiana 99, Maryland 64
Ala.-Birmingham 69, Kentucky 62
Kansas State 50, Oregon State 48
Illinois 67, Wyoming 65
Utah 94, Northeastern 69

North Carolina 74, Pittsburgh 57
Virginia 54, Villanova 50
Tenn. 58, Va. Com'wealth 56 (ot)
BYU 78, UCLA 55
Notre Dame 54, James Madison 45

Regional Semifinals
LSU 72, Arkansas 56
Wichita State 66, Kansas 65
St. Joseph's (Pa.) 42, Bos. Col. 41
Indiana 87, Ala.-Birmingham 72
Kansas State 57, Illinois 52
North Carolina 61, Utah 56
Virginia 62, Tennessee 48
BYU 51, Notre Dame 50

Regional Finals
LSU 96, Wichita St. 85
Indiana 78, St. Joseph's (Pa.) 46
North Carolina 82, Kansas State 68
Virginia 74, BYU 60

Semifinals
Indiana 67, LSU 49
North Carolina 78, Virginia 65

Third Place
Virginia 78, LSU 74

Championship
Indiana 63, North Carolina 50

STATISTICS

1981 INDIANA

Head Coach—Bob Knight   **Final Record—26-9**

Player	Pos.	Hgt.	Wgt.	Cl.	G	FG	FGA	Pct.	FT.	FTA	Pct.	Reb.	Pts.	Avg.
Isiah Thomas	G	6-1	185	So.	34	212	383	.554	121	163	.742	105	545	16.0
Ray Tolbert	F-C	6-9	225	Sr.	35	177	301	.588	74	100	.740	224	428	12.2
Randy Wittman	G	6-6	205	Jr.	35	155	286	.542	53	69	.768	79	363	10.4
Landon Turner	F-C	6-10	241	Jr.	33	138	246	.561	38	53	.717	122	314	9.5
Ted Kitchel	F	6-8	209	Jr.	34	113	243	.465	88	103	.854	113	314	9.2
Jim Thomas	G	6-3	189	So.	33	47	95	.495	27	35	.771	105	121	3.7
Tony Brown	G	6-2	178	So.	28	38	83	.458	15	28	.536	36	91	3.3
Steve Risley	F	6-8	215	Sr.	31	33	73	.452	28	43	.651	71	94	3.0
Glen Grunwald	F	6-9	207	Sr.	27	21	41	.512	8	13	.615	33	50	1.9
Phil Isenbarger	F	6-8	192	Sr.	26	15	25	.600	13	20	.650	30	43	1.7
Steve Bouchie	F	6-8	228	So.	29	18	47	.383	9	11	.818	35	45	1.6
Chuck Franz	G	6-2	160	So.	21	7	12	.583	14	16	.875	7	28	1.3
Craig Bardo	G	6-5	180	Fr.	4	1	3	.333	2	3	.667	1	4	1.0
Mike LaFave	F	6-9	188	Fr.	15	3	8	.375	5	8	.625	13	11	0.7
Team												170		
Indiana					35	978	1846	.530	495	665	.744	1144	2451	70.0
Opponents					35	793	1820	.436	462	645	.716	1104	2048	58.5

1981 NORTH CAROLINA

Head Coach—Dean Smith   **Final Record—29-8**

Player	Pos.	Hgt.	Wgt.	Cl.	G	FG	FGA	Pct.	FT.	FTA	Pct.	Reb.	Pts.	Avg.
Al Wood	F	6-6	193	Sr.	37	274	522	.525	121	156	.776	233	669	18.1
Sam Perkins	C	6-9	220	Fr.	37	199	318	.626	152	205	.741	289	550	14.9
James Worthy	F	6-9	224	So.	36	208	416	.500	96	150	.640	301	512	14.2
Jimmy Black	G	6-2½	157	Jr.	37	89	167	.533	93	118	.788	54	271	7.3
Mike Pepper	G	6-3	184	Sr.	36	98	189	.519	25	32	.781	53	221	6.1
Matt Doherty	F	6-7	208	Fr.	28	57	125	.456	53	75	.707	84	167	6.0
Jim Braddock	G	6-1½	165	So.	37	39	95	.411	19	23	.826	9	97	2.6
Pete Budko	C	6-9	226	Sr.	23	23	48	.479	1	3	.333	74	47	2.0
Dean Shaffer	G	6-4	194	Sr.	10	3	8	.375	7	10	.700	4	13	1.3
Eric Kenny	F	6-6	216	Sr.	35	13	22	.591	10	13	.769	24	36	1.0
Chris Brust	C	6-8½	218	Jr.	35	11	24	.458	14	24	.583	41	36	1.0
Jeb Barlow	F	6-7	207	Jr.	30	6	15	.400	10	12	.833	16	22	0.7
Cecil Exum	G	6-5	192	Fr.	28	8	20	.400	3	5	.600	7	19	0.7
Team												75		
North Carolina					37	1028	1969	.522	604	826	.731	1264	2660	71.9
Opponents					37	975	2128	.458	394	579	.680	1065	2344	63.4

1981 VIRGINIA

Head Coach—Terry Holland   **Final Record—29-4**

Player	Pos.	Hgt.	Wgt.	Cl.	G	FG	FGA	Pct.	FT.	FTA	Pct.	Reb.	Pts.	Avg.
Jeff Lamp	G	6-6	193	Sr.	33	223	406	.549	154	178	.865	137	600	18.2
Ralph Sampson	C	7-4	219	So.	33	230	413	.557	125	198	.631	378	585	17.7
Lee Raker	F	6-5	201	Sr.	31	148	280	.529	56	75	.747	97	352	11.4
Othell Wilson	G	6-0	182	Fr.	32	78	164	.476	55	71	.775	71	211	6.6
Jeff Jones	G	6-4	190	Jr.	33	77	150	.513	43	52	.827	73	197	6.0
Craig Robinson	F	6-8	200	So.	31	62	158	.392	40	63	.635	137	164	5.3
Terry Gates	F	6-8	225	Sr.	33	33	56	.589	34	53	.642	69	100	3.0
Lewis Lattimore	C	6-9	217	Sr.	30	29	60	.483	26	42	.619	57	84	2.8
Ricky Stokes	G	5-10	165	Fr.	33	19	43	.442	30	42	.714	24	68	2.1
Louis Collins	G	6-5	207	Sr.	18	14	42	.333	2	7	.286	11	30	1.7
Jeff Klein	F	6-5	185	Sr.	18	8	27	.296	11	16	.688	11	27	1.5
Team												78		
Virginia					33	921	1799	.512	576	797	.723	1143	2418	73.3
Opponents					33	824	1901	.433	353	514	.687	1032	2001	60.6

1981 LOUISIANA STATE

Head Coach—Dale Brown   **Final Record—31-5**

Player	Pos.	Hgt.	Wgt.	Cl.	G	FG	FGA	Pct.	FT.	FTA	Pct.	Reb.	Pts.	Avg.
Howard Carter	G	6-5	235	So.	36	233	450	.518	110	137	.803	148	576	16.0
Durand Macklin	F	6-7	205	Sr.	36	223	357	.625	127	180	.706	351	573	15.9
Ethan Martin	G	6-0	170	Sr.	34	131	303	.432	129	172	.750	98	391	11.5
Leonard Mitchell	F	6-7	190	Fr.	36	170	333	.511	50	88	.568	258	390	10.8
Greg Cook	C	6-9	230	Sr.	33	119	211	.564	66	93	.710	175	304	9.2
Willie Sims	G	6-3	200	Sr.	35	107	207	.517	84	121	.694	81	298	8.5
Johnny Jones	G	6-2	170	Fr.	36	46	130	.354	25	49	.510	34	117	3.3
Tyrone Black	C	6-8	200	So.	21	31	60	.517	7	12	.583	35	69	3.3
John Tudor	G	6-5	180	Fr.	33	19	43	.442	27	47	.574	27	65	2.0
Matt England	G-F	6-5	180	Fr.	11	3	14	.214	10	16	.625	10	16	1.5
Brian Bergeron	G	6-3	175	Jr.	19	5	16	.313	13	18	.722	10	23	1.2
Andy Campbell	C	7-2	235	Sr.	12	6	11	.545	4	9	.444	7	16	1.3
Joe Costello	G	6-7	200	So.	14	3	4	.750	1	2	.500	4	7	0.5
Brian Kistler	F	6-6	190	Fr.	8	2	3	.667	0	0	.000	2	4	0.5
Team												84		
Louisiana State					36	1098	2143	.512	653	944	.692	1324	2851	79.2
Opponents					36	971	2060	.471	507	705	.719	1180	2449	68.0

(Louisiana State totals include basket scored by opposing player.)

1981 FINAL FOUR

At Philadelphia
Semifinals

Indiana	fg	fga	ft	fta	rb	pf	tp
Kitchel	3	8	4	4	6	3	10
Turner	7	19	6	7	8	1	20
Tolbert	3	7	1	2	6	3	7
I. Thomas	6	8	2	3	2	4	14
Wittman	3	10	2	2	2	0	8
Risley	0	2	1	2	2	0	1
J. Thomas	0	4	2	2	9	1	2
Bouchie	0	1	0	0	2	0	0
Grunwald	1	2	1	2	2	1	3
Brown	0	1	0	1	0	0	0
Isenbarger	0	1	0	0	0	0	0
Franz	0	0	2	2	0	1	2
LaFave	0	0	0	0	2	1	0
Team					3		
Totals	23	63	21	27	44	15	67

Louisiana State	fg	fga	ft	fta	rb	pf	tp
Mitchell	3	10	3	4	10	3	9
Macklin	2	12	0	0	8	1	4
Cook	3	5	0	0	5	5	6
Martin	2	8	3	3	3	4	7
Carter	5	10	0	0	6	3	10
Sims	2	8	1	2	1	0	5
Johnny Jones	0	2	0	1	2	3	0
Tudor	1	3	4	4	2	3	6
Bergeron	0	0	0	0	0	0	0
Costello	0	0	0	0	0	0	0
T. Black	1	1	0	0	1	0	2
Team					4		
Totals	19	59	11	14	42	22	49

Halftime: Louisiana State 30-27. Officials: Turner, Lauderdale and Moser.

North Carolina	fg	fga	ft	fta	rb	pf	tp
Wood	14	19	11	13	10	3	39
Worthy	2	8	4	7	3	2	8
Perkins	4	7	3	5	9	4	11
Pepper	0	4	0	0	1	2	0
J. Black	4	6	2	3	1	4	10
Doherty	0	1	8	9	4	1	8
Braddock	0	1	0	0	0	0	0
Kenny	1	1	0	0	1	0	2
Team					2		
Totals	25	47	28	37	31	16	78

Virginia	fg	fga	ft	fta	rb	pf	tp
Lamp	7	18	4	4	7	5	18
Gates	1	1	0	0	4	4	2
Sampson	3	10	5	7	9	3	11
Wilson	4	7	0	0	2	4	8
Jeff Jones	5	13	1	1	3	3	11
Stokes	0	2	0	1	3	0	0
Raker	5	9	3	5	5	5	13
Lattimore	1	1	0	0	1	0	2
Team					2		
Totals	26	61	13	15	34	27	65

Halftime Score: 27-27. Officials: Dibler, Kelley and Howell.

Championship
March 30

Indiana	fg	fga	ft	fta	rb	pf	tp
Kitchel	0	1	0	0	0	3	0
Turner	5	8	2	2	6	5	12
Tolbert	1	4	3	6	11	0	5
I. Thomas	8	17	7	8	2	4	23
Wittman	7	13	2	2	4	2	16
Risley	1	1	3	4	4	1	5
J. Thomas	1	4	0	0	4	2	2
Team					2		
Totals	23	48	17	22	33	17	63

North Carolina	fg	fga	ft	fta	rb	pf	tp
Wood	6	13	6	9	6	4	18
Worthy	3	11	1	2	6	5	7
Perkins	5	8	1	2	8	3	11
Pepper	2	5	2	2	1	1	6
Black	3	4	0	0	2	5	6
Budko	0	1	0	0	1	0	0
Doherty	1	2	0	1	4	4	2
Braddock	0	2	0	0	0	1	0
Brust	0	0	0	0	0	0	0
Kenny	0	1	0	0	1	0	0
Team					0		
Totals	20	47	10	16	29	23	50

Halftime: Indiana 27-26. Officials: Turner, Lauderdale and Moser.

1982 North Carolina Hits Jackpot

North Carolina Coach Dean Smith (left) finally got his national championship, but not before John Thompson's Georgetown Hoyas had forced the title game to a dramatic conclusion.

At last, big-time college basketball found a home suitable to its aspirations—a place capable of housing the Big Ten, Big Eight, Big East and Big Sky all under one roof. In 1982, they played the Big Event in the Big Gym.

Its official title was the Louisiana Superdome. But to those who spend the best years of their lives in pursuit of a bouncing ball, any building with a court and backboards at each end forever will be a gym. As it was at the Springfield YMCA, where the first baskets were nailed from the balcony of a running track, so it was at the Final Four. Only the seating capacity had changed, from none to 61,612.

That was Jimmy Black's attitude. Black, a senior point guard from North Carolina, took his first look at the massive facility during a practice session the day before the national semifinals in New Orleans.

"It's just another gym," he decided.

Still, when North Carolina and Houston stepped onto the court for the opening tip in the first game of the doubleheader, it represented a quantum leap for a sport that traced its roots to cramped sweatboxes and basement halls, complete with pillars. In such surroundings, Tommy Heinsohn never would have had to develop his flat-trajectory jump shot, not with the ceiling 19 stories above the floor. This was a building created for Kareem Abdul-Jabbar's

Much of Georgetown's firepower came from high-flying Patrick Ewing (left), who swatted at everything in sight. North Carolina's main man was James Worthy (right), a master at taking the ball to the basket.

sky hook.

It was the spectators who marked the event as a milestone in the sport. They reported to the spacious arena in record numbers even though at least a third were guaranteed a brush with vertigo.

Ironically, Houston had provided America with a glimpse of the future when the Cougars scheduled a regular-season game against mighty UCLA in the Astrodome on January 20, 1968. The promise of a contest between the nation's two best teams and a matchup between Abdul-Jabbar (then Lew Alcindor) and Elvin Hayes drew a crowd of 52,693 fans.

Although few actually saw the Houston upset with their naked eyes—the court was far removed from most of the seats—it remained the largest basketball gathering in the country until the Superdome shootout. The 1968 "Game of the Century" also attracted a nationwide television audience on a hastily assembled independent network.

"I thought it changed college basketball tremendously," said Guy Lewis, the Houston coach in both instances.

From that moment, college basketball and the TV networks that supported it began thinking in bigger terms. The Superdome was the biggest thought yet, and as the decade progressed, domes played an increasingly significant role in the development of the sport.

Although Houston pioneered the concept in the Astrodome, the Cougars did not respond well to the mammoth surroundings or the challenge of North Carolina and became the first college basketball team to suffer defeat in front of 61,000 witnesses. The Cougars battled back to forge a 29-29 tie late in the first half after North Carolina scored the game's first 14 points, but they never took the lead and the Tar Heels went on to a 68-63 victory. In the second game, Georgetown held off Louisville, 50-46.

Their victories created an intriguing matchup for the NCAA title between teams coached by the Tar Heels' Dean Smith and the Hoyas' John Thompson, who were the best of friends. They had first met in 1971, when Smith made a trip to Washington, D.C., to recruit a talented youngster named Donald Washington. Thompson happened to be Washington's legal guardian as well as his coach at St. Anthony's High School.

His first impression, Thompson recalled, was not enthusiastic. Smith seemed too smooth for his taste, too carefully packaged. But Washington was sold on the coach and the school and elected to enroll at Carolina.

Washington had a difficult time. He suffered a broken foot. He experienced academic difficulties. He had emotional problems.

"He was not in a position to help the Carolina program," Thompson said.

Nevertheless, Smith was supportive. He steered Washington to the Denver Nuggets, where former Carolina player Larry Brown was coaching, and later to a European club, where he was able to make the adjustment.

As a result, what had been a nodding acquaintance between the coaches grew into an enduring friendship. Thompson, a 6-foot-10 bear of a man who had starred at center for Providence and later served as Bill Russell's understudy with the Boston Celtics, moved up to Georgetown in March 1972, and four years later he served as Smith's assistant with the U.S. Olympic team in Montreal. When Thompson's son was ready for a basketball camp, he sent him to Smith's. And Smith was not reluctant to call Thompson's home at any hour to discuss basketball and a hundred other topics.

The foundation on which the hardened competitors had built a friendship was strong enough to survive a clash for the national championship.

"It's not a coaches game," said Smith, a reserve on Kansas' 1952 NCAA titlists. "It's a players game. It's not Dean Smith versus John Thompson. If it was, he would take me inside and kill me. We played each other one-on-one at the Olympics and he beat me, 6-0."

Their teams were more evenly matched. Carolina had the better record (31-2) and the top ranking in the polls, but Georgetown (30-6) had played devastating defense in the NCAA Tournament and boasted the most intimidating player in the country in 7-foot freshman Patrick Ewing. The Tar Heels had no one so big or strong, but they did have outstanding 6-9 threats in consensus All-America forward James Worthy and center Sam Perkins. They also had a sensational freshman of their own in guard

James Worthy, who produced 28 points against Georgetown, enjoys the traditional net-cutting honor.

The biggest postgame smile belonged to freshman Michael Jordan (23), who connected for North Carolina's game-winning basket.

North Carolina big men Sam Perkins (left) and James Worthy (52) met up with promising Houston sophomore Akeem Olajuwon in a semifinal contest.

Michael Jordan. Add Georgetown guard Eric (Sleepy) Floyd, another consensus All-America, and the two teams would start five players eventually chosen in the first round of the National Basketball Association draft.

It was Ewing who commanded attention at the outset of the game. The Georgetown strategy was to make Carolina hesitate pushing the ball inside, and to that end the young colossus swatted at every shot he could reach. The result was five goaltending calls in the first half.

"We wanted them to be conscious of Patrick," Thompson said.

Ewing also startled a few people with his offensive ability, and his shooting touch helped propel the Hoyas to a 32-31 halftime advantage. The teams then traded leads—a four-point Georgetown advantage, the last with 12:06 to play, was the biggest—through much of a glorious second half. Floyd and senior forward/guard Eric Smith supported Ewing; Jordan's jump shots complemented Worthy's stunning drives to the basket.

A nine-foot jump shot in the lane by Floyd provided Georgetown with its final lead, 62-61, with 57 seconds remaining. Carolina killed 25 seconds, then called a timeout to set up a play. Though Worthy, a

junior, seemed a logical choice to take the shot, Smith picked Jordan. The freshman did not hesitate when he received the pass on the left side.

"I was all kinds of nervous," he said. "But I didn't have time to think about doubts. I had a feeling it was going to go in."

The jump shot, from 16 feet, dropped cleanly through the hoop and Carolina again had the lead. Fifteen seconds remained, plenty of time for Georgetown to work for the winning basket.

Fred Brown, a sophomore point guard, brought the ball upcourt for the Hoyas. He looked to the left baseline for Floyd, but the Carolina defense shifted quickly and the passing lane was closed. Brown looked toward the middle, but both Ewing and Ed Spriggs were covered. Instinctively, he knew that left Smith open on the right wing.

"I thought I saw Smitty out of the right corner of my eye," Brown said later. "My peripheral vision is pretty good. But this time it failed me. It was only a split second, but that's all it takes to lose a game."

The player Brown thought was his teammate, Smith, turned out to be Worthy.

"I thought he'd try to lob it over me or throw it away from me," Worthy said. "I was surprised that it was right in my chest."

The Hoyas had to survive a semifinal encounter with the high-flying Louisville Cardinals. Georgetown's Patrick Ewing (33) shoots over Louisville's Charles Jones (33).

Worthy caught the ball with five seconds left and dribbled for the other end of the court. By the time Smith could reach and foul him, only two seconds remained. It didn't matter that Worthy missed both free throws because Georgetown only had time for a desperation shot by Floyd that was well off the mark.

Worthy led both teams in scoring with 28 points, including five forceful slam dunks, but the biggest play he made in the game was the result of being in the right place at the right time.

Thompson, ever mindful of his players' emotions, threw his arm around Brown as he came off the court.

"He told me that I had won more games for him than I had lost," Brown recalled. "He said not to worry."

Still, he could not help but relive that errant pass. It was the first question on every reporter's mind.

"I knew it was bad as soon as I let it go," Brown said. "I wanted to reach out and grab it back. If I had a rubber band, I would have yanked it back."

The player appeared remarkably composed. Someone asked how that was possible.

"This is part of growing up," he said. "It was a great game. I loved playing it. I just wish the score was reversed at the end."

But the score, 63-62, favored Carolina and granted Smith his first national title after six empty trips to the Final Four.

"This is one we'll always remember," said Worthy, the Final Four's outstanding player. "It was the one that made us and Dean Smith champions."

It also was a contest that measured up to the building. A Big Game for the Big Gym.

1982 Tournament Results

First Round
James Madison 55, Ohio St. 48
St. John's 66, Pennsylvania 56
Northeastern 63, St. Joseph's 62
Wake Forest 74, Old Dominion 57
Boston College 70, San Fran. 66
Kansas St. 77, No. Illinois 68
Houston 94, Alcorn State 84
Marquette 67, Evansville 62
Tennessee 61, SW Louisiana 57
Indiana 94, Robert Morris 62
Mid. Tenn. St. 50, Kentucky 44
Tenn.-Chatt. 58, N.C. State 51
Wyoming 61, Southern Cal 58
West Virg. 102, No. Caro. A&T 72
Iowa 70, Northeast Louisiana 63
Pepperdine 99, Pittsburgh 88
Louisville 81, Middle Tenn. St. 56
Minnesota 62, Tenn.-Ch'tan'oga 61
Georgetown 51, Wyoming 43
Fresno State 50, West Virginia 46
Idaho 69, Iowa 67
Oregon St. 70, Pepperdine 51

Second Round
No. Carolina 52, James Madison 50
Alabama 69, St. John's 68
Villanova 76, N'th'tern 72 (3 ot)
Memphis State 56, Wake Forest 55
Boston College 82, DePaul 75
Kansas State 65, Arkansas 64
Houston 78, Tulsa 74
Missouri 73, Marquette 68
Virginia 54, Tennessee 51
Ala.-Birmingham 80, Indiana 70

Regional Semifinals
N. Carolina 74, Alabama 69
Villanova 70, Memphis State 66
Boston College 69, Kansas St. 65
Houston 79, Missouri 78
Ala.-Birm. 68, Virginia 66
Louisville 67, Minnesota 61
Georgetown 58, Fresno State 40
Oregon St. 60, Idaho 42

Regional Finals
N. Carolina 70, Villanova 60
Houston 99, Boston Col. 92
Louisville 75, Ala.-Birm. 68
Georgetown 69, Oregon State 45

Semifinals
N. Carolina 68, Houston 63
Georgetown 50, Louisville 46

Championship
N. Carolina 63, Georgetown 62

STATISTICS

1982 NORTH CAROLINA

Head Coach—Dean Smith **Final Record—32-2**

Player	Pos.	Hgt.	Wgt.	Cl.	G	FG	FGA	Pct.	FT.	FTA	Pct.	Reb.	Pts.	Avg.
James Worthy	F	6-9	219	Jr.	34	203	354	.573	126	187	.674	215	532	15.6
Sam Perkins	C	6-9	224	So.	32	174	301	.578	109	142	.768	250	457	14.3
Michael Jordan	G	6-5	189	Fr.	34	191	358	.534	78	108	.722	149	460	13.5
Matt Doherty	F	6-8	210	So.	34	122	235	.519	71	92	.772	103	315	9.3
Jimmy Black	G	6-3	162	Sr.	34	100	195	.513	59	80	.738	59	259	7.6
Jim Braddock	G	6-2	171	Jr.	34	28	62	.452	10	12	.833	17	66	1.9
Chris Brust	F	6-9	231	Sr.	33	23	37	.622	10	22	.455	56	56	1.7
Buzz Peterson	G	6-3	165	Fr.	30	16	41	.390	3	7	.429	14	35	1.2
Cecil Exum	F	6-6	206	So.	17	8	21	.381	3	11	.273	17	19	1.1
Lynwood Robinson	G	6-1	176	Fr.	14	7	11	.636	1	5	.200	3	15	1.1
Jeb Barlow	F	6-8	206	Sr.	28	12	31	.387	4	9	.444	23	28	1.0
Warren Martin	C	6-11	220	Fr.	19	7	15	.467	0	5	.000	16	14	0.7
John Brownlee	F	6-10	215	Fr.	13	4	7	.571	1	5	.200	14	9	0.7
Timo Makkonen	C	6-11	202	So.	12	0	0	.000	2	4	.500	4	2	0.2
Team												59		
North Carolina					34	895	1668	.537	477	689	.692	999	2269	66.7
Opponents					34	811	1742	.466	263	407	.646	873	1885	55.4

(North Carolina totals include basket scored by opposing player.)

1982 GEORGETOWN

Head Coach—John Thompson **Final Record—30-7**

Player	Pos.	Hgt.	Wgt.	Cl.	G	FG	FGA	Pct.	FT.	FTA	Pct.	Reb.	Pts.	Avg.
Eric (Sleepy) Floyd	G	6-3	170	Sr.	37	249	494	.504	121	168	.720	127	619	16.7
Patrick Ewing	C	7-0	220	Fr.	37	183	290	.631	103	167	.617	279	469	12.7
Eric Smith	F-G	6-5	185	Sr.	37	131	273	.480	91	134	.679	113	353	9.5
Anthony Jones	F	6-6	185	Fr.	37	102	207	.493	44	73	.603	104	248	6.7
Mike Hancock	F-C	6-7	180	Sr.	36	99	209	.474	38	55	.691	127	236	6.6
Fred Brown	G	6-5	190	So.	37	67	134	.500	62	95	.653	112	196	5.3
Bill Martin	F	6-7	190	Sr.	35	63	126	.500	46	74	.622	84	172	4.9
Ed Spriggs	C	6-9	240	Sr.	36	39	89	.438	31	46	.674	115	109	3.0
Gene Smith	G	6-2	190	So.	21	8	21	.381	13	18	.722	18	29	1.4
Ron Blaylock	G	6-3	185	Sr.	22	13	36	.361	5	12	.417	20	31	1.4
David Blue	F	6-7	180	Jr.	11	7	14	.500	0	2	.000	8	14	1.3
Kurt Kaull	G	6-3	185	Jr.	19	7	21	.333	4	8	.500	7	18	0.9
Elvado Smith	G	6-2	165	Fr.	8	2	13	.154	3	8	.375	7	7	0.9
James Corcoran	G	6-0	185	Sr.	2	0	0	.000	0	0	.000	0	0	0.0
Team												109		
Georgetown					37	970	1927	.503	561	860	.652	1230	2503	67.6
Opponents					37	757	1808	.419	465	669	.695	1076	1979	53.5

(Georgetown totals include basket on tip-in by opposing player.)

1982 HOUSTON

Head Coach—Guy Lewis **Final Record—25-8**

Player	Pos.	Hgt.	Wgt.	Cl.	G	FG	FGA	Pct.	FT.	FTA	Pct.	Reb.	Pts.	Avg.
Robert Williams	G	6-2	175	Jr.	30	240	504	.476	153	193	.793	64	633	21.1
Clyde Drexler	F	6-6	205	So.	32	206	362	.569	73	120	.608	336	485	15.2
Larry Micheaux	C-F	6-9	220	Jr.	33	177	293	.604	55	95	.579	249	409	12.4
Michael Young	F-G	6-6	210	So.	33	158	358	.441	44	64	.688	179	360	10.9
Lynden Rose	G	6-3	185	Sr.	33	126	222	.568	31	56	.554	49	283	8.6
Akeem Olajuwon	C	7-0	240	So.	29	91	150	.607	58	103	.563	179	240	8.3
Rodney Parker	G	6-0	200	Sr.	17	20	31	.645	8	14	.571	5	48	2.8
Bryan Williams	F	6-7	215	Jr.	22	22	36	.611	5	10	.500	44	49	2.2
Reid Gettys	G	6-6	190	Fr.	19	12	29	.414	18	20	.900	10	42	2.2
Eric Dickens	G	6-1	168	Fr.	14	15	32	.469	1	3	.333	8	31	2.2
Benny Anders	G	6-5	188	Fr.	19	16	41	.390	3	11	.273	16	35	1.8
Eric Davis	G	6-2	180	Sr.	24	12	34	.353	16	23	.696	14	40	1.7
Gary Orsak	F	6-7	200	Fr.	4	3	5	.600	0	5	.000	5	6	1.5
David Bunce	C	6-11	225	Jr.	18	7	16	.438	10	14	.714	22	24	1.3
Team												80		
Houston					33	1105	2113	.523	475	731	.650	1260	2685	81.4
Opponents					33	951	2025	.470	515	737	.699	1141	2417	73.2

1982 LOUISVILLE

Head Coach—Denny Crum **Final Record—23-10**

Player	Pos.	Hgt.	Wgt.	Cl.	G	FG	FGA	Pct.	FT.	FTA	Pct.	Reb.	Pts.	Avg.
Derek Smith	F	6-7	205	Sr.	33	204	346	.590	109	162	.673	199	517	15.7
Jerry Eaves	G	6-4	180	Sr.	33	164	322	.509	88	119	.739	74	416	12.6
Lancaster Gordon	G	6-3	185	So.	33	148	301	.492	53	71	.746	77	349	10.6
Rodney McCray	F-C	6-7	220	Jr.	33	112	196	.571	59	84	.702	234	283	8.6
Poncho Wright	G-F	6-5	195	Sr.	33	85	198	.429	33	44	.750	96	203	6.2
Charles Jones	C	6-8	215	So.	31	60	102	.588	65	92	.707	122	185	6.0
Milt Wagner	G	6-5	185	Fr.	32	63	131	.481	11	19	.579	33	137	4.3
Wiley Brown	F-C	6-8	220	Sr.	31	42	117	.359	36	64	.563	63	120	3.9
Scooter McCray	G-F	6-9	215	Jr.	30	37	96	.385	24	34	.706	101	98	3.3
Manuel Forrest	F	6-7	200	Fr.	20	27	53	.509	8	17	.471	28	62	3.1
Marty Pulliam	C	6-9	225	Sr.	1	1	2	.500	0	0	.000	1	2	2.0
James Jeter	G	6-2	160	Fr.	14	8	20	.400	5	9	.555	5	21	1.5
Danny Mitchell	G-F	6-6	185	Fr.	11	5	15	.333	6	13	.462	14	16	1.5
Greg Deuser	G	6-0	175	Sr.	19	6	24	.250	8	14	.571	13	20	1.1
Kent Jones	G-F	6-2	182	Fr.	5	2	4	.500	1	2	.500	2	5	1.0
Team												87		
Louisville					33	964	1927	.500	506	744	.680	1149	2434	73.8
Opponents					33	835	1857	.450	458	642	.713	1094	2128	64.5

1982 FINAL FOUR

At New Orleans

Houston	fg	fga	ft	fta	rb	pf	tp
Drexler	6	12	5	6	9	3	17
Young	1	7	0	1	3	0	2
Micheaux	8	14	2	3	6	2	18
Rose	10	15	0	2	2	2	20
R. Williams	0	8	2	2	1	1	2
B. Williams	0	1	0	0	1	2	0
Olajuwon	1	3	0	0	6	4	2
Davis	1	2	0	0	3	2	2
Anders	0	2	0	0	0	2	0
Team					5		
Totals	27	64	9	14	33	19	63

North Carolina	fg	fga	ft	fta	rb	pf	tp
Doherty	2	7	1	2	1	1	5
Worthy	7	10	0	0	4	3	14
Perkins	9	11	7	7	10	1	25
Black	1	2	4	6	3	4	6
Jordan	7	14	4	4	5	4	18
Peterson	0	0	0	0	1	0	0
Brust	0	0	0	0	1	0	0
W. Martin	0	0	0	0	0	0	0
Braddock	0	0	0	0	0	0	0
Team					2		
Totals	26	44	16	19	26	14	68

Halftime: North Carolina 31-29. Officials: Dabrow, Dibbler and Nichols.

Louisville	fg	fga	ft	fta	rb	pf	tp
W. Brown	2	5	0	0	1	4	4
D. Smith	4	8	2	4	6	4	10
R. McCray	2	5	4	4	5	5	8
Gordon	1	6	0	0	1	2	2
Eaves	4	9	0	0	4	1	8
Wagner	1	4	0	0	2	3	2
Jones	4	7	0	2	6	0	8
S. McCray	0	1	0	0	0	1	0
Wright	1	3	2	2	0	1	4
Team					2		
Totals	19	48	8	12	27	18	46

Georgetown	fg	fga	ft	fta	rb	pf	tp
E. Smith	6	10	2	4	2	2	14
Hancock	1	3	0	0	2	0	2
Ewing	3	8	2	10	2	4	8
F. Brown	1	3	2	3	3	4	4
Floyd	3	11	7	8	5	4	13
Spriggs	2	2	1	3	7	2	5
G. Smith	0	0	0	0	2	0	0
Jones	2	4	0	0	3	1	4
B. Martin	0	0	0	0	1	0	0
Team					1		
Totals	18	41	14	20	34	16	50

Halftime: Georgetown 24-22. Officials: Forte, Rucker and Wortman.

Championship
March 29

Georgetown	fg	fga	ft	fta	rb	pf	tp
E. Smith	6	8	2	2	3	5	14
Hancock	0	2	0	0	1	0	0
Ewing	10	15	3	3	11	4	23
F. Brown	1	2	2	2	2	4	4
Floyd	9	17	0	0	3	2	18
Spriggs	0	2	1	2	1	2	1
Jones	1	3	0	0	0	0	2
B. Martin	0	2	0	0	0	1	0
G. Smith	0	0	0	0	1	0	0
Team					2		
Totals	27	51	8	9	22	20	62

North Carolina	fg	fga	ft	fta	rb	pf	tp
Doherty	1	3	2	3	3	0	4
Worthy	13	17	2	7	4	3	28
Perkins	3	7	4	6	7	2	10
Black	1	4	2	3	2	4	4
Jordan	7	13	2	2	9	2	16
Peterson	0	3	0	0	1	0	0
Braddock	0	0	0	0	1	0	0
Brust	0	0	1	2	1	1	1
Team					2		
Totals	25	47	13	22	30	11	63

Halftime: Georgetown 32-31. Officials: Dabrow, Dibbler and Nichols.

1983 The Wolfpack Devours Houston

Fast-talking Jim Valvano was on top of the world in April 1983 after his North Carolina State team had completed its Cinderella run to the national championship with a 54-52 victory over Houston.

It was more than a nickname. For the Houston basketball team, it was an identity. The Cougars exulted in their image as high fliers who elevated their sport to unprecedented heights.

These were the brothers of Phi Slama Jama, a fraternity invented by a Houston sportswriter and adopted by a group of players who believed the primary object of the game was to dunk the ball as often as possible.

"We figure the team with the most dunks will win," said 7-foot center Akeem Olajuwon, a native of Nigeria and the focal point of the Cougars' airborne attack.

The team with the most dunks invariably was Houston, which arrived at the Final Four with the top ranking in both wire-service polls and a 25-game winning streak, the longest in the nation. Of the 52 teams invited to the NCAA Tournament—the highest number ever—none appeared capable of stopping Houston.

Not only were the Cougars big—freshman point guard Alvin Franklin was the only starter under 6-6—but they also had extraordinary athletic talent, running the floor with the speed and grace of a National Basketball Association team. Still, what separated the Cougars from their peers was their leaping ability, which enabled them to block shots and score over defenders. To them, a dunk represented a psychological weapon as much as the ultimate high-percentage shot.

As chance would have it, Houston's opponent in the national semifinals was Louisville. The Cardinals not only were ranked second nationally, but also had won the NCAA title three years earlier with a team known as the "Doctors of Dunk." They didn't anticipate being awed or dazzled by acrobatics.

"They won't intimidate us," 6-9 senior Scooter McCray predicted.

When the Final Four teams assembled in mile-high Albuquerque, it was assumed that the NCAA champion would emerge from the Houston-Louisville game. The other semifinal matched two surprise teams. One was Georgia, which had finished tied for fourth in the Southeastern Conference but had won the league's postseason championship to earn its first NCAA Tournament bid. The Bulldogs then had stunned top-seeded St. John's and North Carolina in the East Regional. The other entry, North Carolina State, had suffered 10 defeats but had swept the Atlantic Coast Conference Tournament, staggered past Pepperdine in two overtimes and, finally, squeezed past Virginia, 63-62, in the West Regional final.

"Everybody is saying Louisville-Houston is the heavyweight game and we're the JV game," said N.C. State Coach Jim Valvano, whose team would try to become the first NCAA champion with a double-digit loss total.

The N.C. State-Georgia contest certainly looked like a warmup game to witnesses in University Arena, which natives fondly called "The Pit." Suffering from jangled nerves, Georgia made only 27.8 percent of its shots from the field in the first half and 35.1 percent for the game. Meanwhile, seniors Dereck Whittenburg, Sidney Lowe and Thurl Bailey combined for 50 points and the Wolfpack advanced with a pedestrian 67-60 victory.

Then the fun began. The second game was even better than advertised. In a breathtaking display of speed, power and thrust, Houston up-and-overwhelmed Louisville, 94-81. The fact that the Cougars scored 58 points in the second half to eradicate a five-point halftime deficit was almost secondary to the verve with which they operated.

After a slow first half in which they managed only two dunks, the Cougars held a party above the rim for the final 20 minutes. Twenty-two of Houston's points in the second half were the result of stuffs, a few of such uncommon variety they merited style points. Even a Bulgarian judge might have been moved to award a perfect 10 to 6-7 forward

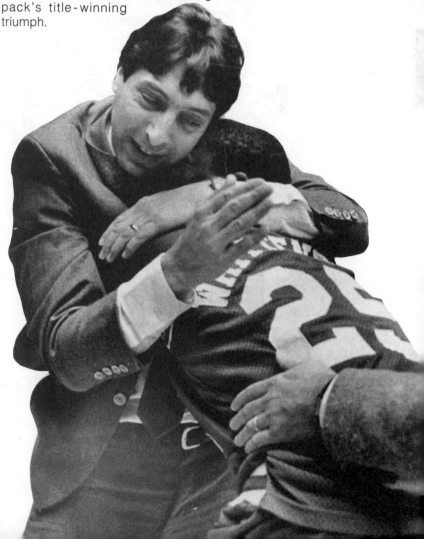

N.C. State Coach Jim Valvano and guard Dereck Whittenburg share an emotional hug after the Wolfpack's title-winning triumph.

Muscular sophomore forward Lorenzo Charles was in the right place at the right time and slammed in Dereck Whittenburg's short desperation jumper as time was running out.

Clyde Drexler and 6-5 forward/guard Benny Anders, who brought down the ball and then brought down the house.

McCray, the Louisville forward/center who thought he had seen everything, reconsidered.

"We've put on a show like that for our fans during preseason," he said, "but never during a real game."

Houston didn't waste its highlights on a preseason or even a pre-game show.

"On behalf of Phi Slama Jama fraternity," said Anders, a sophomore reserve, "we do our best dunks during a game."

Fittingly, a 13-0 Houston run that obliterated the Cardinals' last lead began with successive slams by 6-6 Michael Young, Drexler and Anders. Two free throws by Franklin tied the score at 57-57, and one free throw in two tries by Olajuwon gave the Cougars the lead and set the stage for Drexler, who changed hands on the fly, double-pumped and then threw down a two-handed exclamation point for a 60-57 advantage.

Olajuwon, who had an extraordinary 22 rebounds as well as 21 points, sealed the victory with four stuffs down the stretch. And then Anders provided the finishing touch by completing a three-on-none break with a reverse, two-handed slam.

"I've watched every NCAA Tournament since 1947," said Edward Steitz, secretary-editor of the NCAA Rules Committee, "and that's the most exciting game I've ever seen. And I've never seen so many good athletes, either."

After that astonishing performance, Houston was heavily favored to crush N.C. State and secure its first NCAA basketball title. Of course, the Wolfpack had no intention of getting into a run-and-dunk contest with the Cougars, as Louisville had.

"I've never seen anything like that in 16 years of coaching college basketball," Valvano said. "We'll try to handle their team by playing, shall I say, a slower tempo. If we get the opening tip, we may not take a shot until Tuesday morning."

He was exaggerating, but only slightly. Because of its experience and its outstanding backcourt of Whittenburg and Lowe, N.C. State was superb at controlling the pace of a game. And the Wolfpack had upset so many highly ranked teams en route to the championship game that it appeared unfazed by Houston's pyrotechnics.

"So many things have been happening right for us," said Bailey, a 6-11 forward. "We might be catching them at the right time."

It was clear from the outset that the Wolfpack not only was prepared for the Cougars' high-powered offense, but also had some surprises of its own. For starters, Bailey scored the first basket of

Houston big man Akeem Olajuwon, pictured shooting (left) over N.C. State's Cozell McQueen, was his usual formidable self but couldn't provide enough firepower to give Coach Guy Lewis his first NCAA championship.

the game on, of all things, a dunk. And by limiting fast-break opportunities and packing its zone defense around the basket, N.C. State curtailed Houston's most devastating weapon. Phi Slama Jama didn't manage its first dunk until Olajuwon followed a missed shot with 5:05 left in the first half.

Houston was forced to settle for short jump shots. The frustration was evident in its .313 field-goal percentage in the first half. Meanwhile, after making maximum use of long-range shooting in both the ACC (which was experimenting with the three-point field goal) and throughout the NCAA Tournament, the Wolfpack also was misfiring from outside. But Bailey was superb around the baseline. He scored 11 of his 15 first-half points during a 19-10 stretch that enabled N.C. State to build a 33-25 half-time lead.

More critical to Houston than the deficit were the four personal fouls on Drexler. In the semifinal game against Louisville, Coach Guy Lewis and his staff had lost track of the foul situation on 6-9 Larry Micheaux and allowed the senior forward to foul out with 13:28 remaining. In the title game, Drexler was charged with his third personal just 7:39 into the game but, for some reason, kept playing for almost five more minutes. After being removed with 7:35 left in the half, he was reinserted 98 sec-

onds later, giving him plenty of time to commit his fourth foul.

"I was amazed," Micheaux said.

Drexler began the second half on the bench alongside Micheaux who, for reasons unknown, would play only two of the final 20 minutes. Yet, such was the depth and talent of the Cougars that they outscored the Wolfpack by a 17-2 margin in the first 10 minutes of the second half to assume a 42-35 lead. The upstarts appeared to be reeling when Lewis ordered his team into a delay game.

The coach called it his "locomotion" offense. He wanted the Cougars to spread the court and force N.C. State out of its constrictive zone.

"I have a lot of confidence in that offense," Lewis said. "I felt we could get some layups."

His players did not share in that confidence.

"I felt that we should have kept playing the way we were playing," Micheaux said. "Our game is to get up and down the floor and dunk the ball."

Handcuffed by the slowdown, the brothers of Phi Slama Jama managed only four baskets (one a layup) the rest of the way.

The Wolfpack took advantage of the strategy. Two long jump shots by Lowe sandwiched around a pair of free throws by Drexler pulled the "Cardiac Pack," as N.C. State had become known for its

Georgia's Vern Fleming soars high over North Carolina State's Thurl Bailey for two points in a 1983 semifinal contest won by the Wolfpack, 67-60.

many narrow victories down the stretch, within four, 52-48. Whittenburg took care of that deficit with two jumpers from well beyond the ACC's three-point distance, tying the score at 52-52 with 1:59 to play. Valvano then motioned his players to foul Franklin. The freshman promptly missed the front end of a one-and-one.

Suddenly, the game was N.C. State's to win. It held the ball until the final seconds, hoping to free Whittenburg for an open jump shot. But a pass from Bailey was high, and Drexler managed to slap the ball away. Whittenburg grabbed the ball on the first bounce but was left with a desperation heave of about 30 feet. The shot was short, very short. Olajuwon did not react to the ball, but Lorenzo Charles, a 6-7 sophomore forward who had spent a frustrating night trying to battle the towering center, slid down the lane.

"I knew when Whit let the shot go that it was short," Charles said. "I didn't know where Akeem was, just that he was behind me. I knew I was the closest one to the basketball. I just went up and dunked it."

Actually, he caught the ball in midair and slammed it through with one second remaining. Remarkably, ironically, N.C. State won the game and the championship, 54-52, on a dunk.

"The team with the most dunks wins the game," Lewis had stated on the eve of the final. "That's our slogan."

In the NCAA championship, the team with the most dunks was N.C. State, by the margin of two to one.

1983 Tournament Results

Opening Round
Robert Morris 64, Ga. Southern 54
Alcorn State 81, Xavier 75
Princeton 53, No. Caro. A&T 41
La Salle 70, Boston U. 58
First Round
Maryland 52, Tenn.-Chatt. 51
Lamar 73, Alabama 50
Georgetown 68, Alcorn State 63
Iowa 64, Utah State 59
Purdue 55, Robert Morris 53
Ohio 51, Illinois State 49
Tennessee 57, Marquette 56
Oklahoma 71, Ala.-Birm. 63
Utah 52, Illinois 49
Washington St. 62, Weber St. 52
Princeton 56, Oklahoma State 53
N.C. State 69, Pep'dine 67 (2 ot)
James Madison 57, W. Virginia 50
Va. Com'wealth 76, La Salle 67
Syracuse 74, Morehead St. 59
Rutgers 60, SW Louisiana 53
Second Round
Villanova 60, Lamar 58
Houston 60, Maryland 50
Iowa 77, Missouri 63
Memphis St. 66, Georgetown 57
Kentucky 57, Ohio 40
Arkansas 78, Purdue 68
Indiana 63, Oklahoma 49

Louisville 70, Tennessee 57
Virginia 54, Wash. St. 49
Utah 67, UCLA 61
N.C. State 71, Nev.-Las Vegas 70
Boston College 51, Princeton 42
N. Carolina 68, James Madison 49
Georgia 56, Va. Com'wealth 54
Ohio State 79, Syracuse 74
St. John's 66, Rutgers 55
Regional Semifinals
Villanova 55, Iowa 54
Houston 70, Memphis State 63
Kentucky 64, Indiana 59
Louisville 65, Arkansas 63
N.C. State 75, Utah 56
Virginia 95, Boston College 92
N. Carolina 64, Ohio St. 51
Georgia 70, St. John's 67
Regional Championships
Houston 89, Villanova 71
Louisville 80, Kentucky 68 (ot)
N.C. State 63, Virginia 62
Georgia 82, N. Carolina 77
Semifinals
N.C. State 67, Georgia 60
Houston 94, Louisville 81
Championship
N.C. State 54, Houston 52

STATISTICS

1983 NORTH CAROLINA STATE

Head Coach—Jim Valvano **Final Record—26-10**

Player	Pos.	Hgt.	Wgt.	Cl.	G	FG	FGA	Pct.	FT	FTA	Pct.	Reb.	Pts.	Avg.
Dereck Whittenburg	G	6-1	195	Sr.	22	141	302	.467	64	80	.800	59	385	17.5
Thurl Bailey	F	6-11	214	Sr.	36	250	499	.501	91	127	.717	276	601	16.7
Sidney Lowe	G	6-0	197	Sr.	36	136	295	.461	90	116	.776	134	406	11.3
Ernie Myers	G	6-4	203	Fr.	35	150	336	.446	74	122	.607	89	391	11.2
Lorenzo Charles	F	6-7	225	So.	36	109	201	.542	73	109	.670	215	291	8.1
Terry Gannon	G	6-0	161	So.	36	76	146	.521	56	62	.903	27	261	7.3
Cozell McQueen	C	6-11	215	So.	36	53	123	.431	19	33	.576	200	125	3.5
Alvin Battle	F	6-7	223	Jr.	33	31	74	.419	26	50	.520	66	88	2.7
George McClain	G	6-0	175	Fr.	25	27	72	.375	5	10	.500	13	68	2.7
Mike Warren	F	6-7	177	So.	10	5	8	.625	4	9	.444	11	14	1.4
Quinton Leonard	F	6-8	214	Sr.	8	4	7	.571	3	5	.600	2	11	1.4
Walter Proctor	F	6-8	220	So.	16	7	21	.333	0	4	.000	18	14	0.9
Harold Thompson	F	6-5	213	Jr.	26	6	17	.353	1	2	.500	12	13	0.5
Walt Densmore	F	6-6	203	Fr.	11	0	4	.000	4	11	.363	9	4	0.4
Tommy DiNardo	F	6-5	195	Jr.	4	0	3	.000	0	0	.000	4	0	0.0
Team												102		
North Carolina State					36	995	2108	.472	510	740	.689	1237	2672	74.2
Opponents					36	933	2071	.450	465	664	.700	1214	2435	67.6

Three-Point Field Goals: Bailey 10-15, Gannon 53-90, Whittenburg 39-82, Lowe 44-115, McClain 9-25, Myers 17-51, Warren 0-2, McQueen 0-1; Opponents 104-282.

1983 HOUSTON

Head Coach—Guy Lewis **Final Record—31-3**

Player	Pos.	Hgt.	Wgt.	Cl.	G	FG	FGA	Pct.	FT	FTA	Pct.	Reb.	Pts.	Avg.
Michael Young	F-G	6-6	220	Jr.	34	266	519	.513	56	88	.636	195	588	17.3
Clyde Drexler	F	6-7	210	Jr.	34	236	440	.536	70	95	.737	298	542	15.9
Akeem Olajuwon	C	7-0	240	So.	34	192	314	.611	88	148	.595	388	472	13.9
Larry Micheaux	F	6-9	220	Sr.	34	193	328	.588	82	146	.562	232	468	13.8
Benny Anders	F-G	6-5	188	So.	30	75	150	.500	28	45	.622	48	178	5.9
Alvin Franklin	G	6-2	185	Fr.	30	58	136	.426	28	45	.622	22	144	4.8
David Rose	G	6-3	185	Sr.	31	46	87	.529	18	31	.581	22	110	3.5
Reid Gettys	G	6-7	190	So.	34	46	84	.548	24	34	.706	42	116	3.4
Eric Dickens	G	6-4	170	So.	27	32	84	.381	6	14	.429	10	70	2.6
Derek Giles	G	6-3	175	Jr.	25	14	33	.424	9	19	.474	16	37	1.5
Renaldo Thomas	G	6-4	215	Fr.	13	6	12	.500	6	10	.600	6	18	1.4
Bryan Williams	F	6-7	215	Sr.	23	12	22	.545	3	14	.214	32	27	1.2
David Bunce	C	6-11	225	Sr.	15	6	14	.429	5	7	.714	11	17	1.1
Dan Bunce	C	7-0	235	So.	3	1	2	.500	1	2	.500	4	3	1.0
Gary Orsak	F	6-7	200	So.	11	3	7	.429	4	5	.800	9	10	0.9
Team												78		
Houston					34	1186	2232	.531	428	703	.609	1413	2800	82.4
Opponents					34	883	2037	.433	441	677	.651	1136	2207	64.9

1983 LOUISVILLE

Head Coach—Denny Crum **Final Record—32-4**

Player	Pos.	Hgt.	Wgt.	Cl.	G	FG	FGA	Pct.	FT	FTA	Pct.	Reb.	Pts.	Avg.
Milt Wagner	G	6-5	185	So.	36	227	437	.519	61	86	.709	92	517	14.4
Lancaster Gordon	G	6-3	185	Jr.	36	208	400	.520	76	99	.768	120	492	13.7
Rodney McCray	F-C	6-7	220	Sr.	36	152	259	.587	92	124	.742	304	396	11.0
Charles Jones	C	6-8	215	Jr.	36	134	243	.551	123	184	.668	247	391	10.9
Scooter McCray	F-C	6-9	215	Sr.	36	132	287	.460	65	98	.663	232	329	9.1
Billy Thompson	F	6-8	195	Fr.	36	104	213	.488	53	81	.654	140	261	7.3
Jeff Hall	G	6-4	180	Fr.	36	81	158	.513	17	29	.586	39	179	5.0
Manuel Forrest	F	6-7	200	So.	7	8	28	.286	7	12	.583	21	23	3.3
Robbie Valentine	F	6-6	200	Fr.	19	11	28	.393	2	9	.222	19	24	1.3
Danny Mitchell	G-F	6-6	185	So.	14	5	13	.385	7	11	.636	13	17	1.2
Chris West	G	6-3	175	Fr.	19	4	14	.286	11	17	.647	9	19	1.0
Kent Jones	G-F	6-2	182	So.	5	0	1	.000	4	6	.667	0	4	0.8
James Jeter	G	6-2	160	So.	4	0	1	.000	2	2	1.000	2	2	0.5
Team												83		
Louisville					36	1066	2082	.512	520	758	.686	1321	2654	73.7
Opponents					36	940	2139	.439	409	621	.659	1180	2291	63.6

Three-Point Field Goals: Wagner 2-4, Hall 0-1, Mitchell 0-3, West 0-1; Opponents 2-9.

1983 GEORGIA

Head Coach—Hugh Durham **Final Record—24-10**

Player	Pos.	Hgt.	Wgt.	Cl.	G	FG	FGA	Pct.	FT	FTA	Pct.	Reb.	Pts.	Avg.
Vern Fleming	G	6-5	185	Jr.	34	227	424	.535	121	169	.716	158	575	16.9
James Banks	F	6-6	215	Jr.	33	183	346	.529	95	130	.731	178	461	14.0
Terry Fair	F-C	6-7	210	Sr.	34	174	326	.534	116	175	.663	224	464	13.6
Gerald Crosby	G	6-1	185	So.	34	163	356	.458	44	64	.688	49	373	11.0
Lamar Heard	F	6-5	190	Sr.	34	99	193	.513	41	61	.672	223	240	7.1
Richard Corhen	F-C	6-6	200	So.	34	44	94	.468	54	87	.621	110	142	4.2
Donald Harty	G	6-2	170	Fr.	33	52	100	.520	20	37	.541	25	125	3.8
Derrick Floyd	G	6-3	185	Sr.	30	31	69	.449	25	32	.781	23	87	2.9
Horace McMillan	G-F	6-5	185	Fr.	18	12	29	.414	6	13	.462	18	30	1.7
Troy Hitchcock	C	7-2	190	Fr.	21	10	19	.526	7	17	.412	17	27	1.3
Monroe Jones	G	5-11	170	Jr.	7	2	3	.667	1	2	.500	1	5	0.7
Elfrem Jackson	F	6-6	185	Fr.	2	0	0	.000	1	2	.500	0	1	0.5
Greg Bozman	F	6-7	195	Fr.	5	0	1	.000	0	0	.000	4	0	0.0
Glen Ross	G	6-3	180	So.	2	0	1	.000	0	0	.000	0	0	0.0
Team												105		
Georgia					34	997	1961	.508	531	789	.673	1135	2530	74.4
Opponents					34	909	1894	.480	376	533	.705	1110	2199	64.7

Three-Point Field Goals: Crosby 3, Heard 1, Harty 1; Opponents, 5.

1983 FINAL FOUR

At Albuquerque
Semifinals

N.C. State

	fg	fga	ft	fta	rb	pf	tp
Bailey	9	17	2	5	10	3	20
Charles	2	2	1	2	6	1	5
McQueen	4	5	0	0	13	5	8
Whittenburg	8	18	4	4	0	1	20
Lowe	4	6	2	2	5	3	10
Battle	0	0	0	0	2	0	0
Gannon	1	4	2	2	1	0	4
Team					0		
Totals	28	52	11	15	37	13	67

Georgia

	fg	fga	ft	fta	rb	pf	tp
Banks	5	19	3	5	2	3	13
Heard	3	5	2	3	10	2	8
Fair	2	9	1	2	6	3	5
Crosby	5	15	2	2	1	3	12
Fleming	7	17	0	0	11	4	14
Corhen	3	6	0	1	7	2	6
Hartry	1	3	0	0	0	3	2
Floyd	0	0	0	0	0	0	0
Team					2		
Totals	26	74	8	13	39	20	60

Halftime: North Carolina State 33-32. Officials: Lembo, Weiler and Turner.

Louisville

	fg	fga	ft	fta	rb	pf	tp
S. McCray	5	8	0	0	6	4	10
R. McCray	3	6	2	8	5	4	8
Jones	3	10	6	8	11	3	12
Gordon	6	15	5	6	6	3	17
Wagner	12	23	0	0	2	4	24
Thompson	1	4	4	5	5	4	6
Hall	2	4	0	0	1	0	4
West	0	0	0	0	0	1	0
Valentine	0	0	0	0	0	0	0
Team					4		
Totals	32	70	17	27	40	23	81

Houston

	fg	fga	ft	fta	rb	pf	tp
Drexler	10	15	1	2	7	2	21
Micheaux	4	7	0	1	3	5	8
Olajuwon	9	14	3	7	22	4	21
Franklin	5	8	3	4	1	0	13
Young	7	18	2	3	4	2	16
Gettys	0	0	0	0	1	2	0
Anders	5	9	3	5	6	4	13
Rose	0	2	0	0	0	3	0
Williams	1	1	0	0	0	0	2
Giles	0	0	0	1	0	0	0
Team					1		
Totals	41	74	12	23	45	22	94

Halftime: Louisville 41-36. Officials: Nichols, Housman and Forte.

Championship
April 4

N.C. State

	fg	fga	ft	fta	rb	pf	tp
Bailey	7	16	1	2	5	1	15
Charles	2	7	0	0	7	2	4
McQueen	1	5	2	2	12	4	4
Whittenburg	6	17	2	2	3	1	14
Lowe	4	9	0	1	0	2	8
Battle	0	1	2	2	1	1	2
Gannon	3	4	1	2	1	3	7
Myers	0	0	0	0	1	0	0
Team					2		
Totals	23	59	8	11	34	16	54

Houston

	fg	fga	ft	fta	rb	pf	tp
Drexler	1	5	2	2	2	4	4
Micheaux	2	6	0	0	6	1	4
Olajuwon	7	15	6	7	18	1	20
Franklin	2	6	0	0	0	0	4
Young	3	10	0	4	8	0	6
Anders	4	9	2	5	2	2	10
Gettys	2	2	0	0	2	3	4
Rose	0	1	0	0	1	2	0
Williams	0	1	0	0	4	3	0
Team					1		
Totals	21	55	10	19	44	16	52

Halftime: North Carolina State 33-25. Officials: Nichols, Housman and Forte.

1984 Hoyas Win 'Big' Battle

The 1984 title game revolved around two defensive giants, Georgetown's Patrick Ewing and Houston's Akeem Olajuwon. Ewing rejects a shot (left) by Houston's Rickie Winslow while Olajuwon (right) plays havoc with Virginia's Olden Polynice.

When Patrick Ewing and Akeem Olajuwon walked to the center jump circle for the opening tip of the 1984 NCAA championship game, the situation was familiar even if the opponent was not.

The two most celebrated big men in college basketball were meeting in competition for the first time, but neither was a stranger to the season finale. Two years earlier, when he was named the Big East Conference's Rookie of the Year, Ewing and his Georgetown team had fallen one point short of North Carolina in a thrilling title contest. A year later, Houston had been upset by North Carolina State at the buzzer despite a dominating performance by Olajuwon, then a sophomore. Now the two 7-foot consensus All-Americas were in Seattle's Kingdome to redress the wrongs, to claim the championships that had been denied them.

They had much in common, including a foreign

ancestry, a late introduction to the sport and an assertive court presence that was particularly notable on defense. Ewing was born in Kingston, Jamaica, and his involvement with basketball didn't begin until after he moved with his parents to Cambridge, Mass., at the age of 11. Olajuwon's progress had been even more remarkable. He was a native of Lagos, Nigeria, who hadn't played an organized game until he was 16 and who basically recruited himself for Houston.

Although both players had displayed offensive skills in the course of successful junior seasons, they were at their intimidating best protecting their own baskets.

"They do the same things," Houston Coach Guy Lewis said. "They're close to the same size. They're both good defensive players, rebounders and shot-blockers, and they both cause opposing players to shoot seven or eight percentage points less."

Statistics proved as much. Georgetown had held its opponents to 39 percent field-goal shooting, the lowest mark in the nation, while winning 33 of its first 36 games. With Olajuwon in front of the basket, Houston (32-4 entering the championship game) was not far behind at 42 percent.

"Patrick and Akeem are the two primary figures," Georgetown Coach John Thompson said, "but it won't be just a one-on-one matchup. If you look at team defense, we'd lose a lot of games if Patrick guarded just one person. Those kids are great because they help out a lot of people."

That help was evident in the semifinals. First, Houston held Virginia to a .389 field-goal percentage and defeated the surprising Cavaliers, 49-47, as Olajuwon rose to deflect guard Othell Wilson's driving pass in the lane with two seconds left in overtime. Georgetown was even more efficient and frightening on defense as the Hoyas overcame a seven-point halftime deficit by harassing Kentucky into shooting a dismal 9.1 percent in the second half en route to a 53-40 victory.

The latter exhibition stunned the 38,471 fans, not to mention the confident Kentucky players. The Wildcats had arrived at the Final Four with a stellar front line of 6-8 Kenny Walker, 7-1 Sam Bowie and 6-11 Melvin Turpin, a record of 29-4, realistic expectations of a second title in seven years and a healthy .522 shooting percentage. But after hitting half its field-goal attempts in assuming a 29-22 half-time lead over Georgetown, Kentucky wilted under the application of perhaps the greatest defensive pressure in NCAA Tournament history.

Consider that not a single Kentucky starter made a field goal in the second half. The Wildcats missed

Georgetown seemingly had the championship game well in hand when guard Alvin Franklin began a shooting blitz that brought Houston back.

their first 11 shots after intermission, made one of 22 while the outcome was being decided and finished with three of 33 in the half.

"They took away our inside game," Kentucky point guard Dicky Beal said. "They disguised their defenses well. We'd look for one and they'd switch into another."

With Turpin, Bowie and Walker drifting farther and farther from the basket to avoid Ewing and 6-9 forward Michael Graham, the Wildcats' offense was reduced to perimeter shots. Soon it was reduced to tears.

"Never have we shot or have I seen a team shoot as bad as we did in the second half," Coach Joe B. Hall said. "I can't explain it."

Kentucky preferred to blame itself for its shooting woes rather than credit the Georgetown defense. Even Thompson wasn't sure which came first, the wall or the bricks.

"I don't think our defense can take credit for all of that," he said. "I've never seen a team go that cold."

Still, it was evident that defense boosted the Hoyas into the championship game. Ewing, hampered by foul trouble, scored only eight points on six shots. And Georgetown missed the front end of four consecutive one-and-one situations late in the game. Olajuwon also was quiet on offense, taking just five shots and scoring 12 points in Houston's overtime struggle. The Cougars scored their fewest points of the season against Virginia, while Georgetown's output against Kentucky was its second lowest.

Because these were defensive giants working within a team framework, the individual matchup didn't produce the anticipation surrounding the duels between Houston's Elvin Hayes and UCLA's Lew Alcindor. Hayes and Alcindor were great offensive forces.

"This game doesn't have that feel about it at all," said Lewis, the Cougars' coach even before Hayes arrived in 1964. "It's not the same."

And while Olajuwon expressed an eagerness to test himself against Ewing, the Georgetown pivotman

One of Georgetown's biggest strengths was a deep bench that included Michael Graham, a 6-9 enforcer who hit Houston with an intimidating 14-point effort.

Georgetown Coach John Thompson (left), unemotional as always, cuts the final threads of net after Georgetown's 84-75 victory over Houston in the 1984 championship game. Houston Coach Guy Lewis buries his head in his ever-present towel, reflecting on what might have been.

denied there was any significance to the identity of his opponent.

"It's not Olajuwon against Ewing," he said. "It's Houston against Georgetown."

And so it was. The personal confrontation did not go much beyond the jump ball to start the game. Unlike the semifinal round games, the championship contest was decided by offense and the supporting casts. Georgetown had more of both.

Starting with an 18-foot baseline shot by guard Reid Gettys and three consecutive jumpers by forward Michael Young, Houston connected on its first seven field-goal attempts to take a 14-6 lead. Georgetown then pulled into a 14-14 tie by running off the next eight points. At that stage, Thompson switched the Hoyas into an aggressive man-to-man defense, giving the assignment of Olajuwon to Graham, a freshman who played with a shaved head and a fierce scowl.

After Georgetown had opened a 28-22 lead with the help of three Ewing baskets, the coach removed his center, who had two personal fouls, and ordered his team into a spread offense. The Hoyas weren't stalling. In fact, they went repeatedly to the basket and widened the gap to 40-30 at halftime as Ewing

sat on the bench.

It proved to be a wise decision. Without the benefit of relief, Olajuwon picked up his third foul with 42 seconds left in the half. The problem was compounded 23 seconds into the second half when the Houston star was charged with his fourth personal. Lewis buried his face in his familiar red-and-white polka-dot towel, then benched the center less than two minutes later with his team trailing, 44-34.

But just when it appeared that Georgetown was about to pull away, Alvin Franklin took control of the game. The sophomore guard scored 14 of Houston's next 20 points with an assortment of jump shots, hang-gliding moves down the lane and free throws, rallying the Cougars within three points, 57-54, midway through the half. He finished with a game-high 21 points.

Still, it was not enough. Georgetown had the better reinforcements. Graham and another freshman, 6-7 Reggie Williams, who had been the nation's outstanding high school player the previous year, combined for 11 of the team's 15 field goals in the second half and the Hoyas prevailed, 84-75. The muscular Graham scored 14 points in the game and the slender Williams led Georgetown with 19. Soph-

Georgetown put on a frightening defensive show in the semifinals, holding Kentucky and star Kenny Walker (34) to three second-half field goals.

omore David Wingate added 16 points.

It was little consolation to Olajuwon that he had played Ewing to a standstill on the backboards (both centers had nine rebounds) and outscored his rival, 15-10. At the end, he wept in frustration for the second consecutive year.

Perhaps the happiest Hoya was senior guard Fred Brown, who had made the ill-fated pass in the final seconds of Georgetown's loss to North Carolina two years earlier. He had persevered, and in the final game of his collegiate career, Brown had become a champion.

"I'm just in a very good mood right now," Brown said.

When the last second ticked off the scoreboard, Thompson, who had been quick to console Brown after his 1982 blunder, sought out the senior to hug first. He then faced the media spotlight, at which time a thin smile creased his lips.

"I've had an obsession with winning the national championship—so much so that I'd wake up in the middle of the night saying 'national championship,'" the coach said. "Now I've got the monkey off my back."

1984 Tournament Results

Opening Round
Morehead St. 70, N. Caro. A&T 69
Princeton 65, San Diego 56
Richmond 89, Rider 65
Northeastern 90, Long Island 87
Alcorn St. 79, Houston Baptist 60

First Round
BYU 84, Ala.-Bir'ham 68
Louisville 72, Morehead State 69
West Virginia 64, Oregon State 62
Villanova 84, Marshall 72
SMU 83, Miami (Ohio) 69
Nev.-Las Vegas 68, Princeton 56
Washington 64, Nevada-Reno 54
Dayton 74, LSU 66
Temple 65, St. John's (N.Y.) 63
Richmond 72, Auburn 71
Va. Com'wealth 70, N'eastern 69
Virginia 58, Iona 57
Illinois State 49, Alabama 48
Kansas 57, Alcorn State 56
Memphis State 92, Oral Roberts 83
Louisiana Tech 66, Fresno State 56

Second Round
Kentucky 93, BYU 68
Louisville 69, Tulsa 67
Maryland 102, West Virginia 77
Illinois 64, Villanova 56
Georgetown 37, SMU 36
Nevada-Las Vegas 73, UTEP 60
Washington 80, Duke 78

Dayton 89, Oklahoma 85
N. Carolina 77, Temple 66
Indiana 75, Richmond 67
Syracuse 78, Va. Com'wealth 63
Virginia 53, Arkansas 51 (ot)
DePaul 75, Illinois St. 61
Wake Forest 69, Kansas 59
Memphis St. 66, Purdue 48
Houston 77, Louisiana Tech 69

Regional Semifinals
Kentucky 72, Louisville 67
Illinois 72, Maryland 70
Georgetown 62, Nev.-Las Vegas 48
Dayton 64, Washington 58
Indiana 72, N. Carolina 68
Virginia 63, Syracuse 55
Wake Forest 73, DePaul 71 (ot)
Houston 78, Memphis St. 71

Regional Championships
Kentucky 54, Illinois 51
Georgetown 61, Dayton 49
Virginia 50, Indiana 48
Houston 68, Wake Forest 63

Semifinals
Georgetown 53, Kentucky 40
Houston 49, Virginia 47 (ot)

Championship
Georgetown 84, Houston 75

STATISTICS

1984 GEORGETOWN

Head Coach—John Thompson   Final Record—34-3

Player	Pos.	Hgt.	Wgt.	Cl.	G	FG	FGA	Pct.	FT.	FTA	Pct.	Reb.	Pts.	Avg.
Patrick Ewing	C	7-0	240	Jr.	37	242	368	.658	124	189	.656	371	608	16.4
David Wingate	G-F	6-5	180	So.	37	161	370	.435	93	129	.721	135	415	11.2
Michael Jackson	G	6-1	172	So.	31	115	226	.509	84	103	.816	52	314	10.1
Reggie Williams	G-F	6-7	185	Fr.	37	130	300	.433	76	99	.768	131	336	9.1
Bill Martin	F	6-7	202	Jr.	37	118	232	.509	93	132	.705	219	329	8.9
Michael Graham	F	6-9	210	Fr.	35	69	123	.561	34	74	.459	139	172	4.9
Horace Broadnax	G	6-1	185	So.	35	69	159	.434	29	34	.853	49	167	4.8
Gene Smith	G	6-2	190	Sr.	36	45	88	.511	42	71	.592	74	132	3.7
Fred Brown	G	6-5	208	Sr.	36	36	74	.486	42	65	.646	93	114	3.2
Ralph Dalton	F-C	6-11	240	Jr.	36	37	65	.569	27	47	.574	79	101	2.8
Victor Morris	F	6-9	220	So.	16	10	26	.385	9	15	.600	21	29	1.8
Clifton Dairsow	F	6-7	225	Fr.	18	11	20	.550	9	19	.474	26	31	1.7
Team												92		
Georgetown					37	1043	2051	.509	662	977	.678	1481	2748	74.3
Opponents					37	799	2025	.395	545	821	.664	1129	2143	57.9

1984 HOUSTON

Head Coach—Guy Lewis   Final Record—32-5

Player	Pos.	Hgt.	Wgt.	Cl.	G	FG	FGA	Pct.	FT.	FTA	Pct.	Reb.	Pts.	Avg.
Michael Young	F	6-7	220	Sr.	37	319	637	.501	96	149	.644	231	734	19.8
Akeem Olajuwon	C	7-0	250	Jr.	37	249	369	.675	122	232	.526	500	620	16.8
Alvin Franklin	G	6-2	185	So.	37	160	338	.473	139	173	.803	55	459	12.4
Rickie Winslow	F	6-8	223	Fr.	37	133	233	.571	50	82	.610	203	316	8.5
Reid Gettys	G	6-7	200	Jr.	37	67	136	.493	35	43	.814	66	169	4.6
Benny Anders	F-G	6-5	188	Jr.	27	45	102	.441	24	44	.545	40	114	4.2
Greg Anderson	C	6-10	220	Fr.	35	49	101	.485	19	36	.528	123	117	3.3
Eric Dickens	G	6-1	170	Jr.	34	37	75	.493	23	39	.590	8	97	2.9
Derek Giles	G	6-3	175	Sr.	32	28	63	.444	12	34	.353	24	68	2.1
Braxton Clark	F	6-8	230	Jr.	14	8	20	.400	9	16	.563	23	25	1.8
Renaldo Thomas	G	6-2	190	So.	22	11	24	.458	2	10	.200	11	24	1.1
James Weaver	G	6-4	190	Fr.	11	2	4	.500	7	8	.875	1	11	1.0
Marvin Alexander	G	6-4	190	Jr.	15	4	17	.235	0	1	.000	3	8	0.5
Gary Orsak	F	6-7	220	Jr.	13	2	7	.286	1	3	.333	9	5	0.4
Stacey Belcher	F	6-6	210	Fr.	11	1	4	.250	1	4	.250	9	3	0.3
Team												69		
Houston					37	1115	2130	.523	540	874	.618	1375	2770	74.9
Opponents					37	961	2268	.424	427	620	.689	1282	*2351	63.5

*Includes field goal tipped in by Houston player.

1984 KENTUCKY

Head Coach—Joe B. Hall   Final Record—29-5

Player	Pos.	Hgt.	Wgt.	Cl.	G	FG	FGA	Pct.	FT.	FTA	Pct.	Reb.	Pts.	Avg.
Melvin Turpin	C	6-11	240	Sr.	34	224	378	.593	70	94	.745	217	518	15.2
Kenny Walker	F	6-8	190	So.	34	171	308	.555	80	109	.734	200	422	12.4
Sam Bowie	F-C	7-1	235	Sr.	34	133	258	.516	91	126	.722	313	357	10.5
Jim Master	G	6-5	180	Sr.	33	129	284	.454	60	74	.811	56	318	9.6
Winston Bennett	F	6-7	210	Fr.	34	67	156	.429	88	126	.698	129	222	6.5
Dicky Beal	G	5-11	170	Sr.	30	60	105	.571	70	90	.778	35	190	6.3
James Blackmon	G	6-3	180	Fr.	34	52	114	.456	24	49	.490	42	128	3.8
Roger Harden	G	6-1	165	So.	29	25	68	.368	5	6	.833	36	55	1.9
Tom Heitz	C-F	6-9	220	Jr.	21	10	17	.585	14	20	.700	16	34	1.6
Bret Bearup	F	6-9	230	Jr.	26	13	31	.419	14	21	.667	32	40	1.5
Paul Andrews	G	6-3	180	Fr.	18	9	18	.500	2	4	.500	10	20	1.1
Troy McKinley	F-G	6-6	195	Jr.	11	6	10	.600	0	0	.000	5	12	1.1
Leroy Byrd	G	5-5	145	So.	6	1	2	.500	0	2	.000	1	2	0.3
Team												65		
Kentucky					34	900	1749	.515	518	721	.718	1157	2318	68.2
Opponents					34	796	1894	.420	383	576	.665	1024	1975	58.1

1984 VIRGINIA

Head Coach—Terry Holland   Final Record—21-12

Player	Pos.	Hgt.	Wgt.	Cl.	G	FG	FGA	Pct.	FT.	FTA	Pct.	Reb.	Pts.	Avg.
Othell Wilson	G	6-3	193	Sr.	29	166	337	.493	69	96	.719	111	401	13.8
Rick Carlisle	G	6-5	207	Sr.	33	149	289	.516	67	96	.698	93	365	11.1
Jim Miller	F	6-8	212	Jr.	33	145	302	.480	68	95	.716	125	358	10.8
Olden Polynice	C	6-11	210	Fr.	33	98	178	.551	57	97	.588	184	253	7.7
Tom Sheehey	F	6-9	217	Fr.	33	98	208	.471	45	70	.643	91	241	7.3
Ricky Stokes	G	5-10	169	Jr.	33	69	131	.527	73	92	.793	51	211	6.4
Kenton Edelin	C	6-8	204	Sr.	29	53	78	.679	21	40	.525	185	127	4.4
Ken Lambiotte	G	6-4	185	So.	5	8	14	.571	5	7	.714	7	21	4.2
Tim Mullen	G-F	6-5	194	Jr.	29	46	101	.455	24	37	.649	45	116	4.0
Dan Merrifield	F	6-6	226	Jr.	30	34	82	.415	21	38	.553	51	89	3.0
Kenny Johnson	G	6-0	171	Jr.	7	2	9	.222	3	7	.429	3	7	1.0
Anthony Solomon	G	5-10	160	Fr.	13	2	2	1.000	6	10	.600	3	10	0.8
Team												77		
Virginia					33	870	1731	.503	459	685	.670	1026	2199	66.6
Opponents					33	791	1683	.470	447	635	.704	961	2029	61.5

1984 FINAL FOUR

At Seattle
Semifinals

Virginia	fg	fga	ft	fta	rb	pf	tp
Miller	6	15	0	0	4	2	12
Edelin	1	2	0	0	3	3	2
Polynice	4	7	1	1	7	1	9
Wilson	5	12	2	2	3	2	12
Carlisle	3	14	2	2	6	2	8
Stokes	1	1	0	0	2	4	2
Sheehey	1	3	0	0	1	0	2
Team					3		
Totals	21	54	5	7	29	14	47

Houston	fg	fga	ft	fta	rb	pf	tp
Winslow	4	7	0	0	7	2	8
Young	8	16	1	4	7	1	17
Olajuwon	4	5	4	6	11	3	12
Franklin	2	7	2	2	4	1	6
Gettys	3	7	0	0	3	3	6
Dickens	0	0	0	0	0	0	0
Alexander	0	0	0	0	0	0	0
Totals	21	42	7	12	32	10	49

Halftime: Houston 25-23. End of regulation: 43-43. Officials: Clark, Nichols and Paparo.

Georgetown	fg	fga	ft	fta	rb	pf	tp
Wingate	5	8	1	2	3	0	11
Dalton	0	1	0	0	4	1	0
Ewing	4	6	0	0	9	3	8
Brown	0	1	0	2	4	0	0
Jackson	4	9	4	6	10	2	12
Smith	2	4	1	2	2	5	5
Martin	1	4	0	0	1	1	2
Graham	4	6	0	2	6	3	8
Williams	1	7	0	0	3	3	2
Broadnax	2	4	1	2	1	0	5
Team					2		
Totals	23	50	7	15	43	19	53

Kentucky	fg	fga	ft	fta	rb	pf	tp
Bowie	3	10	4	4	11	3	10
Walker	1	3	2	2	3	3	4
Turpin	2	11	1	2	5	2	5
Beal	2	8	2	2	1	4	6
Master	2	7	2	2	1	1	6
Bennett	1	8	0	0	7	5	2
Blackmon	2	5	1	2	1	3	5
Bearup	0	0	2	2	0	0	2
Harden	0	1	0	0	2	1	0
Team					3		
Totals	13	53	14	16	34	22	40

Halftime: Kentucky 29-22. Officials: Spitler, Tanco and Turner.

Championship
April 2

Houston	fg	fga	ft	fta	rb	pf	tp
Winslow	0	1	2	2	6	4	2
Young	8	21	2	3	5	3	18
Olajuwon	6	9	3	7	9	4	15
Franklin	8	15	5	6	2	3	21
Gettys	3	3	0	0	1	2	6
Anders	2	2	0	2	0	0	4
Clark	0	0	0	0	0	0	0
Anderson	1	1	0	0	2	0	2
Dickens	2	3	1	2	0	5	5
Thomas	0	0	0	0	0	0	0
Giles	0	0	0	0	0	0	0
Weaver	0	0	0	0	0	0	0
Orsak	1	1	0	0	0	0	2
Alexander	0	0	0	0	1	0	0
Belcher	0	0	0	0	0	0	0
Team					3		
Totals	31	56	13	22	29	21	75

Georgetown	fg	fga	ft	fta	rb	pf	tp
Wingate	5	10	6	9	1	4	16
Dalton	0	0	0	0	2	3	0
Ewing	4	8	2	2	9	4	10
Brown	1	2	2	2	4	4	4
Jackson	3	4	5	5	0	4	11
Graham	7	9	0	2	5	4	14
Williams	9	18	1	2	7	2	19
Broadnax	2	3	0	0	0	2	4
Martin	3	6	0	0	2	6	6
Morris	0	0	0	0	0	0	0
Team					7		
Totals	34	60	16	22	37	25	84

Halftime: Georgetown 40-30. Officials: Spitler, Tanco and Turner.

1985 Villanova Pulls A Shocker

The field of teams in the 1985 Final Four was not unlike a Fab Four featuring John, Paul, George and Wayne Newton. One member of the group simply didn't fit.

The sore thumb among the basketball teams was Memphis State, the only surviving club in the NCAA Tournament not affiliated with the Big East Conference. Noting the other regional champions—Georgetown, St. John's and Villanova, all Catholic institutions from the East—Memphis State Coach Dana Kirk claimed a victory of sorts before a shot had been fired.

"We already won the non-Catholic championship of the nation," he declared.

Ironically, the Tigers needed a last-second basket in the Midwest Regional semifinals to overcome Boston College, thereby depriving the Big East of a possible fourth team and a total monopoly of the Final Four. That achievement would have been all the more remarkable in a year when the NCAA Tournament field, reflecting the skyrocketing popularity of the event, inflated to 64 teams, the largest ever.

As it was, no conference ever had advanced as many as three teams to the national semifinals. That this feat was accomplished by the Big East, which had begun competition only five seasons before among schools that never had won an NCAA title, was a tribute to the vision of Big East Commissioner Dave Gavitt. The former Providence coach and athletic director had conceived the idea of a league with ties to the major media markets in the East and then sold it to the administrators of the traditionally independent schools.

The prime locations of the institutions enabled Gavitt to put together a lucrative television package, and before long, the Big East was a financial success. With Georgetown's rise to prominence, the league quickly gained stature for its high quality of play, too. And in 1985, one year after the Hoyas had become the first Big East team to win the national title, the conference had virtually swept the board at the Final Four.

There was no question about the favorite in Lexington, Ky. Georgetown had lost only twice in 36 games, and those losses (to conference rivals St. John's and Syracuse) had come by a total of three points. It was the school's third Final Four appearance in the career of consensus All-America Patrick Ewing, the Hoyas' 7-foot senior center.

"Georgetown is as good a team as has ever been assembled," Villanova Coach Rollie Massimino said on the eve of the semifinals, "and that's only because of Patrick. He's the best to ever play college basketball. When it comes time to make the decision to win or lose in the last four minutes, he's involved in every single defensive play. For that reason, Georgetown is a cut above St. John's and Memphis State." Not to mention Villanova, which had been defeated twice already by Georgetown and three times by St. John's that season. But with their constantly changing defenses, experienced lineup and ability to control the tempo, the Wildcats were a difficult opponent. The absence of a shot clock, which had been utilized during the season but not in the tournament, enhanced their chances.

Villanova faced a test in Memphis State, the Metro Conference champion. The Tigers had won

Standing between Cinderella Villanova and the 1985 national title was Georgetown and big man Patrick Ewing.

The big man in Villanova's drive to the '85 NCAA championship was Ed Pinckney, who is pictured above driving for a basket over Georgetown guard Michael Jackson.

Dwayne McClain, the high-scoring Villanova forward/guard, slams the ball through during championship-game action against Georgetown. McClain finished with 17 points.

31 of 34 games behind 6-10 consensus All-America Keith Lee, 7-foot center William Bedford and 5-10 guard Andre Turner. They had greater firepower than Villanova, but they couldn't solve the Wildcats' defense. And Lee, as he had many times before, spent much of the game in foul trouble and eventually fouled out. Villanova advanced to the championship game, 52-45, holding an opponent under 50 points for the fourth time in five NCAA Tournament games.

Like Memphis State, St. John's was 31-3 entering the national semifinals. The Redmen had been ranked No. 1 in the country after edging Georgetown in January but were overwhelmed, 85-69 and 92-80, in subsequent games against the Hoyas. With 7-foot Bill Wennington and 6-8 Walter Berry up front and consensus All-America Chris Mullin shooting from the perimeter, the Redmen had enjoyed the greatest season in Coach Lou Carnesecca's long tenure.

"We take great pride in our defense," Georgetown Coach John Thompson said, "and Chris Mul-

lin has presented more problems for our defense than any player I've coached against."

But on March 30, before 23,124 fans at Rupp Arena, Georgetown presented one more problem than even Mullin, the college Player of the Year in some quarters, could fathom. His name was David Wingate, and he chased the St. John's star all over the court in the Hoyas' box-and-one defense.

For long stretches of the game, Mullin didn't even touch the ball. He was limited to eight shots and eight points, ending his streak of consecutive games scoring in double figures at 100. He managed one basket in the second half as Georgetown drew away to a decisive 77-59 victory.

More than ever, it appeared that Georgetown was destined to become the tournament's first repeat champion since the final days of the UCLA dynasty.

"I'd have to put them with the great San Francisco teams of Bill Russell and the great Kentucky teams, Alex Groza and that club," Carnesecca said. "I'd also have to put them with the great UCLA clubs and the Indiana team (1976) that had five (future) pros. We tried everything, but when a club like Georgetown is performing at that level of proficiency, there's nothing you can do."

Villanova was not convinced. Although the Wildcats had suffered 10 defeats, they had given Georgetown fits before succumbing, 52-50 in overtime and 57-50. And both of those games were played with a 45-second shot clock.

"Knowing you can take your time is great," said 6-6 Dwayne McClain, the Wildcats' finest marksman. "When you don't have to rush, you can stay fresh. The first two games against Georgetown started like track meets."

On the afternoon of the final, before the team's pregame meal, Massimino addressed his players.

"I told all the kids," he recalled, "to go to their rooms, sit for 15 minutes and tell themselves: 'You're not going to play to lose. You're going to play to win.' I told them: 'You can't play tentative; you can't play scared; you can't play not to lose. You're as good as the team you're playing tonight.'"

For one night, at least, Villanova was as good as any team that ever played the game. That fact began to dawn on the crowd late in the first half as the Wildcats, trailing by only one point, held the ball for a final shot. Thousands of fans rose to applaud the team that had become America's favorite underdog, and they stayed on their feet to celebrate forward Harold Pressley's basket, which boosted Villanova into a 29-28 halftime lead.

The Wildcats had made 13 of their first 18 shots under intense defensive pressure. The obvious question was whether they could maintain that percentage. The answer was no. Instead, they improved upon it. What followed was 20 minutes of near-per-

Guard Gary McLain, who handled the ball flawlessly against the tough Georgetown press, holds up Villanova's hard-earned championship trophy.

fect basketball, as flawless a half as any team had played in the history of the tournament.

The Wildcats attempted 10 field goals in the second half; they made nine. They shot 14 free throws in the final 2:11; they converted 11. And even those numbers don't begin to tell how superbly the Wildcats performed en route to a stunning 66-64 upset.

They had to. Nothing less would have succeeded. Villanova used a 9-2 run early in the second half to build a 38-32 lead. The Wildcats' defense held guard/forward Reggie Williams, who had 10 points in the first half, scoreless and limited Ewing to six points for a game total of 14. Still, the Hoyas came back on the strength of their own defense and Wingate's shooting to take leads at 42-41, 44-43, 46-45 and 54-53, the latter occasion with 4:50 left to play.

In the most crucial stage of the game, Harold Jensen, a 6-5 reserve guard, stepped forward. After the Wildcats had passed the ball around the perimeter for almost 40 seconds, searching for the right man in the right place, Jensen hit an open jump shot from the right wing to reclaim the lead, 55-54, with 2:36 remaining. It was the sophomore's fifth basket in as many attempts, and it was the last field goal Villanova would need.

Wingate was charged with an offensive foul on Georgetown's next possession and the Wildcats went into their delay game, forcing the Hoyas to foul. Ed Pinckney, the senior center who outplayed Ewing in the most important game of his career, hit two free throws to begin Villanova's victory parade. Jensen's four free throws opened a 61-56 lead that Georgetown could not overcome.

Villanova's .786 field-goal percentage was an all-time tournament record—and one team's solution to combating a superior force.

"They're definitely the better team," Pinckney, who was named the Final Four's outstanding player, said of Georgetown. "If we played 10 times, they'd probably win a majority of them."

But only one game is played for the national championship, and on the night of April 1, 1985, Villanova was the equal of anyone. Pinckney had 16 points and six rebounds, McClain knifed through the Georgetown defense for 17 points and senior point guard Gary McLain not only hit all three shots he took from the field, but also turned the ball over just twice against a defense that contested every dribble.

"Without him," Massimino said, "there's no way we win this game."

That the Wildcats did win was a remarkable accomplishment.

"Anytime you shoot that percentage," said Thompson, who had his team stand and applaud the winning players as they mounted the victory stand, "you deserve the praise. You couldn't get much better."

Villanova Coach Rollie Massimino gets a well-deserved victory ride after his team's startling upset of Georgetown in the NCAA title game.

1985 Tournament Results

First Round
Georgetown 68, Lehigh 43
Temple 60, Virginia Tech 57
SMU 85, Old Dominion 68
Loyola (Ill.) 59, Iona 58
Illinois 76, Northeastern 57
*Georgia 67, Wichita State 59
Syracuse 70, DePaul 65
Georgia Tech 65, Mercer 58
Auburn 59, Purdue 58
Kansas 49, Ohio 38
Notre Dame 79, Oregon State 70
N. Carolina 76, Middle Tenn. 57
Michigan 59, FDU-Teaneck 55
Villanova 51, Dayton 49
Maryland 69, Miami (O.) 68 (ot)
Navy 78, LSU 55
Oklahoma 96, N. Carolina A&T 83
Illinois State 58, Southern Cal 55
Ohio State 75, Iowa State 64
Louisiana Tech 78, Pittsburgh 54
Boston College 55, Texas Tech 53
Duke 75, Pepperdine 62
Ala.-Birmingham 70, Mich. St. 68
Memphis State 67, Pennsylvania 55
St. John's (N.Y.) 83, Southern 59
Arkansas 63, Iowa 54
Kentucky 66, Washington 58
Nev.-Las Veg. 85, San Diego St. 80
UTEP 79, Tulsa 75
N.C. State 65, Nevada-Reno 56
Alabama 50, Arizona 41
Va. Com'wealth 81, Marshall 65

Second Round
Georgetown 63, Temple 46
Loyola (Ill.) 70, SMU 57

Illinois 74, *Georgia 58
Georgia Tech 70, Syracuse 53
Villanova 59, Michigan 55
Maryland 64, Navy 59
Auburn 66, Kansas 64
N. Carolina 60, Notre Dame 58
Oklahoma 75, Illinois State 69
Louisiana Tech 79, Ohio St. 67
Boston College 74, Duke 73
Memphis St. 67, Ala.-Birm. 66 (ot)
St. John's (N.Y.) 68, Arkansas 65
Kentucky 64, Nevada-Las Vegas 61
Alabama 63, Va. Commonwealth 59
N.C. State 86, UTEP 73

Regional Semifinals
Georgetown 65, Loyola (Ill.) 53
Georgia Tech 61, Illinois 53
Villanova 46, Maryland 43
N. Carolina 62, Auburn 56
Okla. 86, Louisiana Tech 84 (ot)
Memphis St. 59, Boston Col. 57
N.C. State 61, Alabama 55
St. John's (N.Y.) 86, Kentucky 70

Regional Championships
Georgetown 60, Georgia Tech 54
Vil'nova 56, N. Carolina 44
Memphis State 63, Oklahoma 61
St. John's (N.Y.) 69, N.C. State 60

Semifinals
Villanova 52, Memphis State 45
G'getown 77, St. John's (N.Y.) 59

Championship
Villanova 66, Georgetown 64

*Georgia's participation in the 1985 tournament voided.

STATISTICS

1985 VILLANOVA

Head Coach—Rollie Massimino   **Final Record—25-10**

Player	Pos.	Hgt.	Wgt.	Cl.	G	FG	FGA	Pct.	FT.	FTA	Pct.	Reb.	Pts.	Avg.
Ed Pinckney	C	6-9	205	Sr.	35	177	295	.600	192	263	.730	311	546	15.6
Dwayne McClain	F-G	6-6	195	Sr.	35	206	359	.574	106	137	.774	143	518	14.8
Harold Pressley	F	6-7	210	Jr.	35	166	340	.488	87	135	.644	278	419	12.0
Gary McLain	G	6-0	180	Sr.	35	105	210	.500	69	83	.831	43	279	8.0
Dwight Wilbur	G	6-2	185	Jr.	35	112	240	.467	38	51	.745	69	262	7.5
Harold Jensen	G	6-5	195	So.	32	53	122	.434	39	48	.813	39	145	4.5
Mark Plansky	F	6-7	200	Fr.	30	42	95	.442	16	29	.552	59	100	3.3
Chuck Everson	C	7-1	255	Jr.	32	18	35	.514	13	23	.565	48	49	1.5
Connally Brown	F	6-7	205	So.	21	9	17	.529	10	18	.556	21	28	1.3
Wyatt Maker	C	6-11	245	So.	19	8	22	.364	9	16	.563	19	25	1.3
Veltra Dawson	G	6-1	175	Fr.	18	7	20	.350	2	5	.400	2	16	0.9
Steve Pinone	F	6-4	195	Sr.	9	2	8	.250	1	4	.250	5	5	0.6
Roland Massimino	G	5-10	165	Jr.	17	4	13	.308	0	2	.000	4	8	0.5
Brian Harrington	G	6-0	165	Sr.	11	0	8	.000	3	4	.750	3	3	0.3
Team												70		
Villanova					35	909	1784	.510	585	818	.715	1114	2403	68.7
Opponents					35	904	1932	.468	429	581	.738	1057	2237	63.9

1985 GEORGETOWN

Head Coach—John Thompson   **Final Record—35-3**

Player	Pos.	Hgt.	Wgt.	Cl.	G	FG	FGA	Pct.	FT.	FTA	Pct.	Reb.	Pts.	Avg.
Patrick Ewing	C	7-0	240	Sr.	37	220	352	.625	102	160	.638	341	542	14.6
David Wingate	G-F	6-5	185	Jr.	38	191	395	.484	91	132	.689	135	473	12.4
Bill Martin	F	6-7	215	Sr.	38	196	361	.543	76	117	.650	234	468	12.3
Reggie Williams	G-F	6-7	180	So.	35	168	332	.506	80	106	.755	200	416	11.9
Michael Jackson	G	6-2	180	Jr.	36	104	234	.444	55	75	.733	58	263	7.3
Horace Broadnax	G	6-1	190	Jr.	38	85	197	.431	29	44	.659	65	199	5.2
Perry McDonald	G-F	6-4	190	Fr.	38	64	158	.405	39	86	.453	97	167	4.4
Ralph Dalton	F-C	6-11	240	Sr.	36	39	64	.609	38	59	.644	95	116	3.2
Grady Mateen	C	6-10	210	Fr.	31	30	58	.517	24	40	.600	73	84	2.7
Ronnie Highsmith	F	6-8	225	Fr.	24	23	41	.561	9	22	.409	52	55	2.3
Kevin Floyd	G	6-4	185	Fr.	22	9	23	.391	14	21	.667	18	32	1.5
Tyrone Lockhart	G	5-10	155	So.	15	3	8	.375	3	4	.750	3	9	0.6
Team												133		
Georgetown					38	1132	2223	.509	560	866	.647	1504	2824	74.3
Opponents					38	833	2064	.404	512	733	.698	1160	2176	57.3

1985 ST. JOHN'S

Head Coach—Lou Carnesecca   **Final Record—31-4**

Player	Pos.	Hgt.	Wgt.	Cl.	G	FG	FGA	Pct.	FT.	FTA	Pct.	Reb.	Pts.	Avg.
Chris Mullin	G	6-6	205	Sr.	35	251	482	.521	192	233	.824	169	694	19.8
Walter Berry	F	6-8	215	So.	35	231	414	.558	134	187	.717	304	596	17.0
Bill Wennington	C	7-0	230	Sr.	35	168	279	.602	102	125	.816	224	438	12.5
Mike Moses	G	5-11	160	Sr.	33	70	145	.483	52	66	.788	34	192	5.8
Willie Glass	F	6-6	205	Sr.	35	94	167	.563	58	95	.611	113	246	7.0
Mark Jackson	G	6-4	195	So.	35	57	101	.564	66	91	.725	44	180	5.1
Ron Rowan	F	6-5	210	Jr.	28	37	80	.463	25	33	.758	27	99	3.5
Shelton Jones	F	6-8	200	Fr.	32	32	59	.542	26	42	.619	52	90	2.8
Ron Stewart	F	6-8	212	Sr.	35	24	53	.453	21	38	.553	55	69	2.0
Steve Shurina	G	6-4	185	Fr.	17	4	6	.667	9	11	.818	7	17	1.0
Terry Bross	F	6-8	215	Fr.	17	5	9	.556	7	9	.778	15	17	1.0
Rob Cornegy	C	6-11	210	Fr.	14	2	6	.333	1	2	.500	5	5	0.4
Bob Antonelli	G	6-3	170	Sr.	3	3	5	.600	0	0	.000	3	6	2.0
Team												103		
St. John's					35	978	1806	.542	693	932	.744	1155	2649	75.7
Opponents					35	920	2011	.457	423	603	.701	1043	2263	64.7

1985 MEMPHIS STATE

Head Coach—Dana Kirk   **Final Record—31-4**

Player	Pos.	Hgt.	Wgt.	Cl.	G	FG	FGA	Pct.	FT.	FTA	Pct.	Reb.	Pts.	Avg.
Keith Lee	F	6-10	220	Sr.	35	266	536	.496	156	200	.780	323	688	19.7
William Bedford	C	7-0	220	So.	35	179	330	.542	68	101	.673	265	426	12.2
Andre Turner	G	5-10	165	Jr.	34	154	309	.498	80	112	.714	79	388	11.4
Baskerville Holmes	F	6-7	190	Jr.	35	136	255	.533	63	85	.741	206	335	9.6
Vincent Askew	G	6-5	200	Fr.	35	115	225	.511	59	93	.634	117	289	8.3
Willie Becton	F	6-5	215	Sr.	34	77	148	.520	23	31	.742	114	177	5.2
Dwight Boyd	G	6-3	190	Fr.	34	39	108	.361	22	33	.667	36	100	2.9
John Wilfong	G	6-2	170	So.	28	16	48	.333	18	23	.783	21	50	1.8
Ricky McCoy	G	6-2	180	Sr.	19	7	19	.368	19	25	.760	12	33	1.7
Dewayne Bailey	C	6-9	220	Fr.	27	19	38	.500	6	8	.750	43	44	1.6
David Jensen	F	6-6	215	Fr.	16	7	17	.412	9	11	.818	15	23	1.4
Team												74		
Memphis State					35	1015	2033	.499	523	722	.724	1305	2553	72.9
Opponents					35	911	2152	.423	406	573	.709	1142	2228	63.7

1985 FINAL FOUR

At Lexington, Ky.
Semifinals

Villanova	fg	fga	ft	fta	rb	pf	tp
Pressley	1	8	1	2	6	3	3
McClain	6	9	7	7	4	4	19
Pinckney	3	7	6	9	9	3	12
Wilbur	0	2	0	0	1	1	0
McLain	2	5	5	5	2	1	9
Plansky	1	1	1	3	0	1	3
Jensen	3	6	0	0	4	0	6
Everson	0	0	0	0	0	0	0
Team					1		
Totals	16	38	20	26	27	13	52

Memphis State	fg	fga	ft	fta	rb	pf	tp
Lee	3	9	4	4	7	5	10
Holmes	4	8	0	0	2	5	8
Bedford	4	9	0	0	7	4	8
Turner	5	13	1	2	4	3	11
Askew	1	3	0	1	7	2	2
Wilfong	0	1	0	0	1	1	0
Boyd	0	2	0	0	0	0	0
Bailey	1	1	0	0	0	2	2
Becton	1	4	2	2	5	1	4
Totals	19	50	7	9	33	23	45

Halftime Score: 23-23. Officials: Clougherty, Dibler and McJunkin.

St. John's	fg	fga	ft	fta	rb	pf	tp
Berry	4	8	4	5	6	4	12
Glass	4	4	5	7	2	4	13
Wennington	4	7	4	5	5	2	12
Mullin	4	8	0	0	5	2	8
Moses	3	7	0	0	1	3	6
Bross	0	0	0	0	0	1	0
Jackson	3	4	0	2	2	1	6
Jones	1	4	0	0	2	1	2
Stewart	0	0	0	0	0	2	0
Shurina	0	0	0	0	0	0	0
Cornegy	0	0	0	0	1	0	0
Totals	23	42	13	19	24	20	59

Georgetown	fg	fga	ft	fta	rb	pf	tp
Martin	4	8	4	4	7	4	12
Williams	8	15	4	4	4	1	20
Ewing	7	12	2	4	5	4	16
Jackson	2	5	0	0	4	4	4
Wingate	3	8	6	8	6	2	12
McDonald	0	1	0	0	1	0	0
Floyd	0	0	0	0	1	0	0
Broadnax	3	4	3	4	3	0	9
Lockhard	0	0	0	0	0	0	0
Highsmith	0	1	0	0	1	0	0
Mateen	0	1	0	0	0	0	0
Dalton	2	2	0	0	1	3	4
Totals	29	57	19	24	29	18	77

Halftime: Georgetown 32-28. Officials: Vacca, Rutledge and Burr.

Championship
April 1

Villanova	fg	fga	ft	fta	rb	pf	tp
Pressley	4	6	3	4	4	1	11
McClain	5	7	7	8	1	3	17
Pinckney	5	7	6	7	6	3	16
Wilbur	0	0	0	0	0	0	0
McLain	3	3	2	2	2	2	8
Jensen	5	5	4	5	1	2	14
Plansky	0	0	1	0	1	0	0
Everson	0	0	0	0	0	0	0
Team					3		
Totals	22	28	22	27	17	12	66

Georgetown	fg	fga	ft	fta	rb	pf	tp
Martin	4	6	2	2	5	2	10
Williams	5	9	0	2	4	3	10
Ewing	7	13	0	0	5	4	14
Jackson	4	7	0	0	0	4	8
Wingate	8	14	0	0	2	4	16
McDonald	0	1	0	0	0	0	0
Broadnax	1	2	2	2	1	4	4
Dalton	0	1	2	2	0	1	2
Totals	29	53	6	8	17	22	64

Halftime: Villanova 29-28. Officials: Clougherty, Dibler and McJunkin.

1986 Louisville Uses Secret Weapon

For the seniors on Duke's 1986 basketball team, a humiliating defeat inflicted by Louisville three years earlier was the best gauge of the strides they had made as a team since their freshman year.

"We found out why they were called the 'Doctors of Dunk,'" Duke forward David Henderson recalled. "They put on a clinic."

Louisville, which was tabbed "Doctors of Dunk" in its national championship season of 1980 and was en route to its second consecutive Final Four appearance in 1983, demolished the Blue Devils, 91-76, on Duke's own court. But it wasn't just the score; it was the manner in which the Cardinals manhandled the Blue Devils that made the game unforgettable.

"They really put on a show for the fans," said Mark Alarie, the Blue Devils' other starting forward, "and we were intimidated by their athletic display."

Of the five starters for the 1986 Blue Devils, four were seniors who had suffered through that losing experience as freshmen and gained stature as well as confidence in the intervening years. Henderson, Alarie, guard Johnny Dawkins and center Jay Bilas helped the Blue Devils improve from an 11-17 record that first season to a 37-2 mark and the top ranking in the wire-service polls three years later. On the eve of the 1986 NCAA championship game, Duke already had won more games in one season than any other team in NCAA history.

The Blue Devils no longer looked up to anybody.

"As we've gone through the last four seasons, we've come to realize a dunk is just two points," Alarie said. "We're such a confident group that I don't think athletic skill can intimidate us."

That statement was significant because the next evening, Duke was scheduled to meet none other than Louisville for the national title in Dallas' Reunion Arena. Of course, the Louisville team the Blue Devils were facing wasn't the same one that had overpowered them in 1983. But the Cardinals had plenty of talent, including a strong senior class that featured 6-foot-7 forward Billy Thompson and guards Milt Wagner and Jeff Hall.

The Cardinals had started the season slowly, as

Pervis (Never Nervous) Ellison, a freshman giant, rose to great heights while leading Louisville to its 1986 NCAA Tournament championship-game victory over Duke.

When the 1986 title game got down to the nitty-gritty, Louisville freshman Pervis Ellison took control and made life miserable for Mark Alarie (32) and the other Duke big men.

was their custom, but had qualified for the title game with their 16th consecutive victory, an 88-77 triumph over Louisiana State in the national semifinals. And they had been devastating in the tournament, outscoring opponents by a 99-50 margin over the last six minutes of their previous five games.

Duke had cleared a more difficult obstacle in the semifinals, squeezing past Kansas, 71-67. And for all the Blue Devils' experience, it was the work of a freshman, 6-10 reserve forward Danny Ferry, that ensured their 21st consecutive victory. With the score tied, Ferry nabbed a key defensive rebound that gave the Blue Devils a chance to move in front. He then rebounded an Alarie miss and put it in the basket for a 69-67 lead. He also took a charge with 11 seconds left that spoiled the Jayhawks' last good scoring opportunity.

As it developed, a tall freshman would play a major role in the 1986 championship game, but it would not be Ferry.

At the center of the Louisville offense and defense was a 6-9 youngster named Pervis Ellison. In the course of his high school career in Savannah, Ga., Ellison had acquired a nickname that was both unusual and marvelously appropriate: Never Nervous.

"I'm sure I get nervous at times," he said, "but you've got to get me off the court to get me nervous."

Ellison was 18. He wore braces on his teeth. It seemed almost unfair to send him out against the likes of the 6-8 Bilas and the 6-8 Alarie, who had the shoulders and arms of lumberjacks.

"People say they're not very big," Louisville Coach Denny Crum said, "but stand next to Alarie and Bilas and tell me they're not big. They're men."

It was, however, the smallest of Duke's senior starters who most concerned Crum. The 6-2 Dawkins, a two-time consensus All-America, was an explosive offensive force who was quick enough to play outstanding man-to-man pressure defense. In the team's five previous NCAA Tournament games, Dawkins had scored no fewer than 24 points while

With Louisville's Pervis Ellison (43) towering over him, Duke sharpshooter Johnny
Dawkins scrambles after a loose ball during the 1986 title game.

making 61.5 percent of his field-goal attempts.

He had never been better. And that was fortunate for the Blue Devils because Dawkins' teammates had been mired in a shooting slump. But they continued to play aggressive defense and exercise good judgment on offense. And Dawkins was always there to take control in crucial moments.

The outset of the championship game was one such instance. Dawkins was spectacular. He scored 11 of his team's first 15 points as Duke opened a seven-point gap. In addition, he and junior point guard Tommy Amaker wreaked havoc on defense. They helped force 14 turnovers in the first half (Amaker was credited with five outright steals) as the Blue Devils built a 37-34 lead.

It might have been larger but for the inability of the other Duke players to hit their shots with any consistency and for the persistent inside play of Ellison, whose three baskets late in the half kept the Cardinals within reach. With the play of Wagner and Hall thoroughly disrupted by the Duke backcourt and Thompson fortunate to earn a standoff against Alarie, the freshman suddenly was thrust into the role of leading man.

He responded superbly. Ellison helped the Cardinals gain a 42-41 advantage early in the second half. Dawkins answered that challenge by scoring the next seven points to put Duke ahead, 48-42. Louisville countered by implementing a 1-3 zone defense, with Hall assigned to chase Dawkins around the floor and try to deny him the ball.

"I was happy to see that," Dawkins said. "That leaves other guys open. We've always won in that situation."

In this instance, however, the other guys did not make the open shots. Duke made only 40.3 percent of its shots from the floor in the game. Discounting Dawkins, the other Blue Devils shot a combined 34.9 percent.

"Offense," Duke Coach Mike Krzyzewski said, "is fickle."

Nevertheless, the Blue Devils' defense was consistent enough to maintain a lead for the better part of the second half. It drove Wagner, Louisville's senior leader, to the bench and into an impassioned lecture from Crum. The Cardinals trailed, 61-55, with 7:19 left and appeared incapable of mounting a serious offensive when Ellison began to assert himself.

"I don't think I took charge," he said later in a matter-of-fact tone. "I think it just came my way. There was pressure on Milt and Jeff. That left me mostly man-to-man with my man. They got the ball to me and I just turned and did it."

Smooth and relaxed, Ellison did it to Bilas, who spent much of the game in foul trouble, and Alarie, who eventually fouled out. He made a key layup to pull Louisville within one point, and after the Cards

Duke's Mark Alarie agonizes after being whistled for his fifth foul late in the championship game against Louisville.

finally inched ahead—at 64-63 on Wagner's back-door layup and at 66-65 on Thompson's jump shot from the lane with 2:49 remaining—the freshman made the most significant play of the game.

It occurred after Duke had misfired on seven straight field-goal attempts. Midway through that stretch, Henderson, who sank only five of 15 floor shots in the game, missed a jumper and Dawkins mysteriously, almost heroically, rose above the bigger bodies to snare a vital offensive rebound. But his shot also rolled off the rim. Of his team-high 24 points, Dawkins managed only a pair of free throws in the final 15 minutes.

With Louisville in possession and 48 seconds left to play, Crum called a timeout and diagramed a play for the senior shooters, Wagner or Hall. But once again, Duke's tenacious backcourt forced an ugly shot. Hall's jumper was so far off it didn't even graze the rim. That appeared to confound the Blue Devils' big men, but not the Cardinals' fabulous freshman.

"Ellison got the rebound—as always," Dawkins said in admiration.

Indeed, he plucked the shot out of the air and laid the ball in, boosting the Louisville lead to 68-65. And when Henderson's driving layup rimmed the basket seconds later, Ellison collected another rebound, drew the foul that disqualified Alarie and then sank both ends of a one-and-one with 27 seconds left and only the national title at stake.

The free throws boosted Ellison's game-high total to 25 points. He also grabbed 11 rebounds, second only to teammate Herbert Crook's 12, while leading the Cardinals to a 72-69 victory.

"It's unbelievable a freshman can handle that kind of pressure and play as well as he did," Crum said.

He was so dominating, in fact, that Ellison became the first freshman since Arnie Ferrin of Utah in 1944 to be selected the Final Four's outstanding player. The youngster accepted the award with his usual display of nonchalance.

"I like to take things in stride," he said. "I try not to get too excited because you get too emotional. That tends to wear you down."

It was Duke's seniors who wore down instead. Despite 24 turnovers and only 13 points by Thompson and nine by Wagner, Louisville annexed its second NCAA basketball championship under Crum. The Cards and their coach had a freshman to thank for that.

It was celebration time for Louisville players Milt Wagner (back) and Kevin Walls (front) after the Cardinals' 72-69 title-game victory over Duke.

1986 Tournament Results

First Round

Kentucky 75, Davidson 55	Alabama 58, Illinois 56
Western Kentucky 67, Nebraska 59	LSU 83, *Memphis St. 81
Alabama 97, Xavier (Ohio) 80	Georgia Tech 66, Villanova 61
Illinois 75, Fairfield 51	Auburn 81, St. John's (N.Y.) 65
LSU 94, Purdue 87 (2 ot)	Nevada-Las Vegas 70, Maryland 64
*Memphis State 95, Ball State 63	N. Carolina 77, Ala.-Birm. 59
Villanova 71, Virginia Tech 62	Louisville 82, Bradley 68
Georgia Tech 68, Marist 53	Duke 89, Old Dominion 61
St. John's (N.Y.) 83, Mont. St. 74	DePaul 74, Oklahoma 69
Auburn 73, Arizona 63	Cleve. St. 75, St. Joseph's (Pa.) 69
Maryland 69, Pepperdine 64	Navy 97, Syracuse 85
Nev.-Las Veg. 74, NE Louisiana 51	Kansas 65, Temple 43
Ala.-Birm. 66, Missouri 64	Michigan St. 80, Georgetown 68
N. Carolina 84, Utah 72	N.C. St. 80, Ark.-L'tle R. 66 (2 ot)
Bradley 83, UTEP 65	Iowa State 72, Michigan 69
Louisville 93, Drexel 73	**Regional Semifinals**
Duke 85, Mississippi Valley St. 78	Duke 74, DePaul 67
Old Dominion 72, West Virginia 64	Navy 71, Cleveland St. 70
DePaul 72, Virginia 68	Kansas 96, Michigan State 86 (ot)
Oklahoma 80, Northeastern 74	N.C. State 70, Iowa St. 66
St. Joseph's (Pa.) 60, Richmond 59	Kentucky 68, Alabama 63
Cleveland State 83, Indiana 79	LSU 70, Ga. Tech 64
Navy 87, Tulsa 68	Auburn 70, Nevada-Las Vegas 63
Syracuse 101, Brown 52	Louisville 94, N. Carolina 79
Kansas 71, North Carolina A&T 46	**Regional Championships**
Temple 61, Jacksonville 50 (ot)	LSU 59, Kentucky 57
Michigan State 72, Washington 70	Louisville 84, Auburn 76
Georgetown 70, Texas Tech 64	Duke 71, Navy 50
N.C. State 66, Iowa 64	Kansas 75, N.C. State 67
Ark.-Little Rock 90, Notre Dame 83	**Semifinals**
Iowa St. 81, Miami (Ohio) 79 (ot)	Duke 71, Kansas 67
Michigan 70, Akron 64	Louisville 88, LSU 77
Second round	**Championship**
Kentucky 71, Western Kentucky 64	Louisville 72, Duke 69

*Memphis State's participation in the 1986 tournament voided.

STATISTICS

1986 LOUISVILLE

Head Coach—Denny Crum **Final Record—32-7**

Player	Pos.	Hgt.	Wgt.	Cl.	G	FG	FGA	Pct.	FT.	FTA	Pct.	Reb.	Pts.	Avg.
Billy Thompson	F	6-7	195	Sr.	39	221	384	.576	140	196	.714	304	582	14.9
Milt Wagner	G	6-5	185	Sr.	39	220	444	.495	137	159	.862	122	577	14.8
Pervis Ellison	F-C	6-9	195	Fr.	39	210	379	.554	90	132	.682	318	510	13.1
Herbert Crook	F	6-7	190	So.	39	171	324	.528	119	173	.688	252	461	11.8
Jeff Hall	G	6-4	180	Sr.	39	168	317	.530	65	73	.890	68	401	10.3
Tony Kimbro	F	6-7	190	Fr.	39	91	159	.572	26	44	.591	96	208	5.3
Mark McSwain	F	6-7	220	Jr.	28	32	57	.561	38	53	.717	80	102	3.6
Kenny Payne	F	6-7	195	Fr.	34	52	119	.437	17	22	.773	58	121	3.6
Kevin Walls	G	6-1	170	Fr.	27	16	36	.444	24	32	.750	12	56	2.1
Mike Abram	G-F	6-4	195	So.	17	12	23	.522	5	13	.385	19	29	1.7
Robbie Valentine	F	6-6	200	Sr.	16	9	17	.529	2	4	.500	9	20	1.3
Chris West	G	6-3	175	Jr.	22	6	12	.500	7	14	.500	9	19	0.9
Will Olliges	F	6-9	205	So.	12	2	5	.400	2	2	1.000	7	6	0.5
David Robinson	F	6-8	190	Fr.	5	1	3	.333	0	0	.000	6	2	0.4
Avery Marshall	F-C	6-7	220	Fr.	1	0	1	.000	0	0	.000	1	0	0.0
Team						1	1					89	2	
Louisville					39	1212	2281	.531	672	917	.733	1450	3096	79.4
Opponents					39	1067	2336	.457	560	823	.680	802	2694	69.1

1986 DUKE

Head Coach—Mike Krzyzewski **Final Record—37-3**

Player	Pos.	Hgt.	Wgt.	Cl.	G	FG	FGA	Pct.	FT.	FTA	Pct.	Reb.	Pts.	Avg.
Johnny Dawkins	G	6-2	170	Sr.	40	331	603	.549	147	181	.812	142	809	20.2
Mark Alarie	F	6-8	220	Sr.	40	262	490	.535	162	197	.822	249	686	17.2
David Henderson	F	6-5	195	Sr.	39	217	419	.518	119	160	.744	186	553	14.2
Jay Bilas	C	6-8	225	Sr.	34	76	128	.594	79	134	.590	166	231	6.8
Tommy Amaker	G	6-0	155	Jr.	40	101	225	.449	53	70	.757	80	255	6.4
Danny Ferry	F	6-10	230	Fr.	40	91	198	.460	54	86	.628	221	236	5.9
Billy King	F	6-6	195	So.	40	63	120	.525	35	75	.467	115	161	4.0
Quin Snyder	G	6-2	160	Fr.	32	29	62	.468	16	22	.727	36	74	2.3
Kevin Strickland	G	6-5	190	So.	32	29	78	.372	9	13	.692	37	67	2.1
John Smith	F	6-7	210	Fr.	18	11	24	.458	12	17	.706	26	34	1.9
Weldon Williams	F	6-6	190	Sr.	31	21	46	.457	12	19	.632	39	54	1.7
Martin Nessley	C	7-2	260	Jr.	20	14	36	.389	6	9	.667	38	34	1.7
Team												105		
Duke					40	1245	2429	.513	704	983	.716	1440	3194	79.9
Opponents					40	1082	2268	.477	525	763	.688	1203	2689	67.2

1986 KANSAS

Head Coach—Larry Brown **Final Record—35-4**

Player	Pos.	Hgt.	Wgt.	Cl.	G	FG	FGA	Pct.	FT.	FTA	Pct.	Reb.	Pts.	Avg.
Danny Manning	F	6-11	215	So.	39	279	465	.600	95	127	.748	245	653	16.7
Ron Kellogg	G	6-5	190	Jr.	39	244	442	.552	134	159	.843	132	622	15.9
Calvin Thompson	G	6-6	205	Sr.	39	215	380	.566	94	115	.817	176	524	13.4
Greg Dreiling	C	7-1	250	Sr.	39	180	300	.600	91	128	.711	262	451	11.6
Cedric Hunter	G	6-0	180	Jr.	39	140	249	.562	74	137	.540	141	354	9.1
Archie Marshall	F	6-6	185	Jr.	39	120	233	.515	32	41	.780	149	272	7.0
Mark Turgeon	G	5-10	150	Jr.	39	31	68	.456	30	44	.682	28	92	2.4
Chris Piper	F	6-8	190	So.	39	26	61	.426	25	41	.610	88	77	2.0
Jerry Johnson	F	6-7	190	Fr.	19	7	16	.438	19	32	.594	25	33	1.7
Richard Barry	G	6-2	165	Fr.	17	7	21	.333	9	12	.750	7	23	1.4
Rodney Hull	F	6-7	205	So.	17	6	16	.375	9	14	.643	16	21	1.2
Altonio Campbell	G	5-11	165	So.	15	5	13	.385	4	8	.500	10	14	0.9
Monte Mathis	G	5-10	165	..	5	0	2	.000	2	4	.500	0	2	0.4
Jeff Johnson	F	6-4	175	So.	3	0	0	.000	0	0	.000	0	0	0.0
Team												99		
Kansas					39	1260	2266	.556	618	862	.717	1378	3138	80.5
Opponents					39	1038	2320	.447	557	804	.693	1234	2634	67.5

1986 LOUISIANA STATE

Head Coach—Dale Brown **Final Record—26-12**

Player	Pos.	Hgt.	Wgt.	Cl.	G	FG	FGA	Pct.	FT.	FTA	Pct.	Reb.	Pts.	Avg.
John Williams	F	6-8	237	So.	37	269	540	.498	120	155	.774	313	658	17.8
Derrick Taylor	G	6-0	185	Sr.	38	221	439	.503	81	92	.880	62	523	13.8
Nikita Wilson	F	6-7	200	Jr.	18	90	165	.545	56	71	.789	108	236	13.1
Don Redden	G-F	6-6	213	Sr.	38	197	385	.512	99	117	.846	181	493	13.0
Anthony Wilson	G	6-4	192	Jr.	38	161	332	.485	44	50	.880	109	366	9.6
Ricky Blanton	G	6-6	225	So.	38	94	159	.591	52	80	.650	188	240	6.3
Zoran Jovanovich	C	7-0	247	So.	11	16	34	.471	14	21	.667	31	46	4.2
Jose Vargas	C	6-9	225	So.	37	47	101	.465	17	33	.515	94	111	3.0
Oliver Brown	G-F	6-6	195	Jr.	37	38	79	.481	16	34	.471	78	92	2.5
Bernard Woodside	G-F	6-6	200	So.	31	18	41	.439	11	22	.500	23	47	1.5
Nebosha Bukumirovich	G	6-4	181	So.	28	13	34	.382	12	17	.706	8	38	1.4
Ocie Conley	G	6-1	179	So.	14	4	13	.308	6	10	.600	6	14	1.0
Chris Carrier	F	6-4	208	So.	2	1	1	1.000	0	1	.000	0	2	1.0
Edwin Wilson	G	5-10	150	So.	13	1	4	.250	9	13	.692	0	11	0.8
Team												94		
Louisiana State					38	1170	2327	.503	537	716	.750	1298	2877	75.7
Opponents					38	1113	2257	.493	453	645	.702	1220	2679	70.5

1986 FINAL FOUR

At Dallas
Semifinals

Kansas	fg	fga	ft	fta	rb	pf	tp
Manning	2	9	0	0	5	5	4
Kellogg	11	15	0	0	3	4	22
Dreiling	1	7	4	4	6	5	6
Hunter	2	5	1	4	8	5	5
Thompson	5	12	3	3	5	1	13
Turgeon	1	1	0	0	0	3	2
Marshall	6	10	1	1	2	3	13
Piper	1	1	0	0	1	0	2
Team					3		
Totals	29	60	9	12	33	26	67

Duke	fg	fga	ft	fta	rb	pf	tp
Henderson	3	12	7	8	4	1	13
Alarie	4	13	4	6	8	3	12
Bilas	1	2	5	7	5	2	7
Amaker	2	5	3	4	2	1	7
Dawkins	11	17	2	4	3	3	24
Strickland	0	1	0	0	0	0	0
Ferry	4	5	0	1	3	1	8
King	0	0	0	0	3	3	0
Team					6		
Totals	25	55	21	30	34	14	71

Halftime: Duke 36-33. Officials: Galvan, Clougherty and Finchen.

Louisiana State	fg	fga	ft	fta	rb	pf	tp
Williams	7	17	0	1	9	4	14
Redden	10	20	2	3	6	3	22
Blanton	3	5	3	6	12	4	9
Taylor	7	17	2	2	1	2	16
Wilson	7	15	1	1	3	3	15
Brown	0	1	1	2	3	0	1
Team					1		
Totals	34	75	9	15	35	16	77

Louisville	fg	fga	ft	fta	rb	pf	tp
Crook	8	13	0	1	9	3	16
Thompson	10	11	2	5	10	4	22
Ellison	5	11	1	2	13	3	11
Wagner	8	16	6	6	4	1	22
Hall	6	11	2	2	1	1	14
McSwain	1	2	1	4	2	3	3
Walls	0	2	0	0	0	0	0
Kimbro	0	2	0	0	0	1	0
Team					3		
Totals	38	68	12	17	44	15	88

Halftime: Louisiana State 44-36. Officials: Forte, Paparo and Wirtz.

Championship
March 31

Duke	fg	fga	ft	fta	rb	pf	tp
Henderson	5	15	4	4	4	5	14
Alarie	4	11	4	4	6	5	12
Bilas	2	3	0	0	4	4	4
Amaker	3	10	5	6	2	3	11
Dawkins	10	19	4	4	4	1	24
Ferry	1	2	2	2	4	2	4
Williams	0	1	0	0	0	0	0
King	0	1	0	1	0	2	0
Team					4		
Totals	25	62	19	21	27	22	69

Louisville	fg	fga	ft	fta	rb	pf	tp
Crook	5	9	0	3	12	2	10
Thompson	6	8	1	3	4	4	13
Ellison	10	14	5	6	11	4	25
Wagner	2	6	5	5	3	4	9
Hall	2	4	0	0	2	2	4
McSwain	2	4	1	2	3	1	5
Walls	0	1	0	0	1	2	0
Kimbro	2	4	2	2	2	1	6
Team					1		
Totals	29	50	14	21	39	20	72

Halftime: Duke 37-34. Officials: Nichols, Rutledge and Pavia.

1987 Indiana Passes Bomb Test

The shot heard 'round the nation was not credited to a specific college player or team. It was not notable for the way in which it left a shooter's hands. Nor was it made at a certain stage of a game. All that distinguished this shot was a launching site anywhere behind a line drawn 19 feet, 9 inches from the center of the basket.

The three-point field goal. For the first time since the 1890s, a field goal was worth more than two points—if the shooter was the right distance from the basket.

This radical rule change had many sensible purposes: to unclog the inside under the basket, an area that had become packed by a growing number of zone defenses; to restore the game's traditional balance, which had been thrown out of kilter as teams grew to rely on slam-dunking big men rather than outside-shooting guards, and to increase scoring, which the fans enjoyed watching.

Noble though these intentions were, the rule was praised, cursed, cheered, jeered and hotly debated from the Great Alaska Shootout at Anchorage in November 1986 through the Final Four at New Orleans in March 1987. Virtually everyone associated with the game had an opinion on the subject.

The most common objection to the rule was the shot's length. The National Basketball Association already had instituted a three-point shot, but that line was 22 feet from the center of the basket at its shortest distance.

"Nineteen feet is a Mickey Mouse shot," St. John's Coach Lou Carnesecca said.

Among the three-point shot's most outspoken critics was Indiana Coach Bob Knight. Ironically, Knight coached perhaps the finest marksman in the country, senior guard Steve Alford. Nevertheless, he personalized his dislike by needling Edward Steitz, secretary and editor of the NCAA Rules Committee. Knight identified Steitz as the "father of the three-point field goal" and equated that with being father of the Edsel.

Steitz, the athletic director at Springfield College—the same Massachusetts school where basketball was born—didn't mind the criticism.

"I'm the one that articulates the rules," he said on the eve of the 1987 NCAA championship game.

Indiana's biggest obstacle in the 1987 championship game against Syracuse was 6-foot-10 center Rony Seikaly.

Indiana Coach Bob Knight, the brains behind the Hoosiers' drive to the 1987 NCAA championship, yells instructions to his team during action in the title game against Syracuse.

"I'm also an advocate. I don't deny that."

Early in the season, Steitz noted, the feedback from coaches, fans and the media was largely negative. But he arrived in New Orleans with the results of a recent survey in which 84 percent of those polled endorsed the concept, although not necessarily the distance.

"If it was up to the purists," Steitz said, "we'd still be playing with a jump ball after every basket. I played under that rule, and it was terrible."

The team that made the best use of the three-point shot in its first season was Providence. Top-heavy in backcourt talent and outside shooters, the Friars were suited perfectly to the rule change. To his full-court pressure defense, second-year Coach Rick Pitino added a three-guard offense that stressed the three-pointer. Even on fast breaks, Providence looked to pull up for the jump shot, provided it was beyond the arc.

Providence averaged 8.2 three-point field goals per game, the highest figure in the nation, and in the process underwent a breathtaking transformation. The Friars, who had finished 11-20 only two years earlier, qualified for the NCAA Tournament for the first time since 1978, scored stunning upsets of Alabama and Georgetown in the Southeast Regional and arrived at the Final Four with a 25-8 record.

Nevada-Las Vegas was accustomed to shooting from long range even before the advent of the three-point line. The new rule only enhanced the Rebels' appreciation for the tactic. In the course of a season in which it was ranked No. 1 in the nation and lost only once entering the tournament—and that by a single point at Oklahoma—UNLV averaged 7.9 three-pointers per game, second only to Providence. Trailing Iowa by 18 points with 17:58 remaining in the West Regional final, Coach Jerry Tarkanian's Rebels unleashed a barrage of mortar shots and escaped with an 84-81 victory.

The other two national semifinalists got to New Orleans the old-fashioned way—two points at a time. With 6-foot-10 center Rony Seikaly and 6-9 forward Derrick Coleman dominating the middle, Syracuse upset North Carolina in the East Regional final, 79-75. And Big Ten Conference champion Indiana, which got only a pair of three-pointers from Alford, rallied from nine points down with just over four minutes left to edge Louisiana State, 77-76, in the Midwest final.

Big East Conference rivals Providence and Syracuse met for the third time in the 1987 season in the first game of the semifinal doubleheader, which was staged before an NCAA record crowd of 64,959 fans at the Louisiana Superdome. The result was the same as the first two meetings—Syracuse beat Providence—only worse. The teams combined for 33 turnovers and 18 steals in a sloppy affair. The Or-

Indiana guard Keith Smart goes high to release the dramatic shot that resulted in a 74-73 Hoosier victory over Syracuse in the 1987 NCAA Tournament championship game.

When all was said and done, Keith Smart was riding high and the Indiana Hoosiers were at the top of the college basketball world.

angemen overpowered the Friars on the backboards while limiting the tournament's leading scorer, guard Billy Donovan, to eight points and won in low style, 77-63.

Of utmost significance was the fact that Syracuse triumphed despite taking eight three-pointers and hitting three. Providence attempted 19 from the great beyond, making five. If that statistic eased Knight's fears, it wasn't evident on the sidelines. Spotting Steitz before the Indiana-UNLV semifinal game, Knight told him, "I sure hope your baby doesn't kill us."

On this particular Saturday, however, the three-point field goal was a weapon of self-destruction. The Rebels came out misfiring. They took 14 three-pointers in the first half, just to get loose. Then they added 21 tries in the second half for a total of 35, which represented 42.7 percent of their total field-goal attempts. Thirteen of the bombs were good, including 10 by guard Fred Banks, who scored a game-high 38 points. By contrast, Indiana took four such shots, making two. Indiana won, 97-93, as Alford scored 33 points.

This was a curious Hoosiers team. Alford was the only Indiana native among the starting five, a rare happenstance in a state so proud of its high school programs and basketball heritage. Furthermore, two starters were junior college transfers, a breed of athlete Knight had begun accepting only two years earlier. They were Dean Garrett, a 6-10 center who provided Indiana with its first shot-blocker in years, and point guard Keith Smart, whose quickness and penetration contributed immensely to the team's 29-4 record entering the title game.

Smart's was a remarkable story. He had grown up in Baton Rouge, La., but not nearly as tall as his friends. As a junior in high school, he was only 5-3. He grew to 5-7 as a senior, but that season ended prematurely when he broke his wrist. Not surprisingly, few recruiters were knocking at his door.

"I had the spirit," he said, "but I just didn't have the body."

After a year spent flipping hamburgers at a fast-food restaurant and playing locally, Smart was recommended to the coach at Garden City (Kan.) Community College, where he flourished and grew to 6-1. So after two years of junior college ball and one season at Indiana, he was back home in Louisiana. He had been in the Superdome only once before, he recalled, as a member of a Boy Scout troop that served as ushers at a New Orleans Saints game.

Syracuse (31-6 before the finale) had been a pleasant surprise in the Big East after losing star Dwayne (Pearl) Washington to the pros. In Washington's absence, sophomore Sherman Douglas was a revelation at point guard and the Orangemen became a more balanced team. Seniors Howard Triche and Greg Monroe provided stability, while Coleman

Indiana's Rick Calloway releases some emotion during the postgame awards
presentation that officially proclaimed the Hoosiers 1987 champions.

was a commanding shot-blocker and rebounder. And Seikaly, who had been raised in Lebanon and Greece, had made tremendous progress at center in the course of the tournament.

The biggest task faced by the Orangemen was defending Alford, who moved constantly without the ball and used the screens in Indiana's motion offense to free himself for his accurate jump shot.

"He's gotten more out of his ability offensively than anybody I've ever seen," marveled Knight, who generally reserved his praise for after a player's graduation. "He doesn't tip in shots, he doesn't post, he doesn't drive a lot. He's got 2,400 points and he's just a jump shooter. He totally amazes me."

Alford, a four-year star and two-time consensus All-America, demonstrated how he became Indiana's all-time leading scorer in the first half. He hit four of five three-point attempts, including two in the final two minutes, to lift the Hoosiers to a 34-33 halftime lead against the Orangemen. Syracuse had tried a variety of defenses, switching from a 2-3 zone to a man-to-man to a box-and-one, with the 6-5 Triche shadowing Alford. The latter method proved effective in the second half when he was held scoreless after his layup tied the score at 65-65 with 4:01 left to play.

But Syracuse paid a price for such diligent work on Alford, who finished with 23 points.

"I've said all year long we're too good a team to have people just trying to contain me," Alford said.

The end of the game belonged to Smart, who scored 12 of the Hoosiers' final 15 points.

Still, Smart's heroics would not have been sufficient had the Orangemen been able to hit key free throws. With 38 seconds left and Syracuse leading, 73-70, Triche missed the back end of a one-and-one opportunity. After Smart drove the lane for a leaning eight-foot jumper to bring the Hoosiers within one point, Coleman, the precocious freshman who had a game-high 19 rebounds, was fouled and missed the front end of a one-and-one. Indiana grabbed the uncontested rebound and had a chance to win at the end.

The Hoosiers looked to Alford for the final shot, but he was blanketed. Smart passed to burly forward Daryl Thomas, who had Coleman on his back. As Triche moved inside to double-team Thomas, the forward flipped it back to Smart, who was cutting left toward the baseline. He took the pass and shot over a lunging Triche in the same motion. The 16-foot jumper swished through the net with five seconds left, presenting Indiana with its fifth NCAA championship and Knight with his third, a total exceeded only by John Wooden (10) and Adolph Rupp (four).

"I wasn't surprised I got the ball," the exuberant Smart said. "I was surprised it went in."

The season of the three-point field goal had ended

with a two-point basket and a sensational one-point victory, 74-73. But Indiana did need the three-pointer to win. The Hoosiers hit seven baskets from beyond the line, all by Alford, to just four by Syracuse. That was a net gain of three points.

"If not for the three-pointer," Syracuse Coach Jim Boeheim said, "we'd be national champions."

Knight was amused by the irony. And he recalled a conversation with Steitz back in the spring.

"He told me," Knight related, "'We put in the rule so you could win the national championship with Steve Alford.'"

The coach smiled and said, "Thanks, Ed."

Sharpshooter Steve Alford celebrates with his mother after Indiana's victory.

1987 Tournament Results

First Round

Purdue 104, Northeastern 95	Syracuse 104, W. Kentucky 86
Florida 82, N.C. State 70	DePaul 83, St. John's 75 (ot)
W. Kentucky 64, W. Virginia 62	LSU 72, Temple 62
Syracuse 79, Georgia Southern 73	Georgetown 82, Ohio St. 79
Temple 75, Southern U. 56	Kansas 67, SW Missouri State 63
LSU 85, Georgia Tech 79	Oklahoma 96, Pittsburgh 93
St. John's 57, Wichita St. 55	Iowa 84, Texas-El Paso 82
DePaul 76, Louisiana Tech 62	Notre Dame 58, TCU 57
SW Missouri St. 65, Clemson 60	N. Carolina 109, Michigan 97
Kansas 66, Houston 55	Indiana 107, Auburn 90
Georgetown 75, Bucknell 53	Duke 65, Xavier, Ohio 60
Ohio St. 91, Kentucky 77	Provid'ce 90, Austin Peay 87 (ot)
Iowa 99, Santa Clara 76	Alabama 101, New Orleans 76
Texas-El Paso 98, Arizona 91 (ot)	Nev.-Las Vegas 80, Kansas St. 61
Pittsburgh 93, Marist 68	Wyoming 78, UCLA 68
Oklahoma 74, Tulsa 69	**Regional Semifinals**
TCU 76, Marshall 60	Syracuse 87, Florida 81
Notre Dame 84, Mid. Tenn. St. 71	N. Carolina 74, Notre Dame 68
Michigan 97, Navy 82	LSU 63, DePaul 58
N. Carolina 113, Pennsylvania 82	Indiana 88, Duke 82
Xavier, Ohio 70, Missouri 69	Providence 103, Alabama 82
Duke 58, Texas A&M 51	Georgetown 70, Kansas 57
Auburn 62, San Diego 61	Iowa 93, Oklahoma 91 (ot)
Indiana 92, Fairfield 58	Nev.-Las Vegas 92, Wyoming 78
New Orleans 83, BYU 79	**Regional Championships**
Alabama 88, N. Carolina A&T 71	Syracuse 79, N. Carolina 75
Austin Peay 68, Illinois 67	Indiana 77, LSU 76
Providence 90, Ala.-Birmingham 68	Providence 88, Georgetown 73
Kansas State 82, Georgia 79 (ot)	Nev.-Las Vegas 84, Iowa 81
Nev.-Las Vegas 95, Idaho State 70	**Semifinals**
UCLA 92, Central Michigan 73	Syracuse 77, Providence 63
Wyoming 64, Virginia 60	Indiana 97, Nev.-Las Vegas 93
Second Round	**Championship**
Florida 85, Purdue 66	Indiana 74, Syracuse 73

STATISTICS

1987 INDIANA

Head Coach—Bob Knight   **Final Record—30-4**

Player	Pos.	Hgt.	Wgt.	Cl.	G	FG	FGA	Pct.	FT	FTA	Pct.	Reb.	Pts.	Avg.
Steve Alford	G	6-2	183	Sr.	34	241	508	.474	160	180	.889	87	749	22.0
Daryl Thomas	F	6-7	236	Sr.	34	199	370	.538	136	173	.786	194	534	15.7
Rick Calloway	F	6-6	190	So.	29	146	275	.531	72	97	.742	126	364	12.6
Dean Garrett	C	6-10	222	Jr.	34	163	301	.542	61	96	.635	288	387	11.4
Keith Smart	G	6-1	175	Jr.	34	148	286	.517	74	88	.841	100	382	11.2
Magnus Pelkowski	C	6-10	218	Jr.	14	24	46	.522	3	5	.600	27	53	3.8
Steve Eyl	F	6-6	216	Jr.	34	35	54	.648	31	46	.674	116	101	3.0
Joe Hillman	G	6-2	184	Jr.	32	28	58	.483	23	31	.742	37	80	2.5
Tony Freeman	G	5-7	144	Fr.	16	10	24	.417	14	20	.700	14	35	2.2
Brian Sloan	F-C	6-8	210	Jr.	17	13	29	.448	9	18	.500	19	35	2.1
Kreigh Smith	G-F	6-7	221	Jr.	25	12	24	.500	6	7	.857	19	37	1.5
Jeff Oliphant	G	6-5	200	So.	2	0	0	.000	3	5	.600	4	3	1.5
Todd Meier	F-C	6-8	222	Sr.	29	9	20	.450	13	22	.591	43	31	1.1
Dave Minor	F	6-5	203	Fr.	18	5	20	.250	5	7	.714	15	15	0.8
Team												100		
Indiana					34	1033	2015	.513	610	795	.767	1189	2806	82.5
Opponents					34	937	2077	.451	420	620	.677	1179	2412	70.9

Three-Point Field Goals: Alford 107-202, Smart 12-33, Hillman 1-5, Pelkowski 2-3, Smith 7-8, Freeman 1-4, Sloan 0-1; Opponents 118-307.

1987 SYRACUSE

Head Coach—Jim Boeheim   **Final Record—31-7**

Player	Pos.	Hgt.	Wgt.	Cl.	G	FG	FGA	Pct.	FT	FTA	Pct.	Reb.	Pts.	Avg.
Sherman Douglas	G	6-1	170	So.	38	246	463	.531	151	203	.744	97	659	17.3
Rony Seikaly	C	6-10	240	Jr.	38	216	380	.568	141	235	.600	311	573	15.1
Greg Monroe	G	6-3	195	Sr.	38	181	369	.491	49	67	.731	94	490	12.9
Derrick Coleman	F	6-9	215	Fr.	38	173	309	.560	107	156	.686	333	453	11.9
Howard Triche	G	6-5	215	Sr.	38	185	370	.500	77	107	.720	181	447	11.8
Stephen Thompson	G	6-4	175	Fr.	38	72	155	.465	46	86	.535	70	192	5.1
Rodney Walker	F	6-9	225	So.	14	24	52	.462	14	21	.667	55	62	4.4
Derek Brower	F-C	6-9	230	Jr.	37	47	95	.495	20	48	.417	105	114	3.1
Matt Roe	G	6-5	175	Fr.	13	12	35	.343	3	3	1.000	11	29	2.2
Herman Harried	F	6-7	210	So.	33	27	55	.491	15	35	.429	64	69	2.1
Keith Hughes	F	6-7	205	Fr.	20	14	28	.500	9	12	.750	19	37	1.9
Erik Rogers	C	6-10	205	Fr.	9	5	11	.455	2	3	.667	7	12	1.3
Joel Katz	G	5-11	182	Sr.	8	1	6	.167	3	4	.750	5	5	0.6
Joey Kohm	F	6-3	205	Sr.	8	1	5	.200	0	0	.000	2	3	0.4
Team												170		
Syracuse					38	1204	2333	.516	637	980	.650	1524	3145	82.8
Opponents					38	1049	2428	.432	514	741	.694	1380	2766	72.8

Three-Point Field Goals: Douglas 16-49, Seikaly 0-1, Monroe 79-180, Triche, 0-2, Thompson 2-3, Roe 2-10, Katz 0-1, Kohm 1-2; Opponents 154-431.

1987 NEVADA-LAS VEGAS

Head Coach—Jerry Tarkanian   **Final Record—37-2**

Player	Pos.	Hgt.	Wgt.	Cl.	G	FG	FGA	Pct.	FT	FTA	Pct.	Reb.	Pts.	Avg.
Armon Gilliam	F-C	6-9	230	Sr.	39	359	598	.600	185	254	.728	363	903	23.2
Fred Banks	G	6-2	155	Sr.	39	258	590	.437	92	117	.786	98	760	19.5
Gerald Paddio	F	6-8	196	Jr.	39	194	467	.415	37	55	.673	169	512	13.1
Gary Graham	G	6-4	185	Sr.	39	135	292	.462	88	105	.838	74	393	10.1
Jarvis Basnight	F	6-8	190	Jr.	38	133	204	.652	82	112	.732	184	348	9.2
Mark Wade	G	6-0	160	Sr.	38	60	142	.423	38	49	.776	103	180	4.7
David Willard	C	6-11	195	So.	33	57	107	.533	34	40	.850	83	148	4.5
Eldridge Hudson	G-F	6-6	215	Sr.	39	74	150	.493	12	43	.280	168	163	4.2
Lawrence West	G-F	6-7	205	Jr.	19	27	64	.422	7	14	.500	39	63	3.3
Stacey Cvijanovich	G	6-3	185	Fr.	20	10	37	.270	27	40	.675	12	55	2.8
Richard Robinson	C	6-10	205	Jr.	37	29	67	.433	13	38	.342	101	71	1.9
Leon Symanski	F	6-7	210	Sr.	17	3	16	.188	10	17	.588	17	16	0.9
Team												155		
Nevada-Las Vegas					39	1339	2734	.490	625	884	.707	1566	3612	92.6
Opponents					39	1065	2425	.439	679	1009	.673	1512	2945	75.5

Three-Point Field Goals: Banks 152-358, Paddio 87-237, Graham 35-89, Wade 22-60, Hudson 3-14, Robinson 0-1, West 2-5, Cvijanovich 8-17; Opponents 136-391.

1987 PROVIDENCE

Head Coach—Rick Pitino   **Final Record—25-9**

Player	Pos.	Hgt.	Wgt.	Cl.	G	FG	FGA	Pct.	FT	FTA	Pct.	Reb.	Pts.	Avg.
Billy Donovan	G	6-0	171	Sr.	34	203	467	.435	199	236	.843	102	702	20.6
Delray Brooks	G	6-4	199	Jr.	28	134	310	.432	68	83	.819	110	402	14.4
Ernie Lewis	F	6-4	182	Sr.	34	137	335	.409	32	40	.800	143	401	11.8
Dave Kipfer	F	6-7	212	Sr.	34	145	289	.502	108	147	.735	180	398	11.7
Steve Wright	C	6-9	209	Jr.	34	103	190	.542	62	83	.747	164	268	7.9
James Best	F-G	6-5	190	So.	6	17	30	.567	2	3	.667	14	38	6.3
Darryl Wright	F	6-5	187	So.	33	72	156	.462	38	51	.745	71	201	6.1
Carlton Screen	G	6-0	158	Fr.	25	39	93	.419	52	73	.712	28	131	5.2
Marty Conlan	F	6-9	210	Fr.	34	43	96	.448	64	77	.831	100	150	4.4
Abdul Shamsid-Deen	F	6-10	209	Fr.	33	45	80	.563	27	44	.614	84	117	3.5
Jacek Duda	C	6-11	233	Sr.	34	47	105	.448	21	37	.568	116	115	3.4
Bryan Benham	F	6-3	195	So.	20	5	16	.313	2	4	.500	14	12	0.6
David Snedeker	F	6-8	215	Jr.	24	4	17	.235	0	2	.000	8	8	0.3
Ryan Ford	G	6-0	185	So.	14	0	5	.000	0	1	.000	1	0	0.0
Team												103		
Providence					34	994	2189	.454	675	881	.766	1238	2943	86.6
Opponents					34	862	1918	.449	790	1169	.676	1285	2623	77.1

Three-Point Field Goals: Donovan 97-237, Brooks 66-157, Lewis 95-220, Best 2-6, D. Wright 19-41, Screen 1-2, Ford 0-2; Opponents 109-349.

1987 FINAL FOUR

At New Orleans
Semifinals

Providence	fg	fga	ft	fta	rb	pf	tp
Kipfer	4	10	0	1	5	4	8
Lewis	2	12	2	2	5	3	7
Duda	2	7	0	1	7	4	4
Brooks	4	9	0	0	3	4	9
Donovan	3	12	1	1	1	3	8
Screen	5	6	7	10	2	2	18
Shamsid-Deen	1	2	0	0	2	1	2
Conlan	1	1	0	0	3	4	2
D. Wright	1	4	0	0	0	2	3
S. Wright	1	3	0	0	4	5	2
Snedeker	0	0	0	0	0	1	0
Team					3		
Totals	24	66	10	15	35	33	63

Syracuse	fg	fga	ft	fta	rb	pf	tp
Triche	4	10	4	5	11	3	12
Coleman	4	6	4	7	12	3	12
Seikaly	4	11	8	11	6	3	16
Monroe	4	9	6	10	4	2	17
Douglas	5	11	2	6	11	3	12
Brower	0	1	0	0	4	2	0
Thompson	3	5	1	5	1	7	7
Harried	0	0	1	2	0	0	1
Totals	24	53	26	44	53	17	77

Halftime: Syracuse 36-26. Three-point field goals: Providence 5-19 (Lewis 1-8, Brooks 1-5, Donovan 1-3, Screen 1-1, D. Wright 1-2); Syracuse 3-8 (Monroe 3-7, Douglas 0-1). Officials: Galvan, Grillo and Rutledge.

UNLV	fg	fga	ft	fta	rb	pf	tp
Paddio	2	13	0	0	6	1	6
Gilliam	14	26	4	6	10	3	32
Basnight	3	4	0	1	2	5	6
Wade	1	6	1	2	4	4	4
Banks	12	23	4	6	8	4	38
Robinson	0	0	0	0	1	1	0
Graham	0	5	1	4	2	4	1
Hudson	3	4	0	0	5	2	6
Willard	0	1	0	0	0	2	0
Team					2		
Totals	35	82	10	19	40	26	93

Indiana	fg	fga	ft	fta	rb	pf	tp
Alford	10	19	11	13	4	4	33
Smart	5	7	4	5	2	5	14
Garrett	7	10	4	5	11	2	18
Calloway	6	10	0	0	6	3	12
Thomas	3	5	0	0	4	3	6
Meier	0	0	0	0	3	0	0
Eyl	3	3	1	2	5	4	7
Smith	0	2	0	0	1	0	0
Hillman	3	4	1	3	3	2	7
Team					3		
Totals	37	60	21	28	42	23	97

Halftime: Indiana 53-47. Three-point field goals: UNLV 13-35 (Banks 10-19, Paddio 2-8, Wade 1-6, Graham 0-2); Indiana 2-4 (Alford 2-4). Officials: Cougherty, Herring and Paparo.

Championship
March 30

Syracuse	fg	fga	ft	fta	rb	pf	tp
Triche	3	9	2	4	1	4	8
Coleman	3	7	2	4	19	2	8
Seikaly	7	13	4	6	10	3	18
Monroe	5	11	0	1	2	1	12
Douglas	8	15	2	2	2	3	20
Brower	3	3	1	3	1	3	7
Thompson	0	2	0	0	3	0	0
Totals	29	60	11	20	38	16	73

Indiana	fg	fga	ft	fta	rb	pf	tp
Calloway	0	3	0	0	2	3	0
Thomas	8	18	4	7	7	1	20
Garrett	5	10	0	0	10	4	10
Alford	8	15	0	0	3	2	23
Smart	9	15	3	4	5	2	21
Meier	0	0	0	1	1	0	0
Eyl	0	0	0	0	1	2	0
Smith	0	0	0	0	0	1	0
Hillman	0	1	0	0	2	2	0
Team					4		
Totals	30	62	7	12	35	17	74

Halftime: Indiana 34-33. Three-point field goals: Syracuse 4-10 (Monroe 2-8, Douglas 2-2); Indiana 7-11 (Alford 7-10, Smart 0-1). Officials: Forte, Fine and Silvester.